# WINE TRAILS OF ITALY

## Itineraries through the Vineyards

© Clodio/iStock

## WINE TRAILS OF ITALY

| | |
|---|---|
| **Editorial Director** | Cynthia Clayton Ochterbeck |
| **Editor** | Sophie Friedman |
| **Production Manager** | Natasha George |
| **Original Edition** | Itinerari tra i vigneti. Alla scoperta di 750 cantine in Italia, Canton Ticino, Istria © Michelin Italiana S.p.A. – Carte e Guide |
| **Design, Layout and Translations** | Malerba Editorial & Partners, Milan Francesca Malerba (design), Laura Magda Barazza and Flavia Scotti (update) |
| **Cartography** | Cartographie Michelin Paris and CPZ Press Division |
| **Cover Design** | Francesca Malerba |
| **Contact Us** | Michelin Travel and Lifestyle North America One Parkway South Greenville, SC 29615 USA travel.lifestyle@us.michelin.com |
| | Michelin Travel Partner Hannay House 39 Clarendon Road Watford, Herts WD17 1JA UK ✆01923 205240 travelpubsales@uk.michelin.com www.viamichelin.co.uk |
| **Special Sales** | For information regarding bulk sales, customized editions and premium sales, please contact us at: travel.lifestyle@us.michelin.com |

**Note to the reader**

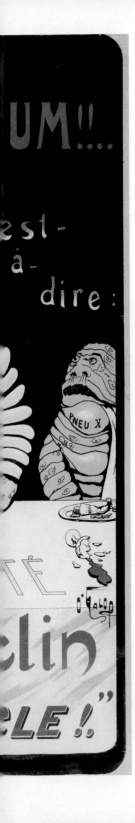

"Now is the time for drinking" exhorted the Michelin Man, quoting Horace back in 1898. And it was due to the success of this advertising campaign that he was nicknamed Bibendum. In this ad, Michelin tyres "drink" (absorb) the "obstacle" (bumps and objects in the road), which seems an appropriate image to accompany this new title, dedicated to lovers of good living: on page after page you will discover itineraries that reveal the artistic, cultural and enological treasures in the most beautiful winemaking areas of Italy, Canton of Ticino in Switzerland, and Istria.

Cheers!

# Contents

*Harvest*
© Robert Paul van Beets/Shutterstock

Wine Trails of Italy
# **Discovering Wine**

# THE WORLD OF WINE

Wine is a marvellous creature, born of expert alchemy in which nature and culture, *terroir* and *savoir-faire* concur. The best wines hail from designated terrain, but the *vignaiolo*'s – or winegrower's – ability to understand it and achieve the best product from each vintage is the wine producer's signature, the individual touch that gives each wine its typical quality and uniqueness. Thus begins our adventure to discover this rich and complex world: at the end of our journey we shall be able to appreciate the nectar of Bacchus, celebrated over the centuries at tables, in culture and in art.

© Davide Bretti/Shutterstock

## Notions of viticulture

From plant to fruit via the terrain and its composition. In order to understand wine we must go from the ground up, as the morphological, chemical and climactic characteristics of the soil the fruit is grown in are the first elements that distinguish it. The typical characteristics of the different vine species then join these to develop the product.

### THE GRAPE

To understand the wine, we must first know the grape, the primary material that it is derived from. A cluster consists of the **grape stalk** (also known as the "**rachis**"), which is the central part of the branched, woody element, and is an extension of the peduncle attached to the cane of the plant, and the **grape berry**, which consists of the skin, or **exocarp**, the flesh, or **mesocarp**, and

the endocarp which is the central fruity part containing the grape seeds.). The grape stalk contains water, tannin, pectin, cellulose, resin, minerals and nitrous substances. Tannin plays an important role. To avoid excessively tannic wine, grapes may be destemmed prior to production.

The **skin**, whether tender or tough, thick or thin, is rich in pectin, cellulose, aromatic substances (terpenes) and **polyphenols**. Among the latter,

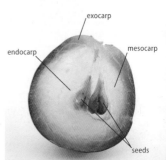

exocarp

mesocarp

endocarp

seeds

© Iwka/Shutterstock

catechins, leuko-anthocyanidins and flavons are responsible for the colour of **white grapes**, while anthocyanins give **red and black grapes** their colour. As the compounds that confer colour are in the skin, contact between the skin and the grape must plays a determining role in the end tint of the wine. The skin, moreover, is coated with a waxy substance called bloom that protects the berries from external agents, while collecting yeasts and microorganisms – borne by the wind and insects – that are important to the activation of alcoholic fermentation.

The **pulp**, which may be soft or compact, juicy or crunchy, is rich in water, acids and sugars, as well as pectin, vitamins and mineral and nitrogen substances. The distribution of these elements is not uniform: the part closest to the skin contains the most tannins, but fewer acids and sugars, the pulp in the middle – the mesocarp – contains the most sugar, but little tannin, while that around the seeds – the endocarp – contains the most acids and least sugars. We may thus deduce that delicate pressing will produce sweeter must, while more aggressive pressing will produce a more acidic and tannic must.

**Grape seeds** are pear-shaped, swollen at one end and pointed at the other. They are composed of water, fatty substances (fundamental to obtaining grape seed oil), tannin, cellulose and mineral salts.

The **cluster** may have different forms (pyramidal, conical, cylindrical, with berries that are more or less compact) and the length varies depending on the vine species. Even the berries may have different shapes – spherical, ellipsoidal, obovoid, ellipsoidal elongated, ovoid, oblate – with varying diameters. Variables that affect the appearance of the berry are its maturity, climatic changes, time of year, grape variety.

## CLIMATE AND SOIL

Vines produce the best when climatic conditions are perfect: sunny, breezy, with a good range of daytime and nighttime temperatures. Water is also important: moderate rain and a good irrigation system allow for ideal vine growth, but it is preferable not to have rain during florescence as this can cause mildew.

Climatic changes can contribute to the creation of a particularly interesting vintage from a winemaking vantage point just as easily as they can jeopardise the quality.

Vineyards are positively affected by thermal variations during the day as well as throughout the season as they can improve the flavours and aromas of wine, and affect acidity and crispness.

## Morphology

Whether the vines cultivated in the mountains, on a plain or in hilly areas, influences their development. Hilly slopes offer ideal conditions for optimum development as they facilitate exposure to the Sun, breezes and optimise drainage.

In choosing the position of a vineyard, the variety of the grapevine must be taken into consideration: in colder climates faster ripening grapes should be cultivated. The vicinity of lakes, rivers, mountains and wooded areas is also important as they can protect the vines from cold winds, by regulating the temperature and providing humidity during drier periods.

Rivers and lakes influence the climate: in dry periods, they make the air less muggy by lowering the temperature and increasing humidity, giving the vines better conditions for growth. Generally speaking, hilly areas benefit from temperatures that are never too high, ideal temperature ranges and good ventilation prevent air and humidity from stagnating, which is to the advantage of the vines, making them less subject to mildew and parasites.

© Yasonya/Shutterstock

© Arman Zenders/Shutterstock

## Soil composition

In addition to morphology, the composition of the soil also plays a fundamental role in oenology. The soil where grapevines grow consists mostly of **sand** (made of particles measuring between 2 and 0.02 mm in diameter), **silt** (with particles measuring between 0.02 and 0.002 mm in diameter) and **clay** (made of particles measuring smaller than 0.002 mm in diameter) in different proportions. Grapevines adapt to just about any soil but the same vine cultivated in different soils produces different grapes. The roots of the vines reach down into the subsoil to provide the plants' nutrients, which influence the characteristics of the grapes and thus the wine.

The composition of the soil affects drainage as well as vine growth: sand makes the earth more porous, while clay absorbs the water, feeding it gradually to the plant's roots; clay also absorbs fertilizing substances and makes the ground compact, but if there is too much, then the ground becomes too plastic and impermeable with a negative influence on the vines. Silt is a substance somewhere between clay and sand.

The soil may contain **limestone**, or calcium carbonate, which when it contains a percentage of clay is considered marly limestone; marl, instead, contains equal proportions of limestone and clay.

**Clayey soil** is good for cultivating the black grape berries used for making long-lived red wines, with intense colours and flavours, good acidity, alcohol and body. **Marly-calcareous soil** pro-

duces wines with intense colour, good body and alcohol, low acidity, finesse, with sharp aromas and inviting hues. From **sandy soil** come pale wines that lack any particular structure, have a delicate bouquet and good acidity. **Calcareous areas** produce wines with a high level of alcohol; **stoney zones** produce refined alcoholic wines; while **marly ferruginous** soil produce wines of excellent quality.

Moreover, it may be added that humid soils produce weak colours, aromas that lack persistence, are very acidic and are short-lived; acid soils offer wines that are not very strong, but fizzy, with good freshness, little alcohol, light body and moderately persistent aromas.

Finally, as particularly fertile soil produces everyday, average quality wines, it is best to cultivate them with fruits and vegetables rather than grapevines.

## PLANTING AND CULTIVATING THE VINEYARD

Once the vine species best adapted to the soil and climate has been chosen, rows are laid out and stakes placed and wired to support the vines. The choice of most appropriate planting, culture and pruning will depend on the slope, the composition of the soil, the microclimate and surrounding environment, and will be made with a goal to guaranteeing optimal sun exposure and drainage for the grapes. Among the determining factors in viticulture are the density of the plantation, the supply of water and nutrition, steps taken to ward off parasites and disease, grape harvesting technique and the monitoring of maturation. In particular the distance between plants and wires plays an important role in the correct development of the vineyard and influences the quality of the wine, as does limiting the load of clusters on each vine stock.

Variables such as climate, soil, and the variety of vine species are fundamental considerations in the planting of a vineyard.

Various vine-management systems exist: tents, pergolas, Guyot, bush, spurred cordon, Casarza, Sylvoz, to cite just a few. These are selected depending on the soil, the climate, and the vine species, and the forms must optimise sun exposure and drainage.

The goal of pruning is to reduce the number of buds and thus the clusters to improve the quality of the grapes.

## THE VINE

The vine grows and changes continuously. The **life cycle** is related to its age and influences productivity. For one to three years following planting it remains unproductive because it is still young. At 4-5 years of age its productivity begins to develop. From 5 to 20-25 years productivity is constant and the vine is at the height of its maturity, while after 30 years it gradually reduces productivity.

With regard to vegetation, each year buds germinate in April and until August the shoots grow while from August to November they change from green to brown. In December the leaves fall and the vines go dormant until the following April.

The vegetative cycle includes the production cycle. Out of each sprout grow clusters that bloom in June. The first grape berries also form in June, developing and changing colour until August: green at first, they become yellow or red depending on the vine species. The maturity of the berries depends on the climate and the variety cultivated, it may end in August or continue to September-October. Once this phase is complete, the grapes are harvested. The beginning of the harvest will influence the type of wine obtained: grapes are harvested earlier for a fresher, more acidic wine, while a smoother wine requires a later harvest, and a very late one for sweet wines.

# Vinification

Now we will enter the alchemic world of fabricating wine out of the must and its yeast. From this point on everything lies in the hands of man, who using age-old *savoir-faire* develops an infinite variety of grape clusters, from white to red, from dry to sweet.

## THE MUST

Wine is the product of the alcoholic fermentation of the grape must thanks to the variety of yeast called *Saccaromyces cerevisiae*. In short, what happens during vinification is that the yeast attack the sugars in the must, transforming them into alcohol and carbon dioxide; the alcohol is left behind while the carbon dioxide is allowed to escape in the production of wines that are not bubbly, while it is trapped for sparkling wines. Every wine grape is capable of producing dry, sweet, flat or sparkling wines; the result depends on whether the sugars in the cluster are completely or only partially fermented, rather than on the grape vine species.

The must is an acidic-sugary solution produced by pressing grapes and consists of water, sugars, acids, minerals, vitamins, polyphenols, aromatic and nitrous substances, pectin, enzymes and other microorganisms.

© Cloudia Spinner/Shutterstock

© Robert Paul van Beets/Shutterstock

© Patricia Hofmeester/Shutterstock

The must contains primarily two sugars: glucose and fructose; unripe grapes contain mostly glucose, while ripe grapes contain fructose. The sugars are the result of chlorophyll photosynthesis, so exposure to sunlight is very important for grapevine cultivation.

The percentage of sugar in the berries increases as they ripen to the detriment of acids, in which the berries are rich: tartaric acid, malic acid and citric acid as well as other acids that are present to a lesser extent.

The **microorganisms present** in grapes are yeasts, bacteria and moulds. The first are responsible for alcoholic fermentation, while the latter cause Malolactic fermentation.

In wine cellars the must may be treated in order to increase its limpidity, sugariness, acidity, colour, concentration of tannins and extract, meaning all the matter (sugars, acids, tannins, salts and nitrogenous substances) dissolved in the must that are not volatile at 100 °C.

## RED WINES

Red winemaking techniques are characterised by the fermentation of the must with the berry skins that contain the substances that give the wine colour (anthocyanides).

For red wines, once the berries have been harvested they are pressed gently to avoid extracting too much tannin from them. Destemming machines eliminate the stems, which are very rich in polyphenolic substances that could confer unpleasant flavours on the wine.

At this point the must and grape skins are allowed to ferment at an ideal temperature of 25-28 °C.

Operations to pump the wine over the must that has risen to the top and **to punch the** must down facilitate the fermentation process and the release of substances that colour the wine and add aroma.

If the goal is a wine rich in colour, body and aroma, fermentation will be longer (ca. 15-20 days), while to produce a wine for drinking young, fresh and fragrant, the process takes 5-7 days.

Next follows **racking – or drawing off –** in which the wine is separated from the vinacce, or vinasses which are the vinification lees, and from the waste residue from vinification (dregs). The vinasses may then undergo further pressing to extract wine residue.

For red wines, alcoholic fermentation, is often followed by **malolactic fermentation** in which bacteria transform malic acid into lactic acid – which has a less sour flavour and softer mouth texture – as well as into carbon dioxide. Malolactic fermentation is useful for filling out the flavour of wine and giving it more body, and is often used for wines that are intended for aging, mostly red. Next follows barrel aging, to make the wine more limpid, to correct eventual imperfections and stabilise it. **Bottling** takes place next, followed by commercialization for wines meant to be drunk young, whereas those intended for aging are left to age in bottles prior to sale.

### Novello

So-called "**novelli**" wines deserve special mention. These wines are obtained through a special technique of "**carbonic maceration**" in which whole grape berries are fermented in a vat along with carbon dioxide without crushing for 5-20 days at around 30 °C in order to promote intracellular fermentation. At the end of carbonic maceration the berries are pressed to obtain a wine that is fresh, fruity, and *beverino*, meaning easy to drink, to be consumed within a few months following production.

## WHITE WINES

To make white wines the must is macerated without the skins of the berries, although some white wines that are aged call for the skins. Since white wine is often a fresh, fragrant wine that should be consumed young, the harvest takes place earlier with respect to reds so that the grapes are more acidic. The harvest must be delicate and the stalks are generally removed prior to pressing.

An important phase in the process is the separation of the juice from the skins and the grape seeds; this makes it possible to obtain white wine from red grapes. The must derived from this process is then crushed and clarified, then fermentation begins at a temperature of 18-22 °C. Next follow **stabilization** and **bottling**.

For wines that are di *pronta beva* – meaning ready to drink, vinification takes place in steel containers, and is briefer compared to red wines and does not include malolactic fermentation or aging in wood barrels. However, there are plenty of white wines for aging that use similar procedures to those for red wines, in which malolactic fermentation takes place and the wine is left to age in barrels and then in bottles. Sometimes a "**cold maceration**" process is used meaning that after pressing, the must and vinasses sit in a vat at a low temperature in order to extract a maximum of aromatic substances from the skins.

### Rosé wines

For rosé wines contact between the must and skins is very brief or partial. They are produced using the process of white wine vinification of red grapes or by mixing red and white grape berries or by macerating only some of the grape berries with the vinasses.

Different techniques and the duration of maceration determine the colour intensities. For this type of wine the preferred vine species are characterised by bunches that are neither highly pigmented nor very tannic. Rosés are appreciated for their freshness, aroma and ready to drink quality; they are not wines for aging.

In terms of colour and structure, the "**cerasuoli**" are the closest to white wines, while "**chiaretti**" are closer to red wines.

© Rachell Coe/Shutterstock

© Zeljka/Shutterstock

## SWEET, LIQUOR-LIKE, PASSITI, AROMATIC WINES

Wines are **sweet** when fermentation is stopped to prevent all the sugars from being transformed into alcohol and carbon dioxide. The process may be interrupted naturally, when the action of yeast is stopped to achieve a certain level of alcoholic content (around 14°) by lowering the temperature or fortifying or "correcting" the wine, by adding alcohol, in this case the wine is **liquor-like**. The best-known liquor-like wines include Porto, Madera, Sherry and the Italian wine Marsala.

**Vino passito** instead, is made from withered grapes so the berries are sugar-rich and the aromatic substances are concentrated; they produce sweet, extraordinarily fragrant wines. The withering may take place either by leaving the grapes on the vine or by harvesting the clusters and leaving them to dry in the sun or in special rooms on racks. The latter method is used to make Tuscan Vin Santo.

Sometimes the concentration of sugars and aromatic substances is due to the growth of *Botrytis cinerea*, a **mold** known as "Noble Rot", on the berries: France's prestigious Sauternes, Hungarian Tokaji and the German Trockenbeerenauslese are a few of the wines that this precious mold contributes to favourably.

Sweet Eccelsi wines are also produced using a natural process called "floral abortion", as in the case of Picolit. This means that only a few of the berries on each grape cluster mature, resulting in high concentrations of sugars and aromas in the ripened few.

Vini aromatizzati, or **flavoured wines**, are made from a base wine that has an alcoholic strength of no less than 10° to which alcohol, sugar and extracts or infusion of herbs and spices are added: one example of such wine is Barolo Chinato.

## SEMI-SPARKLING AND WINES SPARKLING

Carbon dioxide is produced along with alcohol during alcoholic fermentation. When the gas remains imprisoned in the wine and not allowed to wane sparkling and semi-sparkling wines result.

Wines that are semi-sparkling – *frizzante* – have a carbon dioxide pressure of 1 to 2.5 atmospheres at a temperature of 20 °C in a sealed recipient.

"**Spumantes**", or sparkling wines under the same conditions, have a carbon dioxide pressure of at least 3 to 3.5 atmospheres. When the goal is to produce a sparkling wine, the grape berries are generally harvested early in order to have a good level of acidity; the grape berries are lightly pressed and meticulously stemmed to avoid excess tannins and polyphenols which could penalise the product's crispness. Next follows normal vinification off the skins (or in *rosato* – partly on the skins – for sparkling rosé wines). If exclusively white grape berries are used, the sparkling wine will be called "**Blanc des Blancs**", if only black grape berries are used instead, then the wine is called "**Blanc des Noirs**". The base wine may be enriched with wines from previous years, except in the case of vintage spumantes that are necessarily from the same year indicated on the label.

### Types of spumante

Depending on sugar content, spumante wines may be defined as:

Extra Brut: 0-6 g/l of sugar
Brut: less than 15 g/l
Extra Dry: 12-20 g/l
Dry or Secco: 17-35 g/l
Demi-sec or Semisecco: 33-50 g/l
Sweet: more than 50 g/l

© Ken Durden/Shutterstock

Spumante wines are referred to as **natural** if the carbon dioxide comes from refermentation, while they are **artificial** if the carbonation is added. In order to produce natural sparkling wines a variety of systems may be used, the most widespread of which are the Metodo Classico (also called the Méthode Champenoise used to produce Champagne) and the Charmat Method.

## Metodo Classico or Méthode Champenoise

In sparkling wine production using the Metodo Classico, the wine base (often obtained through the assemblage or blending of different grape varieties and/or vintages – hence the term cuvée), then a mixture of wine, sugars, yeasts and other substances – the *liqueur de tirage* – are added to activate a second fermentation. This blend of wine with the liqueur de tirage is then poured into bottles made of especially thick glass able to withstand the internal pressure from the carbonation, and sealed with a plastic stopper with a small cylinder, or *bidule*, – used for catching sediment waste from fermentation known as the dregs or *fecce* – held in place by a crown cap.

The bottles are stored lying down in cool, dark cellars where the second fermentation takes place that produces carbon dioxide and alcohol. Internal pressure is measured constantly using a special instrument (manometer). In order to make the *spuma* (or *perlage*) produce as fine and elegant a stream of bubbles as possible, the external temperature must be low and fermentation slow.

Once the second fermentation process is complete, **maturation** in contact with yeasts begins during which the spumante's bouquet is enriched and develops structure. Fundamental to the evolution of the aromatic heritage is the so-called "yeast autolysis", a process during which the destruction of yeasts causes the release of substances into the wine that can affect the elegance and finesse of the bouquet.

Maturation on yeasts can even last for many years. The bottles are laid in special wine racks called *"pupitres"* by inserting the neck of the bottle in holes that keep the bottles angled down. When **"remuage"** takes place, the bottles are rotated slightly and gradually inclined so that the dregs (dead yeast cells and residue waste) drop down into the plastic cylinder under the crown cap. This operation is carried out by specialised personnel or a mechanical riddler known as a *gyropalette*. From the initial horizontal position, the bottles finish in a nearly vertical position at which point they are removed from the *pupitres* and left upended until *disgorgement*, in which the dregs that have accumulated in the cylinder or on the cork are removed to obtain a clear product. This procedure used to be done *"à la volée"*: the bottle was opened in an inclined position and then quickly straightened to lose as little $CO_2$ and wine as possible; today it is done *à la glace*, meaning the bottle neck is immersed in a cooling solution for a few minutes in order to freeze the part where the dregs are. Then the bottle is opened and the frozen part is pushed out naturally by the internal pressure build up.

Once the dregs are eliminated, the **shipping dosage** (*liqueur d'expédition*) is added to replace the lost liquid and give the product the desired gustatory characteristics. This syrup is made of wine from previous years, must, sugar and sometimes a small amount of distilled alcohol. When dosage does not take place, the spumante is said to be *pas dosé*. The addition of *liqueur* is prohibited in the production of quality aromatic spumantes made from Moscato and Malvasia grape berries.

Finally, the bottle is closed using a traditional mushroom shaped cork, held firmly in place by a wire cage. The bottle is then laid down in the cellar until the wine and liqueur blend and then the cage is wrapped with a capsule, the bottle is labelled and finally marketed.

## Charmat Process

The second fermentation in the Charmat Process (also known as **Martinotti** after the Italian developer of the process) takes place in large tanks rather than bottles as in the Metodo Classico. The result is wines that are particularly fresh with heightened floral and fruity aromas.

In addition to the fact that the process for **producing sparkling wine in an autoclave** is more rapid with respect to the bottled process, another substantial difference between the two systems is that all the phases further to second fermentation take place under isobaric conditions, to prevent the loss of carbon dioxide produced during the second fermentation. In the Charmat Method once the base wine has been prepared and the yeasts selected, the autoclave is filled with wine to which sugar, yeasts and other substances useful to secondary fermentation are added. The latter takes place at a temperature of 12-18 °C, after which it is poured under isobaric conditions into another autoclave in order to separate the wine from the dregs. At this point the wine is stabilised and rendered transparent by refrigerating, clarifying, filtering and centrifuging it. The final phase is isobaric bottling and corking.

**Autoclaves** are stainless steel or enamelled recipients that hold up to 500 hl or even 1000 hl of wine, and are able to withstand 7-8 atm of pressure as well as maintain the fermentation temperature.

As for the **Classic Method**, this process may be used to produce both dry and sweet spumante wines: to produce sweet spumante it is enough to rapidly drop the temperature to block fermentation before all the sugar has been transformed. Dry spumantes produced this way are generally sealed with natural corks while sweet Charmat spumantes may opt for plastic corks. According to the standards developed by the EU for Vini Spumanti di Qualità and Vini Spumanti di Qualità Prodotti in Regione Determinata (quality spumante wine and quality spumante wine produced in a specific area) produced using the Charmat method, the period of time between the second fermentation process and commercialization must not be greater than 6 months.

This system is also used to produce, among others, the well-known Asti Spumante DOCG: the Charmat process is ideal for making the characteristics of aromatic grape varieties stand out, such as the Moscato grape used to make Asti DOCG.

# Tasting

One's approach to wine should offer a moment of pleasure and joy, without excess technicalities that take the fun and hedonist aspects out of tasting. It is true, however, that to better appreciate wine a few basic rules are necessary.

Delighting in the Nectar of Bacchus happens in three fundamental stages: visual, olfactory and then gustatory. The attentive taster will begin to understand the wine as soon as the bottle is uncorked and the wine is poured in the glass, so even the auditory experience plays a role.

## THE VISUAL ASSESSMENT

The visual analysis studies variables such as colour, clarity, fluidity and, in the case of spumante wines, effervescence.

© Sklep Spozywczy/Shutterstock

## The elements

The colour of wine alone can say much about the product because it is determined by elements such as the type of vine species, the maturity of the grape berries, the method used to make the wine – off the skins, on the skins, or partly on the skins – and for sparkling rosé wines, the amount of aging, its state of evolution, typology, area of production.

The terms used most often to describe the colour of white wines are: straw yellow, golden or amber; reds are purplish, ruby, garnet, or may tend towards orange; rosés will be cherry or claret. The intensity and highlights of the colour are evaluated. The latter refer to the shading at the nail, which is the edge or the shallowest part visible when the glass is held at a 45-degree angle. A pale colour may be the result of reduced extraction of colouring substances and may be the producer's choice, either because the year was particularly rainy, because the harvest was too big, because the vines are young or because the grapes were not very ripe. An intense colour is the result of small harvests, older vines, prolonged maceration in contact with the skins as well as vine species that are naturally rich in pigments.

When talking about the **limpidity** of a wine, it is said to be limpid, or even crystal clear or brilliant, when there are no particles suspended in the liquid, otherwise it is considered veiled.

**Fluidity** is revealed by the presence of arcs, legs and tears after turning the glass in a rotary manner: alcohol, sugar and other substances determine their formation. The more slowly a wine goes down the sides of the glass forming arcs, legs and tears, the more body the wine has.

**Effervescence** indicates the presence of carbon dioxide in sparkling wines; the bubbles rising up, or perlage, and the mousse they form are evaluated in terms of size, number, dimension and persistence of bubbles present in the wine.

## Technique

In the visual assessment, it is important to have a transparent, colourless glass with a long stem so that it may be held

© Mountainpix/Shutterstock

by the stem or the base. The glass is first held up to the light to analyse its colour, then at a 45-degree angle against a white background to determine intensity and liveliness. Holding the glass at eye-level and rotating the wine in the glass in order to coat the sides of the glass with wine enables observation of the arcs, legs and tears and thus considerations in function of fluidity.

## OLFACTORY ASSESSMENT

The olfactory assessment reveals the intensity, quality and complexity of the wine's aromas, as well as its eventual defects.

## The elements

The aromas of wines can be **primary** (meaning from the grape itself), **secondary** (due to vinification and in particular the fermentation process), or **tertiary** (determined by aging in barrels or bottles). A further classification of aromas involves the use of adjectives such as **floral** (when a bouquet of flowers can be detected), **fruity** (when aromas of fruits are detected), **aromatic** (from the aromatic components of vines themselves with a marked primary scent such as Moscatos, Brachettos, Gewürztraminers, Malvasias), **herbaceous** (presenting an aroma reminiscent of cut grass or other green vegetables), **spicy** (sensations of spices, such as pepper, cloves, cinnamon, nutmeg, and so on) to cite just a few.

# INTRODUCTION

The most skilled are able to distinguish different scents within a single category, identifying a floral wine's bouquet of white flowers, or a fruity wine's aromas that recall yellow or red fruits and more specifically peach or strawberry through ever more specific levels of knowledge, leading to an increasingly specific and detailed description. In addition to evaluation of the varieties of fragrances is the **intensity and persistence** of these, as well as their finesse and quality.

The fragrance, like the colour, says a great deal about wine; and scenting the glass of wine also makes it possible to make considerations about the vine species and the vine's state of evolution.

A **young white wine** generally has white and yellow fl oral and yellow fruit notes, an **aged white wine**, meanwhile, has more mature fruity notes or even scents of dried or candied fruit or preserves.

A **young red wine may** generally be distinguished by its scents of red fruits, violet flowers, green and vegetable notes, while an **aged red wine** has a more variegated bouquet with scents of dried or very ripe fruits, preserves, spices, roasting and other evolved fragrances.

The olfactory analysis may also reveal defects with vinegary, sulphurous, corky or other unpleasant odours caused by excessive oxygenation of wine.

## Technique

The olfactory assessment is carried out by sniffing the wine first still in the glass and then after rotating the glass; the latter operation frees more fragrant sensations. To prevent foreign scents from interfering with those of the wine, it is preferable to keep hands a certain distance from the nose and not wear perfumes or strong deodorants. So the nose does not grow accustomed to the scent of the wine, inhalations should be deep, not continuous, but repeated at regular intervals.

## GUSTATORY ASSESSMENT

### The elements

Finally, elements Finally, gustatory assessment takes place, which makes it possible to identify the balance, the structure or the body, the intensity, persistence, the quality, the evolution and the harmony of the wine, as well as the eventual presence of defects.

The **balance** of a wine is determined by all the gustatory (sweet, bitter, salty, acidic) and tactile (warmth, freshness, astringency, effervescence) sensations, for there to be a balance there must be a harmonious cohabitation of soft and hard sensations. The first come from sugars, alcohols and polyalcohols, while the latter come from acids, tannins, mineral salts.

Depending on the structure, the wine may be classified as thin, weak, fullbodied, robust, while depending on the state of evolution it may be immature, young, ready, mature or old.

It is appreciable for a wine to be intense and persistent or to delight the palate

© Peter Zurek/Shutterstock

with complex sensations that linger in the mouth.

Finally, a wine is considered fine if it is balanced, pleasant and elegant, while it is harmonious if the visual, olfactory and gustatory analyses concord.

### Technique

Ideally, tasting should take place in the morning, away from meals, in adequate lighting and tranquil, quiet settings. The glass is very important: it must be transparent in order to appreciate the colour, have a stem so hands are not in direct contact with the bowl of the glass, be big enough to facilitate the perception of aromas.

The gustatory assessment is carried out by taking a small quantity of wine in one's mouth, holding it there for a few moments while breathing in some air in order to cause aromas to volatilise; once swallowed, retro-olfactory sensations should be observed.

(*The tasting method proposed herein is inspired by that of the AIS – Associazione Italiana Sommelier*).

# Acquisition

**The best way to buy wine is directly from the producer; in this way the purchase becomes an opportunity to visit the cellar and vineyard, as well as meet the producer. Usually it is also possible to have better prices. Visiting cellars can satisfy personal quests, lead to the discovery territories and people; the pleasure of discovery and travel is priceless. In** recent years, wine tourism has become more widespread and receives increased approval.

It is advisable to prepare the visit prior to departure; one should know the characteristics and types of wines produced in the area one wishes to tour and seek information about the best cellars in the region. Participating in tastings and events in the area is a good, as well as fun, activity that can help expand one's knowledge in the field.

## CELLARS

Before leaving, one should call the cellar ahead to be sure the producer is available to receive visits, and to reserve a tour or a guided tasting as well as to find out if it is possible to make direct purchases. The best moments for buying from the producer are early spring and late autumn; late summer and early fall should be avoided as producers are busy with the grape harvest.

## WINE SHOPS

Visiting wine cellars is not always possible, so wine shops remain key for making purchases. There, specialised personnel can assist clients, guide them in their choices, offer advice and useful information. Bottles of wine are available for every budget. **Vinarius** (www.vinarius.it) is the Associazione Enoteche Italiane with members throughout Italy whose goal is to improve the services available to clients and the spread of the culture of wine.

## SUPERMARKETS

In recent years, the increased number of wine lovers has led to the presence of spaces dedicated to wine in supermarkets and hypermarkets. Here it is possible to find very affordable wines and highly renown wines alike. The value offered is the main reason for choosing mass distribution for one wine versus another. While the offering here can often be advantageous, it is also true that wines at the supermarket are not stored in ideal conditions: under neon lights, exposed to noise, inappropriate temperatures, vibrations. Some points of sale have a specialised consultant available to answer customers' questions and offer advice.

## INTERNET

Recently, e-commerce has begun to spread into the oenological sector, supplanting mail orders, which were popular in the last century.

There are specialised portals that represent veritable brickand- morter shops online. As they do not have consultants available the way real wine shops do, making online purchases is only advisable for those familiar with the wine being purchased and after comparing prices with bottles available in shops or other points of sale, and after receiving guarantees about the good condition of the product and the way it is stored and delivered.

Many producers have opened their own websites on specific platforms that communicate orders directly to the wine cellar.

E-commerce for collector's bottles, precious and hard to find wines, is very interesting. A quick investigation using search engines will lead the buyer to many sites where it is possible to trade wines and participate in veritable online auctions. Before embarking on this virtual adventure it is wise to check out the vendor's credibility.

## AUCTIONS

Another way to stock up on rare connoisseur labels is to attend auctions attended by collectors from around the world. These very specialised auctions are organised by serious houses such as Christie's, Sotheby's, Acker Merral & Condit, Pandolfini, Finarte, Wine Gallery, to cite just a few. Even in this case, before penetrating this fascinating world it is wise to learn about its rules, costs, times and modes, as well as to ask for guarantees regarding the condition of the bottles and learn how to avoid eventual mistakes.

## "EN PRIMEUR"

Finally there is another form of purchase: *"en primeur"*, or in preview. In this case the wine purchased is not delivered immediately but only after a certain period of aging at the producer's. This system, once the exclusive preserve of the chateaux of Bordeaux, now concerns many types of wine. Wines for laying down – in Italy, **Amarone**, **Brunello di Montalcino**, **Barolo**, **Barbaresco** – are the perfect protagonists of this method. Wines *en primeur* allow producers to more easily sustain the investment costs necessary for aging wines and for the buyer to stock up on bottles produced in fairly limited quantities and to get lower prices than those practiced when the wine enters the market, at the risk, however, of overrating the wine.

To make a purchase en primeur one should address specialised operators that are guaranteed trustworthy and opt for prestigious wines, produced in good years, by sought-after producers, with excellent capacities for aging wine, with a view not only to drinking the wine but also (even years after their purchase) reselling them at a higher price (sometimes much higher than the purchase price) thereby enablingenticing proceeds and representing aneconomic investment in all aspects.

# Conservation

**Wine is a product that evolves constantly. Thus, once it has been bought it should be stored and handled properly. It is very important for the areas where the bottles are to be stored to fulfil certain criteria.**

## CRITICAL FACTORS

Among the variables that need to be kept under control, **humidity** is certainly one of the most important; the optimum percentage, measured using an instrument called a "hygrometer", is 70-80%. Too much humidity encourages the growth of mould and fungus and damages labels, while in spaces that are too dry it is the cork that suffers and may lose its elasticity.

Alterations in wine can also be caused by vibrations and noises, thus it is wise to place the bottles away from sources of vibrations, such as household appliances, as well as furnaces and burners that may generate noise and heat.

Cork is porous and thus may absorb external **odours** and transmit them to wine, so foods with strong odours such as salami, cheese, onions, truffles should not be stored near bottles; contact with odorous non-foods such as gasoline, diesel, paint, detergent, bleach and so on should also be avoided.

A room where air can be renewed continuously limits the growth of moulds, so proper **ventilation** of the cellar or storage rooms is very important.

The ideal cellar is nonetheless underground: the etymology of the French word cave derived from the Latin *cavus*, means "sunk". The shelves best adapted to storing wine bottles are wood as these are able to attenuate any eventual vibrations and temperature changes.

## THE ORGANIZATION OF THE CELLAR

The lowest shelves are ideal for sparkling and white wines, with the colours darkening as they go higher: rosés, then reds

| STORAGE TEMPERATURE | |
|---|---|
| Spumante | 5 °C |
| Dry whites and rosés | 7 °C |
| Whites for aging | 8-10 °C |
| Light whites | 8 °C |
| Reds for aging | 12-13 °C |
| Aged reds | 15-17 °C |
| Sweet and liqueur-like wines | 5-12 °C |

for drinking young and finally reds for aging towards the top. Such a disposition takes into consideration that fact that the temperature rises with the levels of the shelves.

The cork should remain in contact with the wine so that it does not lose its elasticity; thus the recommended position for storage of bottles is **horizontal**, which is particularly true for wines intended for aging.

For rapid and efficient identification, a good solution for organizing the home wine cellar is to divide bottles by type (sparkling, white, red, for laying down) or according to place of origin, dividing them by region.

## AGING

Cellar organization should take into consideration the fact that wines differ in their ability to age. It is thus preferable to keep wines that should be drunk young more accessible. In most cases there are indications on the label as to the wine's ability to age. Generally, very inexpensive wines do not age well, while nouveau wines should be drunk soon after purchase, whites and rosés are appreciated for their freshness so it is preferable to drink them young, except for a few cases where refinement causes the wine to develop interesting characteristics, non-vintage spumante wines should be drunk within a few months of disengorgement, while vintage wines may be drunk much later.

The vine species, in the case of both white wines and red wines, is often essential in determining a wine's ability to age, because of this it is good to know its characteristics prior to purchase.

If wines are purchased with the intention to save them it is wise to opt for better years rather than mediocre ones.

Those who do not have a veritable cellar may opt for a special refrigerated cabinet that has temperature controls that regulate sections for each specific wine.

## THE CORK

The Romans sealed their amphorae with cork, but in the Middle Ages there was a preference for fabric, string, skins held on using sealing wax or even glass plugs.

© Kondor83/Shutterstock

Cork became widespread once again from the second half of the 16th century.

Corks are made from the bark of a particular **cork oak tree** found mostly in Sardinia, the south of France and Spain, the north of Tunisia and Morocco as well as the central-southern area of Portugal. It takes forty years for a cork oak to grow bark that is appropriate for making corks, and once removed, it takes about another decade to grow back.

The extraction and elaboration of cork requires laborious and long operations: to begin with the planks are aged for a year. 6 months after their production is complete, the cork reaches optimal conditions for being used. The best quality corks do not require the application of paraffin in order for them to perfectly adhere to the glass.

**Different types** of cork are available: natural single piece corks, granular agglomerated corks, composed of disks laminated to natural cork and agglomerate, multi-piece cork stoppers. Obviously the price varies in function of the quality of the cork. The best are the first and are normally reserved for exclusive wines, the second and third are widely used for sparkling wines.

In addition to variety, it may generally be observed that cork stoppers measuring 4 to 6 centimetres are used for wine for aging while sparkling wines require corks that are especially wide and elastic.

The **quality** of a cork stopper is a function of its lightness, impermeability, adherence, ability to insulate and its elasticity. A mediocre quality of cork is more likely to cause problems, so once it has been uncorked it is wise to verify the condition of the cork, sniffing it before pouring: the cork may, in fact, confer unpleasant aromas to the wine. This can happen if certain fungal or moulds grow on it (in this case the wine is said to "taste corky"), or else because it was cut from unhealthy planks that are not fully mature or insufficiently aged. The cork may also present dripping or an excessive absorption of wine or even leave the scent of wood inside the bottle; in these cases the quality of the cork is debatable.

Alternatives to cork are less expensive screw-on or crown, corona and polyester caps. Since these can sometimes influence the wine's bouquet, the use of **synthetic silicon stoppers** has recently become widespread. These non-toxic thermoplastic stoppers were created in France at the end of the Seventies. They have the advantages of not being affected by mold, not crumbling and efficiently preserving wine from external factors. These stoppers are not adapted

© Alekcey/Shutterstock

© Keith Levit/Shutterstock

to wines for laying down to age as they do not allow for any gaseous exchange which is necessary to the evolution of wine's aromas.

## BOTTLES

In order to protect wine from the oxidizing effects of light, bottles are usually made of **dark glass**, particularly in the case of red wines for aging.

The bottle's **capacity** affects the rapidity of its development: in smaller bottles, wine ages more rapidly, while in larger bottles the evolution is slower; the magnum, which holds 1.5 litres, offers ideal maturation. Bottles should be filled carefully as the less wine there is in the neck of the bottle, the more space there is for air and thus the greater the likelihood of oxidation.

The bottom of the bottle usually has a concave, funnel-shaped bottom, which is useful for making it more stable. The body of the bottle is the central part that goes from the base to its shoulders; the role of the latter is important because they can prevent eventual sediment from being poured into the glass.

The **demijohn** is a fairly large glass container used to transport wine. Recently bag-in-box conditioning has become widespread for wine that is vacuump-acked to prevent oxidation. These plastic and aluminium containers are held inside cardboard or similar boxes and are used for wines that are ready to drink and usually have a spigot. They should not be confused with Tetrabricks, which are plastic-coated cardboard boxes that are also adapted to ready to drink wine.

### On a historic note

Originally wine was kept in containers made of pottery, which were later replaced with wood containers. For serving at the table, smaller recipients were of different shapes and sizes and made of different materials, such as leather, pewter, wood and ceramic. Expensive and fragile, glass was used less often. Only from the 300s, when glass bottles began to be covered with leather or straw to make them more resistant, did the use of glass become more commonplace, but nonetheless these recipients had little in common with today's bottles.

In the 1600s and 1700s in Europe (France and Holland in particular) major innovations developed in the sector of glass-making. In 1652 furnaces with forced ventilation were developed, making it possible to melt a blend of sand, potash and lime, out of which very resistant dark-coloured bottles were made that were the ancestors of today's bottles. At this time the first bottle blowing factories began to spread. Initially they were produced in moulds with square sections to facilitate packaging, then rounded or bubble-shaped bottles, with long necks and convex bases. Only later did the slender, cylindrical form take shape; the mechanical manufacture of bottles dates to the end of the 17th century.

### Types

There are currently available a variety or types of bottles, generally developed out of local traditions in their places of origin, including:

– **Albeisa**: conic-cylindrical shape, created in the area of Alba in the province of Cuneo in the 1970s when a few local producers decided to further characterise their production through the shape of the bottle. It may be observed that the word "Albeisa" is stamped in relief on the glass. This bottle is widely used for great Piedmont wines;

– **Anfora**: used in the Marches for Verdicchio and in Friuli in the area of Cormons, as well as in France for Provence wines.

– **Bordolese**: originally from the French region of Bordeaux, with large shoulders that are useful for catching sediment, often green or brown, it is widely used for red, rosé and white wines for aging or not.

– **Borgognona**: from the region of Burgundy, with a cylindrical-conic shape and sloping shoulders and an indented bottom to create an obstacle for sediment. Fairly dark green or brown, it is widely used for wines that are for aging.

– **Champagnotta**: bottle for spumante, made of particularly thick and resistant glass, adapted to the pressure generated by carbon dioxide. The neck has a thick raised ring to which the wire cage anchoring the mushroom stopper is secured.

– **Fiasco and Chiantigiana**: the first, born in Tuscany in the 14th century, is characterised by its very round form and woven straw covering, created to absorb bumps during transportation. It is now replaced by the Chiantigiana, a bottle that borrows the shape and has a 1.5 litre capacity.

– **Marsalese**: used for liqueur-like wines such as Marsala, as well as for other well-known fortified European wines such as Portuguese Porto, and Spanish Madeira and Sherry.

– **Pulcinella**: a squashed shape, traditionally used for Orvieto wine, but also for Armagnac in France and a few Portuguese wines.

– **Renana (or Alsaziana)**: slim, tapered, shoulderless shape, typical of areas in France and Germany around the Rhine River, traditionally used for white wines with its form that is well-adapted to rapid cooling.

– **Ungherese**: with its 0.5 l capacity, it is the typical container for Hungary's best-known sweet wine called Tokaji Aszù.

# Serving

**The final, but indispensable, consideration for wine, without which all the efforts made and care taken in producing the wine risk being in vain.**

## TEMPERATURE

Temperature is fundamental for serving wine properly. Spumante wines are served at about 8 °C (45 °F), white and dry rosé wines at 10 °C (50 °F), sweeter white and rosé wines 12 °C (55 °F), while red wines should be 14-18 °C (60-65 °F) depending on the amount of tannin and the year. In this regard, more onerous wines, like aged wines, require warmer temperatures than younger wines.

The right temperature optimises the volatilisation of aromatic substances, ideal conditions to fully appreciate the wine's bouquet.

The evaporation of aromas is in fact slowed at low temperatures, while it is favoured by high ones. In the mouth, a wine served at too low a temperature will express "harder" sensations caused by tannin, acidity and sapidity, while a higher temperature will bring out "softer" sensations such as the amount of alcohol and sweetness, thereby creating a different gustatory perception. Higher temperatures can also highlight a wine's defects.

To avoid the temperature rising excessively, it is useful to have a bucket with water and ice or a *glacette* to hold

| BOTTLE FORMATS | |
|---|---|
| Half bottle | 0.375 litres |
| Bottle | 0.75 litres |
| Magnum | 2 bottles - 1.5 litres |
| Jeroboam | 4 bottle - 3 litres |
| Rehoboam | 6 bottles - 4.5 litres |
| Mathusalem | 8 bottles - 6 litres |
| Salmanazar | 12 bottles - 9 litres |
| Balthazar | 16 bottles - 12 litres |
| Nabuchodonosor | 20 bottles - 15 litres |

© Albo/Shutterstock

white, spumante and often rosé wines throughout their service.

If it is necessary to cool a white, spumante or rosé wine rapidly, a handful of salt may be put in the ice bucket to help melt the ice and cool the bottle; specific wine cooling sleeves are also very useful.

Wine should absolutely never be placed in the freezer because doing so may alter the sensorial characteristics of the product. Fast Chillers are rapidly finding their way into restaurants, wine shops and wine bars, where they cool bottles to the desired temperature in just a few minutes.

If wine is too cold, however, the bottle may be sunk into a basin of water at 25 °C (77 °F). Wine should never be placed near sources of high temperatures (ovens, radiators, stoves and others) because the thermal shock could compromise the harmony of the product. In order to preserve the wine's balance it should be brought to the desired temperature slowly and gradually.

Wines are delicate, particularly aged ones, thus in their move from cellar to table brusque movements should be avoided; care is truly important for transport.

## UNCORKING

Opening a bottle begins with cutting around the aluminium or plastic capsule just beneath the raised ring at the end of the bottleneck, followed by a vertical cut to remove the capsule. After cleaning the bottleneck, the corkscrew is carefully inserted in the exact centre and turned until it has reached the full

length of the cork without piercing through it to avoid pieces of cork falling into the wine. Then, if using a sommelier's knife, brace the fulcrum arm on the lip of the wine bottle to use it as a lever to pull the cork out of the bottle. If the fulcrum has two notches, shift to the second notch for more leverage. When most of the cork is out, twist or wiggle it a little to finish removing it without making an inelegant pop. The cork may be sniffed to check for unpleasant odours. Clean the edge of the bottle to remove any cork residue then taste the wine for defects.

For sparkling wines, remove the foil covering on the wire cage, hold the neck of the bottle firmly in the left hand with the thumb on the cork, then untwist the wire cage with the right hand and remove it, rotate the bottle with the left hand while grasping the cork in the right hand with a cloth until it is eased out without a loud pop.

| SERVING TEMPERATURE | |
|---|---|
| Spumante | 7-9 °C |
| Dry whites and rosés | 9-11 °C |
| Whites and rosés with residual sugar | 11-13 °C |
| Reds low in tannin | 13-15 °C |
| Reds with medium tannin | 15-17 °C |
| Reds heavy in tannin | 17-19 °C |
| Passito and liqueur-like wine | 8-18 °C |

# INTRODUCTION

## SERVING

Wine should be served by holding the bottle by the bottom. Women should be served first, and then men respecting age. At a large table guests are served from the right proceeding clockwise around the table. Glasses should be filled no more than two-thirds full.

For a several course meal, white wines are generally served before the reds, young wines before aged wines, light wines before more structured ones. Moreover, wines should be served in order of serving temperatures and alcohol content from the lowest up. In keeping with this rule, sparkling wines are usually served first, followed by whites, then rosés, then light reds before more structured reds and finally sweet and liqueur-like wine.

These rules may even be applied in the varied world of sparkling wines, in which crémant are served first, followed by brut sans année (the *blanc de noirs* follow the *blanc de blancs*), then vintage years or special *cuvées*, and finally *demisec* and sweet.

These are of course general rules that are by no means inviolable: every wine and every meal has its own story and may be evaluated in a case-by-case manner.

## GLASSES

In wine appreciation, the role of glasses should not be underestimated, as they alone are able to valorise or even penalise the bouquet. Moreover, each wine has different characteristics, and thus it is necessary to choose the form of the glass that enhances the experience.

On the table, glasses should be placed to the right of the setting, above the knife and spoon, and they should be arranged in order of height with the smallest outermost, the glass for white wine will thus be closer to one's dining companion on the right, then follow the reds. The water glass should be placed to the left of those for wine.

### On a historic note

Glasses have been used by humanity since very ancient times. At first they were made from a variety of materials such as clay, wood and precious and less precious metals; Egyptians and Persians used cattle horns, the Greeks used shells.

Glass was invented in 4000 BC but the use of glass glasses developed only in the 1st century BC.

The Romans learned the art of glass making from the Syrians and greatly appreciated the use of this material for drinking. Forms, colours and decoration varied over the centuries. Large glasses with long stems and tulip-shaped bowls were very popular in the 12th century especially among the wealthier classes. In the 15th century cylindrical glasses without stems became widespread among all social classes.

In a few cases glass making became a veritable art form, as in Venice which has been recognised for the finesse of the works in glass produced there since the year 1000. Venetian glass production was concentrated on the island of Murano from the end of the 13th century resulting in the Island's becoming the emblem of this type of craftsmanship. The art of glass making also developed in Florence and in Altare, near Savona. Italian skill in this craft was recognised and renowned throughout Europe, but in the 17th century when new tech-

© Zaichenko Olga/Shutterstock

© Zamula Artem/Shutterstock

niques for glass-working developed in Bohemia and England, conquering the European and American markets, the Italian craft lost ground. While in Venice soda continued to be used in glass production, in England lead glass came into use and in Bohemia potassium glass was made, these brighter products were easier to work and led to the realization of precious transparent crystal. In the same period French crystalware flourished. It was in the 19th century that crystalware was at the height of splendour with magnificent table services.

## Materials

Glass is made of sand, lime, soda and sometimes magnesite; crystal, instead, contains potash – rather than soda – and lead compounds. The latter is more precious because this glass wins for its density, brightness, transparency, refractivity and pure colour.

The production of glasses is said to be "hollow glass" and is done by blowing, pressing and centrifuging. The ancient rite is very fascinating: the craftsman takes a blowhose from the annealing pot of molten glass and makes a bubble by blowing, this bubble is then worked and modelled into the desired shape. The need for rapid production and identically shaped objects led to an evolution in the technique and the perfection of special nozzles. In 19th-century England a system for pressing glass was developed to shape glass by using a mold and a plunger to determine the shape and thickness. Centrifuging is a specific moulding operation in which the vitreous mass is poured into a rotating mould.

## The shape

The ideal glass for tasting wine is transparent, thin, colourless, smooth, with a tulip-shaped bowl and a long stem to hold it by. The rim of the bowl should be inclined towards the inside to limit the dispersion of aromas. Its size depends on the wine: the broader the bowl, the easier it is to perceive the aromas, making the *balloon* (particularly large glasses) ideal for very good aged wines, while narrow bowls are indicated for young, white wines. To prevent the wine from being heated by the warmth of one's hand, the glass should be held by the stem or the base of the glass.

© Nikola Bilic/Shutterstock

It should be noted that a glass's shape conditions the drinker's posture: glasses with broad openings encourage large sips, lowering the head, putting the taster in the ideal position for fully appreciating the wine's aftertaste; a narrow opening forces the drinker to recline the head and drink in small sips, limiting the flow of wine and directing it towards specific areas of the tongue.

One could say that large (*balloon*) and bellied glasses are ideal for well-aged, full-bodied wines; slender glasses with long stems and dimensions in proportion to the complexity of the wine are ideal for light wines, young reds and nouveau wines; rosés do well in flared glasses; medium-sized glasses are for whites that are aged or have more body, significant spumantes and reds with good body; elongated slim bowls (flute) for light spumantes and semisparkling wines in order to appreciate the perlage and freshness; apple-shaped with a broad base and a narrow opening for particularly acidic wines; small eggshaped bowls, for dessert wines, including sweet wines, and for aromatic Asti Spumante: the characteristic coupe.

Regardless of shape, glasses should never be filled more than two-thirds to avoid the dispersion of aromas. More precisely, for the best conditions for appreciation, it is estimated that the ideal quantity to pour for red wines is 6 cl; for young reds, whites and rosés 5-5.5 cl; for spumantes 7.5 cl. For water, only 1.2 cl should be poured to avoid it getting too warm or having the carbonation disperse before it is drunk.

## Cleaning

For proper tasting, glasses should be perfectly clean and thoroughly odourless. Proper washing is thus fundamental whether it is done by hand or machine. The first procedure is preferable to avoid damaging the brightness of the glass. It is important to wash and rinse glasses several times with hot water, and rinse aids and abrasives should be avoided. The best detergents are neutral and fragrance-free. Glasses should then be carefully dried with white, perfumefree towels that do not leave lint. If when holding them up to the light the glasses are not perfectly dry and sparkling, they should be wiped with a dry lint-free cloth.

Glasses should be stored in odourless locations away from wood, paper, food and any other sources of fragrances or aromas. When they are removed from the cupboard, to be placed on the table, they should be checked for cleanliness, clearness and odourlessness; in any case it is a good practice to wipe them with a clean, dry cloth before using them.

## ACCESSORIES

Uncorking and serving wine require a series of accessories, some are indispensable such as the corkscrew, others are more decorative. Prices vary depending on the material out of which they are made.

### Corkscrews

Many models exist including, screw and lever models. The professional corkscrew, which is practical, pocket-size and compact, is the most widespread and functional. At the centre of its handle it has a 6 cm long helix (also called a worm) that sticks out perpendicularly when it is open. The handle also has a small knife that opens out to cut the capsule.
Also available are two-lever, spiral, mon-olever and wall-mounted corkscrews as well as many other models to fit all tastes and all budgets. It is no surprise that there are avid collectors.

### Decanter

Another object that comes in captivating forms is the decanter, which is a glass or crystal carafe, with a large base and narrow neck, its goal is to oxygenate wines that need their aromas revived, and to separate the wine from eventual residues and sediments. Decanting is a very fascinating operation: first the outside of the carafe is heated with hot water, then the interior is rinsed with a bit of wine by rotating it onto the sides of the vessel. This priming of the glass or carafe is called *avvinamento*. Finally the contents of the bottle are poured very slowly into the decanter, paying careful attention not to pour out the deposit. To prevent the sediment from finding its way into the decanter, a candle may be used to observe when the residue begins to approach the bottleneck, at which point decanting is stopped.

A special **funnel** may also be used that has a filter precisely for this purpose, making the operation more manageable. A well-aged wine requires more aeration, and thus must be decanted a sufficient number of hours prior to serving.

After use, the decanter, should be washed with water – no detergents – and left to drip dry upside down.

## Everything and then some...

Among the many other accessories available at the wine shop that may be used to serve wine are:

– the **foil cutter**, useful for cutting and removing the capsule covering the cork;

– the **tastevin**, a small, round, usually silver, cup about 8 cm wide and 2 cm deep, it has a thumb rest with a ring underneath it, as well as a convex bottom, some sommeliers wear it on a chain to taste wine to ensure its condition before serving it to guests;

– the **bottle basket**, useful for transporting wines from cellar to table, particularly for wines that have been aged for a long time as it holds the bottle in a horizontal position reducing the risk of sediment shifting in the bottom;

Wolfgang Amri/Shutterstock

– the **cork grip**, useful for extracting mushroom corks from spumante and semi-sparkling wines, has a toothed jaw to firmly grip the cork and eventually wire cutters to cut the metal wires on the cage anchoring the cork;

– the **bucket**, for holding water and ice to keep the bottle cool; it should be filled three-quarters full and a clean cloth should be kept handy to dry the bottle before serving;

– the **glacette**, a double-walled thermal container for maintaining the temperature of the bottle;

– the **wine-cooling sack and the fast chiller** are both capable of rapidly cooling bottles. The first is a folding bag about 25 cm tall containing a cooling liquid that is stored in the freezer until needed, at which point the bottle is inserted and reaches the desired temperature in ten minutes or so. The latter is an electric temperature dropper;

– the **thermometer**, useful for checking the temperature of wine; it is dropped into the neck of the bottle or placed in the glass;

– the **drip catcher** and **drop stop** prevent dripping during service. The first is a metal ring with absorbent felt inside it that is slipped around the bottle neck; the second is a thin round leaf of aluminium and pvc that is rolled and inserted into the bottle neck upon serving.

To seal an unfinished bottle, it is wise to eliminate air using a **vacuum pump** in combination with especially designed corks; there are also special devices for spumante and semi-sparkling wines that maintain and even revive the *perlage*.

# Accompanying wine

There is nothing more satisfying to the taste buds than the harmonious union of food and wine. In this regard there are basic guidelines, although there are no inviolable rules regarding pairing: personal taste must always prime, whether it concerns choosing a main course or a wine. Other variables that should be taken into consideration are the atmosphere, setting, company, mood. Any one dish may be served with a variety of wines depending on whether it is a romantic dinner for two or a business lunch or an evening with friends; being at home or in an elegant versus informal restaurant also affects choice.

## EQUIVALENCES, CONTRASTS AND HARMONY

Beyond these considerations that are all subjective and difficult to evaluate, the first variable to consider in order to make the right choice is the **equivalence** between the intensity, persistence and structure of aromas and perfumes of the food and those of the wine. A complex dish, with an intense and persistent aroma requires a wine with similar characteristics that is just as rich and structured; delicate dishes call for light wines. The goal is to not have the wine overwhelmed by the aromatic strength of a dish and viceversa.

It is noteworthy how food and wine can balance one another through a pairing based on the **contrast** or **similarity** of gustatory perceptions. For example a flavourful or spicy dish may be rounded out by smooth wines, just as a fatty dish will benefit from pairing with a light, acidic wine or better yet a tannic one or a spumante, whose characteristics are able to soften the dish's unctuous quality. When wines are paired based on similarity however, food and wine follow the same trend and sweet dishes are served with sweet wines.

Another recommended praxis to follow is **local-regional pairing** meaning a wine produced in a certain territory is served with dishes and products from the same zone. Thus, a Florentine t-bone steak will be served with a Tuscan wine such as Chianti, *lepre in civet* (jugged hare) with Barbaresco, *risotto alla milanese* with a Franciacorta and so on.

## THE RIGHT CRESCENDO

A meal with several courses and several wines should ideally evolve in a gradual crescendo of gustatory complexity. Starting with the first course and a wine with a strong and persistent flavour could, in fact penalise the dishes and wines that follow. Thus it is best to start with delicate **hors d'oeuvres** and light fresh wines, and continue with richer white, rosé or red wines, served with more complex first courses, followed by a flavourful main course served with pronounced red wines or structured whites, and closing with a dessert wine to accompany sweets. The basic concept of this rule

is simple, it is enough to imagine how difficult it would be to enjoy a delicate white wine after a structured red, just as it would not be very pleasant to drink a tannic red after a sweet wine because due to the order it would taste particularly bitter.

## TO EACH HIS OWN

Delicate *hors d'oeuvres* made of vegetables or fish require fresh white or rosé wines, or better yet a spumante; more complex ones – with meat, coldcuts or mushrooms – should be paired with red wines or persistent whites.

When it comes to **first courses** the sauce will determine the counterpart. Generally speaking if the recipe has fish, vegetables or legumes among the ingredients white or rosé wines should be selected, while with meat, truffles and mushrooms a red wine should be preferred. Caution should be exercised with regard to preparations such as *cacciucco* (fish chowder) and *guazzetto* (fish stew) so the most appropriate choice is a full-bodied rosé or a red. The rule that the condiment is the variable to be considered is also true for pizza, which goes well with wine even if beer is often the beverage of choice.

**Red meats** and game go with red wines of equivalent complexity and structure, while white meats go well with rosés or medium bodied whites.

Delicate **fish-based preparations** go well with an equally fine wine, so white wines are preferred, but if the dish has a sauce or is particularly rich a rosé or light red may be appropriate. Fatty and smoked fish do better with spumante or white wines with more body.

**Cold cuts** call for spumante as the effervescence softens the fattiness otherwise white, red or rosés with sufficient acidity to cleanse the palate of the film of fat usually left behind by coldcuts.

For **eggs** there are white wines that are smooth and rich, while **vegetables** are accompanied well by smooth white wines that have enough body to go with the preparation; tomato-based sauces or dips call for medium-bodied rosés or reds. Salads dressed with wine vinegar or lemon should not be served with wine.

Choosing wines to go with **cheese** is rather complicated: the more intense the flavour of the cheese the more full-

© Svetlana Lukienko/Shutterstock

bodied the wine needs to be, thus ricotta and mozzarella go with delicate white wines, medium ripened cheeses with full-bodied white wines, and well-ripened cheeses with structured red wines that have low tannin, while those with a more pungent flavour, such as veined cheeses, may be served with sweet or liqueur-like wines.

**Desserts** go with sweet wines that are equally intense, persistent and complex. Particularly noteworthy is the fact that cold inhibits taste buds, so ice cream is a dessert that does not go well with wine, but eventually a smooth, sweet, delicate wine would work if required.

**Chocolate**, meanwhile goes well with sweet, liqueur-like wines.

## WINE AS AN INGREDIENT

Wine also plays an interesting role in cuisine in the preparation of sauces and marinades. Since the Middle Ages it has been considered a precious ingredient. In the past it had an antibacterial role and masked odours caused by poor food conservation, unfortunately, however, mediocre wines were used to the detriment of the wholesomeness and flavour of the dish. Today, instead, good wines are used with the result that the dish is even more appetizing. When used in cooking it can soften any sensations that are too sharp, moreover, it is like a solvent with respect to fats which it helps diffuse within the food, and as it evaporates it transports aromas, favouring olfactory sensations.

Its acidity makes dishes fresher and marinating affects the consistency and succulence of food, leaving it more tender, particularly in the case of meat.

The type of wine used in cooking depends on the dish being prepared. Colourful, flavourful and structured dishes suggest the use of red wines, but this is not a steadfast rule.

Recipes in which wine is the protagonist include dishes that have become more commonplace such as *risotto* and *brasato al Barolo* (braised beef in Barolo). Sweet wines, instead, are frequently used to prepare deserts, for example *tiramisù*.

As for accompaniments, the same – or superior – quality of wine should be served as was used to cook.

# Wine and health

**Wine is not just a beverage but also a food and should be treated as such. It should be consumed responsibly and moderately: excess is the enemy of good drink.**

Assumed in a sufficient quantity during meals it can even be an ally of well-being. In particular it stimulates digestion by promoting the secretion of saliva and gastric juices; in small doses it is even able prevent the formation of gallstones, and it stimulates diuresis. It contains potassium – a fundamental element for muscles – iron, copper and other substances that have a positive effect on the circulatory, coronary and cardiovascular systems, reducing the risk of heart attacks.

It has been established that the polyphenols in wine have a benefic effect on blood cholesterol, increasing the "good" cholesterol to the detriment of the "bad" one, thereby preventing arteriosclerosis.

When consumed with good judgment, it prevents cellular aging as it is an enemy of free radicals and stimulates the immune system. It is also an anti-oxidant, antibacterial agent and disinfectant. In excess, instead, wine has negative effects on health: it can irritate the walls of the stomach aggravating ulcers and gastritis, it can cause hepatitis, damage the nervous and circulatory system. Moreover those with weight problems must keep in consideration the fact that ethyl alcohol provides 7 kcal per gram, meaning one litre of wine is a full 700 kcal!

Responsible wine consumption means around 4 glasses of 100 ml a day for men and 2 for women. Obviously it is important to take into consideration the fact that wine is metabolised differently by different organisms, thus each individual has a different limit.

Women and the elderly generally have more problems metabolizing alcohol and thus they are advised to limit consumption.

A final intrigue is that wine, in addition to stimulating the appetite, stimulates, according to some connoisseurs, a desire for foods high in proteins to the detriment of carbohydrates.

# The organic choice

Organic or biodynamic cultivation is increasingly important issues even in the wine world. Organic farming is a method of cultivation that excludes the use of pesticides and synthetic chemical substances and uses only natural systems with a goal to pursuing total environmental respect. This system preserves the fertility of the earth through the use of organic fertilisers, rotating cultivations, sowing to protect the land, non-invasive elaboration, the exclusion of synthetic chemicals, selection of varieties best adapted to this type of farming.

In Europe, legislation began regarding the organic world starting in 1991 with the Regulation CEE 2092. Since then many amendments and integrations have been made necessary, so much so that in July 2000 a new Regulation was enacted: 834-07 that substituted that of 1991 from January 1, 2009. Those countries that acknowledged the European law have provided for the nomination of Authorised certification agencies to guarantee the organic quality of production.

Biodynamic farming is driven by the principal that it is fundamental to take care of land in order to take care of mankind and viceversa, in a global vision in which man, earth, animals and the entire universe in all its forms are part of a single cosmic project in which every element is correlated to the others. In this vision, the fertility of land must therefore be preserved and motivated by carefully maintaining the humus in good condition, to the full advantage of human health.

The seeds used must be vital in order to produce foods that strengthen man's psychic-physical wellbeing. Mineral, vegetable and animal elements all move in unison for the wellbeing of all, operating in nature without damaging, impoverishing or polluting, but rather in an attempt to revitalise the environment, thanks to the strengths that generate and move life. Thus we understand that farming is a true and proper philosophy of life.

The first to lay the foundations for biodynamic farming was the Austrian scholar **Rudolf Steiner** in the Twenties, and in his wake, the Englishman Albert Howard perfected the first forms of organic fertiliser, while the method of organic-biological cultivation was begun in the Thirties by the Swiss **Hans Müller** and then perfected by the German Doctor **Rusch**.

# Speaking wine language

In Italian there are many specific words to talk about wine that have original and evocative sounds that recount all the outstanding subtleties to be found in a glass of wine.

**Abboccato-Demi-sec**: wine that offers a slight sensation of sweetness.

**Acerbo-Sour**: wine that is slightly sour and disharmonious in the mouth because it is too young.

**Acescenza-Ascetic**: an alteration that causes the wine to become vinegar.

**Affinamento-Refinement**: stage in the aging of wine following maturation that coincides with a period of evolution and stabilization in wood barrels or in bottles.

**Allappante-Astringent**: when wine causes puckering due to the presence of excessive tannins.

**Amabile-Mellow**: wine in which one can distinguish a sweet taste.

**Ambrato-Amber**: white wine with amber tones.

**Ampio-Full-bodied**: refers to a complex and varied perfume.

**Antociani-Anthocyanins**: pigments in the berry skins.

**Appassimento-Withering**: dehydration of the grape berries in order to concentrate sugars and aromatic substances.

**Aranciato-Orange coloured**: red-orange tone typical of red wines that have been very well aged.

**Aromatico-Aromatic**: wines with perfumes that stand out, proffering the natural odoriferous characteristics of the vine species it comes from.

**Assemblaggio-Blending**: the combination of different wines or grapes; synonymous with *blend* or *cuvée*.

**Barrique-Oak barrel**: small oak barrel with a capacity of about 225 litres used for aging wine.

**Bouquet**: the array of aromatic components of a wine.

**Brillante-Bright**: wine that is so limpid, luminous and transparent that it reflects light, which is generally related to the presence of *perlage*.

**Caldo-Hot**: wines with high alcohol that give the impression of "heat" when tasted.

**Carente-Empty**: wine lacking bouquet and depth.

© Sjeade/Shutterstock

**Corpo-Body**: related to the extract, or what remains after volatile substances have been evaporated: tannins, acids, mineral salts, sugars and pectic substances.

**Corto-Short**: wine with an aroma and flavour that are not very persistent.

**Cristallino-Crystalline**: wine with no particles in suspension and having its own luminosity.

**Cru**: term of French origin that indicates a plot of vineyard that is particularly good.

**Debole-Weak**: wine with little structure.

**Dorato-Golden**: white wine with a yellow tone tending toward gold.

**Enologia-Enology**: discipline and technique covering the science of wine and winemaking.

**Equilibrato-Balanced**: wine in which the smooth sensations (from sugars, alcohols and polyalcohols) and hard ones (from mineral salts, tannins and acids) are balanced.

**Etereo-Ethereal**: used to describe the fragrance derived from aging.

**Fecce-Lees or dregs**: residue left over from fermentation composed of skins, grape seeds and stalks eliminated through transfers.

# INTRODUCTION

**Fermentazione alcolica-Alcoholic fermentation**: process during which yeasts transform the sugars from the grape berries into alcohol and carbon dioxide.

**Fermentazione malolattica-Malolactic fermentation**: process during which bacteria transform malic acid from the grapes into Lactic acid.

**Fine**: a wine is considered fine when it has a good taste-olfactory quality, is elegant and balanced.

**Floreale-Flowery**: wine with a floral fragrance.

**Franco**: clean and precise fragrance specific to the typology of the vine species.

**Fresco-Fresh**: wine that is sufficiently acidic.

**Fruttato-Fruity**: wine with a fruity fragrance.

**Glicerina-Glycerol**: a member of the family of polyalcohols that plays an important role in determining the consistency and the extract of a wine.

**Granato-Garnet coloured**: particular red tonality typical of moderately aged red wines.

**Immaturo-Immature**: wine that is not yet ready for consumption.

**Leggero-Light**: wine with low alcohol content.

**Limpidezza-Clear**: absence of suspended particles.

**Magro-Thin**: bodiless wine.

**Maturazione-Maturation**: first phase of aging wine that happens in large recipients made of cement, fibreglass, wood or steel.

**Molle-Flaccid**: wine lacking in tannic acid.

**Morbido-Soft**: wine with a good concentration of alcohol and glycerol.

**Oidio-Oidium**: fungus that attacks the vine.

**Ossidazione-Oxidation**: chemical reaction due to contact of wine with oxygen.

**Paglierino-Straw yellow**: white wine with a yellow, straw-coloured hue.

**Pastoso-Pasty**: excessively soft, very alcoholic wine rich in glycerol.

**Peronospora**: parasite that attacks the vine.

**Persistente-Persistent**: said of a wine with a long-lasting perfume and flavour.

**Piatto-Flat**: not very acidic, not very fresh wine.

**Porpora**: reddish-purple tonality that recalls the typical cardinal colour of young red wines. Pronto-Ready: wine in its ideal period to drink.

**Robusto-Robust**: very structured wine.

**Rubino-Ruby**: tone of red like the gem.

**Speziato-Spicy**: wine that has aromas recalling spices.

**Spigoloso-Sharp**: not very soft.

**Stucchevole-Velvety**: an excessively sweet wine.

**Velato-Veiled**: wine with suspended particles.

**Verdolino-Greenish-yellow**: a tone of yellow found in very young, light, fresh white wines.

**Vinoso-Vinous**: a young wine with the typical perfumes of vinification, of fermenting skins and seeds.

# THE ITALY OF WINE

Italy boasts front stage positioning in today's wine production worldwide, amongst the main wine producers. 36% of Italy's territory is mountainous, 42% hilly, 22% planes; viticulture is widespread throughout much of the country, and is particularly concentrated in hilly areas where, moreover, the best wine is produced.

© Valeria/Shutterstock

## On a historic note

The land of Italy, of Miocene origin, is very well adapted to viticulture. Grapevines were already known in prehistoric times and the fact that grape juices fermented naturally was an acquired fact. We only know of viticulture and winemaking techniques from the 2nd millennium BC when first Creto-Mycenaean civilisations and then, Phoenician and Greek ones spread their know-how to many Italian coastal areas, where they introduced sapling cultivation, which is still used in many regions.

### ETRUSCANS AND ROMANS

The **Etruscans made a decisive** contribution to the development of vine cultivation. When Rome was founded in 753 BC Lazio was one of the areas on the peninsula with the fewest vineyards, whereas Greek dominion in the south of Italy and Etruscan in central Italy had been influential even from this point of view. With Rome's gradual rise in power, the **Romans** learned the uses and customs of the populations it controlled and embarked upon viticulture, and even perfected techniques and became great amateurs and promoters. A protagonist of bacchanal pleasures and more cultivated symposia (a term derived from the Greek expression meaning "drink together"), wine became a symbol of social aggregation. For the most part these wines were diluted with water and flavoured with honey and spices. Many Roman scholars wrote about wine, including the poet **Horace** and **Pliny the Elder** who mentioned oenology in *Naturalis Historia*, listing over one hundred wines in the Roman Empire.

The spread of winemaking techniques to populations conquered during the Age of Augustus brought about the capillary spread of grapevines and wine.

### THE MIDDLE AGES

With the fall of the Empire and the advent of Barbarian invasions, vine cultivation came to a sudden halt. Fortunately this tradition was maintained in the monasteries throughout the Middle Ages. It was not until the 9th century, however, that the spread of viticulture picked up again with Charlemagne, who encouraged such cultivation and working the land in general.

In the 900s Arabs in Sicily encouraged the cultivation of grapevines, and table grapes in particular. In 1000 Maritime Republics developed and with these commerce with the Orient, which included wine.

Periods of famine and drought led to a gradual reduction in the consumption of water – often unwholesome – and renewed interest in wine – no longer watered down – and it was considered a veritable food.

The revival of viniviticulture gradually spread, until the 16th-17th century when its renaissance could be felt in every region of Italy.

## THE MODERN ERA

In 1710 Cosimo III de' Medici delimited the principal areas with a vocation for wine growing and production in Tuscany – Carmignano, Pomino, Valdarno, Chianti – anticipating what would become the philosophy on which the definition of today's *denominazione d'origine*, or appellation, is founded. It is difficult to imagine Renaissance and Baroque festivities without wine, a symbol of wealth and social status; among the less well-to-do classes instead spread the frequent use of hostelries, where wine could be drunk by the chalice.

Towards the end of the **18th century** wines from Burgundy and Cyprus were well accepted on the peninsula. Industrialised production of Marsala and Vermouth, a flavoured wine, began at this time as well.

A few great figures who made their mark on Italian history in the 19th century contributed to the relaunch of viticulture: **Camillo Benso di Cavour** was fundamental to Barolo, **Bettino Ricasoli** for Chianti and **Garibaldi**, during his travels up the boot, informed farmers about the risks of oidium, a fungal disease affecting vines that was spreading.

In addition to oidium, between the end of the 19th century and the beginning of the 20th two other scourges plagued vineyards: **phylloxera** and **peronospora**. The crop was almost completely destroyed; this emergency was handled by grafting the vines on American bases – immune to this contagion – and replanting the vineyards, sometimes preferring international vine species over local ones – French ones in particular – such as Merlot, Cabernet, Pinot, Riesling.

At the beginning of the 20th century laws were issued prohibiting the adulteration of wines, but viticulture was plagued again by the two World Wars. Only after 1950 could Italian wines try to find a new identity.

Despite a few scandals and frauds, since the post-war period efforts have been made to recuperate native vine species, with more intense selection of grape berries, experimentation with new vine growing and wine production techniques, as well as research and innovation to improve the quality of production, even to the detriment of quantity.

# A few notions of legislature

European Community regulations lie behind the onset of intense national legislation that lead to the creation of the IGT, DOC and DOCG, in addition to an array of regulations. The situation is evolving even further with the only labels valid in the European Union from August 2009 being the DOP (Denominazione di Origine Protetta-Protected Denomination of Origin) and IGP (Indicazione Geografica Protetta-Protected Geographic Origin), assigned by Brussels rather then on a national level.

© Patricia Hofmeester/Shutterstock

## IGT, DOC, DOCG, VQPRD...

In terms of regulations, wines produced in Italy are classified as **Vini da Tavola**, IGT (Indicazione Geografica Tipica-Priotected Geographic Indication), DOC (Denominazione di Origine Controllata-Controlled Denomination of Origin) and DOCG (Controlled and Guaranteed Denomination of Origin).

Little may be said about the first, there are very good and very mediocre alike, because they are left to the discretion of the producers. **IGT** regulations, instead, require indications of the production area on the label: this offers consumers a guarantee with regard to origin.

**DOC** wines must follow rigid specifications for production regulated by the production area: minimum percentage of alcohol, the duration of refinement, maximum production, vine species and so on.

The most prestigious label is **DOCG**, which in addition to following very precise regulations regarding production, the wines also undergo very rigorous quality controls. DOCG is attributed to very precious wines that are DOC wines at least 5 years old. Today there are just over seventy DOCG wines, while DOC applies to several hundred.

In some cases the name of the denomination of origin makes use of the name of the vine species used to produce the wine, some that come to mind are Picolit and Barbera, in other cases the name comes from the area of production, as in the case of Taurasi, Franciacorta, Chianti,

Bardolino, Conero. Finally references to the vine species and the region may be combined: Fiano di Avellino, Greco di Tufo, Montepulciano d'Abruzzo, Albana di Romagna, Brachetto d'Acqui and so on. On the level of the European Community, DOC and DOCG are among the socalled **VQPRD** (Vini di Qualità Prodotti in Regione Determinata-**Quality Wines Produced in Determined Regions**). Other classifications in force in the European Community are: **VLQPRD** (Vino Liquoroso di Qualità Prodotto in Regione Determinata-**Quality Sweet Wines Produced in Determined Regions**), VSQPRD (Vino Spumante di Qualità Prodotto in Regione Determinata-**Quality Spumante Wines Produced in Determined Regions**) and VFQPRD (Vino Frizzante di Qualità Prodotto in Regione Determinata-**Quality Sparkling Wines Produced in Determined Regions**).

Regarding spumante wines, a further distinction needs to be made: for generic **Vino Spumante** there are no specific limitations as to the duration of the production process, it should have at least 3 atm of pressure and a minimum alcoholic strength of 9.5%. **Vino Spumante di Qualità (VSQ)**, instead, has a minimum production period of 6 months using large vats or 9 months in bottles, secondary fermentation in contact with the lees should last at least 3 months, or if a tank with a mixer is used the time may be reduced to 30 days, the actual alcoholic content should be at least 10% and minimum pressure 3.5 atm. **Vino Spumante di Qualità Aroma-**

tico made with aromatic grape berries without requiring contact with the lees, should have a production period of at least one month and actual alcoholic strength by volume of at least 6%, and a final alcoholic content of at least 10%, with pressure of at least 3 atm. The definition **Vino Spumante di Qualità Prodotto in Regione Determinata (VSQPRD)** follows the same parameters of the VSQ but identifies spumantes as DOC and DOCG. Finally, **Vino Spumante di Qualità Prodotto in Regione Determinata di tipo Aromatico** is a DOC or DOCG spumante wine made using aromatic grape berries.

The case of "**novelli**" wines is also particular. By law they may be defined as such only if at least 30% of the grape berries have undergone carbonic maceration, if they have a total alcoholic content of at least 11° with maximum residual sugar of 10 grams; in addition they must go on sale from November 6, while bottling must take place before December 31 of the production year.

## THE LABEL

The label is a veritable identity card for wine and provides many useful details, so it is important to be able to read it. Its purpose is to provide information and the information on it must follow national and European community legislation in force. Every type of wine must, or may, relate a series of details on the label, some of which are optional and others obligatory, depending on the regulations in force. This is particularly true for wines that are IGT and VQPRD (or DOC and DOCG), as they must respect specific production processes that necessarily have implications on the information provided on the label. For all wines it is **compulsory** to mention the batch number, the volume of the bottle's contents, the European label for packaging, the name or company name and headquarters of the bottler, the Country the wine was bottled in (if destined for export), the actual alcoholic content, indications for disposal of the packaging.

Mentioning the name and colour of the wine, on the other hand, is **optional**, as are the type of product, indications and recommendations of different kinds (regarding food accompaniment, storage, characteristics, aging, history of the wine or its producer), the final alcohol content (calculated by adding the actual alcohol content and the potential from unfermented available sugars), wine brand, the name or company name and headquarters of the wine's producer and distributor if different from the bottler. In addition to the afore-mentioned remarks, for IGT it is also compulsory to indicate the geographic area of production and the eventual sub area, while mentioning the variety of vine species, the year, any terms that may reinforce the prestige of the producer, the mention "novello" are all optional.

Instead of the IGT mention, in the Aosta Valley "*Vin de Pays*" is allowed, while in the Alto Adige "*Landwein*" is used.

The name of the vine species used to produce a certain wine may be mentioned only if it is characteristic, recognised and if the wine is made entirely or at least 85% out of that particular grape. A similar rule applies to the mention of the year, which may be made only if at least 85% of the grapes used in that wine production were harvested in the year on the label.

In addition to what has been established for table and IGT wines, for VQPRD wines it is compulsory to include the name of the region of production on the label, and the mention VQPRD, VSQPRD, VFQPRD, VLQPRD, DOC or DOCG; the latter acronyms may be substituted by

"Asti" and "Marsala" for those wines. The name of the sub-regions of the production, instead, is optional, as is the vine species the grape come from, other complementary remarks, and the type of elaboration.

Also not compulsory are useful indications such as: "**Superiore**" suggesting that the wine has a higher alcohol content than the basic version; "**Riserva**" for wines that undergo a longer aging period than usual; "**Classico**", a reference reserved for wines produced in the sub-regions with the oldest tradition within the denomination.

**Spumante wines** benefit from special regulations so that even the label has its own peculiarities. First and foremost it must say whether it is a Vino Spumante, a Vino Spumante di Qualità, a Vino Spumante di Qualità di tipo Aromatico, Vino Spumante di Qualità Prodotto in una Regione Determinata or Vino Spumante di Qualità Prodotto in una Regione Determinata di tipo Aromatico. Another fundamental piece of information is whether or not it has undergone any artificial carbonation process through the addition of carbon dioxide rather than secondary fermentation. The mention of the type of spumante is also important: Extra Brut, Brut, Extra Dry, Dry or Secco, Demi-sec or Semisecco, Dolce (Sweet).

Providing the year of the harvest on the label is optional, as is the process used to make it such as "Metodo Classico" or other similar mention and the variety of vine species.

For all types of wine the indications on the label must not be presented in such a manner as to deceive the consumer.

Every statement, be it compulsory or optional, is regulated in terms of how it is written and positioned on the label. In some cases, specifications for a certain denomination may require some indications, usually optional ones, to be imperatively mentioned for wines falling under that regulation.

# Italy's main wines and vine species

The array of vine species present in Italy today is broad and variegated: alongside the primary types that are cultivated everywhere, such as Merlot, Cabernet Sauvignon, Cabernet Franc, Pinot Nero, Pinot Bianco, Pinot Grigio, Chardonnay, Sauvignon, Riesling, Gewürztraminer, Syrah. There are many native varieties originating in and typical of certain regions of Italy, such as Nero d'Avola, Marzemino, Nebbiolo. The vine species recommended and authorised by legislation are more than 300, including the most cultivated and widespread Sangiovese, followed by Barbera, Trebbiano Toscano, Moscato Bianco, Malvasia Bianca, Montepulciano.

Sometimes wines bear the same name as the vine species used to make it, for example Aglianico, other times the same vine species results in several different wines with different names, as in the case of Nebbiolo which is used to produce Barolo, Barbaresco and others still. Following is an inexhaustive list of the most characteristic vine species in Italy's oenological panorama:

## AGLIANICO

One of the best vine species producing black grapes in the south, where its best expressions are found in Campania and Basilicata, but they are also successfully cultivated in Puglia and Molise. These grapes produce fresh and fruity rosés and well-structured long-lived red wines. It was brought to Italy by the Greeks in the 8th century BC and its name is derived from the term *Hellenico*, in honour of its origins.

## BARBERA

Vine species bearing black grape berries cultivated throughout much of the peninsula, it is closely linked to the Piedmont region, its elect land. It produces well-structured red wines with a characteristic harsh and acidic note. Its name would appear to be derived from *barba*, a term that represents its intricate origins well, and *albera*, because in the past it was planted in some wooded areas in the place of trees.

## CANNONAU

Red wine species symbolising Sardinia, it is thought to have been introduced to the island by Spaniards in the 15th century. Today in Spain it is called *Garnacha*, while in France and the Aosta Valley it is known as Grenache. It likes climates that are both dry and humid, so it has found its ideal habitat in Sardinia. It produces strong and structured red wines.

## CORVINA

Typically Venetian grape species with red berries that is key, together with Rondinella and Mulinara, to the production of wines such as **Bardolino**, **Valpolicella** and **Amarone**. It results in full-bodied, round wines with a great deal of personality, intense colour.

## FALANGHINA

A white vine species from Campania that produces fresh white wines that are fruity and soft. Already known in the Roman era.

## FIANO

Ancient variety of white grapes from the South of Italy, the region of Avellino in particular. Produces white wines adapted to aging and excellent sweet wines. Confers a typical note of toasted hazelnut.

## LAGREIN

A vine species that grows in the Trentino and Alto Adige regions where it produces fruity red wines with good potential for aging and fresh, fragrant rosé wines.

## LAMBRUSCO

It's name is derived from that of the wild grapes known as *"vitis labrusca"*. This vine species produces red wines – both still and sparkling – very fresh, flavourful and fruity. It is primarily cultivated in Emilia Romagna and the region of Mantova.

## MALVASIA

This name identifies an extensive family of aromatic vine species. Cultivated throughout much of Italy, many of these are white, others are black. While each variety has its own particularity, they all present a characteristic vegetal, floral, as well as musky and fruity scent. The name is derived from Monembasia, a Byzantine city in Peloponnesus. The Venetians first commercialised the sweet wines produced in those regions in Europe and introduced the vine species to Italy.

## MOSCATO

The term Moscato, or Muscat, identifies a large family of aromatic vines, some of which are white and others black. The name would appear to derive from *"muscum"* for its characteristic musky aromatic note that distinguishes the vine species. Moscato Bianco is one of the vine species with white berries that is the most farmed in Italy and contributes to the production of many wines that have Denomination of Origin throughout the peninsula. Some connoisseurs maintain that it was already known and appreciated by ancient Greeks and Romans.

## MONTEPULCIANO

A black grape berry from the Abruzzo region that then spread throughout southern-central Italy. The wines made with Montepulciano (which have nothing to do with Nobile di Montepulciano, which is produced with Sangiovese grapes) are an intense ruby colour, with the aromas of red and black fruit, as well as cinnamon and nutmeg.

## NEBBIOLO

A great vine species from the Piedmont region used to produce wines such as **Barolo**, **Barbaresco**, **Ghemme**, **Gattinara** and **Valtellina** in Lombardy. Its name comes from the word "nebbia" meaning fog because it is harvested between October and November when Autumn fog characterises the Piedmont's hilly landscape. It makes full-bodied, structured wines, with excellent aging potential.

## NEGROAMARO

Pugliese grape variety with an intense deep red colour with nearly black highlights. The name is derived from the dialectal term *"niuru maru"* in reference to its black skin and bitter flavour.

## NERO D'AVOLA

Cultivated almost exclusively in Sicily, produces dark red wines with body, and has accents of liquorice and small red and black fruits. Also called Calabrese.

## PRIMITIVO

This grape variety is called *primitivo* because it ripens early, it is a vine species from Puglia that produces a characteristic deep red wine with accents of fruit and spice.

## PROSECCO

Widespread in the hilly region of the province of Treviso, the origins of prosecco would appear to lie in Trieste whence it moved to the Colli Euganei, where it is known as Serprina, and then it spread to the northeast of the Veneto. Wines made with prosecco grape berries are characterised by its light straw yellow colour, fruity and floral perfume, and savoury and fresh flavour.

## SAGRANTINO

Umbrian vine species with black berries that produces well-structured wines with a tannic flavour and intense aromas of ripe fruit and spice.

## SANGIOVESE

Cultivated in Tuscany since the Etruscans, this is the most common vine species in Italy, particularly in the central regions. It plays a hand in some of the peninsula's most famous wines such as **Brunello di Montalcino**, **Chianti**, **Vino Nobile di Montepulciano**, **Torgiano**. Its name would appear to be derived from the Latin *sanguis Jovis*, meaning "Jupiter's blood".

## TREBBIANO

These include a wide range of white-berried varieties including the better-known Trebbiano Toscano (known in France as Ugni Blanc), the Trebbiano di Soave and Trebbiano Romagnolo. Some scholars maintain that the term comes from the Trebbia River, others that it comes from *Trebulanum*, a name given to some Roman villages.

## VERMENTINO

Imported from Spain towards the end of the 16th century, it arrived in Italy via Liguria and Corsica, and then spread to Sardinia. It produces crisp wines with herbaceous, fruity and aromatic notes. It is at its best when cultivated near the sea.

© Elena Elisseeva/Shutterstock

*Vineyards of Chianti, Tuscany*
© JFL Photography/Fotolia.com

# Italy's greatest wines

## AMARONE

Amarone is characterised by the fact that it is obtained from withered **Corvina**, **Molinara** and **Rondinella grapes**. Clusters destined to produce this wine are harvested and then spread on matting and left to wither for one hundred days. The resulting must is particularly sweet and dense and fermentation is long. The wine produced from it has an impressive structure, a deep red colour, good acidity and elegant tannins, with notes of spices and ripe red and black fruit. Long aging makes it even more elegant and refined.

A sweet wine is also produced using the same procedure and the same grapes: **Recioto della Valpolicella**. Legend suggests that Amarone was created thanks to a mistake in the production of **Recioto** that resulted in the fermentation process not being blocked and the result was a dry wine instead of a sweet one. It is produced in a dedicated hilly area in the region of Verona.

## BRUNELLO DI MONTALCINO

Symbol of Tuscany, Brunello is made from **Sangiovese grape berries**, known as "Brunello" in the medieval city in the province of Siena that lent its name to the wine. An intense ruby-red leaning towards garnet, it boasts a broad array of aromas ranging from underbrush to berry jams, from herbaceous to spicy notes. Persistent and intense, this wine ages well, and is at its best after many years of refinement. It accompanies dishes made with game, red meats, mushrooms, truffles and aged cheeses extremely well. It finds its way into commerce only after aging for four years (five for "riserva"), of which at least two are spent in wood barrels.

Its history is tied to the Biondi-Santi family: Clemente Santi and his grandson Ferruccio Biondi who in the second half of the 19th century began selecting local Sangiovese grape berries to produce a wine from a single vine species.

## BARBARESCO

A very elegant and well-structured wine made from **Nebbiolo grapes**. At first garnet red, it shifts to shades of orange with age. Its aromas include violets, vanilla, berries, underbrush and spice. Sold only after two years of aging, of which at least one is spent in wood barrels, while the "riserva" is aged for a minimum of four years. It was created by **Domiziano Cavazza**, director of the Scuola Enologica di Alba, who towards the end of the 19th century

began experimenting with a few vine species uprooted to Barbaresco. In 1893 he created the Cantina Sociale del Barbaresco and the following year the wine named after its village of origin. The current area of production includes, in addition to the homonymous town, the communes of Treiso, Neive and San Rocco Seno d'Elvio.

## BAROLO

A wine worth waiting for, to be drunk only after long years of aging as it improves with age like few others. Its history is intertwined with that of illustrious figures such as the count and French oenologist **Oudart**, the **Marchesa Falletti di Barolo** and **Camillo Benso count of Cavour**. Before they entered into play, Barolo had been a somewhat sweet wine that sometimes even had a sparkle to it. The Frenchman suggested Bordeaux-style vinification and the result was a dry wine, with body and great potential for aging. The Marchesa and Cavour were passionately dedicated to the production of the progenitor of today's Barolo and laid the foundations for what it later became. Barolo is produced south of the Tanaro River, in the Barolo zone that includes other neighbouring communes identified with its production. Aged at least 3 years, of which at least two are spent in wood barrels, prior to going on sale, its

bouquet is full and ethereal with notes of wild berries, liquorice, wild rose, violets, undergrowth; it is pleasantly warm, tannic and acidic in the mouth.

## SUPER TUSCANS

**Sassicaia**, **Ornellaia**, **Solaia**, **Masseto**, and **Tignanello** are just a few of the celebrated "supertuscans" that have made Tuscany famous worldwide. These wines are obtained from cuts with Bordeaux vine species (**merlot**, **cabernet franc**, **cabernet sauvignon**), aged in barrels and produced using oenological techniques inspired by those in the French region of **Bordeaux**. What led to this phenomenon is Sassicaia: originally a "Vino da Tavola" that has been regulated by the DOC Bolgheri Sassicaia from the 1990s. It is produced in the province of Livorno, in the municipality of Castagneto Carducci. The arrival of *barbatelle* di Cabernet Sauvignon in this zone dates back to the postwar period, and is characterised by pebbly terrain (whence the its name).

The year that marked the turnaround for this wine is 1968, when it drew the attention of experts and began its ascent to popularity. This experience opened the way to what became a veritable revolution within the traditional system of Tuscan winemaking, now adopted by many producers even in different areas of the region.

# Enogastronomic tourism

Enogastronomic tourism is a phenomenon that continues to grow and has led to the birth of associations and organisations that offer a series of services in the sector.

The national organization "**Strade del Vino e dei Sapori**" (Wine and Flavour Routes) has helped every region promote its own winemaking territories. These itineraries link areas with strong vine and wine growing vocations combining the pleasure of discovering vineyards and cellars with natural, cultural and historical attractions to promote oenotourism through the valorisation of vineyard activities with respect to all aspects of their operating context. Each winemaking zone has its own route, a search by region and area is easy.

Search the Web for "Strade del Vino e dei Sapori" in any search engine to find a list of related sites for the area being visited. There are over a hundred throughout Italy. In 1987 the **Associazione Nazionale Città del Vino** (www.cittadelvino.com) was created, followed by the Centro Studi e Servizi Strade del Vino e dei Sapori in 2005. In 1993 the **Movimento Turismo del Vino** (www.movimentoturismovino.it) was founded to promote wine culture through tours of places that produce wine and lead up to the **Cantine Aperte** event, when associated cellars open their doors to wine tourists.

Another important organization related to wine tourism is the Association "**Go Wine**" (www.gowinet.it), founded in Alba in 2001, precisely because wine is increasingly one of the symbols of the country's agro-food culture and able to motivate a vast number of enthusiasts.

# Events

Many local wine-related events and festivals take place year round.

The most popular nationally are **Vinitaly** (www.vinitaly.com) which takes place in Verona each year in April, **Merano Wine Festival** held in Merano in November (www.meranowinefestival.com), **Vinum** (www.vinumalba.com) held annually in Alba at the end of April/beginning of May, **Vitigno Italia** (www.vitignoitalia.it) dedicated to the peninsula's native vine stock held each year in May in Naples. On the last Sunday of May is held **Cantine Aperte**, during which around 800 cellars associated with the Movimento Turismo del Vino open their doors to the public.

The Movimento Turismo del Vino was founded in 1993 with a goal to developing the awareness of places that produce wine, thereby promoting direct contact between the wine tourist and the vine cultivator.

The Association has more than 1000 cellars that are members and promotes initiatives and events year round.

For further information, visit the Website www.movimentoturismovino.it.

# ACROSS THE BORDER: THE CANTON OF TICINO AND ISTRIA

A small excursion outside Italy to two areas that, in their character, display a certain cultural and artistic continuity with the Bel Paese. As far as the enological panorama is concerned, they show steady growth and are characterized by increased attention to quality production and involve wine tourists in activities to discover the territories.

Vineyards of Arogno, Ticino

## The Canton of Ticino

### VITICULTURE IN THE CANTON

The Canton of Ticino is divided into two principal areas, Sopraceneri and Sottoceneri – respectively north and south of Monte Ceneri pass – covering eight districts: Bellinzona, Blenio, Riviera, Leventina, Locarno, Vallemaggia, in Sopraceneri; Lugano and Mendrisio in Sottoceneri. All of these areas have vineyards to some extent.

The **climate**, which is mostly sunny, is marked by abundant precipitation at certain times of the year. The terrain is mostly granite and gneiss and is fairly acidic. Because of pedoclimatic conditions, the best-adapted system for cultivation has proved to be the Guyot system. Because of the frequency of hail, particularly in Mendrisiotto and Malcantone, the vines are protected by anti-hail nets.

The **surface area** planted with vines is around 1,000 hectares and the average annual production of **Merlot**, the grapevine covering most of this surface area, is around 55,000 quintals. The grape harvest season generally runs from end-September to beginning October, depending on the climatic situation from one area to the next.

Vinification mostly (around 75%) takes place in cellars that purchase the grapes from grape growers, although some of these cellars also have their own vineyards, the rest is produced by mediumsmall-sized grape growers (2,000-40,000 bottles) that produce wine exclusively from their own harvests, and by the Cantina Sociale Mendrisio (around 15%), which also owns a large vineyard.

### ON A HISTORIC NOTE

Wild grapes have existed in Switzerland since antiquity, but it was the Romans who introduced wine grapes at the beginning of the Christian era. Thus it is not by chance that the first references to grapevines and wines in Ticino are from around the year 1000 and according to a few scholars vine cultivation was not yet widespread in the year 1200. Charlemagne promoted its development, but in the Middle Ages only monks pursued this type of cultivation, even because farmers could not have their own properties as land purchases were the domain of only Lords and ecclesiastics. Also, ancient documents from that period testify that farmers were taxed if they consumed wines produced with the grapes they cultivated.

In the course of the 17th century, international commerce took root favouring wine imports from other countries to the detriment of national production. Only in the 19th century can any interest in viticulture be observed: in 1850 Swiss grape farming grew to 30,000 hectares, in 1879 a commission was created to study phylloxera, and in 1893 the Department of agriculture was created.

**Phylloxera** scourged the Ticino towards the end of the 19th century, causing vast damage to production; more resistant varieties – but of lower quality – were planted with obvious effects on the wines produced.

In order to manage this situation the government developed the Antiphylloxera Service and the Travelling Agricultural Information Desk. In the 20th century the focus shifted to local vines and vine species; testing began with particular attention to Merlot and the Cantine Sociali were created.

Interest in grape farming gradually grew until, it came to a halt with World War I. In 1921 the engineer Giuseppe Paleari, with the collaboration of the Stazioni Federali d'Esperienze Agrarie, resumed testing of Merlot that led to the affirmation of this variety with respect to others. From the second half of the 19th century to the end of the 20th the surface area of vineyards shrank progressively while planting was rationalised and vine cultivation gained in professionalism and quality.

## VINE SPECIES IN THE TICINO

Today, **Merlot** is the emblematic species of vine cultivation in the Ticino, where it occupies over 80% of vineyards. Originally from France's Bordeaux region, it arrived in Switzerland at the beginning of the 20th century, when it became necessary to recreate the grape farming heritage following the phylloxera blight and it was immediately observed that it adapted well to the climate and the terrain in the canton. Cloned selections and experimentation carefully studied by the Stazione Federale di Ricerche Agronomiche di Cadenazzo from 1955 helped the vine species reach interesting levels of quality as well as good resistance to adverse conditions. Vine shoots were supplied to vine farmers by authorised nurseries and taken from controlled vines.

Merlot is not the only vine species cultivated in the Ticino. **Pinot Nero**, **Bondola** (the only native vine species in the region, cultivated in Sopraceneri), **Cabernet Franc**, **Cabernet Sauvignon**, **Diolinoir**, **Pinot x Cabernet**, **Gamaret**, **Garanoir**, **Ancellotta**, **Syrah** and **Gamay** are also present. At many vineyards testing is done to identify varieties that could complement the traditional vine species in order to improve the quality of the product offering and identify varieties best adapted to the changing climatic conditions.

## LEGISLATION

The introduction of Controlled Denomination of Origin to the Canton of Ticino dates back to 1997. DOC designates a wine meeting qualitative requirements that correspond to conditions set by the Cantons regarding the boundaries of areas for production, grapevines used, cultivation procedures, minimum natural sugar content, yield per surface area, vinification techniques used, organoleptic evaluation and examination.

The Ordine della DOC is the organization in charge of managing and attributing the DOC label. It consists of a commission of qualified tasters, responsible for ensuring quality and typicality by means of organoleptic and analytical controls of vine samples provided by wine producers for study.

Pure grapevines, if they respect the conditions set forth in the regulations, bear the denomination "**TICINO**" DOC, followed by the name of the grapevine and eventual complementary information such as the area, municipality or farm that cultivated the grapes.

The DOC for blends are **Rosso** or **Bianco del Ticino** (or Ticinese) eventually followed by the grape species in the blend. DOC wines must be made within the canton. Wines that do not correspond to criteria defined in DOC specifications bear the denomination "**Svizzera Italiana**" IGT, and may mention the type of vine species, or simply the wine's colour. The term "**nostrano**" may complement the IGT denomination, but such wines may not bear the Ticinese denomination which is reserved for DOC wines.

Bilateral agreements between the EU and Switzerland have made it possible to reserve the denomination "**Grappa**" for Italian-speaking Swiss regions (Ticino and Valli dei Grigioni). This traditional definition has always been used here and in Italy's Alpine and Pre-Alpine valleys.

The **Merlot** that undergo quality control receive the label **Marchio VITI** that is the result of an evaluation system based on a series of parameters introduced by the Council of State in 1948 in order to provide incentives for higher quality standards. In order to boast this label, producers must present wines before a tasting commission that determines pertinence. From 1995 the Marchio VITI has been controlled by a private entity, the Associazione Viti, composed of wine producers that attribute both the Marchio VITI and "Grappa e acquavite ticinese controllata" labels. The criteria for this classification are openly qualitative and expressed in points (80/100). Analytical data for the wines must respect internal regulations.

(*Source: www.ticinowine.ch*)

## ROUTES AND EXHIBITIONS

There are five **Strade del Vino del Canton Ticino** (itineraries to visit cellars and places of interest for nature, culture and history) that cover the following vine and wine growing areas:

– **Mendrisiotto**: from the centre of Mendriso to Chiasso
– **Locarnese**: from Tenero to Ascona
– **Bellinzonese**: from Camorino to Bodio
– **Malcantone**: from Lamone to Termine
– **Piano di Magadino and Valle di Blenio**: from Gudo to Dongio

Wine lovers should visit the **Museo del Vino** at Matasci winemakers in Tenero. Each fall there are many festivals centred on grapes throughout the region. The **Bacchica** is the grape harvest festival in Bellinzona at the beginning of September (*for more information see www. ticino.ch*).

The **wine routes** in the region of **Mendrisio**, particularly those on the slopes of Monte San Giorgio, a UNESCO world heritage site for its fossil deposits, and through the vineyards of Castel San Pietro and Chiasso-Pedrinate are of particular interest (*www.mendrisiotourism.ch*).

# Istria

Some scholars believe this name is derived from the ancient peoples called the Histri who lived in this area in Antiquity, others maintain that it comes from the Latin term *Hister*, referring to the Danube, which marked the confines of the region.

## ON A HISTORIC NOTE

Istria boasts a long winemaking tradition. It is thus not by chance that in the Gulf of Arsa, near the village of Rakalj, there is a bay called Kalavojna, that in Greek means good wine (*kalos oinos*), attesting to how well the Greeks liked the wine of Istria.

But the Romans gave local winemaking the fundamental stimulus, such that Pliny the Elder, referring to Istrian wines in his work *Historiarum mundi*, sang the praises of *vinum Pucinum*, even attributing the long life of Empress Livia to it.

# INTRODUCTION

Histrian wine has also had its vicissitudes: periods of splendour and others of hard times.

The Middle Ages were certainly a historic period in which it gained great fame. Italian Moscati wines were an unavoidable delicacy at royal banquets and the introduction of Malvasia grapes to Europe dates back to the Middle Ages, an era of fruitful and plentiful commerce between the Serenissima Repubblica of Venezia and Peloponnesus, whence this vine species hails. Another period of glory was the epoch of the Austrian Empire when vineyards covered more than 30,000 hectares. Unfortunately from the second half of the 19th century to the beginning of the last century, Phyloxxera brought Istrian viticulture down to its knees. Vineyards were replanted and only today have they returned to their original splendour. Today, Istria's wine is highly considered and is an integral part of the region's identity.

## WINES AND VINEYARDS IN ISTRIA

### Malvasia and more

Istrian winemaking cannot be mentioned without leaving some room for its symbolic vineyard, Malvasia, which is now an integral part of Istria's identity, and occupies nearly two-thirds of the vineyards planted in the region. While Malvasia is the prevalent white grapevine species, its red equivalent is surely **Terrano**, which produces ruby red wines with purple highlights, offering fruity aromas – wild berries in particular – as well as character and acidity. Terrano is the protagonist of one of the most characteristic preparations: supa, a traditional peasant dish consisting of toasted bread soaked with red wine served in an earthenware dish called a *bukaleta*.

Along with Malvasia and Terrano, different types of **Moscato** are cultivated in Istria, in particular **Moscato di Momiano** and **Moscato Rosa di Parenzo**, which are used to produce excellent sweet wines served at the end of the meal.

Finally, **Croata Nera** (*hrvatica crna*), a vine species known in Italy as Croatina, has remained a minor species with respect to better-known black grapes by pure negligence. International white grapevine species that have found ideal conditions for cultivation in Istria include Chardonnay, Pinot Grigio and Pinot Bianco, which are used to make dry wines for drinking young and for aging. International black vine species cultivated there include Merlot, Cabernet Sauvignon and Cabernet Franc.

## LEGISLATION

**IQ (Istrian Quality)** is the label conferred through an articulated system of controls established by **Vinistra**, the Associazione dei viticoltori e dei produttori del vino istriani. In recent years this association elaborated a specific approach to follow to obtain a detailed system of checks to survey the quality of Istrian Malvasia from vineyard to wine cellar, to bottling and sale. The IQ label on bottles is an important guarantee of quality for consumers.

*Motovun, Istria*

© Draconcello/iStock

# QUIZ

### 1. TYRES ARE BLACK SO WHY IS THE MICHELIN MAN WHITE?

Back in 1898 when the Michelin Man was first created from a stack of tyres, they were made of natural rubber, cotton and sulphur and were therefore light-coloured. The composition of tyres did not change until after the First World War when carbon black was introduced. But the Michelin Man kept his colour!

### 2. FOR HOW LONG HAS MICHELIN BEEN GUIDING TRAVELLERS?

Since 1900. When the MICHELIN guide was published at the turn of the century, it was claimed that it would last for a hundred years. It's still around today and remains a reference with new editions and online restaurant listings in a number of countries.

### 3. WHEN WAS THE "BIB GOURMAND" INTRODUCED IN THE MICHELIN GUIDE?

The symbol was created in 1997 but as early as 1954 the MICHELIN guide was recommending "exceptional good food at moderate prices". Today, it features on the MICHELIN Restaurants website and app.

If you want to enjoy a fun day out and find out more about Michelin, why not visit the l'Aventure Michelin museum and shop in Clermont-Ferrand, France:
**www.laventuremichelin.com**

MICHELIN
A better way forward

Wine Trails of Italy
# Itineraries through the vineyards

*Vineyards in Badia a Passignano, Chianti, Tuscany, Italy*
© J. Arnold Images/hemis.fr

# Italy

# AOSTA VALLEY

The mighty presence of Monte Bianco looms over this region, where grapes are grown in extreme conditions. The vines tenaciously climb the steep slopes in some of the highest vineyards in Europe, challenging the often adverse conditions. The fact that viticulture in the Aosta Valley has managed to achieve such high levels of quality is greatly due to the regional administration. The decision to focus on excellence resulted in the replanting of vineyards, the protection of native species of vine, investment in wine cooperatives, and use of sustainable, integrated agricultural methods. This commitment has been repaid: though modest in terms of quantity, today the local wine production is of superior quality.

© fotografiche/iStock

*Matterhorn or Monte Cervino*

## The terroir

There is a single designation of origin, **Valle d'Aosta DOC**, which breaks down into further specifications that identify the production zones (Donnas, Enfer d'Arvier, Arnad – Montjovet, Nus, Chambave, Torrette, Blanc de Morgex et de La Salle), the types of wine (Rosso, Rosato, Bianco, Passito, Superiore and Spumante) and the varieties of grape used (Chardonnay, Cornalin, Fumin, Gamay, Mayolet, Merlot, Nebbiolo, Premetta, Petite Arvine, Petite Rouge, Pinot Nero, Pinot Bianco, Pinot Grigio, Syrah, Müller Thurgau). This system of designations covers a wide range of wines, many of which are of excellent value.

The grape and wine production region in the Aosta Valley can be divided into three areas: the **Upper Valley** (Valdigne), where the vineyards rise to 1200 m and the principal grape is the Prié Blanc; the **Central Valley**, where native varieties such as Premetta, Petite Rouge and Fumin flourish; and the **Lower Valley**, where the vines grow at an altitude of about 300 m and reds predominate, Nebbiolo in particular.

The **reds**, which are well structured and of outstanding acidity, include the zones Donnas, Enfer d'Arvier, Arnad – Montjovet and Torrette; the reds of Chambave and Nus, however, are smoother.

With regard to these last two zones, not to be missed are the Chambave Muscat and Nus Malvoisie (made with a particular clone of Pinot Grigio rather than Malvasia), both in the dry and dried-grape versions (or Flétri as it is called locally).

The **whites** include the highly refined and elegant Blanc de Morgex et de La Salle, obtained from the native Prié Blanc, with vineyards that rise to a height of 1200 m. This vine gives fresh still wines, admirable sparkling wines, and an interesting Vin de glace.

The curious wine tourist should not miss the chance to try the reds and rosé wines of several interesting local varieties, such as Cornalin, Petit Rouge, Vien de Nus and

Premetta. Also of quality are the wines from grapes that are not just local, like Pinot Nero, Gamay, Müller Thurgau, Chardonnay, Moscato, Pinot Grigio, Petite Arvine, Nebbiolo and Dolcetto.

The relaunch of local wine production began in the 1960s and has been strongly supported by the regional administration. The first result was the attribution of the first DOC recognition to Donnas and Enfer d'Arvier in the early 1970s, which were then incorporated in the Aosta Valley regional DOC in 1985.

## Itinerary

*Locations with a winery are indicated by the symbol ♟; for the addresses of the wineries, see p. 66.*

### THE DORA BALTEA VALLEY

**From Pont-Saint-Martin to Courmayeur**

*Itinerary of approximately 90 km along the S 26.*

This valley is a superb tourist area, thanks to the magnificent spectacle of Europe's highest mountains, castles and valleys dotted with houses with wooden balconies and roofs made of *lose*, combined with innumerable excursions and panoramic roads that end at the feet of dazzling glaciers. The grapes are mostly grown on the sunny left side of the river, the Dora Baltea, and the problems often created by the slope of the land are overcome by terracing.

The starting point for the itinerary is the entrance to the valley, **Pont-Saint-Martin**, which takes its name from the 1st-c. BC **Roman bridge** protected by a chapel dedicated to St John Nepomucene. The ruins of the medieval castle

**DOC**
Valle d'Aosta – Vallée d'Aoste (V.d.A.)

**SUB-ZONES**
Arnad – Montjovet
Blanc de Morgex et de La Salle
Chambave Rouge
Chambave Muscat
Donnas
Enfer d'Arvier
Nus Rouge
Nus Malvoisie
Torrette

loom over the town's historic centre. Continue along the state road past **Donnas** ♟, close to which remain traces of the ancient Roman road Via delle Gallie. In the village, the cellars where the Caves Cooperatives de Donnas (*see the Addresses*) were based from 1971 to 1976, were rebuilt in 2003 and today are home to the **Wine and Viticulture Museum**. *Via Roma 97. Open Sun. 10-12, 14-18, ℘ 0125 80 70 96, www.donnasvini.it.*

Set close against the mountain soon after, you come to **Bard**, where the fort★, founded in the Middle Ages, was dismantled in 1800 by Napoleon (whose advance was delayed by it for 2 weeks) and rebuilt during the 19th c., where it dominates the upper Dora Baltea valley. After long restoration, today the building is home to several museums, including the enjoyable and educational **Museum of the Alps**, which illustrates the history, geography, nature, culture and traditions of the region. *Open 10-18 (Sat., Sun. and public hols. 19), closed Mon. (in win.), 24, 25 Dec. ℘ 0125 83 38 11, 0125 80 98 11, www.fortedibard.it.*

## PRINCIPAL VARIETIES CULTIVATED

| WHITE GRAPES | GREY GRAPES | BLACK GRAPES | |
|---|---|---|---|
| Chardonnay | Cornalin | Bonda | Merlot |
| Erbaluce | Mayolet | Crovassa | Ner d'Ala |
| Moscato Bianco | Pinot Grigio | Diolinoir | Neyret |
| Müller Thurgau | Prié Rouge *or* | Fumin | Petit Rouge |
| Petite Arvine | Premetta | Gamaret | Pinot Nero |
| Pinot Bianco | Traminer | Gamay | Roussin |
| Prié Blanc | Aromatico | Granoir | Syrah |
| | | | Vien De Nus |
| | | | Vuillermin |

*Remains of the Roman forum, Aosta*

Several kilometres on you arrive in **Arnad**, renowned as a production centre of lard.On the other side of the river, you will see **Issogne Castle★** (late 15th c.), famous for its courtyard with a wrought-iron fountain crowned by a pomegranate, the arched loggia decorated with farming scenes (15th-c. frescoes), and its locally made furniture. *Piazza Castello. Open 9-19 (Apr.-Sept.), 10-13 and 14-17 (Oct.-Mar.), closed Mon. (in win.), 25 Dec.,1st Jan., ℘ 0125 92 93 73.*

About 2 km north of **Verrès** stands the cubic Verrès Castle. Built in the 14th c., it has no corner towers or donjon. *Open 9-19 (Apr.-Sept.), 10-13 and 14-17 (Oct.-Mar.), closed Mon. (in win.), 25 Dec., 1st Jan., ℘0125 92 90 67.*

Continuing along the state road you will see the ruins of **Montjovet Castle** and then arrive at **Saint Vincent★**, a spa town famous for the popular Casino de la Vallée, situated amidst beautiful grounds. Do not miss the lovely parish Church of **San Vincenzo**, founded in the Middle Ages and decorated with Renaissance frescoes.

Pass **Chambave ♆** to reach **Fénis Castle★**. This fortified home was built in the 13th c. by the Challant family and was soon copied by other castles in the region. It has a fine internal courtyard with frescoes of the Golden Legend, and interiors with very fine locally made furnishings. *Open 9-19 (Apr.-Sept.), 10-13 and 14-17 (Oct.-Mar.), closed Mon. (in win.), 25 Dec., 1st Jan., ℘ 0165 76 42 63.*

## Aosta★

🛈 *Via Porta Pretoria. ℘ 0165 23 66 27, www.regione.vda.it* The regional capital has retained its ancient Roman castrum plan and boasts several Roman **monuments★** in a pleasant pedestrian city centre: the **Porta Pretoria**, the majestic **Augustan Arch★**, the **theatre** and ruins of the amphitheatre, all in an archaeological park *(Open 9-19 Apr.-Sept., 10-13 and 14-17 Oct.-Mar., ℘ 0165 23 16 65, 349 64 36 018).* The Roman walls were built on a rectangular plan during the Augustan age and feature a number of towers.

The large collegiate **Church of Sant'Orso★★** was built over an early Christian church. Dedicated to the Irish saint who came to evangelise the valley in the 11th c., it has beautiful 15th-c. carved wooden stalls and a Baroque jube. Next to the 11th-c. crypt is a door that leads to a charming small Romanesque **cloister★** with capitals historiated with biblical and secular scenes. The **Priorate** is a Renaissance-style building with elegant windows. The ceiling is decorated with a moving cycle of 11th-c. **frescoes★**. The **cathedral** stands over the site of the ancient **Roman forum**, of which various remains can be seen. Built in the 12th c., it has been rebuilt several times and now has a Neoclassic façade (1848). There is a 12th-c. mosaic floor in the choir, 15th-c. Gothic stalls and the tomb of Tommaso II of Savoy (14th c.). The sacristy contains a rich ecclesiastical treasure. The cloister is 15th c.

Housed in an ancient convent, the modern **MAR**, **archaeological museum** displays Roman finds from around the region, including the decoration in bone of the funerary bed in the necropolis of St Roch. *Piazza Roncas 12. Open 9-19 (Apr.-Sept.),10-13 and 14-17 (Oct.-Mar.). Closed 25 Dec., 1st Jan., ℘ 0165 27 59 02.* Leaving Aosta, continue to **Sarre Castle**, the summer residence of the counts of Savoy, and the fort at **Aymavilles** ♟ (14th c.), which has large, round, crenellated corner towers. From Aymavilles, continue for 20 or so kilometres along the lovely R 47 to **Cogne**, one of the most frequently visited villages in **Gran Paradiso National Park**.

Returning to Aosta Valley, **Sarriod de la Tour Castle★**, built between the 10th and 12th c., stands near **Saint-Pierre**. Attractions are the frescoes painted in the chapel in 1250 and the surprising **"Room of the Heads"**, which takes its name from the ceiling supported by 171 brackets carved in the shapes of strange monsters and animals bearing coats of arms, datable to around 1430. *Open 9-19 (Apr.-Sept.), 10-13 and 14-17 (Oct.-Mar.), closed Mon. (in win.), 25 Dec.,1st Jan., ℘ 0165 90 46 89 (guided tour).* The village proper is overlooked by another medieval castle that houses a natural science museum. *Closed at the time of writing, for information ℘ 0165 30 63 23.*

After Saint-Pierre, a road forks left to **Valsavarenche** and passes through **Villeneuve** ♟, where you can see the ruins of a 12th-13th c. castle.

Your itinerary continues towards **Morgex** ♟, the site of a lovely parish church and medieval buildings and towers, and to **Pré-Saint-Didier**, where a thermal spa that has been used since the times of the Romans has recently been restored to its ancient splendour.

The final stop on the itinerary is the famous town of **Courmayeur** (1224 m), which is an excellent starting point for many superb excursions. Leaving from La Palud, take the cable car **over the Mont Blanc massif★** and the Cresta d'Arp. By car you can explore Val Veny, Val Ferret, the Testa d'Arpi and the road of the Piccolo San Bernardo, one of the most important alpine passes, and used by the Romans back in antiquity.

wineries: Cave du Vin Blanc de Morgex et de La Salle in Morgex in Valdigne(www.caveduvinblanc.com), La Crotta di Vegneron in Chambave (www.lacrotta.it) and the Coopérative de l'Enfer (Co-Enfer) in Arvie (www.coenfer.com).

# Addresses

## Tourist information

**Aosta Tourist Office** – Piazza Porta Praetoria 3, Aosta. Open 9-19 (25 Dec. 15-19, 1st Jan. 10-19) ✆ 0165 23 66 27, www.lovevda.it

**Route des Vins Association** – Corso Lancieri 32, **Aosta**, www.routedesvinsvda.it

## The wineries

*The addresses are listed in alphabetical order by location.*

**Co-Enfer** – *Via Corrado Gex 52 - **Arvier** (AO) - ✆ 0165 99 238 - www.coenfer.com - info@ coenfer.it - Winery tours by reservation.* The cooperative manages the entire growing and production activities of Enfer d'Arvier, a full-bodied wine made from grapes grown in the municipality after which it is named. The sobriquet "inferno" – hell – is derived from the area's excellent exposure. The main variety is Petit Rouge, but other red grapes such as Pinot Noir, Vien de Nus, Neyret and Mayolet are also grown. Hectares under vine: 5.
**Wines**: Enfer d'Arvier, Digne du Pape, Clos de l'Enfer, Seigneur Mayolet, Trikell. Other products: Eau de l'Enfer.

**Cave des Onze Communes** – *Fraz. Urbains 14 - **Aymavilles** (AO) - ✆ 0165 90 29 12 - www.caveonzecommunes.it - info@caveonzecommunes.it - Winery tours by reservation.* Inaugurated in 1990, the winery collects and vinifies grapes from vineyards in 11 municipalities in the central area of Valle d'Aosta, on both sides of the

©by Chan/Shutterstock

Dora Baltea. The grapes are supplied by 220 members – true artisans of the land – who manage vineyards divided into extremely small plots, many of which situated on steep slopes, making them difficult to work and impossible to mechanise. Respect for the environment, limited use of pesticides and painstaking vine management yield excellent wines. Hectares under vine: 60.
**Wines**: Petite Arvine, Fumin, Fumin Barrique, Torrette, Torrette Supérieur, Chardonnay, Cornalin, Petit Rouge, Pinot Noir Barrique, Syrah. Other products: grappa, Muscat Petit Grain.

**Les Crêtes** – *SR20, 50 - **Aymavilles** (AO) - ✆ 0165 90 22 74 - www.lescretes.it - info@ lescretes.it - Winery tours by reservation, closed Sun. and public hols.* Bernardin Charrère, the great-grandfather of the winery's current owner, emigrated from Haute-Savoie to Aymavilles around 1750 and constructed the building that is still used today, with wine cellars and a walnut mill. The estate has been handed down from one generation to the next, and today Costantino continues his forefather's work, passionately devoting himself to viticulture and the selection of varieties and wines that would otherwise have been lost. He and a group of friends established Les Crêtes, which in just over a decade has become the region's largest private domaine. Hectares under vine: 25.
**Wines**: Chardonnay, Syrah, Torrette, Petite Arvine, Fumin.

**La Crotta di Vegneron** – *Piazza Roncas 2 - **Chambave** (AO) - ✆ 0166 46 670 - www. lacrotta.it - info@lacrotta.it - Winery tours by reservation.* The cooperative was established in 1980 to safeguard production in the Chambave and Nus areas, as these wines – known and appreciated since the Middle Ages – were gradually disappearing. This work was paralleled by efforts to valorise the local grappa. La Crotta has vineyards in about ten municipalities in the middle valley, an area with a particular microclimate that permits minimal use of pesticides. Hectares under vine: 39.
**Wines**: Chambave Muscat, Chambave Moscato Passito, Nus Malvoisie Flétri, Fumin "Esprit Follet", Cornalin. Other products: grappa.

**Caves Cooperatives de Donnas** – *Via Roma 97 - **Donnas** (AO) - ✆ 0125 80 70 96 - www.donnasvini.it - info@donnasvini.it - Winery tours and tasting by reservation.* Thanks to a mild climate that is ideal for growing grapes and Mediterranean plants, viticulture in Donnas boasts extremely old traditions, despite the difficulties posed by very steep slopes. In 1971 a group of local winegrowers formed a cooperative to protect and guarantee the quality and authenticity of the wine with this appellation. Hectares under vine: 21.

**Wines**: Donnas Superieur, Donnas Napoleone, Donnas Classico, Nebbiolo Barmet, Pinot Grigio. Other products: "Donatium" flavoured wine, grappa.

**Cave du Vin Blanc de Morgex et de La Salle** – *Chemin des Iles 31, La Ruine - **Morgex** (AO) - 🖉 0165 80 03 31 - www.cavemontblanc.com - info@ cavemontblanc.com - Winery tours by reservation, closed Sun.* As part of a policy implemented by the regional government to support and develop viticulture in Valle d'Aosta, the winery was established in 1983 and has devoted enormous energy to reviving Prié Blanc and viticulture on the slopes of Mont Blanc, in order to preserve the area's age-old traditions. Hectares under vine: 20.

**Wines**: Rayon Blanc de Morgex et de La Salle, Plagne Blanc de Morgex et de La Salle, Extrème Blanc de Morgex et de La Salle Metodo Classico, Brut Blanc de Morgex et de La Salle Metodo Classico, Chaudelune Vin de Glace Blanc de Morgex et de La Salle.

**F.lli Grosjean** – *Fraz. Ollignan 2 - **Quart** (AO) - 🖉 0165 77 57 91 - www. grosjeanvins.it - info@grosjeanvins.it - Winery tours by reservation.* The five Grosjean brothers run this estate, which is located on the border of the municipalities of Quart and Saint Christophe, and is profoundly tied to local grape varieties and the region's winemaking traditions. Other varieties – Fumin, Cornalin, Premetta and Vuillermin – have been added to those cultivated initially (Petit Rouge, Gamay, Pinot Noir and Petite Arvine). The excellent results of this respect for the territory are evident in every glass. Hectares under vine: 7.5.

**Wines**: Torrette Vigne Rovetta, Pinot Noir Vigne Tzeriat, Cornalin, Fumin Vigne Rovettaz, Vigne Rovettaz.

**La Source** – *Loc. Bussan Dessous 1 - **Saint-Pierre** (AO) - 🖉 0165 90 40 38 - www.lasource.it - info@lasource.it.* La Source was founded in 2003 from the experience and passion of a group of young Valdostani, all agriculturists for generations and experts in winemaking. The company owns roughly 7 hectares located in the best winemaking areas in Valle d'Aosta, and cultivated with both national (Arvine, Chardonnay, Syrah) and local varietals (Cornalin, Fumin, Petit Rouge, Premetta and Vien de Nus). Grapes are carefully selected, and the company's owners personally follow each step of production, from cultivation to transformation into wine; the operation is conducted according to the most modern technologies and fully respecting Valdostan winemaking traditions. Hectares under vine: 7.

**Wines**: Valle d'Aosta DOC Petite Arvine, Valle d'Aosta DOC Torrette, Valle d'Aosta DOC Torrette Superiore, Valle d'Aosta DOC Cornaline, Valle d'Aosta DOC Gamay. Other products: Grappa and flavoured wine "vin du Paradis".

🐾 **La Vrille** – *Loc. Grangeon 1/a - **Verrayes** (AO) - 🖉 0166 54 3018 - www.lavrille.it - lavrille@gmail.com - Winery tours by reservation.* The winery is set in a lovely area, with views of Mont Avic and Mont Emilius, and enjoys excellent exposure throughout the year, ensuring ideal maturation of the grapes. Although the estate is quite small, its wines are of excellent quality. The sweet ones (Chambave Muscat and Chambave Muscat Flétri) are very good, but the dry Fumin and Cornalin are also a pleasant surprise to the palate. The estate offers accommodation (*6 rooms, €80 and restaurant service*). Hectares under vine: 1.5.

**Wines**: Chambave, Chambave Muscat, Fumin, Cornalin, Vuillermin, Chambave Muscat Flétri, Pinot Noir.

**Maison Anselmet** – *Fraz. Vereytaz 30 - **Villeneuve** (AO) - 🖉 0165 90 48 51 - www. maisonanselmet.it - Winery tours by reservation.* Renato and Giorgio Anselmet, whose family has made wine for generations, have long believed in respecting the environment and enhancing the *terroir*. Their production revolves around the traditional grapes and wines of Valle d'Aosta, but they also grow international varieties such as Chardonnay and Pinot Noir. Passion and devotion yield wines that fully express the qualities of this region. Hectares under vine: 6.5.

**Wines**: Petit Rouge, Torrette, Pinot Noir, Chardonnay, Cornalin.

## Where to stay

### SAINT-PIERRE

**La Meridiana Du Cadran Solaire** – *Loc. Château Feuillet 17, Saint Pierre - 🖉 0165 90 36 26 - www.albergomeridiana.it - 16 rooms, doubles from €75.* A small, elegant hotel redolent of times past, with a profusion of wood and period furniture. The restaurant is run by a successful and imaginative chef.

# PIEDMONT

Piedmont means "at the foot of the mountains", which is an exact description of the geography of the region. But the mountains are just one aspect of Piedmont. The rest of the region has a great deal to offer: hills planted with vineyards, rivers, lakes, modern cities, medieval hamlets, ancient castles and ultramodern buildings. It is home to some of the world's most highly prized wines. They are at times difficult, austere and a little rugged, but gradually they reveal their secret nature in the glass, rewarding the patient wine-lover.

© Argalis/iStock

*Barolo vineyards*

## The terroir

Grapes are grown in much of the region and produce numerous types of wine, many of which are very well known, such as Barolo, Barbaresco, Asti Spumante, Barbera and Nebbiolo, to mention only a few.

Piedmont is one of Italy's most productive regions and has the greatest number of DOC appellations. It is also the area with the highest percentage of VQPRD wines (*Quality Wines Produced in Specified Regions*), a definition that groups the DOC and DOCG zones. Regardless of numbers and statistics, what must be underlined is that wine is an integral part of the culture of the Piedmonts. The preferred varieties are Nebbiolo, Dolcetto, Barbera, Freisa, Arneis, Cortese, Brachetto, Favorita and Moscato. The principal wine production areas are Monferrato, the Langhe, Roero and Alto Piemonte.

**Monferrato** stretches from the hills of Turin to the border with Lombardy, including Asti and parts of the provinces of Alessandria and Cuneo. **Barbera** is

one of the most common local varieties and produces a wine that symbolises the entire region: it is characterised by a very heady bouquet, a good structure and a rugged, slightly acid note that often develops and becomes more harmonious with age. The area is also the home of the famous **Asti DOCG** as well as other well known wines made from Dolcetto, Freisa, Grignolino and Cortese grapes. In the Acquese and Casalese zones to the south of this area, **Brachetto** and **Cortese** are the preferred varieties from which Brachetto d'Aqui DOCG (with a rosé, muscat nose) and Gavi DOCG (a fruity scent and fresh, dry taste) are respectively produced.

The **Langhe and Roero** are areas separated by the river Tanaro in Cuneo province: the Langhe lies on the right bank, Roero on the left. **Nebbiolo** is the most popular grape here, the name of which refers to the November fogs (*nebbie*) that typically cover the area. The grape is used to produce the gems of the local wineries, **Barolo** and **Barbaresco**, both extraordinary reds that will keep for decades without losing their splendour.

## DOCG

Alta Langa
Asti Spumante - Moscato d'Asti
Barbaresco
Barbera d'Asti
Barbera del Monferrato Superiore
Barolo
Brachetto d'Acqui or Aqui
Dogliani
Dolcetto di Diano d'Alba or Diano d'Alba
Dolcetto di Ovada Superiore or Ovada
Erbaluce di Caluso or Caluso
Gattinara
Gavi or Cortese di Gavi
Ghemme
Nizza
Roero
Ruché di Castagnole Monferrato

## DOC

Alba
Albugnano
Barbera d'Alba
Barbera del Monferrato
Boca
Bramaterra
Calosso
Canavese
Carema
Cisterna d'Asti
Colli Tortonesi
Collina Torinese
Colline Novaresi
Colline Saluzzesi
Cortese dell'Alto Monferrato
Coste della Sesia
Dolcetto d'Acqui
Dolcetto d'Alba
Dolcetto d'Asti
Dolcetto delle Langhe Monregalesi
Dolcetto di Ovada
Fara
Freisa d'Asti
Freisa di Chieri
Gabiano
Grignolino d'Asti
Grignolino del Monferrato Casalese
Langhe
Lessona
Loazzolo
Malvasia di Casorzo d'Asti or Casorzo or Malvasia di Casorzo
Malvasia di Castelnuovo Don Bosco
Monferrato
Nebbiolo d'Alba
Piemonte
Pinerolese
Rubino di Cantavenna
Sizzano
Strevi
Terre Alfieri
Valli Ossolane
Valsusa
Verduno Pelaverga

## PRINCIPAL VARIETIES CULTIVATED

### WHITE GRAPES

Arneis
Barbera Bianca
Chardonnay
Cortese
Erbaluce
Favorita
Moscato Bianco
Müller Thurgau
Pinot Bianco
Riesling Italico
Sauvignon
Sylvaner Verde
Timorasso
Traminer Aromatico

### GREY GRAPES

Pinot Grigio

### BLACK GRAPES

Aleatico
Ancellotta
Avanà
Avanengo
Barbera
Bonarda
Brachetto
Cabernet Franc
Cabernet Sauvignon
Ciliegiolo
Croatina
Dolcetto
Doux d'Henry
Durasa
Freisa
Gamay
Grignolino
Lambrusca di Alessandria
Malvasia di Casorzo
Malvasia di Schierano
Merlot
Moscato Nero d'Acqui
Nebbiolo
Neretta Cuneese
Neretta di Bairo
Pelaverga
Pelaverga Piccolo
Pinot Nero
Plassa
Quagliano
Ruché
Sangiovese
Syrah
Uva Rara
Vespolina

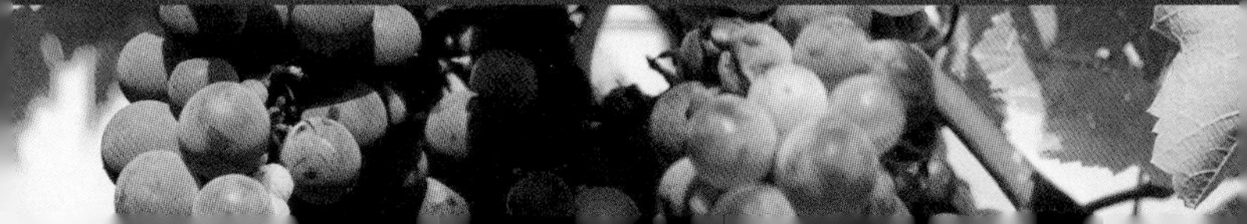

*Langhe vineyards and hazel tree cultivation, Serralunga d'Alba*

© Argalis/iStock

# Itineraries

*Locations with a winery are indicated by the symbol ♟; for the addresses of the wineries, see p. 84.*

## 1. THE LANGHE AND ROERO

A favourite destination of wine and food tourists in Italy, the **Langhe** is a region of undulating hills, sharp ridges, valleys carved out by torrents, vines that stretch to the horizon, perched hamlets and innumerable castles. Made famous by the works of authors Cesare Pavese, Beppe Fenoglio and Nuto Revelli, the Langhe's hedonistic attractions are matched by its intimist spirituality represented by its ancient churches and abbeys.

Lying to the south of Alba, the Langhe is bounded by the rivers Tanaro and Bormida and touches on the provinces of Cuneo and Asti. The geographic definitions of **Alta Langa** and **Bassa Langa** are purely altimetric: lower (*bassa*) Langa covers the gentler hilly region to the north that becomes more wooded and mountainous as it climbs into the Ligurian Apennines. Whereas the vine-covered ridges of Bassa Langa produce some of the greatest Italian reds, Alta (upper) Langa is the region famous for growing **hazelnuts**.

From an enological standpoint we are in a realm of **Nebbiolo**, but also of Barbera, Dolcetto and Moscato. There are many designated wines, all of which are

## THE TERROIR

**Area**: 25,386.70 km$^2$, of which approximately 42,961 hectares are planted to vine
**Production 2019**: 2,569,126 hectolitres of which 2,405,480 VQPRD
**Geography**: the region is 26.5% flat, 30% hilly and 43.5% mountainous

## THE PROTECTION CONSORTIA

Associazione produttori Nizza – c/o Enoteca Regionale, Via Crova 2, Nizza Monferrato, Asti, www.ilnizza.net

Consorzio di Tutela Vini d'Acqui – ✆ 0141 59 48 42, www.brachettodacqui.com

Consorzio di Tutela Alta Langa Metodo Classico – ✆ 0141 59 48 42, www.altalangadocg.com

Consorzio dell'Asti DOCG – ✆ 0141 59 48 42, www.astidocg.it

Consorzio Barbera d'Asti e Vini del Monferrato – ✆ 0141 32 43 68, www.viniastimonferrato.it

Consorzio di Tutela Barolo, Barbaresco, Alba, Langhe e Dogliani – ✆ 0173 44 10 74, www.langhevini.it

Consorzio di Tutela e Valorizzazione Vini DOCG di Caluso e DOC di Carema e Canavese – ✆ 011 98 33 860, www.erbalucecarema.it

Consorzio Tutela Vini DOC Colli Tortonesi – ✆ 392 03 16 625, www.collitortonesi.com

Consorzio per la Tutela del Dolcetto di Ovada – ✆ 339 56 34 721, www.ovada.eu

*Treiso and Barbaresco vineyards*

packed with character. The unquestioned king and queen of the region are **Barolo** and **Barbaresco**, both of which are produced from Nebbiolo grapes. The first is a generous, ethereal wine with hints of berries, liquorice, dog-rose, violet and brushwood, and is pleasantly warm, tannic and acidulous in the mouth. The second is a wine of great elegance and structure, garnet red in colour that tends towards orange with age. It has a bouquet of violet, vanilla, red berries, brushwood and spices. It is refined for a minimum of two years (of which one is in oak barrels) before being bottled, whereas the "Riserva" variant requires a minimum of four years.

To the north of Alba, on the left bank of the Tanaro, lies **Roero**, characterised by a rugged, rocky landscape, turreted hamlets, and ancient patrician residences. In addition to select cultivars (Roero, Arneis, Favorita), the district is noted for its cultivation of fruit, in particular peaches and strawberries.

## South of Alba

### The Langa of Barolo and Dolcetto

*Itinerary of approximately 80 km, starting in Alba.*

**Alba** 🍷 is an unmissable destination for gourmets, who come to taste its superb **white truffles** (*fair in Oct./Nov.*). The skyline of the historic centre is charac-

Consorzio di Tutela Freisa di Chieri – 📞 011 94 25 745, www.freisadichieri.com

Consorzio di Tutela del Gavi – 📞 0143 64 50 68, www.gavi972.it

Consorzio Colline del Monferrato Casalese – 📞 338 90 02 84, www.vinimonferratocasalese.it

Consorzio di Tutela Vino Malvasia Casorzo di Asti – 📞 0141 92 92 29, www.casorzodoc.it

Consorzio di Tutela Nebbioli Alto Piemonte – 📞 0163 84 17 50, www.consnebbiolialtop.it

Consorzio di Tutela Vini DOC Pinerolese – 📞 0121 59 10 5 or 333 77 03 638

Consorzio di Tutela Vini DOC Valsusa

## WINE AND FOOD ROUTES

Strada del Vino Astesana – 📞 0141 96 40 38, www.astesana-stradadelvino.it

Strada del Barolo e dei grandi vini di Langa – 📞 0173 78 71 66, www.stradadelbarolo.it

Strada del Vino dei Colli Tortonesi – www.stradacollitortonesi.com

Strada del Vino del Monferrato Astigiano – 📞 0141 35 71 11, www.stradadelvino-monferratoastigiano.it

Strada Reale dei Vini Torinesi – 📞 011 53 51 81, www.stradarealevinitorinesi.it

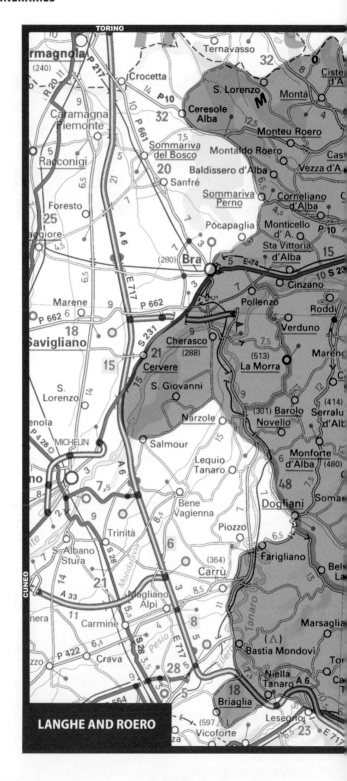

**LANGHE AND ROERO**

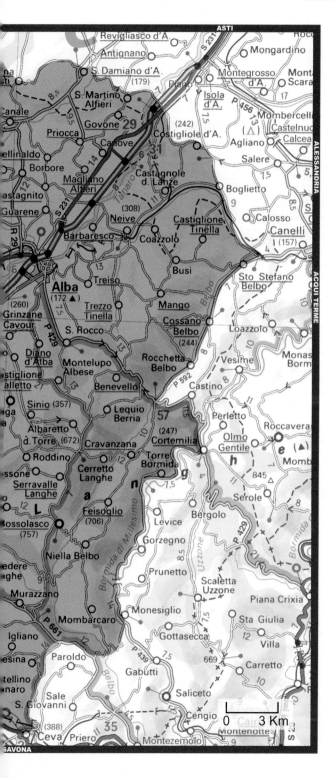

Church of San Giovanni Battista, Diano d'Alba

© cristianoalessandro/iStock

terised by the town's **medieval towers**, while **Via Vittorio Emanuele** is lined by beautiful palaces, including **Casa Do** (15th c.) decorated by a tiled **frieze★** of knights and their ladies. In Piazza Risorgimento, the site of the Roman forum, stand the Town Hall and the **duomo**, originally Romanesque but several times remodelled. The symbols of the 4 evangelists on the façade form the name of the city: **A**ngel, **L**ion, **B**ue (Ox) and **A**quila (Eagle). The town's churches boast some excellent works of art. Traces of the Roman theatre have been found beneath the Church of San Giuseppe; the Teatro Sociale, close to the Church of San Domenico, has a fine Neoclassical auditorium.

**Diano d'Alba** 🍷 *(6 km south of Alba)* was an ancient settlement named after the cult of Diana, the goddess of hunting worshipped by the Liguri and Roman peoples. Remains are visible in the small chapel dug out of the rock at the entrance to the village. There is also the 18th-c. Church of San Giovanni Battista.

**Grinzane Cavour**, whose mayor was Camillo Cavour from 1832 to 1849, is dominated by the **castle★** (13th-15th c.), home of the **Regional Wine Cellar** and the place where the famous Grinzane Cavour literary prize is awarded. *Open 10-18 (Apr.–Oct. 10-19), closed Tue., Jan. and public hols., ℘ 0173 26 21 59, www. castellogrinzane.com.*

**Serralunga d'Alba** 🍷 is a sunny town halfway between the plain and low mountains. It runs in a concentric circle around the stern **castle** built by

the Falletti family, which was used as a garrison due to its strategic **position★**. *Guided tours 10.30-18; for information and reservations ℘ 0173 61 33 58, www. castellodiserralunga.it.*

Now you leave the gentle hills to head south towards the more wooded and mountainous countryside of Alta Langa. **Bossolasco** is an elegant little town adorned by innumerable climbing roses. A set of shop signs made by various artists in the 1960s is displayed in the Town Hall.

After the splendidly sited **Murazzano**, where a famous cheese is made, you head north again to **Dogliani** 🍷, home of Dolcetto and the farm estate developed and run by Luigi Einaudi, the President of Italy from 1948-55, who is buried in the town.

Continue northwards to **Monforte d'Alba** 🍷, one of the strongholds of the Piedmont Cathars. Stormed in 1028 by Archbishop Ariberto, the castle after which the village is named experienced mixed fortunes and was rebuilt in the 18th c. as Palazzo Scarampi.

Head to **Barolo** 🍷, the capital of Piedmont wines. The powerful Falletti family built forts and castles right across the Langhe: the one in Barolo, the family's principal feud conserves the library looked after by Silvio Pellico, and is home to the **Regional Wine Cellar of Barolo and WiMu** (*Wine Museum, www. wimubarolo.it, www.enotecadelbarolo.it; for information ℘ 0173 38 66 97*). It is surrounded by magnificent countryside that pays tribute to the king of Italian wines.

From Barolo you climb to **La Morra** 🍷, where you can see the remains of medieval and Baroque buildings and the splendid **belvedere★★** offers breathtaking views over the Langhe. Hidden between rows of the most prestigious cru at the foot of La Morra stands the small and psychedelic **Brunate Chapel★**, built in the early 20th c. and redecorated recently by David Tremlett and **Sol LeWitt**. *For information on visits* ☎ *0173 28 59 42.*

🐾 From La Morra to **Castiglione Falletto** 🍷, passing through Barolo, a path 8.6 km long crosses a marvellous landscape planted with vines. *Approx. 3 h, direction signs in red and white. Other routes available at the Tourist Offices in Barolo and Alba, and on the site www. langheroero.it.*

## East of Alba

### The Langa of Barbaresco and the white truffle

*Itinerary of approximately 30 km. From Alba head north-east along the winding road to the heart of Barbaresco DOCG.*

Set on the right bank of the Tanaro, **Barbaresco** 🍷 is the birthplace of the other great Piedmont wine made from the Nebbiolo grape. The place-name is linked to the forest (*Barbarica Sylva*) in which the Liguri tribe settled when fleeing from the Romans. The castle built at the end of the 17th c. is now privately owned, whilst the 19th-c. Church of San Donato is the seat of the **Regional Wine Cellar of Barbaresco** (*see p. 84*).

Five kilometres to the east lies **Neive** 🍷, the second largest municipality in Barbaresco. It stands on the boundary between the Langhe and Monferrato and has an attractive historic centre with Baroque churches and fine town residences. Heading down back towards Alba, you come to **Treiso**, Barbaresco's third municipality and one of the places where the hunt for the prized white truffle has a long history.

## Roero

### Wines and castles on the left bank of the Tanaro

*Itinerary of approximately 50 km starting from Alba.*

Since the time of the Ligurian and Roman settlements, this area has seen a continual flux of lords and seigniories, as the many castles in the countryside indicate. With the passing of time their defensive role turned residential, one more suited to the court of the Savoys. The enological jewels of the zone are **Roero** – which, like Barolo and Barbaresco, is made from Nebbiolo grapes and characterised by a delicate aroma and a dry, velvety, balanced taste –, **Arneis**, a fresh, dry, pleasingly bitterish white wine, and **Favorita**.

In the Church dell'Assunta in **Santa Vittoria d'Alba**, immediately to the west of Alba, is the lovely altarpiece painted by Macrino d'Alba, one of the outstanding figures of Renaissance painting in Piedmont. The centre of the town still contains several buildings from the ancient village.

*La Morra and its vineyards*

© LlaneM/iStock

Provana Castle, Guarene

© Ph. Orain/Michelin

▶ **Detour** – a few kilometres separate Cinzano from **Pollenzo**, which still retains its amphitheatrical form from Roman times, while the Agenzia, a Neo-Gothic model farm built by Carlo Alberto in the 19th c., is one of the two seats of the University of Gastronomic Sciences (the other is in Colorno, in the province of Parma).

**Bra★** (*5 km north-west of Pollenzo*) is the birthplace of Beato Cottolengo and – more prosaically – of the **Slow Food** movement that champions the food and wine culture (*piazza XX Settembre 5, ℘ 0172 41 96 11, www.slowfood.com*). The elegant palaces of the town are distributed around Via Vittorio Emanuele II and **Piazza Caduti★**, onto which face the Church of Sant'Andrea designed by Bernini and built by Guarino Guarini, and the Town Hall, originating in the Middle Ages but rebuilt in the 18th c. Close by, Palazzo Traversa (1450, Civic Museum) is the only Gothic building in Bra. Take Via Barbacana (*just behind Sant'Andrea*) to reach the Church of **Santa Chiara**, a masterpiece of Piedmont Rococo. It has an extraordinary **twin cupola★** in which the openings in the lower dome allow sight of the frescoes in the upper one.

**Pocapaglia** (*4 km north of Bra*) is surrounded by a landscape of gullies, ravines and rock formations created by erosion.

The SP 171 passes through **Monticello d'Alba**, where there is a lovely medieval castle refurbished in the 18th c., and then arrives at **Guarene**, where you can visit **Provana Castle★**, a splendid 18th-c. residence with original furnishings (member of Relais&Châteaux from 2016). Guarene is also the home of the **Sandretto Re Rebaudengo Foundation**, which organises cultural events linked to contemporary art in the Palazzo Sandretto Re Rebaudengo. *Information on visits ℘ 011 379 76 00 (Turin office), www.fsrr.org.*

Another hamlet, another castle: **Magliano Alfieri** has a beautiful 18th-c. residence built by the Alfieri di Sostegno family that incorporates parts of an earlier medieval castle. The playwright Vittorio Alfieri (1749-1803), stepson of the then owner, spent several summers of his childhood here. The castle contains an interesting museum devoted to ceiling plaster decorations, a technique popular in the area. *Open Sat.-Sun. 10.30-18.30 (Apr.-Oct.), guided tours upon appointment ℘ 0173 661 17.*

The dramatic Baroque castle in **Govone** designed and built by Guarini and Juvarra has attractive decorated rooms, a sumptuous ballroom, and offers a spectacular view over the village below. Jean-Jacques Rousseau once worked offers there as a librarian. In the 19th c. it was chosen by the Savoys as a summer residence. *Open Apr.-Dec., Fri.-Sat.-Sun. 10-12 and 15-18 (Jul.-Aug. 16-19, closed Fri. in Nov.-Dec.); for other times contact Govone Municipality, ℘ 0173 58 103.*

Head west towards **Canale** ▼, a farming village famous for its succulent peaches and home to the **Regional Wine Cellar of Roero**. The porticoed Via Roma runs through the historic centre, lined by Baroque churches and the ancient castle renovated in the 18th c.

Five kilometres north of Canale you come to **Cisterna d'Asti** 🍷, the only municipality in Roero in the province of Asti rather than Cuneo. The lovely castle contains an interesting ethnographic museum. *Piazza Maggiore Hope 1. Open Sat.-Sun. 15-19, guided tours upon appointment* ☞ *0141 97 90 21, www. museoartiemestieri.it.*

Continuing to **Vezza d'Alba**, a little outside of the town you will see the Sanctuary of the Madonna dei Boschi, the ancient burial place of the counts of Roero in a fine panoramic position.

## Moscato

### The hills between the Langhe and Monferrato

*Itinerary of approximately 30 km starting from Canelli.*

In Piedmont the Moscato grape lies at the base of many wines, including Asti Spumante DOCG, the famous party sparkling wine. But it is not all bubbles: the designated area Moscato d'Asti includes still dried-grape wines with their intoxicating fruity and floral bouquet.

The Moscato variety has been grown at **Canelli** 🍷 since Roman times and the long wine-making tradition has made the town the capital of Italy's most famous white wines. It also brought a series of wonderful Art Nouveau buildings that were constructed when production was at its height. The town is dominated by Gancia Castle, built in 1930 on the site of a 17th-c. residence, but Canelli also boasts the **Underground Cathedrals★**, a network of more than 20 km of tunnels dug in the tufa since the 18th c., where the sparkling wine could be refined at a standard temperature of 12-14 °C. The procedure used was similar to the one used in Champagne in France. *For information* ☞ *0141 82 02 80, and www.comune.canelli.at.it.*

"A village means not being alone, knowing that in the people, in the plants, in the land there is something of you, and that even when you are not there, it is there waiting for you" (*The Moon and the Bonfires*, Cesare Pavese [1908-50]). Pavese was the voice of 20th-c. Italian literature; he wrote about the Piedmont countryside which he saw as an archetypal place of happiness and innocence. The house

where he was born and many places linked to his works can be visited in **Santo Stefano Belbo** 🍷 (*Piazza Confraternita 1. For information* ☞ *0141 84 08 94, www. fondazionecesarepavese.it*). What remains of Santo Stefano's medieval settlement are the ruins of the Benedictine Abbey of **San Gaudenzio** (*on the other side of the river Belbo, north-west of the village*), whose monks introduced viticulture to the village.

**Calosso** offers a marvellous view over the Langhe and Monferrato. The village's castle, founded in the early Middle Ages, is set in a lovely park. The historic centre has ancient flights of steps and *crotin* (wine cellars) carved out of the tufa.

A very ancient hamlet, **Castagnole delle Lanze** 🍷 has a tower that stands on the site of an earlier castle and, in the historic centre, the monumental Baroque Church of San Pietro.

The road that rises from Castagnole to **Castiglione Tinella** 🍷 provides splendid views over the hills.

Pass through **Mango** (seat of the **Regional Wine Cellar of Moscato**) on your way to **Neviglie** 🍷, where you can see a fine altarpiece of the *Marriage of St Catherine* by the outstanding painter of the Piedmont Renaissance, Macrino d'Alba, in the Church of San Giorgio.

## 2. MONFERRATO

Monferrato is bounded to the north by the river Po, to the west by the Langhe, and to the east by the Alessandrian plain. As with the Langhe, the definitions of the two districts, Alto and Basso Monferrato, are based on the gentle hills of the north and the more wooded and mountainous landscape as one approaches the Ligurian Apennines.

## The lands of Barbera

*Itinerary of approximately 60 km starting from Nizza Monferrato.*

Barbera is one of the most common grapes used in Piedmont wine making and represents a good percentage of the region's wine production. It is grown in many appellations, of which the best known are Barbera d'Asti, Barbera del Monferrato and Barbera d'Alba. Barbera wine has a heady aroma, good structure and a characteristic rugged and acidulous note that, with time, becomes soft and velvety, balanced and full. Those are the salient traits of this *grande dame* of Italian wine-production.

A large village in the Belbo valley, **Nizza Monferrato** ♀ has a pleasant historic centre through which the porticoed Via Carlo Alberto – the historic Via Maestra – runs to Piazza Garibaldi. This square has been the site of the covered market since the 19th c. The village has many lovely 18th-c. buildings, the Municipal Hall (in a building dating originally to the Middle Ages), and the **Stabilimento Bersano** where you can visit a "peasantry" museum and see wine prints. *Piazza Dante 21. ℰ 0141 72 02 11, www. bersano.it.*

A point of interest: the village was the birthplace in 1836 of Francesco Cirio, one of the pioneers of industrial preserves.

To the east of Nizza, **Mombaruzzo** ♀ offers excellent macaroons and boasts the beautiful Gothic Church of Sant'Antonio Abate, with its tiled façade crowned by pointed gables, a frequent feature of medieval architecture in Piedmont. The Clock Tower in the middle of the village is the only remnant of the medieval castle.

Returning on your steps, before arriving in Nizza, turn south to **Calamandrana** ♀, which is dominated by its imposing 14th-c., privately owned castle, and **San Marzano Oliveto** ♀, where the castle, also 14th-c., has beautiful vaulted cellars and hosts exhibitions and conventions. Next, go north to **Agliano Terme**, which focuses not only on wine but water too, with its sodium chloride-sulphur-magnesium thermal waters. Agliano was the birthplace of Bianca Lancia, mother of Costanza and Manfredi, the two illegitimate children of Federico II of Savoy. Just outside the town stands the Sanctuary dell'Annunciazione in a lovely panoramic position in **Molizzo**.

**Costigliole d'Asti** ♀ is another village centred around a **castle**, once the residence of the Countess of Castiglione and now seat of the Italian Culinary Institute for Foreigners, where courses and master courses are organised for foreign chefs. The castle is also home to Italy's national wine and oil cellars, which both offer tastings.

The itinerary ends at **Rocchetta Tanaro** ♀, the feud of the Incisa della Rocchetta family since the Middle Ages. Today, the family lives in the palace next to the castle. Just outside the village lies the wooded area of the **Rocchetta Tanaro Regional Park**. The enormous expanse of beech, oak, chestnut and durmast trees is home to many protected creatures, such as badgers, foxes and boar, and many species of birds, including herons. The river still provides a habitat to the freshwater prawn, a fact that serves as an important biological indicator. *Rocchetta Tanaro National Park, Via Salie 19, Rocchetta Tanaro. ℰ 0141 64 47 14, www.comune.rocchettatanaro.at.it.*

## Basso Monferrato, from Asti to Malvasia

*Itinerary of approximately 120 km starting from Asti.*

The gentle hills of Basso Monferrato create a harmonious mosaic featuring vineyards, fortified villages, towers and castles. In Piedmont, Malvasia means sweet red wines. This grape has two designated areas: **Malvasia di Castelnuovo Don Bosco**, whose production zone ranges across several municipalities in Asti, and **Malvasia di Casorzo**, which is produced in several municipalities in Asti and Alessandria.

### Asti★ ♀

The city where Vittorio Alfieri was born was founded in ancient times but is prevalently 18th-c. in layout today. Asti is home to a famous palio and the *Douja d'Or*, a festival that celebrates fine Italian wines. The main street in the historic centre is the Corso Alfieri, around which the city's most important monuments are grouped. Making your way up the street, on the right in Piazza Medici you see the 13th-c. Troyana Tower. On the left, in Piazza San Secondo, are the 18th-c. City Hall and the Collegiate Church of San Secondo (13th-15th c.), the "church of the merchants" who made Asti's fortune in the Middle Ages. Inside the church are fragments of ancient frescoes, the polyptych by Gandolfino d'Asti of the *Adoration of the Magi* (15th c.), and the drapes and *carroccio* (wagon) of the Palio. Take Via Aliberti, pass by the so-called Palazzo del Podestà (13th c.) and enter the ghetto instituted in 1724 (the synagogue is at no. 8 Via Ottolenghi). Shortly after, Piazza Roma lies to your right where the 14th-c. Comentina Tower stands incorporated in a Neo-Gothic palace. Continue down Via Aliberti to Piazza San Martino, turn right into Via Roero and follow it back to Corso Alfieri. Sant'Anastasio Museum is at no. 365/a; this is an archaeological area with Roman and medieval layers, and includes a **crypt**★ (11th c.). *Open 10-19, closed Mon., ☎ 0141 53 04 03, www.fondazioneastimusei.it.*

You will shortly come to Palazzo Alfieri (18th c.), where the poet was born: the house has a lovely trapezoidal courtyard. At the end of the Corso stands a Roman tower (1st c. AD), which was part of the ancient city walls.

The **cathedral**★★ is one of the best examples of Piedmont Gothic (14th c.) and, on its right side, has a fine portico in Ornamental Gothic style decorated with statues and low reliefs. The interior is entirely lined with 17th- and 18th-c. frescoes and has beautiful panels by Gandolfino d'Asti (16th c.) and a terracotta group of the *Lamentation over the Dead Christ* (16th c.). Note the floor mosaic of the earlier Romanesque church (12th-13th c.) by the altar.

At the end of Corso Alfieri (opposite end to the Roman tower) stands the **San Pietro complex** (12th c.), comprising a lovely octagonal baptistery linked to the 15th-c. Church of San Pietro in Consavia. (*same adresses of S. Anastasio Museum, open 10-13 and 16-19, 16-18 in win.*).

*From Asti take the SP 458 north-west, then the SP 119 left.*

The road enters Malvasia territory and leads to **Castelnuovo Don Bosco**, the birthplace of three saints: Giovanni Bosco, Giuseppe Cafasso and Domenico Savio. A small side trip takes you to **Colle Don Bosco**, the site of the house where Don Bosco was born and the sanctuary built (1961-91). In addition to being a place of pilgrimage, the place has a museum illustrating agricultural life in the 19th c. and a missionary ethnological museum. *Open 10.30-12 and 14.30-18 (14.30-17 in win.), closed Mon. ☎ 011 98 77 168, www.memcolledonbosco.it, www.colledonbosco.org.*

*Return to Castelnuovo Don Bosco.*

**Pessione** (*16 km south-west of Castelnuovo Don Bosco and 5 km south of Chieri*): you can visit the **Martini Museum of the History of Enology**★ in the 18th-c. cellars of the first Martini&Rossi plant. *Piazza Luigi Rossi 2. For information ☎ 011 94 191, www.visitcasamartini.it.*

*From Castelnuovo Don Bosco continue north towards **Albugnano**.*

Set in a silent hollow, the **Abbey of Vezzolano**★ is one of the best examples of Piedmont Romanesque-Gothic. The façade of the abbey is decorated with tiles and sandstone and the portal is adorned with reliefs. The splendid **jubé**★★ (1189) has polychrome low reliefs of the Patriarchs and scenes from the life of the Virgin. At the end of the right aisle is the entrance to the elegant **cloister**★, where you can see the remains of 13th- and 14th-c. frescoes. *Open Sat., Sun. and public hols. 10-18 (10-17 in win.), ☎ 333 13 65 812, www.vezzolano.it.*

Asti cathedral

© Flavio Vallenari/iStock

*Piazza della Bollente, Acqui Terme*

Follow the signs to **Cocconato** 🍷 (a fine 15th-c. Town Hall) and then **Montiglio**, an elegant village dominated by a castle. In its park, the Chapel of Sant'Andrea has a cycle of 14th-c. frescoes. The charming Romanesque Church of San Lorenzo, with richly sculpted capitals, stands by the village cemetery.

*Go back to the SS 590 and head in the direction of Casale Monferrato.*

Passing through fields, vineyards and woods you come to **Murisengo**. Here you can see a privately owned castle that retains some elements from the feudal period, and the splendid Rococo **interior★** of the Church of Sant'Antonio Abate. Close by and not to be missed is the Belvedere Castle in **Villadeati**, a striking 18th-c. residence in a panoramic position.

*Go back to the SS 590 and continue towards Casale Monferrato.*

At **Serralunga di Crea** 🍷 a right turn will take you to the Sacro Monte di Crea. The **Sacro Monte** was built on top of one of the highest hills in Basso Monferrato in the late 16th c. A path leaves from the square where the Sanctuary of Santa Maria Assunta stands (15th-c. frescoes and a panel by Macrino d'Alba) and leads to the various chapels on the way to the Chapel of Paradise, from where there are superb views.

*Continue to Casale Monferrato.*

## Casale Monferrato

The capital of Monferrato (1464-1713) under the Paleologues and the Gonzaga family, Casale is a pleasant, 18th-c. town with a historic centre traversed by Via Roma and Via Lanza.

The **duomo** (12th-13th c., restored in the 19th c.) has a large narthex and, inside, a wooden crucifix lined with silver leaf (12th c.), and wall mosaics (also 12th c.) in the ambulatory.

Turn right in Via Lanza to reach the Church of San Domenico, a Gothic construction with an elegant Renaissance portal and a lovely brick cloister on the right.

*Go back to Via Lanza and turn left into Via Paleologhi.*

**Via Mameli★**, the town's most refined street, is lined by fine 18th-c. palaces.

Take Via Cavour on the right. The **Cloister of Santa Croce★** (civic museum) has 16th-c. frescoes painted by Moncalvo, the "Raphael of Monferrato".

*Turn right into Via Roma and then left into Via Alessandria.*

The Baroque **Synagogue degli Argenti★** at no. 44 Vicolo Olper houses a museum of Jewish art and history. *Open 8.30-12.30 only on request, closed Sat., ☎ 0142 71 807, www.casalebraica.info.*

At the end of Via Alessandria (no. 26), the palace that belonged to Anna d'Alençon, marquess of Monferrato, has a splendid Renaissance **courtyard★**.

In Piazza Castello, site of the imposing Paleologues Castle (15th-16th c.), take Via Saffi to reach the small Piazza Santo Stefano, looked onto by the church of the same name (17th c.) and the 19th c. Palazzo Ricci.

Heading south you come to **Vignale** ☂, the home of the **Regional Wine Cellar of Monferrato** (see p. 84) in a castle founded in the 17th c. and a prestigious summer dance festival.

**Moncalvo** ☂ lies in a strategic position between Asti and Casale, 15 km to the west. This was the town where the painter Guglielmo Caccia (called Moncalvo, 1568-1625) chose to spend much of his life. Considered the leading exponent of Mannerism in Piedmont, he left many works in the churches of Monferrato and Turin. The town of Moncalvo has a number of very fine civic buildings from different eras, and the Church of San Francesco, which was founded in the 13th c. (bell tower and apse) and later remodelled. Moncalvo hosts many gastronomic events and festivals.

## Alto Monferrato

### Acquese, Ovada, Gavi and the hills of Tortona

*Itinerary of approximately 50 km starting from Acqui Terme.*

The itinerary takes you through the hills of the Pre-Apennines that mark the boundary between Piedmont and Liguria. The landscape features castles and villages that are Ligurian in appearance, with painted palaces and twisting alleyways. The most favoured grape variety is the **Cortese**, from which the fresh, flowery white wine **Gavi DOCG** is made. **Brachetto** gives delicate, very perfumed, sparkling wines, while the **Timorasso** variety grown on the Tortonesi hills gives white wines of such structure that they can be aged.

### Acqui Terme★

A thermal spa known since the Roman era, Acqui is a very pleasant little town. On the left before the Carlo Alberto Bridge over the river Bormida lie the remains of the Roman aqueduct, and the ancient spa buildings on the right (the new spa is in the historic centre). The main street is Corso Italia, to the right of which lies the square where the duomo stands, originally Roman-

esque but now with a Baroque façade. The castle behind is home to the civic museum and a botanical garden that gives good **views★** over the surrounding hills. Continuing down Corso Italia, on the right stands **Piazza della Bollente★**, a 19th-c. kiosk beneath which the spa water rises at a temperature of 70-75 °C. Head right into the elegant Piazza Conciliazione lined with elegant palaces. Back in Corso Italia, turn left to visit the ancient Basilica of San Pietro, which still has the apses constructed in the 5th-6th c.

Drive on through Morsasco and Cremolino, clustered around their ancient castles, to arrive at **Molare**, whose 13th-c. castle was renovated in Neo-Gothic style by Alfredo d'Andrade in the 19th c.

The long domination of the area by the Genoese has resulted in **Ovada** having a decidedly Ligurian appearance: in addition to winding alleys and painted palaces, the historic centre has several lovely churches. **Dolcetto** is a typical local wine.

Continue to **Tagliolo Monferrato** ☂, where the beautiful castle is now the premises of a wine-making company. Founded in the 10th c., the castle was remodelled in the 15th and 19th c. *Visits by appointment,* ✆ *0143 89 195, www.castelloditagliolo.it.*

The beautiful **Lerma Castle** ☂ (15th c.) is surrounded by an ancient residential area and stands over the sheer drop to the torrent Piota.

The next stop is in **Gavi** ☂, where the famous white wine is made. The village is dominated by the massive medieval **fort★** that was long contested by Genoa and Milan. *For information on guided tours,* ✆ *0143 64 35 54, www.fortedigavi.it.*

Continuing through the vine-clad hills, you come to **Novi Ligure** ☂, a town boasting lovely **painted palaces★** that belonged to the Genoese nobility who resided there. The central Via Roma leads to Piazza Dellepiane, site of the Collegiate Church and Palazzo Cambiaso. The latter has a courtyard featuring a painted architectural backdrop.

**Tortona** ☂ was founded by the Liguri in the 5th c. BC. Lined with lovely 19th-c. porticoes, the Roman Via Emilia leads to Piazza Duomo, faced onto by the majestic cathedral and archbishop's palace, and to Piazza Arzano. Here the medieval Palazzo Guidobono (renovated in the 20th c.) is the setting for the archaeological museum and civic picture gallery. The remains of a medieval fort stand on Savo hill to the east of the town.

To the south-east and east of Tortona stretch the winding hills carpeted with vineyards that produce the dry **Colli Tortonesi DOC** wines whose delicate aroma contains a hint of almond.

## 3. THE LAKES AND CASTLES OF CANAVESE

*Itinerary of approximately 70 km starting from Caluso.*

The Canavese area lies in a curve to the north of Turin. It is dotted with lakes of glacial origin and innumerable castles indicative of its feudal past. A key figure in Canavese history is Arduino, marquis of Ivrea and king of Italy between 1002 and 1014, who, defeated by Henry II of Germany, retired to the Abbey of Fruttuaria. The ruins of the abbey are incorporated in the Church dell'Assunta in **San Benigno Canavese**. This vast area is planted prevalently with **Nebbiolo**, **Barbera**, **Freisa** and **Neretto** grapes for the reds, while the fresh, dry **Erbaluce** is a favourite for the whites, producing a balanced and velvety dried-grape wine.

Founded by the Romans, **Caluso** is justly famous for its Erbaluce and dried-grape wines. Its position on the slopes of a morainic hill give lovely views of **Lake Candia**, a glacial lake in Candia Provincial Park, visited by many species of birds.

Driving 6 km east of Caluso you come to **San Giorgio Canavese** 🍴. Its 14th-c. castle was rebuilt in the 18th c. to turn it into a palace with richly decorated interiors and a surrounding park.

*Continue north to* **Agliè** 🍴. The **castle★** was built in the 17th c. by architect Amedeo di Castellamonte for Count Filippo San Martino di Agliè. In 1763 it passed to the Savoy family, who enlarged it and included the hamlet in the structure of the castle. The castle contains a small but enchanting Neoclassical **theatre★**, mostly 19th-c. furnishings, and a magnificent ballroom decorated with 17th-c. frescoes of the deeds of Arduino. The residence is surrounded by a huge

landscaped park. *Open 8.30-19.30, closed Mon., for information ℘ 0124 33 01 02, www.residenzereali.it.*

In front of the castle run the porticoes of Via Principe Tommaso, near which stands the small Church of **Santa Marta★** (1730-60), whose plan resembles the silhouette of a lady.

You come to Ivrea by passing through **Castellamonte**, a city renowned for its ceramics, as is attested by the arch designed by Arnaldo Pomodoro in the main square. The square is also the site of the Rotonda, an uncompleted basilica that is used each year to host a ceramics exhibition.

### Ivrea

Ivrea is the city where the first typewriter was built and the home of Olivetti, whose headquarters stand on the left bank of the Dora Baltea. Ivrea lies to the south-west of the **Serra di Ivrea★**, the largest morainic wall in Europe. The city skyline is dominated by the 14th-c. castle and its towers. The upper part of the city is where the duomo stands, originally Romanesque but rebuilt in the 19th c. The lower city is the location of the central and elegant Via Palestro, Piazza Vittorio Emanuele (site of the City Hall) and Piazza Ottinetti.

On the other side of the river, Olivetti buildings around Via Jervis have been turned into the **Modern Architecture Museum**, which features interesting examples of civil and industrial architecture from the years 1930-79. *Via Jervis 26. For information ℘ 0125 63 41 55, www.mamivrea.it.*

To the north of the city lie five small glacial **lakes** (Sirio, Pistono, Nero, Campagna, San Michele) surrounded by beautiful vegetation.

From Ivrea, take the S 228 to the foot of the morainic Serra, pass through **Piverone** 🍴 and arrive at **Lake Viverone**, of glacial origin and the site of many Bronze Age lake-dwelling civilisations. Having passed through the village of **Viverone** 🍴, you come to **Roppolo**, where the cellars of the medieval castle are home to the **Regional Wine Cellar of Serra**.

*Go back a few kilometres along the SS 228 and take the left turn to Caravino.*

In a splendidly panoramic **position★★** stands **Masino Castle** (owned by the FAI), built in the 9th c. by the counts Valperga and transformed into an elegant country residence in the 18th c. The interior (with its outstanding ballroom) conserves 17th- and 18th-c. furnishings and, it is said, the remains of King Arduino. You can also visit the park, stables and carriage museum. *For information ℘ 0125 77 81 00, www.fondoambiente.it.*

## 4. THE HILLS OF NOVARA, BIELLA AND VERCELLI

*Itinerary of 30 km starting from Gattinara.*

**Alto Piemonte**, the hilly area close to the ring of mountains traversed by the river Sesia, runs across the provinces of Biella, Novara, Verbania and Vercelli. Here Nebbiolo is the most common variety (locally known as **Spanna**), which is used to produce wines with the Gattinara, Ghemme, Lessona, Boca, Colline Novaresi, Fara, Sizzano, Bramarerra and Coste della Sesia designations.

Situated on the right bank of the Sesia, among the eastern ramifications of the Biella prealps, **Gattinara** ♟ was founded as a free town in the 13th c. by Vercelli. The fame of the dry, well-balanced Gattinara wine, which takes on violet tones with time, is the result of the publicising work carried out by Cardinal Mercurino Arborio di Gattinara, chancellor of Charles V, who made it known right across Europe. The 14th-c. Church of San Pietro, rebuilt on several occasions, has a beautiful tiled façade in Lombard Romanesque style. The 11th-c. Tower of the Castelle looks down on the town

from the hill and was once part of Gattinara's system of defences.

**Rovasenda**, with its impressive 12th-c. castle, lies 11 km south of Gattinara. The road to it passes through stretches of **Baraggia**, a protected woodland zone that was once very large but reduced to isolated patches by the draining of the land to grow rice.

Proceeding north from Gattinara towards Romagnano Sesia you come to the ruins of **San Lorenzo Castle** (12th c.), from where there are fine views.

Crossing the river you come to **Romagnano Sesia** ♟, which, like Gattinara, was also established as a free town, but in this case by Novara. The Church of San Silano was built in the 19th-c. over the remains of an ancient abbey and holds various excellent works of art. Close by, the "cellar of the Saints" is all that remains of the medieval abbey, and has interesting 15th-c. frescoes. In the north section of the town stands the Pretorio, the remains of a 13th-c. defensive system. Monte Cucco is the site of the monumental **Villa Caccia★**, built by Alessandro Antonelli (1798-1888) around 1845. With its tower it looks out over the town of Romagnano. The villa contains the **History and Ethnography Museum of Bassa Valsesia**. *Open by reservation only, ℘ 342 16 31 245.* The birthplace of the great architect Alessandro Antonelli, **Ghemme** ♟ has retained its medieval plan and boasts a huge and articulated 15th-c. **castle and fortified hamlet**. The crypt of the Blessed Panacea designed by Antonelli (1874) can be seen in the Baroque Church dell'Assunta.

*Piazza Cavour, Vercelli*

© M. Saracco/iStock

# Addresses

## Tourist information

**Alba Bra Langhe Roero Tourist Board** – Piazza Risorgimento 2, **Alba**, ☏ 0173 35 833, www.langheroero.it

**Alexala – Province of Alessandria** – Piazza S. Maria di Castello 14, **Alessandria**, ☏ 0131 28 80 95, www.alexala.it

**Asti Tourist Office** – Piazza Alfieri 34, **Asti**, ☏ 0141 53 03 57, www.astiturismo.it

**Roero Turismo** – At the Roero Regional Wine Cellar, Via Roma 57, **Canale**, ☏ 0173 97 82 28, www.roeroturismo.it

**Mon.D.O. Monferrato Casalese** – **Casale Monferrato**, ☏ 0142 45 77 89, www.monferrato.org

**Province of Turin** – Piazza Ottinetti, **Ivrea**, ☏ 0125 61 81 31, Via Duomo 1, **Pinerolo**, ☏ 0121 79 55 89 www.turismotorino.org

## Regional wine cellars

Housed in evocative settings, the Regional Wine Cellars offer an overview of the local production. For further information, *www.piemonteagri.it*

**Acqui Terme e Vino** – Piazza Levi 12, **Acqui Terme** (AL), ☏ 0144 77 02 73, www.termeevino.it

**Barbaresco Regional Wine Cellar** – Deconsecrated church of S. Donato, Piazza del Municipio 7, **Barbaresco** (CN), ☏ 0173 63 52 51, www.enotecadel barbaresco.it

**Province of Turin Regional Wine Cellar** – Palazzo Valperga di Masino, Piazza Valperga 2, **Caluso** (TO), ☏ 011 98 31 041, www.enotecaregionaletorino.wine

**Roero Regional Wine Cellar** – Via Roma 57, **Canale** (CN), ☏ 0173 97 82 28, www.enotecadelroero.it, www.roero turismo.it

**Canelli and Astesana Regional Wine Cellar** – Via G.B. Giuliani 29, **Canelli** (AT), ☏ 0141 82 26 40, www.enotecaregionale dicanelli.it

**Gattinara and Terre del Nebbiolo of Northern Piedmont Regional Wine Cellar** – Corso Valsesia 112, **Gattinara** (VC) - ☏ 0163 83 40 70, www.enotecaregionale digattinara.it

**Cavour Piedmontese Regional Wine Cellar** – Castello di Grinzane Cavour, Via Castello 5, **Grinzane Cavour** (CN), ☏ 0173 26 21 59, www.castello grinzane.com

**Colline del Moscato Regional Wine Cellar** – Castello dei Busca, Piazza XX Settembre 19, **Mango** (CN), www.facebook.com/enotecaregionale collinemoscato

**Nizza Regional Wine Cellar**– Palazzo Crova, Via Crova 2, **Nizza Monferrato** (AT), ☏ 0141 79 33 50, www.enotecanizza.it

**Monferrato Regional Wine Cellar** – Castello del Monferrato, Piazza Castello, **Casale Monferrato** (AL), ☏ 348 04 35 097, www.enotecadelmonferrato.it

The Region of Piedmont, in conjunction with local associations, groups of wine-growers and cooperatives wineries, has promoted the establishment and development of many **Municipal Wine Cellars** and **Wine Shops**. For a complete list, see *www.piemonteagri.it*

## The wineries

*The addresses are listed in alphabetical order by location.*

### LANGHE - BAROLO AND DOLCETTO

🏚 **Boroli** – *Via Brunella 4 -* **Castiglione Falletto** *(CN) -* ☏ *0173 62 927 - www.boroli. it - info@boroli.it - Winery tours by reservation.* "The Brunella cantina is entirely dedicated to the production of Barolo wines. Its position at the centre of Castiglione Falletto valley and its innovative design make this cantina unique. Achille Boroli produces and exalts three grand, historical vines: Villero Cerequio and the Brunella monopoly." Visitors can stay in the 8 rooms of the Locanda del Pilone hotel (€155) and dine at the renowned restaurant of the same name, ☏ *0173 36 66 16, www. locandadelpilone.com.* Hectares under vine: 31.

**Wines**: Barolo, Barolo Villero, Barolo Cerequio, Barolo Brunella, Chardonnay Bel Amì.

**Ceretto Aziende Vitivinicole** – *Loc. San Cassiano 34 -* **Alba** *(CN) -* ☏ *0173 28 59 42 - www.ceretto.com - ceretto@ceretto.com - Winery tours by reservation, visit@ceretto. com.* The Ceretto family have been making wine for 3 generations and over 70 years. It all started with Riccardo, but the real turning point came in the 1960s, with the arrival of his sons Bruno and Marcello, who set about achieving a leap in quality, starting with the terroir by choosing the finest crus of Barolo and Barbaresco. In the space of little more than 30 years they created a network of small independent estates in the Langhe and Roero, with a multitude of wineries producing very well-known wines and grappas. The third generation entered the business in 1999, driven by the same enthusiasm as their forebears. Hectares under vine: 160.

**Wines:** Langhe Arneis Blangé, Dolcetto d'Alba Rossana, Langhe Rosso Monsordo, Barbaresco Asili, Barolo Bricco Rocche. Other products: Barolo Chinato, nougat, grappa.

**Poderi Colla** – *San Rocco Seno d'Elvio 82 - **Alba** (CN) - ☎ 0173 29 01 48 - www.poderi colla.it - info@podericolla.it - Winery tours by reservation.* The desire to continue the family winemaking tradition and build something different drove Tino Colla and his niece Federica to join forces in 1993 to create a new winery. The result was Poderi Colla, comprising the Cascine Drago of Alba, Tenuta Roncaglia of Barbaresco and Dardi Le Rose of Monforte estates. Three estates on prime sites, each specialised in the production of different types of wine, thus offering a range that almost completely covers Alba's entire enological spectrum. Hectares under vine: 27.

**Wines:** Barolo Bussia, Barbaresco Roncaglie, Bricco del Drago, Nebbiolo d'Alba, Barbera d'Alba.

**Cascina Adelaide** – *Via Aie Sottane 14 - **Barolo** (CN) - ☎ 0173 56 05 03 - www.cascinaadelaide.com - wine@ cascinaadelaide.com - Winery tours by reservation, closed Sat. pm and Sun.* This winery is worth a visit, as it is a harmonious blend of tradition and innovation, terroir and technology. Owner Amabile Drocco inherited the passion for wine-growing from his farmer father and has conveyed it to his entire family. Hectares under vine: 8.

**Wines:** Barolo Cannubi, Barolo Fossati, Barolo Preda, Dolcetto di Diano, Barbera d'Alba Superiore.

🍴 **Marchesi di Barolo** – *Via Roma 1 - **Barolo** (CN) - ☎ 0173 56 44 19 o 0173 56 44 91 - www.marchesibarolo.com - reception@ marchesibarolo.com - Winery tours by reservation.* This estate is an authentic piece of Piedmont's history. It has been producing renowned wines for centuries and the old cellars are housed in the Agenzia della Tenuta Già Opera Pia Barolo, overlooking Barolo from the hill opposite to the Falletti Castle. The wine shop features the entire range of Marchesi di Barolo wines. Food also served (booking required). Hectares under vine: 200.

**Wines:** Barolo, Dolcetto d'Alba, Nebbiolo d'Alba, Moscato d'Asti, Barbaresco.

🍴 **Terre da Vino** – *Via Bergesia 6 - **Barolo** (CN) - ☎ 0173 56 46 11 and 0173 56 00 22 (wineshop) - www.terredavino.it - accoglienza@vitecolte.it - Winery tours by reservation, closed Wed.* The winery was founded in 1980 with the aim of increasing the sale of wines produced by co-operatives of Piedmontese wine-growers. The company philosophy is to produce high-quality wines at reasonable prices, as exemplified by the Superbarbera project that led to the creation of the Barbera d'Asti Superiore "La Luna e i Falò". The winery is an interesting example of modern architecture and boasts a spectacular ageing cellar that can hold up to 3000 barriques. A suspended walkway accesses the various production areas, making the tour particularly intriguing. Hectares under vine: 5000 belonging to the 2500 members.

**Wines:** Barbera d'Asti Superiore "La Luna e i Falò", Barolo "Essenze", Piemonte Moscato Passito "La Bella Estate", Barbaresco "La Casa In Collina", Roero Arneis "La Villa". Other products: Barolo Chinato.

**Gigi Rosso** – *Str. Alba-Barolo 34 - **Castiglione Falletto** (CN) - ☎ 0173 26 23 69 - www.gigirosso.com - info@gigirosso. com - Winery tours and tastings (€10) by reservation, closed Sun.* The cellar is situated in the heart of the Barolo zone and produces wines from the grapes grown on the winery's four estates. Each of them is a vineyard attentively chosen from the finest wine-growing country of the Langhe hills. The choice of vineyards, enthusiastic tending of the vines and field selection ensure excellent results. Hectares under vine: 30.

**Wines:** Barolo, Barbaresco, Nebbiolo, Barbera, Dolcetto, Langhe Rosso, Roero Arneis, Langhe Chardonnay, Moscato d'Asti, Langhe Rosato. Other products: grappa.

## ADDRESSES

**Terre del Barolo** – *Via Alba-Barolo 8 - ***Castiglione Falletto** *(CN) - ☎ 0173 26 20 53 - www.terredelbarolo.com - info@ terredelbarolo.com - Winery tours by reservation, closed Sun. pm. (also am in Jan. and Feb.).* On 8 December 1958 Arnaldo Rivera of Castiglione and around 20 wine-growers decided to found a co-operative winery. Today it is one of the best known in the area and in 2001 it launched a quality project that is yielding excellent results while offering good value for money. Hectares under vine: 650.
**Wines**: Barolo, Nebbiolo d'Alba, Dolcetto di Diano d'Alba, Verduno Pelaverga, Barbera d'Alba. Other products: grappa, Barolo Chinato.

**Azienda Agricola Bricco Maiolica** – *Via Bolangino 7 - Fraz. Ricca - ***Diano d'Alba** *(CN) - ☎ 0173 61 20 49 - www. briccomaiolica.it - info@briccomaiolica.it - Winery tours by reservation.* In 1928 Bernardo Accomo, the forebear of the current owners, purchased 5 hectares of land and a farmhouse on the Maiolica hill, attracted by its particularly fine soil. He immediately started to grow Dolcetto grapes, followed over the years by Barbera, Nebbiolo and white varieties. Today the winery has 20 hectares of vineyards and is owned by Angelo Accomo and his son Beppe. Respect for the environment is fundamental and no chemical fungicides or anti-mould agents are used. Hectares under vine: 20.
**Wines**: Barbera d'Alba Vigna Vigia, Dolcetto Diano d'Alba Sorì Bricco Maiolica, Nebbiolo d'Alba Cumot, Langhe rosso, Langhe bianco.

**Marenco Aldo** – *Borgata Pamparato 25 - ***Dogliani** *(CN) - ☎ 0173 72 10 90 - www. marencoaldo.it - info@marencoaldo.it - Winery tours by reservation.* This winery has long been owned by the Marenco family for 4 generations of unbroken tradition and passion. The Marencos have always been fired by their farming spirit, respect for nature, and research in the vineyard and the cellar to avoid artifice and polluting treatments, earning the winery organic certification about 10 years ago. Hectares under vine: 10.
**Wines**: Dogliani, Langhe Barbera, Langhe Favorita, Dujan Rosé, Roero Arneis, Barolo, Barbaresco, Nebbiolo. Other products: *Cugnà* grape-must jam, grappa.

⌂ **Poderi Luigi Einaudi** – *Borgata Gombe 31/32 - ***Dogliani** *(CN) - ☎ 0173 70 191 - www. poderieinaudi.com - lorenza@poderieinaudi. com - Winery tours by reservation.* The history of Poderi Luigi Einaudi commenced in 1897, when the 23-year-old Luigi Einaudi (who would become Italian President in 1948) purchased a farm with vineyards in Dogliani. Today the estate is run by Luigi's granddaughters Paola and Roberta. The wines have always been made following the President's dictate: "innovation while respecting tradition". The winery also boasts an elegant guesthouse with 10 rooms (min. stay 2 days, doubles €140). Hectares under vine: 43.
**Wines**: Dolcetto di Dogliani, Dogliani "Vigna Tecc", Barolo "Cannubi", Barolo "Costa Grimaldi", Langhe Rosso "Luigi Einaudi".

**Azienda Agricola Abbona Anna Maria** – *Fraz. Moncucco 21 - ***Farigliano** *(CN) - ☎ 0173 79 72 28 - www.annamariabbona. it - info@annamariabbona.it - Winery tours by reservation.* Anna Maria and her husband Franco have been making wine on the Moncucco hill since 1989. It was her grandfather Angelo who started wine-growing and the tradition was continued by Giuseppe, Anna Maria's father, and finally Anna Maria herself. The winery has long followed the EC regulations aimed at reducing and eliminating chemical agents in wine-growing. The wines are bottled without refrigeration or filtration in order to preserve the natural aromas of the grapes to the full. Hectares under vine: 10.
**Wines**: Dogliani, Dolcetto di Dogliani, Langhe Nebbiolo, Langhe Rosso, Barbera D'Alba.

**Beni di Batasiolo** – *Fraz. Annunziata 87 - ***La Morra** *(CN) - ☎ 0173 50 130 - www. batasiolo.com - info@batasiolo.com - Winery tours by reservation.* The values of bygone days, ancient traditions, respect for the land and a sense of family have always been the keystones of this winery. The winery's star Barolos and Barbarescos are flanked by wines made from typically Piedmontese varieties such as Dolcetto, Arneis and Brachetto, as well as international varieties like Chardonnay. The monovarietal grappas are also interesting. Hectares under vine: 120.

© Close Encounters Photography/Shutterstock

**Wines**: Barolo, Barbaresco, Barbera, Dolcetto, Moscato. Other products: grappa.

**Damilano** – *Strada Provinciale Alba-Barolo 122* - **La Morra** *(CN)* - ℘ *0173 56 105* - *www. cantinedamilano.it* - *info@damilanog.com*. It was Giuseppe Borgono, the great-grandfather of the current owners, who started to produce wine from the estate's grapes over 100 years ago and the activity has been continued by his children and grandchildren. The estate's vineyards and those under lease are almost completely planted with Nebbiolo, with small plots of Dolcetto, Barbera and Arneis. Hectares under vine: 32.

**Wines**: Langhe Nebbiolo Marghe, Moscato d'Asti, "Lablù" Barbera, Dolcetto d'Alba. Other products: Barolo Chinato, grappa.

**Oddero Poderi e Cantine** – *Fraz. Santa Maria 28* - **La Morra** *(CN)* - ℘ *0173 50 618* - *www.oddero.it* - *info@oddero.it* - *Winery and vineyard tours by reservation*. This old Langhe winery has been making wine since 1878. Its estate includes some of Piedmont's finest *"sorì"* (the sunniest hilltops), including Brunate, Vigna Rionda, Bussia, Villero and Gallina. The Oddero family have owned vineyards since 1700, but started making wine from their own grapes between the 18th and 19th Centuries. Currently, after more than a century of activity, the winery is run by the sisters Mariacristina and Mariavittoria, who took over from their father Giacomo, and are aided by their children. Hectares under vine: 35.

**Wines**: Barolo, Barbaresco, Barbera, Nebbiolo, Dolcetto, Moscato, Langhe Riesling. Other products: grappa.

**Josetta Saffiro** – *Loc. Castelletto 39* - **Monforte d'Alba** *(CN)* - ℘ *0173 78 72 78* - *www.josettasaffirio.com* - *info@ josettasaffirio.com* - *Winery tours by reservation*. In 1977 Ernesto Saffirio asked his daughter Josetta, a wine-growing and enology teacher at the Enology School in Alba, and enologist Roberto Vezza to tend the family vineyards. This marked the start of the estate's wine-growing, experimentation and production activities. Today Sara, Josetta's daughter, is also passionately involved in the winery, fired by her love of wine and the Langhe. Hectares under vine: 5.

**Wines**: Langhe Rosato, Langhe Nebbiolo, Barbera d'Alba, Barolo, Barolo Persiera, Moscato d'Asti, Rossese Bianco.

**Tenuta Cucco** – *Via Mazzini 10* - *Serralunga d'Alba (CN)* - ℘ *0173 61 30 03* - *tenutacucco.it* - *info@tenutacucco.it* - *Winery tours by reservation*. Tenuta Cucco, owned by the Rossi Cairo family, is located in Serralunga d'Alba at the foot of a 14th-century castle that dominates the entire Langhe Albesi area. The company's name was drawn from one of the oldest and highest quality crus in Serralunga, already mentioned in the historical Barolo maps drawn by Renato Ratti. Located at heights varying between 200 and 420 metres above sea level, and cultivated in calcareous terrain, with open-air outcrops caused by heavy erosion on the most exposed slopes, the company's vineyards produce a highly-structured, complex wine with long, intense and persistent bouquets. Hectares under vine: 13.

**Wines**: Barolo, Dolcetto, Langhe Rosso, Nebbiolo, Barbera d'Alba, Chardonnay.

**Ettore Germano** – *Loc. Cerretta 1* - **Serralunga d'Alba** *(CN)* - ℘ *0173 61 35 28* - *www.ettoregermano.com* - *info@ ettoregermano.com* - *Winery tours by reservation*. This family-run winery is situated in Cerretta, one of the crus of the Alba area. The vineyards are planted mainly with Chardonnay, Barbera, Dolcetto and Nebbiolo. Ettore Germano and his father Alberto have always been growers, but in 1975 they started producing wine from small quantities of their own grapes. Since 1993 they have vinified and bottled the entire output of their vineyards. Visitors can participate in the harvest from Sept. to Dec. Hectares under vine: 13.5.

**Wines**: Barolo, Langhe Nebbiolo, Barbera d'Alba, Dolcetto d'Alba, Langhe Bianco Binel.

⌂ **Fontanafredda** – *Via Alba 15* - **Serralunga d'Alba** *(CN)* - ℘ *0173 62 61 11* - *www.fontanafredda.it* - *info@fontana fredda.it* - *Winery tours by reservation*. The history of the Fontanafredda winery commenced in 1878 with Emanuele Guerrieri, Count of Mirafiori. In addition to the vineyards, the old estate of around 100 hectares comprises a hunting lodge, a hamlet and evocative cellars. The production of red and white wines is divided into three ranges (Tradizione, Selezioni, Tenimenti Fontanafredda), which differ by geographical provenance and production size. The estate offers accommodation in its guesthouse *(14 rooms, €170)* and restaurant service by reservation. Hectares under vine: 100.

**Wines**: Barolo Vigna La Rosa, Barolo Serralunga d'Alba, Diano d'Alba La Lepre, Nebbiolo d'Alba Marne Brune, Moscato d'Asti Moncucco. Other products: Cuneesi chocolates, Barolo Chinato, grappa.

**Massolino** – *Piazza Cappellano 8* - **Serralunga d'Alba** *(CN)* - ℘ *0173 61 31 38* - *www.massolino.it* - *visite@massolino.it* - *Winery tours by reservation*. The winery was founded in 1896 by Giovanni Massolino, who was followed by his son Giuseppe, one of the founders of the Protection Consortium for Barolo and Barbaresco.

He was succeeded in turn by his son Giuseppe. The production philosophy is to make wine with passion, in its territory, preserving the typicity of the native grape varieties. Hectares under vine: 21.
**Wines**: Barolo, Nebbiolo, Dolcetto, Barbera, Moscato, Chardonnay.

**Schiavenza** – *Via Mazzini 4* - **Serralunga d'Alba** *(CN)* - ✆ *0173 61 31 15* - *www. schiavenza.com* - *schiavenza@schiavenza. com* - *Winery tours by reservation.* Schiavenza was founded in 1956 by the brothers Vittorio and Ugo Alessandria and is now run by the second generation of the family. The farm and the surrounding land belonged to the Opera Pia Barolo and the work was performed by sharecroppers, known as schiavenza in Piedmontese dialogue, hence the winery's name. The family also owns the Cascina *Schiavenza* trattoria, which opened at the foot of the medieval castle in 1997 and offers the classic dishes of the Langhe and Piedmont. Hectares under vine: 8.
**Wines**: Barolo, Barbera d'Alba, Langhe Nebbiolo, Dolcetto d'Alba, Barolo Chinato.

⌂ **Azienda Agricola Comm. G.B. Burlotto** – *Via Vittorio Emanuele 28* - **Verduno** *(CN)* - ✆ *0172 47 01 22* - *www. burlotto.com* - *burlotto@burlotto.com* - *Winery tours by reservation*. The young Commendatore Giovan Battista Burlotto founded this winery in the second half of the 19th c. He was one of the first in the Langhe to offer wine in bottles instead of demijohns, with French-inspired labels bearing the word Château. The winery occupies a fascinating 19th-c. house and has always been engaged in promoting Pelaverga, a little-known native variety that produces an interesting red wine.
The Locanda dell'Orso Bevitore guest farm, with 10 rooms (€100), also belongs to the estate. Hectares under vine: 12.
**Wines**: Barolo, Verduno Pelaverga, Dolcetto d'Alba, Barbera d'Alba, Langhe Freisa.

♟ **Castello di Verduno** – *SS Via Umberto I 9* - **Verduno** *(CN)* - ✆ *0172 4 70 284* - *www.cantinecastellodiverduno.it* - *info@ cantinecastellodiverduno.it* - *Winery tours by reservation*. After years spent in Eritrea, in 1950 Commendatore Giovanni Battista Burlotto returned to Verduno and started to tend to the 16th-c. castle that his grandfather had purchased at the beginning of the century. In order to bring the complex back to life he decided to create a gourmet meeting place with accommodation. Today his three daughters and their respective families run what the castle has become: the Ca' del Re hotel (*8 rooms., 80 €*), restaurant (✆ *0172 47 02 81*) and the winery. Hectares under vine: 8.
**Wines**: Verduno Basadone, Barbera d'Alba -

Bricco Cuculo, Barolo Massara - Monvigliero, Barbaresco - Rabaja e Faset, Dolcetto d'Alba Campot, Nebbiolo, Bellis Perennis. Other products: grappa.

## SOME OF THE EPOCH-MAKING NAMES OF BAROLO

Here are some of the great names associated with Barolo, whose wineries can be visited in some cases, but do not sell wines to the public.

**Domenico Clerico** – Loc. Manzoni 22/A, Monforte d'Alba (CN), ✆ 0173 78 171, www.domenicoclerico.com, info@domenico clerico.com, winery tours by reservation.

**Conterno Fantino** – Via Ginestra 1, Monforte d'Alba (CN), ✆ 0173 78 204, www.conternofantino.it, info@ conternofantino.it winery tours by reservation (visit@conternofantino.it).

**Elio Altare** – Fraz. Annunziata 51, La Morra (CN) ✆ 0173 50 835, www.elioaltare.com, elioaltare@elioaltare.com, winery tours by reservation.

**Elio Grasso** – Loc. Ginestra 40, Monforte d'Alba (CN), ✆ 0173 78 491, www.elio grasso.it, info@eliograsso.it

**Giacomo Conterno** – Loc. Ornati 2, Monforte d'Alba (CN), ✆ 0173 78 221, www. conterno.it, winery tours by reservation.

**Poderi Aldo Conterno** – Loc. Bussia 48, Monforte d'Alba (CN), ✆ 0173 78 150, www.poderialdoconterno.com, winery not open to public.

**Roberto Voerzio** – Loc. Cerreto 7, La Morra (CN), ✆ 0173 50 91 96, www.robertovoerzio. com, info@robertovoerzio.com, winery not open to public.

**Sandrone Luciano** – Via Pugnane 4, Barolo (CN), ✆ 0173 56 00 23, www.sandroneluciano.com, info@ sandroneluciano.com

**Vietti** – Piazza V. Veneto 5, Castiglione Falletto (CN) ✆ 0173 62825, www.vietti. com, info@vietti.com, winery tours by reservation.

## THE BARBARESCO LANGA

**Bruno Rocca** – *Strada Rabajà 60* - **Barbaresco** *(CN)* - ✆ *0173 63 51 12* - *www.brunorocca.it* - *info@brunorocca.it* - *Winery tours by reservation*. The Roccas of Barbaresco have peasant roots and have always tended their own vineyards. Initially they sold their wines unbottled, but in 1978 Bruno Rocca took charge of the estate and decided to sell bottled wine only. The top of the winery's range is its Barbaresco Rabaja. Hectares under vine: 682.
**Wines**: Barbaresco Rabajà, Barbaresco Coparossa, Barbaresco, Barbera d'Alba, Barbera d'Asti.

**Carlo Boffa** – *Via Torino 17* - **Barbaresco** *(CN)* - ☎ *0173 63 51 74* - *www.boffacarlo.it* - *boffa@boffacarlo.it* - *Tasting by reservation, closed Wed.* The winery was founded in the 1960s by Pietro Boffa. Since 1996 it has been headed by Carlo Boffa and his wife Laura. The winery is situated on the road that leads to the tower of Barbaresco. It is a small estate specialising in the production of red wines from Nebbiolo, Dolcetto and Barbera grapes. Hectares under vine: 4.
**Wines**: Barbaresco, Barbaresco Ovello, Barbaresco Paje, Barbera D'Alba, Roero Arneis, Dolcetto D'Alba. Other products: grappa made from Barbaresco.

**Ca' Romè** – *Via Rabajà 86/88* - **Barbaresco** *(CN)* - ☎ *0173 63 51 26* - *www.carome.com* - *info@carome.com* - *Winery tours by reservation.* The family atmosphere is evident in this little winery, starting with its name. *Ca'* (or "casa") indicates that it is the home of the Marengo family, who have been producing wine on the renowned Rabajà hill, legendary for its Barbarescos, since 1980. The winery's vineyards are located partly in the Barbaresco production zone and partly in Serralunga d'Alba in Barolo territory. Hectares under vine: 5.
**Wines**: Barbera d'Alba La Gamberaja, Barbaresco Rio Sordo, Barbaresco Maria di Brün, Barolo Rapet, Barolo Vigna Cerretta.

**Produttori del Barbaresco** – *Via Torino 54* - **Barbaresco** *(CN)* - ☎ *0173 63 51 39* - *www.produttoridelbarbaresco.com* - *Winery tours by reservation.* The Produttori del Barbaresco co-operative winery, situated in the heart of Barbaresco at the foot of the old tower, has a long history. In 1894 Domizio Cavazza, head of the Royal Enology School of Alba and resident in Barbaresco, where he owned the castle and the adjoining farm, founded the Cantine Sociali di Barbaresco and started to produce wine, naming it after the town. The original co-operative winery was closed during the Fascist period, but in 1958, as soon as the difficulties of the post-war period had been solved, Don Fiorino, Barbaresco's parish priest, revived the tradition by gathering together 19 wine-growers and founding the Produttori del Barbaresco, which now boasts 56 members. Hectares under vine: 110.
**Wines**: Barbaresco, Nebbiolo Langhe. Other products: grappa.

**Tenute Cisa Asinari dei Marchesi di Grésy** – *Loc. Martinenga - Strada della Stazione 21* - **Barbaresco** *(CN)* - ☎ *0173 63 52 21* - *www.marchesidigresy.com* - *Winery tours and tastings by reservation.* The owner Alberto di Grésy grew up with a passion for the land and vineyards, spending much of his free time as a boy on the family's estate on Monte Aribaldo near Treiso. He soon realised that it was a shame to sell the estate's grapes to others and started making his own wines in 1973. Today Tenute Cisa Asinari dei Marchesi di Grésy comprises 3 Langhe and Monferrato estates. Hectares under vine: 35.
**Wines**: Langhe Bianco Sauvignon, Dolcetto d'Alba Monte Aribaldo, Monte Colombo Barbera d'Asti, Camp Gros Barbaresco, Gaiun Barbaresco. Other products: grappa.

**Cantina Negro Giuseppe** – *Via Gallina 22* - **Neive** *(CN)* - ☎ *0173 67 74 68* - *www.negrogiuseppe.com* - *cantina@negrogiuseppe.com* - *Winery tours by reservation.* Situated in one of the finest growing areas for the production of great Piedmontese wines, this winery is run directly by the owner, enologist Giorgio Negro, who has always made quality his production philosophy. The wines are made from the most characteristic local grape varieties.
**Wines**: Barbaresco, Monsù Nebbiolo, Barbera d'Alba, Dolcetto d'Alba, Roero Arneis, Monsú Rosé. Other products: grappa.

**Castello di Neive** – *Via Castelborgo 1* - **Neive** *(CN)* - ☎ *0173 67 171* - *www.castellodineive.it* - *info@castellodineive.it* - *Winery tours by reservation.* This winery belonging to the four Stupino brothers was founded by their father Giacomo, who purchased land and vineyards in the best positions in the municipality of Neive and started producing unbottled wine for domestic consumption and sale. Over the years the number of estates and vineyards has increased, along with production. The castle, with its huge cellars, was purchased in 1964. The winery is also responsible for the revival of the Arneis grape variety. Hectares under vine: 26.
**Wines**: Barbaresco, Barbera d'Alba, Dolcetto d'Alba, Langhe Arneis, Piemonte Spumante.

© Newphotoservice/Shutterstock

**Francone - Antichi Poderi dei Gallina** –
*Via Tanaro 45 - **Neive** (CN) - ☏ 0173 67 068
- www.franconevini.com - francone@francone
vini.com - Winery tours by reservation
Mon.-Sat., Sun. morning Oct.-Nov.* Adriano
Francone was already making wine for
private consumption in the second half of
the 19th c. His son Alberto subsequently
decided to open a wine bar near Turin, to
promote Francone wines outside the family
home and region. The family's passion for
wine has remained constant through the
generations. Visitors can also tour a small
museum. Hectares under vine: 6.2.
**Wines:** Barbaresco "Gallina", Barolo, Barbera
d'Alba, Roero Arneis "Magìa", Moscato d'Asti.
Other products: grappa, Valsellera
Spumante Brut.

**Paitin** – *Via Serra Boella 20 - **Neive** (CN)
- ☏ 0173 67 343 - www.paitin.it - info@
paitin.it - Winery tours by reservation.*
This winery has a very long history, going
back to 1796, when Benedetto Elia
purchased the estate. His son Giuseppe
later extended the vineyards and
purchased the 15th-c. underground cellar.
The first Barbaresco was bottled in 1893
and in 1898 the winery started exporting
its production abroad. The estate is
currently headed by Secondo Pasquero
and his two sons Giovanni and Silvano.
Hectares under vine: 17.
**Wines:** Barbaresco, Barbera d'Alba, Dolcetto
d'Alba, Nebbiolo d'Alba, Langhe Rosso, Roero
Arneis.

## SOME OF THE EPOCH-MAKING NAMES OF BARBARESCO
Here are some of the great names
associated with Barbaresco, although their
wineries **are not open to visitors**.
**Bruno Giacosa** – Via XX Settembre 52,
Neive (CN), ☏ 0173 67 027, www.
brunogiacosa.it
**Gaja** – Via Torino 18, Barbaresco (CN),
☏ 0173 63 51 58.

## ROERO

**Enrico Serafino** – *Corso Asti 5 - **Canale**
(CN) - ☏ 0173 97 94 85 - www.enrico
serafino.it - cristiana.barbero@enrico
serafino.it - Winery tours by reservation.*
Founded in 1878 by businessman and
landowner Enrico Serafino, this winery
soon became one of the most important
in Piedmont. In 2005 it became part of the
Campari Group. An innovative new range,
named "Cantina Maestra", was recently
established. The winery focuses on the
biodiversity of local grape varieties,
focusing production on the emblematic
grapes of Roero - Nebbiolo, Dolcetto,
Barbera and Arneis - as well as typically
Piedmontese grapes such as Cortese,
Grignolino and Moscato. Hectares under
vine: 13.
**Wines:** San Dependente Barbera d'Alba
Superiore, Oesio Roero, Pajena Barbera
d'Alba, Tovasacco Nebbiolo d'Alba, Poggio di
Caro Roero Arneis. Other products: grappa.

☙ **Malvirà** – *Case Sparse Canova 144
- **Canale** (CN) - ☏ 0173 97 81 45 - www.
malvira.com - malvira@malvira.com -
Winery tours by reservation, 8-12, 14-18,
info@malvira.com.* Malvirà is an old
Piedmontese word that indicated the
house where the cellar was situated and is
derived from the position of the courtyard,
which instead of being to the south, as
traditional, lies to the north and is thus
*mal girata* (badly turned) or *malvirà* in the
local dialect. The winery is run by the two
Damonte brothers, assisted by their wives,
and grows and makes wines from the
typical grape varieties of the Alba area:
Arneis, Favorita, Nebbiolo, Barbera,
Bonarda Piemontese, Brachetto and a
small area planted with Chardonnay and
Sauvignon. Villa Tiboldi guest farm offers
accommodation and meals (*10 rooms,
doubles €120, ☏ 0173 97 03 88, www.
villatiboldi.it*). Hectares under vine: 42.
**Wines:** Roero Arneis, Favorita, Barbera
d'Alba, Roero, Birbet.

**Matteo Correggia** – *Via Santo Stefano
Roero 124 - **Canale d'Alba** (CN) - ☏ 0173
97 80 09 - www.matteocorreggia.com -
cantina@matteocorreggia.com - Winery
tours by reservation.* The estate's first
vineyards were planted in 1935 by Matteo
Correggia. The winery gradually expanded
and in 1985 Matteo's grandson, also called
Matteo, took the helm and led it to the
success for which it is known today.
Following Matteo's untimely death in
2001, his wife Ornella continues to run the
winery. Hectares under vine: 20.
**Wines:** Roero Ròche d'Ampsej, Barbera
d'Alba Marun, Nebbiolo d'Alba La Val Dei
Preti, Roero Arneis, Langhe Bianco Matteo
Correggia.

**Pescaja** – *Fraz. San Matteo, Via Cima 59 -* **Cisterna d'Asti** *(AT) - ℘ 0141 97 97 11 - www.pescaja.com - info@pescaja.com - Winery tours by reservation.* Pescaja was founded in 1990 by Beppe Pescaja, a university student who was so fascinated by nature and country life that he decided to produce small amounts of wine, preferring the outdoor life to office work. Over the years the estate has grown and now produces excellent wines based on three principles: Sun, Heart and Soul. Hectares under vine: 16.
**Wines**: Arneis, Barbera.

**Taliano Michele** – *Corso Manzoni 24 -* **Montà** *(CN) - ℘ 0173 97 61 00 - www. talianomichele.com - taliano@libero.it - Winery tours by reservation.* The winery was founded by Domenico Taliano in 1930, but its origins reach back much further, for Domenico belongs to a long line of farmers dedicated to working the vineyards and the land. The estate's vineyards are in Roero and at San Rocco Seno d'Elvio in the Barbaresco area. In addition to Nebbiolo, the vineyards are planted with Sauvignon, Cabernet Sauvignon, Arneis, Brachetto, Barbera, Dolcetto and Moscato. Today it is Michele's son Alberto who runs the winery, aided by his father and his enologist brother Ezio. Hectares under vine: 12.
**Wines**: Barbaresco, Roero, Roero Arneis, Barbera d'Alba, Moscato d'Asti.

🌱 **Tenuta Carretta** – *Loc. Carretta 2 -* **Piobesi d'Alba** *(CN) - ℘ 0173 61 91 19 - www.tenutacarretta.it - info@terremiroglio. com - Winery tours by reservation.* This estate has a long tradition dating back to the early 12th c. and a winemaking vocation spanning hundreds of years. Today it is actively involved in the constant qualitative improvement of its wines and has flanked this activity with first-rate accommodation (*9 rooms, doubles from €140, ℘ 0173 61 92 61*) and restaurant service. Hectares under vine: 70.
**Wines**: Roero Arneis "Cayega", Barolo "Vigneti Cannubi", Barbaresco "Cascina Bordino", Dolcetto d'Alba "Il Palazzo", Langhe Bianco Sauvignon.

## MOSCATO AREA

**Contratto** – *Via Giuliani 56 -* **Canelli** *(AT) - ℘ 0141 82 33 49 - www.contratto.it - elena@contratto.it - Winery tours by reservation (payment required).* Contratto was founded in 1876 and the premises are housed in Art Deco buildings, dating from the period in which the winery's name became famous throughout the world. The courtyard has been restored with splendid cobbles, like the traditional old streets of Canelli, and flower beds. Contratto was the first producer in Italy to show the vintage on the label for Classic Method sparkling

wines with its Extra Dry-Brut Riserva Speciale 1917.
**Wines**: Millesimato Pas Dosé Brut, Cuvée Novecento, Asti Spumante "De Miranda", Bacco d'Oro Brut, Blanc de Blancs, For England Rosé, Riserva Special Cuvée Pas Dosé.

**Coppo** – *Via Alba 68 -* **Canelli** *(AT) - ℘ 0141 82 31 46 - www.coppo.it - visit@coppo.it - Winery tours by reservation.* The winery has always focused on Moscato since its foundation at the beginning of the 20th c., when Piero Coppi started to make sweet sparkling wines from this bountiful grape. It then moved towards Pinot-based brut wines and the great red wines of Monferrato and the Langhe. Piero was succeeded by his son Luigi and then his grandsons Piero, Gianni, Paolo and Roberto. The traditional production is flanked by the cultivation of international grape varieties and the native Freisa, which the Coppo family interpret in a highly personal style in Mondaccione. Don't miss the old cellars, formed by a maze of underground tunnels carved out of the tufa. Hectares under vine: 56.
**Wines**: Barbera d'Asti Pomorosso, Chardonnay Piemonte Monteriolo, Brut Riserva Coppo, Barbera d'Asti Camp du Rouss, Moscato d'Asti Moncalvina, Barolo, Gavi La Rocca. Other products: grappa.

**Gancia** – *Corso Libertà 66 -* **Canelli** *(AT) - ℘ 0141 83 01 - www.gancia.it - franco. ferrero@gancia.it - Winery tours by reservation.* Gancia celebrated its 150th anniversary in 2000. Since its foundation the winery's core business has been sparkling wines. Gancia is a legendary name and one of the oldest all-Italian companies, which has always believed in coupling wine with architecture. Indeed, the Locanda Gancia in Santo Stefano Belbo allows guests to admire a work by architect Tobia Scarpa: the huge roof of the weighing and crushing station, completed in 1989. Gancia has recently renewed this combination of wine and design in its partnership with Pininfarina Extra, which created a "triptych of Spumanti" to contain the finest Italian sparkling wines in a bottle with a special design. Hectares under vine: 2000.
**Wines**: Pinot di Pinot, Vintage Integral, Camillo Gancia, P. Rosé Oltrepò Pavese, Modonovo. Other products: Americano Gancia, vermouth.

**Vittorio Bera** – *Reg. Serramasio 39 -* **Canelli** *(AT) - ℘ 0141 83 11 57 - berav@ libero.it - Winery tours by reservation.* The Bera family has been producing Moscato for many years, using artisanal methods to preserve its purity and naturalness. While Moscato is the flagship wine, the estate also achieves excellent results with Barbera and Dolcetto. Arcese, from Cortese, Favorita and Arneis, is also interesting. The winery is run by Vittorio Bera and his children Gianluigi and Alessandra, who have been using organic methods to tend their vineyards since 1964. Hectares under vine: 10.

**Wines**: Moscato d'Asti, Barbera d'Asti, Barbera del Monferrato, Dolcetto del Monferrato, Arcese Vino Bianco da Tavola.

**La Spinetta** – *Via Annunziata 17 -* **Castagnole Lanze** *(AT) - ℘ 0141 87 73 96 - www.la-spinetta.com - info@la-spinetta.com - Winery tours by reservation.*
The history of the Rivetti family commenced in 1890, when Giovanni, grandfather of Carlo, Bruno and Giorgio, left Piedmont to emigrate to Argentina, with the dream of returning home later to become a great wine-maker. His dream was fulfilled by his son Giuseppe (nicknamed Pin) and his wife Lidia, who purchased vineyards and started making wine. Today the winery has three estates: the original one in Castagnole Lanze, another in Grinzane Cavour and a third in Terricciola in Tuscany. Hectares under vine: 100.

**Wines**: Moscato d'Asti Bricco Quaglia, Pin, Barolo Campè, Barbaresco Gallina, Barbera d'Asti Superiore Bionzo.

**Caudrina** – *Strada Brosia 20 -* **Castiglione Tinella** *(CN) - ℘ 0141 85 51 26 - www.caudrina.it - romano@caudrina.it - Winery tours by reservation.* The winery's history commenced in the 1940s, when Redento Dogliotti started to crush his own grapes to make must for the large local producers of Moscato d'Asti. Together with his son Romano, the current owner, he started focusing on the production, bottling and sale of quality wines under the estate's name in the 1970s. Today the estate is renowned above all for its Moscato d'Asti and Asti Spumante, but it also produces Barbera d'Asti and Chardonnay. Hectares under vine: 25.

**Wines**: Moscato d'Asti La Caudrina, Moscato d'Asti La Galesia, Asti Spumante La Selvatica, Barbera d'Asti La Solista, Barbera d'Asti Montevenere.

**Paolo Saracco** – *Via Circonvallazione 6 -* **Castiglione Tinella** *(CN) - ℘ 0141 85 51 13 - www.paolosaracco.it - info@paolosaracco.it - Winery tours by reservation.* The Saracco family have been tending vineyards, making wine and promoting Moscato, the grape variety that is the symbol of this area of Piedmont, for 4 generations. Enological studies and experience have made the winery one of the best known in the region. Hectares under vine: 50.

**Wines**: Moscato d'Asti, Piemonte Moscato d'Autunno, Prasuè, Riesling, Pinot Nero.

**Forteto della Luja** – *Reg. Candelette Bricco Rosso 4 -* **Loazzolo** *(AT) - ℘ 0141 83 15 96 or 0144 87 197 - www.fortetodellaluja.it - info@fortetodellaluja.it - Winery tours by reservation.* This very small family-run winery is headed by Giancarlo Scaglione and his children Silvia and Giovanni. The first documents that testify to its existence were written in 1826, but the stone cave-cellar dates from the 18th c. The family's efforts have long been aimed at respecting the local cultural and natural heritage. Indeed, the winery, selected as a WWF Oasis, also offers guided tours of the nearby Luja woods to spot wild orchids, the orchard with old varieties of apples and pears, and the butterfly garden. Renowned for its Loazzolo, the winery boasts a cellar powered by solar cells and has adopted eco-friendly organic methods in the vineyard. Hectares under vine: 9.

**Wines**: Piasa Rischei Loazzolo Vendemmia Tardiva, Forteto Pian dei Sogni Brachetto Piemonte, Le Grive Monferrato Rosso, Piasa Sanmaurizio Moscato d'Asti, Mon Ross Barbera d'Asti.

**Isolabella della Croce** – *Reg. Caffi 3 -* **Loazzolo** *(AT) - ℘ 0144 87 166 - www.isolabelladellacroce.it - info@isolabelladellacroce.it - Winery tours by reservation.* Renowned for the production of its Moscato di Canelli-based sweet wines, such as "Solìo" Loazzolo and sparkling "Valdiserre" Moscato d'Asti, the winery is now focusing on the reappraisal of Brachetto, offering an interesting late-harvest version called "Trentasei". The majority of the vineyards are over 50 years old. Hectares under vine: 14.

**Wines**: Solìo Loazzolo Vendemmia Tardiva, 36 Brachetto d'Acqui, Valdiserre Moscato d'Asti, Augusta Barbera d'Asti Superiore Nizza, Solum Monferrato Bianco. Other products: grappa.

**Ca' d'Gal** – *Via Strada Vecchia di Valdivilla 1 - Valdivilla -* **Santo Stefano Belbo** *(CN) - ℘ 0141 84 71 03 - www.cadgal.it - info@cadgal.it - Winery tours by reservation.* With 4 generations of wine-growers, the estate boasts a long history. The winery, guest farm and educational farm - all housed in a recently restored farmhouse - are surrounded by vineyards. The estate's flagship wine is Moscato d'Asti, but it also produces Dolcetto d'Alba, Langhe Chardonnay and Pian del Gaje, a blend of Freisa, Barbera d'Asti and Dolcetto d'Alba. In recent years, work in the vineyard has focused particularly on respect for nature, reducing the use of herbicides and excessive fertilisers. Accommodation is also available at the guest farm (*6 rooms*) with

restaurant. Hectares under vine: 8.
**Wines**: Moscato d'Asti Lumine, Moscato d'Asti Vigna Vecchia, Asti Spumante. Other products: *Cugnà* grape-must jam.

## MONFERRATO: BARBERA AREA

**Michele Chiarlo** – *Strada Nizza-Canelli 99,* **Calamandrana** (AT) - ℘ *0141 76 90 30 - www.chiarlo.it - info@chiarlo.it - Winery tours by reservation.* Michele Chiarlo embarked upon his adventure in the world of wine in 1965, commencing with the 5 hectares of his father's estate planted with Barbera and Moscato. At the beginning of the 1970s he introduced the innovative practice of malolactic fermentation to the production of Barbera. Over the years he has purchased the finest vineyards and today the estate comprises more than 50 hectares of vineyards in important Piedmontese crus in 3 production zones: Monferrato, Langhe and Gavi. Hectares under vine: 110.
**Wines**: Barolo Cerequio, Barbera d'Asti La Court Nizza, Barbaresco Asili, Barbera d'Asti Le Orme, Moscato d'Asti Nivole. Other products: grappa.

**Cascina Castle't** – *Str. Castelletto 6 - Costigliole d'Asti* (AT) - ℘ *0141 96 66 51 - www.cascinacastlet.com - info@ cascinacastlet.com - Winery tours by reservation, closed Sun.* The estate's production is founded on its respect for nature and its determination to keep pace with the times. Large investments in land, technology and research have allowed Cascina Castle't to offer high-quality products at reasonable prices. The estate has belonged to the Borio family for generations and the current owner, Mariuccia, inherited it from her father in 1970. She has brought her experience accrued in the family's wine shop in Turin, and knowing the taste of the clientele has proven very useful for producing wines that satisfy people's expectations. Hectares under vine: 31.
**Wines**: Barbera d'Asti, Moscato d'Asti, Aviè Moscato Passito, Passum. Other products: grappa.

**Malgrà** – *Loc. Bazzana, via Nizza 12 - Mombaruzzo* (AT) - ℘ *0173 61 91 19- www.malgra.it - info@terremiroglio.com - Winery tours by reservation. Malgrà* is the name that was once given to people considered clairvoyants, dreamers or a little mad: in other words, entirely unconventional. The project followed by the founders of the brand is underpinned by the free interpretation of the land and the vineyard, the close relationship between man and the land, sensitivity and humility, and the resulting wines vaunt great character and personality. Hectares under vine: 34.

**Wines**: Barbera d'Asti Superiore Nizza, Barbera d'Asti, Moscato d'Asti, Barolo, Gavi di Gavi. Other products: grappa.

**Bersano Vini** – *P.zza Dante 21 - Nizza Monferrato* (AT) - ℘ *0141 72 02 11 - www. bersano.it - wine@bersano.it - Winery tours by reservation.* The estate's history commenced in the 18th c., when its name became closely bound up with the region (Monferrato) and its principal grape variety (Barbera). Arturo Bersano's motto "If you want to drink well, buy yourself a vineyard" has inspired his winery's choices and today it owns around 230 hectares under vine, scattered over the best wine-growing country in the Langhe and Monferrato. This makes Bersano one of the largest wineries in the country. It also has an impressive museum of rural life, which is well worth a visit. Hectares under vine: 230.
**Wines**: Barbera Generala, Barbera Cremosina, Barolo Badarina, Ruchè S. Petro, Moscato S. Michele. Other products: grappa and spirits.

**Braida di Giacomo Bologna** – *Via Roma 94 - Rocchetta Tanaro* (AT) - ℘ *0141 64 41 13 - www.braida.com - info@braida.it - Winery tours by reservation, closed Aug., Sun. except in autumn.* Braida is the nickname that Giuseppe Bologna earned as a Sunday player of the typical Piedmontese sport known as *pallone elastico*. His son Giacomo inherited his vineyards and nickname, but above all his love for the land and wine, which he also conveyed to his wife Anna and later also his children. Today Anna continues Giacomo's work aided by their children Raffaella and Beppe. The winery has always pursued the goal of achieving the noble and qualitative status that Barbera deserves. Hectares under vine: 48.
**Wines**: Bricco dell'Uccellone, Ai Suma,

© GeorgeS/Shutterstock

Montebruna, Moscato d'Asti, Bricco della Bigotta. Other products: grappa.

**Carussin** – *Regione Mariano 27 -* **San Marzano Oliveto** *(AT) - 𝒫 0141 83 13 58 - www.carussin.it -vinicarussin@gmail.com - Winery tours by reservation.* The winery was founded in 1927 by Ferro Maggiore from nearby Calosso, from which its name, *Carussin* (meaning "from Calosso" in Piedmontese dialect), derives. Over the following years the estate's wine-growing vocation was boosted with new vineyards until reaching the current area. It is currently run by Bruna Ferro and her husband Luigi, and is almost completely planted with Barbera d'Asti, which is their great passion. Additional information: the winery organises educational workshops on bread, as well as trekking and donkey rides. Hectares under vine: 22.

**Wines**: "Il Carica l'Asino", Barbera d'Asti "Asinoi", Barbera d'Asti "Lia Vi", Barbera d'Asti "La Tranquilla", Passito di Barbera "Respiro Di Vigna". Other products: traditionally brewed beer "Clan!Destino?".

**Cantina Sociale di Vinchio** – *Regione San Pancrazio 1 -* **Vinchio** *(AT) - 𝒫 0141 95 09 03 - www.vinchio.com - welcome@vinchio. com - Winery tours by reservation.* The co-operative was founded in 1959 by 19 wine-growers from Vinchio and Vaglio Serra. It currently has 224 contributing members, owners and operators. The vineyards are located mainly in the municipalities of Vinchio and Vaglio Serra, with a few in the outlying municipalities of Incisa Scapaccino, Cortiglione and Nizza Monferrato. Members can draw on technical assistance to cultivate their vineyards, featuring programmes for the integrated protection of the vines. The aim is to implement low-environmental-impact viticulture, limiting the use of plant protection products. Hectares under vine: 420.

**Wines**: Barbera d'Asti Sorì dei Mori, Barbera d'Asti Sup. I Tre Vescovi, Barbera d'Asti Sup. Vigne Vecchie, Barbera d'Asti Sup. Sei Vigne Insynthesis, Barbera d'Asti Sup. Laudana sottozona Nizza. Other products: hazelnut oil, grappa.

### BASSO MONFERRATO

⌂ **Castello di Razzano** – *Fraz. Casarello, Strada Gessi 2 -* **Alfiano Natta** *(AL) - 𝒫 0141 92 25 35 - www.castellodirazzano.it - info@ castellodirazzano.it - Winery tours by reservation.* The estate stands on what was originally a Roman site and consists of a stately home with enclosed courtyard dating from 1697. In the mid-17th c. the estate passed into the hands of the Caligaris family, whose most illustrious member was Valentino, Italy's first Advocate General in the post-war period and a great statesman. It is to Valentino Caligaris that Augusto Olearo, the estate's current owner, dedicated the most important label of its production: Barbera d'Asti Superiore Riserva Valentino Caligaris. Part of the estate is planted with olive groves. Visitors can also enjoy the 13-room Relais di Charme Castello di Razzano (€115-240). Hectares under vine: 30.

**Wines**: Barbera, Grignolino, Merlot, Dolcetto, Chardonnay. Other products: "Chinà" flavoured wine, grappa.

⌂ **Caldera** – *Fraz. Portacomaro Stazione 53 -* **Asti** *- 𝒫 0141 29 61 54 - www. vinicaldera.it - info@vinicaldera.it - Winery tours by reservation.* The family's wine-growing experience dates back to the early 20th c. and today, four generations later, Caldera wines continue to pay tribute to tradition and the region. The estate offers guest accommodation (*rooms from €60, www.dabetty.it*). Hectares under vine: 12.

**Wines**: Barbera d'Asti, Grignolino d'Asti, Ruché di Castagnole Monferrato, Dolcetto di Dogliani, Gavi.

**Castello del Poggio** – *Loc. Poggio 9 - Fraz. Portacomaro Stazione -* **Asti** *- 𝒫 0141 20 25 43 - www.poggio.it - info@poggio.it - Winery tours by reservation.* The estate is named after the medieval fortified house that overlooks it and belongs to the Buneis noble family. It was built in the 11th-14th c. to keep watch over the borders of Asti. Since 1985 the estate has been owned by the Zonin family, who have slowly recomposed the original land holdings. The modern cellar was built in 1988. Hectares under vine: 158.

**Wines**: Barbera d'Asti, Grignolino d'Asti,

Monferrato Dolcetto, Moscato d'Asti, Piemonte Brachetto Spumante.

♀/ **Cascina Moncucchetto** – *Cascina Moncucchetto 50* - **Casorzo** *(AT) - ℘ 0141 92 91 39 - www.moncucchetto.it - info@ moncucchetto.it - Winery tours by reservation.* Giorgio Cantamessa's Cascina Moncucchetto is situated in a prime wine-growing area on south-facing hills with excellent limestone and clay soil. The wines reflect all the aromas and flavours of Monferrato. The estate's most famous wines include Barbera d'Asti "La Pinota", selected and aged in barriques, the sparkling and semi-sparkling Malvasia di Casorzo, and Solatìo, a wine made from partially dried selected bunches of late-harvest Malvasia. Food also served, reservation required. Hectares under vine: 15.

**Wines**: Barbera d'Asti, Grignolino d'Asti, Barbera superiore, Freisa d'Asti, Malvasia di Casorzo, Piemonte Cortese.

**Bava** – *Strada Monferrato 2* - **Cocconato d'Asti** *(AT) - ℘ 0141 90 70 83 - www.bava. com - vino@bava.com - Winery tours by reservation.* Bava is a modern family-run estate that was founded in 1911, although the family has owned vineyards in the town of Cocconato since 1600. The company history boasts almost 100 harvests and 4 generations of toil in the cellar and in the vineyard. Barbera is the main focus of the winery's production, followed by Malvasia, used to produce the Malvasia di Castelnuovo Don Bosco. The winery also stages concerts and art exhibitions in the cellar. Hectares under vine: 50.

**Wines**: Stradivario Barbera d'Asti Superiore, Libera Barbera d'Asti, Barolo Scarrone di Castiglione Falletto Cru Scarrone, Thou Bianc Chardonnay, Rosetta Malvasia di Castelnuovo Don Bosco. Other products: flavoured grappa.

**Cocchi** – *Via Liprandi 21* - **Cocconato d'Asti** *- ℘ 0141 60 00 71 - www.cocchi.it - cocchi@cocchi.com - Winery tours by reservation.* This is the oldest sparkling wine producer in Asti, founded in 1891 by Giulio Cocchi. By the turn of the 20th c. it was already very famous for its flavoured wines, and particularly its Barolo Chinato and Aperitivo Americano. Today, Cocchi is owned by the Bava family and has preserved its artisanal nature associated with high-quality sparkling wines produced using the Classic or Charmat methods, but it is equally renowned for its Asti DOCG. The historic **Bar Cocchi** in Cocconato gives visitors the chance to sample the winery's products and offers guided tastings of sparkling wines at its "sparkling bar".

**Wines**: Toto Corde Alta Langa Metodo Classico, Bianc 'd Bianc Alta Langa Brut, Primosecolo, Chardonnay Brut, Rosa Pinot Nero Brut Metodo Classico. Other products: Barolo Chinato, Aperitivo Americano, grappa, Cru chocolates.

⌂ **Poderi dei Bricchi Astigiani** – *Via Ritane 7* - **Isola d'Asti** *(AT) - ℘ 014 195 89 74 - gaslinialberti.it - info@ bricchiastigiani.it - Winery tours by reservation.* ⊠ Poderi dei Bricchi Astigiani – Acquired at the end of the 1990s by the Gaslini Alberti family, Poderi dei Bricchi Astigiani is located in one of the most beautiful areas of the entire Asti region. The property includes a splendid agriturismo and a small, working cantina. The main vine is Barbera, among the most famous Piedmont grapes. The company's symbol is the family insignia, and the Gaslini Alberti family personally guarantees the quality of the products its company provides. Hectares under vine: 15.

**Wines**: Barbera d'Asti DOC, Barbera d'Asti Superiore DOC, Monferrato Rosso DOC, Piemonte Rosato DOC, Brut metodo classico DOC.

🍇 **Bricco dei Guazzi** – *Via Vittorio Veneto 23* - **Olivola** *(AL) - ℘ 0422 86 45 11 - www.briccodeiguazzi.it - info@genagricola. it - Winery tours by reservation.* This estate was founded in 1979. During the 16th c. the Guazzo family became the bailiffs of the Monferrato lands of the Gonzaga family, a land of rolling hills, known as *bricchi* in Piedmontese dialect, hence the name "Bricco dei Guazzi". The house and the cellars were completely renovated and completed in 2004. The vineyards were replanted with new clonal selections to produce a new Barbera, and indeed Barbera is the grape variety on which the winery has lavished most of its attention. Villa Guazzo-Candiani is a stunning house, named after two illustrious families that once lived there. Hectares under vine: 30.

**Wines**: Barbera del Monferrato, Chardonnay, La Presidenta Rosso del Monferrato, Gavi di Gavi, Albarossa.

**Colle Manora** – *Via Bozzola 5* - **Quargnento** *(AL) - ℘ 0131 21 92 52 - www. collemanora.it - info@collemanora.it - Winery tours by reservation.* Colle Manora stands atop a hill in the centre of an amphitheatre surrounded by acacia, oak and wild cherry woods to the north and east. The area is particularly suited for wine-growing due to its ideal microclimate and clay soil that formed during the Miocene Epoch. Alongside the traditional Barbera vineyards, the winery also grows Chardonnay, Pinot Nero, Cabernet Sauvignon, Merlot and

Albarossa. Hectares under vine: 20.
**Wines**: Barbera Monferrato Pais, Rosso Barchetta, Ray, Manora, Paloalto, Mimosa, Mila, Double Bubble Spumante Brut.

**Vicara** – *Cascina Madonna delle Grazie 5 -* **Rosignano Monferrato** *(AL) - ℘ 0142 48 80 54 - www.vicara.it - vicara@vicara.it - Winery tours by reservation.* Diego Visconti, Carlo Cassinis and Domenico Ravizza have pooled their experience and the potential of their estates to establish this new winery. The vineyards currently cover an area of 35 hectares, located in prime sites in 5 towns: Salabue, Serralunga di Crea, Ozzano, Treville and Rosignano Monferrato. Production follows the principles of integrated vineyard management and eco-friendly farming. Hectares under vine: 40.
**Wines**: Grignolino del Monferrato Casalese, Barbera del Monferrato, Monferrato Freisa, Monferrato Rosso, Monferrato Bianco. Other products: grape-must jellies, brandy, grappa.

⌂ **Marchesi Alfieri** – *Piazza Alfieri 28 -* **San Martino Alfieri** *(AT) - ℘ 0141 97 60 15 - www.marchesialfieri.it - info@ marchesialfieri.it - Winery tours by reservation.* This well-known winery is run by 3 sisters, Emanuela, Antonella and Giovanna San Martino di San Germano, aided by enologist Mario Olivero. The top of the winery's range is its Barbera d'Asti. The estate comprises a spectacular castle and grounds. Today the San Martino di San Germano sisters have equipped the old cellars with the latest technologies, and have maintained and enhanced Marchesi Alfieri's historical heritage and wine-growing traditions. Guests can stay at the Locanda Alfieri (*7 rooms, €100*), an old house in the winery's courtyard, while the Cascina Margherita, in the castle grounds with views over the hills and the nearby towns, is perfect for families or small groups. Hectares under vine: 21.
**Wines**: Barbera d'Asti Superiore Alfiera, Barbera d'Asti La Tota, Pinot Nero San Germano, Nebbiolo Costa Quaglia, Grignolino Sansoero, Monferrato rosso Sostegno, Blanc de Noir Metodo Classico Millesimato.

⌂ **Tenuta La Tenaglia** – *Strada Santuario di Crea 5 -* **Serralunga di Crea** *(AL) - ℘ 0142 94 02 52 - www.tenutatenaglia.it - info@latenaglia.com - Winery tours by reservation, Mon.-Fri. 8-18, Sat. and Sun. 11-18.* Tenuta La Tenaglia was founded by the Governor of Moncalvo Giorgio Tenaglia, a famous condottiere and an adventurous patron with a great passion for Barbera, who decided to found a wine-growing "oasis" in the 17th c. Over the centuries the estate was expanded to comprise 30 hectares of land, 19 in the province of Alessandria (municipalities of Serralunga di Crea and Ponzano) and 11 in the province of Asti (municipality of Grazzano Badoglio). In 2001 the winery was taken over by the German Ehrmann family, who have modernised it while maintaining its strong bond with the region. The estate hosts several art exhibitions and periodically classical music concerts, theatre shows and typical markets. It also offers accommodation (*2 rooms, €100*) Hectares under vine: 30.
**Wines**: Grignolino del Monferrato Casalese, Barbera d'Asti Giorgio Tenaglia, Barbera d'Asti Bricco, Piemonte Chardonnay Oltre, Monferrato Rosso Olivieri "Etichetta d'Autore" (numbered limited edition wine with labels featuring the works of Sabine Ehrmann's partner, artist Giuseppe Olivieri). Other products: grappa.

⌂ **Accornero** – *Via Cà Cima 1 -* **Vignale Monferrato** *(AL) - ℘ 0142 93 33 17 - www.accornerovini.it - info@accornerovini.it - Winery tours by reservation.* The Accornero family have been tending their vineyards for 4 generations with the same passion and commitment to produce quality wines. Their great-grandfather, Bartolomeo, purchased Cascina Cà Cima, where Accornero is still based today. The estate offers guest accommodation (*2 rooms, €85, and 1 apt.*) in a renovated building. Hectares under vine: 20.
**Wines**: Bricco Battista, Centenario, Giulin, Bricco del Bosco, Cima.

**Nuova Cappelletta** – *Cascina Cappelletta 9 -* **Vignale Monferrato** *(AL) - ℘ 0142 93 31 35 - www.nuovacappelletta.it - info@ nuovacappelletta.it - Winery tours by reservation.* The estate's main activity is wine-growing, but it also farms Piedmontese cattle and cereals. The traditional Piedmontese varieties are grown here: Grignolino, Barbera, Freisa, Nebbiolo, Cortese and Chardonnay. The estate has followed the dictates of organic farming for over 20 years and, more recently, the principles of biodynamic farming. Hectares under vine: 20.
**Wines**: Grignolino del Monferrato Casalese, Barbera del Monferrato, Monferrato Rosso and Freisa, Piemonte Chardonnay, Piemonte cortese.

## ALTO MONFERRATO

**Cantina Alice Bel Colle** – *Reg. Stazione 9 -* **Alice Bel Colle** *(AL) - ℘ 0144 74 103 - www.cantinaalicebc.it - info@cantina alicebc.it - Winery tours 8-12 and 14-18, closed Wed.; closed also Sun. in Jan., Feb., Jul. and Aug.* Founded in 1955, this co-operative winery now has around 150 members and is renowned for its Brachetto d'Asti and Moscato d'Asti. It produces wine from approximately 3,800,000 kg of grapes, of which 1,600,000 kg of Moscato d'Asti, 300,000 kg of Brachetto d'Acqui, 500,000 kg of Dolcetto d'Acqui and Barbera d'Asti, 300,000 kg of Cortese dell'Alto Monferrato and Piemonte Chardonnay, and the rest for other types of products. Hectares under vine: 400.

**Wines**: Moscato d'Asti, Brachetto d'Acqui, Barbera d'Asti, Dolcetto d'Acqui, Piemonte Chardonnay.

**Tacchino Luigi** – *Via Martiri della Benedicta 26-* **Castelletto d'Orba** *(AL) - 𝒫 0143 83 01 15 - www.luigitacchino.it - info@luigitacchino.it - Winery tours by reservation.*

The Tacchino family counts 3 generations of wine-growers. The estate was founded during the second half of the 20th c. and focused particularly on Gavi, Dolcetto d'Ovada and Barbera del Monferrato, which are still its leading products today. Hectares under vine: 10.

**Wines**: Gavi del Comune di Gavi, Cortese dell'Alto Monferrato, Dolcetto d'Ovada, Barbera del Monferrato, Monferrato Rosso.

**Broglia - La Meirana** – *Loc. Lomellina 22 -* **Gavi** *(AL) - 𝒫 0143 64 29 98 - www.broglia.it - broglia.azienda@broglia.eu - Winery tours by reservation.* The name Meirana is bound up with the history of Gavi. The first document, dating from 971, the time of the origin of the name Gavi, mentions vineyards and chestnut groves in Meirana. The winery was founded by Bruno Broglia, whose son Piero took over in 1972. Most of the vineyards are planted with Cortese grapes for the production of Gavi di Gavi. Hectares under vine: 47.

**Wines**: Gavi del Comune di Gavi, Spumante Brut, Barbera d'Asti, Nebbiolo d'Alba.

**Ca' dei Mandorli** – *Stradale Alessandria 90 -* **Acqui Terme***(AL) - 𝒫 0144 37 16 00 - www.cadeimandorli.com - info@cadeimandorli.com - Winery tours by reservation.* The Ricagno family's wine-growing history dates back to the first half of the 19th c. with Cristoforo Ricagno who grew vines in the Sezzadio area. His son Paolo gradually started buying up the best land for wine-growing in the municipalities of Alice Bel Colle, Castel Rocchero and Ricaldone. His grandson Paolo Ricagno has continued the family tradition purchasing new land and making radical changes in the vineyard and the cellar. The fourth generation is represented by Stefano, who has followed in his father's footsteps. Hectares under vine: approx. 200.

**Wines**: Brachetto d'Acqui, Moscato d'Asti, Barbera d'Asti, Gavi, Asti Spumante, Valcrös Pinot Chardonnay.

**Castellari Bergaglio** – *Fraz. Rovereto 136R-* **Gavi** *(AL) - 𝒫 0143 64 40 00 - www.castellaribergaglio.it - gavi@castellaribergaglio.it - Winery tours and tastings 9-12 and 14-17 by reservation.* Castellari Bergaglio is a family-run winery that monitors every stage of production, from the vineyard to the cellar, where the wine is made using modern techniques. Mario Bergaglio, his wife Vanda Castellari and their son Marco carefully tend to their product, and aim to valorise the entire heritage of Gavi and relaunch its undoubted historic and cultural potential in various ways, such as through the opening of the Gaviteca, showcasing Gavis, and the use of particularly informative back labels. Hectares under vine: 10.

**Wines**: Gavi di Tassarolo "Fornaci", Gavi di Gavi "Rolona", Gavi di Gavi "Rovereto-Vignavecchia", Gavi "Pilin", Gavi "Saluvii", "Gavium" Vino Passito.

**La Scolca** – *Strada per Rovereto 170/R -* **Gavi** *(AL) - 𝒫 0143 68 21 76 - www.lascolca.net - contatti@scolca.it - Winery tours by reservation.* Scolca is a small family-run winery whose vineyards, cellar and sales are tended and overseen by the owners themselves. Today the winery is headed by Giorgio Soldati, Vittorio's son, who has worked there since 1970. He has been flanked for several years now by his daughter Chiara, who represents the fifth generation of the family. La Scolca has always concentrated on Gavi and is capable of producing versions that retain their freshness and elegance even after 10 or more years in bottle. Hectares under vine: 45.

**Wines**: Gavi, Gavi dei Gavi® La Scolca d'Antan®, RosaChiara, Pinot Nero, Soldati La Scolca Spumante. Other products: grappa.

**Tenuta La Giustiniana** – *Fraz. Rovereto 5 -* **Gavi** *(AL) - 𝒫 0143 68 21 32 - www.lagiustiniana.it - info@lagiustiniana.it - Winery tours by reservation.* Giustiniana's origins are very remote. There are records of a settlement in the hills around the river Lemme as early as 1000 and in 1250 "La Grangia Bassignana" was indicated as a Benedictine wine-growing estate belonging to the Abbey of Rivalta Scrivia. In 1625 it passed into the hands of the Giustiniani, an aristocratic Genoese family that gave its name to the estate and built the Neoclassical villa that dominates the entrance to it. Today the estate belongs to the Bombardini family and covers an area of 110 hectares, of which 40 under vine. Hectares under vine: 40.

**Wines**: Gavi del Comune di Gavi "Lungarara", Gavi del Comune di Gavi "Montessora", Gavi del Comune di Gavi "Terre Antiche".

# ADDRESSES

🏠 **Villa Sparina** – *Fraz. Monterotondo 56 - **Gavi** (AL) - ☎ 0143 63 38 35 - www.villa sparina.it - sparina@villasparina.it - Winery tours by reservation.* The Villa Sparina estate in Monterotondo is a charming place. It comprises 100 hectares of land, of which over half is vineyards, surrounded by woods. Most of the vineyards are planted with Cortese, but there are also other vines like Chardonnay, Müller Thurgau, Sauvignon Blanc, Barbera and Dolcetto. The estate's symbol wine is its Gavi "Monterotondo" made from carefully selected Cortese grapes. The picturesque winery is the ideal setting for various events. Guests can stay in the charming Relais l'Ostelliere (*33 rooms, from €165*) and enjoy the La Gallina restaurant (*Closed at lunch, except Sat. and Sun., ☎ 0143 68 51 32, la-gallina. it*). Hectares under vine: 70.
**Wines**: Gavi del Comune di Gavi, Gavi del Comune di Gavi Monterotondo, Monferrato Rosso Rivalta, Barbera, Montej, Blanc de Blanc Brut.

**Nuova Abbazia di Vallechiara** – *Cascina Albarola 16/B - **Lerma** (AL) - ☎ 0143 87 72 65 - Winery tours by reservation.* This small winery is the result of a great passion for the Ovada area and its grape varieties, particularly Dolcetto. Several old vineyards were selected on particularly well-aspected sites with soils of various composition, in order to achieve varied production that expresses the terroir. In addition to Dolcetto, the estate grows Cortese – from which it makes an interesting Gavi – and Brachetto. Hectares under vine: 3.
**Wines**: Dolcetto d'Ovada "Coste Belletti", Dolcetto d'Ovada "Terrazze dell'Avarena", Brachetto d'Acqui "Rebecca", Vino da Tavola Rosso "Double Face", Gavi.

**Vigneti Massa** – *P.zza G. Capsoni 10 - **Monleale Alessandria** (AL) - ☎ 0131 80 302 - Winery tours by reservation.* Walter Massa is one of the local wine-growers who has most fully understood the potential of the native variety Timorasso and has interpreted it to best effect. Part of the merit for the recognition of the Colli Tortonesi Timorasso DOC zone is his. The winery produces three wines from this grape variety: Derthona (from the old name of Tortona), Costa del Vento and Sterpi. They are sumptuous whites with great potential for ageing. The estate also makes Barbera, Croatina, Freisa and Moscato. Hectares under vine: 20.5.
**Wines**: Colli Tortonesi Monleale, Colli Tortonesi Barbera Sentieri, Colli Tortonesi Timorasso Derthona; Colli Tortonesi Timorasso Costa del Vento, Colli Tortonesi Croatina Pertichetta.

**Il Vignale** – *Via Gavi 130 - **Novi Ligure** (AL) - ☎ 0143 72 715 - www.ilvignale.it - ilvignale@ilvignale.it - Winery tours by reservation.* The winery was purchased in 1984 by the Cappellettis, a couple of pharmacists with a great love of country life and wine. Since 1996 they have made their guest farm their full-time occupation, embracing a philosophy of total respect for nature. A completely natural method has been adopted for both weeding and fertilising, allowing wild geese to graze vineyards and complete the life cycle with their excrement. Hectares under vine: 22.
**Wines**: Gavi Vigne Alte, Gavi selezione Vilma Cappelletti etichetta verde (unoaked) and etichetta nera (1 year older and lightly cask aged), Monferrato Rosso. Other products: grappa.

**La Raia** – *Strada Monterotondo 79 - **Novi Ligure** (AL) - ☎ 0143 74 36 85 - www.la-raia.it - info@la-raia.it - winetour@la-raia.it - Winery tours by reservation.* La Raia, a Demeter-certified biodynamic company owned by the Rossi Cairo family, is located in Novi Ligure, in the heart of Gavi territory. With over 180 hectares of splendid property, the company can boast 45 hectares of Cortese and Barbera vineyards, a fish-filled lake, centenarian woods, cereal grain fields and open fields where Piedmont cows graze. This unique ecosystem is used to produce three different kinds of Gavi and two kinds of Barbera, as well as honey. The property also hosts Fondazione La Raia, which boasts site-specific contemporary artworks by Remo Salvadori and Koo Jeong A. Hectares under vine: 45.
**Wines**: Gavi DOCG, Gavi DOCG Riserva, Gavi DOCG Pisé, Piemonte Barbera DOC, Piemonte Barbera DOC Largé.

🏠 **Marenco** – *Piazza Vittorio Emanuele 10 - **Strevi** (AL) - ☎ 0144 36 31 33 - www.marencovini.com - info@marencovini.com - Winery tours and tastings by reservation.* The winery, situated just 6 km outside the town of Acqui Terme, is owned by the Marenco family, which boasts a long line of farmers and wine-growers. It was the current owner Giuseppe Marenco who transformed the estate's activity from the straightforward cultivation and sale of grapes to the vinification and sale of wine. The product range includes red and white wines, dessert wines, and both still and sparkling wines, made from Brachetto, Moscato, Chardonnay, Caricalasino (an almost forgotten native variety), Cortese, Barbera and Dolcetto grapes. Accomodation available at cascina Valtignosa (347 2878198). Hectares under vine: 80.

**Wines**: Strevi DOC Moscato Passri' Scrapona, Brachetto d'Acqui DOCG Pineto, Barbera d'Asti DOCG Bassina, Vitigno Carialoso, Barbera d'Asti DOCG Superiore Ciresa, Dolcetto d'Acqui DOC Marchesa, Barbera del Monferrato DOC Vivace Masino, Piemonte DOC Albarossa, Moscato d'Asti DOCG Scrapona and Strev, Cortese dell'Alto Monferrato DOC Valtignosa, Brachetto Acqui DOCG Passri' Pineto. Other products: grappa.

**Banfi** – *Via Vittorio Veneto 76* - **Strevi** *(AL)* - 📞 *0144 36 26 00* - *www.castellobanfi.com* - *banfi@banfi.it* - *Winery tours and tastings by reservation*. The Vigne Regali project, aimed at valorising the most prestigious DOC zones of Lower Piedmont, is the result of the merging of the region's age-old traditions of wine-growing and sparkling wine production with the enological experience of the Banfi estate in Montalcino, in Tuscany. The extensive production is inspired by high quality and bonds with the land, taking the form of a varied range of labels that express the principal Piedmontese grape varieties – Cortese, Brachetto, Dolcetto and Barbera – in a total of 14 wines. Hectares under vine: 46.

**Wines**: Cuvée Aurora Rose Alta Langa, Rosa Regale Brachetto d'Acqui, Vigneto Banin Barbera d'Asti, Asti Spumante, Banfi Brut Metodo Talento Classico.

🏠 **Castello di Tagliolo** – *Via Castello 1* - **Tagliolo Monferrato** *(AL)* - 📞 *0143 89 195* - *www.castelloditagliolo.it* - *castello ditagliolo@libero.it* - *Winery tours and tastings by reservation*. The oldest part of the castle is the base of the tower, which was built earlier than the year 1000, while the upper part was constructed between the 15th and the 16th c. The castle was restored at the end of the 19th c. and its current owners, the Marchesi Pinelli Gentile, maintain it in an excellent state of repair. In Tagliolo Monferrato viticulture and the production of quality wines are age-old traditions, documented as early as the 15th c. in the castle's accounts. Today the castle continues to produce wines that have received numerous awards in both Italy and abroad. Visitors can also enjoy the 4 Guest House. Hectares under vine: 24

**Wines**: La Castagnola, L'In…chino, Ambra Nobile, Spumante del Castello, Gentile. Other products: grappa.

**Castello Tassarolo** – *Loc. Alborina 1* - **Tassarolo** *(AL)* - 📞 *0143 34 22 48* - *www.castelloditassarolo.it* - *info@castello ditassarolo.it* - *Winery tours and tastings by reservation*. This organic winery is housed in a perfectly conserved 12th-c. castle that has always belonged to the Spinola, an old noble family. The castle's wines were

© Mars Evis/Shutterstock

already renowned in the Middle Ages and today Massimiliana successfully continues the tradition. The vineyards frame the medieval castle, making the scene even more picturesque. They are planted with Cortese, Cabernet Sauvignon, Barbera and Chardonnay. Manual harvesting, soft crushing and temperature control underpin the estate's high-quality production. Hectares under vine: 20.

**Wines**: Gavi Marchesi Spinola, Gavi Castello di Tassarolo, Gavi Vigneto Alborina, Cuvée Monferrato.

**Tenuta San Pietro in Tassarolo** – *Loc. S. Pietro 2* - **Tassarolo** *(AL)* - 📞 *0143 34 24 22* - *www.tenutasanpietro.it* - *info@ tenutasanpietro.it* - *Winery tours and tastings by reservation*. Tenuta San Pietro is one of the longstanding wineries of the Gavi DOCG zone. It is located in an area particularly well suited to the growing of Cortese grapes and the soil, which was once submerged by the sea, is rich in sea salt, giving the wine its distinctive acidity and zestiness. From the 12th c. the hilltop was home to a Franciscan monastery and the consecrated church of San Pietro, which probably gave its name to the place. Hectares under vine: 35.

**Wines**: Gavi "San Pietro", Gavi "Il Mandorlo", Gavi "Gorrina", Monferrato Rosso "Orma Romea", Monferrato Rosso "Nero San Pietro". Other products: grappa.

**La Colombera** – *Strada Comunale per Vho 7* - **Vho di Tortona** *(AL)* - 📞 *0131 86 77 95* - *www.lacolomberavini.it* - *info@ lacolomberavini.it* - *Winery tours and tastings Sat. 10-12 and 15-18, Sun. 10-12, Mon.-Fri. only by reservation*. Renato Semino arrived at Cascina Colombera in 1937 and decided, together with his father

# ADDRESSES

Pietro and his mother Maria, to tend this land, planting the first vineyards in the 1950s. His son, Piercarlo, worked with him in the vineyard and in the 1970s he decided to start producing his own wine instead of selling his grapes to dealers and the co-operative winery. He soon achieved success, which continues today thanks to the commitment of Piercarlo's entire family. Hectares under vine: 22.
**Wines:** Cortese Bricco Bartolomeo, Timorasso Derthona, Barbera Elisa, Croatina Arché, Nibiò Suciaja. Other products: peaches preserved in syrup and jams made from untreated fruit.

## CANAVESE

**Cantina Sociale della Serra** – *Via Strada Nuova 12 -* **Piverone** *(TO) -* ℘ *0125 72 166 - www.cantinadellaserra.com - info@ cantinadella serra.it - Winery tours and tastings by reservation 9-12.30 and 15.30-19, closed Sun.* This co-operative winery was officially founded on 10 May 1953 with 99 members by Canavese businessman, politician and sociologist Adriano Olivetti. Today it counts over 300 members and has an important influence on the local wine scene due to the high quality of its Erbaluce di Caluso and Canavese wines, produced in various versions. Hectares under vine: 150.
**Wines:** Erbaluce di Caluso, Serra Classic Brut, Caluso Passito, Canavese Rosso, Canavese Nebbiolo.

**Cieck** – *Cascina Castagnola 2-* **San Giorgio Canavese** *(TO) -* ℘ *0124 33 05 22 - www.cieck.it - info@cieck.it - Winery tours and tastings by reservation, 9-12 and 15-18.* Ciek was founded in 1985, when Lodovico Bardesono and Remo Falconieri decided to pool their vineyards and experience.

© Wolfgang Amri/Shutterstock

The estate grows native grape varieties: Erbaluce, Barbera, Nebbiolo, Freisa and Neretto di San Giorgio, a true enological rarity. The jewel in the crown of the winery's production is the sparkling San Giorgio and the dried-grape wine Alladium. Hectares under vine: 20.
**Wines:** Spumante S. Giorgio Brut, Misobolo Erbaluce di Caluso, Passito Alladium, Nebbiolo, Neretto.

**Orsolani** – *Via Michele Chiesa 12 -* **San Giorgio Canavese** *(TO) -* ℘ *0124 32 386 - www.orsolani.it - info@orsolani.it - Tastings by reservation, Tue.-Sat. 9-12 and 15-18.* Orsolani's history commenced at the end of the 19th c., when great-grandfather Giovanni and his wife Domenica returned from America and opened an inn, the Locanda Aurora, with Domenica in the kitchen and Giovanni in the vineyard and the cellar to produce the necessary wine. With the following generation, the estate's principal activity became wine-growing. Today Orsolani is one of the best-known wineries for its commitment to promoting the native Erbaluce grape, and its wines are made exclusively from this varietal. Hectares under vine: 20.
**Wines:** La Rustia Erbaluce di Caluso, Cuvée Tradizione Caluso Spumante, Sulè Caluso Passito, Vintage Erbaluce di Caluso, Acinisparsi Canavese Rosso.

⌂ **Cellagrande** – *Via Cascine di Ponente 21 -* **Viverone** *(BI) -* ℘ *0161 189 22 13 - www.cellagrande.it - info@cellagrande.it - Winery tours and tastings by reservation.* The winery boasts a stunning position on Lake Viverone on the site of a 12th-c. Benedictine monastery, of which the church and the bell tower can still be seen. The estate offers guest accommodation *(9 rooms, €100).* Hectares under vine: 5.
**Wines:** Erbaluce di Caluso, Erbaluce di Caluso Brut Metodo Charmat, Erbaluce di Caluso Brut Metodo Classico, Erbaluce di Caluso vendemmia tardiva, Erbaluce di Caluso passito.

## COLLINE NOVARESI, BIELLESI, VERCELLESI

⌂ **Azienda Agricola Cà Nova** – *Via San Isidoro 1 -* **Bogogno** *(NO) -* ℘ *0322 86 34 06 - www.cascinacanova.it - mailbox@ cascinacanova.it - Winery tours, vineyards tours and tastings by reservation.* The vineyards of this winery, which has chosen to use exclusively eco-friendly treatments, are planted in the morainic soils of the Novara hills. Don't miss the Golf vineyard that not only surrounds the winery, but is also set between the 12th and 13th holes of the Bogogno golf course. The estate also features the Relais

Agriturismo Cà Nova (*Via IV Novembre, 200 m from the Bogogno Golf Club, ☎ 0322 86 34 06, www.cascinacanova.it*) that offers 8 comfortable apartments of various sizes with a kitchenette. Hectares under vine: 10.

**Wines**: Ghemme, Colline Novaresi Nebbiolo, Colline Novaresi Nebbiolo Rosato, Colline Novaresi Bianco Erbaluce, Spumante Brut, Extra Brut.

**Antico Borgo Dei Cavalli di Barbaglia Sergio** – *Via Dante 80 -* **Cavallirio** *(NO) - ☎ 347 09 38 710 - www.vinibarbaglia.it - info@ vinibarbaglia.it - Winery tours and tastings by reservation.* The estate was founded just after WWII by Mario Barbaglia, father of the current owner and enologist Sergio. Love for the land and the country tradition, careful selection, and cutting-edge winemaking and bottling techniques are the cornerstones of the activity of this winery, which has always offered high-quality wines. Hectares under vine: 4.

**Wines**: Boca, Colline Novaresi Bianco, Nebbiolo, Vespolina, Spumante Metodo Classico. Other products: grappa, flavoured wine.

**Travaglini Giancarlo Società Agricola** – *Via delle Vigne 36 -* **Gattinara** *(VC) – ☎ 0163 83 35 88 - www.travaglini gattinara.it - visite@travaglinigattinara.it - Winery tours and tastings by reservation.* The name of this family-run estate has long been associated with Gattinara, a Nebbiolo wine with great structure and complexity, particularly in the Riserva version. The winery is run by Cinzia Travaglini together with her husband Massimo and her mother Liliana. In addition to the winery guests can visit the picturesque vineyard-covered hills surrounding the estate. Hectares under vine: 42.

**Wines**: Gattinara, Gattinara Tre Vigne, Gattinara Riserva, Nebbiolo Coste Della Sesia, Il Sogno Vino da Vendemmia Tardiva.

**Torraccia del Piantavigna** – *Via Romagnano 69/A -* **Ghemme** *(NO) - ☎ 0163 84 00 40 - www.torraccia delpiantavigna.it - info@torracciadel piantavigna.it - Winery tours, vineyards tours and tastings by reservation.* In 1977 the Francoli family planted its first Nebbiolo vineyard on a small plot of land. The first part of the name comes from a local hill called Torraccia and the ruined tower of nearby Cavenago Castle, while Piantavigna is a tribute to the maternal grandfather of the current owner. The estate is home to the Vineria, where you can taste the estate's wines, and the International Library of Aqua Vitae and Liquor. The Distillerie Francoli offer a wide choice of *grappe, Via Romagnano 20, ☎ 0163 84 47 11, www.francoli.it.* Hectares under vine: 40.

**Wines**: Ghemme, Gattinara, Colline Novaresi Nebbiolo, Colline Novaresi Vespolina, Colline Novaresi Bianco, MUFii Vino Muffato.

## Where to stay

### ACQUI TERME

**Acqui & Beauty Center** – *Corso Bagni 46, Acqui Terme (AL) - ☎ 0144 32 26 93 - www. hotelacqui.it - Closed 7 Jan.-7 Mar. - 30 rooms, doubles from €100.* Comfortable, tasteful rooms. There is a small but well-equipped beauty centre on the top floor.

### ALBA

**Agriturismo Villa la Meridiana-Cascina Reine** – *Loc. Altavilla 9, 1 km S of Alba (CN) - ☎ 338 40 06 527 - www.villala meridianaalba.it - 10 rooms, doubles from €100.* Agritourism set in an elegant Art Nouveau villa and the adjacent farmhouse; welcoming interiors and stylish rooms. The suite looks over the vineyard.

### CANDIA CANAVESE

**Residenza del Lago** – *Via Roma 48, Candia Canavese (TO) - ☎ 011 98 34 885 - www.residenzadelago.it - 11 rooms, doubles from €60.* A typical farmhouse skilfully modernised with beautiful, spacious and welcoming rooms with period furniture.

### CANELLI

**Agriturismo La Casa in Collina** – *Loc. Sant'Antonio 54, 2 km NW of Canelli (AT) - ☎ 0141 82 28 27 - www.casaincollina. com - Closed Jan. - 6 rooms, doubles from €110.* Referred to repeatedly in the novels of Cesare Pavese, Canelli is one of the most panoramic places in the Langhe, with a view as far as Monte Rosa. The furnishings in the home are refined and typically Piedmontese.

### GATTINARA

**Dimora del Barone** – *Corso Valsesia 238, Gattinara (VC) - ☎ 0163 82 72 85 - www. dimoradelbarone.it - 22 rooms, doubles from €120.* A master's villa on the edge of town. The building's history has been carefully harmonised with the modernity of the furnishings. Large rooms with frescoed ceilings.

### MONCALVO

**La Locanda del Melograno** – *Corso Regina Margherita 38, Moncalvo (AT) - ☎ 0141 91 75 99 - www.lalocandadel melograno.it - 9 rooms, doubles from €90.* A well-restored, late 19th-c. building that respects its origin but makes clever use of modern comforts. Resale of local wines and products.

# LIGURIA

The sea, with which the history of Liguria is inextricably tied, enabled its people to have dealings with different civilisations for centuries, which in turn influenced their wine production. Ligurian viticulture is varied and original, with cultivars like Bosco, Pigato, Albarola, Bianchetta and many more. Sometimes vineyards exist in places it is difficult to believe possible. In the Cinque Terre area, for example, they perch on terraces hewn with difficulty out of plunging slopes, proving that determination can overcome adverse conditions. Exploring Liguria is a fascinating activity due to the beauty of the region's landscape, above all the scenic combination of its sea and mountains. The presence everywhere of vineyards and olive groves confirms that the production of wine and olive oil is an integral part of the local culture.

© bluejayphoto/iStock

*Vernazza and its vineyards, Cinque Terre*

## The terroir

Liguria runs for 250 km between the Alps and the Ligurian Apennines. **Genoa**, the capital and an ancient sea-faring city with a glorious past, sits between the two Rivieras: the **Levante** (east), which stretches down to the Tuscan border and is characterised by calcareous clayey soil mixed with sand, and the **Ponente** (west), which ranges along the coast to France, formed by red, calcareous and marly soil.

Grapes are also often grown in extreme conditions, on terraces buttressed by small stone walls that step steeply down to the sea. The structure and position of these terraces are so particular that those in Cinque Terre have been declared a World Heritage Site by UNESCO.

It was probably Greek merchants who brought the vine to the Ligurian coast and taught the population how to cultivate it and make wine. Known and appreciated by the Romans, Ligurian wines enjoyed a period of great splendour in the 16th and 17th c., but this was followed by times of difficulty as trade from Genoa began to drop off and ravages were brought by phylloxera.

The region's range of vine species is particularly varied as a result of the exchanges the marine republic had with many countries, some of them very distant. To prevent vines being uprooted in some areas, such as Cinque Terre, public incentives were put in place to encourage newcomers to enter the world of viticulture.

In general the vineyards are very small, as is the scale of individual and cooperative wine production in Liguria as a whole. Most of the varieties are native and the wine-making methods used are solidly traditional, which, with the close link that exists between the people and their local territory, forms the strong point of Ligurian enology. The best known black grapes are the **Dolcetto** (with which Ormeasco is made) and **Rossese**, while **Vermentino** and **Pigato** are celebrated among the whites.

## Itineraries

*Locations with a winery are indicated by the symbol ♀; for the addresses of the wineries, see p. 110.*

### 1. THE RIVIERA DI PONENTE

### From Ventimiglia to Savona

*Itinerary of approximately 250 km with deviations inland.*

The Via Aurelia originally built by the Romans continues to be the principal route along this stretch of Liguria, even if the A 10 motorway runs parallel to it over innumerable viaducts and through countless tunnels. The Via Aurelia is difficult to use because it is winding, narrow and heavily trafficated, but it offers lookout points of great beauty along the coast. The perfect exposure of the Riviera di Ponente has encouraged year-round flower-growing in glasshouses along the hills of the shoreline, but in the interior, which begins immediately behind the coast, a strong contrast is provided by the silence and wildness of the wooded terrain.

From an enological viewpoint, this area includes the designations **Riviera Ligure di Ponente**, **Rossese di Dolceacqua** and **Ormeasco di Pornassio**. The most common varieties are the white Pigato and black Rossese and Ormeasco. The **Ormeasco**, a clone of the Piedmont Dolcetto, is named after Ormea in the province of Cuneo from where it was imported by the Saracens. The wines

| DOC |
| --- |
| Cinque Terre / Cinque Terre Sciacchetrà |
| Colli di Luni |
| Colline di Levanto |
| Dolceacqua *or* Rossese di Dolceacqua |
| Golfo del Tigullio-Portofino *or* Portofino |
| Pornassio *or* Ormeasco di Pornassio |
| Riviera Ligure di Ponente |
| Val Polcèvera |

it produces have character, smelling of spices and red fruit, and leaving a bitterish aftertaste in the mouth. A rosé produced is the **Ormeasco Sciac-trà**, not to be confused with the Sciacchetrà from the Riviera di Levante. Rossese, on the other hand, is a pale ruby colour, with little tannin and delicate aromas of flowers and fruit.

**Pigato** is a particular variety of Vermentino, which probably originated in the south. Its name is likely derived from the term *pigau* (speckled) after the appearance of the grape skin. The **white wines** of the Ponente, which are mostly obtained from this variety, are very scented, floral, fruity and "planty", pleasingly full-flavoured and fresh.

### Ventimiglia

Lying almost on the French border, the medieval city of Ventimiglia still stands. Set amongst its welter of alleys is the duomo (11th-12th c.), an octagonal baptistery (11th c.), the Church of San Michele (11th-12th c.) and the Oratory dei Neri (17th c.).

At Mortola Inferiore (*6 km from the French border*) the **Hanbury Gardens ★★** are set on terraces down to the sea, planted with a great variety of exotic plants. *Corso Montecarlo 43 - La Mortola.*

## PRINCIPAL VARIETIES CULTIVATED

| WHITE GRAPES | | BLACK GRAPES |
| --- | --- | --- |
| Albana | Moscato Bianco | Barbera |
| Albarola | Pigato | Canaiolo |
| Bianchetta Genovese | Rollo | Ciliegiolo |
| Bosco | Trebbiano Toscano | Dolcetto |
| Greco | Vermentino | Merlot |
| Lumassina | | Pollera Nera |
| Malvasia Bianca Lunga | **BLACK GRAPES** | Rossese |
| | Alicante | Sangiovese |

**THE TERROIR**
**Area:** 5,416.15 km², of which approximately 1,624 hectares are planted to vine
**Production 2019:** 81,486 hectolitres, of which 44,553 VQPRD
**Geography:** 65% mountainous, 35% hilly

**WINE AND FOOD ROUTES**
Associazione Strada del Vino e dell'Olio dalle Alpi al Mare – c/o Comunità Montana
Ponenete Genovese, Via Giuseppe Mazzini 28, Albenga (SV), ℘ 0182 55 89 61

*Open 9.30-dusk, closed Mon. (1° Nov.-end
Feb.), ℘ 0184 22 95 07, www.giardini
hanbury.com.*

*Take the SP 65 which leads inland into
the* **Nervia valley** *as far as Pigna and
Triora (50 km from Ventimiglia to Triora).*
Ten kilometres north of Ventimiglia you
come to **Dolceacqua★ 🍷**, a delightful
medieval village split in two sections
by a torrent crossed by a 15th-c. bridge.
The older and more characteristic district,
Terra, is on the left side of the torrent, and
Borgo on the other. The village boasts a
14th-c. castle built by the Doria family
and is the home of the excellent Rossese
di Dolceaqua.

Proceeding north for 8 km you come
to **Apricale★**, another enchanting village founded in the Middle Ages. It is
known as an artists' village because of
the murals that embellish the historic
centre. Built around a network of alleys
that run concentrically around the hill
starting from the central square on the
top, the alleys are linked, like snakes and
ladders, by steep flights of steps and
covered passageways.
The restored Lucertola Castle contains a
local history museum and holds temporary art exhibitions. In summer the village

is the setting for performances by the
Teatro della Tosse from Genoa.

Return to the SP 64 and continue for 11
km till you reach **Pigna★**, another lovely
stone village. The Church of San Michele
(15th c.) has a splendid rose window by
Giovanni Gagini and a fine 16th-c. **polyp-
tych★** by Giovanni Canavesio. There is a
superb **view★** from Piazza Castello.

Continue on the pretty winding road
for another 24 km to **Triora**, known as
the "village of the witches" owing to the
witchcraft trials held there in the late
16th c. Take a walk through the alleyways
and discover Triora's stone houses, fine
religious buildings, hidden courtyards
and flights of steps. The **Witchcraft
Museum** (*Corso Italia 1. For information
www.museotriora.it*) tells the story of
Triora and its link with witchcraft.

*Return to the coast.*

### Bordighera★
Bordighera is a celebrated resort of villas,
hotels, flowering gardens and shade-giv-
ing palms. The old town, with its twisting
alleyways, still features the gates of its
ancient city wall.

*Continue along the Via Aurelia.*

### San Remo★
Set between the sea and the mountains
on a wide bay between Capo Nero and
Capo Verde, the elegant centre of the
Riviera di Ponente enjoys a mild temperature all year round and is the sunniest
spot in all Liguria. Besides its favourable
climate, San Remo has a marina, casino,
horse-racing course and golf course, and
is the setting for annual events, such as
the famous Italian Song Festival. It is also
the most important centre in the Italian
flower business: from here millions of
roses, carnations and mimosa are sent
out across the world every year. The
flower market is held between 6 and 8am
every morning from October to June.

### The Principality of Seborga

*11 km north-east of Bordighera.*
Due to a bureaucratic oversight
this small principality was never
officially registered as one of the
dominions of the Savoy monarchs.
Thus in the 1960s the inhabitants
of Seborga started to claim
independence from the Republic of
Italy, elected a prince, and began to
mint their own coins and print their
own stamps. *To know more: www.
comuneseborga.it*

The seaside Corso Imperatrice, famous for its Canary Island date palms, is one of the most elegant promenades in Liguria. **La Pigna★** (pinecone) is the name given to the old city due to its pointed shape. Its tall, narrow, medieval buildings are threaded by winding alleys. A lovely **view★** over the city and bay can be enjoyed on the walk from Piazza Castello up to the Baroque Sanctuary of the Madonna della Costa.

**Monte Bignone★★**, 13 km north, offers **views★★** from its peak (1299 m) that stretch as far as Cannes.

## Bussana Vecchia

A medieval perched hamlet, Bussana Vecchia was heavily damaged by an earthquake in 1887 and remained uninhabited until the 1960s. Now it is populated by artists, predominantly foreign, who have opened shops along the paved streets.

## Taggia★

Located among orchards, vineyards and olive groves (this is the centre of the **Taggiasca olive**), Taggia is a large village that overlooks the Argentina valley. It was an important art centre in the 15th and 16th c. and welcomed many painters. The Convent of San Domenico has fine **paintings★** by Ludovico Brea, and there are frescoes by Giovanni Canavesio around the cloister. The central Via Soleri is lined by interesting buildings, and the 16-arch medieval bridge should not be missed.

## Imperia ♟

Imperia is formed by two centres separated by the torrent Impero: **Oneglia** is more recent and industrial, and **Porto Maurizio** the typical fishing town with the district of Parasio perched on a promontory. Oneglia has an **olive museum★**, built by the Fratelli Carli oil company to celebrate one of the traditional businesses in Liguria. *Via Garessio 13 (behind the railway station), Imperia Oneglia. Open 9-12.30 and 15-18.30, closed Sun., ℘ 0183 29 57 62, www. museodellolivo.com.*

A deviation inland of about 20 km along the **Impero valley** along the SS 28 – one of the "salt roads" between Liguria and Piedmont – leads to **Pieve di Teco ♟**. This small town has retained its medieval plan, the porticoes on Corso Ponzoni, and the ruins of a castle. **Pieve di Teco** is also interesting for the traditional goods it produces: mountain footwear and cheese.

*Return to the coast.*

## Diano Marina ♟

From the town you can reach the fortified village of **Diano Castello**, where the Chapel of the Cavalieri di Malta (12th c.) is covered by a polychrome wooden roof.

## Cervo★

This lovely village is dramatically set on a hill over the sea. Attractions are its charming alleys, the Piazza dei Corallini, and the Baroque **façade★** of the

© F. Carucci/Shutterstock

*Porto Maurizio, Imperia*

Church of San Giovanni Battista where a prestigious chamber music festival is held each summer.

From Marina di Andora head inland to **Andora Castello**, an attractive and isolated site where the remains of a castle and the medieval church dedicated to Santi Giacomo e Filippo can be seen.

## Alassio★

Alassio is one of the most sophisticated towns on the Riviera di Ponente. It was famous in the 1960s for its *muretto*, a small wall autographed by celebrities of the era. A visit should be paid to the busy *budello*, a good shopping area and evening meeting place. Lying off the coast between Alassio and Albenga is a privately owned island called **Gallinara**, which is kept as a nature reserve.

## Albenga★ ☙

Lying a little inland, in a fertile alluvial plain used for horticulture, Albenga has a **medieval centre★** clustered around its cathedral. This building has an impressive 14th-c. bell tower, and trompe l'oeil frescoes on the vault over the nave. The remarkable octagonal 5th-c. **baptistery★** features a font and enchanting early Christian mosaic in the style of Ravenna. Next to the baptistery stand the municipal tower and loggia, an outstanding set of medieval buildings dating from the 14th c. This point marks the start of the lovely **Via Ricci★**, a medieval street that lies over the Roman decuman.

Roughly 6 km inland you come to **Villanova d'Albenga**, an attractive hamlet of picturesque alleyways surrounded by turreted walls.

## Toirano Grottoes★

*Guided visits (70 min.), 9-12 and 13.30-16.30, closed mid-Dec.-mid-Jan., ☎ 0182 98 062, www.toiranogrotte.it.* This series of caves with stalactites and stalagmites was inhabited during the Neolithic period (human footprints, signs of torches, clay balls used as weapons, and the remains and traces of bears are still visible). The last section is very interesting: the cave was once filled with water, which has created beautiful rounded rock formations.

## Borgio Verezzi

Reached via a winding and spectacular climb from the Via Aurelia, the medieval hamlet of **Verezzi** stands 200 m above the sea and is the setting for a famous theatre festival in summer.

## Finale Ligure ☙

**Finale Marina** still has its basilica with an extravagant Baroque façade and city bastions built in the 14th c. by Castelfranco. The abbey church at **Finale Pia** has a fine late 13th-c. bell tower. Two kilometres inland, the historic **Finale Borgo★** has maintained its ancient fortifications, while the Church of San Biagio has an elegant polygonal 13th-c. bell tower; inside the church is a polyptych of *St Catherine* (1533) and a 16th-c. panel of *St Biagio*.

*Albenga medieval centre*

From **Castel San Giovanni** (*30 min. walk away from Via del Municipio along the Beretta road*) there are **views★** of Finale Ligure, the sea and inland. Higher up, **Castel Gavone** has a lovely round tower (15th c.) with pointed ashlars.

## Noli★

Once you pass the pleasant village of **Varigotti**, you come to Noli, a fishing village, which has conserved several ancient houses, 13th c. towers and the Romanesque Church of **San Paragorio★**, where you can see a coeval painted wooden crucifix.

## Savona

Savona is one of Italy's most important cargo ports but also a stopping place for cruise ships. The old city has a charming centre with Renaissance palaces, and, on the shoreline, **Priamar Castle★** (16th c.) where Giuseppe Mazzini was imprisoned in 1830. Today it is the home of the **History and Archaeology Museum** (*Complesso Monumentale Fortezza del Priamàr, Corso Mazzini 1, www.museoarcheosavona.it*) and the **Sandro Pertini Collection** of modern artworks (*for informations 𝄞 019 83 10 256*). The President of Italy, Pertini was born in Savona.

The Church of Nostra Signora di Castello, beside the 16th-c. duomo, has a fine **polyptych★** by Vincenzo Foppa (late 15th c.) of the Madonna and Saints, while the **City Picture Gallery** in the 16th-c. Palazzo Gavotti offers an opulent display of Ligurian art from the 14th to 20th c. *Piazza Chabrol 1-2. Open Wed.-Sun. 10-13.30, Thu.-Sat. 10-13.30 and 15.30-18.30, 𝄞 019 83 10 256.*

### The 2011 floods

Serious flooding on 25 October 2011 caused enormous damage, particularly in the villages of the Cinque Terre and at Borghetto di Vara, Brugnato, Bonassola, Levanto and Aulla. The delightful historic centres of Vernazza and Monterosso were devastated by the mud, rocks and other detritus swept as far as the sea following the bursting of the river banks. Reconstruction work has, however, reopened some of the trails that attract thousands of keen walkers every year.

## Albissola Marina

The town's production of handmade ceramics perpetuates a tradition that dates from the 13th c. The 18th-c. **Villa Faraggiana**, surrounded by a beautiful exotic **park★**, is home to the Ligurian Centre of the History of Ceramics, and features Empire furniture, tiled floors and a superb **ballroom★** lined with frescoes and stuccoes. *Guided visits Mar.-Sept., 𝄞 019 48 06 22, www.villa faraggiana.it.*

## 2. THE RIVIERA DI LEVANTE

### From Cinque Terre to Lunigiana

*Itinerary of approximately 70 km from Levanto to Sarzana.*

Promontories stretching into the sea, small wind-sheltered coves embracing tiny fishing ports, large luminous bays, cliffs, woods of pine and olive trees, and villages with characteristic alleyways: this is the Levantine landscape that stretches to the Tuscan border through the provinces of Genova and La Spezia. The designated areas in the Levante are **Val Polcèvera**, **Golfo del Tigullio**, **Cinque Terre**, **Colline di Levanto** and **Colli di Luni**, the last of which is shared with neighbouring Tuscany. The **white wines** are full-flavoured, fresh and Mediterranean; the most common varieties cultivated here are **Vermentino**, Albarola, Bosco and Bianchetta Genovese. The most prevalent, Vermentino, seems to have been imported into Italy by the Spanish during the Hapsburg domination of Sardinia. The **reds**, to be drunk young, are obtained from Dolcetto, Sangiovese and Ciliegiolo grapes. The most refined wine in this area is the **Schiacchetrà**, soft and amber-coloured made from the passerillage of Bosco, Albarola and Vermentino grapes, then aged in small wooden casks. The result is exceptional and aromatic, with hints of honey, spices and dried and candied fruit.

### Cinque Terre★★

🔳 *www.cinqueterre.it.* The area known as Cinque Terre (the name refers to five villages) is still difficult to reach, which is why the rocky coastline, with its fishing villages and vineyards, has conserved its wild and beautiful landscape almost

*Vernazza and its terraced vineyards*

intact. With Portovenere and the islands of Palmaria, Tino and Tinetto, Cinque Terre is a **World Heritage Site** and has been a **national park** since 1999. *For information: Parco Nazionale delle Cinque Terre, Via Discovolo c/o Stazione Manarola, Riomaggiore.* ℘ *0187 76 26 00, www.parconazionale5terre.it.*

A path along the shoreline connects the five villages of Monterosso, Vernazza, Corniglia, Manarola and Riomaggiore and offers marvellous views. The villages can be reached by car but the twisting and very busy roads means this option is preferably avoided. It is better to arrive by train or, for those with the time and a good pair of legs, to use the paths that join the villages.

**Monterosso** – comprises the old fishing village and Fegina, a modern seaside resort. In the upper village, the Church of San Francesco has admirable works of art, including a *Crucifixion* attributed to Van Dyck and a *St Jerome Penitent* by Luca Cambiaso.

**Vernazza**★★ – this is the most interesting village of the five. Its church and tall painted houses are set around a well-protected bay, but curiously, it is the apse of the church that faces onto the small square rather than its façade.

**Corniglia** – this is more of an agricultural than fishing village; it stands on a hill crest and is connected to the sea by a long flight of steps.

**Manarola**★ – a fishing village surrounded by terraced vineyards, Man-

arola still has its 14th-c. church. From here the romantic path called the **Via dell'Amore**★★ takes you to Riomaggiore in about 30 minutes, offering superb views of the coast and other villages.

**Riomaggiore**★ 🍷 – the old houses in this medieval village are crammed into the narrow valley of a torrent. The tiny fishing port is squeezed into a bay between strange, stratified black rocks that are typical of the region.

## Portovenere★★

The houses in this severe looking town, dominated by an imposing citadel (12th-16th c.) are very old, some dating from the 12th c., while others were fortified by the Genoese in later centuries. The Church of San Lorenzo was constructed in the 12th c., and that of San Pietro conserves ruins from the 6th c.: from the terrace there is a beautiful **view**★★ of the Cinque Terre and the **Gulf of Poets**, named after the stay there by Byron and Shelley, at the far end of which lies La Spezia.

Ferry trips leave from Portovenere for the islands of **Palmaria**, where you can visit the Blue Grotto. The islands of Tino and Tinetto cannot be visited.

### La Spezia

🛈 *Via del Prione 228.* ℘ *0187 02 61 52, www.turismoprovincia.laspezia.it.* In a setting of great beauty, this prevalently 19th-c. city is an important Italian naval base and commercial port. The dockyard built in the late 19th c. is one of the largest in Italy. The **naval museum**

*Portovenere and its multi-coloured buildings*

there exhibits shipping documents and materials from the past and a collection of figureheads. *Viale Amendola 1. For visits and information ☎ 0187 78 47 63.*

Constructed in the Middle Ages and several times rebuilt, the Castle of San Giorgio was recently restored to hold the **Ubaldo Formentini archaeological museum**, which exhibits finds from the area dating from prehistory to the Middle Ages, including 19 Bronze Age **stelae★** found in Lunigiana. *Via 27 Marzo. Open Winter: Wed.-Sun. 9.30-12.30 and 14-17; Mon. 9.30-12.30. Summer: Wed.-Sun., 10.30-17.30; Mon. 10.30 13.30., closed Tue., ☎ 0187 75 11 42, museodelcastello.spezianet.it.*

Art lovers should not miss the extraordinary **Lia Museum★★** (*Via Prione 234. Open Tue.-Sun. 10-18, ☎ 0187 73 11 00, museolia.spezianet.it*), which has a collection of more than 1100 works from the Roman age to the 18th c. Donated by Amedeo Lia, it is housed in a 17th-c. convent.

## Lerici★

A tiny port and seaside resort, Lerici lies at the end of a well-sheltered bay. Its impressive 13th-c. **castle** was rebuilt 300 years later by the Genoese. From Lerici you can reach the hamlets of **Fiascherino** and **Tellaro** by road or by sea.

## Sarzana★ ♀

At one time a Genoese outpost and a rival to Pisa, this busy little town has many reminders of the past. The cathedral has a finely carved marble **altarpiece★** (1432), and in a chapel to the right of the choir there is an ampulla that is supposed to have contained the blood of Christ. The chapel to the left of the choir contains a splendid Romanesque **crucifix★**.

**Sarzanello Fort★**, built in 1322 by Castruccio Castracani, the *condottiero* from Lucca, stands on a rise to the north-east of the city. It is an interesting example of military architecture with deep moats, solid walls and round towers. A magnificent **view★★** over the city and the first rises of the Apennines is given from the keep. *For visits and information, ☎ 0187 62 20 80, www.fortezzadisarzanello.com.*

**Luni**, 8 km to the south of Sarzana, was a thriving Roman port until the 3rd c. and today is an important archaeological site with an impressive amphitheatre and interesting museum. It is from this town that **Lunigiana** – the surrounding region divided between Tuscany, Liguria and Emilia – takes its name. Running through it is the river Magra, along whose valley various castles have been built, such as those at **Ortonovo** ♀, Nicola and **Castelnuovo Magra** ♀, as well as less important fortifications.

The **Montemarcello Magra River Park** lies at the mouth of the Magra. This oasis covers 4300 hectares and provides a habitat for many species of birds and Mediterranean flora, which can be explored along paths, mule tracks and guided walking routes.

# Addresses

## Tourist Information

**Alassio Tourist Office** – Via Mazzini 68, Alassio, ℘ 0182 64 70 27, www.comune. alassio.sv.it

**Genova Tourist Office** – Calata Molo Vecchio 15, Magazzini del Cotone, Modulo 5, **Genova**, ℘ 010 24 85 711, www.lamialiguria.it

## The wineries

*The addresses are listed in alphabetical order by location.*

### RIVIERA DI PONENTE

**Cascina Feipu dei Massaretti** – *Reg. Massaretti 7 - Fraz. Bastia -* **Albenga** *(SV) - ℘ 0182 20 131 - www.aziendamassaretti.it - mirco.mastroianni.albenga@gmail.com - Winery tours by reservation.* Owned by Agostino and Bice Parodi, the winery planted its first vines in 1965. The vines and wines follow Ligurian tradition, with Pigato and Rossese prevalent, but there are also specialities like Granaccia. The sweet wines are also interesting: the Bice made from sun-dried Pigato grapes, and the Pippo from mixed black varieties. Hectares under vine: 6.
**Wines**: Pigato, Pigato La Palmetta, Rossese, Granaccia IGT, Vino Bianco La Bice (Passito di Pigato), Russu du Feipu.

⌂ **Poggio dei Gorleri** – *Via San Leonardo 1 - Fraz. Gorleri -* **Diano Marina** *(IM) - ℘ 0183 49 52 07 - www.poggiodeigorleri. com - info@poggiodeigorleri.com - Winery tours and tastings by reservation.* The winery was founded in 2003 as a result of the

© GeorgeSi/Shutterstock

passion for wine of Giampiero Merano and his sons Matteo and Davide. They pursue the goal of creating a modern, innovative Ligurian wine representative of the character of the inhabitants and the aromas of the region. Their personal efforts and the innovations they have introduced in the cellar and the vineyard are quickly bringing about results. Accommodation available at the Poggio dei Gorleri Wine Resort *(11 apts.)*. Hectares under vine: 10.
**Wines**: Vermentino, Vermentino "Vigna Sorì", Pigato "Cycnus", Pigato "Albium", Dolcetto "Peinetti", Granaccia "Shalok".

⌂ **Altavia** – *Loc. Arcagna -* **Dolceacqua** *(IM) - www.altavia.im.it - info@altavia.im.it - Winery tours by reservation.* Dolceacqua is famous for the Rossese vine, which is not easy to cultivate as the steepness of the terraces makes the use of mechanical equipment impossible. Passion is required, which, fortunately, is not missing amongst the individuals behind the winery: Deborah Fada, Augusta Gariboldi and Gianni Arlotti. In addition to Rossese, the winery cultivates and produces Carignano, Syrah and Vermentino with excellent results. Accommodation available at the agritourism *(2 farm houses, min. stay one week, ℘ 0184 31 539)*. Hectares under vine: 5.
**Wines**: Rossese Dolceacqua Superiore, Noname, Skip Intro, Dapprimo. Other products: olive oil.

⌘ **Terre Bianche** – *Loc. Arcagna -* **Dolceacqua** *(IM) - ℘ 0184 31 426 - www.terrebianche.com - terrebianche@ terrebianche.com - Winery tours by reservation 8.30-12.30, 14.30-17, closed Sat. and Sun. in Nov. and Feb.* The winery was founded in 1870 when Tommaso Rondelli decided to plant the first Rossese vines next to the olive groves, to which Vermentino and Pigato were added. With time the winery grew and modernised. Management passed from generation to generation down to the current owners: Filippo Rondelli, Paolo Rondelli, Franco Laconi. In addition to wine production the winery offers farm accommodation *(5 rooms, €100, closed Nov. and Feb.)* and produces fruit, vegetables, oil and more. Evening meals available. Hectares under vine: 8.
**Wines**: Rossese di Dolceacqua, Riviera Ligure di Ponente Vermentino, Riviera Ligure di Ponente Pigato, Arcana Bianco, Arcana Rosso. Other products: oil.

**Cascina delle Terre Rosse** – *Via Manie 3/B -* **Finale Ligure** *(SV) - ℘ 019 69 87 82 - www.cascinaterrerosse.it - Winery tours by reservation.* Vladimir Galluzzo's land benefits from the proximity of the sea and a dry, ventilated climate. Pigato is the principal variety and wine of both the winery and this corner of Liguria, but the Cascina brings excellent results with Vermentino, Lumassina, Granaccia, Rossese and Barbera. Hectares under vine: 5.5.

**Wines:** Pigato, Vermentino, Apogeo, Banche, Solitario.

↑ **Tenuta Agricola Colle dei Bardellini** – *Via Fontanarosa 12 - Loc. Bardellini* - **Imperia** - ✆ *0183 29 13 70 - www.colledeibardellini.it - info@colledeibardellini.it - Winery tours by reservation.* Set 300 metres above the sea at Porto Maurizio, this domain produces Vermentino, Pigato and Rossese. The Vermentino Vigna "U Munte" is the pride of the winery and has won important national and international honours. The winery also sells a Vermentino grappa distilled from the marc of the "U Munte" grapes. Don't miss the extravirgin olive oil produced from the first cold pressing of olives grown inland. Accommodation is available at the agritourism, which offers 5 apartments with kitchenette. Hectares under vine: 4.

**Wines:** Vermentino, Pigato, Granaccia, Rossese. Other products: oil, grappa.

**La Baia del Sole Cantine Federici** – *Via Forlino 3 - Fr. Antica Luni di Ortonovo (SP)* - ✆ *0187 66 18 21 - www.cantinefederici.com - info@cantinefederici.com - Winery tours and tastings by reservation.* La Baia del Sole – is located in the Antica Luni di Ortonovo, a territory that has always been rich in art, culture and civilization, as the discover of an ancient Roman amphitheatre buried here has proven. All the cantina's operations are followed with maniacal attention by the owners, from the grape's entrance into the winemaking process, all the way to bottling the final product, which takes place rigorously under cold processing and aging, as the bottles are set in thick stone walls. The vineyards, spread out over several different hilly areas, make it possible for the diverse morphologies of the terroir and excellent sunny exposition to give the company's wines considerable depth and bouquet. Hectares under vine: 30.

**Wines:** Vermentino Colli di Luni Sarticola, Vermentino Colli di Luni Oro d'Isèe, Vermentino Colli di Luni Solaris, Rosso Colli di Luni Terre d'Oriente, Rosso Colli di Luni Eutichiano. Other products: grappa, spumanti, olive oil.

**Durin** – *Via Roma 202 - Ortovero (SV)* - ✆ *0182 54 70 07 - www.durin.it - info@durin.it - Winery tours by reservation.* "Durin" is the nickname of the Basso family, a tradition probably begun two centuries ago with the great-grandfather of the current owner, Antonio Basso. Antonio's father was a farmer and produced Pigato, which he sold in demijohns. He also grew fruit which he sold daily at the fruit and vegetable market in Albenga. Thanks to hard work and dedication, the Durin name is today one of the best known in the region. Hectares under vine: 16.5.

**Wines:** Pigato, Vermentino, Rossese, Ormeasco, Granaccia. Other products: oil, grappa.

**Lupi** – *Corso Mazzini 9 - Pieve di Teco (IM)* - ✆ *0183 36 973 - www.casalupi.it - lupi@casalupi.it - Winery tours by reservation.* In the 1950s and 1960s Tommaso Lupi and his sister Pina opened a bar-tavern in the heart of Oneglia. This soon became a favourite with people wishing to taste the best local wines. With his brother Angelo, in 1965 Tommaso set up as a wine-maker in a building used as a monks' convent in the year 1000. This was the start of the Lupi wine-making business, which today is in the hands of Massimo, Fabio and Tiziana Lupi. They have restarted the family olive business and now offer extra-virgin oil from Taggiasca olives alongside the family wine. Hectares under vine: 10.

**Wines:** Rossese di Dolceacqua, Pigato, Vermentino, Ormeasco di Pornassio, Vignamare. Other products: oil, grappa, preserves in oil.

↑ **A Maccia** – *Via Umberto I 56 - Ranzo (IM)* - ✆ *0183 31 80 03 - www.amaccia.it - info@amaccia.it - Winery tours by reservation.* In addition to producing excellent wines, the winery has launched the "Educational Farm" project, with organised visits for guests to encounter nature and learn about the production of wine and oil, from the plant to the table. Visitors to the company and guests at the agritourism have available a number of itineraries, on foot or bicycle, on the property and in the surrounding area, and are allowed to take part in work activities such as the grape and olive picking or working in the cellar. Independent apartments with kitchenette are also available (*4 apts., from €60, min. stay 2 days*). Hectares under vine: 3.5.

**Wines:** Riviera Ligure di Ponente Pigato, Riviera Ligure di Ponente Rossese, U Rosau Vino Rosato, Ormeasco. Other products: oil.

## RIVIERA DI LEVANTE

**Lambruschi Ottaviano** – *Via Olmarello 28 - Castelnuovo Magra (SP)* - ✆ *0187 67 42 61 or 338 44 13 761 - www.ottavianolambruschi.com - info@ottavianolambruschi.com - Winery tours by reservation.* The winery was founded in the mid-1970s when Ottaviano Lambruschi decided to leave his work at the Carrara marble quarries and buy 2 hectares of woodlands at Costa Marin with his brother Alessandro. With time the winery acquired new vines in particularly suitable zones. Research, tradition and modern techniques have ensured Lambruschi wines have earned themselves a reputation. Hectares under vine: 5.

**Wines**: Colli di Luni Vermentino Costamarina, Colli di Luni Vermentino Il Maggiore, Colli di Luni Vermentino, Colli di Luni Rosso, IGT Bianco.

⌂ **Buranco** – *Via Buranco 72 -* **Monterosso al Mare** *(SP) - ℘ 0187 81 76 77 - www.burancocinqueterre.it - info@ buranco.it - Winery tours by reservation.* Grape-growing in such inhospitable terrain is a challenge that this winery has overcome. They use narrow terraces held in place by dry walls. The soil, much of which is imported, is poor in organic substances but rich in minerals, which ensures the quality of the wines. The whites are produced using the most local varieties: Bosco, Vermentino, Albarola; also interesting is the red made with Cabernet and Syrah. Accommodation available in the agritourism (3 houses, *doubles €120).* Hectares under vine: 1.5.

**Wines**: Cinque Terre, Cinque Terre Sciacchetrà, Cinque Terre Magiöa, Rosso Buranco. Other products: grappa, oil, limoncino, honey.

**Cantine Lunae Bosoni** – *Cà Lunae - Via Palvotrisia 2 -* **Castelnuovo Magra** *(SP) - ℘ 0187 69 34 83 - www.cantinelunae.it - info@calunae.com - Winery tours by reservation.* Continual research has allowed Paolo Bosoni, the owner, to create very modern wines that use tradition as a starting point for evolving towards the new. Hectares under vine: 40.

**Wines**: Colli di Luni Vermentino Etichetta Nera, Colli di Luni Vermentino Cavagino, Colli di Luni Bianco Fior di Luna, Colli di Luni Rosso Niccolò V, Rosso IGT Golfo dei Poeti Horae. Other products: oil, spirits and jams.

**La Pietra del Focolare** – *Via Isola 76 -* **Ortonovo** *(SP) - ℘ 347 95 00439 - www. lapietradelfocolare.it - lapietradelfocolare@ libero.it - Winery tours by reservation (no tour in Sept.).* A small winery run with passion by Laura Angelini, whose attention focuses primarily on Vermentino grapes. Her vineyards are located disparately between Sarzana, Ortonovo and Calstelnuovo Magra, with different terrains and exposures. This enables vines with different colours, flavours and aromas to be obtained. Other varieties, international and Ligurian, are grown. Hectares under vine: 6.

**Wines**: Colli di Luni Vermentino Solarancio, Colli di Luni Vermentino Villa Linda, Colli di Luni Vermentino Augusto, Colli di Luni Vermentino L'Aura di Sarticola, Liguria di

Levante Bianco Vigna delle Rose, Colli di Luni Rosso Saltamasso, Colli di Luni Rosso la Merla dal Becco.

**Cantina Cinque Terre** – *Fraz. Groppo -* **Riomaggiore** *(SP) - ℘ 0187 92 04 35 - www.cantinacinqueterre.com - info5t@ cantinacinqueterre.com - Winery tours by reservation.* Formed in 1982, the cooperative now has 300 members and works to maintain the landscape and appreciation of wine in the Cinque Terre. Currently it is the largest producer in the zone. The aim is to bring out the character of the area in the wines produced, despite being of very limited quantity. Hectares under vine: 43.

**Wines**: 5 Terre, 5 Terre Costa da' Posa, 5 Terre Costa de Campu, 5 Terre Sciacchetrà.

## Where to stay

### RIVIERA DI PONENTE

**La Dimora del Conte Bracco B.** – *Piazza San Francesco 39,* **Albenga** *- ℘ 366 19 70 756 - www.ladimoradibracco.it - 2 rooms, doubles from €90.* In the very heart of the historical centre, this charming hotel offers cozy rooms.

### RIVIERA DI LEVANTE

**Da Ö Vittorio** – *Via Roma 160,* **Recco** *- ℘ 0185 74 029 - www.daovittorio.it - 29 rooms, doubles from €90.* A family-run little hotel with comfortable rooms furnished with different styles. The Bisso family restaurant offers great traditional Ligurian food in a picturesque and elegant atmosphere.

**Agriturismo Villanova** – *Loc. Villanova,* **Levanto** *- ℘ 0187 80 25 17 - www.agriturismo villanova.it - Closed 7 Nov.-Feb. - 13 rooms, doubles from €110.* Set in a rustic building surrounded by nature, ideal for lovers of peace and countryside.

# LOMBARDY

Wine is only one of the many things this region has to be proud of. Grapes have been cultivated in Lombardy since earliest times: archaeological finds of *Vitis vinifera silvestris* near Lakes Iseo and Garda dating to the Bronze Age demonstrate that the vine has been present in Lombardy since prehistory. Viticulture here has also benefited from the contributions of ancient peoples, like the Reti from the north, and the Etruscans and Liguri to the south. It was probably the latter who introduced terracing to Valtellina, which is in fact very similar to the type seen in Cinque Terre. In the 19th-c. the land under vine cultivation was much greater than today as many zones in the provinces of Varese, Como, Lecco and Milan, where today the vineyards are limited, used to produce wine in abundance.

*Valtellina vineyards*

## The terroir

An important wine-producing area in Lombardy is the **Valtellina** in the province of Sondrio, a zone where viticulture is considered "heroic" due to the difficulties posed by working on its steep, rugged terrain. **Nebbiolo** is the main variety grown, from which the great red wines Valtellina, Valtellina Superiore and Sforzato di Valtellina are produced.

**Oltrepò Pavese** is a very rich area enologically. This appellation makes use of many varieties of grape and produces many types of wine: white and red, still and sparkling, dry and sweet. It achieves levels of excellence in its classic method **sparkling wines**, which have recently been recognised with a DOCG appellation.

The province of **Brescia** offers the largest number of designated areas: Franciacorta, Terre di Franciacorta, Botticino, Capriano del Colle, Cellatica, Garda Bresciano, San Martino della Battaglia and Lugana. Franciacorta, which lies close to Lake Iseo, has carved itself out a large share of the Italian sparkling wine market. The **Franciacorta** DOCG wines are classic method *spumanti* made with Chardonnay, Pinot Nero and Pinot Bianco grapes. However, Franciacorta's gamut of products also includes still white wines (from Pinot Bianco, Chardonnay and Pinot Nero vinified in white) and reds (from Cabernet Franc, Cabernet Sauvignon, Barbera, Nebbiolo, Merlot and other varieties).

**San Martino della Battaglia** is an interregional DOC zone shared between Brescia and Verona that produces a wine from Friulano grapes in both a dry and sweet version. **Lugana** is a fresh and approachable white wine made from Trebbiano di Soave or di Lugana varieties and is produced in Spumante and Superiore versions. Wines with the **Garda**

## DOCG

Franciacorta
Oltrepò Pavese Metodo Classico
Scanzo *or* Moscato di Scanzo
Sforzato di Valtellina *or*
  Sfursat di Valtellina
Valtellina Superiore

## DOC

Bonarda dell'Oltrepò Pavese
Botticino
Buttafuoco dell'Oltrepò Pavese
  *or* Buttafuoco
Capriano del Colle
Casteggio
Cellatica
Curtefranca

Garda (with Veneto)
Garda Colli Mantovani
Lambrusco Mantovano
Lugana (with Veneto)
Oltrepò Pavese
Oltrepò Pavese Pinot Grigio
Pinot Nero dell'Oltrepò Pavese
Riviera del Garda Classico
San Colombano al Lambro
  *or* San Colombano
San Martino della Battaglia
  (with Veneto)
Sangue di Giuda dell'Oltrepò Pavese
  *or* Sangue di Giuda
Terre del Colleoni *or* Colleoni
Valcalepio
Valtènesi
Valtellina Rosso *or* Rosso di Valtellina

## PRINCIPAL VARIETIES CULTIVATED

### WHITE GRAPES

Chardonnay
Cortese
Garganega
Invernenga
Kerner
Malvasia bianca
di Candia
Manzoni Bianco
Moscato Bianco
Moscato Giallo
Müller Thurgau
Pinot Bianco
Prosecco
Riesling
Riesling Italico
Sauvignon
Friulano
Trebbiano di Soave
Trebbiano Giallo
Trebbiano Romagnolo
Trebbiano Toscano
Veltliner
Verdea
Verdese

### GREY GRAPES

Pinot Grigio

### BLACK GRAPES

Ancellotta
Barbera
Bonarda
Cabernet Franc
Cabernet Sauvignon
Corvina
Croatina
Dolcetto
Fortana
Franconia
Freisa
Groppello di Mocasina
Groppello di S. Stefano
Groppello Gentile
Incrocio Terzi n.1
Lagrein
Lambrusco di Sorbara
Lambrusco Grasparossa
Lambrusco Maestri
Lambrusco Marani

Lambrusco Salamino
Lambrusco Viadanese
Marzemino
Merlot
Meunier
Molinara
Montepulciano
Moscato di Scanzo
Nebbiolo
Negrara
Pignola
Pinot Nero
Raboso Veronese
Rondinella
Rossola Nera
Sangiovese
Schiava
Schiava Gentile
Schiava Grigia
Schiava Grossa
Teroldego
Uva Rara
Vespolina

# LOMBARDY

**Bresciano** appellation are produced in the hills on the Brescian shore of **Lake Garda**. Garda, Garda Classico Chiaretto and Groppello are the most representative wines of the zone.

**Botticino** and **Cellatica** are red wines produced in the municipalities of the same name from Barbera, Schiava, Marzemino and Sangiovese grapes, while the **Capriano del Colle** appellation signifies white wines, occasionally slightly fizzy, from Trebbiano grapes and reds from Barbera, Marzemino and Sangiovese.

In the province of **Mantova** there are the designated areas **Garda dei Colli Mantovani** (white and red wines) and **Lambrusco Mantovano**, the latter a Lombard variety of the grape that is the symbol of viticulture in neighbouring Emilia.

The hills of **Bergamo** produce red and white wines in the **Valcalepio DOC** zone, as well as the rare red dried-grape wine made from Moscato di Scanzo grapes. The province of Milan also has a small wine-making area, which produces the red **San Colombano** around the village of the same name.

# Itineraries

*Locations with a winery are indicated by the symbol ♈; for the addresses of the wineries, see p. 134.*

## 1. OLTREPÒ PAVESE

Oltrepò Pavese produces a generous range of **white**, **red**, **sparkling** and **still wines**, and the variety of vine types is also extensive. The red wines can be still or lively, and offer scents of blackberries, raspberries, strawberries, roses or violets. They are approachable, pleasingly refreshing and best drunk young.

The great character of the zone's white and rosé **sparkling wines**, obtained with second fermentation in the bottle (Classic Method), has resulted in their DOCG attribution. The **whites** are distinguished by scents of yellow- and white-fleshed fruit, flowers, croissant and bread crust, whereas the **rosés** are attractive for their colour and delicate bouquet of wild strawberries and yeast. The sweet wines made from aromatic grapes go wonderfully with biscuits and cakes.

**Buttafuoco** and **Sangue di Giuda** are both made from Croatina, Barbera

### The wines of Brianza

Although there is no appellation in Brianza, a zone that stretches north from Monza to Lakes Como and Lecco, the area actually has a long-established and glorious past, in particular in the district of Montevecchia Nature Park. At the time of the Romans, the wines on these slopes were recognised and appreciated. In the 19th c. the Milanese poet Carlo Porta sang their praises and, more recently, they won over the two refined gourmets Gianni Brera and Mario Soldati. For information on **Montevecchia Regional Nature Park** and the **Curone Valley Nature Park**, see www.parcocurone.it and **Consorzio Terre Alte**, www.terrealtelecco.it

and Bonarda grapes, but whereas the first is full-bodied and structured, with intense, persistent aromas of spices and fruit jams, the second is delicately sweet, light and fruity.

**Riesling** finds the ideal conditions in Oltrepò Pavese. It is cultivated in the Renano and Italico varieties: the **Renano** comes from Alsace and Germany and gives magnificent white wines that age wonderfully; the **Italico** is a clone that produces not only refined still white wines but also sparkling wines of outstanding character.

Oltrepò Pavese is the leading area for growing **Pinot Nero** in Italy. This variety lies at the base of interesting still reds to be laid down, production of which is increasing, although it is in the sparkling winemaking method that Pinot Nero gives its best in Oltrepò Pavese.

## Pavia★

An important military post in Roman times, Pavia later became the capital of the Lombard kings, a rival to Milan in the 11th c., a noted intellectual and artistic centre in the 14th c. under the Visconti, a fortified city in the 16th c., and one of the most fervent centres of the Risorgimento movement in the 19th c. Its university is one of the oldest and most famous in Europe, welcoming Petrarch, Leonardo da Vinci and Ugo Foscolo, amongst others. Its beauty and pleasantly restricted size make it a city "on a human scale".

**Visconti Castle and the civic museums★★** – Viale XI Febbraio 35. *Open 10-18, closed Tue. and public hols.* ✆ *0382 39 97 70, www.museicivici.pavia.it.* The imposing 14th-c. construction today is home to the city's museums of archaeology, medieval and Renaissance sculpture, and paintings. The many masterpieces of painting include a lovely altarpiece by the Brescian artist Vincenzo Foppa, a *Madonna and Child* by Giovanni Bellini, and an expressive *Christ Carrying the Cross* by the Lombard painter Bergognone. The last room contains a large wooden model of the cathedral made by Fugazza in the 16th c. from drawings by Bramante. Also worthy of note is the 19th-c. section with works from the Neoclassical age to the early 20th c.

**Duomo★** – construction of this vast building and immense cupola was started in 1488: Bramante and Leonardo da Vinci are said to have contributed to its design. However, the façade dates from the 19th c. Facing it is the 16th-c. Bishop's Palace. The municipal tower (16th c.) used to stand to the left but it collapsed in 1989.

The neighbouring Piazza Vittoria is the site of the **Broletto**, the 12th-c. City Hall, which gives an interesting view of the apse of the duomo.

**San Michele★★** – this lovely Romanesque church has a sandstone façade distinguished for the balance and variety of its decoration. There is a Romanesque portal on the right side with an architrave decorated with an image of Christ giving St Paul a *volumen* of papyruses and the keys of the Church to St Peter. Inside you can admire interesting architectural features and, in the apse, the beautiful 15th-c. **fresco★★** of the *Coronation of the Virgin.*

**San Pietro in Ciel d'Oro★** – consecrated in 1132, the church in Lombard Romanesque style boasts a richly decorated portal. In the presbytery the remains of **St Augustus** (354-430) lie in his **sarcophagus★** carved by Campionesi mastermasons.

**San Lanfranco** – *2 km west of the historic centre towards the motorway link to Bereguardo.* The presbytery contains a late 15th-c. **cenotaph★** in memory of Lanfranc, archbishop of Canterbury, who was born in Pavia and died in Canterbury in 1098, where he is buried.

## The Charterhouse of Pavia★★★

*Open 9-11.30 and 14.30-16.30 (18 in summer), closed working Mon.,* ✆ *0382 92 56 13, www.certosadipavia.com.* One of the most representative monuments of Lombard art and the home of a small community of Cistercian monks, the Charterhouse lies 10 km to the north of the city. Ordered in 1396 by Gian Galeazzo Visconti as a family mausoleum, it was mostly built in the 15th and 16th c. The elaborate **façade★★★** is surprising for the refinement and quality of its details, but it retains an elegant sobriety of structure. The lower, more highly wrought half (partly the work of the famous architect-sculptor Amadeo, active mostly in Bergamo) was executed between 1473 and 1499, while the upper section is 16th c. Before entering the church, walk down the left

Charterhouse of Pavia

© RnDmS/iStock

## THE TERROIR

**Area**: 23,863.10 km$^2$, of which approximately 22,093 hectares are planted to vine

**Production 2019**: 1,302,737 hectolitres of which 680,807 VQPRD

**Geography**: mostly mountainous (40.5%) or flat (47.1%). The flat zones are part of the Po-Veneto plain while the mountains are prevalently the Central Alps. The mountainous section is divided into Alps formed by crystalline rocks and Prealps of medium-height composed of calcareous and morainic rocks. Lombardy is the region with the most and largest lakes in Italy

## THE PROTECTION CONSORTIA

As.Co.Vi.Lo. - Associazione Consorzi Tutela Vini Lombardi – www.ascovilo.it

Ente Vini Bresciani (with the associated Consortia: Associazione Produttori del Cellatica, Botticino, Montenetto, Valcamonica, Valtènesi, Provveditoria dei Vini Novelli Bresciani) – ✆ 030 36 47 55, www.entevinibresciani.it

Consorzio di Tutela del Franciacorta DOC – ✆ 030 77 60 477, www.franciacorta.net

Consorzio di Tutela Lugana – ✆ 045 92 33 070, www.consorziolugana.eu

Consorzio Provinciale di Tutela Vini Mantovani – ✆ 0376 23 44 20, www.vinimantovani.it

Consorzio di Tutela Moscato di Scanzo – ✆ 035 65 91 425, www.consorziomoscatodiscanzo.it

Consorzio di Tutela Vini Oltrepò Pavese – ✆ 0383 77028, www.vinoltrepo.it

Consorzio Volontario Vino DOC San Colombano – ✆ 0371 89 88 30, www.sancolombanodoc.it

Consorzio di Tutela Valcalepio – ✆ 035 95 39 57, www.valcalepio.org

Consorzio di Tutela Vini Valtellina – ✆ 0342 20 08 71, www.consorziovinivaltellina.com

## WINE AND FOOD ROUTES

Federazione Strade dei Vini e dei Sapori di Lombardia – ✆ 0376 23 44 20, www.viniesaporidilombardia.it and www.buonalombardia.it

Strada del Vino Colli dei Longobardi – ✆ 030 41 889, www.stradadelvinocollideilongobardi.it

Strada del Vino Franciacorta – ✆ 030 77 60 870, www.franciacorta.net

Strada del Vino e dei Sapori del Garda – ✆ 030 99 90 402, www.stradadeivini.it

Strada dei Vini e dei Sapori Mantovani – ✆ 0376 23 44 20, www.mantovastrada.it

Strada del Vino e dei Sapori dell'Oltrepò Pavese – ✆ 0383 77028 or 349 10 88 317, www.vinoltrepo.it and www.oltrepopavese.com

Strada del Vino San Colombano e dei Sapori Lodigiani – ✆ 0376 23 44 20, www.viniesaporidilombardia.it

Strada del Vino e dei Sapori della Valcalepio – ✆ 035 95 39 57, www.valcalepio.org

Strada del Vino e dei Sapori della Valtellina – ✆ 0342 20 08 71, www.stradadelvinovaltellina.it

Strada del Gusto Cremonese – ✆ 0372 40 67 54, www.viniesaporidilombardia.it

Strada del Riso e dei Risotti Mantovani – ✆ 339 70 46 909, www.stradadelrisomantovano.it

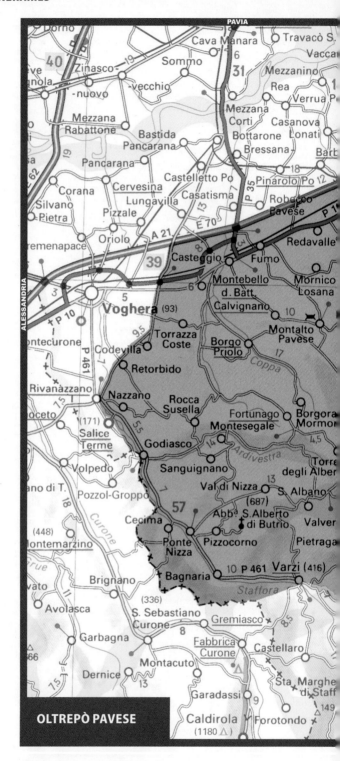

OLTREPÒ PAVESE

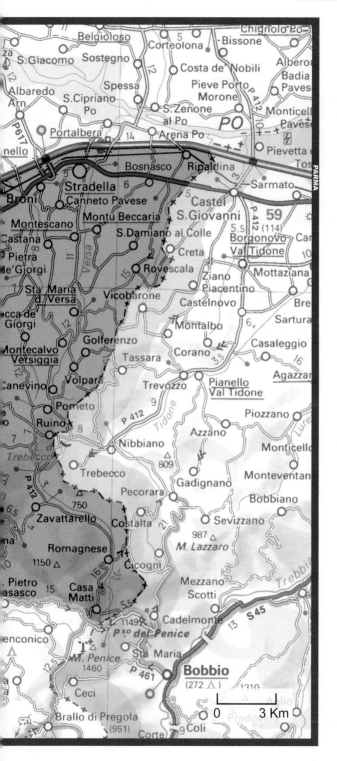

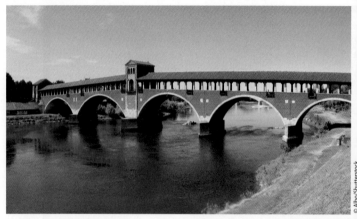

*Ponte Vecchio (Old Bridge), Pavia*

side to admire the superb composition in Late Lombard Gothic style, and the superimposed arcades.

The beautiful but stately **interior** is in Gothic style but some anticipatory signs are apparent of the Renaissance in the transept and presbytery in particular. Once you are inside, look upwards: above the chapels on the right a painted Carthusian spies on visitors from a twin lancet window; higher up, the intense blue of the vaults is illuminated by stars. The church holds many works by Bergognone (1481-1522). The magnificent **great cloister** is a vast space lined with arcades, above which are set the 24 monks' cells (occupied until 1968): despite their extreme plainness, each cell is an individual apartment with a view onto a garden.

In the old sacristy you can see the **triptych** carved by Baldassare degli Embriachi from ivory and hippopotamus tooth for Gian Galeazzo Visconti (late 14th c.).

## Oltrepò Pavese: from Pavia to the Apennines

*Itinerary of approximately 130 km.*
*Leave Pavia on the SS 234 and take the SS 617 to Broni.*

The countryside in the province of Pavia between the Po and the Apennines is remarkably varied: from the alluvial plain planted with cereals you pass to vine-covered hills, and then up into a wooded, mountainous landscape. On the way you pass over the confluence of the Po and Ticino at the **Becca Bridge**, an outstanding engineering work of the early 20th c. The point of reference for exploring the wine-producing areas of Oltrepò is **Broni**, a town through which the Roman Via Emilia Scaura runs. A couple of km east of Broni stands the Art Nouveau building (1923) of the Recoaro water company.

South of Broni is the **Scuropasso valley**, a hilly zone where Riesling Italico in particular is grown. The valley takes in the municipalities of **Cigognola** ♟, **Rocca de' Giorgi** ♟ and **Pietra de' Giorgi** ♟, the site of one of the oldest manors in the zone, **Villa Fornace**, which dates from the 11th c. and takes its name from an old lime furnace.

Proceeding east from Broni on the SS 10 you come to **Stradella**, a town famous for **accordions**, about which there is an interesting museum in Palazzo Garibaldi (*Via Montebello 2, ✆ 0385 48 870*). Its strategic position as a border town has resulted in Stradella having two defensive castles, the ruins of which can still be seen.

From Stradella you come to **Canneto Pavese** ♟ (*5 km south-west*), the home of the prized Buttafuoco. It stands in lovely hilly countryside along the ridge that separates the Scuropasso valley to the west from the Versa valley to the east. Continuing a few more km takes you to Castana, whose ancient castle has been rebuilt in its original form. Several routes leave from the road that runs alongside the left bank of the Versa torrent to other villages mostly situated on the ridges of the vine-covered hills. One of these climbs to **Montù Beccaria** ♟,

120

the name of which refers to the Beccaria family, the local lords who built the castle. Continue to **San Damiano al Colle** 🍷, in a fine panoramic position, and **Rovescala** 🍷, a village with a winemaking tradition that dates right back to the Romans.

Returning to the provincial road, head for **Santa Maria della Versa** 🍷, the capital of sparkling wine, which grew up around an image of the Virgin once displayed in a small rural chapel and now in the parish church. A few more km brings you to **Canevino**, perched on the hill that separates the Versa and Scuropasso valleys. Pilgrims heading for Bobbio monastery founded by St Columbanus in Val Trebbia used to pass through this village.

Once past Canevino you enter the zone of **Oltrepò Montano**. The principal centre here is **Varzi**, which has an attractive ancient village and the Church dei Cappuccini founded in the 14th c. Follow the SP 461 alongside the Stàffora torrent to Ponte Nizza, from where you can reach the **Abbey of Sant'Alberto di Butrio** (11th c.), which enjoyed fame and power until the 14th c.

Continuing along the provincial road, you come to **Salice Terme**, whose spa waters were known to the Romans. Passing through **Retorbido** 🍷 and **Codevilla** 🍷 you arrive at **Voghera**, the largest town in Oltrepò. It boasts a fine porticoed Piazza Duomo, from where Via Cavour leads to the 14th-c. castle, long used as a prison. Next, head east in the direction of Bobbio to Montebello della Battaglia, whose name commemorates the two defeats inflicted on the Austrians in 1800 and 1859, and then to **Casteggio** 🍷, where there are good views from its upper part and the 18th-c. Palazzo della Certosa Cantù, home to an **archaeological museum** (✆ 0383 83 941, www.museocasteggio.it). A few kilometres to the south and east of **Casteggio** lie **Calvignano** 🍷, **Montalto Pavese** 🍷, dominated by its castle, **Borgo Priolo** 🍷, with an interesting medieval centre, and **Corvino San Quirico** 🍷 where wine-lovers can enjoy a peaceful stopover.

Lying slightly off the itinerary (*30 km north-east of Broni, in the province of Lodi*) stands **San Colombano al Lambro** 🍷,

named after the Irish monk who in the 7th c. converted the pagan tribes settled in this area and founded Bobbio Abbey. The vine-covered hill of the same name is to the south. The medieval castle has been permanently demolished, leaving only a few towers. The pleasant ancient town stands outside the castle walls.

About 5 km to the west of San Colombano is **Miradolo Terme**, where the spa centre lies amongst the woods.

## 2. VALCALEPIO

The wine-making area of Valcalepio in the province of **Bergamo** makes white, red and dried-grape wines of interesting quality. The reds are obtained from Cabernet Sauvignon and Merlot grapes and the whites from Chardonnay, Pinot Bianco and Pinot Grigio. These are refreshing wines to be drunk young, which give a pleasant almond-like aftertaste. The pride of Valcalepio is the **Moscato Passito** produced from a local variety of grape, Moscato di Scanzo, which is left to dry for at least 3 weeks on the racks before being pressed. It is a sweet wine with very original aromatic qualities thanks to its scents of rose, sage and acacia honey. If vinified in the municipality of **Scanzorosciate** 🍷 it can use the appellation **Scanzo** or **Moscato di Scanzo**.

### Bergamo ★★★

There is a Bergamo "*de sura*" and another "*de sota*", as is said in the dialect of these parts. The lower city (*de sota*) is modern and busy and lies beneath the Venetian walls of the small, splendid upper town. Bergamo is also known for its traditional recipes, such as *polenta e osei*, actually cornmeal mush with bird meat.

You reach the **Upper City** by car (*park outside the walls*) or the cable railway (*station in Viale Vittorio Emanuele II*) that arrives in the picturesque Piazza del Mercato delle Scarpe. **Piazza Vecchia★** is the city's historic centre.

**Palazzo della Ragione** (the oldest Municipal Palace in Italy) dates from 1199 but was rebuilt in the 16th c. The central balcony crowned by St Mark's lion was a statement of Venice's domination of the city. During the closure of the **Accademia Carrara** (in the Lower City) the palace is displaying a section of the city's art collections. *Winter: 1st Oct.-26th*

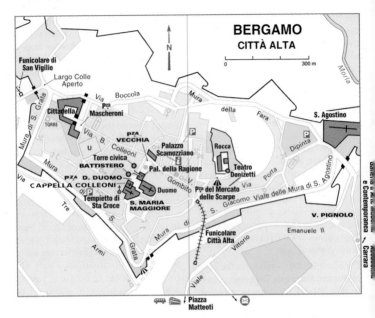

**BERGAMO**
CITTÀ ALTA

*Jan. Wed.-Mon. 9.30-17.30. Summer: 7th May-30th Sept. 10-18. Closed working Tue. ℘ 035 41 22 097 or ℘ 035 23 43 96, www. accademiacarrara.bergamo.it.*

Opposite, Palazzo Scamozziano is in Palladian style. The fountain at the centre of the square was offered to the city in 1780 by the doge of Venice, Alvise Contarini.

Pass through the arches of Palazzo della Ragione to reach **Piazza del Duomo★★**, onto which the city's most important monuments face.

**Colleoni Chapel★★★** – *Open 9-12.30 and 14-18.30 (16.30 in Nov.-Feb.), closed Mon., ℘ 035 21 00 61.* A jewel of Lombard Renaissance architecture, the mausoleum of the *condottiere* Bartolomeo Colleoni was built between 1470 and 1476 by Amadeo, architect of the Charterhouse of Pavia. The burial chapel is attached to the side of the Basilica of Santa Maria Maggiore; the main body, topped by a cupola, is joined to the north atrium of the church which is masterfully used as a counterpart to the kiosk. The façade is lined with polychrome marble, enlivened by animated decoration and adorned with delicate sculptures: *putti*, fluted and spiral columns, sculpted pillars, vases and candelabras, medals and low reliefs are blended with, in the taste of the time,

sacred and profane images, for example, allegories, episodes from the Old Testament, effigies of famous figures from antiquity, and scenes from the legend of Hercules, with whom the *condottiere* liked to identify. The magnificent interior is embellished with low-relief sculptures of great refinement, frescoes by Tiepolo and Renaissance stalls. **Colleoni's tomb**, also by Amadeo, is topped by an equestrian statue of the man made from gilded wood. Colleoni's favourite daughter, Medea, who died at the age of 15, lies next to him in a tomb also designed by Amadeo.

**Santa Maria Maggiore★★** – *Mon.-Wed. 9-12.30 and 14.30-18, Thu.-Sun. 9-18, ℘ 035 22 33 27.* The building dates from the 12th c. but two centuries later Giovanni da Campione added the north and south porches that stand on lions in typical Lombard Romanesque style. The interior, renovated in Baroque style at the turn of the 17th c., is richly decorated with stuccoes and gilding. The walls of the choir and the left and right aisles are lined with superb Florentine **wall-hangings★★** (1580-86) displaying scenes from the life of the Virgin, while the magnificent late 17th-c. tapestry from Flanders on the wall at the end of the nave represents the **Crucifixion★★**. This part of the church also contains the tomb of composer Gaetano Donizetti (Bergamo, 1797-1848). In the choir pews there are 4 superb early 16th-c. **tarsias**★★ designed by Lorenzo Lotto.

Leaving the church, admire the **Tempietto di Santa Croce** in Piazza Santa Maria Maggiore. This four-sided building was constructed around 1000 in Romanesque style. Also note the 14th-c. south portal of Santa Maria Maggiore. Return to Piazza Duomo and walk around the basilica to admire the **apse**★ and its elegant arches.

The **baptistery**★ is an octagonal building architecturally lightened by a small loggia in red Verona marble, slender columns and 14th-c. statues of the Virtues. It is in fact a reconstruction of the work by Giovanni da Campione (1340) originally built at the end of the nave of Santa Maria Maggiore. However, it was judged too intrusive, demolished in 1660 and rebuilt in 1898 in its current position. The duomo has a rich 18th-c. interior with very beautiful Baroque stalls carved by the Sanzi family.

The house belonging to Bartolomeo Colleoni stands at nos. 9-11 in Via Colleoni that runs from Piazza Vecchia. Lovely **views**★ over Upper and Lower Bergamo can be had from the Rocca (fort), built in the 14th c. and renovated by the Venetians.

In the **Lower City**★ picturesque streets surround the **Accademia Carrara**★★ (*see p. 121*). (*see p. 121*).

The **old district**★ stretches along **Via Pignolo**★, a winding street lined by ancient palaces (16th-18th c.) and elegant churches, for example, San Bernardino (contains the altarpiece *Madonna and Child with Saints* by Lorenzo Lotto, 1521) and Santo Spirito.

Lying in the modern city centre, the immense **Piazza Matteotti**★ is the setting for the Teatro Donizetti and Church of San Bartolomeo. Inside you can see the superb **Martinengo Altarpiece**★ by Lorenzo Lotto (*Holy Conversation*). The favourite city walk of the Bergamaschi is the **Sentierone**, which runs along the square.

## Valcalepio: from Bergamo to the river Oglio

*Itinerary of approximately 40 km from Bergamo to Credaro. Leave Bergamo east towards Seriate and follow the SS 42.*

A beautiful zone of vine-covered hills lies between the rivers Serio and Oglio. **Trescore Balneario**, a spa known since ancient times, has several interesting religious buildings and above all a cycle of **frescoes**★ executed by Lorenzo Lotto in 1524 on the walls of the oratory of Villa Suardi. *Mar.-Nov. Sun. 15-15.45 and 16.15-17 or visits by reservation at Trescore tourist office,* ☏ *035 94 47 77.*

At **Carobbio degli Angeli** 🍷, on the top of Monte degli Angeli, stand the remains

Colleoni Chapel and the baptistery, Bergamo

© vale_t/iStock

of a 14th-c. complex, originally a fort but later turned into a Carmelite convent and today a winery. A small detour south takes you to **Costa di Mezzate** and the imposing Camozzi-Vertova castle, with buildings dating from the 13th-14th c.

Return to Carobbio to continue to **Grumello del Monte** 🍷, where there is an ancient manor (the summer residence of Bartolomeo Colleoni) that was transformed into an aristocratic villa in the 17th c.

*Continue along the SP 91.*

Passing through Castel de' Conti, you reach **Credaro**, an ancient village whose Church of San Giorgio has frescoes by Lorenzo Lotto. The 11th c. **Trebecco Castle** has recently been rebuilt to conserve the form of the fortified medieval village.

## 3. FRANCIACORTA

"Franca Corte" ('free court') was once a tax-free zone, whence its name. This strip of land to the **north of Brescia** stretches between Lake Iseo and the Garza torrent and is the home of Lombardy's most famous **sparkling wines**. The terrain, climate and the dedication shown produce classy wines of great elegance and character, the best of which are in no way inferior to French champagnes. They are produced in white and rosé versions. The sugar residue determines if a wine is *pas dosé, extra brut, brut, sec or demisec*; and wines made using only white grapes (Chardonnay and Pinot Bianco) are referred to as **satèn**.

Obtained using refermentation in the bottle (Classic Method), Franciacorta wines stand out for their complex and lingering scents of croissant, yeast, citrus fruits, flowers, honey and bread crust. The area where **Franciacorta DOCG** wines are produced is also responsible for still white and red wines with the appellation **Curtefranca DOC**: they are best drunk young and give pleasant aromas of flowers, fruit and grass.

## Brescia★ 🍷

Standing at the feet of the Prealps of Lombardy, Brescia occupies the regular 4-sided plan of the ancient Roman *castrum* and its emblem is still the noble winged lion of Venice. With the 14th-c. Visconti **castle** on the north side, the history of the city is recounted in buildings of great beauty. Brescia is surrounded by vine-covered hills and lies close to Garda, "the most Mediterranean of the alpine lakes". After the splendours of the imperial Roman city of Brixia, attested by its Capitoline temple and the remains of the ancient forum, in the 8th c. Brescia became a Lombard dukedom and in the 12th and 13th c. a free commune and member of the Lombard League. It was especially prosperous due to the manufacture of armour and arms that it sold right across Europe until the 18th c. From 1426 to 1797 it lived under the rule of the Serenissima and constructed itself magnificent civic and religious buildings. Great painters such as Vincenzo Foppa, Romanino, Moretto and Savoldo in the 15th and 16th c. gave rise to the **Brescian School**, characterised by rich tonality and solid and balanced composition. A display of the work of this school is given by the **Tosio Martinengo Picture Gallery★** (*Tue.-Fri. 9-17, Sat., Sun. and public hols. 9-18, closed working Mon., Piazza Moretto, for information ☏ 030 29 77 833/4, www.bresciamusei.com*).

**Piazza della Loggia★** takes its name from the splendid 16th c. building that is today the City Hall. The design of the upper floor was contributed to by, among others, Sansovino and Palladio. On the east side of the square is the Clock Tower, topped by two figures that strike the hours. On the south side are the Palazzi del Monte di Pietà Vecchio (1484) and Nuovo (1497), and on the north side is the start of a picturesque popular district featuring porticoes and ancient houses. In addition to its beauty, the square is sadly remembered for the terrorist bomb of 1974 that cost the lives of 9 people.

Piazza Paolo VI is the setting for the 17th c. white marble Duomo Nuovo. Next to it stands the **Duomo Vecchio★**, a late 11th-c. Romanesque building constructed over an earlier sanctuary and known, due to its circular plan, as the Rotonda. Inside there is a magnificent pink marble sarcophagus with a statue of a bishop, and, in the presbytery, canvases by the Brescian painters Moretto and Romanino. To the left of the Duomo Nuovo is the austere Romanesque **Broletto**, crowned by a solid square tower and adorned by a lovely balcony known as the Loggia delle Grida.

**Via Musei★** offers an interesting walk by the **Capitoline Temple★** (73 AD) and the **Roman theatre**.

Next you come to the monastic complex founded in 753 by the Lombard king Desiderio and his wife Ansa, and in which, according to Manzoni, Ermengarda is buried. The ancient monastery also comprised the Lombard Basilica of San Salvatore, the Romanesque Church of Santa Maria in Solaio and the Renaissance Church of **Santa Giulia**. The entire complex has been transformed into the **City Museum★** that recounts the history of Brescia since the Bronze Age. Note the fresco of the starry sky with God the Father in the dome of Santa Giulia, and **Desiderio's Cross★★** (8th-9th c.). In addition to being set with gems, cameos and coloured glass, the cross is decorated with the supposed portrait of Galla Placidia with her children (3rd-4th c.). *Via Musei 81/bis. Open 9-17 (Sat., Sun. and public hols. 18), closed working Mon., ☏ 030 29 77 833/4, www.bresciamusei.com.*

**Churches★** – Brescia boasts many Romanesque, Renaissance and Baroque churches rich with works of art, especially by the local school. Behind the Loggia, Sant'Agata has a polyptych of the *Madonna of the Misericordia* (Brescian School, 16th c.) and the *Virgin of the Coral*, a charming 16th-c. fresco. *Follow Via Fratelli Porcellaga and Via Martiri della Libertà*. The 13th-c. Church of **San Francesco★** contains Moretto's **Three Saints**, a Giottoesque **Pietà** and a **Madonna and Saints** by Romanino. Santa Maria dei Miracoli (15th-16th c.) has a lovely marble façade. The Church of Santi Nazaro e Celso holds a masterpiece by Moretto, the *Coronation of the Virgin*, and a polyptych by Titian.

To the north of Piazza della Loggia you will find the churches of San Giovanni Evangelista with panels by Moretto and Romanino, the Madonna delle Grazie with a Baroque interior, and the "oriental" Madonna del Carmine.

In via Moretto, close to the Tosio Martinengo Picture Gallery stands the Church of Sant'Alessandro where there is a 15th- c. *Annunciation* by Jacopo Bellini and a *Deposition* by Civerchio.

## Franciacorta: from Brescia to Lake Iseo

*Itinerary of approximately 100 km. Leave Brescia in a north-westerly direction.*

Pass through **Gussago**, close to which you can find (*at Piè del Doss*) the 15th-c. Church of Santa Maria, with frescoes and an early Christian sarcophagus. Next you come to **Rodengo**, famous for the Abbey of San Nicola founded in the 11th c. by the Cluniacs. This lovely complex comprises a series of cloisters, the church and the guesthouse with frescoes by Romanino. **Passirano** 🍷 conserves a fine example of a fortified enclosure wall (13th-14th c.) used as a refuge in times of danger but also as an ordinary residence. **Erbusco** 🍷 lies between vineyards and Lake Iseo. It was once a country resort of the Brescian and Milanese nobility and has admirable historic monuments, such as the Church of Santa Maria (13th-15th c.) and the Palladian Villa Lechi (16th-17th c.).

Pass **Adro** 🍷 and arrive at **Capriolo** 🍷, the final municipality in Franciacorta, just by the river Oglio. There is a **Farming and Wine Museum** at the Ricci Curbastro domaine. *Via Adro 37. Open by reservation 9-12 and 14-18, ☏ 030 73 60 94, www.riccicurbastro.it.*

*Return to Adro and turn left towards the lake.* After **Corte Franca** 🍷, an ancient village after which the entire zone was probably named, just past the **Sebino peat bogs** (nature reserve) you arrive at **Provaglio** 🍷, where the **Monastery of San Pietro in Lamosa** stands just outside the village going towards Lake Iseo. Founded in the 11th c. by the Cluniacs, it gives views over the peat bogs. *Via Monastero 5. Open Sat., Sun. and public hols. 10-12 and 15-18 (in Nov.-Mar. 10-12 and 14-17), guided visits by reservation, ☏ 030 98 23 617, www.sanpietroinlamosa.org.*

## Lake Iseo★

Although it is less famous than the other lakes of Lombardy, Iseo (also called **Sebino**) is striking for the variety of its surrounding terrain: tall mountains on three sides and the Franciacorta plain on the other. At the centre of the intensely blue lake lies **Monte Isola★★** *(frequent ferry connections from Iseo and Sulzano; for information contact Iseo and*

FRANCIACORTA

Franciacorta tourist office, Lungolago Marconi 2c, ℰ 030 37 48 733), which offers a spectacular **panorama★★** over the lake and Bergamo Alps from the Church of the Madonna della Ceriola.

**Iseo★** – Already in existence in the 9th c., the town is beautifully laid out around a series of medieval squares. The Church of Sant'Andrea (in the charming Piazza del Sagrato) was built in the 5th c. and rebuilt in the 11th in Cluniac style. The bell tower is 13th-c.

From Iseo head east towards Polaveno. Climb to the Pass of the Tre Termini (701 m) and then descend to the junction with the road that leads to Val Trompia. **Sarezzo** lies in the area that historically has produced arms, as testified by the furnace-museum **I Magli di Sarezzo**. For information ℰ 030 83 37 494/5.

Drive south towards Brescia through **Concesio**, the birthplace of Pope Paul VI (1897-1978), where there is a museum that exhibits nativity scenes. Frazione San Vigilio. Open on public hols. 14.30-18.30 or by appointment ℰ 030 21 85 081 or 333 29 82 936, www.presepiopaolo sesto.it. The pope's family was originally from **Monticelli Brusati** ☗, a municipality of Franciacorta close to the shores of Lake Iseo. Continue towards Brescia, passing through the famous wine-production areas of **Collebeato** and **Cellatica**.

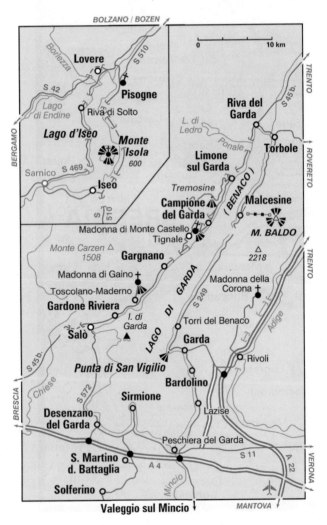

Lake Iseo

## 4. VALTELLINA

*Itinerary of 70 km from Sondrio to Bormio.*

The Tellina valley runs through a broad region of varied alpine landscape. Its mountains, some of which rise to 4000 m, look down on magnificent long valleys. Set in the heart of the Alps, Valtellina is threaded by the river Adda. To the east Valtellina borders Trentino Alto Adige, to the south it reaches to the provinces of Brescia and Bergamo, and to the north the Swiss canton of Grisons. It takes in the high mountains of the Retic Alps, the Orobic Prealps and Stelvio National Park. The principal passes are Stelvio Pass towards Alto Adige, the San Marco Pass towards Val Brembana, and Zappelli Pass at Aprica towards Val Camonica. It is a favourite region with lovers of winter-sports, good cooking and spa treatments, and the dynamic nature and traditions of its many famous towns make it a rewarding destination. The designated areas **Valtellina**, **Valtellina Superiore** and **Sforzato (Sfursat) della Valtellina** produce important red wines from Nebbiolo grapes, which are locally known as Chiavennasca. This is the home of such ageable wines as **Sforzato**, **Sassella**, **Grumello**, **Inferno**, **Vagella** and **Maroggia**, enriched by intense scents of spices, and black- and red-fruit jam. They are wines with character, made in difficult environmental conditions using ingenious terracing and wheeled transportation systems. Carducci dedicated an ode to the wines of Valtellina, and to Sassella in particular, so if they are able to inspire poets, they can certainly excite the palates of even the most demanding wine-lovers. Other very representative varieties grown in Valtellina are Prugnola, Rossola and Pignola. The Sforzato, obtained from selected, rack-dried grapes, have exceptional body and structure; racking concentrates the sugar and aromatic component of the grapes and gives a wine of great power.

### Sondrio

Valtellina's principal city has Roman and Lombard origins, and has retained several historic buildings. Looking down from its rocky perch, the **castle** is the location of a documentation centre and historical exhibition. The collegiate church has ancient origins but was completely rebuilt in the 18th c. Historic palaces, like Palazzo Sertoli, line Piazza Quadrivio. The small Church of the Madonna della Sassella, surrounded by terraces of vines, stands just outside the city gates.

In Montagna in Valtellina, a little distance from Sondrio, you can see the remains of **Grumello Castle**, a building divided into a residential and a military section. Built in 1326, it was destroyed by the Swiss of Grisons when they invaded in the 16th c. The castle was restored and donated to the Fondo Ambiente Italiano by the Valtellina Enological Society in 1987. *Via S. Antonio 645, Montagna in Valtellina; Open 10-18*

*(Oct.-mid-Jan. 17), closed Mon. and mid-Jan.-mid-Feb., guided tours by reservation*
℘ *0342 38 09 94.*

*Take the S 38, drive through* **Chiuro** 🍷 *and* **Teglio** 🍷 *and continue to Tirano (30 km east of Sondrio).*

## Tirano 🍷

Construction of the **Sanctuary of the Madonna di Tirano** began in 1505, the façade is from 1676. The magnificent Baroque interior has frescoes (1575-78, *in the nave)* by Cipriano Valorsa di Gro-sio, who was known as the "Raphael of Valtellina", the fresco of the *Apparition* (1513, *on the left above the confessional),* canvases by a pupil of Morazzone (*pres-bytery and apse),* and the superb 17th-c. organ in a case made by Giuseppe Bul-garini. The panels on the parapet by G.B. Salmoiraghi are of the *Birth of Jesus,* the *Adoration of the Magi,* and the *Circumci-sion* (1638).

*Continue along the S 38 passing through Grosio and Sondalo.*

## Bormio★

In addition to the town's modern ski and sports facilities, Bormio's visitors can enjoy its thermal waters. There are **three spas**: the Bagni Nuovi, Bagni Vecchi and Terme di Bormio. The **Rezia Alpine Botanic Garden** in Via Sertorelli grows the principal plant species found in Stelvio National Park, plus Arctic, Antarctic and non-European species. *Via Sertorelli. Open Jun.-Sept., variable timetable,* ℘ *0342 92 73 70, free entrance.* The town centre is lined with elegant rural houses and a few historic buildings, in particular the Clock Tower and the crenellated towers of the Quadrilatero degli Alberti, a 14th-c. fortified quarter owned by the powerful Alberti family.

## 5. LAKE GARDA

The largest lake in Italy and one of the most harmonious, Garda features a vari-ety of geographical features: a low, flat shoreline of alluvial origin in the south; sheer, rocky drops from the mountains on the west shore, and the Monte Baldo chain that lies along the east shore in the province of Verona. The barrier of the Dolomites to the north helps block cold winds, favouring a mild climate that since antiquity has earned Garda the nickname "the beneficent lake" (it was called Lacus Benacus by the Romans).

It has been a relaxation spot since the Roman era and there are still many vil-lages and towns that offer rest, comfort, sports, good food and of course good wines.

The winemaking area around Lake Garda is long established and its products were appreciated by such figures as Virgil, Strabo, Suetonius and Pliny. The **Garda DOC** zone is an interregional appellation that lies across the provinces of Brescia, Mantova and Verona. It produces white, red, rosé, still, sparkling, dry and sweet-ish wines from a multitude of different varieties.

The hilly area between Desenzano and Salò inland from the lake on the Brescian side is called **Valtènesi** and is carpeted with olives and vines. Its pride is the **Garda Classico Chiaretto** made from Groppello, Sangiovese and Barbera grapes. It is pinkish and has scents of rose, violets, wild strawberries and raspberries. The red **Garda Groppello** is also interesting for its intriguing floral and fruity nose.

## Along the lakeshore from Sirmione to Salò

*Itinerary of 40 km.*

### Sirmione★ 🍷

Situated on the tip of a long, narrow peninsula, the town has been a famous spa for the past 100 years, in particular beneficial to sufferers of respiratory dis-eases. The town used to be protected by the 13th-c. **Scaliger Castle★**, from whose walkways there is a fine view over the dock. *Piazza Castello 34. Tue.-Sat. 8.30-19.30 (Sun. and public hols. 8.30-13.30), closed Mon.,* ℘ *030 91 64 68.* The small 15th-c. Church of Santa Maria Maggiore has interesting frescoes from the 15th and 16th c. The remains of the Basilica of San Salvatore can be reached from the apse.

At the end of the rocky promontory an archaeological zone encloses the **Grottoes of Catullus★** in which, in an **enchanting location★★**, there are the remains of many buildings, including a huge Roman villa from the imperial age. Built over an earlier construction from the republican era, the later building has been identified as the home of the poet Catullus. The site also contains an archaeological museum. *Piazzale G. Orti*

*Manara 4. Open summer 8.30-19.30 (public hols. 9.30-14), winter 8.30-17 (public hols. 8.30-14), closed Tue., ℘ 030 91 61 57.*

*Take the SS 11 west to Desenzano del Garda (5 km).*

## Desenzano del Garda ♟

The "capital" of Lake Garda and dominated by its castle, Desenzano has an Old Port where one of Europe's most important grain markets used to be held. Other attractions are the picturesque Piazza Malvezzi and the adjacent medieval quarter. The 16th-c. duomo that stands on the square conserves a very expressive **Last Supper★** by Tiepolo.

Close to the town centre lies a **Roman villa** in Via Scavi Romani with a set of polychrome **Roman mosaic floors★**. *Open 8.30-19.30 (8.30-17 in Nov.-Feb.), closed Mon., ℘ 030 91 43 547.*

*Continue north along the lakeshore on the SP 26.*

**Maguzzano** is the site of an abbey founded by the Benedictines and later renovated. **Padenghe sul Garda** ♟ retains its appearance of a medieval village in a beautiful position on the lake. A few km west of Padenghe stands the impressive **Drugolo Castle**, built for defensive purposes but later transformed into an aristocratic residence.

A pretty stretch of countryside separates Padenghe from **Moniga del Garda** ♟, where there is a medieval castle with Ghibelline merlons and lookout towers. Inside the village you can see the 17th-c. Villa Brunati-Ferrari.

As you continue along the lakeshore, take the turn-off to **Manerba**, set among vines and olive trees, where the ruins of an old **fort** offer **lovely views★★** of the lake. A few km north of Manerba the hamlet of **Pieve Vecchia** is named after its 12th-c. parish church.

*Head inland.*

**Polpenazze** stands around its ancient castle and boasts several fine buildings, like the Romanesque Church of San Pietro in Lucone, the name of which refers to a lake of the past, now dried up, in the area where the remains of a Bronze Age settlement were found. Once past **Puegnago del Garda** ♟ you are at the gates of Salò.

## Salò★

A Roman settlement and the capital in the 14th c. of the "Magnifica Patria" (an association of about 40 hamlets and villages in the area), and then the residence of the "Capitano" of Venice, this elegant town was also home to several ministers in the Fascist government of the Repubblica Sociale Italiana between October 1943 and April 1945. From its period of greatest splendour, Salò has conserved its 15th-c. **duomo**, where there is a large **polyptych★** in gilded wood (1510) and several works by Moretto and Romanino of Brescia. The oldest district of the town is set around the skirts of the duomo, with Renaissance houses and arched underpasses. On the lakeside stands the Palazzo della Magnifica Patria (16th c.), which is connected by a portico to the Palazzo del Podestà rebuilt after the 1901 earthquake.

*Scaliger castle, Sirmione*

© bbsferrari/Marka/iStock

## The province of Mantova

### The morainic amphitheatre of Lake Garda

*Itinerary of approximately 30 km starting from Castiglione delle Stiviere.*

The morainic amphitheatre formed by concentric waves of hills in the province of Mantua lies to the south of Lake Garda. Its strategic position in relation to important cities like Brescia, Verona and Mantova has made it a battleground over the centuries and resulted in its being dotted with defensive constructions. From an enological viewpoint the zone includes the designated areas Garda, Garda Colli Mantovani and Lambrusco mantovano. In the territory of Mantua the interregionale **Garda DOC** zone produces a dry red wine from Rondinella, Merlot and Rossanella (or Molinara) grapes for early drinking. The appellation **Garda Colli Mantovani** produces a wide range of white, red and rosé wines from many different varieties. A very well known wine, which conjures up images of convivial good cheer, is **Lambrusco mantovano**, a light, fruity wine with notes of rose and violet, different degrees of fizziness, and sometimes a delightful sweetness. Traditionally it is added to the broth in the recipe for *"sorbir d'agnoli"* (pasta in meat broth).

**Castiglione delle Stiviere** has an illustrious history: it was ruled variously by the Visconti and Gonzaga, became a principate in the 17th c., and was devastated during the War of Spanish Succession in 1703. The town has a museum dedicated to the **Red Cross** (*Via Garibaldi 50. Open 9-12 and 15-18 (14-17 in Nov.-Mar.), closed working Mon., ✆ 0376 63 85 05, www.micr.it*), the origin of which is linked to the battle at nearby Solferino. The Basilica of San Luigi (17th-18th c.) is devoted to the saint who was a member of the Gonzaga family to which Castiglione belonged; his skull is conserved in the basilica.

Close to Castiglione are places closely linked to the Italian Risorgimento: at **Solferino** and **San Martino della Battaglia** ♟ the decisive battles of the Second War of Independence took place on 24 June 1859; both are commemorated in each place by an ossuary chapel and museum. The heavy losses (11,000 dead and 23,000 wounded) persuaded Henri Dunant to found the **Red Cross**, a development celebrated at Solferino by a commemorative monument.

Passing through vine-covered hills, you reach **Cavriana**, where a tower from the old castle and the town's medieval fortifications can be seen. A nearby Gonzaga villa was used by Napoleon III as his headquarters and is today used as a local archaeological museum (*Piazza Castello 8. ✆ 0376 80 63 30, www.museo-cavriana.it*). Continuing east towards the river Mincio and turning right you reach **Volta Mantovana** ♟, where there are two lovely Gonzaga residences: Villa Cavriani and Villa Venier. Heading north, you reach **Monzambano** ♟, which lies on the river in the shadow of its 12th-c. castle.

*Mantua*

# QUIZ

**1**  TYRES ARE BLACK SO WHY IS THE MICHELIN MAN WHITE?

Back in 1898 when the Michelin Man was first created from a stack of tyres, they were made of natural rubber, cotton and sulphur and were therefore light-coloured. The composition of tyres did not change until after the First World War when carbon black was introduced. But the Michelin Man kept his colour!

**2**  FOR HOW LONG HAS MICHELIN BEEN GUIDING TRAVELLERS?

Since 1900. When the MICHELIN guide was published at the turn of the century, it was claimed that it would last for a hundred years. It's still around today and remains a reference with new editions and online restaurant listings in a number of countries.

**3**  WHEN WAS THE "BIB GOURMAND" INTRODUCED IN THE MICHELIN GUIDE?

The symbol was created in 1997 but as early as 1954 the MICHELIN guide was recommending "exceptional good food at moderate prices". Today, it features on the MICHELIN Restaurants website and app.

If you want to enjoy a fun day out and find out more about Michelin, why not visit the l'Aventure Michelin museum and shop in Clermont-Ferrand, France:

**www.laventuremichelin.com**

*A better way forward*

# Addresses

## Tourist information

**Region of Lombardy** – See the leisure section at www.regione.lombardia.it

**Bergamo Tourist Office** – Via Gombito 13 (Upper City), ℘ 035 24 22 26, www.visitbergamo.net
P.le Guglielmo Marconi (Lower City), ℘ 035 21 02 04

**Brescia Tourist Office** – Via Trieste 1/ Piazza Paolo VI, ℘ 030 24 00 357, www.turismobrescia.it - www.provincia.brescia.it

**Infopoint Città di Mantova** – Piazza Andrea Mantegna 6, ℘ 0376 43 24 32, www.mantovatourism.it

**Lake Iseo and Franciacorta Tourist Office** – Lungolago Marconi 2 C/D, Iseo, ℘ 030 37 48 733, www.iseolake.info/it/

**Pavia Tourist Office** – Palazzo del Broletto, Via del Comune 18, ℘ 0382 39 97 90, www.comune.pv.it

**Sondrio Tourist Office** – Via Tonale 13, Sondrio, ℘ 0342 21 92 46, www.valtellina.it

## Transport

### LAKE ISEO

Departures each morning in high season from Sarnico, Iseo and Lovere for a lake tour returning in the late afternoon. Option of lunch aboard and stopover at Monte Isola (*duration: 7h*). From Iseo, afternoon tour of the 3 islands (*duration: 2h*). From Sarnico, Iseo, Lovere and Monte Isola, lake tour with afternoon departure. Night cruises and guided tours available Thu. and Fri. in summer. Contact the Lake Iseo and Franciacorta Tourist Office (*see above*) for information.

### LAKE GARDA

Full lake tour from Desenzano, Peschiera and Riva del Garda with the option of lunch aboard. Boat trips to Sirmione, Gardone, Garda, Salò and Limone. Car ferries from Maderno to Torri and vice versa, and from Limone to Malcesine and vice versa. One-day tickets valid on all boats can be purchased. Information: ℘ 800 55 18 01, www.navigazionelaghi.it.

## The wineries

*The addresses are listed in alphabetical order by location.*

### OLTREPÒ PAVESE

**Fattoria Olmo Antico** – *Via Marconi 8 - **Borgo Priolo** (PV) - ℘ 0383 87 26 72 - www.olmoantico.it - info@olmoantico.it - Winery tours by reservation.* The winery is situated in a partly restored medieval village dating from the early 14th c. on which the little town of Borgo Priolo (*priolo* means "stone") grew up. The cellar is perhaps the oldest in the Oltrepò region, dating from 1678. The "old elm" (Olmo Antico) of the name is found on the estate, atop a hill that divides 2 valleys; set in a strategic position, it is visible from all the surrounding hills. The winery is owned by the Bagaggini family and was founded in 1996. Hectares under vine: 22.
**Wines:** 14 Ottobre Croatina, Rè Nano, Marty Rosé, La P… Nera, Giorgio Quinto. Other products: grappa, honey, confectionery.

🍇 **Tenuta Scarpa Colombi** – *Via Groppallo 24 - **Bosnasco** (PV) - ℘ 0385 27 20 81 - www.colombiwines.com - info@colombiwines.com - Winery tours by reservation.* From the beginning of the 20th c. Salvatore Colombi focused his winegrowing activities increasingly on research and selection in order to make quality wines. Over the years he expanded his estate by purchasing vineyards in 2 zones that are very different in terms of soil composition and microclimate, but equally suited to viticulture, here in Bosnasco and in Nizza Monferrato in Piedmont, achieving excellent results in both. Today it is his descendants who run the winery. The estate pursues a philosophy of sustainable agriculture and respect for the environment. Accommodation at the Tenuta Scarpa Colombi Country Inn (*6 rooms, €110*) and meals at La Buta restaurant, housed in the estate's old stables. Hectares under vine: 18.
**Wines:** Teresco Spumante Brut, Merlino Pinot Nero, Ariolo Pinot Nero, Bonarda Marubbio.

🍇 **Azienda Agricola Travaglino** – *Loc. Travaglino 6/a - **Calvignano** (PV) - ℘ 0383 87 22 22 - www.travaglino.com - info@travaglino.it - Winery tours and tasting by reservation, Mon.-Fri. 8-12 and 14-18, Sat.-Sun. 10-17.* The winery dates back to the year 1111. It has been belonged to the Comi family since 1880. During the 1960s, under the management of Vincenzo Comi, the winery commenced a gradual restoration process in order to achieve constant product improvement. It grows and produces wine from typical native grape varieties and international cultivars, such as Cabernet Sauvignon, Merlot and Syrah. Overnight stays (5 rooms, €80) and restaurant service available. Hectares under vine: 80.

**Wines**: Oltrepò Pavese Riesling Campo della Fojada, Oltrepò Pavese Pinot Nero Grand Cuvée Brut, Oltrepò Pavese Pinot Nero Poggio della Buttinera, Oltrepò Pavese Pinot Nero Pernero, Oltrepò Pavese Pinot Nero Monteceresino Brut Rosé. Other products: grappa.

**Frecciarossa** – Via Vigorelli 141 - **Casteggio** (PV) - ☏ 0383 80 44 65 - www.frecciarossa. com - info@frecciarossa.com - Winery tours by reservation. The history of the winery commenced in the early 19th c., when Genoa-born Mario Odero decided to change lifestyle, leaving England where he was a coal merchant and returning to Italy. He settled in the Oltrepò Pavese area and purchased the Frecciarossa estate following WWI, dedicating himself to the world of winemaking. The winery's success has steadily grown ever since. Hectares under vine: 34.

**Wines**: Pinot Nero "Giorgio Odero", Pinot Nero (white vinification) "Sillery", Uva Rara IGT Rosso, Oltrepò Pavese Barbera "Le Praielle", Riesling "Gli Orti".

**Le Fracce** – Via Castel del Lupo 7 - **Mairano di Casteggio** (PV) - ☏ 0383 82 526 - www. lefracce.it - commerciale@lefracce.com -Winery tours by reservation. The winery, founded in 1905, has always been oriented towards the valorisation of the natural resources of the estate and complete respect of the environment, avoiding the use of chemical fungicides and herbicides, and limiting the use of fertilisers. Today it is engaged in the reappraisal of the old vineyards and the revival of the typical grape varieties of the Oltrepò area – Barbera, Croatina, Pinot Nero – and the creation of contemporary, modern wines. Hectares under vine: 40.

**Wines**: Bonarda Vivace, Barbera, Rosso Oltrepò, Riesling, Pinot Nero, Spumante.

🏠 **Prime Alture wine resort** – Strada Madonna Vicinale per Campone - Casteggio (PV) - ☏ 0383 83 214, 348 77 02 271 - www. primealture.it - info@primealture.it - Winery tours by reservation. The company also cultivates gardens and fruit orchards, and visitors can try high-quality food along with the company's wines. Freshly harvested vegetables, seasonal fruit, fresh eggs from hens raised directly on the property and meat from local producers are all ingredients that find their way onto the menu. The tasting area overlooks the aging room and cantina. Overnight stays (6 rooms, 120 €) and restaurant service (35-45 €) available. Tasting menu 48 €.

**Wines**: Pinot Nero, Merlot, Bonarda Il Rosso, Il Bianco, Rosato, Chardonnay, Spumante, Riesling Passito.

🏠 **Montelio** – Via Domenico Mazza 1 - **Codevilla** (PV) - ☏ 0383 37 30 90 - www. montelio.it - cantine@montelio.it - Winery tours by reservation. Vines were grown in the area as early as the second half of the 13th c. and the winery is housed in the old grange of a monastery. The current estate, founded in 1848, grows and makes wine from Cortese, Chardonnay, Riesling Italico, Riesling Renano, Müller-Thurgau, Barbera, Uva Rara, Croatina, Freisa, Dolcetto, Pinot Nero and Merlot grapes. Accommodation at guest farm (6 apts., €70). Hectares under vine: 30.

**Wines**: Oltrepò Pavese Riesling, Oltrepò Pavese Rosato, Oltrepò Pavese Bonarda, Oltrepò Pavese Pinot Nero Costarsa, Oltrepò Pavese Riserva Solarolo. Other products: grappa, fruit in wine syrup.

**Tenuta Mazzolino** – Via Mazzolino 34 - **Corvino San Quirico** (PV) - ☏ 0383 87 61 22 - www.tenuta-mazzolino.com - info@ tenuta-mazzolino.com - Winery tours and tasting Mon.-Fri. 10-12 and 14-17, Sat. by reservation. The business philosophy of the Braggiotti family, who have owned Tenuta Mazzolino since the 1980s, is rooted in the old Borgo Mazzolino in Corvino San Quirico. Over 20 of the 30 hectares of hills are constituted by vineyards, planted with the most suitable grape varieties for the soil and farmed using specialised techniques. Low yields per hectare, short pruning and natural grassing of the vineyards without the use of chemical fertilisers are the basis for the production of quality wines. Hectares under vine: 22.

**Wines**: Pinot Nero "Noir", Chardonnay "Blanc", Bonarda "Mazzolino", Moscato "Mazzolino", Spumante.

**Finigeto** – Loc. Cella 27 - Montalto Pavese (PV) - ☏ 328 70 95 347 - www.finigeto.com - info@finigeto.com - Winery tours by reservation. Aldo Dallavalle, a young agriculturalist who nurtures a passion for winemaking, first founded this company in 2005. The property is located 300 metres above sea level, where the microclimate, soil and excellent exposition all constitute ideal conditions for growing vines. The company, surrounded by natural woods between one vineyard and the next, is run by Aldo, his wife Diana and their daughter Beatrice, all of whom work with full respect for the natural seasons. The vines are cultivated in high density per hectare and low production levels in order to obtain an extremely high quality grape. The company's wines exalt the characteristics of the surrounding terrain. Hectares under vine: 42.

© LIUJIXIN/Shutterstock

**Wines:** Bonarda, Barbera, Pinot Nero, Riesling, Chardonnay, Moscato, Pinot Nero Frizzante, Spumante.

🍷 **Calatroni** – *Loc. Casa Grande 7 –* **Montecalvo Versiggia** *(PV) - ℘ 0385 99 013 - www.calatronivini.com - info@ calatronivini.it - Winery tours Sat. and Sun. 10-16.* Calatroni was founded in 1964, when Luigi Calatroni decided to acquire the vineyards from his ex-employer, and has expanded and developed ever since. Now the third generation of Calatroni vintners are at the helm, and the company continues to blend traditional winemaking experience with modern production methods. Restaurant service available for lunch, and the company owns and runs an agriturismo. Visitors can organize wine tastings and company tours by appointment. Every month the restaurant offers a different menu, pairing local and Piacentino cuisine with its wines. Hectares under vine: 13.
**Wines:** Pinot Nero, Metodo Classico, Riesling, Bonarda, Sangue di Giuda.

🍷 **Cantina Storica di Montù Beccaria** – *Via Marconi 10 -* **Montù Beccaria** *(PV) - ℘ 0385 26 22 52 - www.ilmontu.com - ilmontu@ilmontu.com - Winery tours by reservation.* The Cantina Sociale di Monù Beccaria was one of Italy's first co-operative wineries, founded in 1902 to help local vinegrowers and give dignity to the wines of this region. After years of neglect, the commitment of Franco Tonalini and Riccardo Ottina has allowed the winery to return to its old splendour, thanks also to painstaking archaeological restoration. In addition to the winery, the complex features a distillery and a restaurant, La Locanda dei Beccaria

*( ℘ 0385 26 23 10, closed Mon. and Tue.),* which serves local specialities. Hectares under vine: 100.
**Wines:** Bonarda, Buttafuoco, Sangue di Giuda, Pinot Nero, Barbera, Chardonnay, Riesling, Croatina, Spumante. Other products: grappa, fruit spirits.

**Vercesi del Castellazzo** – *Via Aureliano Beccaria 36 -* **Montù Beccaria** *(PV) - ℘ 335 545 63 20 - www.vercesidelcastellazzo.it - vercesicastellazzo@libero.it - Winery tours by reservation.* The winery was founded in 1808 by the great-grandfather of current owner Franco Vercesi. It is a typical Oltrepò Pavese estate, whose vineyards are planted with the area's most popular grapes: Barbera, Bonarda (Croatina), Pinot Nero, Vespolina, Uva Rara and Cabernet Sauvignon. The wines are packed with character and successfully reflect the terroir. Hectares under vine: 18.
**Wines:** Oltrepò Pavese Rosso Pezzalunga, IGT Rosso Prov. di Pavia Vespolino, Oltrepò Pavese Barbera Clà, Oltrepò Pavese Pinot Nero Luogo dei Monti, Oltrepò Pavese Bonarda Fatila.

**Conte Vistarino** – *Fraz. Scorzoletta 82/84 -* **Pietra de' Giorgi** *(PV) - ℘ 0385 85 117 - www.contevistarino.it - info@conte vistarino.it - Winery tours by reservation.* The Giorgi family of Vistarino has owned this large estate for many centuries. It comprises 828 hectares of land, mostly situated in the municipality of Rocca de' Giorgi. The 180 hectares of vineyards, all registered under the Oltrepò Pavese denomination, are flanked by 200 hectares of wild woodland, 10 of sowable land and 100 allocated for forestation. It is an unspoiled oasis with fascinating scenery and wildlife. The Pinot Nero vineyards were planted by Carlo Giorgi di Vistarino at the turn of the 20th c. and the winery has been handed down to his successors. Hectares under vine: 188.
**Wines:** Pinot Nero "Pernice", Oltrepò Metodo Classico, Bonarda "L'Alcova", Riesling "Rïes", Pinot Nero Bertone.

**Marchese Adorno** – *Via Garlassolo 30 -* **Retorbido** *(PV) - ℘ 0383 37 44 04 - www.marcheseadorno-wines.it - info@ marcheseadorno-wines.it - Winery tours and tastings Mon.-Sat. by reservation.* The Adorno family – of whom Marchese Marcello, the winery's current owner, is the last descendant – has very old roots. Some of the most important figures of Genoese public life, including 7 doges, were members of this aristocratic family. It was in Spain that the Adornos forged a connection with the production of Generalife, a sherry-like wine, of which the family still has many bottles that are over a century old in their Genoa cellars. The

Retorbido estate was purchased by the Adornos in 1834 and has been using traditional techniques to make wines from local grape varieties ever since. Hectares under vine: 80.

**Wines**: Pinot Grigio, Barbera, Pinot Nero, Bonarda, Riesling Superiore, Merlot.

### 🍇 Castello di Luzzano – *Via Luzzano 5 - Rovescala (PV) - ☏ 0523 86 32 77 - www.castelloluzzano.it - info@castelloluzzano.it - Winery tours by reservation.* The Fugazzas are an old Oltrepò Pavese family of landowners and cannery owners. At the beginning of the 20th c. the existing estates were merged with those of Luzzano and Romito (in Ziano Piacentino in Emilia Romagna), which were equipped with new and more modern vineyards and cellars. Today the business is run by Maria Giulia and Giovannella Fugazza. A small museum of local history has been created in the old cellar. Accommodation at the "Locanda Dogana"(*4 rooms and 5 apts., from €95*) and restaurant service by reservation. Hectares under vine: 70.

**Wines**: Colli Piacentini Gutturnio, Colli Piacentini Malvasia, Colli Piacentini Chardonnay, Colli Piacentini Ortrugo, Oltrepò Pavese Pinot Nero, Oltrepò Pavese Bonarda, Merlot.

### Cantina Pietrasanta – *Via P. Sforza 55/57 - San Colombano al Lambro (MI) - ☏ 346 72 19 996 - www.cantina pietrasanta.com - info@catinapietrasanta.com - Winery tours by reservation.* The winery occupies the outhouses of a mid-18th-c. residence owned by the Milanese Pietrasanta family. The family's land has always been home to vineyards. The winery produces sparkling, semi-sparkling and still red and white wines. The grapes used to make the wines are the typical ones of the area: Barbera, Croatina, Cabernet, Merlot and Uva Rara for red wines, and Verdea, Riesling, Chardonnay and Pinot for white and sparkling wines. You can enjoy tastings and lunches in the picturesque barrique cellar. Hectares under vine: 6.

**Wines**: San Colombano Rosso Fermo, San Colombano Rosso Riserva Podere Costa Regina, Rosso della Costa IGT Collina del Milanese, Verdea IGT, San Colombano Bianco della Costa. Other products: honey, grana cheese, charcuterie.

### Azienda Agricola Manuelina – *Fr. Ruinello di Sotto 3 - Santa Maria della Versa (PV) - ☏ 0385 27 82 47 - www.manuelina.com - info@manuelina.com - Winery tours by reservation. Restaurant "Al Ruinello" nearby.*This company was established halfway through the 20th century, when Luigi Achilli and his brother Guido decided to extend production beyond what they needed for personal consumption and turn their passion into a profession: Azienda Agricola Achilli Luigi. This same passion was passed on the Luigi's sons Paolo and Antonio. Today the company's name has been modified with "Manuelina," after Manuela, one of Paolo Achilli's daughters. Hectares under vine: 22.

**Wines**: Barbera, Bonarda, Pinot Nero, Sangue di Giuda, Chardonnay, Riesling Italico, Pinot Grigio, Spumante. Other products: grappa.

### La Versa – *Via Crispi 15 - Santa Maria della Versa (PV) - ☏ 0385 79 84 11 - www.laversa.it - info@laversa.it or mt.paone@laversa.it - Winery tours by reservation.* Founded in 1905 by Cesare Gustavo Faravelli and 22 other landowners to make top-quality wines able to embody the characteristics of the best grapes in their home region, today the winery has 750 members, including 480 winegrowers. Famous for the production of sparkling wines, it is situated in Valle Versa, which is considered the leading Italian area for the production of Pinot Nero, a variety that lends itself beautifully to making sparkling wines. In autumn 2019, La Versa once again became an asset of the Oltrepò Pavese region thanks to the full acquisition of the brand by Terre d'Oltrepò In 2020 winemaker Riccardo Cotarella returned to the winery to study a brand new qualitative product line. Hectares under vine: 1200.

**Wines**: Testarossa Brut Metodo Classico, Testarossa Cruasé Metodo Classico, Metodo Classico Collezione 2007, Pinot Nero Charmat, Riesling Spumante. Other products: grappa.

© Newphotoservice/Shutterstock

# ADDRESSES

**Azienda Agricola Monsupello** – *Via San Lazzaro 5* - **Torricella Verzate** *(PV)* - ℘ *0383 89 60 43* - *www.monsupello.it* - *monsupello@monsupello.it* - *Winery tours by reservation, closed Sun.* The winery's origins can be traced back over a century to 1893, when the Boatti family already cultivated its own vineyards in Cà del Tava. In 1914 the Boattis purchased another estate in the municipality of Torricella Verzate, a few kilometres away. Here they founded the winery, which has now been expanded and modernised to vinify the grapes of the original estates and those purchased subsequently. Hectares under vine: 50.

**Wines**: I Germogli Bianchi and Rosa from Pinot Nero, Bonarda Vaiolet, Barbera I Gelsi, Monsupello Spumante Nature. Other products: grappa.

## VALCALEPIO

**Castello degli Angeli** – *Via Scalette* - **Carobbio degli Angeli** *(BG)* - ℘ *035 95 10 56* - *www.castellodegliangeli.com* - *info@castellodegliangeli.com* - *Winery tours by reservation.* The winery is housed in very picturesque premises: the medieval castle of Santo Stefano degli Angeli, built on the hilly spur of Carobbio that dominates the plain. The recent restoration by the current owner Marco Taiariol has salvaged and valorised the medieval structures: the outer walls, the pointed-arch entrance portal, the monastery cloister, the ruins of the keep and the oldest part of the fortification. Already in the 18th c. the Carmelite monks produced wine and the current owner faithfully continues this old tradition. Accommodation at the elegant Relais in Charme (*6 suites, closed Jan.*) and meals at the Barbariccia restaurant (*open Fri.-Sat., Sun. at noon; May-Oct., Thu.*). Hectares under vine: 2.

**Wines**: Valcalepio Rosso Amedeo, Valcalepio Rosso Barbariccia, Chardonnay della Bergamasca IGT Estereta, Chardonnay della Bergamasca IGT Dildarra dei Gobbi.

**Il Calepino** – *Via Surripe 1* - **Castelli Calepio** *(BG)* - ℘ *035 84 71 78* - *www.ilcalepino.it* - *info@ilcalepino.it* - *Winery tours by reservation.* Angelo Plebani founded the winery in 1972. Calepino's vineyards are situated on morainal terraces (*surúe*), where the soil and climate have always been ideal for vine growing. Today the business is run by Marco and Franco Plebani. In addition to the Valcaleipio DOC wines it also produces particularly interesting Classic Method sparkling wines. Hectares under vine: 15.

**Wines**: Valcalepio Rosso, Valcalepio Bianco, Kalos Cabernet Sauvignon IGT, Epias Chardonnay IGT, Merlot, Il Calepino

Brut Metodo Classico, Fra Ambrogio Metodo Classico.

**Tallarini** – *Via Fontanile 10* - **Gandosso** *(BG)* - ℘ *035 83 40 03* - *www.tallarini.com* - *info@tallarini.com* - *Winery tours by reservation.* The Tallarini family have been restaurant owners for 3 generations and vignerons for over 20 years. In 1983 Vincenzo Tallarini purchased il Fontanile with its vineyards and appurtenances, a group of old buildings in the historic village. He started to make wine to much acclaim, and today his winery is one of the most renowned in the area. The Tallarini group now covers the world of catering, accommodation and prestigious corporate gifts, and the estate's vineyards have been expanded about 30 times over. Accommodation available (*4 rooms, €100*). Hectares under vine: 30.

**Wines**: San Giovannino, Moscato di Scanzo, Brut Tallarini, Arlecchino, Sèrafo.

**Castello di Grumello** – *Via Fosse 11* - **Grumello del Monte** *(BG)* - ℘ *348 30 36 243* - *www.castellodigrumello.it* - *info@castellodigrumello.it* - *Winery tours and tastings by reservation.* The castle was probably built around the year 1000 as a military fortress with the purpose of a lookout and a defence post. Since 1953 it has belonged to the Reschigna Kettlitz family of Milan, who successfully continue the local winemaking tradition. The castle belongs to the Associazione Castelli e Ville Aperti in Lombardia. The estate's wines are aged in the centuries-old cellars of the castle, beneath whose ancient vaults modern technologies are flanked by traditional wine presses. Accommodation in the castle's guesthouse (*12 single rooms, 2 double rooms*) and restaurant service by reservation. Hectares under vine: 20.

**Wines**: Valcalepio Bianco, Valcalepio Rosso, Il Castello, Merera Brolo dei Guelfi, Colle Calvario, Moscato Passito.

**La Brugherata** – *Via Giovanni Medolago 47 - Loc. Rosciate* - **Scanzorosciate** *(BG)* - ℘ *035 65 52 02* - *www.labrugherata.it* - *info@labrugherata.it* - *Winery tours and tastings by reservation.* La Brugherata, owned by the Bendinelli family, is an estate with several hectares of vineyards planted with Moscato di Scanzo, Chardonnay, Pinot Grigio, Pinot Bianco, Cabernet and Merlot and 2 hectares of olive groves. To mark the winery's 10th anniversary, 20 years ago, it released Doglio, whose label depicts details from different paintings by Bergamo artists – from Caravaggio to Lotto and Moroni – each year, attesting to the owners' love of art. Hectares under vine: 10.

**Wines**: Moscato di Scanzo "Doge", Valcalepio Bianco "Vescovado del Feudo",

Valcalepio Rosso "Vescovado", Valcalepio Rosso Riserva "Doglio", Cabernet della Bergamasca "Priore" IGT, Spumante. Other products: olive oil, honey, grappa, confectionery.

**Tenuta Le Mojole** – *Via Madonna delle Vigne* - **Tagliuno di Castelli Calepio (BG)** - ✆ *338 99 53 632 - www.lemojole.it - info@lemojole.it - Winery tours by reservation*. This company was born in 2002, and in just a few short years it has made a name for itself in wine production in the Bergamo region. The numerous prizes the company has earned, both nationally and internationally, demonstrate the excellence of its wines and the reliability of the company's efforts. Hectares under vine: 3.
**Wines**: Donna Marta Brut, Donna Marta Rosa, Donna Marta Rosso, Merlot, Cabernet Sauvignon, Rosso Le Mojole.

## FRANCIACORTA

**Contadi Castaldi** – *Via Colzano 32* - **Adro** (BS) - ✆ *030 74 50 126 - www.contadicastaldi.it - contadicastaldi@contadicastaldi.it - Winery tours by reservation*. The winery premises were once a brickworks and the building has maintained its old charm. The name is derived from the fact that the Contadi were once the counties, or divisions, of the lands of the Castaldi, the lords who were entitled to the best fruits of each harvest. Hectares under vine: 100.
**Wines**: Franciacorta Brut, Franciacorta Rosé, Franciacorta Zèro, Franciacorta Satèn, Franciacorta Soulsatèn S.R.

**Fratelli Muratori - Tenuta Villa Crespia** – *Via Valli 31* - **Adro** (BS) - ✆ *030 74 51 051- www.fratellimuratori.it - villa.crespia@fratellimuratori.it - Winery tours and tastings by reservation*. In medieval Lombardy the term *crespie* was used to designate the earliest Po Valley experiences with second fermentation. The winery's production philosophy is to maintain a close bond between the land and the wine. Consequently all the production decisions are based on the aim of bottling the full expression of the terroir from which the grapes come, respecting the owners' beloved philosophy of the "local cru". Hectares under vine: 60.
**Wines**: Cisiolo Franciacorta Dosaggio Zero, Numerozero Franciacorta Dosaggio Zero, Cesonato Franciacorta Satèn, Brolese Franciacorta Rosé Extra Brut, Novalia.

**Cantine Biondelli**– *Via Basso Castello 2* - **Bornato di Franciacorta** ✆ *030 775 98 96 - www.biondelli.com - info@cantinebiondelli.com. Winery tours by reservation*. The Biondelli family is connected with Piacentino nobility, starting at the time of the Ducato di

© Dasilvafarias/Shutterstock

Parma, Piacenza and Guastalla. During the Second World War, Giuseppe Biondelli, then Ambassador of Italy, first discovered Franciacorta, and decided to make his home in Bornato, following his marriage to Clementina dei Conti Maggi di Gradella. Giuseppe Biondelli had been deeply struck by the beauty of that area. The Biondelli story continues today, as Giuseppe's son Carlottavio Biondelli, who has always overseen the family's agricultural activities, has focused on the vineyards and developed the cantina's activities, including a complete renovation of the 16th-century cantina located at the heart of the family's property. The cantina was officially opened in 2010. Joska Biondelli, Carlottavio's son, currently runs the family wine company.
**Wines**: Biondelli Franciacorta Brut, Biondelli Franciacorta Saten, Biondelli Première Dame Franciacorta millesimato, Biondelli Franciacorta Rosé.

⌂ **Ricci Curbastro** – *Via Adro 37* - **Capriolo** (BS) - ✆ *030 73 60 94 - www.riccicurbastro.it - info@riccicurbastro.it - Winery tours and tasting by reservation*. This historic Franciacorta winery has an agricultural and wine museum and offers accommodation on site (*8 apts. from €79*). Hectares under vine: 27.5.
**Wines**: Franciacorta Extra Brut, Franciacorta Dosaggio Zero, Franciacorta Brut, Terre di Franciacorta Rosso Curtefranca, Terre di Franciacorta Bianco Curtefranca, IGT Sebino. Other products: grappa.

🍷 **Tenuta Quadra** – *Via S. Eusebio 1* - **Cologne** (BS) - ✆ *030 71 57 314 - www.quadrafranciacorta.it - info@quadrafranciacorta.it - Winery tours by reservation*. The winery of the Ghezzi

# ADDRESSES

family was founded in 2003 in an old farmhouse that was completely rebuilt, incorporating state-of-the-art winemaking equipment. Restaurant service offered (*closed Mon. and Sun.-Tue. evening*). Hectares under vine: 20.
**Wines**: Franciacorta Brut, Franciacorta Satèn, Franciacorta Rosé, Extra Brut Quvée 72, Pinot Nero Acchiappasogni.

⚲ **Berlucchi Guido** – *Piazza Duranti 4 - Loc. Borgonato* - **Corte Franca** (BS) - ✆ *030 98 43 81 - www.berlucchi.it - info@berlucchi. it - Winery tours and tasting by reservation.* In the 1950s Guido Berlucchi made his Pinot del Castello, a still white wine. In 1955 his encounter with enologist Franco Ziliani changed the winery's destiny. He was fascinated by the elegant figure of Berlucchi, by his handsome mansion, Palazzo Lana Berlucchi, and by its ancient underground cellars. Ziliani dreamt of producing in Franciacorta a sparkling wine capable of vying with champagne. The challenge was taken up and the foundations for his dream were laid: in 1961 the first 3000 bottles of Classic Method sparkling Pinot di Franciacorta wine were made. The dream came true and today, after Guido Berlucchi's death in 2000, it is Franco Ziliani's children, Cristina, Arturo and Paolo, who run the winery. Accommodation and meals at the Relais Franciacorta (*50 rooms, www. relaisfranciacorta.it*), a charming late-18th-c. country house set in its own grounds and surrounded by the Franciacorta hills. Hectares under vine: 550.
**Wines**: Cuvée Imperiale, Cuvée Imperiale Brut, Cuvée Imperiale Max Rosé, Cuvée Imperiale Demi Sec, Berlucchi Vintage, Berlucchi '61, Berlucchi Vintage, Berlucchi '61 Nature Blanc De Blancs Millesimato, Berlucchi '61 Nature, Berlucchi '61 Nature Millesimato Rosé, Palazzo Lana Extrême Riserva.

**Fratelli Berlucchi** – *Via Broletto 2 - Loc. Borgonato* - **Corte Franca** (BS) - ✆ *030 98 44 51 - www.fratelliberlucchi.it - info@ fratelliberlucchi.it - Winery tours by reservation.* The winery belongs to 5 brothers (Francesco, Gabriella, Marcello, Roberto and Pia Donata), who continue the work of their forefathers. The winery is in the heart of Franciacorta, surrounded by the morainic hills of the prealpine lanscape. The wine is made in the painstakingly restored old buildings, which are adorned with beautiful 16th-c. frescoes. The name "Casa delle Colonne" (house of columns) refers to the family villa and is used for the top range. Hectares under vine: 70.
**Wines**: Brut 25, Freccianera Brut

Millesimato, Freccianera Rosa Millesimato, Freccianera Satèn Millesimato, Freccianera Nature Millesimato,Casa delle Colonne Brut Riserva, Casa delle Colonne Zero Riserva, Curtefranca Bianco DOC Ca' Brusade and Dossi delle Querce, Curtefranca Rosso DOC Mandola.

**Bellavista** – *Via Bellavista 5* - **Erbusco** (BS) - ✆ *030 77 62 000 - www.bellavistawine.it - info@bellavistawine.it - Winery tours and tasting by reservation.* Situated on the hill after which it is named and which looks out over Lake Iseo and the entire Po valley, the estate has belonged to Vittorio Moretti since 1977. Its philosophy is to capture the potential of the terroir and its vineyards to create top-class wines. Consequently, it lavishes particular care on selecting the land for its vineyards, their aspect and the bunches of grapes. Modern techniques have been combined with old customs and traditions to find the right balance that has resulted in impressively consistent quality. Its hectares are distributed among ten townships in Franciacorta, for a total of 107 vineyards. Hectares under vine: 190.
**Wines**: Alma Brut, Alma Non Dosato, Pas Operé, Rosé, Satèn, Nectar, Brut 2013 Vittorio Moretti, Meraviglioso, Arzente, Zuanne, SS. Annunciata, Uccellanda, Alma terra.

**Cà del Bosco** – *Via Albano Zanella 13* - **Erbusco** (BS) - ✆ *030 77 66 111 - www.cadelbosco.com - cadelbosco@ cadelbosco.com - Winery tours and tasting by reservation.* This renowned winery has contributed to establishing the identity of the wines of Franciacorta, allowing them to compete with their French cousins. Hectares under vine: 154.
**Wines**: Franciacorta Cuvée Prestige, Franciacorta Cuvée Annamaria Clementi, Chardonnay, Maurizio Zanella, Pinèro.

**Distillerie Peroni Maddalena** – *Via Alcide De Gasperi 39* – **Gussago** (BS) – ✆ *030 27 70 640 –distillerieperoni.it – info@ distillerieperoni.it - Winery tours and tasting by reservation.* In 1969 in Gussago, Giuseppe Andreoli and his wife Maddalena Peroni acquired part of the property on which the company currently sits. Following the death of their father, Carlo, Paola and Sandro took an active part in the company, while their mother Maddalena remained an irreplaceable point of reference. For grappa production, the distillery guarantees use of raw materials selected from the most representative vineyards, in particular pinot and chardonnay for single-vine Franciacorta, Lugana for Lago di Garda and Amarone for the Valpolicella. These are distilled employing the discontinuous steam method in small copper stills.

**Wines**: Grappa Chardonnay Invecchiata Riserva Oro, Grappa Pinot di Franciacorta, Grappa Lugana del Garda, Grappa Chardonnay Millesimata '99, Grappa Cuvée Millesimata Morbida 2004.

**La Manega** – *Via Manica 8/B* - **Gussago** *(BS)* - ℘ *030 25 22 627 or 338 36 46 759 - www.lamanega.it - info@lamanega.it - Winery tours 9-19 by reservation.* The true wealth of La Manèga agricultural company is its vineyard, which extends across the hills of Gussago, in the eastern Franciacorta region, just below the villa that houses the company cantina. Developed in terraces, the vineyards are always well-exposed and ventilated, favouring the maturation of its grapes already in the first days of August, when they are harvested. The cantina is a gem, a model of the business in which every detail of the winemaking process is monitored in detail, keeping the passion for this business told through the stories of Signor Rizzini. Hectares under vine: 3.
**Wines**: Franciacorta DOCG Brut/Saten/Rosé/Pas Dosè.

**La Montina** – *Via Baiana 17* - **Monticelli Brusati** *(BS)* - ℘ *030 65 32 78 - www.lamontina.it - amministrazione@lamontina.it - Winery tours 10 and 15.30, reservation suggested.* La Montina's name is derived from Benedetto Montini, the ancestor of Pope Paul VI, who owned the estate in 1620. It was purchased in the early 1980s by the Bozza brothers, who built a beautiful cellar in keeping with the winemaking vocation of the area, where they produce their prized Franciacorta wines. The cellar is dug out of the hill behind the estate and covers an area of around 5000 m². Hectares under vine: 72.
**Wines**: Franciacorta Satèn, Brut, Rosé, Extra Brut, Millesimato Brut DOCG.

🏠 **Villa Franciacorta** – *Fraz. Villa 12* - **Monticelli Brusati** *(BS)* - ℘ *030 65 23 29 - www.villafranciacorta.it - info@villafranciacorta.it - Winery tours and tasting by reservation.* The history of the Bianchi family winery is closely associated with the medieval hamlet of the same name, located in the municipality of Monticelli Brusati. The cellar is composed of 4 adjoining rooms, built in different periods, with a stunning central basement area dating from the 16th c. The beautiful refermentation cellar, built in 1989, is entirely underground and adorned with arches and vaults. Accommodation at the Villa Gradoni farmhouse, situated in the medieval centre of the hamlet of Villa di Monticelli Brusati (*21 apts., from €190, www.villagradoni.it*), meals also available. Hectares under vine: 37.

© Boettcher & Petoe/Shutterstock

**Wines**: Franciacorta Brut Millesimato, Franciacorta Satèn Millesimato, Franciacorta Demi-Sec Rosé, Franciacorta Brut Cuvette Millesimato, Franciacorta Pas Dosé Diamant Millesimato.

🏠 **Al Rocol** – *Via Provinciale 79* - **Ome** *(BS)* - ℘ *030 68 52 542 - www.alrocol.com - info@alrocol.com - Winery tours and tastings by reservation.* The estate and guest farm, run by the Vimercati Castellini family, has agricultural traditions reaching back to the 17th c. and was one of the first guest farms opened in Franciacorta. Founded in 1996, it has flanked its winegrowing activities with a guest farm, offering accommodation, meals and a range of genuine products, such as honey of different kinds, grappa and extra virgin olive oil. Accommodation at the Al Rocol guest farm (*15 rooms*) and restaurant service. Hectares under vine: 12.
**Wines**: Franciacorta Cà del Luf Brut, Franciacorta Martignac Satèn, Franciacorta Le Rive Rosé, Terre di Franciacorta Borbone, IGT Sebino Rosso Vignalta. Other products: Sebino olive oil, vinegar, grappa, honey, charcuterie.

**Majolini** – *Via Manzoni 3 - Loc. Valle* - **Ome** *(BS)* - ℘ *030 65 27 378 - www.majolini.it - majolini@majolini.it - Winery tours and tasting by reservation.* Everything started in the early 1980s, when the Maiolini brothers, the descendants of an old farming family, decided to renovate the old family cellar and purchase their first vineyard, continuing a project that their father Valentino has already commenced at the end of the 1960s. Today the brothers' enthusiasm has also led to the return of the old and almost extinct native grape variety known as Majolina, from which the family name is derived. Don't miss the "I Quaderni di Cantina" series of limited edition books that recount years of laborious activity in the vineyard and the cellar. Hectares under vine: 20.

**Wines:** Franciacorta Brut Satèn Ante Omnia, Franciacorta Brut Millesimato Electo, Franciacorta Pas Dosé Aligi Sassu, Franciacorta Brut Rosé Altera, Curtefranca Rosso. Other products: olive oil and grappa.

**Il Mosnel** – *Via Barboglio 14 - Loc. Camignone* - **Passirano** *(BS)* - ℘ *030 65 31 17 - www.mosnel.com - quellicheilvino@ mosnel.com - Winery tours and tastings Mon.-Fri. by reservation, Sat.-Sun. 11 and 15.30.* Il Mosnel is derived from an old place name of Celtic origin, which means "heap of stones". Indeed, this was once a stony area, which was slowly and laboriously cleared by the Cistercian monks who settled here and started to grow vines. Il Mosnel once belonged to the powerful Cacciamatta family and passed into the hands of the Barboglio family, its current owners, in 1836. The oldest part of the winery is its 16th-c. cellars. Hectares under vine: 41.

**Wines:** Franciacorta Brut, Franciacorta Satèn, Franciacorta Pas Dosé, Franciacorta Extra Brut Ebb, Franciacorta Rosé Pas Dosé "Parosé".

**Barone Pizzini** – *Via San Carlo 14* - **Provaglio d'Iseo** *(BS)* - ℘ *030 98 48 311 - www.baronepizzini.it - info@baronepizzini.it*

© Svetlana Lukienko/Shutterstock

- *Winery tours and tastings by reservation (payment required).* Founded in 1870, Barone Pizzini is one of Franciacorta's oldest wineries. Baron Giulio Pizzini, the last descendant of the aristocratic family that ran the estate, played an important role in the development of viticulture in Franciacorta and in 1971 produced the first bottle of sparkling wine. At the end of the 1980s a small group of local businessmen took over the winery. The old headquarters are housed in the 18th-c. buildings of Borgo Barone Pizzini, while the nearby new cellar is an example of eco-friendly architecture. Barone Pizzini was the first winery in the area to produce Franciacorta from organically grown grapes. The winery also has an agricultural museum and a wine bar with shop and tastings. Accommodation in Borgo Santa Giulia (wich is not part of the winery), surrounded by vineyards and a stone's throw from the Torbiere del Sebino Nature Reserve (*rooms from €90*), and meals at Ristorante Santa Giulia in the oldest part of the Borgo complex (℘ *030 98 28 348*). Hectares under vine: 47.

**Wines:** Franciacorta Satèn, Franciacorta Brut, Terre di Franciacorta Curtefranca Rosso and Bianco.

**Bersi Serlini** – *Via Cereto 7* - **Provaglio d'Iseo** *(BS)* - ℘ *030 98 23 338 - www. bersiserlini.it - visite@bersiserlini.it - Winery tours and tasting by reservation.* The estate was purchased by the Bersi Serlini family in 1886, after having belonged to the Church for centuries. The first bottle of brut was produced in 1970. The vineyards are reflected in the wetlands of Lombardy's spectacular Torbiere Nature Reserve. Accommodation available (*4 rooms*). Hectares under vine: 32.

**Wines:** Franciacorta Brut Cuvée N. 4, Franciacorta Rosé Rosa Rosae, Franciacorta Satèn, Franciacorta Brut Anteprima, Franciacorta Anniversario Blanc de Blanc, Franciacorta Extra Brut, Nuvola Demi Sec. Other products: grappa.

## VALTELLINA

**Sesterzio** – *Via Ere 345* - **Berbenno di Valtellina** *(SO)* - ℘ *0342 59 05 37 - www. cantinasesterzio.it - info@cantinasesterzio.it - Winery tours and tasting by reservation.* This company was born from the desire to recover and reuse the terraced vineyards that run down from the monastery into Pedemonte. The cantina and its agriturismo set at the feet of Mount Maroggia. Eco-sustainability, a harmonious synthesis of tradition and technology as well as respect for the environment are all values that guide this winemaking reality, which is working to return not only an environmental and productive perspective to the surrounding territory, but also one of quality and technological development. Visitors can stay overnight in the agriturismo (*11 rooms, 80€*), and the restaurant is open from Thu. to Sun. (*menu 35 €*). Hectares under vine: 4.

**Wines**: Valtellina Superiore Maroggia, Sforzato di Valtellina, Cuvée Sesterizo Brut, Gaudia, Aurum.

**Aldo Rainoldi** – *Via Stelvio 128* - **Chiuro** *(SO)* - ☎ *0342 48 22 25* - *www.rainoldi.com* - *rainoldi@rainoldi.com* - *Winery tours and tastings by reservation*. Founded in 1925, Rainoldi has always been active in promoting Nebbiolo, the principal grape variety of Valtellina. Consequently, it is one of the most renowned wineries for the production of Sforzato Valtellinese and also makes excellent Valtellina Superiore wines. Hectares under vine: 10.

**Wines**: Valtellina Sfursat Ca' Rizzieri, Valtellina Superiore Il Crespino, Valtellina Superiore Inferno Riserva, Valtellina Superiore Sassella Riserva, Valtellina Superiore Prugnolo.

**Caven Camuna** – *Via Stelvio 40/A* - **Chiuro** *(SO)* - ☎ *0342 48 26 31* - *www. cavencamuna.it* - *info@cavencamuna.it* - *Winery tours and tasting by reservation*. Founded in the 1980s, the winery is owned by brothers Stefano and Simone Nera. It stands out for its particular vineyard management techniques, which feature the use of natural fertilisers and substances with low environmental impact, combined with several clonal experiments on the Nebbiolo grape variety. The name Caven refers to the location of the winery, while Camuna harks back to the remote times in which the area was home to the Camunni people. Hectares under vine: 30.

**Wines**: Sforzato della Valtellina Messere, Valtellina Superiore Inferno Al Carmine, Valtellina Sup Inferno La Martellina, Valtellina Sup Sassella La Priora, Valtellina Sup Giupa, Valtellina Sup Le Coppelle, Terre Retiche di Sondrio Tellino Nebbiolo.

♀/ **Nino Negri** – *Via Ghibellini 3* - **Chiuro** *(SO)* - ☎ *0342 48 52 11* - *www.ninonegri.net* - *n.negri@giv.it* - *Winery tours and tasting by reservation*. The winery was founded in 1897 by Nino Negri and is housed in the prestigious setting of Castel Quadrio, built in 1432 by Filippo Visconti for the local *condottiero* Stefano Quadrio. Today Nino Negri is the leading winegrower in Valtellina. Red wines account for the lion's share of production and the main grape variety is Chiavennasca (Nebbiolo), used to

make Sassella, Grumello, Inferno, Fracia and Sfursat. Ca' Brione, a unique white wine, is also made from the same grapes, sometimes together with other varieties, using different winemaking techniques. Meals at the Fracia restaurant (*loc. Fracia, Teglio*, ☎ *0342 48 26 71, closed Wed.*), an old country house set among the vineyards, which was long used as a guesthouse and *fruttaio* for the partial drying of the grapes employed in the production of Sfursat. Hectares under vine: 31.

**Wines**: Sfursat di Valtellina 5 Stelle, Sfursat di Valtellina Carlo Negri, Valtellina Superiore Vigneto Fracia, Valtellina Superiore Mazér, Ca' Brione.

♀/ **Mamete Prevostini** - *Via Don Primo Lucchinetti 63* - **Mese** *(SO)* - ☎ *0343 41 522* - *www.mameteprevostini.com* - *info@ mameteprevostini.com* - *Winery tours and tastings by reservation*. Mamete Prevostini's history is a love affair with wine and the Valtellina that commenced over 70 years ago. Each of its wines reflects the Valtellina. The winery places great emphasis on work in the vineyard, dedicating painstaking care to the selection of grapes during harvest, when only evenly ripe bunches are chosen and unhealthy fruit is rejected. The vineyard is located in Sassella, one of the best winegrowing areas of the Valtellina. Meals available at the Crotasc restaurant(*closed Mon. and Tue.*). Hectares under vine: 18.

**Wines**: Sassella Valtellina Superiore, Opera IGT Bianco Terrazze Retiche di Sondrio, Sommarovina Sassella Valtellina Superiore, Corte di Cama Valtellina Superiore, Albareda Sforzato di Valtellina.

**Azienda Agricola Fay** – *Via Pila Caselli 1* - *Loc. San Giacomo di Teglio* - **Teglio** *(SO)* - ☎ *0342 78 60 71* - *www.vinifay.it* - *info@ vinifay.it* - *Winery tours and tasting by reservation*. The estate was founded in 1973 by Sandro Fay, who decided to expand his family's small wine production. Over the years the winery grew until becoming a benchmark for Valtellina winegrowers. Since 1991 Sandro has been supported in his work by his children Elena and Marco. The winery's efforts are aimed at emphasising the peculiarities of each of its vineyards, which produce very different wines due to their unique soil and climate conditions. Hectares under vine: 15.

**Wines**: Rosso di Valtellina Tèi, La Faya, Valgella Ca' Morei, Valgella Carteria, Sforzato Ronco del Picchio.

♀/ **Conti Sertoli Salis** – *Via Stelvio 18* - **Tirano** *(SO)* - ☎ *0342 71 04 04* - *www. sertolisalis.com* - *info@sertolisalis.com* - *Winery tours Sat. 10.30-17.30, other days by* reservation; Jun.-Sept. also Mon.-Sat. 11-16. According to legend, the Salis came from Etruria, together with Raeto, the mythical hero and Etruscan leader. What is certain is that the De Salicibus family settled in Tirano around the middle of the 17th c., building an imposing family palace. The "Fratelli Salis" were the first wine bottlers of the Kingdom of Italy. Bottles dated 1881 and 1890 have been found in the family cellars, and it appears that the first bottle produced dates from 1869. Don't miss the spectacular old cellars. Food tasting also available. Hectares under vine: 8.

**Wines**: Sforzato di Valtellina Canua, Terrazze Retiche di Sondrio IGT Il Saloncello, Valtellina Superiore Grumello, Valtellina Superiore Riserva Corte della Meridiana, Rosso della Valtellina Petram. Other products: preserves, honey, confectionery, vinegar, *pizzoccheri*.

**Rivetti&Lauro** - *Via Nazionale 121 -* **Villa di Tirano** *(SO) - ☎ 031 33 50 068 - www.rivettielauro.it - info@rivettielauro.it - Winery tours and tastings by reservation.* Rivetti & Lauro started from tradition, then introduced new biological and biodynamic cultivation techniques that fit in harmoniously with the surrounding mountain environment. The company has cultivated new vines, adding their grapes to the existing Nebbiolo with extraordinary results. Harvests are conducted by hand, selecting and collecting only the best grapes in baskets. The homogeneity of the product is preserved based on the vines each comes from: wines are made in wood containers and then aged in bottles, tonneaux and French durmast wood barrels. With Lècia, Emanuele Urbani undertook a new and unique experience in winemaking: experimenting with vine-aging grapes above 1,500 metres above sea level, and bottle aging above 2,000 metres above sea level. The goal of this adventure is biodynamic production. Hectares under vine: 11.

**Wines**: Uì, Sforzato dell'Orco, Sotamà, Cormelò, Calis, Gias, Uì Sassella, Uì Inferno.

**F.lli Triacca** – *Via Nazionale 121 -* **Villa di Tirano** *(SO) - ☎ 0342 70 13 52 - www.triaccavini.eu - info@triacca.com - Winery tours and tasting by reservation at Tenuta La Gatta in* **Bianzone**, *Via Gatta 33, ☎ 0342 72 00 04 or lagatta@triacca.com.* The Triacca family have been making wine for over 100 years and the family business spans 4 generations. At the end of the 19th c. the ancestors of the current owners bought a small vineyard in the Valgella area. After 1950 Fratelli Triacca completely transformed their business, switching

from unbottled to bottled wines. Make sure you visit the picturesque cellar under the former La Gatta convent, which has belonged to the Triaccas since 1969. Hectares under vine: 40.

**Wines**: Terrazze Retiche di Sondrio IGT La Contea, Valtellina Superiore Sassella, Valtellina Superiore Riserva La Gatta, Valtellina Superiore Prestigio, Sforzato di Valtellina San Domenico. Other products: grappa.

## LAKE GARDA

### 1. From Desenzano to Salò

**Azienda Agricola Cantrina** – *Via Colombera 7 - Loc. Cantrina -* **Bedizzole** *(BS) - ☎ 030 68 71 052 - www.cantrina.it - info@cantrina.it - Winery tours and tasting by reservation.* Cantrina is a tiny rural village of the Valtènesi, in the furthest reaches of the Lombard hinterland of Lake Garda. The family-run winery was founded in the early 1990s. It grows several international varieties and other local ones, in accordance with the company philosophy of interpreting the unique characteristics that the terroir gives the different grape varieties. Cristina Inganni, the owner, describes work in the vineyard and the winery as a "freestyle exercise" to be carried out with the utmost respect for nature. Hectares under vine: 5.8.

**Wines**: Riné IGT Bianco, Nepomuceno IGT Rosso, Zerdì IGT Rosso, Valtènesi, Valtènesi Chiaretto, Rosanoire, Vino da Tavola Rosso Eretico, Sole di Dario, a white dried-grape wine.

**Azienda Agricola Citari** – *Loc. Citari 2 - San Martino della Battaglia -* **Desenzano del Garda** *(BS) - ☎ 030 99 10 310 - www.citari.it - info@citari.it - Winery torus by reservation.* Established in 1975 by Francesco Gettuli, the company has grown over time thanks to the love and passion the founder passed on to his daughter Giovanna, who now runs the company together with her husband and children. A strong connection with the territory and respect for tradition are elements that make it possible for Citari to produce two highly valued DOC wines like the Lugana and San Martino. The small vineyards, harvesting by hand, careful selection of only the best grapes and modern cantina techniques exalt the particular characteristics of these wines. Hectares under vine: 21.

**Vini:** San Martino della Battaglia, Lugana Vigneto La Torre, Lugana Vigneto La Conchiglia, Garda Classico Rosso, Garda Classico Chiaretto, Citari Lugana Brut.

**Azienda Agricola Cà Maiol** – *Via dei Colli Storici 119* - **Desenzano del Garda** *(BS) - ℘ 030 99 10 006 - www.camaiol.it - visite@ camaiol.it - Visit to the showroom by reservation.* The winery was founded in 1967 by Walter Contato and its name is derived from the old Provençal origins of the Contato family. Today the business is managed by his wife Cesarina and his children Fabio and Patrizia. The winery has 4 estates: the main one, where the headquarters are based, is called Maiolo (or Ca Maiol by locals), the others are Molino, Rocchetta and Storta. The historical records of the property go back a long way. The name of the founder, Desenzano notary Sebastiano Maioli, and the year of construction, 1710 (MDCCX), are carved above the entrance to the owner's house. Hectares under vine: 120.
**Wines**: Lugana, Valtènesi, Garda Classico Chiaretto, IGT Benaco Bresciano Rosso, Spumante. Other products: olive oil, grappa.

**Costaripa** – *Via della Costa 1/A* - **Moniga del Garda** *(BS) - ℘ 0365 50 20 10 - www.costaripa.it - Winery tours Tue.-Fri. 14.30-18; Sat. 10-12.30 and 15.30-18.* Tending vineyards is a family tradition for the Vezzolas, who commenced in 1936 and have now reached the third generation of growers. The cellar has been designed to respect the landscape and to maximise the efficiency of the production processes. The estate's sparkling wines are exceptionally elegant.
**Wines**: Chiaretto, Groppello, Marzemino, Brut, Lugana.

⌂**Azienda Agricola Cobue** – *Loc. Cobue Sopra - Pozzolengo (BS) - ℘ 030 91 08 319 or 335 76 80 734 - www.cobue.it - info@cobue.it - Winery tours and tasting by reservation.* The company is located in an area where Mediterranean macchia mixes with alpine vegetation. This area has been inhabited since Neolithic times, is rich in history and has witnessed important events. For example, on 24 June 1859 the battle of San Martino was held here, a decisive event during which the French-Italian armies defeated the Austrians. As testimony for this important victory and a memorial for its victims, in 1893 a 74-metre tower known as the Spia d'Italia - Spy of Italy -, was erected, and is still open to visitors today. The monument is just a few minutes away from Cobue. Accomodation available at the estate (*6 apts.*). Hectares under vine: 17.
**Wines**: Lugana Monte Lupo, San Martino della Battaglia DOC, Garda Classico DOC, Garda Marzemino DOC, Zero Metodo Classico.

**Tenuta Roveglia** – *Loc. Roveglia 1* - **Pozzolengo** *(BS) - ℘ 030 91 86 63 - www. tenutaroveglia.it - info@tenutaroveglia.it - Winery tours and tastings by reservation, closed Sun.* Tenuta Roveglia was founded in the 1930s by the Swiss textile industrialist Federico Zweifel. Over the years it was extended, transformed and modernised. It currently covers an area of over 100 hectares, including 60 hectares of vineyards, making it Lugana's largest area under vine. Hectares under vine: 110.
**Wines**: Lugana, Lugana Superiore, Lugana Spumante, Garda Classico Chiaretto, Garda Cabernet Sauvignon, Garda Merlot. Other products: mixed flower honey, grappa, spirits.

**Pasini** – *Via Videlle 2 - Fraz. Raffa* - **Puegnago del Garda** *(BS) - ℘ 0365 65 14 19 - www.pasinisangiovanni.it - info@ pasinisangiovanni.it - Winery tours and tastings by reservation, closed Sun. pm.* In 1958 Andrea Pasini (b. 1914) decided to dedicate himself to wine and found his own winery. Over the following few years he transformed his trattoria in the heart of Brescia into a wine shop, which soon became a small winery. As his three children grew up they fell in love with their father's business. Today Luca and Paolo Pasini represent the third generation and pursue the path of high-quality production with increasing tenacity, seeking to combine the originality of native grape varieties with the qualitative guarantee of the best-known international ones. Hectares under vine: 36.
**Wines**: Lugana, Chiaretto, Groppello, Ceppo 326 Brut Metodo Classico. Other products: olive oil.

# ADDRESSES

♔ **Cà dei Frati** – *Via Frati 22 - Fraz. Lugana - Sirmione (BS) - ℘ 030 91 94 68 - www. cadeifrati.it - info@cadeifrati.it - Winery tours 8.30-12.30 and 14.30-18.30, closed Sun.* In 1939 the great-grandfather of the current owners moved to Sirmione, leaving his farm to start a winery. The business has been handed down through the generations and after 30 years it managed to vinify and bottle its entire harvest with the name Cà dei Frati. Today it is one of the best-known wineries in the area. Accommodation at the *Aquila d'oro Hotel* in Desenzano (*21 rooms, from €180*) with restaurant overlooking the lake. Hectares under vine: 100.

**Wines**: Lugana I Frati, Lugana Brolettino, Benaco Bresciano IGT Pratto and IGT Ronchedone. Other products: grappa.

♀ **Ca' Lojera** – *Via 1866 - Loc. Rovizza - Sirmione (BS) - ℘ 030 91 95 50 - www. calojera.com - info@calojera.com - Winery tours anda tastings by reservation, ℘ 045 755 19 01.* It is told that once, when Lake Garda and little Lake Frassino were connected by a network of waterways, a boat arrived from the north carrying merchants who used the lakeside houses to hide smuggled goods, and that these hideaways were guarded by packs of wolves. The name of the Tiraboschi family's estate, Tenuta Ca' Lojera, refers to these "houses of wolves". Restaurant service available. Hectares under vine: 18.

**Wines**: Lugana, Monte della Guardia Chardonnay and Rosato, Garda Merlot, Garda Cabernet Sauvignon, Passito Ravel, Spumante. Other products: olive oil, honey, grappa.

© Szasz-Fabian Ilka Erika/Shutterstock

## 2. The Province of Mantova

**Cantina Bertagna** – *Via Madonna della Porta 14 – Cavriana (MN) - ℘ 0376 82 211 – www.cantinabertagna.it – info@cantinabertagna.it - Winery tours and tastings by reservation, closed Sun. pm.* Cantina Bertagna has been producing prized and award-winning red and white wines, spumantis and passitos for four generations. Inside the company, Gianfranco oversees the entire production process, transferring his love and passion into the family's wines. The cantina is located in the heart of the Moreno hills, extending between Garda Lake, Solferino and Castellaro Lagusello, a UNESCO World Heritage site. Hectares under vine: 13.

**Wines**: Passito Rosso Alto Mincio, Brut Classico, Montevolpe Rosso Mincio Alto, Lugana, Garda Colli Mantovani Bianco.

**Ricchi** – *Strada Festoni 13/d - Monzambano (MN) - ℘ 0376 80 02 38 - www.cantinaricchi.it - info@cantinaricchi.it - Winery tours and tastings 8.30-12 and 14-19, closed Sun. afternoon.* The Stefanoni family have passed their winegrowing tradition down through the generations. They successfully manage 40 hectares of vineyards using innovative techniques while following the natural growth rhythms of the grapes. Various wines are produced with the Garda and Colli Mantovani designations, while the grappa and sparkling wines are also interesting. Hectares under vine: 40.

**Wines**: Spumante "Ricchi" Met. Classico, Garda Chardonnay Meridiano, Garda Cabernet "Ribò", Garda Merlot "Carpino", Passito IGT "Le Cime". Other products: olive oil and grappa.

♔ **Podere Selva Capuzza** – *Loc. Selva Capuzza - Desenzano del Garda (BS) - ℘ 030 99 10 381 - www.selvacapuzza.it - ufficio@selvacapuzza.it - Winery tours and tasting by request.* Selva Capuzza is the name of a little place hidden among the vineyards in the highest part (hence the name "capuzza") of the San Martino della Battaglia hills. The estate is dedicated to the cultivation of native grape varieties for the production of the DOC wines of the area. In additon to the cellar, it comprises 2 old farms: Cascina Capuzza, which serves traditional dishes accompanied by the estate's wines (*closed Mon.-Wed.*) and the Borgo San Donino guest farm, which grew up around the church of the same name built in 1280 (*11 rooms and apartments, from €92*). Hectares under vine: 25.

**Wines**: Lugana Superiore, Campo del Soglio San Martino della Battaglia, Madèr

Garda Classico Rosso Superiore, San Donino Garda Classico Chiaretto, Lume sweet dried-grape wine. Other products: olive oil and grappa.

**Reale di Boselli** – *Strada Volta - Monzambano 34 -* **Volta Mantovana** *(MN) - ℰ 0376 83 409 - www.cantinareale.it - info@cantinareale.it - Winery tours and tasting by reservation, 8-12 and 14-19, closed Sun.* Cantine Boselli has been present on the morainic hills of Mantua since 1442. The family's commanding coat of arms is featured on the labels. The main grape varieties grown are Merlot, Cabernet, Pinot Nero, Sangiovese and Molinara for red wines and Garganega, Sauvignon, Chardonnay, Trebbiano for whites. The extensive product range features still and sparkling red, white and dessert wines. Hectares under vine: 18.

**Wines**: Matteo Spumante Metodo Classico, Crestale Sauvignon, Balasso Rosso, Vigna del Moro Merlot, Rosso del Ciano red dessert wine. Other products: grappa, salami, Grana Padano.

### BRIANZA

♟/ **Terrazze di Montevecchia** – *Via Alta Collina 12 bis - Cascina Ghisalba -* **Montevecchia** *(LC) - ℰ 333 88 54 020 - www.terrazzedimontevecchia.com - terrazze@terrazzedimontevecchia.com - Winery tours (Vinicola Ghezzi, Via S. Caterina 6d, Rovagnate) 8-12.30 and 14-19, Sun. 10-12.* The estate is an open terrace onto the scenery of the park and valley of Curone and the Lecco mountains, situated 400 metres from the sanctuary of the same name. The winery grows and makes wine mainly from Syrah, Merlot, Sauvignon and Viogner grapes. The star of its production is the elegant and original Classic Method brut sparkling wine from Viogner and Sauvignon. Meals at the Cascina Ghisalba guest farm *(open Thu., Fri., and Sat. evening and Sun. lunch).* Hectares under vine: 9.

**Wines**: Pincianell Rosso, Pincianell Bianco, Munciar Bianco, Passito Pasii, Vino Rosso CEPP, Terrazze Brut Spumante Metodo Classico.

## Where to stay

### BERGAMO

**La Valletta Relais** – *Via Castagneta 19 - ℰ 035 24 27 46 - www.lavallettabergamo.it - 8 rooms, doubles from €85.* Small villa in Parco dei Colli. A few carefully decorated rooms and a refined, gracious atmosphere.

© Alistair Scott/Shutterstock

### BORGO PRIOLO

**Agriturismo Cascina Casareggio** – *Loc. Casareggio,* **Fortunago** *(PV), 10 km S of Borgo Priolo (PV) - ℰ 0383 87 52 28 - www.cascinacasareggio.it - 6 rooms, doubles from €80.* Set in an isolated and peaceful position, the holiday farm offers pleasant rooms and an inviting swimming pool in its surrounding grounds. The cooking is based on simple regional dishes.

### CORTE FRANCA

**Ulivi** – *Viale Madruzza 11,* **Paratico** *(BS), 8 km NW of Corte Franca - ℰ 035 91 29 18 - www.ulivihotel.it - 22 rooms.* In a quiet comfortable oasis by Lake Iseo, the unusual single-storey, horseshoe-shaped building encloses the garden and swimming pool and overlooks the lake. The interior is new and welcoming.

### SAN MARTINO DELLA BATTAGLIA

**Antica Locanda del Contrabbandiere** – *Loc. Martelosio di Sopra 1,* **Pozzolengo** *(BS), 5 km N of San Martino della Battaglia - ℰ 030 91 81 51 - www.locandadelcontrabbandiere.com - Closed Mon. - 3 rooms, doubles from €100.* The two intimate rooms are furnished with antique furniture and have views over open countryside. The meals offered are based on local, traditional recipes.

### TIRANO

**Alta Villa** – *Via ai Monti 46,* **Bianzone** *(SO), 6 km SW of Tirano - ℰ 0342 72 03 55 - www.altavilla.info - 14 rooms, doubles from €50.* Located in the upper section of the village among woods and vineyards; the restaurant serves local dishes in a rustic, informal atmosphere. There is a lovely panoramic terrace.

# VENETO

Viticulture in Veneto is closely linked to the region's history: the wine "de Venegia" was known since the Middle Ages not only in the Italian peninsula, but also beyond its borders, thanks to the far-reaching trade practised by the Serenissima Republic of Venice. It is not surprising, therefore, that wine is an integral part of the culture and daily life of the Veneto. As the goal of local vintners is to make wines of the highest quality, it is not surprising that Venetan production is remarkable not only for its volume (the region is one of the largest producers in Italy) but also for its excellence. The number of designated areas that Veneto boasts also puts the region in the high end of the table, attesting the importance viticulture has in the life of the population and in the regional economy.

*Valdobbiadene town and Prosecco vineyards*

## The terroir

Archaeological finds in the Lessini mountains confirm the close bond the Veneto has with the vine. It is perhaps due to this millenary tradition that the region has such a diverse and rich range of varieties of both white and black grapes.

This ampelographic diversity has given rise to a very broad array of wines: youthful reds and whites, sparkling wines, full-bodied reds and high quality dried-grape wines.

The territory differs widely in terms of its soil, cultural traditions and vine varieties, thus local production can fluctuate strongly even in just a few kilometres. The most commonly cultivated grape is the Merlot, followed by Garganega and Trebbiano.

In the **western part** of Veneto Garganega, Trebbiano, Corvina Veronese and Rondinella are grown; in the **east-ern part** Tocai Friulano, Pinot Bianco, Pinot Grigio and Sauvignon, as well as Prosecco, Cabernet Franc, Merlot and Raboso.

To choose just one outstanding wine of each type, among the reds **Amarone** is certainly the most structured.

Made from sun-dried Corvina, Rondinella and Molinara grapes, it is a wine to be laid down and which ages increasingly well.

Among the whites the **Soave DOC** zone lays claim to more than one record: it is the largest grape-growing area in Europe and one of the oldest DOC areas, having been created in 1936.

Among the **sparkling wines** the Prosecco di Conegliano Valdobbiadene is the most representative, and even among the **sweet wines** there is an embarrassment of choice among the Recioto di Soave, Recioto della Valpolicella and Torcolato di Breganze.

## DOCG

Amarone della Valpolicella
Bagnoli Friularo or Friularo di Bagnoli
Bardolino Superiore
Colli Asolani Prosecco
   or Asolo Prosecco
Colli Euganei Fior d'Arancio
   or Fior d'Arancio Colli Euganei
Colli di Conegliano
Conegliano Valdobbiadene - Prosecco
Lison (with Friuli-V. G.)
Montello Rosso or Montello
Piave Malanotte or Malanotte del Piave
Recioto della Valpolicella
Recioto di Gambellara
Recioto di Soave
Soave Superiore

## DOC

Arcole
Bagnoli di Sopra or Bagnoli
Bardolino
Breganze
Colli Berici

Colli Euganei
Corti Benedettine del Padovano
Custoza
Gambellara
Garda (with Lombardy)
Lessini Durello
Lison Pramaggiore (with Friuli-V. G.)
Lugana (with Lombardy)
Merlara
Montello - Colli Asolani
Monti Lessini
Piave
Prosecco
Riviera del Brenta
San Martino della Battaglia (with Lombardy)
Soave
Valdadige (with Trentino Alto Adige /
   Südtirol)
Valdadige Terradeiforti or Terradeiforti
   (with Trentino Alto Adige)
Valpolicella
Valpolicella Ripasso
Venezia
Vicenza
Vigneti della Serenissima or Serenissima

---

## PRINCIPAL VARIETIES CULTIVATED

### WHITE GRAPES

Bianchetta Trevigiana
Boschera
Chardonnay
Cortese
Durella
Flavis Verdiso
Garganega
Incrocio Manzoni Bianco
Italica
Malvasia Bianca
Malvasia Istriana
Marzemina Bianca
Moscato Bianco
Moscato Giallo
Müller Thurgau
Nosiola
Pedevana
Pinella
Pinot Bianco
Pinot Grigio
Prosecco
Riesling
Riesling Italico
Sauvignon
Serprino

Sylvaner
Tocai Friulano
Traminer Aromatico
Trebbiano di Lugana
Trebbiano Giallo
Trebbiano Toscano
Veltliner
Verduzzo Friulano
Verduzzo Trevigiano
Vespaiola

### BLACK GRAPES

Ancellotta
Barbera
Cabernet Franc
Cabernet Sauvignon
Ciliegiolo
Corvina Gentile
Corvina Veronese
Corvinone
Croatina
Enantio
Fertilia
Franconia
Freisa
Groppello Gentile

Incrocio Manzoni Rosso
Lagrein
Lambrusco
Malbech
Marzemino
Merlot
Molinara
Negrara
Nigra
Pavana
Petit Verdot
Pinot Nero
Prodest
Raboso Del Piave
Raboso Veronese
Refosco dal
   Peduncolo Rosso
Rondinella
Rossignola
Sangiovese
Schiava
Syrah
Teroldego
Tocai Rosso
Trevisana Nera
Turca
Wildbacher

# Itineraries

*Locations with a winery are indicated by the symbol 🍷; for the addresses of the wineries,* *see p. 177.*

## 1. WEST OF VERONA

### Valpolicella and Bardolino

The province of Verona is the one that produces the largest quantity of wine. Between Lake Garda and Verona we find **Bardolino** (also produced in Classico and Chiaretto versions) and **Bardolino Superiore DOCG**. The best known red wine is **Valpolicella** (also produced in Superiore, Classico and Valpantena versions).

The pride of the appellation are **Amarone** and **Recioto della Valpolicella**, both made from Rondinella, Molinara and Corvina grapes left to dry for about 3 months so they have a higher sugar content and are more complex. The wine derived is very firm-bodied, dark red in colour, of good acidity and elegant tannins, with notes of spices and mature red and black fruit. Their bouquets provide a real explosion of scents. Whereas the Amarone is vinified to offer a degree of dryness, the Recioto is a full-blown sweet wine. Another interesting wine is the **Valpolicella Ripasso**, which is a basic Valpolicella given an added boost with the sun-dried marc used in the production of Amarone and Recioto.

In this part of Veneto we also find the designated areas **Custoza** and **Garda**. The latter is an interregional DOC zone shared between Veneto and Lombardy. Other shared appellations with Lombardy are **Lugana**, which produces the white wine of the same name from Trebbiano di Lugana grapes, and **San Martino della Battaglia**, which uses Tocai Friulano. **Valdadige**, on the other hand, is shared with Trentino Alto Adige/Südtirol.

### THE TERROIR

**Area:** 18 345.37 km$^2$, of which approximately 92,042 hectares are planted to vine

**Production 2019:** 11,333,452 hectolitres, of which 7,841,537 VQPRD

**Geography:** 29% mountainous, 15% hilly and 56% flat. The climate causes a large temperature range and becomes increasingly continental the greater the distance from the sea. The coast is hot and sultry in the summer but winter temperatures are mild. The terrain in the north of the region is mountainous and calcareous, while the hill zone is calcareous and volcanic

### THE PROTECTION CONSORTIA

U.VI.VE. Unione Consorzi Vini Veneti DOC –Via Sommacampagna 63 D/E, (VR), ✆ 045 59 52 38, www.uvive.it

Consorzio di Tutela vini Arcole DOC – c/o Casa del Vino, Vicolo Mattielli 11, Soave (VR), ✆ 045 76 81 578, www.arcoledoc.com

Consorzio di Tutela vini DOC Bagnoli – Piazza Marconi 63, Bagnoli di Sopra (PD), ✆ 049 53 80 008, www.consorziovinidocbagnoli.it

Consorzio di Tutela vini Bardolino – Piazza Matteotti 8, Bardolino (VR), ✆ 045 62 12 567, www.ilbardolino.com

Consorzio di Tutela vini DOC Breganze – Piazza Mazzini 18, Breganze (VI), ✆ 0445 30 05 95, www.stradadeltorcolato.it

Consorzio di Tutela vini Colli Berici Vicenza – Piazza Garibaldi 1, Lonigo (VI), ✆ 0444 89 65 98, consorzio.bevidoc.it

Consorzio di Tutela Colli di Conegliano DOCG – Viale XXVIII Aprile 22, Conegliano (TV), www.colliconegliano.it

Consorzio di Tutela vini DOC Colli Euganei – Piazza Martiri 10, Vo (PD), ✆ 049 52 12 107, www.collieuganeidoc.com

Consorzio di Tutela vini DOC Corti Benedettine del Padovano – Via Padova 68, Conselve (PD), ✆ 049 53 84 433, www.cortibenedettine.it

Consorzio di Tutela vino Custoza DOC – c/o Villa Venier, Via Bassa 14,

# Verona★★★ 🍷

The elegance and grace of Verona is seen everywhere: in the surrounding hills, the two gentle curves of the river Adige as it passes through the city, and Verona's ancient, understated churches. In summer its music festival in the Roman Arena is unforgettable. Verona enjoyed its greatest splendour under the Scaliger seigniory, who ruled on behalf of the Holy Roman Emperor from 1260 to 1387. It then suffered the domination of the Visconti of Milan and in 1405 fell into the hands of the Republic of Venice. Occupied by the Austrians in 1814, in 1866 the city joined the kingdom of Italy with the rest of the Veneto.

"Two households, both alike in dignity, In fair Verona, where we lay our scene…". Thus begins the most famous story of love and death of all time. Verona is the setting for the story of Shakespeare's star-crossed lovers, **Romeo and Juliet**, against the backdrop of the struggles of the Guelphs and Ghibellines at the start of the 14th c.

**S. Zeno Maggiore★★** – one of North Italy's most beautiful Romanesque churches stands on the edge of the historic centre. The exterior is noted for its decorative vertical bands and delicate small arches on the façade, and the alternation of brick and stone on the sides and bell tower. The porch supported on crouching lions encloses beautiful **bronze doors★★★** (11th-12th c.) decorated with biblical scenes. The interior is striking for its simplicity and height, the frescoes in the right aisle, and the processional cross attributed to Lorenzo Veneziano. There is a superb **triptych★★** (1495) by Mantegna above the altar. Two 14th-c. statues look down on the iconostasis. An unusual polychrome statue of the "Laughing St Zeno" (13th c.) stands in the left aisle. Other wall frescoes in

Sommacampagna (VR), ☎ 045 55 45 857, www.custoza.wine

Consorzio di Tutela vini Gambellara DOC – Piazza Garibaldi 1, Lonigo (VI), ☎ 044 48 96 598, www.consorziogambellara.com

Consorzio di Tutela vini Garda DOC – c/o Villa Venier, Via Bassa 14, Sommacampagna (VR), ☎ 045 55 45 857, www.gardadocvino.it

Consorzio di Tutela Vino Lessini Durello DOC – c/o Casa del Vino, Vicolo Mattielli 11, Soave (VR),

☎ 045 76 81 578, www.montilessini.com

Consorzio di Tutela Lugana DOC – Parco Catullo 4, Peschiera del Garda (VR), ☎045 9233070, www.consorziolugana.it

Consorzio di Tutela vini Merlara DOC – Casa del Vino, Via A. Mattielli 11, Soave (VR), www.ilmerlara.com

Consorzio di Tutela vini Montello e Colli Asolani DOC – Via San Gaetano 35, Montebelluna (TV), ☎ 331 57 30 216, www.asolomontello.it

Consorzio di Tutela Prosecco DOC di Conegliano Valdobbiadene – Villa Brandolini, Piazza Libertà 7, Pieve di Soligo (TV), ☎ 0438 83 028, www.prosecco.it

Consorzio di Tutela Riviera del Brenta DOC – Via Brentabassa 30, Dolo (VE), ☎ 041 41 04 30, www.cantinerivieradelbrenta.it

Consorzio di Tutela vini Soave – Vicolo Mattielli 11, Soave(VR) ☎ 045 76 81 578, www.ilsoave.com

Consorzio di Tutela vini Terradeiforti DOC – Via Dante 14 - Avio (TN), ☎ 339 8514907, www.terradeifortivini.it

Consorzio di Tutela vino Valpolicella – Via Valpolicella 57, San Pietro in Cariano (VR), ☎ 045 77 03 194, www.consorziovalpolicella.it

Consorzio Vini Venezia – Via Businello 3, 31040 Portobuffolè (TV), ☎ 0422 850045, www.consorziovinivenezia.it – Voluntary Consortium for the Protection of DOC "Venezia", "Lison-Pramaggiore", "Piave" and DOCG "Lison" e "Malanotte del Piave"

## Visit

**Churches** The visit to the churches of Sant'Anastasia, San Fermo, the Duomo and San Zeno Maggiore requires an entrance ticket. For information, contact the Associazione Chiese Vive, ℘ 045 59 28 13, www.chieseverona.it

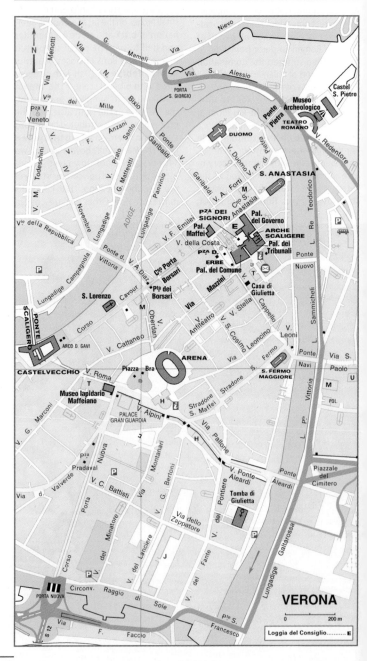

Byzantine style include a Crucifixion attributed to Altichiero (14th c.) and *Christ Enthroned between St John the Baptist, the Mother of God, Archangels and Saints* (12th c.). A charming Romanesque cloister stands on the left of the church.

**Arena★★** – *Piazza Bra. Open 8.30-19.30, Oct.-Jun. closed Mon. morning,* ℘ *045 80 03 204, museomaffeiano.comune. verona.it.* Able to seat 22,000 spectators, this splendid amphitheatre is one of the largest in the Roman world. The structure, built in pink marble and a flint-brick agglomerate, allows the construction to be dated to the end of the 1st c. AD. It is the setting for a famous summer opera festival and from its top tiers offers a broad **view★★** of the city and hills beyond, which, on a clear day, extends as far as the Alps.

*Head down Via Roma.*

**Castelvecchio and the Scaliger Bridge★★** – this beautiful complex of fortified buildings was constructed in 1354 by Cangrande I and is connected to the other bank of the Adige by the Scaliger Bridge. They are a marvellous example of 14th-c. military architecture. The castle was built in two parts separated by a passage protected by a large tower. Inside the castle the **Art Museum★★** is a masterpiece of design by Carlo Scarpa and holds works by the great names of Veronese art from the 12th-16th c. *Open 8.30-19.30, closed Mon. morning,* ℘ *045 80 62 611, www.comune. verona.it/castelvecchio/cvsito.*

Take Corso Cavour to the Church of **San Lorenzo★** (1117), its tufa and ceramic façade flanked by towers. The interior has a hieratic beauty, with pillars alternating with columns topped by Roman and Carolingian capitals.

On the other side of Porta dei Borsari (1st c. AD) follow Corso Porta Borsari to **Piazza delle Erbe★★**. Originally the site of the Roman forum, today it is a busy market square lined by lovely palaces and ancient houses, some of which are still adorned with frescoes and marble columns. On the north side, note the Baroque Palazzo Maffei. In no. 23 Via Cappello you will find the "supposed" **House of Juliet**, a Gothic palace said to have belonged to the Capulets, with the famous interior balcony. The **presumed** tomb of the young girl is in the cloister of the Church of San Francesco al Corso in Via del Portiere, where the two youngsters' marriage is said to have taken place.

Next to Piazza delle Erbe is the elegant **Piazza dei Signori★★**. To the right stands the 12th-c. Palazzo della Ragione (City Hall) and the Lamberti Tower made of brick and stone. An arcade connects it to the Palazzo dei Tribunali (previously Palazzo del Capitano) beside the massive brick Scaliger Tower. On the other side of the square the Loggia del Consiglio is an elegant building in Venetian Renaissance style. The square is closed off by the **Palazzo del Governo** (late 13th c.) where the Scaliger family lived, followed by the Venetian Podestà. Crowned with merlons, it has a beautiful classical portal designed by Sanmicheli in 1533.

*Arena*

© RnDmS/iStock

Set against the palace are the **Scaliger Tombs★★**. These Gothic mausoleums are decorated with sculpted religious scenes and statues of saints, while the sarcophaguses bear the family's coat of arms featuring the Scaliger symbol, a ladder (*scala*).

Continue to the **Sant'Anastasia ★** (13th-15th c.). The wide, soaring interior has a floor made from slabs in three colours: white, black (the colour of the Dominican robe) and red (colour of blood of the martyr, in this case St Peter of Verona). It also features several masterpieces such as the **fresco★** (14th c.) by Altichiero in the Cavalli Chapel, 24 **terracottas★** by Michele da Firenze, and the fresco of **St George and the Princess★★** (15th c.) by Pisanello in the Pellegrini Chapel, an unreal scene in which fantasy and precision are combined. Also note the stoup (1495) by Veronese's father, with the small statue of a hunchback.

*Take Via Duomo on the left.* In spite of a Romanesque choir and a Gothic nave, the **duomo★** was completed with a classic Renaissance bell tower. It has a very fine main door adorned with sculptures and low reliefs. Divided by pink marble pillars, the interior has two treasures: *Our Lady of the Assumption* by Titian (*1st altar on the left*) and the choir enclosure by Sanmicheli (16th c.). The Romanesque font has been carved from a single piece of marble.

The canonical district around the duomo is a pleasant place for a stroll.

*Villa della Torre, Fumane*

© Flavio Vallenari/iStock

Cross the Adige on the **Pietra Bridge** (1st c. AD). On the other side is the Roman **theatre★** (1st c. AD). Close by, the appearance of the **Giusti Garden** has not altered since it was created in the 16th c. by Agostino Giusti, a Knight of the Veneto Republic. In addition to the flowers, the garden features fountains, grottoes, statues, Roman finds and an ancient maze and gives a marvellous **view★** of Verona. *Via Giardino Giusti 2. Open 9-19, ℘ 045 80 34 029, www.giardinogiusti.com.*

Return to Piazza delle Erbe, then walk down the street where Juliet's house is till you reach the river. On the right you will see the Church of **San Fermo Maggiore★** (11th-12th c., later remodelled). The façade combines Romanesque and Gothic, while the open interior has a superb vault like an upturned hull on which 400 saints are portrayed. The walls are decorated with a series of 14th- and 15th-c. frescoes by various artists, including the **Annunciation★** by Pisanello on the Brenzoni mausoleum (1430). The lower church (1065) is very beautiful, with frescoed pillars and a lovely 14th-c. wooden *Crucifix*.

## Valpolicella

*Itinerary of approximately 50 km starting from Verona.*

Valpolicella is a hilly zone to the north of Verona. Three torrents run through it from the Lessini mountains down to the river Adige, forming three parallel valleys. The area is characterised by vineyards and elegant 17th- and 18th-c. villas, typically built with a porch and loggia. Leave Verona west on the SS 12 and pass through Parona di Valpolicella and **Arbizzano**. Shortly after you will see the 18th-c. Villa Mosconi.

Driving up the attractive, cypress-lined valley, you come to the town of **Negrar** ♆. Go back on your steps and turn right for **Pedemonte** ♆, where you will see the beautiful Villa Serego-Boccoli (16th c.) designed by Palladio, with a chapel from an earlier period. Continuing, you come to **San Floriano**, where the 12th-c. parish church has incorporated epigraphs from a Roman temple in its façade.

Carry on up the Marano valley to **Marano di Valpolicella** ♆ and its medieval castle. A little way out of the town you will see a small road that leads up Monte Castellon to the Sanctuary of Santa Maria di Valverde. Founded in a panoramic position in very early times, the shrine was rebuilt in Baroque form.

Pass through **Fumane** 🍷 and descend the valley to the Villa della Torre, an imposing property built in the mid-16th c. taking as its model the forms of the Roman *domus*. You arrive in **San Pietro in Cariano** 🍷, Valpolicella's political and administrative centre, which has retained various fine buildings from past centuries, including several villas. Pass through Gargagnano to reach **San Giorgio di Valpolicella**, a delightful village in a commanding position that boasts an early medieval parish church with 11th-c. frescoes and charming cloister.

Continue in the direction of the Adige to **Sant'Ambrogio di Valpolicella**, which is famous for its wines and the pink marble of Verona.

## From Verona to Malcesine along Lake Garda

*Itinerary of approximately 120 km.*
*The route along the lakeside continues from Malcesine under the heading Trentino Alto Adige/Südtirol, see p. 194.*
Like Valpollicella, the area between the Adige and Lake Garda has many country residences built in the 16th-19th c. by the Veronese and Venetian nobility. The surrounding farmland is used to grow grapes, cereals, fruit and vegetables. Another very common crop, especially in the zone just inland of the lake (**Calmasino di Bardolino** 🍷, **Cavaion**

## WINE AND FOOD ROUTES

Strada del vino Arcole DOC – c/o Casa del Vino, vicolo Mattielli 11, Soave (VR), ☎ 045 76 81 578, www.arcoledoc.com

Strada dell'Asparago Bianco di Cimadolmo IGP – Piazza Martiri 2, Cimadolmo (TV), ☎ 340 61 07 542, www.stradadellasparago.it

Strada del Vino Bardolino, www.stradadelbardolino.com

Strada dei vini dei Colli Berici – c/o Palazzo del Vino, piazza Garibaldi 1, Lonigo (VI), ☎ 0444 89 65 98, www.stradavinicolliberici.it

Strada del vino Colli Euganei – Vial Stazione 60, Montegrotto Terme (PD), ☎ 331 99 24 777, www.stradadelvinocollieuganei.it

Strada del vino Custoza – www.stradadelcustoza.com

Stradon del Vin Friularo – www.stradonvinfriularo.it

Strada del vino Lessini Durello – c/o Casa del Vino, vicolo Mattielli 11, Soave (VR), ☎ 045 76 81 578, www.montilessini.com

Strada dei vini DOC Lison-Pramaggiore – Piazza Libertà 74, Pramaggiore (VE), ☎ 389 45 84 662, www.stradavini.it

Strada dei vini del Piave, www.stradavinidelpiave.com

Strada del Prosecco e vini dei Colli Conegliano Valdobbiadene – Villa Brandolini, Via Roma 7, Pieve di Soligo (TV), ☎ 0423 97 40 19, www.coneglianovaldobbiadene.it

Strada del Radicchio Rosso di Treviso IGP e Variegato di Castelfranco IGP – Via Guidini 50, Zero Branco (TV), ☎ 328 59 47 185, www.stradadelradicchio.it

Strada del Recioto e dei vini di Gambellara DOC – Via Borgolecco 2, Gambellara (VI), ☎ 0444 44 41 83, www.stradadelrecioto.com

Strada del Riso Vialone Nano Veronese IGP – Via Cavour 3, Isola della Scala (VR), ☎ 380 89 34 314, www.stradadelriso.it

Strada del vino Soave, www.stradadelsoave.com

Strada del vino e dei prodotti tipici Terradeiforti – Via Brennero 30, Peri in Dolcè (VR), ☎ 045 72 70 521

Strada del Torcolato e dei vini di Breganze – Piazza Mazzini 18, Breganze (VI), ☎ 0445 30 05 95, www.stradadeltorcolato.it

Strada del vino Valpolicella – Via Ingelheim 7, San Pietro in Cariano (VR), ☎ 346 32 02 167, www.stradadelvinovalpolicella.it

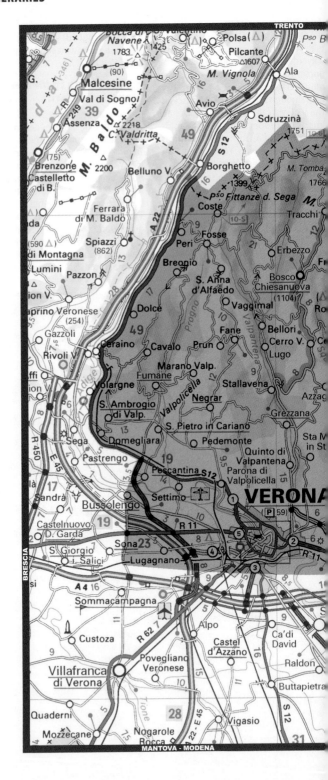

VALPOLICELLA AND SOAVE

**Veronese** ), is olives, which have won this stretch of the shoreline the name Riviera degli Olivi.

**Sommacampagna** is remembered for the defeats at the hands of the Austrians during the Risorgimento in nearby Custoza in 1848 and 1866, where an ossuary commemorates and holds the remains of the dead. The town stands up high on the hills overlooking the vineyards.

The town of **Peschiera del Garda** was built where the river Mincio flows out of Lake Garda. Its strategic position on the border between the territories of Mantua and Verona prompted the Venetians to build a large fortress, the walls of which ring the town centre.

**Valeggio sul Mincio**, 11 km south of Peschiera, is worth a visit for the lovely **Sigurtà Garden Park★★**, whose 50 hectares can be toured on foot, bike, golf car or in the park's visitors' train. Set on the banks of the Mincio, the garden has Mediterranean flora, vast lawns and interesting architectural features. *Open 7 Mar.-8 Nov. 9-19 (9-18 Mar., Oct., Nov.),  045 63 71 033, www.sigurta.it.*

*Return to Peschiera and follow the SS 249 (the Gardesana Oriental).* Not far from Peschiera are the entertainment parks **Gardaland** ( *045 64 49 777, www. gardaland.it*), **Gardaland Sea Life Aquarium** ( *045 64 49 777, www. gardaland.it*), **CanevaWorld** (a water and medieval theme park, *045 69 69 900, www.canevaworld.it)* and **CanevaWorld's Movieland Studios**, in which stuntmen perform spectacular shows.

*Return to the SS 249 along the lake shore.*

**Lazise** is a pleasant walled town that was of strategic importance to the Scaligers and later also the Venetians, who kept their fleet there. Note the 16th-c. Venetian Customs building in the port. The small Church of San Nicolò (12th c.) has Romanesque frescoes, and the Scaliger castle stands nearby.

Continue along the lake through **Cisano**, where the 12th-c. Church of Santa Maria is a fine example of Veronese Romanesque with Neoclassical remodelling.

Famous for its red wine, the nearby town of **Bardolino** boasts the lovely Carolingian Church of San Zeno (11th-c. frescoes) and the elegant Romanesque Church of San Severo (12th c.) decorated with a cycle of frescoes.

A detour of 5 km from Bardolino takes you to the **Eremo dei Camaldolesi** (a Camaldolite hermitage, 17th c.), which gives an excellent view over the lake.

*Return to the lake road.*

**Garda★** is a popular lake resort after which the lake is named. It has retained a few traces of Venetian rule, such as the Palazzo dei Capitani del Lago and the Palazzo Fregoso, both from the 15th c. A short distance north you arrive at the delightful **Punta di San Vigilio★★**, a romantic spot set amongst cypresses and lemon trees. The 16th-c. Villa Guarienti (*not visitable*) was built from a design by Sanmicheli.

Continue to **Torri del Benaco**, in a lovely panoramic spot in the heart of the Riviera degli Olivi. Its 14th-c. castle

Lago di Garda at Malcesine

© Yasonya/iStock

stands by the tiny port at the entrance to the village. *Open 9.30-12.30 and 14.30-18 (9.30-13 and 16.30-19.30 in Summer), closed Mon., ℘ 045 62 96 111, www.museodelcastelloditorridelbenaco.it.*

**Malcesine★** is a typical little town at the foot of Monte Baldo that also boasts a **Scaliger Castle★**. Constructed in the 13th-14th c. by the lords of Verona, today it is home to a museum dedicated to the territory of Monte Baldo and Lake Garda (*Open 9.30-19.30, ℘ 045 65 70 333*). On the lakeshore there is the Venetian-style Palazzo dei Capitani del Lago. The **cable car** from the village takes you to the top of **Monte Baldo**, from where the views over the lake and the Brenta and Adamello massifs to the north are **spectacular★★★**. *Operative 8-18, closes at end of skiing season and end of summer, www.funiviedelbaldo.it.*

After another 10 or so km, you leave Veneto and enter Trentino (*see p. 194*).

## 2. EAST OF VERONA
### Soave and the Lessini Mountains
*Circular itinerary of approximately 100 km starting in Verona.*

The eastern section of Lessinia lies between the Illasi valley to the west and the border with the province of Vicenza to the east. The hills here have a great winemaking tradition, which centres on the Valpolicella and **Soave** designated areas. Soave wine is produced around the town of the same name, predominantly from Garganega grapes and also in the Classico and Superiore versions. The sun-dried version of the same grapes is used to make **Recioto di Soave DOCG**. In the area that straddles the Verona-Vicenza border, Durella grapes are used to produce **Lessini Durello** in sparkling, Superiore and dried-grape versions. On the Veronese side, the appellation lies in the upper Illasi valley, Tramigna valley and municipalities north of the Alpone valley; in Vicentina it falls in the Chiampo, Leogra and Agno valleys.

The **Arcole** appellation produces different wine types that are produced in a vaguely triangular area to the south of Soave that takes in a strip of land in the province of Vicenza.

*Leave Verona to the east along the SR 11 towards* **San Martino Buon Albergo** ♟.
**Caldiero** has been a spa town since the time of the Romans. The Terme di Giunone are fed by two sources and still feature baths built during the Roman age.

### Soave ♟
This walled and turreted little town is dominated by its castle in a beautiful landscape of hills and vineyards. The central Via Roma cuts the historic centre in two and is lined by the town's most important buildings: the Church of San Lorenzo (14th c.), Palazzo Cavalli (built in the 15th c. in Venetian Gothic), and Palazzo di Giustizia (14th c.). Continuing along the road you come to Palazzo Scaliger, now the Town Hall. The **castle** stands among gardens and vines and exhibits a collection of ancient weapons and armour. *Open 9-12 and 15-18.30 (9-12 and 14-16 in winter), closed working Mon., ℘ 045 76 80 036, www.castellodisoave.it.*

On the other side of the motorway and SR 11 stands **San Bonifacio**, where there is the Benedictine Abbey of San Pietro Apostolo, rebuilt in the 12th c.

*Head north.*

**Monteforte d'Alpone** ♟ is a winemaking town founded by the Romans, with the remains of a castle and a 15th-c. bishop's palace. Next drive along the Arpone valley and turn right to **Roncà** ♟, on the easternmost part of the Lessini mountains (the volcanic cone of Monte Calvarina). The village has several villas in different states of conservation. The nearby village of **Santa Margherita** is famous for its Durello wine.

Return to the road that runs along the Arpone torrent and pass through **Montecchia di Crosara** ♟, another wine town. At San Giovanni Ilarione, head left into the Illasi valley and to **Tregnano** to admire the remains of a medieval castle, a fine historic centre, several ancient churches and some 18th-c. villas.

Continue to **Illasi** ♟, where another medieval castle was contested between rival seigniories. The attractive 18th-c. Villa Carlotti was built in Palladian style and the lovely **Villa Perez Pompei-Sagramoso★** (15th-18th c.) is richly decorated with frescoes.

Before returning to Verona, make a small detour to **Mezzane di Sotto** ♟ in the Mezzane valley. This is another important wine-producing town with some admirable villas.

# 3. THE PROVINCE OF VICENZA

## Vicenza★★

This hard-working city, known for its textiles and goldsmithery, well deserves its tag "the city of gold and Palladio". Peaceful and refined, the Roman city *Vicetia* became a free commune in the 12th c. After various conflicts with nearby Padua and Verona, in the 15th c. it placed itself under the protection of Venice, under whose rule the city was enriched with a large number of palaces built by ambitious and generous benefactors.

The centre and its places of major interest are arranged around the busy, elegant Corso Palladio. It runs from Piazza Matteotti (where it is easy to park and just a stone's throw from the Teatro Olimpico and Palazzo Chiericati) to the Salvi Garden.

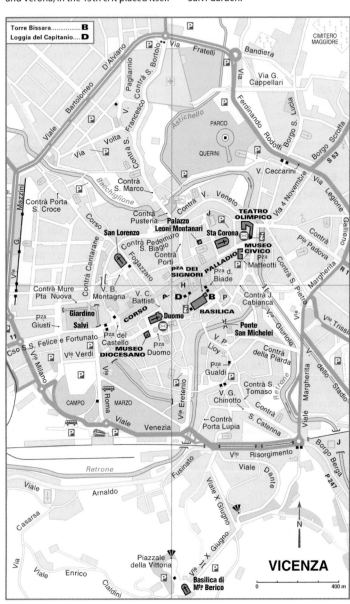

© Giuseppe Masci/iStock

*Teatro Olimpico, with its spectacular architectural scenery*

**Teatro Olimpico★★** – *Open 10-18 (9-17 in winter), closed Mon., ℘ 0444 96 43 80, www.teatrolimpicovicenza.it.* The visit begins with the Odeo Olimpico which Scamozzi designed to hold auditions. It is decorated with monochrome portraits of the gods of Olympus. Even in this first "antechamber" we see the motto of the Accademia Olimpica founded in 1555. It was taken from the words spoken by the Sibyl at Cumae to Aeneas: *HOC OPUS HIC LABOR* (All work requires hard labour), which is also found in the Antiodeo and theatre proper above the stage.

Palladio's model for this splendid wood and stucco theatre (1580) was ancient open-air theatres. It is considered his spiritual testament as the architect died shortly after its completion. It was opened in 1585 with a performance of Sophocles' *Oedipus the Tyrant*, of which the theatre has conserved the superb **perspective stage sets★★★** designed by Scamozzi to represent the seven streets of Thebes, which he depicted as an elegant Venetian city. The frontage of the stage has a double Corinthian order with three arches, while the corona is a false attic featuring scenes from the life of Hercules. The central figure among the illustrious individuals portrayed by the statues at the top of the tiers of seats is of course Palladio.

**Corso Andrea Palladio★** is the main street in Vicenza. Busy and elegant, it is lined by many palaces designed by Palladio and his pupils. At the start of the street is the Palladian Palazzo Chiericati, home to the **civic art gallery★**. *Piazza Matteotti. Open 9-17 (10-18 in*

## Andrea Palladio

The most outstanding buildings in Vicenza were principally designed by Andrea Palladio. Born in Padua in 1508, Palladio was the last great architect of the Renaissance to achieve, in a style of supreme harmony, a combination of the art of antiquity with the needs of modern life. Encouraged by the humanist Gian Giorgio Trissino, Palladio made several trips to Rome, thought deeply on the teachings of Vitruvius and in 1570 published the fruits of his research: the treatise *The Four Books of Architecture*, which made his architectural work known all over Europe.

Palladian style has two predominant characteristics: a rigorous plan based on simple, symmetrical forms, and a perfectly balanced façade that incorporates a porch and a pediment. Palladio worked a great deal for the wealthy members of Venetian society, designing and building elegant villas for them in the Venetian countryside. In these isolated buildings, the architect added to the orderliness of the plan and the nobility of the design by making a science of the placement of each building in its individual setting. He also raised them on high bases so that each villa that he built along the banks of the Brenta or on the slopes of the Monti Berici appeared like a temple.

Andrea Palladio died in Vicenza in 1580, but one of his pupils, **Vincenzo Scamozzi** (1552-1616), completed several unfinished works by the master and continued his style.

Summer), closed Mon., ✆ 0444 22 28 11), www.museicivicivicenza.it.

On the other side of the corso stands the Church of **Santa Corona★** built in the 13th c. to hold the Holy Thorn donated to the Bishop of Vicenza by St Louis, king of France. There are also two masterpieces: a **Baptism of Christ★★** by Giovanni Bellini (5th altar on the left) and an **Adoration of the Magi★★** (1573) by Veronese (3rd chapel on the right). Palladio was buried here before being transferred to the cemetery, and it was for this church that he designed the Valmarana Chapel.

At no. 147 Corso Palladio, Palazzo Da Schio (15th c. in Venetian Gothic) was once known as the Ca' d'Oro (House of Gold) as it was covered with frescoes with a gold ground.

**Piazza dei Signori★★** is built over the ancient Roman forum. As in Venice, there are two columns topped by the lion of St Mark and the Redeemer. One side of the square is occupied by the **Basilica Palladiana★★** (1549-1617) and the **Bissara Tower★** (12th c.). The basilica is one of the architect's greatest works, with the superimposed loggias remarkable for their vigour, proportions and purity. The large vaulted roof damaged by a bombing raid in World War II was rebuilt. The building was not originally religious in function but a meeting place for the VIPs of Vicenza. For information, ✆ 0444 22 28 55), www.museicivicivicenza.it.

Opposite, the 15th-c. Monte di Pietà, whose buildings stand on either side of the Baroque façade of the Church of San Vincenzo, is decorated with frescoes. To the left, in the corner of the Contrà del Monte, stands the **Loggia del Capitaniato★**, once the residence of the Venetian governor. It was begun in 1571 to a design by Palladio but remained unfinished. It has an order of composite capital columns and statues and stuccoes that celebrate the victory at the Battle of Lepanto.

At no. 98 Corso Palladio, **Palazzo Trissino** is one of Scamozzi's most successful works (1592).

From Corso Palladio take Corso Fogazzaro.

At no. 16 you see the stately **Palazzo Valmarana**, built by Palladio in 1566. **San Lorenzo** is a Franciscan church with a fine portal (1344). Inside there are fres-

coes by Mantegna and, in the left aisle, the lovely Lamentation of the Marys.

Return to Corso Palladio and turn left into Via Battisti. Constructed in the 14th-16th c., the **duomo** has a two-tone Gothic façade and a Renaissance apse. Inside you can admire a fine polyptych (1356) by Lorenzo Veneziano.

In Contrà San Gaetano Thiene, at the bottom of Corso Palladio, the east side of **Palazzo Thiene** is by Palladio, but the principal Renaissance façade dates from the late 15th c. (at no. 12 Contrà Porti). Opposite stands **Palazzo Porto-Barbaran**, another of Palladio's works.

The **Salvi Garden** is enclosed on two sides by canals in which charming loggias in Palladian style are reflected (16th-17th c.).

## The valleys north of Vicenza

### Gambellara and Breganze

Itinerary of 160 km from Vicenza to Bassano del Grappa.

A series of parallel valleys formed by the rivers Chiampo, Agno, Astico and Tesina stretches to the east of the Lessini mountains. This is the zone of designated areas **Gambellara DOC** (Classico, Spumante, Vin Santo), **Recioto di Gambellara DOCG** and **Breganze DOC**. This last produces several types of wine, amongst which Torcolato from the raisining of Vespaiolo grapes. The wines of appellation **Arcole** (shared with Verona) and **Vicenza** are also of interest.

Leave Vicenza west on the SR 11. After Tavernelle, a right turn takes you to Montecchio Maggiore. **Villa Cordellina-Lombardi★**, built in Palladian form in the mid-18th c., stands in a garden planted with lemon trees, oleanders and geraniums. The reception room is decorated with frescoes by Tiepolo. On either side the barchesse (porticoes typical of Venetan villas) contained the guesthouse and the stables (with original flooring and pink marble columns). Open Apr.-Oct. Tue.and Fri. 9-13, Wed., Thu., Sat.-Sun. 9-13 and 15-18, rest of the year by reservation. Closed Mon., ✆ 0444 90 82 14, www.provincia.vicenza.it/villa-cordellina-lombardi.

At **Montecchio** the remains of two castles that dominate the village are named after Romeo and Juliet and give a fine **view★**.

Continue to **Montebello Vicentino** 🍷, at the heart of the Lessini Durello DOC zone (*see p. 159*), where there are several villas and a castle. A few km to the east, on the border between Vicenza and Verona, stands the town of **Gambellara** 🍷, after which the appellation is named. From Montebello drive up the Chiampo valley, passing **Montorso Vicentino**, where the impressive 17th-c. Villa Da Porto Barbaran stands, and then **Arzignano**, the main town in the valley, protected by the characteristic castle and fortifications.

Head to **Chiampo**, famous for its red marble quarries, where there are several buildings from the past worthy of attention. Once past San Pietro Mussolino a detour right will take you to **Altissimo**, which stands (as its name suggests) high over the valley. Continuing east you leave the Chiampo valley and enter Val d'Agno.

It was at **Valdagno** 🍷 that the first Marzotto wool mill was set up. The Marzotto family were also responsible for the construction (1927-46) of the Città Sociale, a town built on the principles of the ideal 19th-c. worker city.

The **Montagna Spaccata**, a fissure 90 m long from which a small waterfall gushes, can be seen 3 km to the north-west.

Continue along the pretty road till you come to **Recoaro Terme**. For centuries this has been a renowned thermal spa as its gushing spring-water is low in mineral content.

Drive over the Xon Pass to the Pasubio state road. *Turn right.*

## Schio

With Valdagno, this industrial city was one of the capitals of Italian wool production. It is the home of the company Lanificio Rossi, later Lanerossi, which was bought up by the Marzotto group. One of the testaments to its industrial past is the majestic "Fabbrica alta" (1862) (*Via Pasubio*). The Neoclassical duomo dominates the town and offers a fine view over the countryside.

After Marano Vicentino you come to **Thiene**, a manufacturing town. Built in the 15th c. in the late Gothic style that was then fashionable in Venice, the lovely **Villa Da Porto-Colleoni** stands 3 km to the south. *For information and reservation, ℘ 329 85 41 962, www. castellodithiene.com.*

Once through **Breganze** 🍷, a celebrated winemaking town, take a left to **Lusiana** through a landscape of vineyards and chestnut trees.

The **Villa Godi Malinverni★**, built in 1542 to a design by Palladio, is situated 10 km south-west of Lusiana, in **Lonedo Lugo di Vicenza**. The interior has superb painted decorative work by various 16th-c. artists and exhibits a collection of 19th-c. Italian works. *Via Palladio 44. Mar., Apr., Oct. and Nov., Tue. 14-18, Sat. 9-14, Sun. and public hols. 14-18 ; May-Sept., Tue. 15-19, Sat. 9 -14, Sun. and public hols. 10-19, ℘ 0445 86 05 61, www.villagodi.com.*

*Old bridge in Bassano del Grappa with its mountainous background*

© Meinzahn/iStock

*Return to Breganze and then head for Marostica.*

## Marostica

A medieval walled town, Marostica is famous for its cherries and **Piazza Castello★**. A gigantic chessboard lies in the middle of the square on which the famous **Chess Game** is played in the second week of September each year, using people in 15th-c. costume as pieces. Facing onto the square is the lower castle, which contains the Town Hall and **Chess Costume Museum** (*Info and reservations, ℘ 0424 72 127 www. marosticascacchi.it*). The upper castle can be reached by car or on foot (*20 mins.*) following the walls. Good views are given over Vicenza and the river Brenta.

## Bassano del Grappa★ ⚐

Situated on the banks of the Brenta, the small, intimate Bassano del Grappa is famous for its bridge. The picturesque streets and portico-lined squares bustle with activity linked to the distillation of grappa, the cultivation of the town's excellent asparagus, and the production of pottery. The Loggia dei Podestà (15th c.) and Town Hall stand in **Piazza Libertà**, watched over by the omnipresent Venetian lion.

**Piazza Garibaldi**, dominated by the square Civic Tower (14th c.) is the setting for the Church of San Francesco (12th c.); notice an unusual 15th-c. *Annunciation* on the façade to the right of the porch in which the Child flies towards the Madonna. The convent next door to the church is the home of the **Civic Museum★** (*open Mon.-Sun. 10-19. Closed Tue. ℘ 0424 51 99 01, www.musei bassano.it*), where works by the Da Ponte family (local painters) can be seen. **Jacopo Bassano** (16th c.) was the family's most eminent member, whose popular realism was underpinned by an exceptional use of light and contrast.

**Ponte Vecchio (degli Alpini)** – This was once the site of a 12th-c. bridge. The attractive, flexible wooden bridge that stands here today was rebuilt by the Italian Alpine Corps in 1948 from a design by Palladio. The Poli Grappa Museum (*Via B. Gamba 6. Open 9-19.30, ℘ 0424 52 44 26, www.poligrappa.com*) and the long-established Nardini distillery stand on the east side of the bridge. The Alpine Corps Museum is on the west side.

Following the direction of the river towards the town, you will soon arrive at the **G. Roi Ceramics Museum** in the 18th-c. Palazzo Sturm. *Via Schiavonetti 40. Open Mon.-Sun. 9-19 (closed Tue., 1 Jan., Easter and 25 Dec. Open on holidays Tue.), ℘ 0424 51 99 40, www.museibassano.it.*

# South of Vicenza

## The Colli Berici

*Circular itinerary of 100 km starting and ending in Vicenza.*

The Berici hills form a continual alternation of plain and hills to the south of Vicenza. This area is the setting for some of Palladio's most beautiful villas and the zone of the **Colli Berici DOC**, known in particular for its Tocai Rosso.

## Villa Valmarana ai Nani★★

*2 km south on the road to Este, then first right. Stradella dei Nani 8. Open 7 Mar.-1 Nov. 10-18. (Nov.-Mar. by reservation), ℘ 0444 32 18 03, www.villavalmarana.com.* Your arrival at the villa (17th-18th c.) is observed carefully by dwarfs that seem to have climbed up on the wall to watch what is going on outside. The pride of the villa is the extraordinary cycle of **frescoes★★★** by Giovan Battista Tiepolo and his son Giandomenico. In the palace their theme is sacrifice and renunciation, as embodied by Iphigenia, Briseis, Orlando, Aeneas and Rinaldo. In the guesthouse, the frescoes of rustic scenes are particularly animated, for example, a depiction of a family eating polenta painted by Giandomenico. The portraits of peasants and bored ladies on holiday are psychologically acute. The carnival room is noted for the scene of the *New World*.

## La Rotonda - Villa Almerico Capra★★

*2 km south on the road to Este, then 2nd road on the right. Open mid-Mar.-mid-Nov. 10-12 and 15-18 (interior visits only Wed. and Sat.), closed Mon., ℘ 333 64 09 237, www.villalarotonda.it.* This is one of Palladio's most successful works, which merges geometric volumes (a cube and a sphere), nature and artistic creation. Crowned by a dome (for which Palladio drew on Roman models), it has four identical sides, a pronaos and Ionic columns. The building was completed by Scamozzi after 1580. Inside, the frescoes are by Alessandro Maganza (ceiling) and Louis Dorigny (walls).

## Basilica of Monte Berico★

*2 km south, take Viale Venezia and then Viale X Giugno.* Running alongside Viale X Giugno to the top of the hill is an 18th-c. portico with chapels. The Baroque basilica and dome stands on top of the hill. The church was built in the 15th c. on the spot where the Madonna appeared, though its appearance dates to the 17th-18th c. The impression of magnificence is softened by the intimate atmosphere inside. *The Pietà* by Bartolomeo Montagna (1500) is especially moving. The room on the lower floor holds the **The Supper of St Gregory the Great★★** by Veronese. The huge square offers a wide **view★★** over Vicenza, the Venetan plain and the Alps.

A road from the basilica leads south in a landscape of volcanic hills amongst which stand patrician villas occasionally transformed into farms.

Once past Longare, you arrive at **Costozza** ☙, an ancient village numbering several villas, amongst which the striking **Ville da Schio**, a set of three buildings at different levels on a terraced garden (17th-18th c.).

Continue to **Nanto**, passing through Castegnero along the **Tocai Rosso Route**.

After several km along the S 257, take a right turn to **Barbarano Vicentino**, a municipality with a long winemaking tradition situated on the south-east slopes of the Berici hills. There are various important buildings, including villas from the 17th-18th c.

*Return to the S 257.*

At the limit of the province, **Noventa Vicentina** is home to the magnificent **Villa Barbarigo**, the Town Hall that dates from 1590. Further west you come to **Poiana Maggiore**, where the lovely Villa Pojana is another 16th-c. Palladian work.

The last stop on the itinerary is **Lonigo**, a large farming village with lovely historic buildings, such as the 16th-c. Palazzo Pisani in Piazza Garibaldi, Villa Giovanelli, surrounded by a fine park, and above all **Villa Pisani**, designed by Scamozzi on the model of Palladio's Rotonda.

*Return to Vicenza on the SP 500.*

## 4. THE PROVINCE OF PADOVA

The province of Padova is known for its wines from Bagnoli, Corti Benedettine del Padovano, Riviera del Brenta, Merlara and the Euganean Hills, where a very special wine by the name **Fior d'Arancio** is produced from Moscato grapes.

Excellent results are gained in the **Colli Euganei** with international varieties like Merlot, Cabernet, Riesling, Pinot, Chardonnay and Sauvignon, as well as local grapes such as Garganega, Tocai Friulano, Pinello and Serprino (a variety of Prosecco). The designated area **Bagnoli** produces the wine Friularo from a very particular local grape called Raboso.

Piazza Prato della Valle, Padua

## The Caffè Pedrocchi

At the end of the 18th c. there were no fewer than 77 coffee-houses in Padua for a population of just 35,000 people. The Gran Caffè was opened in 1831 with a bar, billiards room and a business room. In 1837 the *piano nobile* and the Pedrocchino (the Neogothic building opposite) were opened. The coffee-house was kept open all day and all night, and even those who did not order anything were allowed to read the newspapers and receive a glass of water. And if it rained, umbrellas were provided to the patrons. In 1848 the coffee-house was a setting for revolutionary Risorgimento debates, and one wall is still marked with the hole of a bullet fired by an Austrian. Some of the great names of the past who frequented the Caffè Pedrocchi were Stendhal (who loved the *zabaione* there), Georges Sand, Teophile Gautier, Gabriele d'Annunzio, Eleonora Duse and Tommaso Marinetti. *Via VIII Febbraio 15. Piano nobile 9.30-12.30 and 15.30-18, closed Mon. and public hols.,* ☏ *049 87 81 231, www.caffepedrocchi.it*

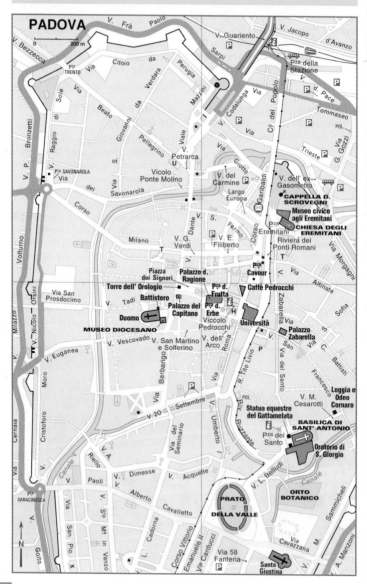

# Padua★★

Padua (the city, as opposed to Padova the province) offers much to the eye and mind. *"Padovani gran dottori"* (The Paduans are great scholars) goes a Venetan saying, and its university, founded in 1222, is the second oldest in Italy after Bologna. Its students have included Pico della Mirandola, Niccolò Copernico (Copernicus) and Torquato Tasso, while Galileo Galilei was a teacher. Biting irony and wit are important facets of the local character, as a glance at the posters of caricatures of recent graduates will confirm. Spending a little time in the city, perhaps seated at the historic Caffè Pedrocchi, is a stirring experience. Destroyed by the Lombards in the 7th c., Padua established itself as a free commune from the 11th to 13th c., a period in which many civic and religious buildings were erected. The city enjoyed its greatest economic and cultural splendour in the 14th c. under the enlightened seigniory of the Da Carrara family, and in 1405 it passed into the hands of the Serenissima, to which it remained faithful until the abolition of the republic's constitution by Napoleon in 1797.

Although **St Anthony** was originally from Lisbon, where he was born in 1195, the city of Padua, near where he died at the age of 36, remains linked to this Franciscan monk and prodigious worker of miracles. His name was invoked in the past to save the shipwrecked and to free prisoners. He is usually represented with a book in one hand and a lily in the other.

Padua is also an art city. Besides the great artists who worked there (Giotto and Donatello first and foremost), the city was the birthplace of **Palladio** (*see box on p. 161*) and **Andrea Mantegna** (1431-1506). Mantegna was a painter of powerful originality, a passionate student of anatomy and archaeology, and an innovator in perspectival representation.

**Piazza delle Erbe★** – the vegetable market in the Middle Ages, today it is still filled with stalls every day. Standing between this square and **Piazza della Frutta★** is the **Palazzo della Ragione★**, once a courthouse, distinguished for its loggias and vaulted roof. It was frescoed by Giotto but these were lost

in a fire in 1420. A **room★** on the 1st floor has a cycle of 15th-c. frescoes that draws on the astrological theme developed by Giotto. or information about your visits *Open 9-19 (9-18 in winter), closed Mon., ✆ 049 82 05 006.*

The huge **Piazza dei Signori** is lined by the Palazzo del Capitanio (14th-16th c.), built as a residence for the Venetian governor, the **Clock Tower★**, and the Renaissance Loggia del Consiglio or della Gran Guardia, where the city council used to meet.

Not far away, on the site of earlier churches, stands the **duomo**. Michelangelo was one of those who worked on its original design, but what you see today dates from the 16th-18th c.

Dating from the late 12th c., the **Baptistery** is a triumph of frescoes, the masterpiece of the Florentine Giusto de' Menabuoi.

Situated in Palazzo del Bò (named after an inn whose symbol was an ox skull, *bove*), the **University** was founded in 1222. It has a lovely 16th-c. court and Europe's first anatomy room, the Teatro Anatomico of 1594 (*for information on visits, ✆ 049 82 73 939*). The presence in the city of the university is very strong, and the improvised "performances" staged by students wearing their traditional pointed hats on graduation day are very amusing.

*Take Corso Garibaldi north.*

**Scrovegni Chapel★★★** – *Arena Gardens. Reservation is compulsory. It is possible to make an online reservation through the call-centre until the day before the visit if you pay by credit card (or a minimum of 3 days before if you want to pay by bank transfer). Tickets should be collected 1 hour before the scheduled time of visit. You are allowed to remain inside the chapel for a maximum of 15 minutes. Open 9-19, in the summer also in the evening, ✆ 049 20 10 020, www.cappelladegliscrovegni.it.* Around 1305-10, **Giotto** decorated the walls of the Scrovegni Chapel (built in 1303) with a cycle of 39 frescoes that tell the story of the life of Joachim, Anne, Mary and Jesus. In the lower order, the powerful figures in chiaroscuro on the left are the Vices, and those on the right the Virtues.

The *Universal Judgement* on the back wall concludes the work. Due to their exceptional unity of style, dramatic power, harmony of composition and intense religious sentiment, this pictorial cycle shows Giotto at the apex of his powers. See the **Madonna★** by Giovanni Pisano at the altar.

**Church degli Eremitani★★** – built in the 13th c. but heavily damaged in a bombing raid in 1944, the church was rebuilt in its original Romanesque style. Many of the frescoes were lost and only photographs remain. Note works by the Florentine Giusto de' Menabuoi (1370 ca.) and the Paduan painter Guariento (active 1338-70) in the Sanguinacci Chapel. But the artistic interest in the church is given by the **Ovetari Chapel**, where fragments remain of frescoes by **Mantegna**. The exceptional use of perspective and the precision in the archaeological details are clearly indicative of the artist's inventive power.

**Civic Museum (at the Eremitani)★** – *Piazza Eremitani 8. Open 9-19, closed working Mon., ℘ 049 82 04 551.* Set in the Convent degli Eremitani di Sant'Agostino, the Civic Museum includes an archaeological museum and the Museum of Medieval and Modern Art. The latter has superb **Venetan works★★** (15th-18th c.) by the region's greatest painters. *Take Via Zabarella and then Via del Santo.*

**Basilica del Santo★★** – *Open 6.20-18.45 (19.45 in Summer), ℘ 049 82 25 652, www.basilicadelsanto.org.* Dedicated to St Anthony, the basilica is an important place of pilgrimage. Built between 1232 and 1300 in a style in transition between Romanesque and Gothic, with its 8 Byzantine domes the basilica is reminiscent of St Mark's in Venice. There are several works of art inside: in the left aisle, the **Chapel of the Saint★★** is a Renaissance masterpiece containing the tomb of St Anthony and magnificent 16th-c. **high reliefs★★** by various artists on the walls. In the choir there is the famous **high altar★★** with bronzes by Donatello (1450). The 3rd chapel in the right aisle is decorated with **frescoes★** by the Veronese artist Altichiero da Zevio (14th c.). Outside, a fine **view★** of the building as a whole is given from the cloisters to the right of the basilica. In the square in front of the building, Donatello erected the splendid **equestrian statue of Gattamelata★★**, the first work of such size to be fused in bronze in Italy.

In the square you will also see the **Oratory of San Giorgio** (with frescoes by Altichiero) and the **School of St Anthony★** (with 16th-c. frescoes, 4 by Titian). *For information on visits ℘ 049 87 55 235, www.arciconfraternita santantonio.org.*

Close by, the **Prato della Valle** is a large oval square from the late 18th c. ordered by the Venetian procurator Andrea Memmo as a site for fairs. At the centre is the "Memmia Island", a grassy area with statues reflected in the canal. The Basilica of **Santa Giustina** is a 16th-c reconstruction of a 5th-c. building with domes similar to those in the Basilica of St Anthony. A fine **altarpiece★** by

Vineyards of the Euganean hills

© Fauxware/Shutterstock

Veronese can be seen at the back of the choir inside.

Founded in 1545, the **Botanic Garden** is one of the oldest in Europe. Filled with exotic flora, you can see the palm tree that inspired Goethe to write his considerations on the metamorphosis of plants. *Open Apr. -Sept. 9-19, Oct. 9-18, Nov.-Mar. 9-17, closed Mon., ℘ 049 82 73 939, www.ortobotanicopd.it.*

## Colli Euganei

*A circular itinerary of 140 km starting and ending in Padua.*

Separated from the Prealps and Monti Berici, the Euganean hills (max. height 600 m) form a pleasantly undulating region lined with orchards and vineyards to the south of Padua. It was appreciated by the Romans for its wine and many thermal waters. In Abano and Montegrotto, south of Padua, the 240 thermal pools, treatment centre and hotels offer a relaxing and comfortable stay. Since 1989 the zone has been administered by the **Euganean Hills Regional Park** based in Este (*Via Rana Cà Mori 8, ℘ 0429 63 29 11, www.parcocollieuganei.it*) and a **Euganean Hills Wine Route** has been established (*www.stradadelvinocolli euganei.it*).

At the foot of the hills, **Abano Terme★** is an elegant hydrotherapy station of Art Nouveau buildings. Its waters emerge from the ground at the temperature of 70-80 °C. The town's main street is Viale delle Terme.

The **Sanctuary of Monteortone** was built in the 15th c. on the site of a miraculous apparition 3 km to the west of the town. It contains some admirable works of art.

A short distance to the south of Abano is another important thermal station, **Montegrotto Terme**. In addition to its springs, the Roman *Mons Aegrotorum* (literally "mountain of the sick"), of which archaeological remains can be seen, offers an interesting park dedicated to butterflies, the Butterly Arc (*for information ℘ 049 89 10 189, www. micromegamondo.com*).

From **Torreglia** (*4.5 km west of Montegrotto*) a road takes you the 4 km to the **Hermitage of Monte Rua**. This was founded in the 14th c. and gives lovely views over the Euganean hills. Return to Torreglia and drive through Galzignano Terme to **Villa Barbarigo**, with its monumental Baroque entrance and fountains, pools, woods, maze and ornamental gardens.

It was at **Arquà Petrarca★ ♟**, a quiet, medieval hill-town, that Francesco Petrarca (Petrarch) spent the last four years of his life (d. 1374). The poet's **house★** has 16th-c. frescoes and an interesting lacunar ceiling. It contains personal effects and handwritten tributes by such illustrious visitors as Carducci and Lord Byron. *Via Valleselle 4. Open 9-12.30 and 14.30-17.30 (Mar.-Oct. 9-12.30 and 15-19), closed Mon., ℘ 0429 71 82 94, www.arquapetrarca.com.*
Erected in 1380, a pink marble monument to Petrarch stands in the church square.

## Monselice★ ♟

The town's Latin name, *Mons Silicis* ("mountain of flintstone") is indicative of the quarrying that took place there in the Roman period. Much of the town's walls and castle (13th-14th c.) have survived. Via del Santuario runs from Piazza Mazzini to the **castle** (*for information, ℘ 0429 72 931, www.castellodimonselice. it*), to the Villa Nani-Mocenigo (with its curious statues of dwarves), the Romanesque duomo and the **Sanctuary of the Seven Churches**. The sanctuary is a 16th-c. set of 6 chapels designed by Vincenzo Scamozzi and the Church of San Giorgio. At the end of the avenue stands Villa Balbi, another work by Scamozzi. It has an Italian garden and a fine **panorama★** is given from its upper terrace.

## Este

Set beside the last rises of the Euganean hills, Este was the town of origin of the famous d'Este family. The town is walled on the north side with impressive **turreted bastions★** that belonged to the castle built by the Carrara family in 1340. The **Atestino National Museum★** in the 16th-c. Palazzo Mocenigo has a collection of archaeological objects and finds dating from between the Paleolithic period and the Roman era. *Via Negri 9/c. Open 8.30-19.30, ℘ 0429 20 85, www.atestino.beniculturali.it.*

The elliptical **duomo** contains a large canvas by Tiepolo (1759). The town is the site of the offices of the Euganean Hills Regional Park.

*Follow the S 10 west.*

## Montagnana★

Montagnana is completely encircled by huge 14th-c. **walls★★**, with 24 polygonal towers and 4 gates. Just outside of the walls stands Palazzo Pisani, built in the mid-16th c. from a design by Andrea Palladio. Close to Porta Padova is San Zeno Castle, constructed in the 13th c. by Ezzelino da Romano and now the home of the civic museum.

The **duomo** (15th c.) stands in the porticoed Piazza Vittorio Emanuele. It has a portal attributed to Sansovino, a *Transfiguration* by Veronese on the high altar, frescoes and 16th-c. wooden stalls. Close to the walls is the Church of **San Francesco**, with its lovely Gothic bell tower.

Return to Este and turn left. Pass through **Baone** ⚑, **Valle San Giorgio**, where there is a Museum of the Euganean Hills in Villa Beatrice (☎ 049 89 10 189), **Cinto Euganeo** ⚑, where an interesting paleontological museum of the Euganean Hills can be visited in the former furnace of Cava Bomba *(Via Bomba 48, ☎ 049 89 10 189)*, **Vo**, **Teòlo**, and then the Abbey of Praglia.

## Abbey of Praglia★

*Guided visits Mon.-Fri. 10-12, closed Mon. and public hols., ☎ 049 99 99 452, www.praglia.it.* Stately and unadorned, the abbey appears peaceful and isolated. Of medieval origin (11th-12th c), it was rebuilt in the 16th c. and is now the home of an active community of Benedictine monks. The abbey has **four cloisters**: rustic, botanic (where officinal plants were grown but which is now an Italian-style garden), the hanging cloister (which stands on columns and collects the rainwater) and the double cloister (with two orders of arcades). Features of the abbey are a chapterhouse, the refectory (with 16th-c. canvases by Zelotti and 18th-c. wooden furnishings), the beautiful loggetta (which looks over the countryside and the seclusion zone), the library and the church designed by Tullio Lombardo (1490, with dome frescoed by Zelotti). The wooden choir is 16th-c.

# 5. THE PROVINCE OF TREVISO

## Treviso★

Set inside its ancient walls, Treviso has a history that features water, mills, art and… chicory! With hidden corners reminiscent of Venice, it is a delightful place to walk, whether along the canals in the Pescheria district or in the shopping area of Via Calmaggiore between Piazza dei Signori and the Duomo. Treviso was where the Benetton company was founded.

**Piazza dei Signori★** lies at the centre of the old city and is lined by various important buildings: the Palazzo del Podestà, with the high municipal tower, the **Palazzo dei Trecento★** (1207) and the Renaissance Palazzo Pretorio. The ancient **Monte di Pietà** stands in the piazza of the same name, and the two churches, **Santa Lucia** and **San Vito** are in Piazza San Vito. The first has very fine 14th-c. **frescoes★** by Tommaso da Modena.

Behind Piazza del Monte di Pietà lies the **Peschiera** district. Bridges over the Cagnàn river, the remains of ancient water mills and the traditional fish market all feature in this enchanting area. There is also the **Santa Caterina Civic Museum★** *(Piazzetta Mario Botter 1, open Tue.-Fri. 9-18, Sat.-Sun. 10-19, ☎ 0422 65 84 42, www.museicivicitreviso.it)* in the Church of Santa Caterina dei Servi di Maria and its annexed convent. Rebuilt after World War II, the church has a series of splendid **frescoes★** detached from various local churches.

On this side of the Cagnàn visit the Romanesque-Gothic Church of **San Francesco** to admire its wooden ceiling, the gravestone of Petrarch's daughter, the tomb of a son of Dante, and frescoes by Tommaso da Modena *(1st chapel on the left of the choir)*.

*Return to Piazza dei Signori.* Follow the porticoes in Via Calmaggiore to the Duomo. Dating from the 15th c., it is covered by 7 domes. The façade is Neoclassical but the crypt is part of the original Romanesque church. At the far end of the right aisle there are frescoes by Pordenone and an *Annunciation* by Titian in the Chapel of the Annunziata.

*Treviso canals*

The **Baptistery** (11th-12th c.) stands to the left of the duomo.

*From Piazza Duomo take Via Risorgimento.*

**San Nicolò★** is an impressive Gothic church. Inside there are frescoes by Tommaso da Modena on massive pillars and various works by Andrea Vicentino (1544-1619) and Palma il Giovane (1548-1628). In the right aisle the fresco of *St Christopher* by Antonio da Treviso (1410) is particularly striking. The Monigo Chapel, to the right of the choir, has portraits by Lorenzo Lotto and a *Christ Risen* by Sebastiano del Piombo. The altarpiece in the high chapel was completed by Savoldo in the 16th c. The funeral monument of the Roman senator Agostino Onigo, an expression of Renaissance taste, stands by the left wall.

In the adjacent **seminary**, the **Chapterhouse** features a cycle of paintings of 40 illustrious Dominicans by Tommaso da Modena (14th-c.). Note the one with a magnifying glass in his hand: this is one of the earliest representations of such a reading tool.

## Piave

*Circular itinerary of 80 km starting and ending in Treviso.*

On the old bed of the river Piave close to the Friuli border, **Piave DOC** wines are produced in various municipalities in the provinces of Venice and Treviso. These are mostly obtained from international varieties like Cabernet, Pinot, Chardonnay and Merlot, though there are also local grapes like Verduzzo and Raboso. The soil in this area is very particular: sandy, stony, clayey and marly in differing quantities, giving the wines unique characteristics. Starting in the eastern Dolomites, the river Piave flows for 220 km to its outlet just behind Venice. A historic natural border, the river was strategically important during World War I, when it was made the Italian line of defence and dreadful trench warfare took place there for a year.

*Leave Treviso to the north and then turn right towards Maserada sul Piave. Once through the town you come to the river.* This zone is called **Grave del Piave** due to the presence of surface pebbles. After the 1832 flood, a large river island called **Grave di Papadopoli** was formed here that divides the river in two. The **Piave** appellation begins on the other side of the river.

Drive to **Vazzola**, an important winemaking centre with beautiful 18th-c. palaces, and then to **Codognè**, where the imposing 18th-c. Villa Toderini has included Ugo Foscolo among its visitors.

*Return to the S 15 and head for Oderzo.*

**Oderzo** ♟ is a lovely village with ancient porticoed buildings and elegant Renaissance residences decorated with frescoed façades. The **duomo** in Piazza Vittorio Veneto was built in a transitional style between Gothic and Renaissance, and the interior is adorned with fine frescoes and paintings. The bell tower was constructed over one of the towers in the medieval walls.

Oderzo is ringed by zones that specialise in viticulture, such as **Ormelle** 🍷, **San Polo di Piave** 🍷 (site of the Neo-Gothic Villa Papadopoli and a splendid park), **Tezze di Piave** 🍷 and, to the south, **Ponte di Piave** and **Salgareda** 🍷. Once past Salgareda, the river flows more regularly, partly due to the building up of the banks and creation of artificial beds.

## The Prosecco zone

*Itinerary of 60 km from Vittorio Veneto to Valdobbiadene.*

The zone is known for the Prosecco variety, which is used to make **Prosecco di Conegliano Valdobbiadene**, the jewel in the crown of which is the **Superiore di Cartizze**. This is produced in limited quantities in the area of the same name and from cru in particular geo-climatic conditions. This wine has been known since the days of the Romans (2nd c. BC): it can be sparkling or semi-sparkling and is made with second fermentation in pressurised vats. It can be vinified in Brut, Extra Dry and Dry versions, in which Brut is the driest, Extra Dry has an intermediate sugar residue, and Dry the most sugar. It is straw-coloured and has a light, fruity bouquet and leaves a citrussy taste in the mouth.

In the environs of Conegliano there is also the **Colli di Conegliano** DOCG zone, where two rare and sought after wines are produced: **Torchiato di Fregona** (from Prosecco, Verdiso and Boschera grapes) and **Refrontolo Passito** (from Marzemino grapes).

### Vittorio Veneto★ 🍷

Named as a tribute to the first king of Italy, Vittorio Emanuele II, to mark the Veneto's annexation to the Kingdom of Italy in 1866, the place name also evokes the great victory won during World War I. It was here, from 24-31 October 1918, that the decisive battle was fought that brought Italy final victory over Austria. The city is long and narrow and divided into two distinct parts: **Serravalle** in the north, and **Cèneda** in the south following the union of the two villages in 1866. The district of Serravalle has retained its ancient layout. The Ospedale della Scuola is a porticoed building from the 14th c. that incorporates the Oratory of San Lorenzo and an interesting 15th-c. cycle of frescoes (*Sat.-Sun. 10-12 and 15-18*

or by reservation, 📞 *0438 55 42 17*). Via Martiri della Libertà is lined by ancient palaces and porticoes and runs through the district to the Loggia Serravallese, a fine construction from the late 15th c. The Duomo has an altarpiece by Titian.

Outside the city centre, the Church of San Giovanni (*reached from Via Roma, then Via Mazzini*) has interesting frescoes attributed to Jacobello del Fiore and Gentile da Fabriano (15th c.).

In **Cèneda** the **Battle Museum** (*open Tue.-Fri. 9.30-12.30, Sat.-Sun. 10-13 and 15-18, closed Mon., 📞 0438 57 695, www. museobattaglia.it*) displays its moving collections in the 16th c. Loggia del Sansovino (also known as the Loggia Cenedese). The exhibition is respectful of the sad mood conjured up by the 1915-18 war, which is recounted through photographs, private letters, period magazines, uniforms, books, bureaucratic documents and equipment.

The medieval San Martino Castle stands in the upper section of the district, and is now the palace of the bishop.

*From Vittorio Veneto head south on the S 51.*

### Conegliano 🍷

Set among hills lined with orchards and vineyards, Conegliano lies at the junction of the **Prosecco Route** itineraries. It is the hometown of the painter Cima da Conegliano (1459-1518), a disciple of Giovanni Bellini and talented colourist who placed his figures against landscapes idealised by a crystalline light. The serenity of the hills, the many works of art, and the taste for good living – appreciable in nature as well as in art – make Conegliano a pleasant place to visit.

The portico-lined Via XX Settembre is lined with ancient palaces and leads to the duomo and its tower. Inside the **duomo** is a **Sacra Conversazione★** painted by Cima. The building façade that hides the entrance to the duomo belongs to the Scuola dei Battuti and is adorned with biblical frescoes in the upper section. A room inside is decorated with **frescoes★** by Francesco da Milano (16th c.) with stories from the Old and New Testaments. *For information on visits* 📞 *0438 22 606.*

The **Rocca di Castelvecchio** is a park in the upper part of the city that offers fine

**views★** over the city and its surroundings and where there is a museum (picture gallery, lapidarium and an archaeological section). *Piazzale San Leonardo 8. Closed Mon., for information on opening hours ✆ 0438 22 871.*

At the gates of the town in the direction of Treviso, the **Enological School of Conegliano** stands at the start of the **Wine Route**. Founded as the Royal School of Viticulture in 1876, it is a very active institution. It has about 1000 students who study the six-year Enology course after secondary school.

Wine tastings and purchases can be made in the cellar. *Via XXVIII Aprile 20, ✆ 0438 61 421, www.isisscerletti conegliano.gov.it.*

Leaving Conegliano north-west on the S 635 brings you to a true winemaking zone set in rolling hills. In **San Pietro di Feletto** the ancient parish Church of San Pietro has frescoes from the 12th-15th c. The pretty road then takes you to Valdobbiadene through **Refrontolo**, **Solighetto** and **Soligo**. Interesting sights in this last town are the 18th-c. Villa De Toffoli and the Church of St. Maria Nuova with 14th-c. frescoes. Continue on the route through **Farra di Soligo**, **Guia** and **Guietta**.

The home of the Prosecco DOC zone, **Valdobbiadene** 🍷 lies in a green yet hilly valley. The parish church was founded in the 14th c. but remodelled in Neoclassical forms. Inside there are works by the Venetan school.From here a lovely road runs for 11 km to **Pianezza**, a summer and winter holiday resort.

Another road from San Pietro di Feletto will take you to Valdobbiadene passing through **Revine** (6 km north-west of Vittorio Veneto), then alongside the Revine lakes, through **Cison di Valmarino** 🍷, Valmareno (where there is the ancient Brandolini Castle), and **Follina**. Follina was the seat of a community of Cistercians to whom the Church of Santa Maria and its lovely cloister belonged.

## The Asolani hills

*Itinerary of 36 km from Valdobbiadene to Maser.*

The Asolani hills are an isolated group that ring Asolo to the north-west. The highest point is less than 500 m. Inhab-ited since ancient times, the villages on the hills have often retained their medieval fortifications.

From Valdobbiadene cross the river Piave at San Vito, turn left and take the S 348 to Pederoba, from where a panoramic road will take you to Asolo.

Pass through **Possagno**, home of the Neoclassical sculptor Antonio Canova, whose house and gallery of plaster casts can be visited. *Via Canova 74. Open Tue.-Sat. 9.30-18, Sun. 9.30-19, closed Mon., ✆ 0423 54 43 23, www.museocanova. it.* The **Canovian Temple**, which was designed by the master, stands on a rise. It contains his tomb and his last sculpture, a **Deposition★**, as well as works by Palma il Giovane and Luca Giordano. *For information ✆ 0423 54 43 23, www. museocanova.it.*
*Continue to the left turn for Paderno del Grappa and Pagnano.*

## Asolo★

Overlooked by the **Castle** founded in very ancient times, the pretty town of Asolo was a seigniory of Caterina Cornaro, who received it in exchange for ceding Cyprus to the Republic of Venice. Famous visitors to the town's frescoed palaces, fountains and villas have been the English poet Robert Browning, who stayed there several times and made it a fashionable destination among the English, and the actress Eleonora Duse, who is buried in the cemetery of Santa Anna. Several of the town's most important monuments stand around **Piazza Maggiore**: the duomo, with paintings by Lorenzo Lotto and Jacopo Bassano, and the 15th-c. Loggia del Capitano, now the home of the civic museum. Take Via Cornaro to reach the ruins of the Queen's Castle, which was the seat of the Venetian podestà and partly demolished in the 19th c. Browning's residence, Villa Beach, stands in the garden.

The busy **Via Browning**, which runs out of Piazza Maggiore, is lined with shops and workshops. Turning left into Via Marconi takes you to the Foresto Vecchio, a romantic pedestrian street that passes the home of the composer Francesco Malipiero and leads to **Casella** (2 km), a village where the lovely 17th-c. Baroque Villa Rinaldi stands on the road to Maser. *Continue to Maser.*

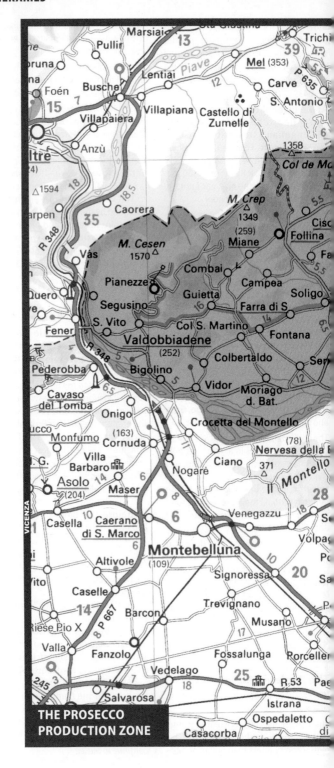

THE PROSECCO
PRODUCTION ZONE

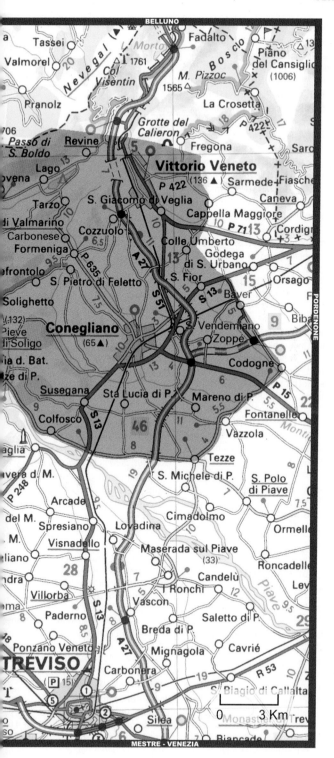

### Villa Barbaro a Maser★★★ ♜

*Via Cornuda. Open Apr.-Oct. Tue.-Sun. 10-18, public hols. 11-18, Nov.-Mar., Sat., Sun. and public hols. 11-17, ℘ 0423 92 30 04, www.villadimaser.it.* This famous villa was built in 1560 by Palladio for Daniele Barbaro (Patriarch of Aquileia) and his brother Marcantonio (ambassador of the Republic of Venice). The interior was decorated in 1566-68 with a notable cycle of **frescoes★★★** by **Veronese**, who made use of all his skills in perspective, foreshortening and false relief, which he combined with colourism and a sense of movement. The stuccoes are by Alessandro Vittoria, a pupil of Sansovino.

Close by is the **Tempietto**, a graceful round chapel topped by a dome, also designed by Palladio.

The cellar founded in 1850 stands next to the villa (*see the Addresses*).

## Montello

*"Monticellus"* is a series of flat hills whose geological nature has prompted the formation of several karstic phenomena. In the past its woodlands supplied the Venetian dockyards. During World War I Montello acted as a hinge between the Piave and Grappa fronts. Lying at the foot of Montello, **Montebelluna** ♜ specialises in the production of mountain boots, a product to which it has dedicated a museum in the 16th-c. Villa Binetti-Zuccareda.

From Montebelluna, pass alongside Montello on the S 248 through **Venegazzu**, **Giavera del Montello** and **Nervesa della Battaglia**.

## 6. LISON PRAMAGGIORE

### From Portogruaro to Annone Veneto

*Itinerary of 25 km from Portogruaro to Annone Veneto.*

The production zone in the Lison Pramaggiore designated area covers many of the municipalities of eastern Veneto and stretches as far as Friuli. The vineyards lie between the two rivers Livenza and Tagliamento in the provinces of Treviso, Venezia and Pordenone. They produce interesting whites, reds, sweet and sparkling wines from international varieties, but also from local grapes like **Verduzzo**. The appellation produces 14 single-variety wines and 4 other types. The DOC has won itself renown for its specialisation in organic cultivation. With 400 hectares of organic vineyards it is one of the largest such production areas in Italy.

### Portogruaro★

Portogruaro lies at the centre of the appellation. It is a river port that grew up from the 11th c. by trading on the river Lemene. Two beautiful porticoed streets run parallel to the river, both lined by palaces built in Venetian style that date from the Middle Ages and Renaissance (14th-16th c.). The most commercial street, **Corso Martiri della Libertà★★**, runs close to the 19th-c. duomo and its leaning Romanesque bell tower. It is also the site of the **Municipal Hall★** built with Ghibelline merlons in late Gothic style (14th c.). Behind the palace there are two restored watermills and a small **Oratory della Pescheria** (17th c.) with a wharf. At 26 Via del Seminario, the other main street, you can visit the **Concordiese National Museum** where there are collections of Roman objects (a small bronze of Diana the Huntress) and early Christian finds from Concordia Sagittaria (*3 km south*), a Roman colony founded in 40 BC. *Via del Seminario 26. Open 8.30-19.30, ℘ 042 17 26 74, www. polomusealeveneto.beniculturali.it.*

Proceeding north to **Sesto al Règhena** (formerly in Friuli), you reach the Benedictine Abbey of **Santa Maria in Sylvis★**. It was founded in the 7th c. and the basilica has frescoes from the 11th-15th c.

Head west through the most important winemaking villages in the zone, such as Pramaggiore and **Annone Veneto** ♜. **Pramaggiore** ♜ used to supply the Venetian nobility with wine, which is why the winged lion features in the logo of the Lison Pramaggiore consortium of vintners. For more than 50 years the small town has hosted the National Wine Fair and the **Regional Wine Cellar of Veneto** (*see the Addresses*).

In **Belfiore** along the banks of the river Loncon, the Old Mill is the setting for an ethnographic museum dedicated to bread and wine. *Via Belfiore 38. For information or reservation, ℘ 0421 20 03 17.*

# Addresses

## Tourist information

**Padua Tourist Office** – Vicolo Pedrocchi, Padova, ✆ 049 52 07 415, www.turismopadova.it

**Treviso Tourist Office** – Via Fiumicelli 30, Treviso, ✆ 0422 54 76 32, www.visittreviso.it

**Verona Tourist Office** – Via degli Alpini 9, Verona, ✆ 045 80 68 680, www.turismoverona.eu

**Vicenza Tourist Office** – Piazza Matteotti 12, Vicenza, ✆ 0444 32 08 54, www.vicenzae.org

## Transport

### LAKE GARDA

Full lake tour from Desenzano, Peschiera and Riva del Garda with option of lunch aboard. Boat trips to Sirmione, Gardone, Garda, Salò and Limone. Car ferries from Maderno to Torri and vice versa and from Limone to Malcesine and vice versa. One-day tickets valid on all boats available. Information: ✆ 800 55 18 01 or 030 91 49 511, www.navigazionelaghi.it

## Regional wine cellars

**Veneto Regional Wine Cellar** – Palazzo Mostra Nazionale Vini, Via Cavalieri di Vittorio Veneto 13, Pramaggiore (VE), ✆ 0421 79 90 36, www.mostranazionalevini.com

## The wineries

*The addresses are listed in alphabetical order by location.*

### VALPOLICELLA AND BARDOLINO

**F.lli Zeni** – *Via Costabella 9 - **Bardolino** (VR) - ✆ 045 72 10 022 - www.zeni.it - info@ zeni.it - Winery tours and tastings by reservation.* The winery's history commenced in 1800, when Bartolomeo Zeni, a carter and amateur painter, transported local products (fish, olive oil and wine) to the various towns on the shores of Lake Garda and to Lombardy. Under his son Gaetano and his grandsons Faustino and Ernesto, wine became the focus of the company, which started to cultivate its own vineyards. Today Fausto, Elena and Federica maintain the philosophy of their predecessors with the same enthusiasm. The estate is home to a wine museum dedicated to the history of winegrowing in the Verona area. Hectares under vine: 25.

**Wines**: Amarone della Valpolicella, Bardolino, Bianco di Custoza, Lugana, Soave. Other products: olive oil, vinegar and grappa.

**Vigneti Villabella** – *Loc. Cà Nova 2 - Fraz. Calmasino - **Bardolino** (VR) - ✆ 045 72 36 448 - www.vignetivillabella.com - info@ vignetivillabella.com - Winery tours by reservation.* Founded in 1971 by Walter Delibori and Giorgio Cristoforetti, the winery still belongs to the two families, which manage it personally. It is situated in one of the finest winegrowing areas of the Bardolino Classico zone, due to the beneficial influence of Lake Garda. It is thus no surprise that the estate is one of the most representative producers of Bardolino. It also makes the classic wines of the Verona area (Amarone, Valpolicella, Soave and Lugana) and wines in a more modern style from international grape varieties. A few kilometres from the winery, the old town of Cordevigo is the home of the 18th-c. villa that is now the company headquarters. It stages wine tastings, conventions and cookery courses. A recent rinovation has converted the villa in a luxurious Wine Relais. Hectares under vine: 100.

**Wines**: Amarone della Valpolicella Classico, Bardolino Chiaretto Classico, Bardolino Classico Morlongo, Lugana, Valpolicella

© Bornholm/Shutterstock

# ADDRESSES

Classico, Montemazzano. Other products: grappa and olive oil.

**Cesari** – *Loc. Sorsei 3* - **Cavaion Veronese** *(VR)* - ☎ *045 62 60 928 - www.cesariverona. it - info@cesariverona.it - Winery tours by reservation.* Gerardo Cesari founded the winery in 1936 and his successors have continued the business with the same passion and perseverance. Over the years the classic Amarone, Valpolicella, Bardolino and Soave wines have been joined by others from international varieties, such as Pinot Grigio, Chardonnay, Merlot and Cabernet. Hectares under vine: 109.
**Wines**: Amarone della Valpolicella Bosan, Amarone della Valpolicella Classico Il Bosco, Lugana Cento Filari, Valpolicella Superiore Ripasso Bosan, Valpolicella Superiore Ripasso Mara.

⌂ **Le Fraghe** – *Loc. Colombare 3* - **Cavaion Veronese** *(VR)* - ☎ *045 72 36 832 - www.fraghe.it - info@fraghe.it - Winery tours by reservation.* The driving force behind the business is Matilde Poggi (b. 1962), the third of 6 children. The first vintage was 1984; prior to that the grapes were harvested and distributed to other wineries for vinification. Accomodation available in the estate guest farm (*2 apts., min. stay 2 nights*). Hectares under vine: 28.
**Wines**: Bardolino, Bardolino Chiaretto, Camporengo Garganega, Chelidon Rondinella, Quaiare Cabernet. Other products: grappa.

**Allegrini** – *Villa della Torre - Via della Torre 25* - **Fumane** *(VR)* - ☎ *045 68 32 070 - www.allegrini.it - ospitalita@allegrini.it - Winery tours and tastings by reservation.* The Allegrini family have inhabited this corner of land for 5 centuries, growing vines and making wine from the grapes. Giovanni was the person who made the greatest contribution to the qualitative shift of the winery, which commenced in the 1960s and 1970s. Today it is headed by his three children, Walter, Franco and Marilisa. Hectares under vine: 100.
**Wines**: Amarone della Valpolicella, La Poja, La Grola, Palazzo della Torre, Valpolicella. Other products: olive oil, vinegar and grappa.

⌂ **Masi** – *Via Monteleone 26* - **Gargagnago di Valpolicella** *(VR)* - ☎ *045 68 32 532 - www.masi.it - wine. experience@masi.it - At Masi Tenuta Canova (Via Delaini 1, Loc. Sacro Cuor, Lazise) winery tours by reservation, canova@masi.it or 045 75 80 239 and wine shop open 10.30-22 (Sun. 10.30-16).* Masi's vineyards are located exclusively on the finest winegrowing hills of the area, explaining why its wines are so renowned, particularly its Amarone and Recioto della Valpolicella. The winery plays an active role in the cultural field and in 1981 it founded the Masi Award, based on an idea by Verona writer Cesare Marchi, which is presented to illustrious figures in literature, art, science, show business and economics who have given prominence to Veneto culture and everything that gravitates around wine. Accommodation at the Serego Alighieri guesthouse (*www. seregoalighieri.it, 8 apts.*), an old estate purchased in 1353 by Dante Alighieri's eldest son. Twenty generations later, it still belongs to the Serego Alighieri family. Hectares under vine: 70.
**Wines**: Amarone della Valpolicella Classico Costasera, Soave Classico Levarìe, Bardolino Classico Frescaripa, Recioto Angelorum, Valpolicella Classico Bonacosta. Other products: grappa, olive oil, balsamic dressing, rice, honey, preserves.

**Bertani** – *Via Asiago 1* - **Grezzana** *(VR)* - ☎ *045 86 58 444 - www.bertani.net - bertani@bertani.net - Winery tours and tastings by reservation, ☎ 045 86 58 424 or ospitalita@bertani.net.* The winery was founded in 1857 by the Bertani brothers and is one of the most renowned Valpolicella wine producers. Painstaking attention to the typicity of native grape varieties, valorisation of the *terroir* and the regular modernisation of the production plant are among the winery's distinctive features. The old winery is housed in the prestigious setting of Villa Novare, an evocative complex built in the first half of the 18th c. Hectares under vine: 200.
**Wines**: Due Uve, Soave Sereole, Valpolicella Valpantena, Secco Vintage, Valpolicella Superiore Villa Novare Ognisanti, Amarone Classico Valpolicella. Other products: olive oil.

**Giuseppe Campagnola** – *Via Agnella 9 - Fraz. Valgatara* - **Marano di Valpolicella** *(VR)* - ☎ *045 77 03 900 - www.campagnola. com - campagnola@campagnola.com - Winery tours by reservation, hospitality@ campagnola.com.* The Campagnola family have been running the estate founded by Carlo in 1886 for 4 generations. Today Luigi Campagnola works actively with over 50 other vintners who own the finest vineyards in the municipality of Marano di Valpolicella. Hectares under vine: 80.
**Wines**: Valpolicella Classico Superiore Ripasso, Valpolicella Classico "Le Bine", Valpolicella Classico Superiore Caterina Zardini, Amarone Classico Caterina Zardini, Amarone Classico Giuseppe Campagnola, Recioto Casotto del Merlo.

**Azienda Agricola Viviani** – *Via Mazzano 8* - **Negrar** *(VR)* - ☎ *045 75 00 286 - www.cantinaviviani.com - viviani@ cantinaviviani.com - Winery tours by* reservation. The Viviani family have been engaged in protecting the environment for many years and manages their vineyards with techniques that allow the vines to achieve the ideal balance for the various grape varieties. Work in the cellar is inspired by the same philosophy and is aimed at respecting the grapes and the regional tradition. Hectares under vine: 14.

**Wines**: Valpolicella Classico, Valpolicella Classico Superiore Ripasso, Valpolicella Classico Superiore "Campo Morar", Amarone della Valpolicella Classico "Della Casa dei Bepi", Recioto della Valpolicella Classico.

**Quintarelli** – *Via Cerè 1 -* **Negrar** *(VR) - ℘ 045 75 00 016 - vini@giuseppe quintarelli.it - Winery tours by reservation.* Quintarelli has been growing vines for around 100 years and its wines are among the finest expressions of the terroir. The secret of this success lies in the estate's ability to respect tradition while remaining in touch with the times and following the rhythms of nature. This yields extraordinarily balanced wines. Hectares under vine: 12.

**Wines**: Primofiore IGT, Valpolicella Classico Superiore, Amarone Classico, Recioto Classico, Alzero Cabernet IGT, Bianco Secco IGT. Other products: olive oil.

**Roberto Mazzi** – *Via Crosetta 8, Fraz. San Peretto -* **Negrar** *(VR) - ℘ 045 75 02 072 - www.robertomazzi.com - info@roberto mazzi.it - Winery tours by reservation.* The estate has been owned by the Mazzi family since the early 20th c. and its wine has been bottled under the name Sanperetto, after the vineyard, since the 1960s. Wine production is now flanked by the "Antica Corte al Molino" relais and guest farm that offers accommodation and

meals (*2 rooms and 2 apts., from €85*). The estate also comprises a 16th-c. water mill. Hectares under vine: 7.

**Wines**: Valpolicella Classico Superiore "Sanperetto", Valpolicella Classico, Valpolicella Classico Superiore "Poiega", Amarone della Valpolicella "Punta di Villa", Amarone della Valpolicella "Castel", Recioto della Valpolicella "Le Calcarole". Other products: grappa and olive oil.

**Villa Spinosa** – *Via Jago dall'Ora 14-* **Negrar** *(VR) - ℘ 045 75 00 093 - www. villaspinosa.it - info@villaspinosa@.it - Winery and vineyards tours by reservation.* Villa Spinosa is a modern winery housed in a prestigious building that has been sensitively restored to respect the old complex. Surrounded by an elegant Italian-style garden, the main house was built in the early 19th c. by the engineer Giacomo Guglielmi, the ancestor of the Spinosa family. The outhouses behind the villa are the traditional country buildings of the Valpolicella, made from the local tuff. Accommodation at the Corte Spinosa guest farm (*2 apts.*). Hectares under vine: 18.

**Wines**: Valpolicella Classico, Valpolicella Cl. Sup. Ripasso "Jago", Amarone della Valpolicella Classico, Amarone della Valpolicella Classico "Guglielmi di Jago", Recioto della Valpolicella Classico "Francesca Finato Spinosa". Other products: olive oil.

**F.lli Speri** – *Via Fontana 14 -* **Pedemonte** *(VR) - ℘ 045 77 01 154 - www.speri.com - info@speri.com - Winery tours by reservation, closed Sat. pm and Sun.* The business was founded during the second half of the 19th c. Despite the estate's considerable subsequent expansion of the estate, the winery retains its family management, which it considers a fundamental resource, without ever forgetting the precious lessons of the experience of the past generations. In order to valorise the complexity of the individual zones and distinguish their unique territorial and microclimatic features, the production is divided by plot. This has enabled the creation of crus named after the vineyard of origin. Hectares under vine: 60.

**Wines**: Valpolicella Classico, Valpolicella Classico Superiore Ripasso, Valpolicella Classico Superiore "Sant'Urbano", Amarone Classico "Sant'Urbano", Recioto Classico "La Roggia". Other products: grappa.

**Tommasi Viticoltori** – *Via Ronchetto 4 -* **Pedemonte** *(VR)- ℘ 045 77 01 266 - www. tommasiwine.it - wine@tommasi.com - Winery tours by reservation, emily.riolfi@ tommasi.com.* Tommasi Viticoltori is a family business founded in 1902. Starting with a tiny vineyard owned by grandfather Giacomo, Tommasi Viticoltori has grown

© Mashe/Shutterstock

over the years. It is now run by the fourth generation of the family. Hectares under vine: 205.

**Wines**: Tommasi Amarone della Valpolicella Classico, Amarone della Valpolicella Classico "Ca' Florian", Valpolicella Classico Superiore "Ripasso", Recioto della Valpolicella Classico, Lugana "Le Fornaci". Other products: olive oil and grappa.

**La Sansonina** – *Loc. Sansonina* - **Peschiera del Garda** *(VR)* - ℰ *045 75 51 905* - *www.sansonina.it* - *info@sansonina.it.* The winery's name is derived from Samson, as the old owner had a particularly strong and assertive character. La Sansonina is housed in a picturesque 18th-c. farm near Peschiera, an area traditionally destined for the production of Lugana. Today the estate is owned by Carla Prospero, who purchased it with the intention of challenging this tradition and producing a great red wine with the grapes from an old Merlot vineyard. Hectares under vine: 12.

**Wines**: Sansonina (merlot 100%), Evaluna Garda Cabernet, Lugana.

⌂ **Ottella** – *Loc. Boschetti - San Benedetto di Lugana* - **Peschiera del Garda** *(VR)* - ℰ *045 75 51 950* - *www.ottella.it* - *info@ottella.it* - *Winery tours by reservation, closed Sun.* It was the current owners' great-grandfather who founded the business. It is told that octuplets were born in Lugana in 1500: the coat of arms in the courtyard of the winery refers to this event, from which the name "Ottella" is derived. Old documents mention the winery as the only Verona producer of Lugana at the end of the 9th c. Accommodation available *(5 rooms, doubles from €90)*. Hectares under vine: 30.

**Wines**: Lugana, Lugana Le Creete, Lugana

Riserva Molceo, Campo Sireso Rosso IGT, Prima Luce Bianco IGT. Other products: olive oil and grappa.

⌂ **Musella** – *Via Ferrazzette 2* - **San Martino Buon Albergo** *(VR)* - ℰ *045 97 33 85* - *www.musella.it* - *relais@musella.it* - *Winery tours with food and wine tasting by reservation (payment required, €25-30).* The winery is housed in a rural courtyard complex dating from 1500, which originally served as the stables of the stately home of the estate. The old hayloft above the stables is now used to dry the grapes used to produce Amarone. The estate is home to the 17th-c. villa that belonged to the aristocratic Muselli family. Accommodation available *(8 rooms, 4 apts., 3 suites)*. Hectares under vine: 29.

**Wines**: Valpolicella Sup., Valpolicella Ripasso, Amarone, Recioto. Other products: olive oil, grappa, balsamic condiment, honey.

**F.lli Tedeschi** – *Via Giuseppe Verdi 4* - **Pedemonte di Valpolicella** *(VR)* - ℰ *045 77 01 487* - *www.tedeschiwines.com* - *info@tedeschiwines.com* - *Winery tours by reservation, Mon.-Fri. 9-12 and 14-18, Sat. 9-12.* The Tedeschi family have been growing vines in Valpolicella for 5 generations. The founder was Nicolò Tedeschi, who signed the first purchase deed for several vineyards in 1824. The latest generation is represented by Antonietta, Sabrina and Riccardo, who have put their heart and soul into producing wines with great personality and style. Hectares under vine: 39.

**Wines**: Recioto della Valpolicella Capitel Fontana, Amarone della Valpolicella Capitel Monte Olmi, Valpolicella Superiore Ripasso Capitel San Rocco, Valpolicella Superiore Capitel Nicalò Leggero Appassimento, Valpolicella Superiore La Fabriseria. Other products: olive oil and grappa.

**Nicolis Angelo e Figli** – *Via Villa Girardi 29* - **San Pietro in Cariano** *(VR)* - ℰ *045 77 01 261* - *www.vininicolis.com, info@vinicolis.com* - *Winery tours 8.30-18.30, Sat. 9-17 by reservation, closed Sun.* The art of winegrowing is a trade that the Nicolis family has handed down through the generations. It was in 1951 that Angelo, aided by his wife Natalia, started to extend the estate's production range. The expansion process continued under his children. Hectares under vine: 42.

**Wines**: Valpolicella Classico, Rosso Verona, Valpolicella Classico Superiore Ripasso, Amarone della Valpolicella Classico, Recioto della Valpolicella Classico. Other products: olive oil and grappa.

**Santa Sofia** – *Via Ca' Dede' 61 - Fraz. Pedemonte di Valpolicella* - **San Pietro in Cariano** *(VR)* - ℰ *045 77 01 074* - *www.santasofia.com* - *info@santasofia.com* -

*Winery tours and tastings 9.30-12 and 14-17, Sat. 9.30-13, closed Sun. Booking required, comunicazione@santasofia.com.* Founded in 1811, Santa Sofia winery has its headquarter and cellars in Pedemonte, north of Verona close to the city of Romeo and Juliet, and in the noble villa realized by Andrea Palladio in XVI century in one of the most beautiful and mildest zone of the Valpolicella Classica. Villa Santa Sofia (previously known as Villa Sarego) is listed in the UNESCO World Heritage. Already in the mid of '800 the winery was known for the fine quality of its wines. Since 1967 it is run by the Begnoni family with passion and spirit of innovation with respect of the wine tradition. Hectares under vine: 38.
**Wines**: Amarone della Valpolicella Classico, Recioto della Valpolicella Classico, Ripasso Valpolicella Superiore, Soave, Custoza, Lugana, Bardolino. Other products: grappa of Amarone and olive oil.

**Villa Bellini** – *Via dei Fraccaroli 6 - Loc. Castelrotto di Negarine -* **San Pietro in Cariano** *(VR) - ☎ 045 68 50 108 - www. tenutavillabellini.com - villabellini@ riellobioagri.com - Winery tours by reservation.* The winery's vineyard is cultivated on terraces supported by dry-stone walls, known as marogne, which characterise the Valpollicella landscape. Since 1990 the company follows the dictates of organic viticulture. Hectares under vine: 3.5.
**Wines**: Valpolicella Classico Superiore, Valpolicella Ripasso Classico, Amarone.

**Cavalchina** – *Via Sommacampagna 7 - Fraz. Custoza -* **Sommacampagna** *(VR) - ☎ 045 51 60 02 - www.cavalchina.it - info@cavalchina.com - Winery tours by reservation, closed Sat. and Sun.* Cavalchina is the name of the area in which the winery stands, and is probably derived from the fact that it was the home of Count Cavalchini. The winery was founded at the beginning of the 20th c. and was a milestone in the history of Bianco di Custoza, for it was the first to give the name "Custoza" to the local white wine made from Fernanda, Trebbiano and Garganega grapes, and to contribute to its commercial success. Hectares under vine: 27.
**Wines**: Amedeo, Custoza, Chiaretto, Bardolino, Santa Lucia.

**Le Vigne di San Pietro** – *Via San Pietro 23 -* **Sommacampagna** *(VR) - ☎ 045 51 00 16 - www.levignedisanpietro.it - info@levigne disanpietro.it - Winery tours by reservation, experience@levignedisanpietro.it.* Le Vigne di San Pietro is the result of the efforts of two nature lovers, Sergio and Franca Nerozzi, the parents of the current owner, Carlo Nerozzi. In 1980 their quest for the ideal place to live took them to Vigne di San Pietro, a huge country estate on the morainic hill of San Pietro in Sommacampagna, between Verona and Lake Garda. Hectares under vine: 10.
**Wines**: Custoza, Bardolino, Bardolino Chiaretto, Refolà, Duecuori. Other products: vinegar and grappa.

**Pasqua Vigneti e Cantine** – *Via Belvedere 135 -* **Verona** *- ☎ 045 84 32 111 - www. pasqua.it - italia@pasqua.it - Winery and vineyards tours and tastings by reservation.* In the 1920s Nicola Pasqua moved to Verona from Trani to open a wine bar and shop selling unbottled wines. Joined by his brothers and encouraged by the success of the shop, he decided to make the transition from the sale to the production of wine. Several generations of Pasquas have succeeded him at the head of a company that has gradually grown in terms of quality and size. Hectares under vine: 200.
**Wines**: Villa Borghetti Amarone della Valpolicella, Villa Borghetti Valpolicella Ripasso, Valpolicella Classico, Soave Classico, Lugana, Bardolino, Bardolino Chiaretto. Other products: olive oil, grappa, spirits.

## SOAVE AND THE LESSINI MOUNTAINS

**Romano Dal Forno** – *Loc. Lodoletta 1 - Fraz. Cellore -* **Illasi** *(VR) - ☎ 045 78 34 923 - www.dalfornoromano.it - info@ dalfornoromano.it - Winery tours by reservation.* Dal Forno produces the best-known Amarone, not only in Italy but throughout the world. Romano Dal Forno grew up among wine and vineyards, for his family have been vintners for 3 generations. Over the years he has succeeded in producing highly concentrated wines with great structure and elegance, and his name is now among the elite circle of the finest producers. The high price of each bottle is justified by the very low yields and the painstaking attention paid to every stage of production. Hectares under vine: 25.

© Keith Levit/Shutterstock

## ADDRESSES

**Wines**: Amarone, Valpolicella Superiore, Vigna Seré IGT Veneto.

**Tenuta Sant'Antonio** – *Via Monti Garbi - Loc. San Briccio -* **Lavagno** *(VR) - 𝄚 045 874 06 82 - www.tenutasantantonio.it - info@ tenutasantantonio.it - Winery tours and tastings by reservation.* Brothers Armando, Tiziano, Massimo and Paolo Castagnedi have cultivated a passion for wine and vines since they were children working in their father's vineyards. In those years the grapes were destined for the co-operative winery of Colognola ai Colli, which their father Antonio helped to found. In 1989 the brothers decided to purchase more land and dedicate themselves to vine growing and the production of wine from their grapes. Hectares under vine: 100.

**Wines**: Amarone della Valpolicella "Campo Dei Gigli", Amarone della Valpolicella "Selezione Antonio Castagnedi", Valpolicella Superiore Ripasso "Monti Garbi", Valpolicella Superiore "La Bandina", Soave "Monte Ceriani". Other products: grappa.

**Roccolo Grassi** – *Via San Giovanni di Dio 19 -* **Mezzane di Sotto** *(VR) - 𝄚 045 88 80 089 - www.roccolograssi.it - info@ roccolograssi.it - Winery tours by reservation.* The family-run artisanal winery is headed by owner and young enologist Marco Sartori, whose painstaking work in the vineyards and cellar allows him to produce powerful but elegant wines, which are achieving ever greater success. Hectares under vine: 14.

**Wines**: Soave, Valpolicella Superiore, Amarone della Valpolicella, Recioto della Valpolicella, Recioto di Soave.

**Ca' Rugate** – *Via Pergola 36 -* **Montecchia di Crosara** *(VR) - 𝄚 045 617 63 28 - www.carugate.it - carugate@carugate.it - Winery tours and tastings by reservation.* The history of Ca' Rugate commenced in the early 20th c., when Amedeo Tessari, great-grandfather of the current owner,

rented a wine bar, where he started to sell the wine produced by the family's estate. The business has since expanded and the qualitative level of its products grown, acquiring an excellent reputation among connoisseurs. Hectares under vine: 90.

**Wines**: Valpolicella Superiore, Soave Classico, Valpolicella, Amarone, Recioto. Other products: olive oil and grappa.

**Anselmi** – *Via San Carlo 46 -* **Monteforte d'Alpone** *(VR) - 𝄚 045 76 11 488 - www. anselmi.eu - anselmi@anselmi.eu - Winery tours by reservation.* Roberto Anselmi's family originally bottled table wine purchased from third parties. However, Roberto decided to break with the past and embark upon the difficult path of making wine from grapes of his own production and pursuing quality at all costs. Today Anselmi is one of Veneto's most renowned wineries both in Italy and abroad. Hectares under vine: 70

**Wines**: San Vincenzo, Capitel Foscarino, Capitel Croce, I Capitelli, Realda.

**Corte Moschina** – *Via Moschina 1 -* **Roncà** *(VR) - 𝄚 045 74 60 788 - www.corte moschina.it - info@cortemoschina.it - Winery tours by reservation.* This family-run winery is housed in a grand old villa and continues the local enological tradition by producing the most representative wines of the area. The company headquarters are housed in an old farm enclosed by ancient walls. The villa dates from the 16th c. and was recently restored to its original splendour. Hectares under vine: 22.

**Wines**: Cabernet, Durello Brut, Recioto, Soave.

**Balestri Valda** – *Via Monti 44 -* **Soave** *(VR) - 𝄚 045 76 75 393 - www.vinibalestrivalda. com - info@vinibalestrivalda.com - Winery tours and tasting by reservation.* A family-run business headed by the experienced enologist Guido Rizzotto. Its vineyards, planted with 70% Garganega and 30% Trebbiano di Soave, are situated on the finest winegrowing slopes of the Soave area. Here the efforts of the family, the agronomists and the enologists are directed at the quest for superior quality, and Balestri Valda's wines are the result. Hectares under vine: 13.

**Wines**: Soave Classico, Recioto di Soave, Recioto di Soave Spumante, Volcanus Spumante, Scaligio Rosso. Other products: olive oil and honey.

**Cantina Coffele** – *Via Roma 5 -* **Soave** *(VR) - 𝄚 045 76 80 007 - www.coffele.it - info@ coffele.it - Winery tours by reservation.* The origins of this business are very old, for the Visco family already had its premises and cultivated vines here at the end of the 19th c. In 1971 Giovanna Visco and Giuseppe Coffele founded the current

© Javier Tuana/Shutterstock

winery. Today they are flanked by their children Chiara and Alberto. Hectares under vine: 25.

**Wines**: Soave Classico, Soave Spumante Brut, Nuj Veneto Rosso IGT, Recioto di Soave. Other products: olive oil.

**Cantina del Castello** – *Corte Pittora 5 -* **Soave** *(VR) - 📞 045 76 80 023 - www. cantinacastello.it - cantinacastello@ cantinacastello.it - Winery tours by reservation.* The winery was founded in the 1960s, but it was under Arturo Stocchetti, who has headed it for over 20 years, that it has reached full maturity. Its production is driven by the aim to valorise Soave, its typicity and its terroir. The winery is housed in the palace of the Sanbonifacio counts, known as Corte Pittora and located in the heart of the old medieval town of Soave, at the foot of the Scaliger Castle. Hectares under vine: 12.

**Wines**: Soave Classico "Castello", Soave Classico "Pressoni", Soave Classico "Carniga", Valpolicella superiore Ripasso, Amarone della Valpolicella, Recioto di Soave Classico "Cortepittora". Other products: olive oil and grappa.

**Cantina di Soave** – *Viale Vittoria 100 -* **Soave** *(VR) - 📞 045 61 39 811 - www. cantinasoave.it - cantina@cantinasoave.it*

In 1898 the first co-operative winery was founded in Soave with 115 members. Today the Cantina di Soave has retained its original structure, but over the years it has continued to grow in terms of both membership and production. In 1996 the Valtramigna co-operative winery was merged with it and in 2006 the proposed merger with the Illasi winery was approved. Hectares under vine: 6000.

**Wines**: Soave Classico, Recioto di Soave Mida, Amarone di Valpolicella, Equipe 5 Brut Riserva, Ripasso della Valpolicella.

🏠 **Monte Tondo** – *Via San Lorenzo 89 -* **Soave** *(VR) - 📞 045 76 80 347 - www. montetondo.it - info@montetondo.it - Winery tours and tastings 9.00-18 (Sun. 9-13) by reservation.* The Magnabosco family has been enthusiastically making wine and growing grapes for more than 3 generations. Today work in the vineyard and cellar has been flanked by accommodation and hospitality, equipping the winery with an elegant shop and a beautiful B&B *(5 rooms, doubles €82, 5 apts., €130).* The architecture, with its terracotta bricks and archways, is in the rural style of farming towns. Hectares under vine: 35.

**Wines**: Soave Classico "Monte Tondo", Soave Superiore Classico "Foscarin Slavinus", Valpolicella "San Pietro", Amarone della Valpolicella, Recioto di Soave. Other products: olive oil and grappa.

**Pieropan** – *Via Camuzzoni 3 -* **Soave** *(VR) - 📞 045 61 90 171 - www.pieropan.it - info@ pieropan.it - Winery tours by reservation.* The winery was founded by Leonildo Pieropan in 1890. Today it is his grandchildren Leonildo and Teresita, with their sons Andrea and Dario, who run it with competence and enthusiasm. The bond with the land, and respect for traditions and the culture of the area merge with the history of the Pieropan family and infuse all the winery's activities. The winery has been using innovative growing systems for years, and has been active in the research into and protection of disappearing grape varieties and in the promotion of Garganega. It is housed in the perfectly renovated Palazzo Pullici, built in 1460, which was the childhood home of Ippolito Nievo. Hectares under vine: 43.

**Wines**: Soave Classico Calvarino, Soave Classico La Rocca, Recioto di Soave Le Colombare, Valpolicella Superiore Ruberpan, Amarone della Valpolicella, Ghes Rosè Spumante. Other products: olive oil.

### THE VALDADIGE DOC ZONE

🍃 **Cantina Roeno** – *Via Mama 5 - Loc. Belluno Veronese -* **Brentino Belluno** *(VR), 40 km NW of Verona along the A 22 - 📞 045 72 30 110 - www.cantinaroeno.com - info@ cantinaroeno.com - Winery tours by reservation.* The Fugatti family, who own the business, have completely renovated and expanded the winery, structured to allow easier tours of the cellar, product tastings and wine sales. It also boasts a guest farm with comfortable rooms and a dining room where you can enjoy Signora Giuliana's local specialities. Hectares under vine: 25.

**Wines**: Enantio Terradeiforti, Roeno Rosso Vallagarina IGT, Cristina Vendemmia Tardiva, Pinot Grigio Rivoli, "Le Fratte" Chardonnay Valdadige.

### THE PROVINCE OF VICENZA

**Villa Angarano** – *Via Contrà Corte S. Eusebio 15 -* **Bassano del Grappa** *(VI) - 📞 0424 50 30 86 - www.villaangarano.com - info@villaangarano.com - Winery tours and tastings by reservation.* This area has a long winegrowing tradition, documented as far back as the 13th c. The vineyards are located in the easternmost area of the Breganze DOC zone and reach to the right bank of the Brenta river. This area of rolling hills enjoys breezes from the Valsugana, which create particularly beneficial conditions for both vines and olives. After 700 years of winemaking, in 2000 Villa Angarana started to reorganise its vineyards and winery in order to produce quality wines. The winery has always been associated with women and today it is run by the 5 Bianchi Michiel sisters. Hectares under vine: 8.

**Wines**: Angarano Rosso - Breganze Rosso Merlot, Cà Michiel Veneto Bianco Chardonnay IGT, Angarano Bianco - Breganze Vespaiolo, Quare di Angarano Cabernet Sauvignon. Other products: olive oil.

**Maculan** – *Via Castelletto 3* - **Breganze** *(VI)* - ☏ *0445 87 37 33 - www.maculan.net info@maculan.net - Winery tours by reservation.* Fausto Maculan was born in the rooms that have now been made into his office, and this probably marked his destiny. After having graduated from the Enology School in Cornegliano Veneto, Fausto's in-depth studies, trips to the best winemaking regions of the world and daring experimentation enabled him to take his business to great heights in terms of quality and image, until offering his discerning fans a complete range of renowned whites, important reds and the finest dessert wines. In 2007 his daughters Angela and Maria Vittoria Maculan entered the business. Hectares under vine: 50.

**Wines**: Vespaiolo, Palazzotto, Fratta, Torcolato, Dindarello. Other products: olive oil, grappa, cheeses, Christmas and Easter cakes.

**Costozza dei Conti da Schio** – *Piazza da Schio 4* - **Costozza di Longare** *(VI)* - ☏ *0444 95 31 95 or* ☏ *340 48 54 568 - www.costozza-villadaschio.it - Winery tours by reservation (payment required).* At the end of the 19th c., the da Schio counts decided to boost wine production by introducing Cabernet and Pinot Nero vines from France and in 1905 Count Giulio da Schio published the important book entitled Enologia e Viticoltura della Provincia di Vicenza. The winery's bottles are still aged in the evocative old cellars of the villa. Hectares under vine: 10.

**Wines**: Cabernet Franc, Cabernet Sauvignon. Pinot Bianco. Other products: mushrooms cultivated in caves in the Costozza quarries.

**Cantina di Gambellara** – *Via Mazzini 2* - **Gambellara** *(VI)* - ☏ *0444 49 13 60 - www.cantinagambellara.com - info@vitevis.com - Winery tours by reservation.* Cantina di Gambellara was built in 1947 by a group of 26 founding members and was the first co-operative winery in the province of Vicenza. Production has since grown, along with the number of members. The grapes are mainly from the Gambellara DOC zone, but also from the neighbouring zones of Soave and Colli Berici. The extensive product range comprises red and white wines, sparklers and dessert wines. Hectares under vine: 600.

© Elena Elisseeva/Shutterstock

**Wines**: Recioto Spumante, Vin Santo, Recioto Passito, Gambellara Classico, Cabernet, Merlot. Other products: grappa and olive oil.

🌳 **Palazzetto Ardi** – *Via Ciron 4* - **Gambellara***(VI)* - ☏ *0444 44 04 50 or* ☏ *347 85 91 509 - www.palazzettoardi.it - palazzetto.ardi@libero.it - Winery tours by reservation.* This organically certified estate is run by Michela Cariolaro and Carlo Sitzia, who made a life-changing decision about 10 years ago, abandoning the city and moving to the country to re-establish the deepest human bond with the land. In addition to vines, the estate now also has orchards and raises free-range poultry and pigs. It is also an teaching farm and a guest farm (*double rooms from €100, restaurant service*). Hectares under vine: 2.

**Wines**: Cabernet Franc, Cabernet Sauvignon, Garganega. Other products: preserves, sausages and salami, fruit, vegetables, pickles and jams.

**Zonin** – *Via Borgolecco 9* - **Gambellara** *(VI)* - ☏ *0444 64 01 11 - www.zonin1821.it - info@zonin1821.it - Winery tours by reservation:* ☏ *0444 64 01 60, hospitality@zonin.it.* The Zonin family have been making wine among the rolling hills of Gambellara for 7 generations. This region was the cradle of one of Italy's leading wineries, which now boasts 11 estates in the finest winegrowing areas. From the 1960s Zonin's aim has been to "allow as many consumers as possible to drink better", adopting a policy in which value for money plays a fundamental role. Hectares under vine: 2000.

**Wines**: Recioto Passito, Gambellara Il Giangio, Valpolicella Ripasso, Prosecco, Amarone. Other products: olive oil and grappa.

**Casa Cecchin** – *Via Agugliana 11* - **Montebello Vicentino** *(VI)* - ☏ *0444 64 96 10 - www.casacecchin.it -*

info@casacecchin.it - *Winery tours by reservation.* Casa Cecchin grows and makes wine from two grape varieties only: Garganega and Durella. Its pride and joy is the traditional Classic Method sparkling wine from Durella grapes. The cellar has been designed and built to blend in with the natural profile of the hill and extends below ground. Hectares under vine: 3.5.

**Wines:** Lessini Durello Spumante Metodo Classico, Veneto Durello Passito "Montebello", Veneto IGT. Other products: olive oil.

**Masari** – *Contrada Bevilacqua 2/a* - **Valdagno** *(VI)* - ✆ *0445 41 07 80* - *www.masari.it - info@masari.it - Winery tours by reservation, 9-18, Sat. 9-13, closed Sun.* In 1998 Massimo Dal Lago and Arianna Tessari's passion for winegrowing and nature led to the foundation of this estate, which currently grows both international varieties (Cabernet and Merlot) and local ones (Durella and Garganega). The cellar is housed in the rooms, formerly used to store wine, of the old home of the Dal Lago family. Hectares under vine: 4.

**Wines:** Agno Bianco, San Martino, Masari, Doro.

↑ **Piovene Porto Godi** – *Via Villa 14 - Fraz. Toara -* **Villaga** *(VI)* - ✆ *0444 88 51 42* - *www.piovene.com - info@piovene.com* - *Winery tours and tastings by reservation.* The estate has belonged to the Babaran counts for centuries and it is from this family that its current owners, Marioantonio and Tommaso Piovene Porto Godi, are descended. Wine has always played a fundamental role in the history of the estate, which had long produced an easy-drinking wine for sale unbottled. However, at the beginning of the 1990s it decided to bottle and produce higher quality wines, which it achieved by reorganising the vineyards and the cellar. The grape varieties cultivated are Tocai Rosso, Cabernet Franc, Cabernet Sauvignon, Merlot, Sauvignon, Pinot Bianco and Garganega. The old mill and the dovecote of the house have been converted into lodgings (✆ *340 85 43 966*). Hectares under vine: 28.

**Wines:** Colli Berici Tocai Rosso Riveselle, Colli Berici Tocai Rosso Thovara, Rosso IGT Veneto Polveriera, Sauvignon IGT Veneto Campigie, Colli Berici Merlot Fra' i Broli. Other products: oil.

## THE PROVINCE OF PADOVA

**Vignalta** – *Via Scalette 23 -* **Arquà Petrarca** *(PD)* - ✆ *0429 77 73 05 - www. vignalta.it - info@vignalta.it - Winery tours by reservation.* Founded in 1980, the winery has always strived to enhance the distinctive characteristics of its various plots in order to grow the different grape varieties in conditions that enable them to express themselves to the full. The current owners are Lucio Gomiero and Graziano Cardin, who pioneered the planting of high-density vineyards in the Colli Euganei zone. The beautiful cellar is carved entirely out of the rock. Hectares under vine: 55.

**Wines:** Sirio Moscato Secco, Rosso Riserva, Rosso Gemola, Cabernet Riserva, Passito Fior d'Arancio Alpianae. Other products: olive oil, vinegar, flavoured salt, spirits.

☖ **Dominio di Bagnoli** – *P.zza Marconi 63* - **Bagnoli di Sopra** *(PD)* - ✆ *049 53 80 008* - *www.ildominiodibagnoli.it - info@ ildominiodibagnoli.it - Winery tours by reservation.* Apart from the Papal State, Dominio di Bagnoli has had only 3 owners since 954: the Widmann counts, the Princes of Aremberg and the Borletti counts, the current owners. The estate's products comply with regulations on low environmental impact and organic farming. Consequently, particular attention is paid to techniques aimed at eliminating the use of herbicides and pesticides, while maintaining the highest qualitative standards. Tours of the old cellars and gardens of Villa Widmann-Borletti and accommodation on guest farm (*3 apts., min. stay depending from the season*) with restaurant service available by reservation (*min. 30 pers.*). Hectares under vine: 58.

**Wines:** Bagnoli Classico Friularo, Spumante Brut Metodo Classico Millesimato, Bianco San Lorenzo. Other products: rice, organic flour, vinegar, honey, confectionery, Limousin beef, spirits.

↑ **Ca' Orologio** – *Via Ca' Orologio 7/a* - **Baone** *(PD)* - ✆ *0429 50 099 - www. caorologio.it - caorologio@caorologio.com* - *Winery tours by reservation.* The winery is the result of the entrepreneurial skills of Maria Gioia Rosellini, who decided to change her life by going to live in the country with her husband and children. The 16th-c. Ca' Orologio, which formerly belonged to the Dondi dall'Orologio family, with its "Brolo" vineyard and the *barchessa* (traditional rural building) now house the "Brolo di Ca' Orologio" guest farm (*7 apt., from €90*). Hectares under vine: 11.

**Wines:** Calaòne, Relògio, Lunisòle, Salaròla. Other products: olive oil.

**Vignale di Cecilia** – *Via Croci 14 -* **Baone** *(PD)* - ✆ *042 95 14 20 - www.vignale dicecilia.it - info@vignaledicecilia.it - Winery tours by reservation.* The owner Paolo Brunello inherited the estate from his grandfather Nello, one of the first members of the Protection Consortium for Colli Euganei DOC wines. Paolo has always wanted to produce wines that are "music to the palate" and it is thus no coincidence that the winery is a tribute to the mountain on which it stands and to Cecilia, the patron saint of musicians. Indeed, Paolo is not only an expert vintner, but also an admired cellist. Hectares under vine: 10.

**Wines**: Colli Euganei Rosso Passacaglia, Colli Euganei Rosso Còvolo, Colli Euganei Moscato Folìa, IGT Veneto Bianco Benavides. Other products: biscuits.

**Ca' Lustra** – *Via San Pietro 50 - Loc. Faedo* - **Cinto Euganeo** (PD) - *☏ 0429 94 128 - www.calustra.it - info@calustra.it - Winery tours by reservation.* Ca' Lustra is located in the Colli Euganei Regional Park. Franco Zanovello has been running this solid firm for 30 years, paying particular attention to respecting the naturally rich nature of the grapes that he vinifies. He has thus planted high-density vineyards (5-6000 vines/ha), worked to protect the old local grape varieties and uses non-aggressive wood for ageing in made-to-measure barrels. Hectares under vine: 25.

**Wines**: Colli Euganei Merlot Sassonero, Cabernet Girapoggio, Rosso Natìo, Fior d'Arancio Passito, Moscato Secco A' Cengia. Other products: olive oil, vinegar, honey, spirits, chocowine.

**Monte Fasolo** – *Via Monte Fasolo 2* - **Cinto Euganeo** (PD) - *☏ 0429 61 30 88 - www. montefasolo.com - info@montefasolo.eu - Winery tours by reservation.* Fattoria Monte Fasolo has been a single estate for over 40 years, with a total area of more than 160 hectares on the high hills in the Colli Euganei Regional Park, including 60 hectares of vineyards, 4000 olive trees and several hectares of woodland with paths and marked trails. Hectares under vine: 60.

**Wines**: Bianco Montefasolo IGT Veneto, Cabernet Veneto, Colli Euganei Fior d'Arancio, Chardonnay, Spumante Brut Metodo Classico. Other products: olive oil and grappa.

⌂ **Castello di Lispida** – *Via IV Novembre 4* - **Monselice** (PD) - *☏ 0429 78 05 30 - www. lispida.com - booking@lispida.com - Winery tours by reservation.* During the second half of the 19th c. the Corinaldi counts of Livorno decided to engage in large-scale winegrowing. They expanded the existing structures of a 13th-c. monastery to build the current cellar, whose 9 bays (the longest of which is 55 metres) makes it one of the largest old cellars in Veneto. The ceilings and floors are made of unplastered bricks and local stone. The soil in the vineyards is not treated with chemical herbicides or fertilisers.

Accommodation available (*8 apts. from €145*). Hectares under vine: 8.
**Wines**: Amphora, Terralba, Terraforte, Montelispida, H Spumante.

⌂ **Conte Emo Capodilista "La Montecchia"** – *Via Montecchia 16* - **Selvanazzano Dentro** (PD) - *☏ 049 63 72 94 - www.lamontecchia.it - lamontecchia @lamontecchia.it - Winery tours by reservation.* Winegrowing has been practised here since the Middle Ages. The current owner, Count Umberto Emo Capodilista, started to renovate the vineyards and cellars at the beginning of the 1990s, and subsequently left his son Giordano to run the entire estate. The estate grows the black grape varieties Cabernet Franc, Cabernet Sauvignon, Carmenere, Merlot and Raboso, and the white Chardonnay, Moscato Fior d'Arancio and Pinot Bianco. Guest-farm accommodation available in the medieval farm and castle (*see website for prices and details*). Tours of Villa Emo Capodilista (16th c.) for groups of min. 15 people by reservation *☏ 049 63 72 94* (including the visit to the Museum of rural life). Food and wine tasting on demand. Hectares under vine: 30.

**Wines**: Fior d'Arancio Spumante Colli Euganei, Donna Daria Fior d'Arancio Passito Colli Euganei, Godimondo Cabernet Franc Colli Euganei, Irenèo Cabernet Sauvignon Colli Euganei, Villa Capodilista Rosso Colli Euganei. Other products: olive oil and grappa.

## THE PROVINCE OF TREVISO

### 1. Piave

⌂ **Tessère** – *Via Bassette 51 - Loc. Santa Teresina* - **Noventa di Piave** (VE) - *☏ 0421 32 04 38 - www.tessereonline.it - info@ tessereonline.it - Winery tours by reservation.* The winery, founded in 1979 by passionate wine lover Ilario Biancoletto, is a prominent name today among the producers of Piave DOC wines for the quality of its products. Its finest expressions can be found in the vinification of Raboso, a native grape variety capable of yielding very characterful red wines. Teaching farm and accommodation available at the holiday farm (*3 rooms from €80 or 1 apt., €200*). Hectares under vine: 15.

**Wines**: Spezièr Raboso, Rebecca Raboso Passito, Redentor Spumante Rosato di Raboso, Galión Merlot, Alimante Chardonnay. Other products: Passito di Raboso grappa.

⌂ **Rechsteiner** – *Via Frassenè 2 - Fraz. Piavon* - **Oderzo** (TV) - *☏ 0422 75 20 74 - www.rechsteiner.it - rechsteiner@ rechsteiner.it - Winery tours and tastings by reservation.* The winery is housed in a

17th-c. building that suffered artistic but not structural damage during WWI. It is the oldest nucleus of the winery and is divided up into 3 areas: the outer one, where the grapes are pressed and fermented, and the two inner ones, which are used for storing wine in tanks and barrel-ageing reds respectively. Accommodation available on the guest farm (*10 rooms, from €65, and 4 apts., from €88/night*) and restaurant service on Fri., Sat. and Sun. (*reservation suggested*), also Thu. for groups by reservation. Hectares under vine: 45.

**Wines**: Prosecco, Manzoni Bianco, Pinot Nero, Cabernet Sauvignon, Maschera Rosa. Other products: radicchio digestif, grappa, preserves, salami, sauces.

**Italo Cescon** – *Piazza dei Caduti 3 - Fraz. Roncadelle* - **Ormelle** *(TV)* - ☎ *0422 85 10 33 - www.cesconitalo.it - cesconitalo@ cesconitalo.it - Winery tours by reservation.* The history of the winery commenced in the 1950s, when winegrowing became the main activity of the Cescon family. It was founded by Italo and today his children pursue the path marked out by their father with commitment and passion. Their 6 estates are situated in various areas of Veneto, and are planted with Cabernet, Merlot, Verduzzo, Chardonnay, Tocai, Pinot Grigio, Pinot Nero, Incrocio Manzoni, Riesling, Raboso, Pinot Bianco, Sauvignon, Refosco, Marzemino and Prosecco. Hectares under vine: 95.

**Wines**: Manzoni Bianco 6.0.13, Manzoni Bianco "Madre", Sauvignon, Raboso, Amaranto 72, Prosecco. Other products: Amaranto 72 spirit.

🍷 **Ornella Molon Traverso** – *Via Risorgimento 40 - Fraz. Campo di Pietra* - **Salgareda** *(TV)* - ☎ *0422 80 48 07 - www. ornellamolon.it - info@ornellamolon.it - Winery tours by reservation.* The estate was founded by the passion of a couple entrepreneurs who dedicated themselves to agriculture with the aim of producing personal, unique and unrepeatable wines. Since 1982 Ornella Molon Traverso has become a leading winery and has won important national and international awards. The winery is housed in an old 17th-c. country villa, which was the prestigious home of Doge Giustinian. The solemn central building with a *barchessa* on either side is home to the winery, the barrel-ageing cellar, the bottling plant and the storage room for the subsequent bottle ageing. It also houses a tasting room and a small museum of country traditions. Restaurant service (*Closed Sun. evening and Mon.*). Hectares under vine: 40.

**Wines**: Merlot, Cabernet, Raboso, Chardonnay Frizzante, Pinot.

**Sutto** – *Via Arzeri 34/1* - **Arzeri** *(TV)* - ☎ *0422 74 40 63 - www.sutto.it - info@ sutto.it - Winery tours by reservation.* The winery has a 100-hectare estate, all planted to vine with the latest training criteria, and employs modern technologies in the cellar. The old *barchessa* of a 17th-c. Veneto villa has been renovated to house a wine shop, which caters to both connoisseurs and novices alike. Hectares under vine: 100.

**Wines**: Merlot Riserva, Dogma Rosso, Raboso Piave, Cabernet, Manzoni Bianco. Other products: olive oil, grappa and vinegar.

**Casa Roma** – *Via Ormelle 19* - **San Polo di Piave** *(TV)* - ☎ *0422 85 53 39 - www. casaroma.com - info@casaroma.com - Winery tours by reservation, wine shop open 8.30-12 and 14-18, closed Sun.* The Peruzzetto family has been engaged in winegrowing for generations. Luigi and Adriano Peruzzetto have tried to valorise the resources of the territory, particularly the native variety Raboso. A talent for experimentation has led to the development of an interesting Raboso Piave dried-grape wine. But Casa Roma is not only Raboso, for the winery also produces other excellent wines. Hectares under vine: 30.

**Wines**: Raboso del Piave, Manzoni Moscato, Manzoni Bianco, Marzemina Bianca, Raboso Passito.

**Bonotto delle Tezze** – *Via Duca d'Aosta 36 - Tezze di Piave* - **Vazzola** *(TV)* - ☎ *0438 48 83 23 - www.bonottodelletezze.it - info@ bonottodelletezze.it - Winery tours by reservation.* The Bonotto delle Tezze family have been farming the land, raising livestock and trading grain since the 15th c. The Borgo di Mezzo premises are home to the winery's fermentation and ageing cellars. The winery is housed in a

© X Jakub Pavlinec/Shutterstock

# ADDRESSES

2-storey *barchessa* and another more modern cellar designed by specialised architects is currently being built. Hectares under vine: 43.

**Wines**: Raboso Potestà, Merlot Spezza, Carmenère Barabane, Manzoni Bianco Novalis, Prosecco Col Real.

**Cecchetto** – *Via Piave 67 - Tezze di Piave - **Vazzola** (TV) - ℘ 0438 28 598 - www.rabosopiave.com - info@rabosopiave.com - Winery tours by reservation*. The winery is closely associated with Raboso, the iconic grape variety of the area. Indeed, its owner Giorgio Cecchetto is one of the founding members of the Confraternity of Raboso Piave, which aims to promote awareness of the only native red grape variety of the March of Treviso and the wine made from it. Hectares under vine: 43.

**Wines**: Raboso Piave, IGT Marca Trevigiana Merlot /Manzoni Bianco /Cabernet Sauvignon, Cabernet Franc (Carmenère).

## 2. Prosecco, Colli Asolani, Montello

**Vigne Matte** – *Via Tea 8 - Loc. Rolle - **Cison di Valmarino** (TV) - ℘ 0438 97 57 98 - www.vignematte.it - info@vignematte.it - Winery tours by reservation*. The winery dedicates itself mainly to the production of Prosecco, but does not neglect red wines made from Merlot, Cabernet Franc and Cabernet Sauvignon grapes. The soil in which the vines grow has a peculiar composition of clay, marl and a stone locally known as "ru" and gives particularly elegant and highly aromatic wines. The vineyards are terraced and are evenly exposed to the sun in order to allow optimum ripening of the bunches of grapes and limited use of chemical treatments. Hectares under vine: 30.

**Wines**: Prosecco di Conegliano Valdobbiadene brut/extra dry/dry, Spumante Brut "Riserva 007", Rosso Colli di Conegliano "Rugai".

© Carole Castelli/Shutterstock

**Follador** – *Via Gravette 42 - Col San Martino (TV) - ℘ 0438 89 82 22 - www.follador prosecco.com - info@folladorprosecco.com - Winery tour by reservation*. In 1769 Giovanni Follador received an honorary title from the Doge in Venice in recognition of the quality of his wines. His descendent Gianfranco Follador brought innovation to the family, concentrating on spumante Among the top ten families that focus on spumanti in the Valdobbiadene area, Gianfranco and his wife Italia continued this tradition of quality, passion and excellence in winemaking. Follador Proseccos are a synonym of refined spumanti, with delicate, persistent perlages, rich bouquets and a dry, elegant finish. These wines are the result of skills passed down over more than two centuries. The Follador vineyards are located within the Prosecco terroir. Hectares under vine: 40.

**Wines**: Prosecco Superiore di Valdobbiadene DOCG, Prosecco DOC Treviso, Prosecco DOC Aeris, Prosecco DOC Renana, Rosè.

**Carpenè Malvolti** – *Via Antonio Carpenè 1 - **Conegliano** (TV) - ℘ 0438 36 46 11 - www.carpene-malvolti.com - info@carpene-malvolti.com - Winery tours by reservation, closed Sat. and Sun*. The winery was founded in the Prosecco area and has a strong association with that grape variety, wine and zone. Conegliano Veneto, the town of wine, is home to its headquarters and production premises. Over 100 local winegrowers bring their quality-controlled grapes to the winery each year, allowing the production of the famous Carpenè Malvolti wines. Hectares under vine: 26.

**Wines**: Conegliano Valdobbiadene Prosecco Superiore Dry/Extra Dry/Brut, Conegliano Valdobbiadene Prosecco Superiore PVXINVM, Rosé Spumante Brut, Tarvisium Brut, 1868 Cartizze Valdobbiadene Superiore. Other products: grappa and brandy.

**Astoria** – *Via Crevada 12/a, SP 38 Conegliano-Pieve di Soligo - **Susegana** (TV) - ℘ 0438 45 43 33 - www.astoria.it - info@astorialoungestore.it - Winery tours by reservation, closed Sun*. Astoria, owned by Paolo and Giorgio Polegato, was founded in 1987 by a historic family of winegrowers and distributes the wines made in its Tenuta Val de Brun estate in Refrontolo. The winery's name is associated with the key products of the Treviso winegrowing tradition, such as Prosecco DOC and Refrontolo Passito. The public is received in the Lounge Store, while Fashion Wine is a space for intercultural encounters and events, as well as for tastings and purchases of the estate's wines. Hectares under vine: 40.

**Wines**: Prosecco di Valdobbiadene, Fervo Passito di Refrontolo, Fashion Victim Astoria Brut, Mina Colli di Conegliano Bianco, Croder Colli di Conegliano Rosso. Other products: "Cà Foresto" selections of food, grappa, vinegar, olive oil.

🍇 **Villa Sandi** – *Via Erizzo 113/A* - **Crocetta del Montello** *(TV) - ℰ 0423 8607 - www.villasandi.it - info@villasandi.it - Sales at the "Botteghe del Vino" in Crocetta del Montello and Valdobbiadene - Winery tours by reservation, closed Sun.* The company premises are housed in a striking Palladian villa dating from 1622, which is a splendid example of a harmonious combination of art and winegrowing. The driveway is adorned with sculptures by Veneto sculptor Orazio Marinali. Villa Sandi organises jazz and blues evenings, and events of various kinds. Restaurant and accommodation at the Locanda Sandi in Valdobbiadene *(6 rooms, doubles €105, www.locandasandi.it)*. Hectares under vine: 50.

**Wines**: Prosecco di Valdobbiadene Spumante Extra Dry, Prosecco di Valdobbiadene Superiore di cartizze Dry, Marinali Raboso, Merlot Venezia, Prosecco di Valdobbiadene Superiore Millesimato. Other products: grappa and spirits.

🍷 **Villa di Maser** – *Via Cornuda 7* - **Maser** *(TV) - ℰ 0423 92 30 04 - www.villadimaser.it - visite@villadimaser.it - Winery not open to public, wine and food tasting by reservation.* The winery dates back to 1850 and was erected by the then-owner Sante Giacomelli next to the villa, built between 1550 and 1560 by Andrea Palladio, and decorated by Paolo Veronese and Alessandro Vittoria. The villa has a wine-bar. Hectares under vine: 30.

**Wines**: Maserino Rosso, Maserino Bianco, Andrea Palladio Rosso, Prosecco Montello e Colli Asolani, Verduzzo Colli Trevigiani. Other products: olive oil.

🍇 **Vini Costa** – *Via Cimitero 24 - Loc. Biadene -* **Montebelluna** *(TV) - ℰ 0423 19 03 782 - www.vinicosta.it or www.facebook. com/vinicosta.asoloprosecco - info@vini costa.it - Winery tours by reservation, shop open Mon.-Sat.- 8.30-12.30 and 14.30-18.30, closed Sun.* The estate was founded more than sixty years ago by Luigi Costa and it is now run by the third generation of the Costa family. Though limited in quantity, the production of high-quality wines is guaranteed by the climate (dry in summer and harsh in winter), the vineyard soil (clayey with red colouring and goo mineral content) and a perfect exposure (south). Hectares under vine: 22.

**Wines**: Asolo Prosecco Superiore DOCG Pra' Grande, Sottocroda, Ardiva, Il Frizzante and Il Tranquillo, Colli Trevigiani IGT Il Rosso del

Bosco, DOC Montello e Colli Asolani Merlot, Cabernet Franc, Cabernet Sauvignon and Chardonnay, Col Fondo.

🍇 **Azienda Agricola Le Colture** – *Via Follo 5 -* **Santo Stefano di Valdobbiadene** *(TV) - ℰ 0423 90 01 92 - www.lecolture.it - info@lecolture.it - Winery tours Mon.-Fri. 8-18, sa. 9-13.* Le Colture is both an active farm and a cantina that has been run by the same family since 1500. In 1983 the Ruggeri family began producing spumanti, and today Cesare Ruggeri can boast an extraordinary patrimony of experience, great and little production secrets, knowledge of the territory and his grapes, as well as an innate sensitivity for the health of the vineyard and atmosphere in the cantina. The vines are taken care of through guided interventions in different batches, using products that have the least environmental impact and natural techniques for plant management. Inside the cantina, a great deal of attention is paid to energy savings: recently the family installed solar panels in order to utilize renewable energy sources. Viewed from outside, the building looks traditional, with a hilltop villa and recently restored cantina, but inside the equipment is entirely avant-garde. The company has preserved a great deal of the traditions and methods inherent to the place, while at the same time casting a constant eye to innovation. The Ruggeri family also owns the agriturismo Prime Gemme, a structure created through the restoration of a 1920s farm located in Nervesa della Battaglia (TV), in the area between the last foothills beneath the Veneto Alps, the Piave River and the hills of Montello. Overnight stays are possible *(8 rooms; 75 €)*, and the structure is located just a few kilometres from the company headquarters. Wine-tasting organized in the family's vineyards are available, as well as mountain bikes for travelling along nearby paths. A restaurant and gym are nearby. Hectares under vine: 40.

**Wines**: Valdobbiadene DOCG Spumante Brut, Valdobbiadene DOCG Spumante Extra Dry, Valdobbiadene DOCG Spumante Dry, Spumante Brut Rosé.

**Collalto** – *Via XXIV Maggio 1* - **Susegana** *(TV) - ℰ 0438 43 58 11 - www.cantine-collalto.it - info@cantine-collalto.it - Winery tours by reservation, closed Sun.* The current winery dates from 1905 and consists of a complex formed by the cellar, offices, houses, and *barchesse* for horses, machinery and farm implements. The basement houses the barrel cellars where the wines are aged. Don't miss the rooms for drying the Verdiso grapes used in spring to make the estate's sweet dried-grape wine. Hectares under vine: 150.

# ADDRESSES

**Wines**: Prosecco di Conegliano Spumante Extra Dry, Wildbacher IGT Colli Trevigiani, Incrocio Manzoni Rosso 2.15 IGT Colli Trevigiani, Cabernet Piave Ris. Torrai, Verdiso Colli Trevigiani.

⚐ **Bisol** – *Via Follo 33 - Loc. Santo Stefano - **Valdobbiadene** (TV) - ℘ 042 39 00 138 - www.bisol.it - info@bisol.it - Winery tours by reservation at 11 and 16 (Sun. only 11), ℘ 042 39 04 737 or accoglienza@bisol.it.* The winery is situated in the heart of the Upper March of Treviso, where the Bisol family, Valdobbiadene winegrowers since 1542, harvest and process the grapes for their Prosecco from vineyards covering an area of over 100 hectares, located in 21 estates. Three of these hectares are situated in the prestigious Cartizze area. Bisol produces high-quality wines and sparkling wines that are strongly associated with the terroir. Accommodation available at the Relais Duca di Dolle (*www.ducadidolle.it, 9 rooms, from €120; 4 apts., from €145, min. stay 3 nights*). Hectares under vine: 100.
**Wines**: Valdobbiadene Prosecco Crede, Valdobbiadene Superiore di Cartizze, Rive di Campea Millesimato, Valdobbiadene Prosecco Superiore Jeio.

**Bortolomiol** – *Via Garibaldi 142 - **Valdobbiadene** (TV) - ℘ 0423 97 49 - www.bortolomiol.com - info@ bortolomiol.com - Winery tours by reservation, ℘ 345 24 98 969 or visitedegustazioni@bortomiol.com* This sparkling wine producer, founded in Valdobbiadene in 1949 by Giuliano Bortolomiol, was established in the old Via Garibaldi cellar, where bottle fermentation is still carried out today. The heart of the town, next to the bell tower, is the site of the fermentation cellar, vineyard, grounds with stone amphitheatre and tasting room, which occupies part of what was once known as the piccola filanda ("small spinnery"). Hectares under vine: 5.
**Wines**: Banda Rossa Valdobbiadene Prosecco Millesimato, Extra Brut Millesimato Riserva del Governatore, Valdobbiadene Prosecco Superiore di Cartizze, Filanda Rosé Brut Millesimato Riserva, Prior Brut Valdobbiadene Prosecco. Other products: grappa.

**Col Vetoraz** – *Strada delle Treziese 1 - Loc. Santo Stefano - **Valdobbiadene** (TV) - ℘ 0423 97 52 91 - www.colvetoraz.it - Winery tours by reservation.* The Miotto family, who own the winery, settled in this area in 1838, when they started to grow Prosecco. Francesco Miotto, Paolo De Bortoli and Loris dall'Acqua founded Col Vetoraz in 1993. It has since become a well-established winery that has won numerous awards and boasts an excellent

© Dusliarfote/Shutterstock

reputation among consumers and the trade alike. Hectares under vine: 13.
**Wines**: Valdobbiadene Prosecco Brut, Valdobbiadene Prosecco Extra Dry, Valdobbiadene Prosecco Millesimato, Valdobbiadene Prosecco Superiore Cartizze.

**Drusian Francesco** – *Via Anche 1 - Loc. Bigolino - **Valdobbiadene** (TV) - ℘ 0423 98 21 51 - www.drusian.it - drusian@drusian.it - Winery tours by reservation, Mon.-Fri. 14-16.* The Drusian family have been making Prosecco for 3 generations. Grandfather Giuseppino was the first in the mid-19th c. He produced 60,000 litres a year and was one of the largest winegrowers of the age of still Prosecco. Bottle fermentation was not yet practised, and the winery didn't start to use the process until 1986. Today the winery is run by Giuseppino's grandson Francesco Drusian and produces around 500,000 bottles of Prosecco and Cartizze each year. Hectares under vine: 45.
**Wines**: Prosecco di Valdobbiadene Spumante Extra Dry/Brut/Millesimato Dry, Prosecco di Valdobbiadene Spumante Gujot Extra Dry, Valdobbiadene Superiore di Cartizze Dry.

**Fasol Menin** – *Via Fasol Menin 22B - **Valdobbiadene** (TV) - ℘ 0423 97 42 62 - www.fasolmenin.com - myprosecco@fasol menin.com - Winery tours and tastings by reservation (payment required).* The road leading to the new cellar, built just below the outer walls of the village, is named after the old village of Fasol Menin. The estate is run by husband-and-wife team Silvana Curto and Massimo de Nardo. The main grape variety grown is Prosecco, used to make 2 Valdobbiadene DOC sparkling wines and a still Colli Trevigiani IGT. Fasol Menin has been designed to host art exhibitions, concerts and literary encounters aimed at promoting the area and its culture, with special focus on children's entertainment. Hectares under vine: 10.

**Wines**: Valdobbiadene Prosecco Extra Dry and Brut, Raboso Piave, Rebelot Vino Bianco, Glera Vino Frizzante.

↑ **Nino Franco Spumanti** – *Via Garibaldi 147* - **Valdobbiadene** *(TV)* - ✆ *0423 97 20 51* - *www.ninofranco.it* - *info@ninofranco.it* - *Winery tours by reservation*. In 1919 Antonio founded the Cantine Franco in Valdobbiadene, which subsequently expanded under his son Nino, although it was under Primo in the 1970s that the winery was restructured according to modern criteria. After having graduated from the Enology School in Coneglian Veneto he eliminated all the products that were not related to the Valdobbiadene area, modernised the equipment, revised the techniques, redesigned the labels and maintained close relations with his grape suppliers. The end result is a Prosecco that reflects its terroir. Accommodation at the Villa Barberina hotel (*Via Roma 2, Valdobbiadene, www.villabarberina.it, doubles from €175*). Hectares under vine: 2.5.

**Wines**: Spumante Prosecco Rustico, Spumante Prosecco di Valdobbiadene Brut, Spumante Prosecco di Valdobbiadene "Riva di San Floriano", Spumante Prosecco di Valdobbiadene amabile "Primo Franco", Spumante Valdobbiadene Superiore di Cartizze.

**Sorelle Bronca** – *Via Martiri 20 - Fraz. Colbertaldo* - **Vidor** *(TV)* - ✆ *0423 98 72 01* - *www.sorellebronca.com* - *info@ sorellebronca.com* - *Winery tours Mon.-Sat. 9-12 and 14-18 (Sat. closes at 16)*. The winery was founded in the mid-1980s by Antonella and Ersiliana Bronca, inspired by their father Livio, who had worked in the Treviso viticultural sector for over 30 years. They have recently been joined by Ersiliana's daughter Elisa, a young enologist who trained at the University of Padua. The cellar is controlled by modern technology that monitors every movement of the wine, while respecting the age-old production tradition. Hectares under vine: 23.

**Wines**: Prosecco Spumante Extra Dry, Prosecco Spumante Brut, Prosecco Spumante Particella 68, Colli di Conegliano Bianco Delico, Colli di Conegliano Rosso "Ser bele".

↑ **Bellenda** – *Via Gaetano Giardino 90 - Loc. Carpesica* - **Vittorio Veneto** *(TV)* - ✆ *0438 92 00 25* - *www.bellenda.it* - *info@ bellenda.it* - *Winery tours by reservation*. The winery was founded in 1986 and is run by the Cosmo family. One of the best expressions of Bellenda's high-quality

production is its sparkling wines, made using both the Charmat and the Classic methods. The Charmats are pleasantly fresh, floral and fruity, while the Classic Method sparklers have an impressive bead and sensory characteristics. The winery is also an Italian distributor for fine foreign wines. B&B accommodation available at the Alice Relais nelle Vigne (*www.alice-relais.com*). Hectares under vine: 35.

**Wines**: Prosecco Spumante, Colli di Conegliano Rosso, Metodo Rurale, Prosecco DOC Treviso.

↑ **Le Vigne di Alice** – *Via della Chiesa 20* - **Vittorio Veneto** *(TV)* - ✆ *0438 92 08 18* - *www.levignedialice.it* - *info@levigne dialice.it* - *Winery tours by reservation*. The winery is run by Cinzia Canzian and Pier Francesco Bonicelli. The feminine element is a fundamental feature in the production of these wines, which reflect and express the strong bond with the area and its traditions. The first harvest was in 2004. The sparkling wines, produced using the cuve close method, are designed and produced to valorise and enhance the typical characteristics of the Prosecco grape. Accommodation at the Alice Relais nelle Vigne (*www.alice-relais.com*). Hectares under vine: 6.

**Wines**: Alice Prosecco Superiore Extra Dry, Doro Prosecco Superiore Brut, Tajad Cuvée Brut, Osé Rosé Brut.

**Conte Loredan Gasparini-Venegazzù** – *Via Martignago Alto 23* - **Volpago del Montello** *(TV)* - ✆ *0423 87 00 24* - *www. loredangasparini.it* - *info@ loredangasparini.it* - *Winery tours by reservation*. The winery was founded in the 1950s by Count Piero Loredan, the descendant of Venetian doge Leonardo Loredan. In 1973 it was taken over by the

© Luis Louro/Shutterstock

current owner, Giancarlo Palla. From the outset the estate has distinguished itself for its wines made from typical Bordeaux varieties such as Cabernet Sauvignon, Cabernet Franc, Merlot and Malbec. Hectares under vine: 80.

**Wines**: Capo di Stato, Venegazzù della Casa, Prosecco. Other products: grappa.

## LISON PRAMAGGIORE

**Cantine Paladin-Bosco del Merlo** – *Via Postumia 12* – **Annone Veneto** *(VE) - ☏ 0422 76 81 67 - www.paladin.it - paladin@paladin.it - Winery tours by reservation, Mon.-Fri. 9-13 and 14-19, Sat. 9-17.* The history of the winery commenced in 1962, when Valentino Paladin managed to make his dream of growing grapes and making wine come true, following the family tradition commenced by his grandfather. Over the years the business has grown, as has the quality of its products. The name "Bosco del Merlo" is a tribute to the oak forests that once covered the area. Hectares under vine: 128.

**Wines**: Refosco dal Peduncolo Rosso, Malbech Gli Aceri, Pralis, Pinot Grigio, Cabernet. Other products: grappa, spirits, liqueurs, olive oil.

**Tenuta Sant'Anna** – *Via Mons. P.L. Zovatto 71 - Loc. Loncon* – **Annone Veneto** *(VE) - ☏ 0422 86 45 11 - www.tenutasantanna.it - info@genagricola.it - Winery tours by reservation.* The estate stands out for the attention that it has long dedicated to greeting visitors. Its old farmhouses have been renovated to accommodate guests and a room has been equipped as a kitchen in order to supply the tasting areas. A traditional fisherman's hut made entirely from reeds has been renovated to house guests during the summer. Hectares under vine: 140.

**Wines**: Bianco di Lison, Prosecco Spumante Charmat, Pinot Grigio, Merlot, Refosco dal Penduncolo Rosso. Other products: grappa and spirits.

**Borgo Stajnbech** – *Via Belfiore 109 - **Belfiore di Pramaggiore** (VE) - ☏ 0421 79 99 29 - www.borgostajnbech.com - info@borgostajnbech.com - Winery tours and tastings by reservation.* Giuliano Valent started working in his father's winery at a very early age, learning the secrets of the art of winemaking. Following a subsequent period training at other wineries, he decided to take the big step and open his own cellar. The winery is distinguished by its founder's propensity for research and wish to experiment, with the aid of his wife Adriana Marinato. Hectares under vine: 13.

**Wines**: Sauvignon Lison Pramaggiore, Pinot Grigio Lison Pramaggiore, Stajnbech Bianco Chardonnay, Refosco dal Peduncolo Rosso Lison Pramaggiore, Malbech IGT Veneto, Other products: grappa.

**Le Carline** – *Via Carline 24* - **Pramaggiore** *(VE) - ☏ 0421 79 97 41 - www.lecarline.com - info@lecarline.com - Winery tours and tastings by reservation (payment required).* Daniele Piccinin, flanked by his wife Diana and their children, has made the winery an admirable example of the use of organic farming methods, which yield fine wines packed with personality, renowned throughout the world. The cellar has recently been expanded using carefully chosen materials and architectural features in order to blend with the surrounding area, embracing the philosophy that "wine is poetry of the land and the sublime expression of those who produce it". Hectares under vine: 30.

**Wines**: Prosecco di Valdobbiadene, Pinot Grigio, Cabernet Franc Carline Rosso, Dogale bianco passito. Other products: grappa and olive oil.

🏛 **Venissa** – *F.te S.Caterina 3* - **Isola di Mazzorbo** - *Venezia - ☏ 041 52 72 281 - www.venissa.it - info@venissa.it - Wine tasting by reservation.* Years of historical and winemaking research, the result of the Bisol family's love for and commitment to Venice, together with the winemaking skills of Desiderio Bisol and the famous winemaker Roberto Cipresso, have brought back to life the precious Dorona di Venezia grape from the Venissa terroir. The vineyard is located on Mazzorbo, an island which – together with Torcello and Burano – is part of native Venice: an archipelago of nature, colours, flavours and art. Venissa is one of the last walled vineyards. The entire vineyard is surrounded by medieval walls,

© Wolfgang Amri/Shutterstock

rebuilt in 1727 as indicated on the marble placards set at opposite ends of the property. This peaceful, quiet location is made even more suggestive by the presence of a 14th-century bell tower at the Chiesa di San Michele Arcangelo, a church built in the 11th century. Overnight stays are available (6 rooms, starting at 145 €), and a restaurant is open for lunch and dinner (*restaurant with 1 Michelin star located inside the vineyard, starting at 60 €, excluding wines*). Hectares under vine: 0.8.

**Wines**: Venissa 2015.

## Where to stay

### ABANO TERME

**Terme Milano** – *Viale delle Terme 169, Abano Terme (PD), 13km/8mi SW of Padova - ☎ 049 86 69 444 - www.termemilano.it - 90 rooms*. In the pedestrianised area of Abano, this hotel offers indoor and outdoor pools to help you make the most of the thermal waters. Gym and tennis court.

### ASOLO

**Hotel Duse** – *Via Browning 190, Asolo (TV) - ☎ 0423 55 241 - www.hotelduse.com - Closed Jan. - 14 rooms, doubles €100*. A stone's throw from the central square, with small but cosy and well-furnished rooms.

### LONGARE

**Agriturismo Le Vescovane** – *Via San Rocco 19, 4 km W of Longare (VI) - ☎ 0444 27 35 70 - www.levescovane.com - 7 rooms, doubles from €100*. A 16th-c. hunting tower set in the silence of the Berici mountains.

### MAROSTICA

**Hotel-ristorante La Rosina** – *Via Marchetti 4, Valle San Floriano, 2 km N of Marostica (VI) - ☎ 0424 47 03 60 - www. larosina.it - 10 rooms, doubles from €90*. An elegant restaurant with a monumental chimney and rooms with relaxing views of the lush hills.

### MONSELICE

**Albergo Ca' Rocca** – *Via Basse 2, SR 104, 4 km SE of Monselice (PD) - ☎ 0429 76 71 51 - www.carocca.it - 19 rooms, doubles from €80*. A recent building with a swimming pool and large, well-appointed rooms.

### ODERZO

**Postumiahoteldesign** – *Via Cesare Battisti 2, Oderzo (TV) - ☎ 0422 71 38 20 - www. postumiahoteldesign.it - 29 rooms, doubles from €145*. A hotel in the town centre and along the river, personalised with works by Treviso artists and truly rare accessories.

© Szasz-Fabian Ilka Erika/Shutterstock

### PADOVA

**Al Cason** – *Via Frà Paolo Sarpi 40 - ☎ 049 66 26 36 - www.hotelalcason.com - 48 rooms*. A little out of the centre but close to the railway station. Family run with fairly basic facilities and simple but high-quality cooking.

### SANT'AMBROGIO DI VALPOLICELLA

**Locanda-trattoria Dalla Rosa Alda** – *Strada Garibaldi 4, San Giorgio, 1,5 km NW of Sant'Ambrogio di Valpolicella (VR) - ☎ 0457 70 10 18 - www.dallarosalda.it - Closed Nov.-mid-Mar. - 10 rooms, doubles from €90*. Simple cuisine featuring local produce. The comfortable rooms are furnished with antiques. Guests can enjoy their meals in a nice garden overlooking the lake, or taste wines in the rustic winery adjacent the Locanda.

### TEOLO

**Villa Lussana** – *Via Chiesa 1, 35037 Teolo, 21km/13mi SW of Padova- ☎ 391 79 19 975. www.villalussana.com - Closed Nov.-Feb. - 7 rooms. Restaurant*. An attractive hotel in an Art Nouveau villa with fine views over the Colli Euganei.

### TREVISO

**Agriturismo Il Cascinale** – *Via Torre d'Orlando 6/b, 3 km SW of Treviso - ☎ 0422 40 22 03 - www.agriturismoilcascinale.it - 17 rooms, doubles from €40*. Formerly immersed in the countryside, this hospitable cottage has comfortable new rooms. Restaurant service available in the evenings of Fri., Sat.; Sun. also for lunch.

### VERONA

**Scalzi** – *Via Carmelitani Scalzi 5 - ☎ 045 59 04 22 - www.hotelscalzi.it - 19 rooms*. Inside this neoclassical early 19th-century hotel you'll find various rooms, each different from the next, and (during warm months) a small, beautiful courtyard for breakfasts.

# TRENTINO ALTO ADIGE/SÜDTIROL

Trentino is a region of immense appeal to all lovers of nature and the mountains. Viticulture has been practised with excellent results along the course of the river Adige for centuries. International varieties such as Chardonnay, Riesling, Sauvignon, Pinot, Cabernet, Merlot, Gewürztraminer, Müller Thurgau and Sylvaner are cultivated with great success, but it is the native varieties, such as Schiava, Nosiola, Lagrein and Marzemino, that are more interesting as they are more representative of the territory and part of its culture and tradition. Sparkling wines known around the world are produced under the appellation Trento DOC. Another of the region's enological treasures is Vino Santo, a sweet wine of great charm produced in very limited quantity. Proud and strongly rooted in its traditions and culture, Alto Adige/Südtirol has two faces, Italian and Mitteleuropean. Grapes are the zone's principal crop and its magnificent landscape is spread with rows of vines. Here the wines develop intense, complex aromas as a result of the large and sudden swings in temperature, daily and seasonally. In Alto Adige/Südtirol sharing a bottle of wine in company is a long established and deeply appreciated pleasure, and in autumn it is wine that provides the theme for a traditional series of convivial meetings: the Törggelen – a name derived from the Latin word *torculum*, meaning wine press – is the custom of touring the local cellars to taste the new wine and enjoy roast chestnuts, homemade bread, charcuterie, cheeses and other local foods.

© Antonioscarpi/iStock

*Mountains in Mezzolombardo*

## Trentino

Here, in a landscape of lakes, mountains, rivers, plains, small towns and tiny villages, viticulture has been practised for centuries, as discoveries of ancient wine-related objects in the Cembra valley has shown. Today Trentino is one of Italy's most famous zones for sparkling wine. It can be argued that the production of sparkling wine in Italy began in the zone designated as **Trento DOC**. The region's **sparkling wines**, whether white or rosé, are produced using the classic method.

Fine and elegant, they are made using Chardonnay, Pinot Nero, Pinot Bianco and Pinot Meunier grapes.

Another very important appellation is **Teroldego Rotaliano**, a zone in one of the region's few flat areas, and home of the native vine of the same name that gives full-bodied red and rosé wines of great character, with intense and lingering scents of red fruit, flowers and spices. In **Casteller DOC** a refreshing, delicately fruity red wine with a moderate alcohol content is made from Schiava and Enantio grapes (Enantio is a variety of Lambrusco). Schiava is the most important variety in the **Caldaro DOC** zone, which is shared with Alto Adige. **Valdadige DOC**, on the other hand, is an interregional zone that lies across certain municipalities in the provinces of Trento, Bolzano and Verona.

The **Trentino** appellation comprises a wide range of grape varieties and wines, one of which is **Vino Santo**, an excellent dried-grape wine made from Nosiola grapes. Also of excellent quality are sweet wines from the aromatic varieties Moscato Giallo and Moscato Rosa.

**Nosiola**, the name of which comes from *nocciola* (hazelnut) due to the colour of its skin and its slightly toasted, bitter flavour, is used to make fruity and flowery dry wines.

Among the black grapes, **Marzemino**, the most commonly cultivated variety in Vallegarina, is perhaps better known as it is mentioned in Mozart's opera *Don Giovanni*. Another local variety is **Rebo**, which is a cross between Marzemino and Merlot.

International varieties represent a large proportion of the grape crop, which here have found the ideal environment to enable wines of subtlety and depth to be made. The quality of the region's wines is partly due to the large rises and falls in temperature that occur each day, and between the seasons. These variations stimulate the aromatic enrichment of the grapes and thus benefit the taste and bouquet of the wines. The best time to drink Trentino sparkling wines is 1-3 years after disgorgement,

### DOC ZONES AND THEIR SUB-ZONES

Casteller
Lago di Caldaro *or* Caldaro
   (with Alto Adige/Südtirol)
Teroldego Rotaliano
Trentino
   Sorni
   Marzemino
   Vino Santo
Trento
Valdadige *or* Etschaler
   (with Alto Adige/Südtirol and Veneto)
Valdadige Terradeiforti *or* Terradeiforti
   (with Veneto)

1-2 years for the reds, and 1 year for the whites and rosés.

## 1. FROM TRENTO TO LAKE GARDA

*Locations with a winery are indicated by the symbol ♈; for the addresses of the wineries, see p. 206.*

for the addresses of the wineries, see p. 206.

### Trento★ ♈

Trentino's chief town stands on the river Adige surrounded by an amphitheatre of mountains, hills and valleys close to the Brenta group. Walking through its streets the blend of the town's Italian and Germanic natures is evident. Between 1545 and 1563 Trento was the setting for the famous Council of Trent, which was the Catholic Church's attempt to resist the growing wave of Protestantism and marked the beginning of the Counter-Reformation. Following

## PRINCIPAL VARIETIES CULTIVATED

| WHITE GRAPES | GREY GRAPES | BLACK GRAPES |
|---|---|---|
| Bianchetta | Trebbiano Toscano | Marzemino |
| Chardonnay | Trevigiana | Merlot |
| Kerner | Veltliner | Meunier |
| Manzoni Bianco | | Negrara |
| Moscato Giallo | **GREY GRAPES** | Pavana |
| Müller Thurgau | Moscato Rosa | Pinot Nero |
| Nosiola | Pinot Grigio | Rebo |
| Pinot Bianco | | Schiava Gentile |
| Riesling | **BLACK GRAPES** | Schiava Grossa |
| Riesling Italico | Cabernet Franc | Schiava Grigia |
| Sauvignon | Cabernet Sauvignon | Syrah |
| Sylvaner | Enantio or Lambrusco | Teroldego |
| Traminer Aromatico | a Foglia Frastagliata | |
| | Lagrein | |

*Duomo and the Neptune fountain, Trento*

the end of Napoleonic domination, in 1814 Trento was given to Austria and it was only after bitter struggle that it and the region were liberated by Italian troops in 1918.

Ringed by the duomo, Palazzo Pretorio (13th c., restored), the Civic Tower and fresco-covered Rella houses, **Piazza del Duomo★** lies at the heart of the city. The majestic **duomo★** was constructed in the 12th-13th c. in Lombard Romanesque style. The allegory of Fortune, which supposedly governs man's fate, is represented in the rose window in the façade of the north transept. Inside, note the original stairs that climb to the towers. On the right, the 17th-c. Chapel of the Crucifix is the setting for the large Christ before which the decrees of the Council were proclaimed. Beneath the choir the remains of a 5th-c. basilica have been uncovered.

**Diocesan Museum★** – *Piazza del Duomo 18. Open 10-13 and 14-18, closed Tue. and hols., ℘ 0461 23 44 19, www. museodiocesanotridentino.it.* The museum in Palazzo Pretorio contains the most outstanding items of the duomo's treasure: paintings, carved wooden panels, an altarpiece and eight Flemish wall-hangings made in the early 16th c. by Pieter Van Aelst.

Via Manci mixes the architecture of the Veneto (loggias and frescoes) with that of the mountains (projecting roofs), and the 17th-c. Palazzo Galasso stands at no. 63. Piazza Battisti, just behind Via Manci, is the starting place to explore

**Tridentum, the underground city**, where you can investigate the remains of the Roman city. *Piazza Battisti Cesare 1, for information on opening times ℘ 0461 23 01 71.*

**Castello del Buon Consiglio★★** – *Via Bernardo Clesio 5. Open May-Nov. 10-18, rest of the year 9.30-17, closed working Mon., ℘ 0461 23 37 70, www.buonconsiglio.it.* This castle was the seat of the prince-bishops of Trento from the 13th-19th c. As its name suggests, Castelvecchio is the old part, of which the Aquila Tower is a section (*to visit, see the keepers in the Loggia del Romanino*). Here a 15th-c. Bohemian painter frescoed the **months★★** in international Gothic style: in January the lords of the castle throw snowballs at one another, May is the season of love, the harvest takes place in October, in December firewood is gathered, etc.

Bernardo Cles, a prince-bishop in Trento in the 16th c., enlarged the castle by adding the Great Palace. Cles was a true Renaissance prince and invited famous artists from afar to decorate his residence. Dosso and Battista Dossi, two brothers from Ferrara, painted the most important rooms, such as the Sala Grande, while the Brescian artist Gerolamo Romanino frescoed the biblical and mythological scenes (Phaeton on his Sun carriage) on the vaults and in the lunettes of the loggia. A visit to the castle is also a chance to see art, coin and archaeological collections, and to visit the Risorgimento Museum.

**MART (Modern and Contemporary Art Museum of Rovereto and Trento)** – *Corso Bettini 43, Tue.-Sun. 10-18 (Fri. 21), www.mart.trento.it.* The 16th-c. Palazzo delle Albere is one of the homes of the MART, where the permanent collection of Italian art from the 19th and early 20th c. are displayed. It is also used to mount temporary exhibitions.

**MUSE - Museo delle Scienze** – *Corso del Lavoro e della Scienza 3. Tue.-Fri. 10-18, Sat.-Sun. 10-19, closed Mon., ℘ 0461 27 03 11, www.muse.it.* Designed by Renzo Piano and inaugurated in 2013, this museum is located in one of the city's former industrial zones and constitutes a magnificent setting in which visitors can explore the sciences. Themes include: glaciers, the alpine habitat and geology.

## Along the rivers Adige and Sarca

*Leave Trento south and take the S 12 to Rovereto.*

The Abetone and Brennero state road passes through the enchanting **Lagarina** valley, with its many castles, orchards and vineyards. Close to Calliano, the huge **Beseno Castle** (12th-18th c.), where there is a lovely cycle of frescoes that illustrates the months, is the setting for historical re-enactments in summer. *Open. 10-18, winter only Sat. and Sun. 9.30-17, closed working Mon., ℘ 0464 83 46 00, www.buonconsiglio.it.*

There are also villages of winemaking interest on the right bank of the Adige, such as **Aldeno**, **Nomi**, **Nogaredo** and **Isera** ♟.

In **Rovereto**, the local premises of the **MART★ (Modern and Contemporary Art Museum of Rovereto and Trento)** is a futuristic and multi-functional building designed by Mario Botta. It holds temporary exhibitions and a permanent collection of works by Italian artists from Futurism to the present day. – *Corso Bettini 43. Open 10-18, Fri. 10-21, closed*

### THE TERROIR

**Area**: 6,206.86 km², of which approximately 9,815 hectares are planted to vine

**Production 2019**: 838,000 hectolitres, of which 770,000 VQPRD

**Geography**: mixed, with flat areas (like the Rotalian Plain) and mountainous zones (like the Dolomites). Similarly the composition is mixed from zone to zone. Even the climate is varied: alpine in the north, continental in the central zones, and mild in the south

**Zones, wines and vines**: Marzemino is popular in the Lagarina valley whereas the Trento plain is planted with Schiava, Merlot, Enantio, Cabernet, Moscato Giallo, Pinot Bianco and Chardonnay. The Adige valley is the natural habitat for Teroldego, while the Cembra valley is known for Schiava, Müller Thurgau, Pinot Bianco and Chardonnay. Finally, the Sarna valley is the centre of production of Nosiola and Vino Santo. Right across the region the most cultivated black variety is Schiava, while their white equivalent is Chardonnay, partly due to its widespread use in making sparkling wines

### WINE AND FOOD ROUTES

Strada del Vino e dei Sapori del Trentino – Via della Villa, 6 - Villazzano di Trento (TN) c/o Villa de Mersi, ℘ 0461 92 18 63, www.tastetrentino.it

Strada del Vino e dei Sapori Colline Avisiane – Via Rodolfo Psaro Belluno (BL) – ℘ 0437 94 03 00, www.dolomiti.it

Strada del Vino e dei Sapori dal Lago di Garda alle Dolomiti di Brenta – Via Cesare Battisti, 38/d, Ponte Arche (TN) ℘ 0465 70 26 26, www.dolomiti.it

Strada dela Mela e dei Sapori delle Valli di Non e di Sole – Via Lorenzoni 27, Cles (TN), ℘ 0463 42 15 84, www.tastetrentino.it

Strada dei Formaggi delle Dolomiti – Via Battisti 4, Predazzo (TN), ℘ 349 54 99 902, www.tastetrentino.it

Strada del Vino e dei Sapori della Piana Rotaliana – Piazza della Chiesa 1, Mezzocorona (TN), ℘ 346 37 29 618, 618, www.dolomiti.it

Strada del Vino e dei Sapori Trento e Valsugana – www.tastetrentino.it

*Mon., ☎ 800 39 77 60 or ☎ 0464 43 88 87, www.mart.trento.it.*

Rovereto's 14th-c. castle has an interesting **museum** dedicated to World War I. *Via Castelbarco 7. Open 10-18, (Sat.-Sun. 10-19 in Summer), closed working Mon., ☎ 0464 43 81 00, museodellaguerra.it.*

To the south of Rovereto the **memorial in Castel Dante** holds the remains of the fallen in the Great War. A fine view is given over the Lagarina valley from **Lizzana Castle**, where Dante is thought to have stayed. On Miravalle hill to the east of Rovereto, the magnificent **Peace Bell**, cast in 1924, strikes 100 times every evening at 9 to commemorate the victims of war.

Continuing south you arrive at **Marco**, known for the rocks that slid down Monte Zugna in prehistoric times, leaving visible layers impressed with dinosaur prints.

Cross the river and head towards Lake Garda, passing through **Mori**, near which an archaeological site dating to the Bronze Age has been found. **Torbole** is an elegant holiday resort much appreciated by windsurfers, from which, taking the road towards Nago, you can see the Marmitte dei Giganti ("Giants' Stockpots"), a geological phenomenon).

**Riva del Garda★** 🍷, at the northern tip of the lake, is a small holiday town overshadowed to the west by massive rock walls. Since antiquity it has been an important trading centre due to its strategic position on the road that connected Verona to the Alps. There is still a small **old town★**, formed by a tangle of narrow shop-lined alleys. The town revolves around Piazza III Novembre, where the Town Hall, Palazzo Pretorio and Apponale Tower stand. Surrounded by the lake, the Rocca (fort), built in the 12th c., renovated several times, and eventually turned into a prison in the 19th c., is the home of the **Alto Garda Museum** (archaeology and history sections). *Piazza Cesare Battisti 3a. Open 10-18, closed Mon., ☎ 0464 57 38 69, www.museoaltogarda.it.*

*For the itinerary in the Venetan part of the lake, see p. 155.*

*Take the S 45 bis that runs up the* **Sarca valley**.

## Arco 🍷

The mild climate enjoyed by Arco, the birthplace of the painter Giovanni Segantini (1858-99), encourages lush vegetation and, in past centuries, made the town a popular resort among the aristocracy of Verona and Brescia. The centre of the town is the lovely **public garden**, around which Arco's principal monuments are ranged. Follow Via Segantini towards the river to find Palazzo dei Panni, an ancient nobleman's house that was later turned into a cloth factory and is today a centre for art exhibitions and workshops.

In the opposite direction to Via Segantini, Via Vergolano leads to Villa Arciducale, a large park that rings the winter residence built in 1873 for Archduke Albert of Austria. A demanding 20-min. walk through the olives takes you to the remains of the 13th-c. **castle** that belonged to the counts of Arco, where a cycle of frescoes is dedicated to games and tournaments.

Continue on the S 45 north, passing **Dro**, celebrated for its Vino Santo, after which the road passes through unusual masses of morainic detritus created in the Ice Age. A little to the north of Dro you pass **Lake Cavedine** 🍷 to arrive at **Sarche** 🍷. Next you come to the charming **Lake Toblino★** set against a backdrop of rock walls. A romantic castle, which used to be a residence of the prince-bishops of Trento but today is a restaurant, stands on a small peninsula. The lake is joined by a canal to Lake Santa Massenza.

Return to Trento through **Vezzano**, a village surrounded by vineyards.

## 2. FROM TRENTO TOWARDS THE NON VALLEY

*Itinerary of 50 km from Trento to Molveno. Leave Trento north on the S 12.*

This route takes you through one of the most beautiful areas of Trentino and one of the most dedicated to winemaking. **Lavis** 🍷 is a lovely village with an interesting Baroque parish church. Several km later you arrive at **San Michele dell'Adige** 🍷, a winemaking village on the junction of the S 42 and the road to Bolzano where you can visit an interesting **ethnographic museum**. *Via Mach 1. Open 9-12.30 and 14.30-18, closed Mon., ☎ 0461 65 03 14, www.museosanmichele.it*

*Take the S 42 for the Non valley.*

After **Mezzocorona** 🍷 cross the **Campo Rotaliano**, a wide fertile plain planted to vine which produces the excellent Teroldego. In 1271 the plain was divided between the prince-bishop of Trento, who received Mezzolombardo, and the Count of Tyrol, who got Mezzocorona. A fine view of the plain can be had from the Gothic Church of San Pietro in **Mezzolombardo** 🍷.

Having left the town, a detour to the left winds up to the holiday resort of **Fai della Paganella**. It stands on a plateau at almost 1000 m overlooked by the Paganella massif (2125 m). The remains of a village called Doss Castel have been found close by, which dates originally back to the Bronze Age.

From Fai, you can either return to Mezzolombardo or continue to **Andalo**, a popular holiday destination in the middle of an immense forest of conifers beneath the peaks of the Brenta group. Even further on is **Molveno**, situated in gentle sloping meadows at the tip of a pretty **lake★**.

# Alto Adige/Südtirol

Viticulture in mountainous areas like Alto Adige (a.k.a. South Tyrol) is not a simple business. The local vine-growers need determination and perseverance as nature here is on the one hand a valuable friend, but on the other sometimes a hindrance.

Almost all the local wines (98%) lie within the designated zones, which puts Alto Adige/Südtirol at the top of the table. The names of the appellations are as follows: Alto Adige/Südtirol, Lago di Caldaro (shared with Trentino) and Valdadige (shared with Trentino and Veneto). Alto Adige/Südtirol is also subdivided into geographical areas.

**Alto Adige/Südtirol** is the principal DOC zone. It produces many types of white, red, rosé, sparkling and sweet wines that are divided between the sub-zones of Val Venosta, Meranese, Terlano, Colli di Bolzano, Santa Maddalena and Valle Isarco.

The most common varieties are Schiava, Lagrein and Traminer Aromatico (or Gewürztraminer). **Schiava** is cultivated in different sub-varieties and gives light, refreshing wines with delicate fragrances of cherries, almonds and violets. **Lagrein** produces an intensely ruby-red wine, full-bodied and characterised by notes of red and black fruits, such as blackberries and plums, but also of violets. Lagrein can also produce a rosé version called Kretzer: this is a thirst-quenching wine with an intriguing colour and pleasant hints of wild strawberries and red soft fruit. **Gewürztraminer** gives a white wine of enticing, heady aromas from which lingering and often mature notes of fruit, flowers and spices arise, with strong hints of litchees and cloves. Its most successful *terroir* is around Termeno.

## PRINCIPAL VARIETIES CULTIVATED

### WHITE GRAPES
Chardonnay
Kerner
Moscato Giallo
Müller Thurgau
Pinot Bianco
Riesling
Riesling Italico
Sauvignon
Sylvaner
Traminer Aromatico
Veltliner

### GREY GRAPES
Moscato Rosa
Pinot Grigio

### BLACK GRAPES
Cabernet Franc
Cabernet Sauvignon
Lagrein
Malvasia
   (Rotermalvasier)
Merlot
Pinot Nero
Portoghese
Schiava Gentile
Schiava Grigia
Schiava Grossa

© Razvan Chirnoaga/Shutterstock

*Rows of Moscato vines*

The international varieties, too, have acclimatised so well that they are able to produce high quality wines.

The **sweet wines** of the South Tyrol are a delight for the palate, above all those made from sun-dried Moscato Rosa and **Moscato Giallo** grapes. The latter is also vinified with surprising results in the "dry" version. Moscato Giallo gives a dessert wine with golden glints and nuances of ripe fruit, jam and flowers. **Moscato Rosa**, however, produces a wine of an intense pink that leaves lingering flavours of rose, spices, ripe fruit and jam in the mouth.

## 1. OLTRADIGE AND THE WINE ROUTE

*Circular itinerary of approximately 80 km.*

### Bolzano/Bozen★ 🍷

**Piazza Walther**, which is the heart of the city, is named after a great medieval German poet. The **duomo★** is built in pink sandstone and covered with polychrome tiles, and is the result of successive building phases: 5th-6th c., early Christian basilica; 8th-9th c., Carolingian building; 12th c., Romanesque construction; 14th c., a Gothic version. The 16th-c. bell tower (62 m tall) has Late Gothic aper-

**THE TERROIR**

**Area**: 7,397.86 km², of which approximately 5,551 hectares are planted to vine

**Production 2019**: 307,880 hectolitres, of which 295,582 VQPRD

**Wines**: approximately 45% of the vines produce white wine. The most common cultivars are Pinot Bianco, Chardonnay and Rulander (Pinot Grigio), followed by Gewürztraminer, Silvaner, Müller Thurgau, Riesling, Sauvignon, Veltliner and Kerner. Black varieties represent the remaining 55%: in addition to the local Schiava and Lagrein, the most important international varieties are grown, such as Pinot Nero, Merlot, Cabernet Franc and Cabernet Sauvignon

**THE PROTECTION CONSORTIA AND WINE ROUTES**

Consorzio Tutela Produzione Vino Santa Maddalena – Via Alto Adige 60, Bolzano (BZ), ✆ 0471 09 41 10, www.magdalener.com

Strada del Vino dell'Alto Adige – Associazione "Südtiroler Weinstraße", via Cantine 10, Caldaro (BZ), ✆ 0471 86 06 59, www.suedtiroler-weinstrasse.it

Associazione Turistica di Termeno/Raiffeisen sulla Strada del Vino – Via Mindelheimer 10A, Termeno sulla Strada del Vino (BZ), ✆ 0471 86 01 31, www.tramin.com

tures. The decoration of the intrados of the "wine door" on the north side with themes linked with vines and the grape harvest is a reminder of the privilege enjoyed by the parish church for the exclusive sale of wine, which occurred in front of the door. Inside there are traces of 14th- and 15th-c. frescoes and a Late Gothic sandstone **pulpit★** (1514).

Constructed in Gothic style at the start of the 14th c., the **Church dei Dome-nicani** (*Piazza Domenicani*) has a deep presbytery separated from the nave by a gallery. It has undergone various altera-tions and suffered damage, in particular after it was secularised in 1785. Beyond the jube, the Chapel of San Giovanni lies on the right, adorned with frescoes by Giottoesque painters of the 14th c. The **cloister** (*Sat. 10-12, ☎ 0471 98 20 27*) is reached from the conservatory for the religious education of young girls to the right of the church, and is decorated with a cycle of frescoes painted by Friedrich Pacher in the 15th c.

The main commercial street in Bolzano is the attractive **Via dei Portici★**, lined by ancient houses, which leads to **Piazza delle Erbe**, the site of the fruit and veg-etable market.

Following the fire in 1291 the **Church dei Francescani** was rebuilt in the 14th c. in Gothic style and had Gothic vaults added a century later. Worthy of note is the elaborate wooden **Nativ-ity Altar★** with doors made by Hans Klocker (16th c.). The **cloister** has traces of Giottoesque-Riminese frescoes.

**Archaeological Museum of Alto Adige, "the Ötzi Museum"★** – *Via Museo 43. Open 10-18, closed working Mon., ☎ 0471 32 01 00, www.iceman.it.* The museum offers a chronological account of the history of Alto Adige/Südtirol from the end of the last Ice Age (15,000 BC) to the Carolingian period (800 AD). The star attraction, "the iceman", more familiarly known as Ötzi, is on the first floor. He was found by a pair of Ger-man climbers on the Similaun glacier in the Ötztal Alps in 1991.

At the end of Via Museo, the **Lungotàl-vera Bolzano** (the riverside promenade) provides an enjoyable walk, on the right of which stands the medieval Mareccio Castle.

*Cross the river Tàlvera and continue along Corso Libertà, past the Abbey Church of Sant'Agostino.* The ancient parish **Church of Gries** was originally built in Roman-esque but reconstructed in the 15th c. in Gothic style. Opposite the entrance is a Romanesque wooden Crucifix. In the chapel to the right of the high altar you can see the **altar with doors★** made by Michael Pacher (ca. 1430-1498), a Tyro-lean painter and sculptor. It is decorated with the *Coronation of the Virgin*. Note the eyeglasses worn by the figure at bottom right.

An attractive and panoramic ride on the funicular railway from Via Sarentino (to the north of the historic centre) takes you to **San Genesio** (Jenesien) on the Salto plateau, which offers splendid **views★** over the city.

## Along the Wine Route

*Leave Bolzano west on the S 42.*

Cross the fertile floor of the Adige valley and, once you have passed over the river, take the left turn to **Firmiano Castle** (Schloss Sigmundskron). This houses the **MMM Firmian★**, the nucleus of the mountain museum created by Reinhold Messner, the famous climber from Alto Adige/Südtirol (there are 5 satellite sites, see the box). *Open 10-18, closed Thu. and mid-Nov.-mid-Mar., ☎ 0471 63 12 64, www.messner-mountain-museum.it.*

Passing through vineyards and orchards, you rise to **Appiano sulla Strada del Vino ♀ (Eppan an der Weinstrasse)**, which is split into several sections. The main one is the architecturally attrac-tive San Michele. A 4-km drive by **Monte** (**Berg**) and a 20-min. walk take you to the

## MMM - Messner Mountain Museum

The museum is based on a novel concept: that of having a central premises (at Castel Firmiano) and five "satellite" buildings that deal with specific topics linked to mountains. In Reinhold Messner's private castle at Naturno, **MMM Juval** is devoted to the religious aspects of mountains; **MMM Dolomites**, in a fort on Monte Rite to the south of Cortina, tackles the theme of rock; **MMM Ortles** in Solda in the Venosta valley, is an underground site dedicated to ice; **MMM Corones**, on the summit plateau of Kronplatz, is dedicated to traditional mountaineering; and **MMM Ripa** in Brunico Castle in the Pusteria valley deals with anthropology, presenting mountain peoples from Asia, Africa, South America and Europe. For information on opening times and visits www.messner-mountain-museum.it

remains of Appiano Castle (12th c.) next to the Chapel of Santa Maddalena (13th c. frescoes). There are several wine-shops in nearby **Cornaiano** ♆ (**Girlan**).

Continue on the S 14 to **Caldaro** ♆ (**Kaltern**), the most important town in Oltradige. Here you can visit the **Wine Museum** (*Via dell'Oro 1, open Apr.-Nov. Tue.-Sat. 10-17, Sun. and hols. 10-12, ℘ 0471 96 31 68, www.museo-del-vino. it*) and admire beautiful Gothic-Renaissance buildings. A funicular leaves from Sant'Antonio, climbing 800 m to the panoramic Mendola Pass. **Lake Caldaro** lies about 4 km from the town of the same name.

**Termeno** ♆ (**Tramin**) has an interesting cycle of 15th c. frescoes in its parish church. Once past **Cortaccia** ♆ (**Kurtatsch**), you come to **Magrè** ♆ (**Magreid**) where the church square is lined by ancient houses in Venetian style dating from the 15th-18th c.

The last municipality on the Wine Route is **Cortina** (**Kurtinig**). A few km later you run alongside the motorway before crossing it to **Salorno** ♆ (**Salurn**), where you take the S 12 in the direction of Bolzano.

**Egna** ♆ (**Neumarkt**) is an old village with porticoed streets. Next comes Villa (Vill), with a lovely Gothic church, and **Montagna** ♆ (**Montan**), and finally **Ora** ♆ (**Auer**), an important junction at the start of the road that runs through the Dolomites.

## 2. FROM BOLZANO TO MERANO AND NATURNO ALONG THE ADIGE

*Itinerary of 45 km from Bolzano to Naturno.*

Leave Bolzano west on the S 38 that runs along the valley floor through vines and fruit trees.

**Terlano** ♆ (**Terlan**) is an important winemaking town with a fine frescoed Gothic church. Continue along the S 38 to Merano.

### Merano/Meran★★ ♆

Lying at the mouth of the Venosta valley, Merano is a renowned spa, ski town and elegant tourist resort. It is ideal for walking: either strolling beneath porticoes, or taking the Winter and Summer *Passeggiate*, or following the Tappeiner Route or Sissi Path, the latter leading to the magnificent gardens of Trauttmansdorff Castle.

The long, straight **Via Portici★** (**Laubengasse**) is entirely lined with porticoes, old houses and 15th-c. shops with carved façades. **Piazza Duomo** lies at the end of the road. The Gothic duomo is dedicated to St Nicholas, of whom a 14th-c. statue stands on the right side with a gigantic St Christopher repainted at the end of the 19th c. The church has a massive bell tower and crenellated façade. The interior features fine ribbed Gothic vaults, two 15th-c. windows, two Gothic panels and paintings by the 18th-c. Tyrolean artist Knoller.

The **Chapel of Santa Barbara** stands at the start of the old path to Tirolo, where there is a 16th-c. high relief of the *Last Supper*.

**Castello Principesco★** – *Via G. Galilei 21, Open 10.30-17 (Sun. and public hols. 10.30-13), closed Mon., Feb. and Mar., ℘ 329 01 86 390, www.comune.merano.bz.it*. Built in the 14th-15th c., the embattled castle and watchtower was the residence of the princes of Tyrol when they stayed in the city. The charming and intimate rooms make it particularly appealing.

Two small but interesting museums are the **Women's Museum** (*Via Mainardo 2, open 10-17 (Sat. 10-12.30), closed Sun.,*

0473 23 12 16, www.museia.it), which exhibits women's clothing and accessories through the ages, and the **Jewish Museum** (Via Schiller 14, not far from the spa, open Tue. and Wed. 15-18, Thu. and Fri. 9-12, 0473 23 61 27) in Merano synagogue, built at the start of the 20th c.

**Terme di Merano**★ – Piazza Terme 9. 0473 25 20 00, www.termemerano.it. The new spa buildings are on the opposite bank of the Passirio. This health facility, which will be appreciated by all fitness and treatment enthusiasts, offers a number of covered and open-air swimming pools, lawns to laze on and a modern relaxation room. The building is almost entirely glazed, allowing swimmers views over the surrounding mountains.

The **Winter and Summer Walks**★★ run alongside the river Passirio and are Merano's most attractive feature. The tree- and flower-lined winter walk (Passeggiata d'Inverno) takes you past shops, coffee shops and terraces. It is the more animated of the two and continues into the Passeggiata Gilf to end by a waterfall. On the other bank, the summer walk takes you into a shady park.

The magnificent **Passeggiata Tappeiner**★★, 4 km long, winds along 150 m above the city, offering fine views as far as the village of Tirolo.

The long **Sissi Path** crosses the city and the river at Passirio Bridge, then continues to the wonderful Trauttmansdorff Castle (approx. 2 km east of the historic centre).

**Trauttmansdorff Castle Gardens**★★ **and Touriseum**★ – Via San Valentino 51/a. Open Apr.-Oct. 9-19 (Fri. till 23 in Jun.-Aug.), 16-31 Oct. 9-18, 1-15 Nov. 9-17, 0473 25 56 00 (Trauttmansdorff), 0473 25 56 55 (Touriseum), www.trauttmansdorff.it, www.touriseum.it. The Botanic Gardens and Touriseum are a pleasant, educational experience to be enjoyed at leisure. During the walk you are asked to try and guess the names of plants that give off a certain smell, you can get lost in the maze, enter the aviary, look over Merano from a belvedere, and visit the Lily Pond.

The **Touriseum** gives a lively and amusing account of the history of 200 years of alpine tourism in a realistic setting.

**Viticulture at Rametz Castle** – Via Labers 4 (Maia Alta), 0473 21 10 11, www.rametz.com. In 1980 the Schmidt family fitted out 4 rooms in Rametz Castle as a museum dedicated to winemaking. It displays tools used to work the ground, bring in the harvest, transport the grapes and make the wine, as well as the oldest techniques for dealing with parasites. The visit passes through the historic stone cellars and ends in the modern winemaking premises.

**Tirolo**★ stands 4 km north of Merano and can also be reached by chairlift. The charming, flower-decked village is surrounded by vines and fruit trees and dominated by **Tirolo Castle** (**Schlosstirol**), which was built in the 12th c. by the counts of the Venosta valley. The

Santa Magdalena, Alto Adige/Südtirol

castle can be reached with a 20 min. walk. It is the home of the **History and Culture Museum of the Province of Bolzano**, which tells the history of the Tyrol and Alto Adige in permanent and temporary exhibitions. *Open 10-17, closed Mon. and Dec.-Feb., ✆ 0473 22 02 21, www.casteltirolo.it.*

Not far away is the bizarre **Castel Fontana** (**Brunnenburg**), an imaginative reconstruction of ruins of 13th-c. fortifications, where Ezra Pound worked on his Cantos. A farming museum is dedicated to the local way of life. *Via Ezra Pound 3. Open Apr.-Nov. 10-17, closed Fri.-Sat., ✆ 339 18 03 086.*

Follow the S 38 from Merano to **Venosta valley★** and the Resia Pass. The Venosta valley is long, sunny and covered by apple orchards, and becomes increasingly wide as you travel west and rise towards the Resia Pass. Shortly after passing the Forst brewery, you come to **Naturno** (**Naturns**), which stands on the meeting point of the Venosta and Senales valleys. The most famous inhabitant of the latter is Ötzi, who lies at rest in Bolzano archaeological museum (*see above*). Looking down on this valley "junction" is the 13th-c. **Juval Castle**, owned by the mountaineer Reinhold Messner, who has made it one of the satellite locations of the Messner Mountain Museum (*see p. 202*). *Open end of Mar.-Jun. and Aug.-Oct. 10-16, closed Wed., ✆ 348 44 33 871, www.messner-mountain-museum.it.*

Before entering the village, you will see the small Church of **San Procolo★** set slightly back from the road amongst orchards. It is decorated with the oldest frescoes (8th c.) in the German-speaking world. Note the saint cheerfully swinging on a rope; he is thought to be Procolo, the bishop of Verona, who fled from the city. The fresco represents his flight but what is strange is that he is shown on a swing being watched in surprise by the men looking out of the "window" above (the rope that supports the saint runs across the shoulders of the figure on the left) and the figures on the right. *Open Apr.-Oct. 9.30-12 and 14.30-17.30, closed Mon., ✆ 0473 67 31 39.*

After Naturno the road continues along the valley, passing by such lovely places as **Castelbello Ciardes** 🍷, **Sluderno**, **Glorenza**, **Malles**, **Burgusio** and **Lake**

**Resia** (*60 km north-west of Naturno*). Rising mysteriously above the lake surface is the bell tower of the old church of Curono, which was submerged in 1950 when the valley was turned into a reservoir and flooded.

## 3. FROM BOLZANO TO BRESSANONE ALONG THE ISARCO VALLEY

*Itinerary of 50 km from Bolzano to Novacella.*

The largest tributary of the river Adige has created a winding valley between Bolzano and Bressanone flanked by vine-covered slopes. *Leave Bolzano east and take the S 12.*

The road alternately runs alongside both banks of the river, passing through Cardano, Prato all'Isarco and Ponte Gardena, from which a detour to the right will take you to **Castelrotto** (**Kastelruth**). This town has fine old buildings and stands in a splendid position on a plateau. *Return to the S 12 and continue towards Bressanone.* Shortly you come to **Chiusa** 🍷 (**Klausen**), set in a narrow stretch at the foot of Sabiona convent. The village has a remarkable core of ancient houses (15th-16th c.) along the street that runs from the Gothic parish Church of Sant'Andrea to the Church dei Dodici Apostoli. Dominating the village

*Church of Sant'Andrea, Chiusa/Klausen*

is the Torre del Capitano, a tower built in the 13th c. A 30-min. walk from the village will take you to **Sabiona convent**. This was originally the seat of a bishopric but was transformed into a fort, and finally turned into a convent for Benedictine nuns.

In **Velturno** (**Feldthurns**) you can visit the Renaissance castle that was once the summer residence of the bishops of Bressanone. It contains decorations, furnishings, works of art and items related to local history. *Via Paese 1. Guided visits Mar.-Nov., closed Mon. For information on opening times ℘ 0472 85 55 25, www. schlossvelthurns.it.*

## Bressanone/Brixen★ ♟

Enjoying a dry climate and exceptional exposure to the Sun, this elegant and typically Tyrolean town stands at the point where the river Isarco meets the Rienza. It was conquered by the Romans in 15 BC, became the seat of the prince-bishop between 1027 and 1803, was made a Bavarian dominion from 1806 to 1813, passed into the hands of the Austrians, and finally became an Italian city after World War I. The beautiful Via Portici Maggiori, lined by ancient houses, leads to the parish Church of San Michele built in the 15th c. To the left of the church stands a lovely Renaissance residence that combines Italian and German architectural features. On the right of the church is the Baroque **duomo** founded in the Middle Ages. It has a Neoclassical pronaos and is flanked by two bell towers. The quality of the light inside is emphasised by the gold decoration. The Romanesque **cloister★** has a 14th-c. cross vault and 14th- and 15th-c. frescoes. The 11th-c. Chapel of San Giovanni Battista has frescoes dating from the 13th c. Built by Prince-bishop Bruno de Kirchberg after 1250, the **bishop's palace** has undergone several reconstructions. Note the **courtyard★** with three orders of loggias. Today the building holds the **Diocesan Museum★**, which exhibits collections of polychrome wooden sculptures in Tyrolean Romanesque and Gothic styles, carved altarpieces from the Renaissance period, the treasure of the duomo and Christmas cribs from the 18th-20th c. *Piazza Palazzo Vescovile 2. Open 10-17, closed Mon., Feb.-mid-Mar., Nov., ℘ 0472 83 05 05, www.hofburg.it.*

*Bressanone/Brixen cathedral*

© Luca Orio/Shutterstock

## Novacella Abbey★★ ♟

*3 km north of Bressanone. For information on opening times ℘ 0472 83 61 89, www.abbazianovacella.it.* Novacella is the northernmost winemaking zone in Italy. The slopes around the abbey are lined with vineyards that for centuries have produced the white grapes vinified in the abbey cellar. Founded in 1142 by the Bishop of Bressanone, Novacella comprises a set of buildings constructed in different eras.

The **historic garden** at the entrance contains a fish pond, an aviary and more than 70 varieties of aromatic herbs.

The **Well of Wonders** (decorated with the "eight" wonders of the world, one of which is the abbey) can be seen in the courtyard.

The striking Bavarian Baroque **church** surprises with its magnificence, brilliance and curious features, such as the leg of a painted figure that literally emerges from the fresco.

The **cloister**, which was originally Romanesque, was covered by layers of frescoes, then whitewashed after the plague in the 17th c. The plaques were set in place in the 18th c., and it was only in the 19th that an attempt was made to reveal the original frescoes. The **library**, with 76,000 volumes, including illuminated manuscripts and incunabola, is set in a magnificent Rococo room.

# Addresses

## Tourist information

**Trentino Tourist Office** – Piazza Dante 24, **Trento**, ☎ 0461 21 60 00
www.discovertrento.it

**Trentino Wine Consortium** – Via del Suffragio 3, **Trento**, ☎ 0461 98 45 36, www.vinideltrentino.com

**Provincial Wine Cellar of Trentino** – Palazzo Roccabruna, Via SS. Trinità 24, **Trento**, ☎ 0461 88 71 01, www.palazzoroccabruna.it

**Alto Adige Tourist Office** – Via Alto Adige 60, **Bolzano**, ☎ 0471 99 99 99, www.suedtirol.info

**Alto Adige Wine Promotion** – Via Crispi, 15, **Bolzano**, ☎ 0471 97 85 28, www.vinialtoadige.com

## The wineries

*The addresses are listed in alphabetical order by location.*

### TRENTINO

♀/ **Madonna delle Vittorie** – *Via Linfano 81 - **Arco** (TN) - ☎ 0464 50 54 32 - www. madonnadellevittorie.it - info@madonna dellevittorie.it - Winery tours and tasting by reservation, closed Sun.* The winery, established by Iginio Mandelli in the late 1950s, is named after an ancient chapel built nearby in the early 16th c. to celebrate a victory by the Counts of Arco.
A small church dedicated to Our Lady was later built nearby as a votive offering from the local population for salvation from danger. Hectares under vine: 45.
**Wines**: D'Eva Brut, Vigneti delle Dolomiti IGP Summo Laco Rosso, Teroldego, Rebo, Gewürztraminer Capoalago, Trento DOC. Other products: olive oil.

🍷 **Azienda Agricola Vallarom** – *Via Masi 21 - **Avio** (TN), 25 km S of Rovereto on the A 22 - ☎ 0464 68 42 97 - www.vallarom.com - info@vallarom.com - Winery tours by reservation.* The farmstead that is home to the winery was purchased in 1963 by Ezio Scienza and his wife Giuseppina, who gradually renovated it and planted the first rooted vines. Now the winery is run by their grandson Filippo and his wife Barbara. Climate and soil conditions well suited to winegrowing, combined with cultivation of the most appropriate varieties, control over yields, the quality of the grapes and sheer passion have allowed the Scienzas to reap the rewards of their long and painstaking work. Overnight stays are possible (*3 rooms, from €45* ). Hectares under vine: 8.

**Wines**: Cabernet Sauvignon, Chardonnay, Foglia Frastagliata, Marzemino, Vadum Caesaris, Pinot Nero, Campi Sarni, Syrah, Vò.

**Tenuta San Leonardo** – *Loc. San Leonardo - **Borghetto all'Adige** (TN), 6 km S of Avio on the A 22 - ☎ 0464 68 90 04 - www. sanleonardo.it - info@sanleonardo.it - Winery tours and tasting Mon.-Fri. by reservation (payment required).* The estate was first documented in 900 and the Guerrieri Gonzaga took it over in 1784. Their love for ancient farming traditions inspired the owners to establish a large collection of objects and documentation in what has become a fully fledged ethnographic museum of farm life. The museum, housed in an old barn, has a display of all types of objects used in different eras, as well as a rich agricultural archive from 1500 to 1960 concerning the winery and the history of the family of the Guerrieri Gonzaga marquises.
Hectares under vine: 30.
**Wines**: Carmenère, San Leonardo, Villa Gresti, Riesling, Terre di San Leonardo, Vette di San Leonardo. Other products: grappa.

♀/ **Azienda Agricola Gino Pedrotti** – *Via Cavedine 7 - Lago di **Cavedine** (TN) - ☎ 0461 56 41 23 - www.ginopedrotti.it - info@ginopedrotti.it - Winery tours by reservation.* The family-run winery is especially sensitive to the environment and biodynamic agriculture. The Pedrottis are also famed for the warm welcome they extend to winery visitors, who are offered tastes of authentic Trentino products (charcuterie, cheese, confectionery).
Hectares under vine: 5.
**Wines**: Chardonnay, Vino Santo Trentino, Merlot, Nosiola, L'Aura, L'Auro, Rebo, Schiava Nera. Other products: grappa.

**Pojer e Sandri** – *Loc. Molini 4 - **Faedo** (TN), 6 km E of San Michele all'Adige - ☎ 0461 65 03 42 - www.pojeresandri.it - info@ pojeresandri.it - Winery tours Mon.-Fri. at 10 or 15, Sat. at 10. Reservation and payment required (€10 ).* The winery was established in 1975 when Fiorentino Sandri and Mario Pojer met. Sandri had just inherited about 2 hectares of vineyards and Pojer had recently graduated from the prestigious enology school of San Michele all'Adige. This serendipitous encounter led to a winery that makes outstanding whites and reds – still, sparkling and dessert wines – as well as excellent spirits. Hectares under vine: 26.
**Wines**: Rosso Faye, Essenzia, Bianco Faye, Müller Thurgau Palai, Pinot Nero Selezione, Traminer aromatico, Chardonnay. Other products: aceto, grappa, fruit spirits, brandy.

**Cantina d'Isera** – *Via al Ponte 1* - **Isera** *(TN) - ℘ 0464 43 37 95 - info@cantinaisera.it - Wine shop closed Sun.* Thanks to the commitment of local vintners, a winegrowers' cooperative was established in Isera in 1907, when Trentino was still part of the Habsburg Empire. Today it has more than 200 members, with an area of over 200 hectares. Great attention is paid to work in the vineyard, as the winery is convinced that a good wine originates from the terroir. Expert agronomists and enologist follow the process, from the choice of new plantings to monitoring the entire growth cycle and making high-quality wines. Marzemino is the pride of the winery's range. Hectares under vine: 220.
**Wines**: Trentino Marzemino, Trentino Superiore Marzemino di Isera, Trentino Chardonnay, Trentino Pinot Grigio, Müller Thurgau, Rebo, Sauvignon, Trento DOC Extra Brut, Gewürztraminer.

**Azienda Agricola De Tarczal** – *Via G.B. Miori 4 - Loc. Marano* - **Isera** *(TN) - ℘ 0464 40 91 34 - www.detarczal.com - info@detarczal.com - Winery tours by reservation.* The winery is housed in a rural mansion dating from the 1700s and for more than a century the land has been owned by the Dell'Adami de Tarczal family. It began to develop under Austro-Hungarian rule, when Marzemino was one of the wines most in demand on royal tables. La Vineria, the restaurant annexed to the guest farm, offers traditional Trentino cuisine (*closed Sun. evening and Mon.*). An old barn has been transformed into a cosy *stube*, where guests can enjoy the estate's wines as well as local cheeses and charcuterie. Hectares under vine: 17.
**Wines**: Marzemino Trentino Superiore, Cabernet Franc, Chardonnay, Pinot Bianco, Merlot, Belvedere, Felix, Husar, Pinot nero. Other products: grappa.

**Cantina La Vis e Valle di Cembra** – *Via Carmine 7 - **Lavis** (TN) - ℘ 0461 44 01 11 - www.la-vis.com - cantina@la-vis.com - Winery tours by reservation.* Established in 1948 by a group of local vignerons, the winery boasts far older origins: it was the year 1850 when the Cembran family built the first portion of the today's production structure. Cantina La Vis e Valle di Cembra was established in 2003. Today it unites 1300 winegrowers with vineyards in the Adige river valley. Hectares under vine: 1450.

**Wines**: Sauvignon, Cabernet, Chardonnay, Müller Thurgau, Pinot Nero, Gewürztraminer, Nosiola, Riesling, Lagrein.

**Cantine Mezzacorona** – *Via del Teroldego 1* - **Mezzacorona** *(TN) - ℘ 0461 61 63 00 - www.mezzacorona.it - visite@mezzacorona.it - Winery tours Mon.-Sat. by reservation.* Mezzacorona cultivates its vineyards by planting only single varietals strictly in the areas where they grow best: 14 different native and international varieties, which are carefully selected and managed, are used to make monovarietal wines. Notably, Mezzacorona was the first Italian producer of Pinot Grigio and Chardonnay. Hectares under vine: 2600.
**Wines**: Teroldego Rotaliano, Pinot Grigio, Gewürztraminer, Müller Thurgau, Merlot, Chardonnay, Marzemino, Moscato Giallo.

**F.lli Dorigati** – *Via Dante 5* - **Mezzocorona** *(TN) - ℘ 0461 60 53 13 - www.dorigati.it - vini@dorigati.it - Winery tours by reservation.* The Dorigati family have worked as vignerons and winemakers for 5 generations. Indeed, their winery was established in 1858. The grapes are grown in part on the estate and in part in the vineyards of several small farmers, i.e. historic growers, with whom the winery has established an enduring and ongoing rapport. Hectares under vine: 13.
**Wines**: Teroldego Rotaliano Diedri, Rebo, Trentino Cabernet Grener, Pinot Grigio, Lagrein Dunkel, Lagrein Kretzer, Methius.

**Cantina Rotoliana di Mezzolombardo** – *Via Trento 65/b* - **Mezzolombardo** *(TN) - ℘ 0461 60 10 10 - www.cantina rotaliana.it - info@cantinarotaliana.it - Wine shop open Mon. 8-12 and 15-18, Tue.-Sat. 8-12 and 15-19, closed Sun. (tasting in the shop, winery tours by reservation).* Located in the heart of the Rotaliana plains, in one of the most beautiful winemaking areas in Europe, the Rotaliana di Mezzolombardo cantina is considered the longstanding cantina of Teroldego Rotaliano, the crown jewel of the Trentino region. Established in 1931, the company makes wine from grapes gathered across its 330-hectare vineyards, producing a remarkable selection of red and white wines that can boast unique characteristics thanks to the particular environment in which they are cultivated and the skills of the people who work here: vintners who have been passionately cultivating this

© Catalin Plesa/Shutterstock

terroir for generations, respecting the environment and traditions inherited from their forefathers. Hectares under vine: 400.
**Wines**: Teroldego Rotagliano, Lagrein Cortvta, Chardonnay Cortvta, Müller Thurgau, Pino Grigio, Pinot Nero, Gewürztraminer, Spumante Trento DOC Riserva Brut. Other products: grappa monovitigno.

**Foradori** – *Via Damiano Chiesa 1 -* **Mezzolombardo** *(TN) - ☎ 0461 60 10 46 - www.elisabettaforadori.com - info@ agricolaforadori.com - Winery tours by reservation, closed Fri. pm, Sat. and Sun.* The winery was built in 1901 in a square near a Franciscan monastery established in 1664, and it was subsequently purchased by Vittorio Foradori in 1935. Today it is run by Elisabetta Foradori. The façade of the building and the ageing cellars are lovely. Another cellar was created in 1999 beneath an old barn and it is used exclusively to age Teroldego, a wine and variety that is representative not only of the Foradori winery but the territory itself. Hectares under vine: 24.
**Wines**: Teroldego Rotaliano Foradori, Morei, Sgarzon, Granato Teroldego Vigneti delle Dolomiti IGT, Fontanasanta Nosiola, Fuoripista Pinot Grigio.

**Cantina Sociale Mori Colli Zugna** – *Strada Provinciale 90, Loc. Formigher 2 - Mori (TN) - ☎ 0464 91 81 54 - www.cantinamorico llizugna.it - info@cantinacollizugna.it - Wine shop Mon. 15-20, Tue.-Thu. 9 - 13 and 15 - 20 (Fri.-Sat. 15-21). Winery tours by reservation.* The cantina was founded at the end of the 1950s by just a few partners and with very little capital, and has grown thanks to a powerful cooperative spirit that has helped turn it into a reality that now harvests and transforms roughly 90% of the production in the surrounding area. The Mori Colli Zugna cantina is located in the Vallagarina territory, where vineyards spread out in a systematic manner starting already in the late 1800s. Vineyards cover over 700 hectares in an area that extends from Vallagarina and lower Sarca to the high plains of Brentonico in the south, and Val di Gresta in the north. This vast land area, which varies between 200 and 700 metres above sea level, offers a multiplicity of terroirs and microclimates that the cantina takes advantage of from a winemaking point of view to produce numerous varietals boasting intimate connections with the land. In 2011 the company completed its most recent headquarters, designed with respect for the surrounding land and a rational utilization of natural resources. This innovative structure was built underground so that it could take advantage of renewable energy sources like geothermal heating and solar panels. Hectares under vine: 700.

**Wines**: Trento DOC Spumante Morus dal 1957, Trentino DOP Gewürztraminer, Trentino DOP Müller Thurgau, Trentino Superiore Isera DOP Marzemino, Trentino DOP Lagrein, Moscato Giallo Trentino DOP.

**Maso Poli Azienda Agricola** – *Strada del vino 33 - Pressano di Lavis (TN) - ☎ 0461 87 15 19 - www.masopoli.com - info@masopoli.com - Wine shop open by reservation. Tours and tasting by reservation.* Maso Poli is a traditional, 18th-century maso, or farmstead, that has been recently restored and is surrounded by a 15-hectare property, 11 of which have been transformed into vineyards. Giving wines a soul, making them unique and intimately connected with the surrounding land is at once the motivation and philosophy behind Maso Poli. The Togn family, which began renewing these vines at the end of the 1970s, levelled off and drained the terrain in order to obtain grapes and wines with bouquets and flavours that celebrate the extraordinary nature of the surrounding land. Hectares under vine: 11.
**Vini**: Pinot Grigio, Nosiola, Pinot Nero, Riesling, Riserva TrentoDoc, Gewürztraminer, Marmoram. Other products: spirits.

**Agraria Riva del Garda** – *Via S. Nazzaro 4 - Riva del Garda (TN) - ☎ 0464 55 21 33 - www.agririva.it - info@agririva.it - Winery tours and tasting by reservation.* The Agraria Riva del Garda co-operative was established in 1926. In 2007 it built a modern winery as well as a mill that produces excellent olive oil. There are two shops where visitors can purchase the estate's products and local specialities. Hectares under vine: 280.
**Wines**: Créa, Gère, Loré, La Préa, Müller Thurgau, Sasèra, Maso Élesi, Maso Lizzone. Other products: olive oil.

**Azienda Agricola Roberto Zeni** – *Via Stretta 2 - Grumo - San Michele all'Adige (TN) - ☎ 0461 65 04 56 - www.zeni.tn.it - info@zeni.tn.it - Winery tours by reservation (€10), closed Sun.* The Zeni family's love affair with wine goes back to 1882 and Grandfather Roberto, but the groundwork for the winery's current success was laid between 1973 and 1975, when the Zeni brothers Roberto and Andrea, students at the San Michele all'Adige enology school, decided to expand their father's winegrowing business and established two new companies: Azienda Agricola R. Zeni and Distilleria Zeni. Today the winery is well-known and highly respected. Hectares under vine: 20.
**Wines**: Nosiola, Müller Thurgau, Teroldego Rotaliano, Moscato Rosa, Rossara IGT, Pinot Grigio Ramato IGT, Pinot Bianco, Pinot Nero Rosato IGT, Chardonnay, Ternet, Gewürztraminer. Other products: monovarietal grappa and fruit aqua vitae.

**Cantina Endrizzi** – *Loc. Masetto 2 -* **San Michele all'Adige** *(TN) - ☏ 0461 65 01 29 - www.endrizzi.it - info@endrizzi.it - Winery tours by reservation (from €10 ).* In 1885, when the Endrici family moved to San Michele all'Adige, they were subjects of the Austro-Hungarian Empire under Francis Joseph. Francesco Endrici, the great-grandfather of the current owners, was a true pioneer and in the early 20th c. he brought in the world's most prestigious varieties, such as Cabernet Sauvignon and Merlot, but did not overlook native varieties such as Lagrein and Teroldego. Today the winery is run by the fourth generation, represented by Paolo, Francesco's great-grandson, and his wife Christine. Hectares under vine: 40.
**Wines:** Müller Thurgau, Gewürztraminer, Teroldego, Masetto Bianco, Masetto Nero, Masetto Doré, Masetto Privé, Piancastello Rosé. Other products: grappa.

♀/ **Cantina Toblino** – *Via Longa 1 -* **Sarche - Madruzzo** *(TN) - ☏ 0461 56 41 68 - www.toblino.it - marketing@toblino.it - Winery tours 10-12 and 14-17 by reservation.* The estate is near Lake Toblino and produces wine exclusively from grapes grown by its 560 members. The quality of the wines is guaranteed by the origins of the grapes grown in the hills around Vezzano, the Cavedine valley and Calavino-Toblino. In addition to the delightful Vino Santo Trentino, it produces excellent dry whites and reds. The modern but charming winery merits a visit. Restaurant service at the Hosteria Toblino. Hectares under vine: 700.
**Wines:** Vino Santo Puro Trentino, Nosiola Sel. L'Ora IGT, Vigneti delle Dolomiti Nosiola Trentino, Rebo Trentino, Kerner, Goldtraminer, Lagrein Kretzer. Other products: grappa.

**Azienda Agricola Francesco Moser**– *Via Castel di Gardolo 5 - Trento - ☏ 0461 99 07 86 - www.cantinemoser.com - info@ mosertrento.com. Winery and vineyard tours by reservation.* Diego and Francesco Moser, who were born and raised in a farming family and began working in vineyards when they were barely teenagers, produced their first bottles in the 1970s in the famous Palù di Giovo cantina, using grapes obtained from family-owned terrain located in the foothills of Valle di Cembra. The Moser family's longstanding agricultural identity has been handed down today to a new generation – Carlo, Francesca and Matteo. Maso Villa Warth is a historical bishop's residence and the production centre of the Moser company, boasting modern cantinas for winemaking, traditional cantinas for aging and a welcoming wine-tasting hall. The terrace overlooking Valle dell'Adige and the natural amphitheatre created by the surrounded vineyards all help make Maso Villa Warth a particularly suggestive destination. Hectares under vine: 15.
**Wines:** Gewürztraminer, Lagrein, Moscato Giallo, Müller Thurgau, Riesling, Teroldego, Moser 51,151, Moser Rosé, Moser Brut Nature, Chardonnay.

**Cantina Sociale di Trento** – *Via dei Viticoltori 2/4 - Trento - ☏ 0461 92 01 86 - www.cantinasocialetrento.it - contatti@ cantinasocialetrento.it - Closed Sun.* On 17 October 1956, eleven local farmers registered their decision to create the Cantina Sociale di Trento with a notary deed. In 2009, the company they built inaugurated a new cantina built according to eco-sustainable and environmentally-friendly criteria, designed to provide clear qualitative improvements in the wines it produces. The idea is to offer small, craftsman production drawn directly from the surrounding territory, an area rich in enological value and individuality. The vineyard territory covered by the 480 agricultural businesses that are partners with the Cantina Sociale di Trento is located primarily on the hills surrounding the city, where Guyot and Pergola Trentina are cultivated. Hectares under vine: 50.
**Wines:** Heredia Pinot Nero Trentino DOC, Heredia Pinot Grigio Trentino DOC, Zell Trento DOC, Zell Rosé Trento DOC, Santacolomba, Chardonney Trentino DOC, 1339 Gewürztraminer. Other products: grappa 1339.

**Cavit (Cantina Viticoltori del Trentino)** – *Via del Ponte 31 -* **Trento** *- ☏ 0461 38 17 11 - www.cavit.it - cavit@cavit.it - Winery tours by reservation, closed Sat. pm and Sun.* Cavit is a large co-operative founded in 1950 and composed of numerous small concerns. Today it represents more than 4500 winegrowers associated with 10 wineries and 65% of Trentino's wine production, making it one of Italy's leaders in this industry. It produces a wide range of high-quality wines. Hectares under vine: 6500.
**Wines:** Trento Alterasi Brut Millesimato, Spumante Müller Thurgau Cuvée Speciale IGT, Trentino Pinot Grigio Bottega Vinai, Trentino Superiore Marzemino Maso Romani, Teroldego Rotaliano Maso Cervara. Other products: grappa.

♀/ **Ferrari F.lli Lunelli** – *Via Ponte di Ravina 15 -* **Trento** *- ☏ 0461 97 23 61 - www. ferraritrento.it - visit@ferraritrento.it. Winery tours by reservation, closed Sun. (from €20).* The winery established by Giulio Ferrari pursued the dream of creating a wine inspired by the finest French champagnes. Bruno Lunelli took it over in 1952 and, working with Ferrari, he helped establish the label's reputation. Today the winery produces only Classic Method sparkling wines and is run by the third Lunelli generation. It is not only Italy's leading producer of Classic Method sparkling wines, but is also one of the top 10 in the world. Meals are served at the nearby Locanda Margon, the Ferrari restaurant located at Via Margone 15 in Ravina ( ☎ *0461 34 94 01, closed Sun. pm and Tue.*), which offers various menus, including one matched with Ferrari sparkling wines. Villa Margon, a Renaissance complex surrounded by vineyards and the Ferrari showcase, can be toured by reservation. Hectares under vine: 120.

**Wines:** Spumante Metodo Classico Ferrari Brut, Ferrari Rosé, Ferrari Demi-Sec, Ferrari Maximum Blanc de Blancs, Ferrari Perlé, Giulio Ferrari Riserva del Fondatore.

## ALTO ADIGE

**Cantina produttori San Michele Appiano** – *Via Circonvallazione 17/19 -* **Appiano/ Eppan** *(BZ) -* ☎ *0471 66 44 66 - www. stmichael.it - wineshop@stmichael.it - Winery tours by reservation, closed Sat. pm (Nov.- Apr.) and Sun.* The co-operative was founded in 1907 to promote quality production starting in the vineyard and guarantee winegrowers an appropriate income. Today it has about 340 members, more than 380 hectares under vine and annual sales of 2.5 million bottles. The "St. Valentin" range is one of the most famous and sought-after by connoisseurs of the wines of Alto Adige. Cellarman Hans Terzer is also one of the region's most renowned enologists and winemakers, and he has contributed enormously to valorising the wines of Alto Adige, particularly the whites. Hectares under vine: 385.

**Wines:** Appius, Pinot Bianco, Pinot Grigio, Sauvignon The Wine Collection, Sanct Valentin, Gewürztraminer, Pinot Nero.

🌳 **Stroblhof** – *Via Pigenoer 25 -* **Appiano/Eppan** *(BZ) -* ☎ *0471 66 22 50 - www.stroblhof.it - hotel@stroblhof.it - Winery tours Mon. by reservation.* Stroblhof boasts a long winegrowing tradition and is cited in ancient documents dating from before the 17th c. It produces approximately 27,000 bottles a year, divided evenly between whites and reds. The estate grows and vinifies Pinot Bianco, Chardonnay, Sauvignon, Gewürztraminer, Schiava and Pinot Nero. There is also an elegant 4-star hotel (*37 rooms, doubles from €124, April– Oct.*) with restaurant service. Hectares under vine: 5.

**Wines:** Pinot Bianco, Chardonnay, Sauvignon, Pinot Nero Pigeno, Pinot Nero Riserva. Other products: vinegar and grappa.

**Tenuta Ansitz Waldgries** – *S. Giustina 2 -* **Bolzano** *-* ☎ *0471 32 36 03 - www. waldgries.it - info@waldgries.it - Winery tours by reservation, closed Sat. pm and Sun.* The estate, dating back to the 13th c., was originally owned by a monastery. This means that winemaking has a 800-year-old tradition here. The complex has a small wine museum displaying ancient equipment, illustrating how demanding the work of winegrowers is in these inaccessible areas, particularly in the past. Hectares under vine: 6.

**Wines:** Sauvignon Blanc MYRA, Santa Maddalena, Lagrein, Moscato Rosa, ISOS Pinot Bianco, Roblinus de' Waldgries.

**Muri-Gries** – *Piazza Gries 21 -* **Bolzano** *-* ☎ *0471 28 22 87 - www.muri-gries.com - info@muri-gries.com - Wine tasting and wine shop 8-12 and 14-18, closed Sat. and Sun.* In the late 11th c. the counts of Bolzano established a fortified outpost in the centre of modern-day Gries. Muri-Gries was founded in 1845, when Benedictines driven out of Muri in the Swiss canton found shelter at the Gries monastery. This opened up a new chapter in the viticultural history of the Gries monastery that continues today. Hectares under vine: 35.

**Wines:** Alto Adige Terlano Pinot Bianco, Alto Adige Lagrein Riserva Abtei Muri, Alto Adige Moscato Rosa Abtei Muri, Lagrein Vigna Klosteranger.

**Cantina Produttori Bolzano** – *Via San Maurizio 36 -* **Bolzano** *-* ☎ *0471 27 09 09 - www.cantinabolzano.com - info@ kellereibozen.com - Winery tours Tue., Fri. 15.00, Sat. by reservation.* In 2001 Cantina Gries (founded in 1908) and Cantina Santa Maddalena (established in 1930) joined forces to form Cantina Produttori Bolzano. It has 200 members, with a total of about 300 hectares of vineyards. Native varieties such as Lagrein, Gewürztraminer and Schiava are grown, but the winery also vinifies international varieties like Merlot, Pinot Bianco and Müller Thurgau, which have found an outstanding microclimate in this area. Hectares under vine: 300.

**Wines:** Alto Adige Gewürztraminer, Alto Adige S. Maddalena Classico, Alto Adige Lagrein, Alto Adige Pinot Nero.

**Azienda Agricola Taschlerhof** – *Loc. Mara 107 -* **Bressanone/Brixen** *( BZ ) -* ☎ *0472 85 10 91, 335 69 14 480 - www.taschlerhof.com - info@taschlerhof.com - Winery tours and retail sales by appointment.* According to the proprietor Peter Wachtler, a young winegrower and member of the Free Winegrowers of South Tyrol Association, the key ingredient of a good wine is character, with a pinch of creativity to make it unique. He has decided to concentrate exclusively on 4 white varieties (Sylvaner, Kerner, Gewürztraminer and Riesling), with which he produces wines with a lingering, intriguing, fruity and intense nose. Hectares under vine: 3.8.

**Wines**: Sylvaner, Sylvaner Lahner, Kerner, Gewürztraminer, Riesling.

**Manincor** – *San Giuseppe al Lago 4 -* **Caldaro/Kaltern** *(BZ) - ☎ 0471 96 02 30 - www.manincor.com - info@manincor.com - Winery tours by reservation, closed Sun.* Hieronymus Manincor zu Ehrenhausen founded the estate in 1608 and in 1662 the Manincors married into the noble Goëss-Enzenberg family, the current owners. The modern winery, surrounded by vineyards, respects the environment and boasts stunning architecture. In 2006 it began to use biodynamic methods for its 50 hectares of vineyards, extending this to the 600 hectares of apple orchards in 2008. Hectares under vine: 50.
**Wines**: La Manina, Réserve del Conte, Réserve della Contessa, Sophie, Mason, Cassiano, Moscato Giallo, Lieben Aich.

**Ritterhof** – *Strada del vino 1 -* **Caldaro/Kaltern** *(BZ) - ☎ 0471 96 32 98 - www.ritterhof.it - info@ritterhof.it - Winery tours, Mon. 10.30 (Apr.-Sept.) or by reservation.* Owned by the Roner family, the winery respects ancient traditions handed down from generation to generation. A harmonious rapport with nature is fundamental, as is the use of modern technology to guarantee high quality. Gewürztraminer, Lagrein and Pinot Nero are the pride of the winery. Hectares under vine: 40.
**Wines**: Gewürztraminer, Vigneto delle Dolomiti Rosè, Lago di Caldaro Novis DOC, Pinot Nero Jansen, Manus Lagrein, Sonus.

**Erste & Neue** – *Via Cantine 10 -* **Caldaro/Kaltern** *(BZ) - ☎ 0471 96 46 06 - www.erste-neue.it - weindiele@erste-neue.it - Winery tours by reservation.* In the year 1900, 70 local winegrowers united to form *Erste Kellereigenossenschaft Kaltern,* Kaltern's first wine co-operative. The new co-operative, called "Neue Kellereigenossenschaft", was established in 1925. The two co-operatives merged in 1991 to form Erste & Neue, and today just under 500 vignerons bring their harvest here each year. Hectares under vine: 280.
**Wines**: Gewürztraminer, Müller Thurgau, Lagrein, Sauvignon, Pinot Bianco, Puntay Kalterersee, Puntay Lagrein Riserva.

⌂ **Niklaserhof - Weingut Niklas** – *Via delle Fontane 31 -* **Caldaro/Kaltern** *(BZ) - ☎ 0471 96 34 34 - www.niklaserhof.it - wine@niklaserhof.it - Winery tours and tasting by reservation.* The winery has built a new cellar with natural stone walls, where the wines are barrel-aged. The Sölva family, which owns the winery, loves to receive visitors and regales guests with stories about their experience in the vineyard and as winemakers. Accommodation available at the winery (*4 apts., from €65*). Hectares under vine: 5.

**Wines**: Alto Adige Pinot Bianco, Alto Adige Pinot Bianco Riserva Klaser, Alto Adige Kerner, Alto Adige Sauvignon, Alto Adige Lagrein-Riserva Mondevinum. Other products: grappa and spirits.

⌂ **Lieselehof** – *Via Kardatsch 6 -* **Caldaro/Kaltern** *(BZ) - ☎ 0471 96 50 60 or ☎ 329 90 11 593 - www.lieselehof.com - info@lieselehof.com - Winery tours by reservation (Mon.-Fri.).* The winery grows and produces Schiava, Cabernet Sauvignon, Carmenere, Cabernet Franc, Pinot Bianco and Bronner, and is test-growing small amounts of the Chambourcin Johanniter, Solaris and Helios varieties. Visitors can enjoy the fascinating "guide path" to the vineyards, along which they can see more than 300 different varieties from around the world, and the Spice Garden, with 100 world spices. The estate offers guest accommodation (*5 apts. from €70*). Hectares under vine: 3.
**Wines**: Amadeus, Lieselehof Brut, Pinot Bianco, Julian, Sweet Claire, Feldherr, Vino del Passo, Gewürztraminer.

**Unterortl** – *Via Juval 1 B -* **Castelbello Ciardes/Kastelbell Tschars** *(BZ) - ☎ 0473 66 75 80 - www.unterortl.it - info@unterortl.it - Winery and vineyards tours by reservation.* Owner Reinhold Messner and leaseholders Gisela and Martin Aurich established the estate in 1992, as they share the same vision regarding production: wines and spirits that express the unique character of Juval Hill. Different grape varieties and fruits for the distillery are grown in an area of more than 5 hectares. Hectares under vine: 4.
**Wines**: Castel Juval Müller Thurgau, Riesling Gletscherschliff, Castel Juval Riesling Windbichel, Castel Juval Blauburgunder, Gneis. Other products: grappa, fruit spirits.

♈/ **Labyrinthgartner Tenuta Kraenzel** – *Via Palade 1 -* **Cermes** *(BZ) - ☎ 0473 56 45 49 - www.kraenzelhof.it - info@kraenzelhof.it - Restaurant mill (closed Sun. and Mon., ☎ 0473 56 37 33). Winery tours by reservation (payment required), closed Sun. and Mon. (Nov.-Mar.).* The earliest documentation of a winegrowing estate in Cermes dates back to 1182; today Pinot Bianco, Chardonnay, Sauvignon Blanc, Gewürztraminer, Vernatsch, Pinot Nero, Lagrein, Merlot and Cabernet Sauvignon are grown here. The estate boasts a spectacular "garden maze" inspired by the desire to create something enduring and delightful for all those who stroll in it. Every year different artists decorate the garden sculptures, based on themes that change annually (*€8*). Hectares under vine: 6.
**Wines**: Helios, Baslan Schiava, Pinot Nero, Sagittarius, Dorado.

**Cantina Produttori Valle Isarco** – *Via Coste 50 -* **Chiusa/Klausen** *(BZ) - ☎ 0472 84 75 53 - www.eisacktalerkellerei.it - info@cantinavalleisarco.it - Wine shop open Mon.-*

*Fri. 9-13 and 14-18, Sat. 9-13.* Cantina Produttori Valle Isarco was founded in 1961. Respect for strict quality standards and constant improvement of vinification techniques guarantee high-quality wines. There is also a small wine museum on site that offers a historical overview of the development of viticulture in the valley. Hectares under vine: 130.

**Wines:** Alto Adige Valle Isarco Sylvaner, Alto Adige Valle Isarco Veltliner, Alto Adige Valle Isarco Müller Thurgau, Alto Adige Valle Isarco Kerner, Alto Adige Valle Isarco Gewürztraminer, Isaras Brut, Sabiona Sylvaner, Aristos Riesling.

**Cantina Colterenzio Soc. Agr. Coop.** – *Strada del Vino 8 -* **Cornaiano/Girlan** *(BZ) - ℘ 0471 66 42 46 - www.colterenzio.it - info@colterenzio.it - Winery tours by reservation, closed Sat. pm (except in Autumn) and Sun.* The co-operative was established in 1960, when 28 local winegrowers decided to join forces to maximise and promote their work in the vineyard and the cellar. Today it has 300 members who cultivate over 300 hectares of vineyards. The wines are produced with the overriding desire to cater to those who taste them, rising above passing trends. Hectares under vine: 306.

**Wines:** Sauvignon Blanc, Cabernet Sauvignon, Gewürztraminer, Chardonnay, Lagrein, Merlot, LR 2015.

**Cantina Girlan - Cantina Sociale Cornaiano** – *Via San Martino 24 -* **Cornaiano/Girlan** *(BZ) - ℘ 0471 66 24 03 - www.girlan.it - info@girlan.it - Winery tours by reservation, closed Sat. pm (except Sept.-Oct.) and Sun.* The co-operative winery was established in 1923 and was one of the first to pay growers according to the quality of their produce and identify 3 product lines based on quality level. The co-operative has grown over the years and now counts 200 members. The pursuit of quality relies on natural cultivation, careful vinification and specifically targeted production. Hectares under vine: 215.

**Wines:** Pinot Bianco Alto Adige Flora Riserva, Sauvignon Alto Adige Flora, Chardonnay Alto Adige Flora, Schiava Alto Adige Gschleier Vecchie Vigne, Trattmann Pinot Nero Riserva.

🌳 **Gert Pomella** – *Via Milla 3 -* **Cortaccia/ Kurtatsch** *(BZ) - ℘ 335 60 46 037 - gert. pomella@yahoo.it - Winery tours by reservation.* This small winery has concentrated in particular on growing and producing two varieties: Cabernet and Merlot. The move to vinify estate-grown grapes is relatively recent and goes back to 1996. It produces approximately 22,000 bottles annually. Gert Pomella wines have good structure and complexity, but also offer delicate and elegant aromas.

Accommodation available at the Schwarz Adler Turmhotel, at Vicolo Chiesa 2 ( ℘ 0471 09 64 00, www.turmhotel.it, 24 rooms, doubles from €154). Hectares under vine: 3.5.
**Wines:** Cabernet Merlot Centa, Cabernet Merlot Milla.

♀/ **Tiefenbrunner** – *Via Castello 4 - Fraz. Niclara -* **Cortaccia/Kurtatsch** *(BZ) - ℘ 0471 88 01 22 - www.tiefenbrunner.com - jausenstation@tiefenbrunner.com - Winery tours by reservation (Easter-Aug. Tue., Thu. at 16.30); wine shop closed Sun.* The Tiefenbrunner Castel Turmhof estate is named after both the castle that has stood in Niclara since the 12th c. and the family that has lived there for generations. Owners Herbert and Christof Tiefenbrunner produce approximately 700,000 bottles annually. Whites constitute the lion's share, accounting for 70% of the production. Restaurant service Apr.-Oct., closed Sun. Hectares under vine: 25.

**Wines:** Feldmarschall von Fenner, Turmhof Gewürztraminer, Racht Sauvignon Riserva, Lagrein Riserva Linticlarus, Pinot Nero Riserva Linticlarus. Other products: grappa.

♀/ **Tenuta Alois Lageder** – *Via Casòn Hirschprunn 1 -* **Magrè/Magreid** *(BZ) - ℘ 0471 80 95 80 - www.aloislageder.eu - paradeis@aloislageder.eu, info@aloislageder. eu - Winery tours and tasting by reservation, closed Sun.* Alois Lageder firmly believes in the symbiosis between nature and technology, earth and sky, history and future, and his wines strive to respect these balances. The cycles of nature determine the work in the vineyard, from pruning to harvesting. The focus here is on natural and renewable sources, such as solar and geothermal energy, and natural ventilation. In the winery, the vinification process exploits the natural force of gravity. Meals available at Vineria Paradeis (*closed Sun.*). Hectares under vine: 163.

**Wines:** Haberle Pinot Bianco, Rain Riesling, Mimuèt Pinot Noir, Cor Römigberg Cabernet Sauvignon, Löwengang, Römigberg Schiava.

**Arunda** – *Via Prof. Josef Schwarz 18 -* **Meltina/Melton** *(BZ), 13 km N of Terlano - ℘ 0471 66 80 33 - www.arundavivaldi.it - info@arundavivaldi.it - Winery tours Wed. at 10 and Thu. at 11 (Apr.-Oct.).* The family-run winery produces only Classic Method sparkling wines. Annual production averages 70,000 bottles, representing approximately 50% of Alto Adige's Classic Method sparkling wine. Pinot Nero, Pinot Bianco and Chardonnay are used. Hectares under vine: none owned by the estate; trusted winegrowers bring their harvests to the winery.

**Wines:** Spumante Brut, Extra Brut, Riserva, Cuvée Marianna, Brut Rosé, Excellor.

**Cantina Merano Burggräfler** – *Via Cantina 9 -* **Marlengo- Merano** *(BZ) -*

*0473 44 71 37 - www.kellereimeran.it - info@cantinamerano.it - Winery tours by reservation, info@kellereimeran.it.* The winegrowers' co-operative was established in 1952 to improve the quality of the wines and bolster its members' sales. Today it has more than 200 members, with approximately 140 hectares under vine. The region's most widespread varieties are grown, such as Gewürztraminer, Sauvignon, Pinot Bianco, Chardonnay, Riesling, Moscato Giallo, Müller Thurgau, Merlot, Cabernet, Lagrein, Schiava and Pinot Nero. Hectares under vine: 140.

**Wines:** Alto Adige Gewürztraminer, Alto Adige Sauvignon, Alto Adige Lagrein, Val Venosta Schiava Sonnenber, Alto Adige Val Venosta Pinot Nero Sonnenber.

**Franz Haas** – *Via Villa 6 -* **Montagna/ Montan** *(BZ) - 0471 81 22 80 - www.franz-haas.it - info@franz-haas.it - Winery tours and tasting Mon.-Sat. by reservation.* The estate has been making wine since 1880 and this art has been handed down to the eldest for 7 generations. Its wines are of exceptional quality and age-worthy, respecting typicity and boasting great personality. One of the most noteworthy is the rare Moscato Rosa, an aromatic sweet wine that is especially appealing and is produced in limited quantities. Hectares under vine: 55.

**Wines:** Pinot Bianco Lepus, Manna, Pinot Nero, Moscato Rosa, Lagrein, Istante.

*♈* **Abbazia di Novacella** – *Via Abbazia 1 -* **Novacella** *(BZ) - 0472 83 61 89 - www.abbazianovacella.it - info@kloster-neustift.it - Winery tours and tasting 10-19 by reservation (from €6), closed Sun. and religious hols.* This enormous complex traces its origins to 1142, when Bishop Hartmann made it the seat of the Augustinian order. From the very beginning it welcomed pilgrims travelling to the Holy Land and was an important spiritual and cultural centre known throughout Europe. Even today it is known for its rich library, numerous cultural initiatives and wine production. Cold lunch available, with barley soup in winter. Hectares under vine: 70.

**Wines:** Müller Thurgau, Sylvaner, Kerner, Gewürztraminer, Omnes Dies. Other products: monovarietal spirits, Amaro dell'Abbazia liqueur, apple juice, herbal teas, cosmetics.

*♈* **Köfererhof** – *Via Pusteria 3 -* **Novacella** *(BZ) - 347 47 78 009 - www.koefererhof.it - info@koefererhof.it - Winery tours by reservation.* The Kerschbaumer Günther winery is located in Italy's northernmost winegrowing area. The terroir yields particularly fresh-tasting, elegant and zesty whites with intense fruity aromas. Consequently, the winery produces only white wines made from the region's most common varieties: Riesling, Sylvaner, Müller

Thurgau, Gewürztraminer, Pinot Grigio and Veltliner. Restaurant service. Hectares under vine: 5.

**Wines:** Sylvaner, Kerner, Gewürztraminer, Riesling, Veltliner, Müller Thurgau.

*⌂* **Strasserhof** – *Via Unterrain 8 -* **Novacella** *(BZ) - 0472 83 08 04 - www.strasserhof. info- info@strasserhof.info - Winery tours by reservation.* The winery grows and produces typical local varieties, focusing on white varieties such as Müller Thurgau, Kerner, Sylvaner, Veltliner, Riesling and Gewürztraminer. The grapes ripen in the sunny vineyards of Novacella, cultivated with passion and using techniques designed to bring out the best of these varieties. The guest farm makes the winery especially appealing in terms of food and wine tourism. Accommodation available (*Feb.-Dec.*) at the Strasserhof guest farm (*6 rooms, doubles from €80*), with restaurant service (*mid-Sept.-Nov., closed Mon.*). Hectares under vine: 5.

**Wines:** Müller Thurgau, Sylvaner, Kerner, Veltliner, Riesling. Other products: apples.

*⌂* **Pacherhof** – *Via Pacher 1 -* **Novacella** *(BZ) - 0472 83 57 17 - www.pacherhof.com - wein@pacherhof.com - Winery tours by reservation.* This dynamic and spirited winery is set alongside an inn and restaurant, and is surrounded by vineyards as far as the eye can see (*22 rooms, half board from €90/person*). Hectares under vine: 8.

**Wines:** Sylvaner, Gewürztraminer, Kerner, Pinot Grigio, Riesling, Grüner Veltliner, Private Curvée.

**Laimburg** – *Via Laimburg 6 -* **Ora-Vadena/ Auer-Pfatten** *- 0471 96 95 00 - www. laimburg.bz.it - landesweingut-cantina@ laimburg.it - Winery tours by reservation, closed Sat. and Sun.* When the Autonomous Province of Bolzano created the Laimburg Research Centre for Agriculture and Forestry in 1975, it also decided to establish a winery, one of whose main goals is research and experimentation in winegrowing and enology for the entire region. The wines that are produced, all of which of top quality, strive to bring out the characteristics of the terroir and grape varieties. Hectares under vine: 50.

**Wines:** Müller Thurgau, Sauvignon, Riesling, Schiava, Lagrein, Pinot Bianco.

**Haderburg** – *Via Albrecht Dürer 3, Fr. Pochi -* **Salorno/Salurn** *(BZ) - 0471 88 90 97 - www.haderburg.it - info@haderburg.it - Winery tours by reservation, closed Sat. pm and Sun.* In the mid-1970s the farm converted from a grape and apple grower into a winery, and now it is one of the most famous in Alto Adige, above all for sparkling wines made with the Classic Method from Chardonnay and Pinot Nero. The estate puts enormous effort into cultivating its grapes with the most natural methods possible, using fertilisers only if strictly necessary and relying instead on compost. Hectares under vine: 12.8.

**Wines**: Spumante Haderburg, Chardonnay Hausmannhof, Pinot Nero Hausmannhof, Gewürztraminer Obermairlhof, Sylvaner Obermairlhof.

**Cantina Produttori Terlano** – *Via Silberleiten 7 -* **Terlano/Terlan** *(BZ) - ℘ 0471 25 71 35 - www.cantina-terlano.com - office@cantina-terlano.com - Winery tours by reservation, closed Sat. pm and Sun.* Founded in 1893, today the Terlano winery has more than 100 members. Hectares under vine: 190.

**Wines**: Terlaner cuvée, Pinot Bianco, Sauvignon Winkl, Lagrein, Merlot Siebeneich Riserva.

**Elena Walch** – *Via Andreas-Hofer 1 -* **Termeno/Tramin** *(BZ) - ℘ 0471 86 01 72 - www.elenawalch.com - visite@walch.it - Winery tours by reservation (from €18).* Elena Walch, who trained as an architect, became a winemaker in 1985 after she married Werner Walch, a descendant of one of Tramin's oldest wine dynasties.
The winery has two estates: Castel Ringberg, across from Lake Caldaro (Kalterersee), and Kastelaz, a hillside vineyard overlooking the centre of Tramin. Elena transformed the vineyards to focus on quality, largely replanting them and working to ensure low yields per hectare with carefully selected clones, maintaining both native and international varieties. Hectares under vine: 30.

**Wines**: Müller Thurgau, Gewürztraminer, Lagrein, Cabernet Sauvignon Castel Ringberg, Chardonnay Cardellino.

🍽 **J. Hofstätter** – *Piazza Municipio 7 -* **Termeno/Tramin (BZ)** *- ℘ 0471 86 01 61 - www.hofstatter.com - info@hofstatter.com - Winery and vineyards tours Mon.-Fri. by reservation (from €12), enoteca@hofstatter.com* - These vineyards keep their doors open to the public from the morning till late at night. Visitors find not only a sine shop, but also a winebar and vineyard garden, a place in which to explore the secrets of winemaking. Take the Gewürztraminer for example: visitors can learn about the best growing conditions for this kind of wine and the ways a winemaker can intervene to improve the quality of the product. There are comfortable benches in the vineyard garden, allowing people to relax and enjoy the spectacular mountain landscape. Restaurant services for lunch and dinner, menu à la carte. Hectares under vine: 50.

**Wines**: Kolbenhof Gewürztraminer, Joseph Hofstätter Gewürztraminer, Riserva Mazon Pinot Nero, Barthenau Vigna S. Urbano Pinot Nero, Barthenau Brut Rosé, de ViTE Curvée. Other products: grappa and honey.

**Tramin - Cantina Produttori Termeno** – *Strada del Vino 144 -* **Termeno/Tramin** *(BZ) - ℘ 0471 09 66 33 - www.cantinatramin.it - info@cantinatramin.it - Winery tours and sales Mon.-Fri. 9-18 (9-19 in summer), Sat. 9-17.* The name Tramin – Termeno in Italian – is inseparably linked with the famous Traminer or Gewürztraminer variety. It was in 1898 that Christian Schrott, a pastor from Tramin and a deputy to the Austrian parliament, decided to establish a winegrowers' co-operative in Tramin, one of the first established in the region. Over a century later, the Kellerei-Cantina Tramin is a winery that, with an area of 260 hectares, coordinates 300 winegrowers who cultivate grapes according to the strictest standards. Hectares under vine: 260.

**Wines**: Gewürztraminer, Lagrein, Pinot Nero, Sauvignon, Pinot Grigio, Schiava.

# Where to Stay

### ARCO

**The Sole Hotel and Apartments** – *Via Foro Boario 5, Arco (TN) - ℘ 0464 51 66 76 - www.soleholiday.com - 20 rooms, doubles from €95; apts. from €100.* This modern family-run hotel is situated in the centre of Arco, between the lake and the mountains. Snack service and wine bar.

### DRO

**Agriturismo Maso Lizzone** – *Via Lizzone 3, Loc. Ceniga, 1.5 km S of Dro (TN) - ℘ 0464 50 47 93 - www.masolizzone.com - Closed Nov.-mid-Mar. - 5 rooms, doubles from €80, 1 apt. €100, and Agricamping with 7 pitches for camper/roulotte €15.* A completely renovated traditional country house set amidst olive groves and vineyards.

### BOLZANO

**Albergo Belvedere-Schönblick** – *Pichl 15, San Genesio (BZ) - ℘ 471 35 41 27 - www.schoenblick-belvedere.com. Closed mid-Jan.-mid-Mar.* - 43 rooms. A short drive from Bolzano, this hotel has fine views over the city. An oasis of calm with cheerful, Tyrolean-style interior decor. High standard of cooking; local fare.

### LAGUNDO

**Agriturismo Plonerhof** – *Via Peter Thalguter 11, Lagundo (BZ) - ℘ 0473 44 87 28 - www.plonerhof.it - 6 rooms, doubles from €80, apts. from €96.* The 13th-c. farmhouse is in a lush natural setting.

### NOVACELLA

**Hotel Ponte-Brückenwirt** – *Via Dolomiti 16A 2, Montagna (BZ) - ℘ 0471 81 98 41 - www.hotelbrueckenwirt.com - 29 rooms, doubles from €80.* Set close to the abbey, it is surrounded by a small park and has a heated swimming pool.

# FRIULI VENEZIA GIULIA

Situated in the extreme north-east of Italy, Friuli has a wide range of geographical attractions, including mountains, glaciers, beaches, hills, plains and the sea. Its grapes are mainly grown in the central-southern section of the region, where the clayey soil with excellent drainage is particularly suited to winegrowing. Friuli is especially known for white and sweet wines, but its reds are equally enjoyable. The DOCG appellations have been given to Ramandolo and Picolit, voluptuous and velvety dessert wines produced in modest quantities from local grapes. The region's most representative varieties – ten in all – are Tocai Friulano, Ribolla Gialla, Verduzzo Friulano, Picolit, Vitovska and Malvasia Istriana among the whites; Refosco dal Peduncolo Rosso, Schioppettino, Pignolo, Tazzelenghe and Terrano for the reds.

© Bosca78/iStock

*Friuli vineyards*

## The terroir

The three DOCGs **Picolit**, **Rosazzo** and **Ramandolo** are in the province of Udine. This same province is also home to **Friuli Colli Orientali** (with the renowned subzones Cialla, Pignolo di Rosazzo, Ribolla Gialla di Rosazzo, Refosco di Faedis and Schioppettino di Prepotto), **Annia**, **Aquileia**, and **Latisana**, while it shares the appellation **Grave** with the province of Pordenone. **Collio**, **Isonzo** and part of **Carso** lie in the province of Gorizia, whereas the rest of Carso is in Trieste. **Lison** is an interregional DOCG that straddles the border between Friuli and the Veneto.

What makes Friuli's wines unique is the composition of the soil. Once the flattish area of the region was covered entirely by water. Over the centuries the detritus, sand and clay settled and telluric movements raised the land to create hills of marl, clay and sand. Today these are the zones of the Ramandolo, Colli Orientali and Collio Goriziano appellations. At the same time the alpine glaciers generated gravel, sand, pebbles and detritus that make the soil composition of the Grave and Isonzo zones so unique. Elsewhere, in the Aquileia, Latisana and Annia designated areas, water was pushed up to the surface. A unique soil composition is also found in Carso Triestino, where the land is described as being "red" owing to the extensive presence of iron-rich clayey rocks.

It is the soil that nourishes vines and when the nutriments are of such excellence the grapes necessarily follow suit – that is why Friulan wines are of such natural high quality.

The peaks of the Carnic and Julian Alps have been modelled by **karstification**, the smoothing action of glaciers and other atmospheric agents. Besides having created the particular terrain of Grave, the mountains provide a bar-

**DOCG**
Colli Orientali del Friuli Picolit
Lison (with Veneto)
Ramandolo
Rosazzo

**DOC**
Carso
Collio Goriziano *or* Collio
Friuli Annia
Friuli Colli Orientali
Friuli Aquileia
Friuli Grave
Friuli Isonzo *or* Isonzo del Friuli
Friuli Latisana
Lison Pramaggiore (with Veneto)
Prosecco

© igor1/iStock

rier against the cold north winds, thus benefiting vine cultivation, to which the mitigating effect of the sea is added.

# Itineraries

*Locations with a winery are indicated by the symbol* ♟ *; for the addresses of the wineries, see p. 229.*

## 1. GRAVE BETWEEN UDINE AND PORDENONE

This is a vast area (roughly 6500 hectares) that straddles the river Tagliamento and falls in the provinces of Udine and Pordenone. It is the largest winemaking area in the region and produces a large proportion of Friuli's wines.

The soil conditions, exposure and climate are ideal for grape-growing and thus also for quality wine production. The name, Grave, is a reference to the French zone Graves, which has a very similar soil composition. The most intriguing characteristic is that the soil in both zones can absorb and release moisture and heat, so that the pedoclimate remains almost constant. The zone was heavily affected by the earthquake of 1976.

## PRINCIPAL VARIETIES CULTIVATED

### WHITE GRAPES
Chardonnay
Garganega
Malvasia Bianca
Malvasia Istriana
Manzoni Bianco
Moscato Giallo
Müller Thurgau
Picolit
Pinot Bianco
Prosecco
Ribolla Gialla
Riesling
Riesling Italico
Sauvignon
Sciaglin
Semillon
Sylvaner
Tocai Friulano
Traminer Aromatico
Ucelut
Verdiso
Verduzzo Trevigiano
Verduzzo Friulano
Vitovska

### GREY GRAPES
Moscato Rosa
Pinot Grigio

### BLACK GRAPES
Ancellotta
Cabernet Franc
Cabernet Sauvignon
Forgiarin
Franconia
Gamay
Lambrusco Maestri
Malbech
Marzemino
Merlot
Piccola Nera
Pignolo
Pinot Nero
Raboso Piave
Raboso Veronese
Refosco dal
    Peduncolo Rosso
Refosco Nostrano
Schioppettino
Tazzelenghe
Terrano

## Udine★

The seat of the Patriarchs of Aquileia from 1238 to 1420 before it passed under the rule of Venice, Udine grew up around the hill on which the castle was built and around which the picturesque alley Vicolo Sottomonte runs. The Gothic and Renaissance monuments, secluded squares, and narrow porticoed streets give beauty to the small city, which with difficulty rebuilt itself after the earthquake. During his stay in the city, the artist Tiepolo was commissioned to decorate several monuments.

Various buildings were constructed in Venetian style around the harmonious and central **Piazza della Libertà★★**, which itself retained its Renaissance appearance. The **Loggia del Lionello**, the old municipal palace of 1457, shows a touch of Venetian Gothic in the lightness of the arches and its white and pink stone lining. Opposite, on a raised plaza, the 16th-c. **Loggia di San Giovanni** is a Renaissance portico topped by the Clock Tower (16th c.) in which the Moors strike the hours. Standing in front of it are the columns of St Mark and Justice, the statues of Hercules and Cacus, and an elegant 16th-c. fountain.

Behind the Loggia del Lionello, the characteristic pedestrian street, the **Via Rialto**, leads to the refined, square **Piazza Matteotti**, lined with porticoed houses, the elegant Baroque Church of San Giacomo (16th c.), a fountain (also 16th c.) and the 15th-c. Column of the Virgin.

From Piazza della Libertà, pass under the Palladian Arco Bollani, follow the Porticato del Lippomano, and climb to the **castle**. This solid 16th-c. construction, preceded by an esplanade offering lovely **views★**, was the seat of power of the Republic of Venice. The building today holds the **Civic Museums** and the **Gallery of History and Ancient Art★**. *Piazzale Patria del Friuli 1. Open 10-18, closed Mon. and hols.* ℘ *0432 12 72 591, www. civicimuseiudine.it.*

Just beside it stands the 13th-c. Church of **Santa Maria del Castello** topped by the archangel Gabriel, with a 16th-c. façade and bell tower. A 13th-c. fresco of the *Deposition* can be seen inside.

The **Archbishop's Palace** (16th-18th c.) has **frescoes★** by **Tiepolo**: the *Fall of the Angels* on the vault of the main stairway, and splendid compositions of scenes from the Old Testament in the private apartments. *Piazza Patriarcato 1. Open 10-13 and 15-18, closed Tue.,* ℘ *0432 25 003, www.musdioc-tiepolo.it.*

The **duomo** is a 14th-c. Gothic building refurbished in the 18th c. The façade is embellished with a lovely ornamental Gothic portico. The solid bell tower features statues of the Annunciation and the archangel Gabriel (14th c.) on one of the faces, and the interior is decorated

*Renaissance architecture of Piazza della Libertà, Udine*

in Baroque style. Tiepolo painted the vaults of the Chapel of the Santo Sacramento with frescoes that make use of false perspective.

To the right of the duomo, the **Oratory della Purità** has a ceiling painted in 1757 by Tiepolo. *Open 10-12 and 16-18, Sun. 16-18, ℘ 0432 50 68 30.*

## The Tagliamento plain

*Itinerary of approximately 160 km from Udine to Passariano.*

Leave Udine north on the S 49 in the direction of Pagnacco and **Colloredo di Monte Albano**. Colloredo is another town that grew up around the feet of a castle (heavily damaged by the 1976 earthquake) owned by the Colloredo Mels family. A member of this family was Ippolito Nievo, who here wrote part of his *Confessions of an Italian.* Continue north to **Osoppo**, where you should visit the interesting hilltop fort founded in the early Middle Ages, or head west towards **San Daniele del Friuli**. The town boasts interesting monuments but is most famous for its ham. Pass through Ragogna to arrive in **Pinzano al Tagliamento**, set around the foot of a hill and the remains of a castle. Next head south to **Spilimbergo**. The town stands on the right bank of the river Tagliamento in a landscape of vines and orchards. It has a fine Gothic duomo with the remains of frescoes in the apse and crypt. On the left of the duomo, the castle boasts a lovely façade adorned by late 15th-c. frescoes. The town is famous for its school of mosaics.

Features of the area between Tagliamento and Livenza are the *magredi*, zones in which the water of the torrents Cellina and Meduna sink into the water table and create an arid and very permeable terrain. The stony countryside here is characterised by vineyards and fields of cereal.

Continuing west on the S 464, you come to **Maniago** on the edge of the Prealps. It is famous for its knives, as the museum in a former spinning mill demonstrates (*Via Maestri del Lavoro 1, open 9:30-12.30 and 15.30-18.30, closed Tue. pm and Wed. pm, ℘ 0427 70 90 63*). The town has several Renaissance buildings set around Piazza Italia and a late 15th-c. duomo.

*Take the S 251 to Pordenone.*

## Pordenone

Starting in Piazza Cavour, take the porticoed **Corso Vittorio Emanuele**, lined with beautiful old houses, to the City Hall, built in Gothic style at the turn of the 13th-14th c., and to the **Duomo** constructed at the start of the 16th c. but showing a 19th c. façade. The bell

## THE TERROIR

**Area**: 7,932.48 km², of which approximately 24,019 hectares are planted to vine.

**Production 2019**: 1,595,272 hectolitres of which 610,332 VQPRD.

**Geography**: 43% mountainous, 38% flat and 19% hilly. The climate varies widely between the different zones: in the coastal strip it is mild due to the sea, in the central area it is continental, and in the mountains the climate is alpine. The region receives different winds

## THE PROTECTION CONSORTIA AND WINE ROUTES

Federdoc Friuli Venezia Giulia- Federazione Consorzi Tutela Vini – ℘ 0432 51 06 19, www.federdoc.com

Consorzio di Tutela Vini DOC Collio e Carso – Via Gramsci 2, Cormòns (GO), ℘ 0481 63 03 03, www.collio.it

Consorzio di Tutela Vini DOC Friuli Aquileia – Via dei Patriarchi 3, Aquileia, ℘ 331 21 40 996, www.viniaquileia.it

Consorzio di Tutela Vini DOC Friuli Colli Orientali, Ramandolo – Piazza XXVII Maggio 11, Corno di Rosazzo (UD), ℘ 0432 73 01 29, www.colliorientali.com

Consorzio di Tutela Vini DOC Friuli Grave – Via A. Altan 83/3, San Vito al Tagliamento (PN), ℘ 0434 18 36 034, www.docfriuligrave.com

Consorzio di Tutela Vini DOC Friuli Isonzo – www.consorziodocfvg.it

Consorzio di Tutela Vini DOC Friuli Latisana – www.consorziodocfvg.it

Consorzio di Tutela Vini DOC Lison Pramaggiore – ℘ 389 45 84 662, www.stradavini.it

© Hi-X/Shutterstock

*Statues on one of the* barchesse *at Villa Manin, in Passariano*

tower stands separate from the rest of the building and dates from the 13th c. The interior boasts superb artworks, amongst which the *Madonna della Misericordia* by Pordenone, a leading Italian Renaissance painter, born in the city in 1484.

**Sacile** 🍷, a lovely ancient village built on two islands in the Livenza, is 13 km west of Pordenone. Its Renaissance palaces overlooking the water are reminiscent of Venice. The centre of the village is the porticoed Piazza del Popolo, onto which faces the City Hall built in the 14th c. Close by are the Baptistery and Duomo, restored to their original Renaissance appearance after the 1976 earthquake. Return to Pordenone and take the S 13 east in the direction of Udine, passing through **Casarsa della Delizia**, a famous winemaking village in which frescoes by the painter Pordenone can be seen in the Church of Santa Croce. The village is also linked to Pier Paolo Pasolini as it was the birthplace of his mother. The film director spent many years in Casarsa and is buried beside his family in the local cemetery. *For information, contact the Centro Studi Pier Paolo Pasolini, Via G. Pasolini 4, ☎ 0434 87 05 93, www.centrostudipierpaolopasolini-casarsa.it.*

Pass through **Codroipo** and take a detour to the right to Passariano and Villa Manin.

## Villa Manin★★

This 16th-c. villa was the summer residence of the powerful Manin family, to whom it belonged until the end of the 20th c. Rebuilt in the 17th c., it features two *barchesse* (porticoes, typical of Veneto villas) that ring the main courtyard and are joined to the horseshoe-shaped exedra. This grandiose setting, which is suggestive of Versailles and St Peter's Square, was chosen by Napoleon to prepare the Treaty of Campoformio (*8 km south-west of Udine*) that ended the existence of the Republic of Venice and was signed here, in the residence of the last doge, Ludovico Manin, on 17 October 1797. The villa has a magnificent chapel and sacristy and, in summer particularly, organizes numerous art and photographic exhibitions, as well as events and concerts by internationally known artists. The park around the villa covers 19 hectares. *Open 9-19, closed Mon. ☎ 0432 82 12 11, www.villamanin.it.*

## 2. COLLI ORIENTALI DEL FRIULI (COF)

The hills cover a broad swath of countryside that stretches east of Udine, from Tarcento (in the north) to San Giovanni al Natisone and **Corno di Rosazzo** 🍷 (to the south) touching on Cividale del Friuli. Protected by the Julian Alps, here the vines are sheltered from the cold northerly winds and benefit from good ventilation. Excellent white and red wines are produced from local and international grape varieties. Special mention is given to **Picolit**, a sweet wine made from grapes of the same name, due to millerandage or abnormal fruit set, as a result of which many of the berries fail to develop fully, giving the ones that remain exceptional sugar content and

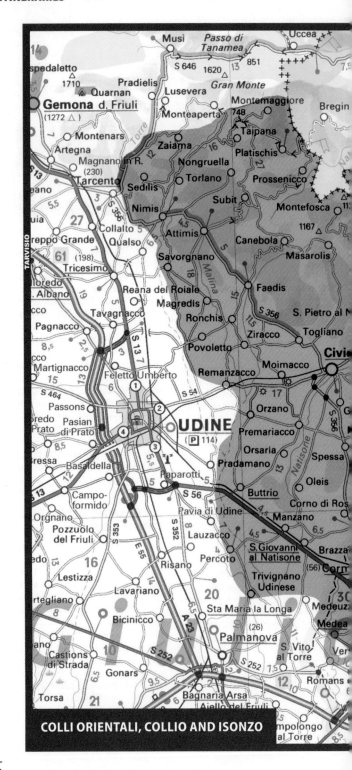

**COLLI ORIENTALI, COLLIO AND ISONZO**

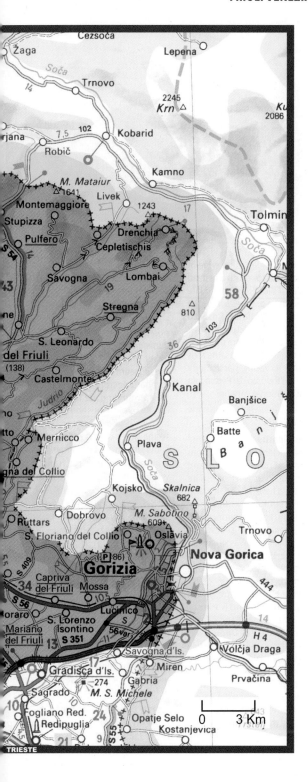

*Region's vineyards in their unspoilt setting*

aromas. The other great white wine of the area is **Ramandolo**, which is instead produced using a slight raisining or late harvest of Verduzzo grapes. Within the designated area, the **Cialla** and **Rosazzo** subzones have always stood out for their quality: whereas the whites are traditionally the most exalted products, the reds too have much to vaunt, particularly those made from Refosco dal Peduncolo Rosso and international varieties.

*Itinerary of approximately 65 km starting from Cividale del Friuli.*

## Cividale del Friuli★

Cividale is the ancient *Forum Julii*, from which the name Friuli is derived, and stands over the river Natisone. The Lombards settled here in the 6th c. and founded the first of many dukedoms in northern Italy. Long independent, Cividale later became the seat of the Patriarchs of Aquileia but was subjected by Venice in the 15th c. Struck by the earthquake in 1976, the town has gone intense reconstruction.

The heart of the historic centre, which lies over the Roman forum, is **Piazza Duomo**, site of the Town Hall and Palazzo dei Provveditori Veneti. The **Duomo** was rebuilt in the 16th c. in Renaissance style but conserves its partially Gothic façade and Gothic elements inside. The building contains the small **Christian Museum★** of Lombard art (*in the right aisle*), where you can see the 8th-c. baptistery of Patriarch Callistus and the 7th-c. marble altar of Duke Ratchis, the sides of which are carved with scenes of the life of Christ.

*Via Candotti 1. Open 10-13 and 15-17, closed Mon. and Tue., ℘ 0432 73 04 03, www.museocristiano.it.*

**National Archaeological Museum★★** – *Piazza del Duomo 13. Open 8.30-19.30, closed Mon. pm, ℘ 0432 70 07 00, www. museoarcheologicocividale.beniculturali. it.* Set in a lovely late 16th-c. palace, the museum exhibits many finds from Lombard necropolises in Cividale and the surrounding area. Do not miss the Roman sarcophagus and funerary goods of Duke Gisulfo (7th c.).

To the north of Piazza Duomo, Piazza Paolo Diacono is a busy marketplace.

Continue west towards Natisone and you will reach the elegant **small Lombard temple★★** built in the 7th c. (*open Mon.-Fri. 10-13 and 15-18, Oct.-Mar. 14-17, Sat., Sun. and public hols. 10-18, Oct.-Mar. 17, ℘ 0432 70 08 67, www.tempiettolongobardo.it*). This is formed by a square room with an ogival cross and is decorated with admirable stuccoes and frescoes. The wooden choir is 14th-c.

From **Ponte del Diavolo**, built in the 15th c. but rebuilt after World War I, there is a good view over the town. Close by is the **Celtic hypogeum**, consisting of various underground rooms dug out of the rock, the function of which remains unknown. They may have been a prison or funerary in nature.

## North towards Tarcento

*Leave Cividale to the north-west taking the S 356.* Along the way you pass through villages of artistic and enological interest, such as **Faedis** ♛, with the ruins of three castles, and **Attimis**, which also boasts exceptional monuments like the 11th-c. Partistagno Castle, soon to be fitted out as a commercial and museum space. An archaeological park is being set up in this zone to draw attention to the area's cultural and environmental assets.

Continue to **Nimis** ♛, in which the ancient parish Church of Santi Protasio and Gervasio dates originally from the 8th c. Some traces of ancient frescoes inside. The town's pride is the DOCG wine made from Ramandolo grapes.

Drive on to **Tarcento** and the first hills of the Prealps. The town was renowned as a resort in the late 19th and early 20th c. Continue further north-east towards Lusevera till you come to **Villanova delle Grotte**, where you can enter a vast network of underground karstic caves. *For information on opening days and times, ☎ 0432 78 79 15, www.grotte divillanova.it.*

## South of Cividale

The wine area of Colli Orientali dei Friuli also stretches to the south of Cividale, and includes many interesting places in terms of both art and wine, such as **Prepotto** ♛, **Premariacco** ♛, and **Buttrio** ♛ (**Wine Civilisation Museum** in the lovely Villa di Toppo Florio, *open by reservation, ☎ 0432 67 33 11*), **Manzano** ♛ and **San Giovanni al Natisone** ♛, from where you can visit **Rosazzo Abbey**, founded in the Middle Ages.

## 3. COLLIO AND ISONZO

**Collio** is a lovely hilly zone covered by vineyards and orchards to the west of Gorizia. It follows the course of the river Judrio along the border with Slovenia.

The **Isonzo** DOC zone, on the other hand, follows the river from Gorizia northwards.

In Collio, **Pinot Grigio**, **Friulano** and **Ribolla Gialla** are the leading wines, whereas in Isonzo **Schioppettino**, **Cabernet** and **Franconia** produce outstanding reds.

## Gorizia ♛

Gorizia was a place of crucial importance during World War I, a frontier town between Italy and Yugoslavia in the past, and between Italy and Slovenia

today. Starting in Piazza della Vittoria, take Via Rastello to the Duomo, which was originally built in the 14th c. but later rebuilt several times. The city centre is dominated by the characteristic **Borgo Castle★** ringed by 16th-c. walls. Built in the 11th c., it was rebuilt after World War I. The cellars of several houses in the castle hamlet hold the **Great War Museum** dedicated to the First World War (*Borgo Castello 13, open 9-19, closed Mon., ☎ 0481 53 39 26*), whereas the rooms of the castle are the setting for the **Gorizian Middle Ages Museum** (*Borgo Castello 36, open 10-19, 9.30-11.30 Mon., ☎ 0481 53 51 46*).

The Renaissance **Palazzo Coronini Cronberg** (north of the historic centre) is surrounded by a splendid park and contains some fine art collections. *Viale XX Settembre 14. For information on opening days and times, ☎ 0481 53 34 85, www. coronini.it. The park is always open.*

Temporary exhibitions are held in the beautiful **Palazzo Attems-Petzenstein** in Piazza de Amicis.

## Collio

*Itinerary of 40 km from Gorizia to Dolegna del Collio.*

Just north of the city the **Sacrario di Oslavia** contains the remains of 57,740 of those who fell in World War I. *Open 9-12 and 14-17, Sat.-Sun. and public hols. 9-12.30 and 13.30-18 (closed Oct.-mid-Mar.), closed Mon. ☎ 0481 53 17 88.*

Close by stands **San Floriano del Collio** ♛, a lovely village in a panoramic position, whose wines were appreciated at the time of the Austro-Hungarian empire. The castle has conserved some of the parts of the ancient building. Next to it is the **Museum of Wine and the Farming Life**.

Return to Gorizia and take the S 56 west to **Capriva del Friuli** ♛ and **Cormons** ♛ along the "Wine and Cherry Route". The village has retained its walls around the historic centre and 18th-c. duomo. The "**Peace Vineyard**" was started here in 1983: grapes representing 550 varieties, donated from around the world, are harvested each year by the association of Cormons vintners. The Peace Wine, whose labels are designed by three famous artists, is sent to each head of state and a number of religious leaders. Palazzo Locatelli in Piazza XXIV Maggio is the seat of the **Municipal Wine Cellar of Cormons**, which brings the producers of Collio and Isonzo together, ✆ 0481 63 03 71, www.enoteca-cormons.it.

Driving north, you come to **Dolegna del Collio** ♟, another important wine-producing village in the area.

## Isonzo

*Itinerary of 35 km from Gorizia to Farra d'Isonzo.*

Several municipalities like Capriva del Friuli and Cormons are represented in both the Collio and Isonzo designated areas. A little to the south, **Mariano del Friuli** ♟ is devoted to two sorts of product: wine and chairs. A few km to the west lies **Gradisca d'Isonzo** ♟, an ancient fortress built to defend the right bank of the river and to which Leonardo da Vinci also contributed. The town has several very fine buildings, such as the Palazzo Torriani, the duomo and the castle. A 15th-c. palace in the historic centre is the seat of the **Regional Wine Cellar of Friuli** (*see the Notes*).

Leave Isonzo and pass through **Sagrado** ♟ to reach the monumental **Sacrario di Redipuglia**, which holds the remains of 100,000 soldiers killed in World War I. *For information* ✆ 0481 48 90 24.

Return towards Gradisca and continue towards Gorizia through **Farra d'Isonzo** ♟.

## 4. THE CARSO

The Carso (Kras in Slovenian) is a limestone plateau that stretches as far as the Julian Alps on the Italian side and into Slovenia and Croatia in the other direction. The calcareous rock is easily eroded by water, with the result that the area is covered with caves, cliffs, dolinas and sinkholes. The wine-producing area of the Carso includes the province of Trieste and the Carso in Gorizia. The landscape is extremely varied, with plenty of vines. In the more temperate zones these are often grown with olives. The Carso is influenced by nearby Slovenia: the most representative grapes here are **Malvasia Istriana**, **Vitovska** and **Terrano**.

## Trieste★

Lying at the end of the gulf of the same name, Trieste is a border town, port and a city of Mitteleuropa. After being subjected by the Patriarchs of Aquileia, Trieste was annexed to Venice in 1202 but, after rebelling against the Serenissima, placed itself under the protection of Austria in 1382. In 1719 Emperor Charles VI declared it a "free port" and made it the seat of the Compagnie d'Oriente e del Levante. The city entered a new period of prosperity, constructed many new buildings and provided refuge to numerous exiles. Trieste was reunited with the kingdom of Italy in 1919 after ferocious fighting.

---

### Coffee-houses and coffee in Trieste

Coffee is of crucial importance to Trieste as the city handles approximately 40% of the product imported into Italy and has two very famous milling companies in **Hausbrandt** and **Illy**. Like Austrian coffee-houses, the cafés of Trieste are places to pass the time of day, discuss, play billiards and read (newspapers are always available). The first coffee-house in Trieste was opened in 1768. At one time each one was linked to a particular nationality but later the divisions were based on social issues: there were cafés for those who wanted to talk politics, others for businessmen and some that functioned as literary salons. The oldest coffee-house in Trieste is the **Caffè Tommaseo** in Piazza Tommaseo 4/c (*www.caffetommaseo.it*). It was popular with irredentists, was frequented by Umberto Saba and today is Viennese in atmosphere. The **Caffè degli Specchi** at Piazza Unità d'Italia 7 was the theatre of fervent political debate. The **Caffè San Marco** at Via Cesare Battisti 18 was also an irredentist hangout (during World War I they even made false passports there), and today, as it always has been, it is a meeting-place for literati and intellectuals. It was frequented by Saba, Joyce, Rilke and Svevo, and its decor is Art Nouveau and Art Deco.
Other addresses: **Caffè Pasticceria Pirona** (*Largo Barriera Vecchia 12, www.pirona1900. com*), patronised by Joyce, **Caffè Tergesteo** (*Piazza della Borsa 15*), **Caffè Stella Polare** (*Via D. Alighieri 14*), **Antico Caffè Torinese** (*Corso Italia 2, www.anticocaffetorinese.ts.it*), **Pasticceria La Bomboniera** (*Via XXX Ottobre 3, www.pasticcerialabomboniera.com*).

*Miramare Castle from the sea*

The notorious *bora* is to all purposes an inhabitant of the city. The wind, which can exceed 100 kph, blows down from the Carso in winter and out to sea with such force that at times the locals are obliged to sit or lie down so as not to be blown over.

**San Giusto Hill★★** – At the top of the city, the **Piazza della Cattedrale★** is the setting for the ruins of a Roman basilica, the castle (15th-16th c.), a Venetian column from 1560, the World War I monument (1929) and the Basilica of San Giusto.

**Basilica of San Giusto★** – founded in the 5th c., the basilica was constructed over a Roman building but much of the modern basilica dates from the 14th c. The façade has a lovely Gothic rose window and is decorated with a low relief and busts in bronze. The sturdy bell tower incorporates fragments of Roman columns in the lower half and is adorned with a statue of St Justus (14th c.). From the top there is a marvellous **view★** over Trieste. Inside, the right apse has a fine 13th-c. mosaic and 11th-c. frescoes of the life of St Justus. In the left apse, there is a magnificent 12th-c. **mosaic★★** of the *Madonna Enthroned, Archangels Michael and Gabriel and the Apostles*.

The museum in the **Castle of San Giusto** exhibits vintage arms, objects and furnishings. There are also temporary exhibitions and the Tergestino *lapidarium. Open 10-17, closed Mon.,*

℘ *040 30 93 62, www.castellodisangiustotrieste.it.*

The **Museum of History and Art** displays a remarkable collection of red-figure **Greek vases★** and lovely archaic Roman **bronzes★**. *Open 10-19 (Nov.-Mar. 10-17), closed Mon.* ℘ *040 31 05 00.*

Lying at the foot of San Giusto hill are the remains of a **Roman theatre** built at the start of the 2nd c.

**The Borgo Teresiano** – on the north side of San Giusto hill and Corso Italia stands the well-ordered 18th-c. town built at the instigation of Emperor Charles VI and his daughter Maria Theresa. It was designed around a series of canals, of which only the **Grand Canal** was actually dug. Revolving bridges allowed sailing ships to enter the centre of the city and reach commercial depots. Today the canal is crossed by fixed bridges, of which the most famous is the **Red Bridge**, after which the market square adjacent is named. To the left of the mouth of the Grand Canal stands the **Palazzo Carciotti** (1800), one of the city's loveliest Neoclassical buildings. Opposite stand the Red Skyscraper (1928) and the 19th-c. Palazzo Gopcevic.

Corso Italia joins Piazza Goldoni to **Piazza della Borsa**, the latter dominated by the columned façade of the 19th-c. Palazzo della Borsa Vecchia. Next door, the Palazzo del Tergesteo (1840) is occupied by a covered shopping gallery. Teatro Verdi, opened on 21 April

1801, stands in Piazza Verdi and offers a celebrated theatre season each year.

**Piazza dell'Unità d'Italia★ and the promenade** – Three Art Nouveau palaces face onto the square: Palazzo del Governo, Palazzo Comunale and Palazzo del Lloyd Triestino. The promenade in Trieste stretches from Molo Audace (a wharf named after a World War I destroyer) to the elegant Rive lined with elegant palaces. The Maritime Station (1930), now used for exhibitions, is located on the Molo dei Bersaglieri.

The **Sea Museum★** (*Magazzino 26, Porto Vecchio, open Thu.-Sun. 11-17, ℘ 345 71 59 132, www.museodelmaretrieste.it*) is well worth a visit. This relates the history of ships from their origins to the 18th c. Of particular interest are the fishing section and the instrumentation of the *Elettra*, Guglielmo Marconi's boat.

### Risiera di San Sabba

*Via Giovanni Palatucci 5, to the south of Trieste along the S 202, take the Val-maura/Stadio/Cimitero exit.* In 1943 this former rice mill was turned into a Nazi extermination camp. *Via G. Palatucci 5. Open 9-19 (Nov.-Mar. 9-17) ℘ 040 82 62 02, www.risierasansabba.it.*

### Foiba di Basovizza

A memorial tablet on the S 14 at the entrance to Basovizza sinkhole records the tragic events linked to the occupation of Istria and Trieste by Tito's partisans in 1945, when the communist militias executed thousands of Italians and Istrians suspected of links with the Fascist regime and threw their bodies into the karstic sinkholes.

### The Carso

*Itinerary of approximately 45 km from Trieste to Duino.*

The Carso plateau forms a rocky coastline of magnificent white cliffs between Trieste and Duino. Leave Piazza della Libertà in the direction of Prosecco and Villa Opicina and follow the sign for Monte Grisa. The modern **Sanctuary del Monte Grisa** is dedicated to the Madonna; the terrace provides **spectacular views★★** over the Gulf of Trieste.

Continue through **Villa Opicina** (*access also via cable railway starting from Piazza Oberdan*). The villa stands at a height of 348 m on the edge of the Carso plateau. The lookout point, marked by an obelisk, gives a magnificent **view★★** over Trieste and its gulf.

*In Opicina, continue left in the direction of Borgo Grotta Gigante.*

The **Giant Grotto★**, which you reach via an impressive flight of steps, is formed by a single enormous cavern lined with extraordinary concretions. There is a **Speleology Museum** at the entrance to the grotto. *For information on opening times ℘ 040 32 73 12, www.grottagigante.it.*

At Sgonico 🍴 you can visit the **Carsiana Botanic Garden** and its huge variety of Carso flora in its natural environment inside a dolina. *For information on opening times, ℘ 389 58 70 090, www.giardinobotanicocarsiana.it.*

Take the S 14 coast road to reach **Miramare Castle and garden★★**. Situated at the end of a promontory, the castle has a charming terraced garden, and an aviary for tropical birds and butterflies. The castle was built in 1860 for Archduke Maximilian of Austria (executed in Mexico in 1867) and his wife Charlotte of Belgium (who went mad and died in 1927). The interior contains the original furnishings. *Open 9-19, for park times ℘ 040 22 41 43, www.castello-miramare.it.*

Continuing along the coast road you come to **Duino** 🍴, once a fishing village. It has the remains of an ancient castle destroyed by the Turks and the solid new castle rebuilt several times in

## Osmizze

The *osmizze* in the Carso are places where wine is sold for consumption directly on the premises of the producer. The name comes from the Slovenian word *osmica*, which refers to the eight (*osem*) days a year they were allowed to open. In 1784 an imperial decree allowed anyone to sell homemade foodstuffs, wine or fruit-must throughout the year as long as the *osmizza* was clearly advertised with a leaf frond along the road or on the house, on pain of closure.

*Mosaic floor, Aquileia Basilica*

different epochs. It is surrounded by a splendid park from which there are views of the landscapes that inspired Rilke to write the *Duino Elegies* when he stayed here in 1911. A marvellous walk from the castle towards Sistiana is named after the great poet.

Continuing towards Monfalcone, you arrive at **Timavo springs**, a place worshiped in ancient times. This is the unusual site where a river returns to the surface after travelling underground for almost 40 km.

## 5. AQUILEIA - ANNIA - LATISANA

The production zone of these three appellations lies in the southern part of the province of Udine, just behind the coastal strip. The finest wines in the **Aquileia DOC** zone, where the terrain is rich in sand, are the reds. The most common variety here is the **Refosco dal Peduncolo Rosso**: it seems that this grape was already known as Pucinum at the time of the Romans. Wines derived from Pinot Grigio and Gewürztraminer are also very interesting. The zone takes in the municipalities that lie north of Aquileia towards Udine, stretching to Gonars, Palmanova and Santa Maria la Longa.

**Annia** is a DOC zone in the plain that produces fresh wines with an intriguing nose, made from Chardonnay, Malvasia, Pinot Bianco, Pinot Grigio, Sauvignon, Friulano, Traminer Aromatico, Verduzzo Friulano, Cabernet Franc, Cabernet Sauvignon, Merlot and Refosco dal Peduncolo Rosso grapes, and they are best enjoyed young. The DOC zone also produces brut and demi-sec **sparkling wines** from Chardonnay and/or Pinot Bianco. The zone is spread across several municipalities in the province of Udine to the west and north-west of Aquileia: Bagnaria Arsa, **Carlino** ☻, Castions di Strada, Marano Lagunare, Muzzana del Turgnano, Porpetto, San Giorgio di Nogaro and Torviscosa.

The **Friuli Latisana** zone is characterised by mineral- and clay-rich soil, and a mild climate thanks to the proximity of the sea. The wines are velvety, full-flavoured and moderately acidulous, with a rich bouquet and a hefty alcohol content. The territory includes various municipalities on Udine's west border, from **Lignano Sabbiadoro** (the leading coastal resort in Friuli) northwards along the banks of the river Tagliamento: Latisana, Ronchis, Rivignano and Varmo are just a few of the towns worth visiting.

### Aquileia Basilica★★

This Roman colony was named after an eagle (*aquila* in Latin) that flew across the sky just as the city was being founded in 181 BC. A flourishing market in the imperial age and Augustus's headquarters during the Germanic wars (when the population of the city reached 100,000), Aquileia later became the seat of one of Italy's most important Patriarchs (554-1751).

Built in the 9th c. over the ruins of a 6th-c. building, the Romanesque **church**, preceded by a portico and separate bell tower, was reworked in the 14th c. The 4th-5th c. baptistery, rebuilt in the 9th c., is very beautiful. The interior is decorated with one of the largest and most splendid **mosaic floors★★** (4th c.) in the Western Christian world. The framework of the roof and the arches are 14th-c., the capitals Romanesque and the decoration of the transept Renaissance. The 9th-c. Carolingian crypt is adorned with 12th-c. **frescoes★★**. The crypt (entrance in the left aisle) contains objects found during excavations, in particular more excellent 4th-c. **mosaic flooring★★**. *Open Apr.-Sept. 9-19 (Nov.-Feb. 10-16, rest of the year 9-18), ℘ 0431 91 067, www. basilicadiaquileia.it.*

**Archaeological areas★** – *Open 8.30 to 1 hour before sunset, ℘ 0431 91 035, www.aquileia.net.* Excavation work close to the basilica has unearthed a section of Roman Aquileia: the Sacra Via (behind the basilica) that led to the river port, several houses and the forum. The **Archaeological** (*open 10-19, closed Mon., ℘ 0431 91 035, www.museoar-cheologicoaquileia.beniculturali.it*) and **Paleochristian museums** (*Piazza Pirano 1, open Thu.-Sat. 8.30-13.30*) contain important collections of excavated objects.

**Grado★**

About 10 km south of Aquileia, in the heart of the lagoon, Grado is a small fishing port, bathing resort and spa. The old district is a tangle of narrow alleys (called *calli*) between the canal-port and the **Duomo** di Sant'Eufemia. Founded in the 6th c., it has several marble columns with Byzantine capitals, a 6th-c. mosaic floor, a 10th-c. ambo (lectern), and an exceptional gilded silver altarpiece made in Venice in the 14th c. Next to the duomo there is a row of sarcophaguses and tombs, and the 6th-c. baptistery decorated with mosaics.

Close by stands the Basilica di Santa Maria delle Grazie (6th c.), which has several original mosaics and fine capitals.

Continuing from Aquileia northwards on the S 352, you pass through **Cervignano del Friuli** 🍷 (fine 17th-c. villa) and Strassoldo (two castles), and arrive at **Palmanova**. This town was built as a 9-pointed star by the Venetians at the end of the 16th c. Radiating out from the central Piazza Grande are 6 streets that lead to the bastions.

# 6. LISON PRAMAGGIORE

Straddling the Veneto and Friuli border is the wine production zone of Lison Pramaggiore. In the Veneto it falls within the provinces of Venezia, Treviso and Pordenone. In Friuli it lies in the provinces of Chions, Cordovado, Pravisdomini and part of Azzano Decimo, Morsano al Tagliamento and Sesto al Reghena. It successfully cultivates many international varieties but excellent results are also obtained with the local Verduzzo, Tocai Italico and Refosco dal Peduncolo Rosso. *For more information see p. 229.*

*Small fishing port of Grado*

# Addresses

## Tourist information

**Aquileia Tourist Office** – Via Iulia Augusta 11, Aquileia, ℘ 0431 91 94 91, www.turismofvg.it

**Gorizia Tourist Office** – Corso Italia 9, Gorizia, ℘ 0481 53 57 64

**Pordenone Tourist Office** – Palazzo Badini Via Mazzini, 2, Pordenone, ℘ 0434 52 03 81

**Trieste Infopoint** – Piazza Unità d'Italia 4/b, Trieste, ℘ 040 34 78 312

**Udine Tourist Office** – Piazza I Maggio 7, Udine, ℘ 0432 29 59 72

**Federdoc Friuli Venezia Giulia** – Federazione Consorzi Tutela Vini - Camera di Commercio Industria Artigianato and Agricoltura di Udine - Via Morpurgo 4, Udine ℘ 0432 51 06 19, www.federdoc.com

## The wineries

*The addresses are listed in alphabetical order by location.*

### GRAVE

**Azienda Agricola Vistorta** – *Via Vistorta 82 -* **Sacile** *(PN) - ℘ 0434 71 135 - www. vistorta.it - vistorta@vistorta.it - Wine shop, closed Sat.-Sun.* The estate has been in the Brandolini family since 1780, but boasts far older origins. Tellingly, two Roman capitals have marked the boundaries since the 2nd c. In the 19th c. Guido Brandolini transformed Vistorta into an efficient farm. Brandino Brandolini d'Adda has run it since 1980. Exploiting the experience of the family's other winery, Château Greysac in Bordeaux, Brandino decided to base Vistorta's production on the French model and focus on making outstanding reds. Hectares under vine: 40.
**Wines:** Merlot Vistorta, Treanni rosso IGT.

### COF (EASTERN HILLS OF FRIULI), COLLIO, ISONZO

**Conte D'Attimis-Maniago** – *Tenuta Sottomonte - Via Sottomonte 21 -* **Buttrio** *(UD) - ℘ 0432 67 40 27 - www.contedattimismaniago.it - info@ contedattimismaniago.it - Winery tours 8.30-12 and 13.30-17.30 by reservation, closed Sat. pm, Sun. and 2 weeks in mid-Aug.* The estate covers 110 hectares, nearly all of which planted to vine, and has been owned by the D'Attimis Maniago family for over 500 years. Ancient documents kept in the winery's archives have numerous historical annotations, such as the one testifying to the fact that 10 farming contracts were granted to a Benedictine monastery in 1140 so that the monks could make wine and oil. The 17th-c. family palazzo, which was recently restored, is especially significant. Hectares under vine: 110.
**Wines:** Refosco dal Peduncolo Rosso, Tazzelenghe, Ribolla Gialla, Sauvignon, Picolit, Friulano, Schioppettino.

🏰 **Castello di Spessa** – *Via Spessa 1 -* **Capriva del Friuli** *(GO) - ℘ 0481 80 81 24 - www.castellodispessa.it - info@castello dispessa.it - Winery tours and tasting by reservation.* The winemaking tradition of the castle of Spessa goes back centuries and its history is documented as early as 1559. Giacomo Casanova, a guest at the castle in the second half of the 1700s, praised the quality of its wines. The ageing cellar, once an army bunker, is worth visiting. It was built in the late 1930s and was used as a shelter during the war. Today a descent of 70 steps connects it to the original cellar that runs east-west through the heart of the castle, which stands in the middle of a golf course. Accommodation available at Castello di Spessa Resorts *(8 rooms, from €170 )*. Restaurant service at Tavernetta al Castello *(Via Spessa 7, ℘ 0481 80 82 28, closed Sun. evening and Mon., 10 rooms)*. Hectares under vine: 28.
**Wines:** Friulano, Ribolla Gialla, Pinot Bianco and Grigio, Collio Merlot, Pinot Nero. Other products: grappa and brandy.

© Boettcher & Petoe/Shutterstock

# ADDRESSES

⌂ **Russiz Superiore** – *Via Russiz 7 -*
**Capriva del Friuli** *(GO) -* ℘ *0481 80 328 -*
*www.marcofelluga.it - info@marcofelluga.it*
*- Winery tours by reservation,* ℘*335 70 80*
*590 or rp@marcofelluga.it.* The estate faces
the splendid hills of Collio Goriziano and
has 96 hectares, 50 of which planted to
vine and divided as follows: 70% white
varieties and 30% red varieties. The area is
particularly suited for the production of
white wines, notably Collio Bianco Col
Disôre (a blend of Pinot Bianco and
Friulano, Sauvignon and Ribolla Gialla),
Sauvignon and Friulano. The estate was
purchased by Marco Felluga in the 1960s.
Accommodation available at the Relais
Russiz Superiore *(7 rooms, double from*
*€136).* Hectares under vine: 50.
**Wines**: Collio Bianco Col Disôre, Collio
Sauvignon, Collio Pinot Grigio, Collio
Friulano, Collio Rosso Riserva degli Orzoni.
Other products: olive oil.

© Luis Louro/Shutterstock

**Villa Russiz** – *Via Russiz 6 -* **Capriva del
Friuli** *(GO) -* ℘ *0481 80 047 - www.
villarussiz.it - villarussiz@villarussiz.it -
Winery tours and tasting by reservation (from
€12).* Gianni Menotti has followed in the
family tradition: his father Edino ran Villa
Russiz for 35 years and Gianni took it over in
1988. From the very beginning, his goal
was to make the winery a virtuous model of
public investment, and he has achieved his
objective. The history of Villa Russiz is
connected with that of the French count
Theodore de La Tour, who in 1869 decided
that the sunny Collio hills would be the
perfect place to live with his wife Elvine
Ritter and indulge his passion for
winegrowing. Hectares under vine: 45.
**Wines**: Graf de la Tour, Sauvignon de la
Tour, Gräfin de la Tour, Pinot Grigio,
Friulano, Defì de la Tour.

**Schiopetto** – *Via Palazzo Arcivescovile 1*
*-* **Capriva del Friuli** *(GO) -* ℘ *0481 80 332 -*
*www.schiopetto.it - azienda@schiopetto.it -*
*Winery tours by reservation.* The Schiopetto
family has been making wine for three
generations and this makes it one of Collio's
most historic wineries: Mario Schiopetto,
the son of Giorgio, who owned a tavern in
Udine, has been producing wine since
1965. Today his children continue the
family tradition at the winery's
headquarters, housed in the old palazzo of
the diocesan curia of Gorizia. Hectares
under vine: 20.
**Wines**: Friulano, Pinot Bianco, Pinot Grigio,
Sauvignon, Mario Schiopetto, Blanc des
Rosis.

⌂ **Zorzettig** – *Via Strada Sant'Anna 37,*
*Fraz. Spessa -* **Cividale del Friuli** *(UD) -*
℘ *0432 71 61 56 - www.zorzettigvini.it -*
*info@zorzettigvini.it - Open Mon.-Fri. 8-12.30*
*and 13.30-18, Sat. 8-17.* Accomodation

available at *Agriturismo Relais La Collina,*
*Premariacco (9 rooms, € 80).*The name
Zorzettig has been connected with
winemaking activities in the Friuli region
for centuries. The Zorzettig family has
been a protagonist in this sector since the
early post-war period, in the midst of
industrial development when only a few
courageous Italians decided to invest
money, resources and effort in working the
land. In addition to the family's own
property, the Zorzettigs also cultivated
lands owned by Cividale hospital,
bequeathed to the institution as
inheritance from its own patients. When
the hospital decided to sell these lands,
the Zorzettig family bought them, marking
the start of a slow but continuous growth
for the family business that has led them
to become one of the most important
realities in the region. Hectares under
vine: 115.
**Wines**: DOC Friuli Colli Orientali Pignolo,
Friulano, Sauvignon, Ribolla Gialla, Refosco
dal Peduncolo Rosso, Schioppettino.
Other products: olive oil, grappa.

⌂ **Borgo San Daniele** – *Via San Daniele 38*
*-* **Cormòns** *(GO) -* ℘ *0481 60 552 - www.
borgosandaniele.it - info@borgosandaniele.
it - Winery tours by reservation, closed Sun.*
"Minerality above all" is the winery's motto
and, in effect, the wines that it produces
fully reflect this philosophy. The winery has
chosen to focus on only a few labels,
maintain high vine density and low yields,
harvest late, and use fermentation on the
skins even for whites, as well as malolactic
fermentation, extended lees contact and
micro-oxygenation to make wines with
plenty of personality. Accommodation
available at the winery *(3 rooms).* Hectares
under vine: 18.

**Wines**: Friulano, Pinot Grigio, IGT Venezia Giulia Bianco Arbis Blanc, IGT Venezia Giulia Rosso Arbis Ròs, Gortmarin.

**Cantina Produttori Cormòns** – *Via Vino della Pace 31* - **Cormòns** *(GO)* - ☏ *0481 62 471* - *www.cormons.com* - *info@cormons. com* - *Winery tours and tasting by reservation, closed Sun.* Cantina Produttori Cormòns was established in the late 1960s and today it has over 120 member winemakers. Its philosophy is based on the assumption that good wine originates in the land and, as a result, special attention is paid to the vineyards. The "Vino della Pace" (Peace Wine) is produced using over 500 grape varieties from all over the world that are harvested in the "World Vineyard" by the winery. The labels are created by leading contemporary artists. Hectares under vine: 400.

**Wines**: Collio Friulano, Isonzo Vendemmia Tardiva, Vino della Pace, Trevenezie Ribolla Gialla IGT, Collio Pinot Grigio. Other products: grappa, spirits, olive oil and vinegar.

🏠 **La Boatina** – *Via Corona 62* - **Cormòns** *(GO)* - ☏ *0481 63 93 09* - *www.laboatina.it* - *www.castellodispessa.it* - *info@laboatina.it* - *Winery tours by reservation.* La Boatina, which is part of Pali Wines, was purchased in 1979 by Loretto Pali; it produces wines with the Collio and Isonzo appellations. The winery boasts high-quality production, as its well-aspected land is particularly suited for winegrowing. The winery also has a guest farm with 5 simple but well-appointed rooms, and a restaurant that serves Italian and international cheeses and charcuterie. Accommodation available at La Boatina guest farm *(5 rooms)* with restaurant service *(closed Wed)*. Hectares under vine: 55.

**Wines**: Pinot Bianco and Grigio, Chardonnay, Sauvignon, Friulano, Merlot.

🏠 **Livio Felluga** – *Via Risorgimento 1 - Fraz. Brazzano* - **Cormòns** *(GO)* - ☏ *0481 60 203* - *www.liviofelluga.it* - *Tasting by reservation.* Wines sold at Locanda Orologio tavern and inn. Livio Felluga is considered a patriarch of Friulian enology. In the 1950s he founded the Brazzano winery and purchased his first vineyards in Rosazzo. His devotion to the land has been the driving force behind his every success. Today the winery owns over 160 hectares in the hills of Collio and eastern Friuli. In 1956 Livio invented the original label with a map of the hills and even today it is the unmistakable symbol of Felluga wines. Accommodation and meals available at Locanda Orologio, across from the winery ( ☏ *0481 60 028, www.terraevini.it*). Accomodation available also at Abbazia di Rosazzo *(14 rooms, www.abbaziadirosazzo.*

*it)*, with its historical wine cellar *(visit by reservation, info@liviofelluga.it)*. Hectares under vine: 160.

**Wines**: Abbazia di Rosazzo, illivio, Rosenplatz, Friulano, Sossò, Vertigo.

⌂ **Polencic** – *Loc. Plessiva 12* - **Cormòns** *(GO)* - ☏ *0481 60 655* - *www.polencic.com* - *info@polencic.com* - *Winery tours by reservation.* Isidoro Polencic relies on young, state-of-the-art viticulture, using clones that ensure high quality. His vineyards are distinguished by different types of soil and microclimates - Cormòns, Ruttars, Flessiva, Novali, Mossa and Castelletto - allowing them to yield grapes with very different characteristics. He produces whites from Pinot Bianco, Pinot Grigio, Fisc, Sauvignon, Friulano, Chardonnay, Ribolla Gialla and Picolit grapes, and reds from Merlot, Cabernet Franc, Cabernet Sauvignon, Pinot Nero. The estate offers accommodation. Hectares under vine: 23.

**Wines**: Ribolla Gialla Collio, Pinot Grigio Collio, Sauvignon Collio, Picolit Collio, Friulano Collio, Pinot Nero Collio, Merlot.

**Tenuta di Angoris** – *Loc. Angoris 7* - **Cormòns** *(GO)* - ☏ *0481 60 923* - *www. angoris.com* - *info@angoris.it* - *Winery tours by reservation (Tue.- Fri.).* The Angoris estate has been making wine for more than 300 years. It is now run by the Locatelli family, who are committed to making excellent wines that reflect a skilful combination of tradition, experience and innovation. Claudia and Massimo are firmly convinced that wines must express terroir and allow those who taste them to experience the sensations of these lands. Hectares under vine: 130.

**Wines**: Pinot Grigio, Friulano, Sauvignon, Chardonnay, Ribolla Gialla. Other products: grappa.

© GeorgeS/Shutterstock

# ADDRESSES

♀/ **Collavini** – *Via della Ribolla Gialla 2 -* **Corno di Rosazzo** *(UD) -* ☎ *0432 75 32 22 - www.collavini.it - collavini@collavini.it - Winery tours by reservation.* The Collavini family began to make wine in 1896, when Eugenio supplied his wines to Udine's leading families: a century later his bottles would be sold around the world. In the 1970s the winery expanded thanks to the purchase of the picturesque 16th-c. manor in Corno di Rosazzo, which became the family home and the company headquarters. Restaurant service Osteria della Ribolla (*closed Mon.*). Hectares under vine: 150.

**Wines**: Pinot Grigio Villa Canlungo Collio, Broy Bianco Collio, Merlot dal Pic Collio, Forresco Friuli Colli Orientali, Ribolla Gialla Spumante Brut. Other products: grappa.

⌂ **Gigante** – *Via Rocca Bernarda 3 -* **Corno di Rosazzo** *(UD) -* ☎ *0432 75 58 35 - www. adrianogigante.it - info@adrianogigante.it - Winery tours by reservation (Gigante Wine & Welcome 8 rooms from €100).* It was in 1957 that Ferruccio Gigante grasped the winemaking potential of Friuli's eastern hills and decided to become a vintner after 40 years as a miller. Today the winery is run by his grandchildren Adriano, Giuliana and Ariedo. Gigante makes a large range of wines, notably Verduzzo, Friulano, Pignolo and Schioppettino. Hectares under vine: 25.

**Wines**: Verduzzo Friulano, Friulano, Friulano Vigneto Storico, Schioppettino, Pignolo.

⌂ **Venica & Venica** – *Loc. Cerò 8 -* **Dolegna del Collio** *(GO) -* ☎ *0481 61 264 - www.venica.it - venica@venica.it - Winery tours by reservation (from €25).* Everything began more than 70 years ago with grandfather Daniele, who in 1930 purchased a farmhouse – now the main body of the Venica winery – and surrounding vineyards. The winery has continued to work, thanks also to a smooth generational turnover. Gianni, Giorgio and Giampaolo Venica are "native" vintners who are committed to valorising local traditions through constant research and innovation, and by striving to learn and understand the qualities of the numerous microclimates present on their estate. Accommodation available at the "Casa Vino e Vacanze" guest farm (*6 rooms, doubles from €130, and 2 apts, from €180, min. stay 3 nights*). Hectares under vine: 33.

**Wines**: Friulano Collio Ronco delle Cime, Sauvignon Collio Ronco del Cerò, Ribolla Gialla L'Adelchi Collio, Pètris Malvasia Collio, Refosco DGT Venezia Giulia Bottaz.

⌂ **Comelli** – *Case Colloredo 8 - Fraz. Soffumbergo -* **Faedis** *(UD) -* ☎ *0432 71 12 26 - www.comelli.it - comelli@comelli.it - Winery tours by reservation.* Comelli makes excellent "Colli Orientali del Friuli" DOC wines. The vineyards are in the hills: to the north they are protected by the Prealps, and to the south they enjoy the mitigating effect of the Adriatic. The soil is composed of arenaceous-marly rock rich in lime, potassium, phosphorous, magnesium and many other minerals. Thanks to this unique microclimate and care lavished in the vineyard and cellar alike, Comelli produces wines of undisputed quality. Accommodation available at L'Uva e le Stelle (*4 apts., from €72*), an agritourism structure housed in a renovated old farmhouse. Hectares under vine: 12.

**Wines**: Friulano, Pignolo, Eoos Picolit, Jacò Merlot, Sauvignon. Other products: olive oil.

**Bressan** – *Via Conti Zoppini 35 -* **Farra d'Isonzo** *(GO) -* ☎ *0481 88 81 31 - www. bressanwines.com - bressanwines@tin.it - Retail sales and winery tours by reservation.* Bressan, which has made wine for centuries, has always staunchly followed a specific philosophy: great grapes make great wines, and vinification is an ancient art that must not be at the mercy of excessive innovation. Respect for nature and rejection of anything that levels and standardises are also two of the winery's cornerstones. Hectares under vine: 20.

**Wines**: Carat, Verduzzo Friulano, Pinot Grigio, Schioppettino, Pignol, Pinot Nero.

**Tenuta Villanova** – *Via C.Beretta 29 -* **Farra di Isonzo** *(GO) -* ☎ *0481 88 93 11 - www.tenutavillanova.com - info@tenuta villanova.com - Winery tours by reservation.* The estate, which boasts a history going back to 1499, was purchased in 1932 by Arnaldo Bennati, a farseeing businessman who transformed it into an efficient winery. Today his wife Giuseppina Grossi oversees the winery with profound passion and enthusiasm. Hectares under vine: 130.

**Wines**: Chardonnay Isonzo, Sauvignon Collio Roncocucco, Friulano Collio Roncocucco, Malvasia Isonzo, Ribolla Gialla Collio, Villanova Brut, Villanova Rosé. Other products: grappa and spirits.

**Gravner** – *Loc. Lenzuolo Bianco 9 - Fraz. Oslavia -* **Gorizia** *-* ☎ *0481 30 882 - www. gravner.it - info@gravner.it - Winery tours by reservation.* Josko Gravner applies his own philosophy of life to his work: respect for the rhythms and rules of nature, symbiosis between man, earth and sky, unwavering commitment, humility and honesty in everyday life and in the vineyard. The moon dictates the timing of his work and the result is unforgettable wines not to be missed. Hectares under vine: 18.

**Wines**: Ribolla, Bianco Breg, Rosso Breg, Rosso Gravner, Rujno.

**Radikon** – *Loc. Tre Buchi 4* - **Gorizia** - ☏ *0481 32 804* - *www.radikon.it* - *info@ radikon.it* - *Winery tours by reservation.* Since 1980 the winery has been run by Stanko Radikon, assisted by his wife Suzana and their son Saöa, who has a degree in viticulture and enology. The family is committed to producing natural wines that fully respect the territory and the environment. Consequently, in 1995 they decided to abandon all chemicals and minimise treatment at much as possible, in the vineyard as well as the cellar. They use only natural products that are not harmful to human health or the environment. Hectares under vine: 13.

**Wines:** Ribolla Gialla, Jakot, Oslavje, Merlot, Pinot Grigio, Slatnik.

⌂ **Marco Felluga** – *Via Gorizia 121* - **Gradisca d'Isonzo** *(GO)* - ☏ *0481 99 164* - *www.marcofelluga.it* - *info@marco felluga.it* - *Winery tours by reservation at Azienda Russiz Superiore, Capriva del Friuli, rp@marcofelluga.it*, ☏ *335 70 80 590.* The winery has over 100 hectares of vineyards, of which 70% planted with white varieties and 30% with red. All the whites are vinified at a controlled temperature and are steel-fermented. Part of the white wine is also barrel-aged, as are the reds. The winery boasts the most advanced equipment, yet fully respects tradition. Accommodation available at Relais Russiz Superiore (*7 rooms, doubles from €136*) Hectares under vine: 100.

**Wines:** Collio Pinot Grigio Mongris, Collio Bianco Molamatta, Collio Ribolla Gialla Maralba, Moscato Rosa, Collio Rosso Carantan. Other products: olive oil.

**Le Vigne di Zamò** – *Via Abate Corrado 4* - *Loc. Rosazzo* - **Manzano** *(UD)* - ☏ *0432 75 96 93* - *www.levignedizamo.com* - *info@ levignedizamo.com* - *Winery tours by reservation Mon.-Fri.* The Zamò family have always loved wine, but this adventure began when Tullio Zamò bought 5 hectares of vineyards on the hill of Rocca Bernarda. The winery expanded over the years and can now exploit three terroirs: Rosazzo, Buttrio and Rocca Bernarda. It works chiefly with local varieties, although international ones are also employed. About 40% of the vineyards are planted with red varieties, bucking the trend of the rest of the region, where whites predominate. Hectares under vine: 65.

**Wines:** Ribolla Gialla, Friulano Vigne Cinquant'anni, Pinot Grigio Ramato, Ronco delle Acacie, Pignolo, Picolit, Merlot.

**Torre Rosazza** – *Loc. Poggiobello 12* - **Oleis di Manzano** *(UD)* - ☏ *0422 86 45 11* - *www. torrerosazza.com* - *info@torrerosazza.com* - *Winery tours by reservation.* The winery is situated in the Palazzo De Marchi, built by

© Mashe/Shutterstock

Antonini Perusini in 1800. Torre Rosazza is derived from the ancient Latin Turris Rosacea (Tower of the Roses). Owned by Genagricola since 1974, the winery has devoted its energies to rediscovering and preserving the most characteristic varieties grown on the hills of Rosazzo, e.g. Ribolla Gialla and Picolit. Hectares under vine: 90.

**Wines:** Picolit, Verduzzo Friulano, Ribolla Gialla, Merlot, Refosco dal Peduncolo Rosso.

⌂ **Vinai dell'Abbate** – *Piazza Abbazia 5 -Loc. Rosazzo* - **Manzano** *(UD)* - ☏ *0432 75 90 91* - *www.abbaziadirosazzo.it* - *info@ liviofelluga.it* - *Winery tours by reservation* (*14 rooms*). The company produces wines from Rosazzo Abbey, a true religious and artistic gem of Friuli, and visitors can visit both the abbey and the cantina, which is the oldest in Friuli, dating back to the end of the 1200. When the weather is nice, visitors can also take the "Sentiero delle Rose" (rose path) route, which winds alongside the vineyards among both heritage and new rosebushes. Hectares under vine: 12.

**Wines:** Pignolo, Ribolla Gialla, Friulano, Sauvignon, Rosazzo.

**Vie di Romans** – *Loc. Vie di Romans 1* - **Mariano del Friuli** *(GO)* - ☏ *0481 69 600* - *www.viediromans.it* - *viediromans@ viediromans.it* - *Winery tours Mon.-Fri. by reservation (payment required).* The Gallo family's commitment to grapes and wine commenced over a century ago. Gianfranco Gallo has headed the winery since 1978. The Vie di Romans labels list not only the name of the variety, but also the vineyard, as each wine has a strong bond with its terroir and the grapes used to make it. Hectares under vine: 60.

**Wines:** Chardonnay, Pinot Grigio, Sauvignon, Malvasia, Dolée Friulano.

# ADDRESSES

**Dario Coos** - *Via Ramandolo 5 -* **Nimis** *(UD) - ☎ 0432 79 03 20 - www.dariocoos.it - info@dariocoos.it - Winery tours and tasting by reservation.* The Coos family have made wine since the early 19th c. and their passion for this land, grapes and wine has been handed down through 5 generations. The Coos philosophy revolves around lending significance to old traditions and methods, and the quest for the true and original Ramandolo, testing new paths and old materials. Hectares under vine: 14.
**Wines**: Ribolla Gialla, Ramandolo, Picolit, Refosco, Schioppettino, Pignolo. Other products: olive oil.

**Giovanni Dri – Il Roncat** – *Via Pescia 7 - Loc. Ramandolo -* **Nimis** *(UD) - ☎ 0432 79 02 60 - www.drironcat.com - info@drironcat.com - Winery tours by reservation.* Giovanni Dri is a vigneron who has no love for sophisticated technologies and has always turned to tradition. He defines his wines as "simple and imperfect"; in reality, however, they are complex and utterly seductive. The success of the company is also attributable to his wife, Renata, and his daughters, who have assisted him from the outset. Hectares under vine: 10.
**Wines**: Ramandolo, Picolit, Refosco, Schioppettino, Pignolo. Other products: grappa, spirits, olive oil.

**La Roncaia** – *Via Verdi 26 - Fraz. Cergneu -* **Nimis** *(UD) - ☎ 0432 79 02 80 - www. laroncaia.com - Winery tours by reservation.* La Roncaia is known for its typically Friulian wines, with their strong and original personality. Established in the 1960s and run by a family with a long line of winegrowers, it is now part of the Fantinel group. The winery's best-known and most popular product is Ramandolo, but its Picolit, Friulano and blends of international varieties are also excellent. Hectares under vine: 22.
**Wines**: Refosco dal Peduncolo Rosso, Fusco, Cabernet Franc, Friulano, Ramandolo, Picolit.

**Dorigo** – *Via Case Sparse Campo 1 -* **Premariacco** *(UD) - ☎ 0432 63 41 61 - www.dorigowines.com - info@dorigowines.com - Winery tours and tasting by reservation (€20).* The winery was established in 1966 when two vineyards, Ronc di Juri in Buttrio and Montsclapade in Premariacco, were purchased. These ancient toponyms mean "the 'Juris' vineyard", after the family that cultivated this land for generations, and "split mountain", due to the road that cuts the highest hill in two. A great deal has been done since then, in a crescendo of quality that has now reached its apex. Hectares under vine: 40.

© Elena Elisseeva/Shutterstock

**Wines**: Montsclapade, Ronc di Juri, Pignolo, Picolit, Ribolla Gialla, Schioppettino.

**Ermacora** – *Via Solzaredo 9 - Fraz. Ipplis,* **Premariacco** *(UD) - ☎ 0432 71 62 50 - www.ermacora.it - info@ermacora.it - Winery tours by reservation, closed Sun.* The first bishop of Aquileia, who lived around the mid-3rd c., was named Hermagorus – Ermacora in Italian – and it was the Romans who built the historic bridge over the Natisone, along the route that still leads to Ipplis. It is in this ancient Lombard town that Dario and Luciano Ermacora oversee their family-run winery, where hands-on work is as fundamental as respecting the timing and rhythms of nature. Hectares under vine: 47.
**Wines**: Friulano, Pinot Bianco, Refosco dal Peduncolo Rosso, Schioppettino, Pignolo.

**La Tunella** – *Via del Collio 14 - Fraz. Ipplis -* **Premariacco** *(UD) - ☎ 0432 71 60 30 - www.latunella.it - info@latunella.it - Winery tours by reservation, closed Sun., visite@latunella.it.* Over 50 years ago, Min and Livio Zorzettig, father and son, embarked on an adventure that has been taken up by Livio's sons Massimo and Marco, who – with their mother – have continued these family traditions. White varieties are grown on approximately 70% of La Tunella's vineyards, and the balance is devoted to red varieties. The wines range from classic whites and reds to blends, dried-grape wines and single varieties. Hectares under vine: 70.
**Wines**: Friulano, Biancosesto, Sauvignon, Refosco dal Peduncolo Rosso, Schioppettino.

**Rocca Bernarda** – *Via Rocca Bernarda 27 -* **Premariacco** *(UD) - ☎ 0432 71 69 14 - www.sagrivit.it - roccabernarda@sagrivit.it - Winery tours by reservation.* The winery has been owned by the Sovereign Military Order of Malta since 1977. Formed about 900 years ago in Jerusalem to defend the

Holy Land, it is recognised under international public law as a sovereign body; the Order's institutional aims are to provide help and assistance. The farming businesses owned by the Order are conducted to further those aims. Hectares under vine: 38,5.

**Wines**: Merlot Centis, Picolit, Sauvignon Blanc, Cabernet Franc, Ribolla Gialla, Refosco. Other products: grappa.

⚐ **Grillo Iole** – *Via Albana 60* - **Prepotto** *(UD)* - ☎ *0432 71 32 01 - www.vinigrillo.it - info@vinigrillo.it - Winery tours and tasting by reservation*. The winery is located in a beautifully renovated 18th-c. manor and its terrace affords a splendid view of the vineyards. Guest-farm accommodation has recently been set up in the facilities for visitors who would like to spend time relaxing at the winery *(2 rooms and 1 apt)*. Hectares under vine: 9.

**Wines**: Friulano, Sauvignon, Ribolla Gialla, Refosco dal Peduncolo Rosso, Schioppettino, Verduzzo Friulano.

⚐ **la Viarte** – *Via Novacuzzo 51* - **Prepotto** *(UD)* - ☎ *0432 75 94 58 - www.laviarte.it - laviarte@laviarte.it - Winery tours and tasting by reservation (€15), (4 rooms)*. In 1973 Giuseppe Ceschin purchased a plot of land and planted a vineyard so that he could make wine, the passion that had brought him to Friuli in 1960. For him, it was "a beginning, a spring": hence the name La Viarte, meaning openness and, in a broader sense, spring. Ties with the local traditions and culture couldn't be stronger: old artefacts from Friulian country life are displayed in various parts of the winery. Hectares under vine: 27.

**Wines**: Pignolo Riserva, Friulano Liende, Ribolla Gialla, Schioppettino, Tazzelenghe, Siùm. Other products: grappa.

**Ronchi di Cialla** – *Via Cialla 47* - **Prepotto** *(UD)* - ☎ *0432 73 16 79 - www.ronchidicialla.it - info@ronchidicialla.it - Winery tours by reservation*. In 1970, the passion of Paolo and Dina Rapuzzi – taken up by their sons Pierpaolo and Ivan – inspired them to establish a family winery whose goal is to valorise ancient Friulian varieties, based on a philosophy of producing only top-quality wines. In 1976 Paolo and Dina were awarded the prestigious "Risit d'Aur" prize for saving the Schioppettino variety from extinction. Ageing in barriques – with a custom blend of wood (French oak) and toasting of the staves – has made Ronchi di Cialla one of the first producers in Italy, and the first for white wines (1977), to adopt this ancient method for naturally stabilising the wine. Hectares under vine: 25.

**Wines**: Schioppettino di Cialla, Ribolla Gialla, Ciallabianco, RoseDiCialla, Picolit.

⚐/ **Tenuta di Blasig** – *Via Roma 63* - **Ronchi dei Legionari** *(GO)* - ☎ *0481 47 54 80 - www.tenutadiblasig.it - info@tenutadiblasig.it - Winery tours by reservation (Restaurant Wed.-Fri. 18-23, Sat.-Sun. 12-15 and 18-23)* Established in 1788, the estate welcomes visitors with a fascinating tour of the 18th-c. cellars and the new production wing. It is famed for its Malvasia, which it supplied to the noblemen of the Venetian Republic. The main villa, set in an age-old park and open by appointment, vaunts period furnishings and frescoes; Gabriele D'Annunzio often stayed here and departed from Ronchi dei Legionari for the March on Fiume (Rijeka). Hectares under vine: 18.

**Wines**: Pinot Grigio, Friulano, Malvasia, Merlot, Refosco dal Peduncolo Rosso.

⚐/ **Castelvecchio** – *Via Castelnuovo 2* - **Sagrado** *(GO)* - ☎ *0481 99 742 - www.castelvecchio.com - info@castelvecchio.com - Winery tours by reservation Mon.-Fri. 8-18*. This noble and ancient estate boasts a Renaissance villa and a park filled with cypresses and age-old oaks. The first vines were planted in the 1970s. Red wines represent 70% of its production. Meals available at the guest-farm *(open Fri. 17.30-21.30, Sat. and Sun. also 11-14, closed Jul.-Aug.)* Hectares under vine: 35.

**Wines**: Vitovska, Malvasia Istriana, Traminer Aromatico, Terrano, Refosco dal Peduncolo Rosso, Cabernet Sauvignon, Merlot Dileo. Other products: olive oil, grappa.

⚐ **Zuani** – *Loc. Giasbana 12* - **San Floriano del Collio** *(GO)* - ☎ *0481 39 14 32 - www.zuanivini.it - info@zuanivini.it - Winery tours and tasting by reservation (from €10) (Casa Zuani, 4 rooms, doubles €120, hospitality@zuanivini.it)*. Patrizia Felluga and her children set a challenge for themselves: putting all their energy into making wines typical of this region, Collio. Friulano, Chardonnay, Pinot Grigio and Sauvignon are cultivated in the vineyards. Meticulous selection has led to the production of two versions of Zuani Collio Bianco: "Zuani Vigne" is fresh and fruity, and steel-fermented at a controlled temperature; "Zuani Zuani" is selected from late-harvest grapes and is aged in small casks. Hectares under vine: 10.

**Wines**: Vigne Collio Bianco, Zuani Zuani Collio Bianco, Pinot Grigio Sodevo, Ribolla Gialla Sodevo.

⚐ **Livon** – *Via Montarezza 33* - **Dolegnano** *(UD)* - ☎ *0432 75 71 73 - www.livon.it - info@livon.it - Winery tours by reservation*. Care, passion, respect for traditional winemaking processes and constant attention to new technologies are the cornerstones of the company philosophy. The logo is a winged woman, an emblem that represents the pleasures of the palate as well as the 1000-year-old culture and tradition of this region to which the Livon family is profoundly tied. Accommodation at the Villa Chiopris (*www.villachiopris.it, 9 rooms, doubles €115, and 3 apts., €150*). Hectares under vine: 240.

**Wines**: Braide Alte, Tiare blu, Ribolla Gialla, Riul, Picotis, Soluna Malvasia.

**Lis Neris** – *Via Gavinana 5* - **San Lorenzo Isontino** *(GO)* - ✆ *0481 80 105 - www. lisneris.it - lisneris@lisneris.it - Winery tours and tasting by reservation*. The entire Pecorari family are involved in the business, which is characterised by a natural penchant for experimentation and innovation, but always safeguarding tradition and terroir. The goal is to produce increasingly elegant fine wines, and so far the Pecorari family has succeeded beautifully. Hectares under vine: 70.

**Wines**: Gris Pinot Grigio, Picol Sauvignon Blanc, Jurosa Chardonnay, Lis, Confini.

**Castello di Rubbia** – *Grad Rubije - Fraz. San Michele del Carso* - **Savogna d'Isonzo** *(GO)* - ✆ *349 79 57 889 - www.castellodi rubbia.com - info@castellodirubbia.it - Winery tours by reservation*. The winery was established in the late 1990s and takes up the old winemaking tradition established in the 16th c. by the Counts of Egg. The estate's historic castle, which is being renovated, is surrounded by 170 hectares of woods and 16 km of trenches and underground embrasures from WWI. The winery has focused on local Kras plateau varieties such as Terrano, Vitovska and Malvasia. Hectares under vine: 13.

**Wines**: Malvasia, Vitovska, Terrano, Trubar, Rosso della Bora, Bianco della Bora.

🏠 **Volpe Pasini** – *Via Cividale 16 - Loc. Togliano* - **Torreano** *(UD)* - ✆ *0432 71 51 51 - www.volpepasini.it - info@volpepasini.it - Winery tours by reservation*. This is one of the oldest wineries in north-east Italy. It is based in a manor, whose original layout dates back to 1596, surrounded by a complex of buildings. The estate also comprises a park and a small vineyard planted with Ribolla Gialla. The production is divided between 60% white varieties and 40% red. Accommodation available (*7 rooms, €107*). Hectares under vine: 52.

**Wines**: Pinot Grigio Zuc di Volpe, Ribolla Gialla Zuc di Volpe, Sauvignon Zuc di Volpe, Focus Merlot Zuc di Volpe, Refosco dal Peduncolo Rosso Zuc di Volpe, Grivò DOC Friuli Orientali, Friulano DOC Friuli Orientali.

## THE KRAS PLATEAU

🔶 **Lupinc** – *Loc. Prepotto 11/b* - **Duino Aurisina** *(TS)* - ✆ *040 20 08 48 or* ✆ *345 71 71 274- www.lupinc.it or www.facebook. com/lupinc.it - info@lupinc.it - Winery tours and tasting by reservation*. The cellar of this small estate dates back to 1913. Matej, third-generation family owner of Lupinc, works with the classic native varieties of Carso: Vitovska, Malvasia Istriana, and Terrano. Restaurant and accommodation available (*4 apts*). Hectares under vine: 4.

**Wines**: Vitovska, Malvasia, Stara Brajda, Terrano, Dulcis in Fundo Passito Malvasia and Terrano.

**Zidarich** – *Loc. Prepotto 23* - **Duino** *(TS)* - ✆ *040 20 12 23 - www.zidarich.it - info@ zidarich.it - Winery tours by reservation*. The winery was established in 1988 thanks to Benjamin Zidarich's passion and tenacity. With great determination, as well as modern ideas and strategies, he revolutionised his father's business, expanding the hectares of vineyards and focusing on native varieties. This was no mean feat, as the land is covered with stone but very little red soil, thus requiring continuous efforts and considerable energy. Dug into the rock underneath the vineyards and built using local resources, the cellar (20 meters deep, with a total of five floors) was officially inaugurated on 2009. Hectares under vine: 8.

**Wines**: Vitovska, Malvasia, Prulke, Terrano, Ruje, Martina, Vitovska Verde, Roz Rosso, Zi-Da.

**Vodopivec** – *Loc. Colludrozza 4* - **Sgonico** *(TS)* - ✆ *040 22 91 81 - www.vodopivec.it - vodopivec@vodopivec.it - Winery tours by reservation*. Paolo and Valter Vodopivec were born into a family that had been involved in nursery gardening for generations, but decided to change all that

by devoting themselves entirely to winegrowing. The winery has focused on a single native variety with enormous potential: Vitovska. This wine has exceptional body, structure and character. Hectares under vine: 4.5.

**Wines**: Vitovska.

## AQUILEIA-ANNIA-LATISANA

⌂ **Cav. Emiro Bortolusso** – *Via Oltregorgo 10 -* **Carlino** *(UD) - ☏ 0431 67 596 - www.bortolusso.it - info@bortolusso.it - Wine shop open Mon.-Sat. 8.30-12 and 14-18; Sun. 9-12 (only Nov.-May), tasting by reservation.* The winery was established by Cavaliere Emiro Bortolusso and is now run by his children Sergio and Clara, who have made the most of their father's experience and teachings. It is set in a beautiful natural landscape, as it borders on the wildlife reserve of Marano Lagunare, known worldwide for the aquatic birds that flock there. Accommodation is available at the Casasola guest farm *(www.agriturismocasasola.it, 10 rooms, ☏ 338 10 33 681)*. Hectares under vine: 45.

**Wines**: Friulano, Malvasia, Sauvignon, Refosco dal Peduncolo Rosso, Ribolla Gialla, Schioppettino, Traminer Aromatico.

**Tenuta Ca' Bolani** – *Via Gradisca 22- Loc. Strassoldo -* **Cervignano del Friuli** *(UD) - ☏ 0431 32 670 - www.cabolani.it - info@cabolani.it - Winery and vineyard tours, tasting by reservation (see website).* Tenuta Ca' Bolani includes the vineyards of Ca' Vescovo and Molin di Ponte, respectively purchased in 1980 and 1998. Once owned by the Bolani family, whose most eminent member was Count Domenico Bolani, Procurator of the Venetian Republic in Friuli during the first half of the 16th c., the estate was purchased by the Zonin family in 1970. The family have restored it to its former glory, reorganising and replanting the vineyards, renovating its buildings and building a state-of-the-art winery. Hectares under vine: 550.

**Wines**: Refosco dal Peduncolo Rosso, Friulano, Sauvignon, Chardonnay, Traminer Aromatico, Aquilis. Other products: grappa.

🍇 **Isola Augusta** – *Casali Isola Augusta 4 -* **Palazzolo dello Stella** *(UD) - ☏ 0431 58 046 - www.isolaugusta.com - info@isolaugusta.com - Winery tours and tasting by reservation (from €8).* Owner Massimo Bassani has fulfilled the dream of his father Renzo: producing high-quality wines in this area. The Isola Augusta estate was established centuries ago, but was taken over by the Bassani family in the 1950s. Surrounded by greenery, the 74-hectare estate extends between the Tagliamento and Stella rivers, with 42 hectares of vineyards and 2 of olive groves. It is farmed

© Dasilvafarias/Shutterstock

exclusively with systems ensuring minimal environmental impact. Accommodation available at the guest farm *(10 apts., doubles €75)*, meals at the restaurant *'900 All'Isola*. Hectares under vine: 74.

**Wines**: Pinot Grigio, Augusteo Cabernet, Prosecco, Sauvignon, Ribolla Gialla, Schioppettino, Merlrose, Les Iles Chardonnay. Other products: grappa, olive oil, honey.

## Where to stay

### TRIESTE

**Hotel Abbazia** – *Via della Geppa 20 - ☏ 040 36 94 64 - www.hotelabbaziatrieste.it - 21 rooms, doubles from €80 -* Centrally located with simple but comfortable rooms. Opened in 1855.

### SESTO AL REGHENA

**Hotel In Sylvis** – *Via Friuli 2,* **Sesto al Reghena (PN)** *- ☏ 0434 69 97 76 - www.hotelinsylvis.com - 37 rooms, doubles from €79.* Lovely accommodation not far from the Benedictine abbey of Santa Maria. Simple and functional décor.

### UDINE

**Hotel Suite Inn** – *Via di Toppo 25 - ☏ 0432 50 16 83 - www.suiteinn.it - 18 rooms, doubles from €150.* A tastefully renovated Art Nouveau villa with custom-decorated rooms.

### VILLA VICENTINA

**Ai Cjastinars** – *Borgo Pacco 1, SS 14, 1 km S of Villa Vicentina - ☏ 0431 97 02 82 - www.hotelcjastinars.it - Closed 10-30 Nov. - 15 rooms, doubles from €75.* It originated as a family trattoria along one of the town's main roads. The rooms overlook the basilica of Aquileia.

# EMILIA-ROMAGNA

In Emilia-Romagna the pleasure had from food and wine is part of the local culture. There are many delights to be enjoyed: filled handmade pasta following traditional recipes, tasty charcuterie, and cheeses known around the whole world, among others. And of course to accompany these delicacies only wine will do, with those from the region often refreshing, sparkling and easy to drink. The region has fully 20 appellations. Heading towards the sea you come to the vineyards of the Colli Piacentini, followed by the Colli di Parma, then the Colli di Scandiano and the flat lands of Lambrusco (Modena and Reggio). Climbing again you reach the Colli Bolognesi, the Colli di Imola and Faenza, then the Colli di Rimini, and finish your trip in the other areas of Romagna planted to vine.

© Fauxware/Shutterstock

*Vineyards around Forlì*

## The terroir

With regard to wine production, there are many differences between Emilia and Romagna. To begin with, in **Emilia** Barbera, Croatina, Lambrusco and Fortana are some of the black varieties cultivated, while Malvasia di Candia, Montu, Ortrugo, Moscato Giallo, Pignoletto and Sauvignon are among the whites. In **Romagna**, on the other hand, you find Sangiovese and Montepulciano for the reds, while the whites include Albana, Trebbiano Romagnolo, Chardonnay and Bombino Bianco. In addition, the two areas differ by the fact that in Emilia the wines are predominantly sparkling, whereas they are still in Romagna.

**Lambrusco** is the most representative grape in Emilia. Cultivated in different varieties (Di Sorbara, Grasparossa, Maestri, Marani, Montericco, Salamino, Viadanese), it produces a refreshing, fragrant and very pleasing wine, especially in the sparkling version.

The grape that symbolises Romagna is the **Albana**, used to make Romagna Albana DOCG, which is best in the sweet, passito version and gives heady aromas of honey, candied apricot, peach jam and vanilla.

The traditional Emilian wines are Pignoletto from the hills of Bologna, Ortrugo and Gutturnio (from Barbera and Croatina grapes) around Piacenza, and Malvasia Bianca di Candia, which is produced in many appellations.

Traditional Romagnolo wines are Cagnina (from the Refosco Terrano variety), and Pagadebit (made from Bombino Bianco, Sangiovese and Trebbiano di Romagna). Wine cooperatives are common, especially in Emilia.

## Itineraries

*Locations with a winery are indicated by the symbol ♈; for the addresses of the wineries, see p. 253.*

**DOCG**

Colli Bolognesi Classico Pignoletto
Romagna Albana

**DOC**

Bosco Eliceo
Colli Bolognesi
Colli di Faenza
Colli d'Imola
Colli di Parma
Colli di Rimini
Colli di Scandiano e di Canossa

Colli Piacentini
Colli Romagna Centrale
Gutturnio
Lambrusco di Sorbara
Lambrusco Grasparossa di Castelvetro
Lambrusco Salamino di Santa Croce
Modena *or* di Modena
Ortrugo-Colli Piacentini
Reggiano
Reno
Romagna

## PRINCIPAL VARIETIES CULTIVATED

**WHITE GRAPES**

Albana
Alionza
Berverdino
Biancame
Bombino Bianco
Chardonnay
Malvasia Bianca di Candia
Malvasia di Candia
    Aromatica
Marsanne
Melara
Montù
Moscato Bianco
Mostosa
Müller Thurgau
Ortrugo
Pignoletto
Pinot Bianco
Riesling
Riesling Italico
Santa Maria
Sauvignon

Friulano
Trebbiano Modenese
Trebbiano Romagnolo
Trebbiano Toscano
Verdea
Verdicchio Bianco

**GREY GRAPES**

Malvasia Rosa
Pinot Grigio

**BLACK GRAPES**

Alicante
Ancellotta
Barbera
Bonarda
Cabernet Franc
Cabernet Sauvignon
Canina Nera
Ciliegiolo
Croatina
Dolcetto
Ervi

Fortana
Groppello Gentile
Lambrusco di Sorbara
Lambrusco Grasparossa
Lambrusco Maestri
Lambrusco Marani
Lambrusco Montericco
Lambrusco Salamino
Lambrusco Viadanese
Malbo Gentile
Marzemino
Merlot
Montepulciano
Negretto
Pinot Nero
Raboso Veronese
Sangiovese
Sgavetta
Syrah
Terrano
Uva Tosca

*Vigoleno and its panoramic view*

## 1. COLLI PIACENTINI AND COLLI DI PARMA

Many wines fall under the appellation **Colli Piacentini**. Among the reds, made from Barbera and Croatina varieties, the **Gutturnio** stands out, a full-bodied and tannin-rich wine, whilst among the whites **Ortrugo** is made from the eponymous variety and has greenish highlights, a fresh, floral and fruity palate with a slightly bitter aftertaste. The sparkling wines are also interesting, including, among the sweet ones, the **Vin Santo and Vin Santo di Vigoleno** made from Marsanne, Berverdino, Sauvignon, Ortrugo and Trebbiano varieties.

In the **Colli di Parma** area white wines are made from Malvasia and Sauvignon varieties, and reds from Barbera, Croatina and Bonarda.

### Piacenza★

Restrained and hospitable, Piacenza is a city on a human scale that offers the visitor art treasures from an illustrious past and, on its hills, medieval villages where you can enjoy good food, good wine and fine views.

The city's ancient political and commercial centre, **Piazza dei Cavalli★** is named after the **equestrian statues★★** of Dukes Alessandro and Ranuccio I Farnese, both Baroque masterpieces by Francesco Mochi. The square is dominated by the massive **"Gotico"★★**, the ancient City Hall and an admirable example of Lombard Gothic architecture (13th c.). The building's severe yet harmonious appearance is given by the contrast between the lower section in marble and the brick lining on the upper floors, and between the large arches and the light decorative work around the windows.

### THE TERROIR

**Area**: 22,444.54 km², of which approximately 53,408 hectares are planted to vine

**Production 2019**: 6,235,750 hectolitres, of which 1,270,297 VQPRD

**Geography**: mostly flat with the exception of the hill and mountain area along the Tuscan-Emilian Apennines. The soils are mostly alluvial and in part formed by limestone, clay and marl. The interior of the region enjoys a sub-continental climate but on the coast it is milder

### THE PROTECTION CONSORTIA

Consorzio Tutela Vini DOC Bosco Eliceo – ✆ 0532 32 80 53, consorzioboscoeliceo.it

Consorzio Tutela Vini Colli Bolognesi – ✆ 051 67 07 752, www.collibolognesi.it

Consorzio Tutela Vini DOC Colli di Parma – ✆ 0521 20 70 66, www.viniparma.it

Consorzio Tutela Vini DOC Colli Piacentini – ✆ 0523 59 17 20, www.piace-doc.it

Consorzio Tutela Lambruschi di Modena – ✆ 059 20 86 10, www.lambrusco.net and www.tutelalambrusco.it

Consorzio Tutela Vini Reggiani e Colli di Scandiano e di Canossa – ✆ 0522 79 65 65, www.vinireggiani.it

Consorzio Tutela Vini del Reno – Via Veneto 76, Castelfranco Emilia (Modena), ✆ 059 92 43 20

Consorzio Vini di Romagna – Via Tebano 45, Faenza (Ravenna), ✆ 0546 28 455, www.consorziovinidiromagna.it

To the left of the square rises the façade of the 13th-c. Church of **San Francesco**, an interesting example of Franciscan Gothic architecture.

*Take Via XX Settembre past the side of San Francesco to Piazza Duomo.* The **duomo★** is a building in Lombard Romanesque style (12th-13th c.), with the façade embellished by a rose window and three portals with a Lombard porch. The Latin cross interior of great simplicity is adorned with superb 17th-c. frescoes in the cupola painted by Guercino and Morazzone, and in the web of the presbytery by Camillo Procaccini and Ludovico Carracci.

*From Piazza Duomo take Via Chiapponi on the left.* **Sant'Antonino**, the early Christian cathedral rebuilt in the 11th c., is interesting for its octagonal bell tower 40 m tall, and the spire-topped pronaos (1350) that is the atrium to the "Gate of Paradise".

*Return to the duomo and continue to Via Roma, then turn right for* **San Savino**. This 12th-c. church has very pure architectural lines. Inside, the capitals of the columns and elegant **mosaic floors★** survive from the original construction.

*Return down Via Roma and turn right at the junction with Via Cavour.* **Palazzo Farnese**, an imposing late-Renaissance building designed by Vignola but

*Sant'Antonino, Piacenza*

© Tupungato/iStock

unfinished, is the home of the **civic museums★**, which contain the Deeds of the Farnese Family (a cycle of 17th-c. frescoes), the Liver of Piacenza (an ancient bronze "haruspex", 2nd-1st c. BC), and works from Emilia, Lombardy and Liguria (16th-19th c.). *Open Tue.- Thu. 9-13, Fri. and Sat. also 15-18, Sun. 9.30-13 and 15-18, closed Mon., ℘ 0523 49 26 58, www.palazzofarnese.piacenza.it.*

*Go to Via Borghetto (continuation of Via Roma) and turn right into Via San Sisto.*

## WINE AND FOOD ROUTES

Strada dei Vini e dei Sapori dei Colli di Forlì e Cesena – ℘ 0543 44 45 88, www.stradavinisaporifc.it

Strada del Prosciutto e dei Vini dei Colli di Parma – ℘ 339 22 64 887 (mobile), www.stradadelprosciutto.it

Strada dei Vini e dei Sapori dei Colli di Rimini – ℘ 0541 78 70 37, www.stradadeivinidirimini.it

Strada dei Vini e dei Sapori delle Colli Piacentini – ℘ 0523 71 69 68, www.stradadeicollipiacentini.it

Strada dei Vini e dei Sapori delle Colline di Faenza – ℘ 0546 74 660 and 0546 69 12 98, www.stradadellaromagna.it

Strada dei Vini e dei Sapori Colline di Scandiano e Canossa – ℘ 0522 87 43 26, www.stradaviniesapori.re.it

Strada dei Vini e dei Sapori delle Corti Reggiane – ℘ 0522 27 23 20, www.stradavinicortireggiane.it

Strada dei Vini e dei Sapori della Provincia di Ferrara – ℘ 0532 20 58 69, www.stradaviniesaporiferrara.it

Terre Piane - Strada dei Vini e dei Sapori della Pianura Modenese – ℘ 059 64 95 41

Strada del Fungo Porcino di Borgotaro – ℘ 0525 92 18 12, www.stradadelfungo.it

Strada del Culatello di Zibello – ℘ 0524 93 90 81, www.stradadelculatello.it

The 16th-c. Church of **San Sisto** has a curious design by Alessio Tramello from Piacenza, with the façade preceded by a portal (1622) that leads into a 16th-c. atrium. The interior has interesting Renaissance decorations and a superb 16th-c. wooden choir. It was for this church that Raphael painted the famous *Madonna Sistina*, which has now been replaced with a copy.

*Follow Via San Sisto and Via Sant'Eufemia, then take Via Campagna on the right.* The Church of the **Madonna di Campagna**★ was designed by Alessio Tramello with a Greek cross plan in a style heavily influenced by Bramante. It is one of Italy's most important Renaissance buildings. The interior has splendid frescoes by Pordenone (1484-1539).

## From the Colli Piacentini to Parma

*Itinerary of approximately 220 km from Parma to Piacenza, with a detour inland to Bobbio.* Heading west from Piacenza towards the Lombardy border, you enter the Tidone valley, a winemaking area strongly oriented to producing Gutturnio and fine white wines. The leading winemaking sites include **Castel San Giovanni**, where there is the lovely 14th-c. Collegiate Church of San Giovanni, **Borgonovo Val Tidone**, with an ancient stronghold that is today the Town Hall, and a Gothic collegiate church from the 15th c., and **Ziano Piacentino** ♟, **Pianello Val Tidone** and **Gazzola** ♟.

Leaving Piacenza southwards along the SP 6, you come to **San Giorgio Piacentino**, where a 17th-c. villa called La Rocca and the ruins of an ancient castle can be seen. Shortly before entering the village, a detour to the right leads to the SP 654 and Grazzano Visconti in the municipality of **Vigolzone** ♟. The pseudo-medieval village was built around a real medieval castle in the early 20th c. by the Milanese businessman Giuseppe Visconti di Modrone.

A few km to the west, along the S 45 in the Trebbia valley, stands **Rivergaro** ♟. Past this you come to **Montechiaro Castle**, built by the Malaspina family in the 12th c., which has an unusual keep isolated in the middle of the court. After Travo the road becomes panoramic and takes you to **Bobbio** (20 km), the site

of the famous and powerful monastery founded in the 7th c. by the Irish monk Columban. The **Abbey of San Colombano** has some of its original elements but its current form is predominantly from the 15th-16th c. There is also an interesting **museum**. *Open Sat. 16.30-18.30 (Nov.-Mar. 15-17), Sun. and public hols. also 10.30-12.30 (Jul. and Aug. also Wed.- Sat. 16.30-18.30), ✆ 340 54 92 188, www.piacenzamusei.it.*

Return to San Giorgio Piacentino. The itinerary continues east through **Carpaneto Piacentino** ♟ and **Vigolo Marchese** (a fine church and medieval baptistery) to reach **Castell'Arquato**★. The attractive medieval village is split into a lower and upper section. The upper part includes the **Piazza del Municipio**★, the Palazzo Pretorio and Romanesque collegiate church (12th c.), and the commanding Rocca (castle). Heading towards Costa Stradivari from Castell'Arquato you come to Vigoleno, a typical walled village.

The Stirone torrent marks the boundary between the provinces of Piacenza and Parma. Cross the torrent to visit the famous **Salsomaggiore Terme**, a spa town that was very fashionable in the early 20th c., as is indicated by the superb Art Nouveau architecture of the Terme Berzieri (1923).

A few km north of Salsomaggiore, **Fidenza** has a very fine **duomo**★ (12th-13th c.), whose central porch has lovely sculptural decoration by Antelami. The three Romanesque portals are decorated with lions, a typically Emilian feature.

*Continue on the S 9.*

## Parma★★

In addition to its rich musical history (the city's many famous musicians have included conductor Arturo Toscanini), Parma boasts a gastronomic tradition that numbers among its many renowned delicacies two world-famous ambassadors of Italian cuisine – Parmesan cheese and Parma ham.

After the reigns of first the Visconti and Sforza families, and then the French, in 1513 Parma was annexed to the Papal States but in 1545 Pope Paul III Farnese detached Parma and Piacenza and turned them into a duchy that he gave to his son, Pier Luigi Farnese, who was

*Hills around Castell'Arquato*

assassinated two years later. However, the Farnese dynasty continued until 1731, numbering amongst its rulers patrons, protectors and collectors of the arts. After the marriage of Philip Bourbon (son of Philip V of Spain and Elisabetta Farnese) to Luisa Elisabetta (the favourite daughter of Louis XV of France), the city enjoyed a period of French influence administratively, artistically and culturally between 1748 and 1801. Many Frenchmen worked in Parma, while others chose to live there, such as Stendhal, who set one of his novels in the city (*The Charterhouse of Parma*, a non-existent building). The Bourbons of Parma had their Versailles at Colorno, to the north of the city. The city's favourite meeting place is the elegant and animated **Piazza Garibaldi**.

The extraordinarily harmonious **Romanesque episcopal complex★★★** consists

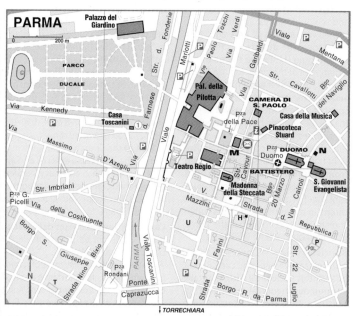

Antica spezieria di San Giovanni Evangelista ........ **N**      Museo Glauco-Lombardi .................................. **M**

*Romanesque duomo, campanile and baptistery in Parma*

of the duomo and baptistery, to which the nearby Baroque Church of San Giovanni is annexed.

**Duomo★★** – *Open 8-19, www.piazza duomoparma.com.* This masterpiece of Paduan Romanesque was constructed between 1090 and 1130 and is flanked by an elegant Gothic campanile. In front of the façade is a lovely porch with lions topped by a kiosk. The apse is richly decorated with small arches, pilasters and sculpted figures, and the interior is lined with a series of 15th- and 16th-c. frescoes. The **dome★★** is the work of Correggio (1530): the theme of the *Assumption of the Virgin* (whose figure is enwrapped by a whirling throng of angels) is the pretext for an ascending spiral of movement. The perfection of the perspective and body in movement contributes to a richness of invention that already heralds the Baroque. The right transept contains the **Deposition from the Cross★★★** (1178) by the great Romanesque sculptor Benedetto Antelami. Another of his works is the bishop's throne in the apse. The inlaid wooden choir from the second half of the 15th c. is another outstanding work of art.

**Baptistery★★★** – *Open 9.30-18.30, www.piazzaduomoparma.com.* Begun in 1196, this is the most architecturally harmonious medieval monument in northern Italy. The architecture and sculptural decoration, which are closely linked, date from the 13th c. Made from Veronese pink marble on an octagonal plan, the building is unquestionably the work of Antelami, whose hand is recognisable in the sculptures and whose name appears on the architrave of the north door dedicated to the Virgin. The 16-sided interior contains a fine cycle of Byzantine-style frescoes (13th c.) of scenes from the *Life of Christ* and the *Golden Legend*.

**San Giovanni Evangelista★** – the building is Renaissance but the façade Baroque. Inside, the **dome★★** is painted by Correggio with the *Vision of St John at Patmos* (1520-24). The frescoes in the intradoses of the chapels on the left are by Parmigianino. The **Renaissance cloisters** in the convent next door are worth a visit. *Piazzale S. Giovanni. Open 8.30-11.45 (convent 9-11.30, closed Thu. and Sun.) and 15-18 (Sun. 8.30-13), ℘ 0521 23 53 11, turismo.comune.parma. it.* Next to the Church of San Giovanni stands the **Antica spezieria di San Giovanni★**, a 13th-c. pharmacy founded by the Benedictine monks, with furnishings that date to the 16th c. *Borgo Pipa 1/a. Open Sat. 14-18, ℘ 0521 50 85 32.*

**Camera di San Paolo★ (or del Correggio)** – *Via Melloni 3/a. Open 13.10-18.20, closed Sun. and public hols., ℘ 0521 28 71 95, www.polomusealeemiliaromagna. beniculturali.it.* This is the dining room of the abbess of the Convent of San Paolo. The frescoes on the vault were the first monumental decoration by Correggio (1520). The influence of Mantegna, with whom he worked in Mantua when young, is evident in the garlands of fruit and pergolas, and the reliefs and architectural details at the base of the vault.

Next to the Camera di San Paolo is the **Puppet Castle**, which exhibits puppets, marionettes, theatrical backdrops and other materials related to this form of entertainment. *Castello dei burattini, Via Melloni 3/a. Open 10-17 (Sat. and Sun. 10.30-18.30), closed Tue., ☎ 0521 03 16 31, www.castellodeiburattini.it.*

Returning to Via Garibaldi, you arrive at **Palazzo della Pilotta**, so called because pelota used to be played in its courtyard. It is a plain building built for the Farnese between 1583 and 1622. It contains several museums. In a modern setting the **national gallery★★** has works from the Emilian, Tuscan and Venetian schools from the 14th to 16th c. The magnificent **Teatro Farnese★★** was built entirely from wood in 1619 after the model of the Teatro Olimpico in Vicenza. Destroyed almost totally in 1944, it was rebuilt in the 1950s faithful to the original. *Open 8.30-19 (Sun. and public hols. 13-19), closed Mon., ☎ 0521 23 33 09.* On the other side of the Parma torrent lies the **Ducal Park★**, designed by the French architect Ennemond Petitot. Continuing down Via Garibaldi you arrive at the 16th-c. Church of the **Madonna della Steccata**, which conserves fine **frescoes★** by Parmigianino. It also contains the tombs of the Farnese family and Parma Bourbons. *Piazza Della Steccata 9. Open 7.30-12 and 15-18.30, ☎ 0521 23 49 37, www.santuari.it/steccata.*

## Colli di Parma

*Circular itinerary of 80 km from Parma.*

In relatively recent times winemaking has spread across the hills that ring the south side of the city resulting in the late 1970s with the assignation of the **Colli di Parma DOC** appellation. The most common variety is the famous Malvasia, followed by Sauvignon, and then Rosso Colli di Parma. Many of the wine-producing villages are strung along the water courses in the hills: the Taro (**Ozzano Taro ▼**), Baganza (**Sala Baganza, San Vitale di Baganza**) and Parma. Gourmets will not miss a visit to **Felino**, renowned for its salami, to which a **museum** has been set up in the local castle. *Open Sat. and Sun. and public hols.*

*10-13 and 14-18, closed Dec.-Feb., ☎ 340 19 39 057, www.museidelcibo.it.*

Along the river Parma there are places of touristic, as well as gastronomic, interest, such as the 15th-c. **Torrechiara Castle★**, built with a double wall, square corner towers, a keep and crenellations. The upper rooms in the castle are decorated with excellent **frescoes★**. Marvellous **views★** of the area as far as the Apennines are given from the terrace. *Open Mon.-Sat. 8.10-13.20, Sun. and public hols. 10-15.30, ☎ 0521 35 52 55, www.castellidelducato.it.*

Continue south from Torrechiara along the S 665 to find another famous gastronomic centre: **Langhirano ▼**, the capital of Parma ham, the history and production of which are recounted in the museum dedicated to Parma ham and charcuterie. *Via Bocchialini 7. Open Sat., Sun. and public hols. 10-18, closed Dec.-Feb., ☎ 0521 86 43 24, www.museidelcibo.it.*

Returning to Torrechiara and taking a right, you come to **Mamiano di Traversetolo**, home of the **Magnani Rocca Foundation★**. The splendid early 20th-c. villa and park are the setting for an extraordinary collection of artworks that range from the Gothic period to the 20th c. *Open mid-Mar.-Nov. 10-18, closed Mon., ☎ 0521 84 83 27, www.magnanirocca.it.*

## 2. FROM REGGIO EMILIA TO BOLOGNA

The variety that is most representative of lower Emilia, in particular around Reggio and Modena, is **Lambrusco**. Its grapes produce Lambrusco Reggiano in the province of Reggio Emilia, Lambrusco di Modena, Lambrusco Salamino di Santa Croce, Lambrusco di Sorbara and Lambrusco Grasparossa di Castelvetro in the province of Modena. Also excellent are the wines of the **Colli di Scandiano e Canossa** in the province of Reggio Emilia. The grapes grown on the **Colli Bolognesi** are Barbera, Cabernet Sauvignon, Merlot, and the whites Sauvignon, Riesling Italico, Pinot Bianco, Chardonnay and the interesting Pignoletto. The **Reno DOC** appellation produces only white wines, amongst which the unusual Montuni from Montù grapes.

## The "Terre Matildiche"

*Itinerary of 30 km from Sant'Ilario d'Enza to Canossa.*

The two wine-producing villages **Sant'Ilario d'Enza** 🍷 and **Gaida** 🍷 lie on the S 9 between Parma and Reggio Emilia. Turning right here takes you into the "Terre Matildiche", named after Matilda of Canossa (1046-1115), an area of many castles, ancient churches and hamlets. For more information on the area see *matildedicanossa.galmodena-reggio.it.* **Montecchio Emilia** has a fort, perhaps founded by Matilda, the appearance of which today dates from the 13th c. **Quattro Castella** 🍷 is named after the four hills that ring the town, each of which used to be topped by a fortress. Today only ruins remain except in the case of Bianello Castle, where Henry IV stayed on the last stage of his trip to Canossa.

Pass through San Polo d'Enza to reach **Canossa**. Only romantic ruins remain of the castle from which Matilda kept up her thirty-year conflict with the Holy Roman Emperor on behalf of the Pope. In 1077 Emperor Henry IV arrived barefoot and dressed only in a shirt to submit to Pope Gregory VII and was made to wait three days before being pardoned for his sins. This is the origin of the Italian saying "to go to Canossa", which means to act contritely and ask forgiveness, i.e., to eat humble pie.

To the west (*4.5 km*), **Rossena**, a village huddled around a castle on a hill, is set among an attractive landscape of rises and gullies.

## From Reggio Emilia to Modena

### Reggio Emilia

*Itinerary of 52 km.*

Charming, warm and hedonistic like all the cities in Emilia, Reggio, like Modena and Ferrara, belonged to the Este family from 1409 to 1776. It was in the City Hall at Reggio in 1797 that what is today the tricolour of Italy was declared the flag of the newly created Cispadane Republic. The following century this standard was taken up by Carlo Alberto during the wars of the Risorgimento and since then has always been the symbol of Italy.

The political, religious and commercial centre, **Piazza Prampolini**, is the site of the cathedral (ancient but rebuilt in the 15th c.), the Romanesque baptistery and the City Hall with the 16th-c. Bordello Tower.

To the right of the cathedral stands an arch behind which runs the busy **Via Broletto**. This leads to Piazza San Prospero, lined by the 18th-c. façade and unfinished bell tower of the Church of San Prospero (16th c.). The church is decorated by a fine cycle of frescoes by Camillo Procaccini and Bernardino Campi in the apse, and has an outstanding wooden choir. *For information ℘ 0522 43 46 67.*

Not far away (*down Via San Carlo*) you will see the lovely **Piazza Fontanesi** lined by antique shops and art galleries.

On Corso Garibaldi stands the lovely Church of the **Madonna della Ghiara★**, built in the early 17th c. to commemorate a miraculous event. Its impressive frescoes, altarpieces and panel offer an anthology of 17th-c. painting in Emilia. One of the most important works is the dramatic *Crucifixion* by Guercino. *Open 7.15-12 and 16.30-19.30, ℘ 0522 43 97 07.* Leave Reggio Emilia south-east on the SP 467 and head to **Scandiano** 🍷, which lies in a lovely hilly setting. This was the birthplace of the Renaissance poet Matteo Maria Boiardo, one of the three exceptional talents (with Ariosto and Tasso) at the court of the Este. The town boasts the wine **Colli di Scandiano e di Canossa DOC**, and an imposing medieval castle whose architecture was softened by its feudatories, the Boiardo family.

Continue to **Sassuolo**, seat of the **Ducal Palace★** and summer residence of the Este family. Reconstruction and enlargement of an earlier noble residence made this a masterpiece of Emilian Baroque. *Piazzale della Rosa. Open 10-13 and 15-19 (in win. by reservation), closed working Mon. ℘ 389 26 73 365, www.sassuolo-turismo.it.* The town is also known for its ceramics factories that use clay taken from the banks of the river Secchia.

About 7 km east of Sassuolo is a veritable shrine for motor-racing fans: **Maranello**, the home of Ferrari. The **Ferrari Museum** commemorates the history of one of the world's most famous automobile companies with cars, trophies and photographs of its successes.

*Piazza Prampolini in the heart of Reggio Emilia*

*Via Dino Ferrari 23. Open 9.30-19 (Nov.-Mar. 18), ℘ 0536 94 97 13, www.galleria.ferrari.com.*

The road to Modena takes you through **Formigine**, a small village of porticoed houses set around a castle rebuilt after 1945, and **Baggiovara** ⯨.

## Modena★ ⯨

Modena is a city for all tastes: for art lovers, car enthusiasts (Ferrari, Maserati, Bugatti and Lamborghini are based near here), and of course gourmets, who find endless delights in the succulent dishes of its hearty cuisine. The renowned local specialities include the famous *zampone* (seasoned pork encased in a pig's foot) accompanied by sparkling Lambrusco and the wonderful balsamic vinegar that is another Modena tradition.

**Duomo★★★** – *Open 7-19 (Mon. 7-12.30 and 15.30-19), ℘ 059 21 60 78, www.duomodimodena.it.* A masterpiece of Lombard Romanesque worked on by the architect Lanfranco, the sculptor Wiligelmo (12th c.) and mastermasons from Campione. Wiligelmo's name appears on the stone to the left of the Lombard porch with the date the church was founded (1099). The façade, supported by the angel of death with a fleur-de-lys, is the work of masons from Campione, while the central portal by Wiligelmo features stylophorous lions (i.e., which support the columns). The architecturally "busy" side that faces the square features, from the left, the Princes Gate (decorated by Wiligelmo), the Royal Gate (a 13th-c. marvel by the Campionesi) and the 16th-c. pulpit adorned with symbols of the four evangelists. Passing beneath the Gothic arches that connect the duomo to the **Ghirlandina** (a Romanesque bell tower named for the garland of columns that ring the octagonal part), you reach the north side of the duomo. Here stands the Fish-market Gate, named after the 'Bishop's Fish-market' held close by. The interior of the duomo blends the vertical thrust of Gothic churches with the simplicity and luminosity of the Romanesque. The **jube★★★** is a masterpiece by Campionesi mastermasons (12th-13th c.) that rests on columns supported by stylophorous lions and telamons. The beautiful crypt contains the tomb of St Geminianus, the patron saint of Modena to whom the duomo is dedicated, and the 15th-c. terracotta sculpture of the *Holy Family* by Guido Mazzoni. Before leaving, visit the 16th-c. terracotta manger in the right aisle.

The **Duomo Museum** displays the famous **metopes★★** (12th c.), low reliefs that once crowned the building's buttresses. They are decorated with dancing and leaping figures and symbols that today are incomprehensible; their modelling, balance and stylisation are almost classical. *Via Lanfranco 4. Open 9.30-12.30 and 15.30-18.30, closed Mon., ℘ 059 43 96 969, www.duomodimodena.it.*

**Palazzo dei Musei** – *Piazza S. Agostino 337. From Piazza Grande take Via Emilia on the left.* The 18th-c. building holds the most important art collections of the Este family. The **Galleria Estense★** exhibits works by masters mostly from

*Romanesque duomo in Modena*

Emilia and the Veneto between the Middle Ages and the 18th c., but there are also exhibits from foreign schools. In addition to paintings the gallery has some excellent terracotta figures typical of Modenese sculptors of the 15th and 16th c., and collections of majolicas and musical instruments, including a splendid harp from 1581. *Largo Porta Sant'Agostino 337. Open 8.30-19.30 (Sun. and public hols. 10-18), closed Mon., ℰ 059 43 95 711, www.palazzodeimusei modena.it.*

The **Biblioteca Estense★** holds 600,000 books and 15,000 manuscripts, and is one of the most important libraries in Italy. Its most outstanding work is the **Bible of Borso d'Este★★**, consisting of 1020 pages illuminated by artists from Ferrara in the 15th c. *All tours, guided or free, must be booked in advance at the ℰ 059 43 95 711.*

The stately **Ducal Palace★** (*Piazza Roma, take Via Rismondo from Piazza Grande*) was begun in 1634 during the rule of Francesco I d'Este. Today is it the home of the Italian Military Academy.

Don't leave Modena without visiting the new **MEF - Museo Enzo Ferrari** (*Via Paolo Ferrari 85, 9.30-18, Apr.-Oct. 9.30-19, ℰ 059 43 97 979, www.museiferrari.com*), a futuristic architectural structure that extending 2,500 m² in the shape of a car bonnet, built alongside the mechanical shops where Alfredo Ferrari, Enzo's father, once worked. The museum displays cars, objects and multimedia materials to detail the legendary life of the engineer and race car driver who founded the Ferrari automobile company.

## North of Modena

*Itinerary of 60 km from Modena to Nonantola.*

Passing through **Ganaceto** 🍷 you come to **Carpi★**, a refined town whose Renaissance cathedral stands in Piazza dei Martiri. **Pio Castle★** is an impressive turreted building with a court designed by Bramante. It hosts the Castello dei Ragazzi cultural centre for under-16s, the Palace Museum and the Civic Museum, dedicated to art and local history respectively. *Piazza dei Martiri 59. Open 9-13 and 15-19, clodes Mon. morning, ℰ 059 64 99 88, www.castellodeiragazzi.carpidiem.it.* Behind the castle, the Church della Sagra (Santa Maria in Castello, 12th-16th c.) has a slender Romanesque bell tower called the Torre della Sagra.

Continuing east you enter the territory of **Lambrusco di Sorbara DOC**, a wine produced in various municipalities between the rivers Secchia and Panaro. Several waterways meet at **Bomporto** 🍷 as its name, meaning "good port", suggests. The stretch between Bomporto and **Solara** is referred to as the *Riviera del Panaro*; it is lined by villas built by the nobility of Modena in the 17th and 18th c.

**Nonantola Abbey** is about ten or so km to the south. It was founded in the 8th c. and flourished in the Middle Ages. The portal of the abbey church (12th c.) has admirable Romanesque sculptures carved in 1121 by the workshop of Wiligelmo. *Open Mon.-Thu. 9-12.30, Fri., Sat. and Sun. also 14-18 ☎ 059 54 90 25, www. abbazianonantola.it.*

## From Modena towards Bologna

*Itinerary of 80 km from Modena to Casalecchio di Reno.*

Leave Modena on the S 9 to the east and pass through Castelfranco Emilia. Turn south to **San Cesario sul Panaro**, which boasts a very ancient church (10th-11th c.) later rebuilt. On the other side of the river Panaro stands **Spilamberto** with its medieval castle. Continue to **Vignola**, famous for its cherry orchards that transform the countryside when the trees blossom. And of course there is a castle, a plain and solid construction of 15th-c. appearance but founded much earlier. Inside the chapel you can admire a cycle of 15th-c. frescoes. *For information ☎ 059 76 59 79, www.fondazione-divignola.it.*

About 7 km to the west along a pretty road you find **Castelvetro di Modena** 🍷, the home of **Lambrusco Grasparossa di Castelvetro DOC.**

Returning to Vignola and heading towards Bologna, you pass through a series of winemaking districts that fall in the **Colli Bolognesi DOC** zone, like **Savignano sul Panaro**, with its ancient section surrounded by medieval walls, and **Monteveglio**, with the abbey Church of Santa Maria that dates from the 11th-12th c. and frescoes from the 15th and 16th c. The hilly, wooded countryside characterised by gullies that surrounds the municipality falls within the Monteveglio Abbey Regional Historic Park. A little to the south lies the winemaking village of **Castello di Serravalle** 🍷.

You reach the outskirts of Bologna passing **Bazzano**, which has a lovely historic centre, and **Zola Predosa** 🍷.

## The Reno Valley

*From Casalecchio di Reno for approximately 50 km.*

The S 64 winds along the valley of the region's largest river as far as Porretta Terme, touching on such places of interest as **Pontecchio**, where you can see the mausoleum of Guglielmo Marconi. It was designed by Marcello Piacentini and stands beside the villa where the Bolognese scientist made his earliest experiments. In addition there is **Sasso Marconi** 🍷, named after the enormous rock that commands the river Reno, **Marzabotto**, originally an Etruscan city named Misa and more recently known for the massacre of 1830 of its citizens by the Germans in 1944 (ossuary in the parish church). The archaeological area retains the plan of the 6th-5th c. BC Etruscan city and the remains of the necropolis, and includes a commendable

*Vineyards in the countryside around Imola*

archaeological museum. *Archaeological zone and museum (reduced hours) Tue.-Thu. 9-16, Fri.-Sun. 11-18.30, closed Mon., ✆ 051 93 23 53, www.archeobologna. beniculturali.it/Marzabotto.*

Continuing along the state road, pass through **Riola**, where the parish church was designed in 1978 by the Finnish architect Alvar Aalto, and arrive at **Porretta Terme**, a popular spa town.

## 3. FROM IMOLA TO CESENA

*Itinerary of approximately 200 km from Dozza to Verucchio.*

This is the area of **Sangiovese di Romagna**, **Trebbiano Romagnolo** and **Albana**. You will also find here the sweetish red, Cagnina, which is made in the zone that lies between Cesena, Faenza and Forlì, and the white Pagadebit. There are several types of **Romagna Albana DOCG**: dry, sweetish, sweet and passito; there is also a sparkling version which is classified as Romagna Albana Spumante.

The itinerary continues along the S 9, Via Emilia, with quick detours into the side valleys to discover the more artistically and enologically interesting towns. Nine km west of Imola, **Dozza** looks out over the vineyards from a height of 190 m. The lovely Sforzesca Castle, which still has its ancient furnishings and decorations, is home to the **Regional Wine Cellar of Emilia-Romagna**, which brings together all the wines of the region. *Piazza Rocca Sforzesca. Open Tue.-Fri. 10-12.30 (Sat., Sun. and public hols. 9.30-13) and 14.30-19, closed Mon., ✆ 0542 67 80 89, www.enotecaemiliaromagna.it.* The houses are enlivened by frescoes painted by contemporary artists.

The last Emilian bulwark on the route is **Imola** ♟, which naturally has a large **castle★** built in the Middle Ages and rebuilt in the 15th c. Inside there are collections of weapons, ceramics and majolicas. *Piazzale Giovanni dalle Bande Nere. Open Sat. 15-19, Sun. 10-13 and 15-19, Tue.-Fri. 9-13 by reservation, ✆ 0542 60 26 09, museiciviciimola.it.* The historic centre is cut in two by the Via Emilia, on the left of which stands the beautiful **Palazzo Tozzoni★** (18th c.), a fascinating example of a nobleman's residence, complete with furnishings. *Via Garibaldi 18. Open Sat. 15-19, Sun. 10-13 and 15-19, Tue.-Fri. 9-13 by reservation, ✆ 0542 60 26 09, museiciviciimola.it.*

Soon after Imola you enter Romagna. **Castel Bolognese** ♟ is one of the municipalities that produces Cagnina di Romagna. Shortly before you enter the village a right turn will take you to Riolo Terme, a spa town in the valley of the Senio torrent, where the ancient centre nestles around the castle.

After passing through Villa San Giorgio a lovely stretch of road takes you to **Brisighella** ♟ in the Lamone valley. The village is spread across three rocky heights where a 14th-c. fort, an ancient "clock" tower and a shrine stand. The village has an intricate tangle of alleyways and walls protected by the unusual **Via del Borgo★** or Via degli Asini. This is a raised and covered walkway, built in the 12th c. and illuminated by half arches. Lovely paintings by Marco Palmezzano from Forlì (active 16th c.) can be seen in the churches of Santa Maria degli Angeli and San Michele Arcangelo.

*From Brisighella take the SP 302 to Faenza.*

---

### Bosco Eliceo DOC

The appellation **Bosco Eliceo** affects a number of municipalities in the provinces of Ferrara and Ravenna where there are a number of canals and rivers and the soil is predominantly sandy. This area produces white wines – **Sauvignon** and **Bianco** from Trebbiano, Romagnolo, Sauvignon and Malvasia Bianca di Candia grapes – and reds like Fortana and Merlot.

An ancient vine, the **Longanesi**, has recently been rediscovered in the province of Ravenna. It produces wines of character and powerful body that are suitable for long ageing. It was in 1913 that Antonio Longanesi bought a property at Bagnocavallo, in which close to an oak he found an old vine with unique characteristics. This was named after him, not only with his surname but also with his nickname, "Bursòn". Since the 2007 harvest, Bursòn has been able to display the IGT attribute (a geographic denomination).

*Façade of Faenza cathedral*

# Faenza 🍷

The name of the city has become the Italian word for tin-glazed pottery, as it has in many other languages (English and French *faïence*, German *Fayence*, Portuguese *faiança*). The painted or enamelled ware of Faenza has been famous since the 15th c. for the delicacy of the ceramic, the high quality enamel, the vividness of the colours and the variety in the decoration.

An international competition and an international biennial show of the ceramic art perpetuate the vocation in the city among its many artists and artisans. The collections in the **International Ceramics Museum★★** tell the story of pottery around the world, with works by artists of international fame. *Viale Baccarini 19. Open Apr.-Oct. 10-19, rest of the year Tue.-Fri. 10-16, Sat., Sun. and public hols. 10-17.30, closed Mon., ℘ 0546 69 73 11, www.micfaenza.org.*

**Piazza del Popolo★** and **Piazza della Libertà** are continuations of one another. Piazza del Popolo, lined by the Palazzo del Podestà (12th c.) and the City Hall (13th-15th c.), is long and narrow with porticoes crowned by loggias. Piazza della Libertà, announced by a beautiful 17th-c. fountain, is the setting for the **cathedral**, with its uncompleted façade. Built in the 15th c. by the Florentine architect Giuliano da Maiano, it contains the tomb of Bishop-Saint Savino, which was designed in 1471 by Benedetto da Maiano.

**Bagnacavallo** 🍷 lies 17 km north of Faenza. The town's name (literally "bathe horse") refers to the legend in which the Roman emperor Tiberius is supposed to have healed his horse in a curative spring. More probably, however, it is a reference to a torrent that needed to be forded. You should see the **Piazza Nuova**, an 18th-c. elliptical market place surrounded by porticoed shops. Just outside the town stands the parish Church of **San Pietro in Sylvis** (7th c.), which conserves some very fine 14th-c. frescoes. *For information ℘ 0545 28 08 98.*

*Return to the Via Emilia.*

# Forlì

In the 13th and 14th c. Forlì was an independent seigniory. The heart of the city is Piazza Aurelio Saffi, looked down upon by the **Basilica di San Mercuriale**, its tall Romanesque bell tower, and its portal whose lunette features a marvellous low relief from the 13th c. Inside there are many works of art, amongst which the 15th-c. tomb of Barbara Manfredi and paintings by the Renaissance artist Marco Palmezzano. Also facing onto the square are the 14th-c. City Hall, the Palazzo del Podestà and the Palazzina degli Albertini, both 15th c.

The medieval duomo behind City Hall was rebuilt in the 19th c. Corso Garibaldi is lined with ancient houses, such as the 18th-c. Palazzo Gaddi at no. 96, which contains several museums.

Leaving Forlì on the S 67 south-west, you

*Countryside near Longiano*

come to **Terra del Sole**, a small town built in 1564 by Cosimo de' Medici when this stretch of Romagna was part of the Grand Duchy of Tuscany. Several of the buildings on Piazza Garibaldi are Tuscan in style.

A little to the south, **Castrocaro Terme** 🍷 is known for its springs and the music contest that has been held there since 1957. The town has an attractive medieval centre with ancient buildings like the Baptistery of San Giovanni and the castle.

Continue through San Lorenzo in Noceto, then turn right along the Rabbi valley. After about 14 km you arrive at **Predappio**, the birthplace of Benito Mussolini, who is buried in the local cemetery. From Predappio a panoramic road passes through Rocca delle Caminate, Mussolini's summer residence, and leads to **Meldola**, which boasts a lovely historic centre ringed by walls built by the Malatesta family.

Back on the Via Emilia, pass through **Forlimpopoli**, with its 14th-c. castle, and take a short diversion to **Bertinoro** 🍷, a walled, medieval village famous for its **Romagna Albana DOCG** wine. Here there stands the "Column of Hospitality", fitted with rings, each of which corresponded to a family in the village. The ring to which a traveller used to tie his horse decided where the traveller would be lodged. The terrace gives a wide **view**★★ that justifies the village's title as the "Balcony of Romagna".

Continuing 6 km south you will find Polenta, the attractive site of the ancient Church of San Donato praised by Carducci.

*Return to Via Emilia.*

## Cesena

The city lies at the foot of the hill on which the vast Malatestian Fort (15th c.) stands, overlooking the central Piazza del Popolo, site of the City Hall. The Renaissance **Malatestian Library**★★ (*Piazza Bufalini*), built by Novello Malatesta in the mid-15th c., has three long aisles like a basilica. It contains precious manuscripts, some of which are from the famous school of miniatures at Ferrara, and a gilded silver missorium, probably made in the 6th c. *Guided visits 9-16 (Sun. 10-16), closed Mon. morning, ✆ 0547 61 08 92, www.malatestiana.it.*

About 3 km south, a pretty road climbs to the **Basilica della Madonna del Monte**, a Benedictine abbey church rebuilt in the 15th-16th c.

Proceeding on the Via Emilia towards Rimini, you reach interesting places such as **Longiano**, an appealing medieval village built around a fort. In the lovely setting of the Church of Santa Maria delle Lacrime there is an interesting museum of cast-iron urban furniture (*S.S. Emilia 1626, ✆ 0547 65 21 71, www.museoitalianoghisa.org*).

**Santarcangelo di Romagna** has a beautiful walled historic centre that surrounds the castle built by Sigismondo Malatesta in 1447. In the ancient part of the town a series of artificial grottoes dug in late antiquity was perhaps used as a place of worship or as a deposit. Today some can be visited (*for information ✆ 0541 62 42 70, www.iatsantarcangelo.com*).

**Verucchio**, 13 km south, stands in a panoramic and strategic location in the Marecchia valley, as the presence of two castles attests. The town was the Malatesta's principal defence against the troops of the Duchy of Urbino.

# Addresses

## Tourist information

**Emilia-Romagna Turismo** – www.emiliaromagnaturismo.it

**Bologna and area Tourist Office** – Via Benedetto XIV n. 3, ✆ 051 6598111 www.cittametropolitana.bo.it/turismo

**Cesena Tourist Office** – Piazza del Popolo 9, Cesena, ✆ 0547 35 63 27, www.comune.cesena.fc.it

**Faenza and area Tourist Office** – Voltone della Molinella 2, Faenza, ✆ 0546 25 231, www.prolocofaenza.it, www.terredifaenza.it

**Forlì and area Tourist Office** – Piazzetta della Misura 5, Forlì, ✆ 0543 71 24 35, www.turismoforlivese.it

**Imola and area Tourist Office** – Galleria del Centro Cittadino, Via Emilia 135, Imola (BO), ✆ 0542 60 22 07, www.visitareimola.it

**Province of Modena** – Piazza Grande 14, Modena, ✆ 059 20 32 660, www.visitmodena.it

**Parma Tourist Office** – Piazza Garibaldi 1, Parma, ✆ 0521 21 88 89, turismo.comune.parma.it

**Province of Piacenza Tourist Office** – Piazza Cavalli, 10 (corner via Calzolai), Piacenza, ✆ 0523 49 20 01 www.comune.piacenza.it

**Reggio Emilia Tourist Office** – Via Farini 1/a, Reggio Emilia, ✆ 0522 45 11 52, turismo.comune.re.it

## Regional wine cellars

**Emilia-Romagna Regional Wine Cellar** – Piazza Rocca Sforzesca, Dozza (BO), ✆ 0542 36 77 00, www.enotecaemiliaromagna.it

## The wineries

*The addresses are listed in alphabetical order by location.*

### COLLI PIACENTINI AND COLLI DI PARMA

**Montesissa** – *Via XXV Aprile 91, Loc. Buffalora - Fraz. Rezzano -* **Carpaneto Piacentino** *(PC) - ✆ 0523 85 01 23 - www. vinimontesissa.it - vinimontesissa@libero.it - Winery tours and tasting by reservation.* Montesissa has been active in the winemaking world for 5 generations, for it has a long history and was founded when Bartolomeo Montesissa purchased the estate in the second half of the 19th c. The extensive production range comprises reds and whites: sweet and dry, still and sparkling. The wines and grape varieties are among the most characteristic of the Piacenza area, including Gutturnio and Ortrugo. Hectares under vine: 30.

**Wines:** Gutturnio Riserva Cuccon, Ortrugo Frizzante, Malvasia Passito Rosa Ronco della Santa, Bonarda Riserva Al Ladar, Spumante Amanar, Barbera Frizzante.

🍷 **Lamoretti** – *Strada della Nave 6 - Casatico -* **Langhirano** *(PR) - ✆ 0521 86 35 90 or ✆ 342 74 33 775 - www.lamoretti.eu - info@lamoretti.eu - Winery tours and tasting by reservation.* The Lamoretti family has been engaged in winegrowing since 1930. The vineyards cover an area of approximately 20 hectares planted with Barbera/Bonarda (20%), Sauvignon, Moscato Bianco (10%) and Malvasia di Candia Aromatica (50%). In addition to Colli di Parma DOC wines, the estate also produces several table wines and IGT wines. Hectares under vine: 20.

**Wines**: Colli di Parma Malvasia, Colli di Parma Sauvignon, Colli di Parma Rosso Frizzante, Moscato, Vinnalunga '71.

🏠 **Monte delle Vigne** – *Via Monticello 22 - Fraz. Ozzano Taro -* **Ozzano Taro** *(PR) - ✆ 0521 30 97 04 - www.montedellevigne.it - info@montedellevigne.it - Winery tours and tasting by reservation.* In his medieval chronicles Fra' Salimbene called the hills where the winery is located *li monti de le vigne* (the "vineyard hills"), from which the name of the estate is derived. During the early 1970s the winery owned just 7 hectares of vineyards, which have now become 60. They are planted with Barbera, Bonarda, Merlot, Lambrusco, Sauvignon, Chardonnay and Malvasia, which are used to make different types of still, semi-sparkling and sparkling wines. Accommodation at L'Antico Casale (4 rooms, €72). Hectares under vine: 60.

**Wines:** Nabucco, Malvasia Callas, Rubina Brut Rosé, Lambrusco, Rosso Monte delle Vigne Colli di Parma, Sauvignon Colli Parma.

🍷 **Tenuta Villa Tavernago** – *Fraz. Frassineto 1,* **Pianello Val Tidone** *(PC) - ✆ 02 51 65 04 22 - www.tenutavilla tavernago.it - info@tenutavillatavernago.it - Winery tours by reservation.* This company was acquired in 1978 by the Pirovano family, and has always been run according to bioethical principles, with the aim of producing a high-quality, genuine wine while respecting the environment. Agricultural development that respects the

environment, combined with careful winemaking techniques, have given the wine superior organoleptic characteristics. In 2002 the farmstead earned ICEA and NOP (USDA Organic) certificates. Options for overnight stays ( 📞 *0523 97 69 56, 13 rooms, starting from €80*) and a dinner restaurant (*menu from €30*). Hectares under vine: 27.
**Wines**: Ortrugo, Bonarda, Malvasia dolce frizzante, Gutturnio DOC Frizzante, Gutturnio DOC.

**La Stoppa** – *Loc. Ancarano* - **Rivergaro** *(PC)* - 📞 *0523 95 81 59 - www.lastoppa.it - info@ lastoppa.it - Winery and vineyards tours, tasting by reservation*. The estate covers an area of 58 hectares, of which 30 under vine, dominated by an elegant medieval tower. In 1973 La Stoppa was purchased by the Pantaleoni family, which modernised the plant and the cellar. The wines are very distinctive, born in the vineyard and not dulled by excessive work in the cellar. La Stoppa makes only a few wines, some from the native grape varieties – Malvasia, Barbera and Bonarda – and others from vines long present on the estate, such as Cabernet Sauvignon, Merlot and Pinot Nero, which were already grown over 100 years ago by the previous owners. Hectares under vine: 30.
**Wines**: Malvasia, Passito Vigna del Volta, Emilia Rosso Macchiona IGT, Emilia Bianco Ageno IGT, Barbera della Stoppa.

**Il Poggiarello** – *Scrivellano di Statto -* **Statto di Travo** *(PC), 4 km W of Rivergaro* - 📞 *0523 95 72 41 - www.ilpoggiarello. fpwinegroup.it - info@ilpoggiarellovini.it - Winery tours by reservation*. Purchased by the current owners in 1980, the winery's central building, housing the cellar and the wine shop, dates from the mid-19th c. It boasts a handsome old portico and a terrace with breathtaking views. The winery has always dedicated particular attention to gourmet tourism and wine enthusiasts. Hectares under vine: 13.
**Wines**: Gutturnio, Malvasia, Ortrugo, Sauvignon IGT, Pinot Nero IGT, Barbera IGT.

**Cantine Ceci** – *Via Provinciale 99 -* **Torrile** *(PR), 15 km N of Parma* - 📞 *0521 81 02 52 - www.lambrusco.it - info@lambrusco.it - Winery tours by reservation*. The winery was founded in 1938 by Otello Ceci, a well-known local innkeeper. His children continued along the same path and today the winery is run by his grandchildren. Situated in the foggy area that stretches north of Parma to the Po, its wines are inspired by the great composer Giuseppe Verdi, who also came from this magical region. Hectares under vine: 13.
**Wines**: Otello Nero di Lambrusco, Otello Ducati, Lambrusco Terre Verdiane 1813, Gutturnio Frizzante DOC, Decanta Rosso.

🍷 **La Tosa** – *Loc. La Tosa -* **Vigolzone** *(PC)* - 📞 *0523 87 07 27 - www.latosa.it - info@ latosa.it - Winery tours by reservation*. The Pizzamiglio family, driven by their love of wine, infuse their work with the desire to probe, reveal and develop the hidden potential of their terroir and its grape varieties. Their motto is "We're happy but never satisfied with the results we have achieved, and want to keep improving". Their wines need no explanation to be appreciated, because they are the faithful reflection of the land and the grapes. The winery is also home to the **Museum of Vine and Wine**, which has collection of over 300 items. Meals by reservation at La Tosa guest farm. Hectares under vine: 19.
**Wines**: Cabernet Sauvignon Luna Selvatica, Malvasia Sorriso di Cielo, Gutturnio Vignamorello, Sauvignon, Colli Piacentini Terrafiaba, Riodeltorto Valnure.

**Torre Fornello** – *Loc. Fornello -* **Ziano Piacentino** *(PC)* - 📞 *0523 86 10 01 - www.torrefornello.it - vini@torrefornello.it - Winery tours and tasting by reservation*. In 1982 the estate was taken over by the Sgorbati family, who have always tended vineyards on the surrounding hills, and since 1992 Enrico Sgorbati has revived the winery's age-old winegrowing tradition, while gradually reorganising the cellar. Under the main house is a very handsome 17th-c. cellar where wines are aged in barriques. Hectares under vine: 73.
**Wines**: Ortrugo, Malvasia Dolce Donna Luigia, Emilia IGT Pratobianco, Gutturnio Superiore Sinsäl, Gutturnio Riserva Diacono Gerardo 1028, Bonarda.

**Zerioli** – *Loc. Pozzolo Grosso 253 -* **Ziano Piacentino** *(PC)* - 📞 *0523 75 12 29 - www.zeriolivini.com - info@zeriolivini.com - Winery tours and tasting by resevation*. Founded in 1890, the winery is over a century old and has been run by 4 generations of winegrowers. Today it covers an area of 77 hectares, 64 of which under vine, divided into 3 estates: Pozzolo, Montecucco and Poggio. The cellar produces around a dozen wines, mainly traditional Piacenza ones. Hectares under vine: 64.
**Wines**: Gutturnio, Ortrugo, Pinot Grigio Rosé, Bonarda, Malvasia, Barbera.

## FROM REGGIO-EMILIA TO BOLOGNA

**Villa di Corlo** – *Strada Cavezzo 200 -* **Baggiovara** *(MO)* - 📞 *059 51 07 36 - www.villadicorlo.com - info@villadicorlo.com - Winery tours by reservation*. Villa di Corlo dates from the late 17th c. It is part of the 100-hectare estate of the same name, which has belonged to the Munari family for almost a century. The winery is renowned for its Lambrusco di Sorbara and Lambrusco Grasparossa di Castelvetro, but it also makes a wine from Cabernet and Merlot grapes.

Traditional Balsamic Vinegar of Modena PDO (Extra-old and Refined) is made in the vinegar room housed in the attic of the villa. Hectares under vine: 25.

**Wines**: Corleto Lambrusco Grasparossa di Castelvetro, Lambrusco di Sorbara Primevo, Lambrusco Grasparossa di Castelvetro Villa di Corlo, Cabernet Merlot Giaco, Cabernet Sauvignon Gelsomoro, Spumante Brut Rosè Elettra. Other products: Traditional Balsamic Vinegar of Modena, grappa.

**Francesco Bellei** – *Via Nazionale 130/132 - Cristo di Sorbara -* **Bomporto** *(MO) - ☏ 059 90 20 09 - www.francescobellei.it - info@francescobellei.it - Winery tours by reservation.* The winery was founded by Francesco Bellei in 1920 and is now run by the fourth generation of winegrowers. In 1979 Giuseppe Bellei started flanking his Lambrusco production with a classic method sparkling wine (Chardonnay and Pinot Nero). His many trips to Champagne convinced him to concentrate production exclusively on wines made using the classic or traditional method with bottle fermentation, even for Lambrusco. Since 2000 the estate's grapes have been certified organic. Hectares under vine: 5.

**Wines**: Cuvée Brut Rosso, Cuvée Brut Rosé, Cuvée Brut Classico, Cuvée Blanc de Noirs.

**Vallona Fattorie** – *Via Cantagallo 37 - Fraz. Fagnano -* **Castello di Serravalle** *(BO) - ☏ 051 67 03 333 - www.fattorievallona.it - info@fattorievallona.it - Winery tours by reservation.* Maurizio Vallona, the winery's owner, has a unique sensitivity and is capable of analysing nature, the environment, the sky, the soil and plants. These are virtues typical of country dwellers who love rural life and are the result of the passion that was born in Maurizio when, as a student, he preferred the Colli Bolognesi, with its woods and fields, to life in the bustling city of Bologna. Hectares under vine: 40.

**Wines**: Vivace D.O.C. Pignoletto Classico, Primedizione Cuvée Bianco, Permartina Vendemmia Tardiva Pignoletto, Affederico Colli Bolognesi Merlot, Diggioanni Colli Bolognesi Cabernet Sauvignon.

**Cleto Chiarli Tenuta Agricola** – *Via Belvedere 4 -* **Castelvetro di Modena** *(MO) - ☏ 059 31 63 311 or 059 70 27 61 - www.chiarli.it - italia@chiarli.it - Winery tours by reservation.* Born of the Chiarli family's desire to unify direction of the different farm properties, the family owns and create a new cantina dedicated to producing superior wines. In 2001 the Chiarlis founded Cleto Chiarli Tenute Agricole in Castelvetro, in the heart of the Modena countryside. The company is the crown jewel of an entrepreneurial winemaking story that began in 1860, the year of Italian

unification, when Cleto Chiarli – great-grandfather of brothers Anselmo and Mauro, who today represent the family's fourth generation of winemakers – began producing Lambrusco wine in Modena, marking the start of what would become the family's successful business then and in the future. Hectares under vine: 100.

**Wines**: Premium Mention Honorable Lambrusco di Sorbara DOC, Vigneto Cialdini Lambrusco Grasparossa di Castelvetro DOC, Lambrusco del Fondatore, Brut de Noir Rosè, Modèn Blanc Brut.

**☙ Corte Manzini** – *Via Modena 131/3 -* **Castelvetro di Modena** *(MO) - ☏ 059 70 26 58 - www.cortemanzini.it - cantinamanzini@gmail.com - Winery tours by reservation.* The family-run winery was founded in 1978 and covers an area of over 25 hectares, with 13 under vine. It makes DOC wines, including Lambrusco Grasparossa di Castelvetro, its flagship product. Accommodation at the Corte Manzini guest farm, Via Modena 147/A, Settecani di Castelvetro, ☏ 059 70 10 49 *(8 rooms, €100)* with restaurant service Fri.-Sat. evening and Sun. Hectares under vine: 13.

**Wines**: Corte Manzini Secco, Amabile, L'Acino, Spumante Brut Bollicine Corte, Spumante Brut Diamante. Other products: preserves, grappa and nocino liqueur.

**Medici Ermete** - *Via Newton 13/a -* **Gaida** *(RE) - ☏ 0522 94 21 35 - www.medici.it - Vinegar loft tours by reservation.* The Medici family have been making high-quality Lambrusco for over 100 years. At the turn of the 19th c. Remigio, their ancestor, opened a winery to produce Lambrusco in order to make the most of the harvest from the family's vineyards. His son Ermete then propagated the winery's reputation. Today the family has been growing grapes for 4 generations. Hectares under vine: 75.

**Wines**: Reggiano Lambrusco Concerto, Reggiano Rosso Assolo, Lambrusco Grasparossa Bocciolo, Malvasia Secco Daphne, Spumante Brut Rosé Metodo Classico Unique. Other products: Traditional Balsamic Vinegar of Reggio Emilia.

**Poderi Fiorini** – *Via Puglie 4 -* **Savignano Sul Panaro** *(MO) - ☏ 059 73 31 51 - www.poderifiorini.com - fiorini@poderifiorini.com - Winery tours by reservation (from €10).* The winery, founded in 1919 and now run by the third generation of the Fiorini family, stands on the hills that were once the land of Matilda of Canossa, with its rich history and tradition. The main grape is Lambrusco, in the Sorbara and Grasparossa varieties. The wish to differentiate and valorise the wines from the most suitable land of the area has led to the creation of authentic Lambrusco vineyard selections: Sorbara Corte degli

Attimi, Castelvetro Terre al Sole and Modena Vigna del Caso. Fiorini have also been making excellent traditional balsamic vinegar for over 100 years in their vinegar room. Hectares under vine: 12.

**Wines**: Corte degli Attimi, Terre al Sole, Spazzavento Pignoletto Frizzante, Cà Mombrina Cabernet Sauvignon, La Torre Barbera Riserva. Other products: Traditional Balsamic Vinegar of Modena.

**Chiarli 1860** – *Via Manin 15* - **Modena** - ℘ *059 31 63 311 - www.chiarli.it - italia@chiarli.it - Winery tours by reservation.* Chiarli is one of the oldest and most renowned producers of Lambrusco. It was founded in 1860 by Cleto Chiarli, who ran the Artigliere trattoria in the centre of Modena and made his own Lambrusco for his clients. Their esteem drove him to expand his business and establish the winery. Hectares under vine: 110.

**Wines**: Prestigio Lambrusco Sorbara, Il Baluardo Lambrusco Grasparossa di Castelvetro Abboccato, Vecchia Modena Brut Millesimato, Vecchia Modena Pignoletto Extra Dry, Lambrusco Salamino di Santa Croce. Other products: spirits and local specialities.

🍇 **Tenuta Bonzara** – *Via S. Chierlo 37/A* - **Monte San Pietro** *(BO), 12 km SW of Zola Predosa* - ℘ *051 67 68 324 or* ℘ *328 08 15 765 - www.bonzara.it - info@bonzara.it - Winery tours by reservation (from €18).* In the 16th c. the land was already worked by the skilled hands of the Berghetti family of expert vine growers. In 1963 Angelo Lambertini founded Tenuta Bonzara, which he made into one of the leading wineries in the area. He was followed by his son Francesco, who shared his same passion. In the vineyard, short pruning and limited yields have ensured a considerable drop in yields. In the cellar the winery has adopted a philosophy of valorisation, aimed at enhancing the distinctive features of the grape varieties by extracting more fragrance and flavour. These choices have led the winery to play an active role in the promotion of the wines of the Colli Bolognesi. Accommodation available *(4 apts.)*. Hectares under vine: 16.

**Wines**: Vigna Antica Pignoletto Classico, Le Carrate Sauvignon Superiore, Borgo di Qua Pignoletto Superiore, Bonzarone Cabernet Sauvignon, Rocca di Bonacciara Merlot.

🍇 **Venturini Baldini** – *Via F. Turati 42 - Loc. Roncolo* - **Quattro Castella** *(RE)* - ℘ *0522 24 90 11 - www.venturinibaldini.it - info@venturinibaldini.it - Tasting tours by reservation (11 rooms, €150).* The winery was founded in 1975 and is run by the Venturini family, particularly Donata, who dedicates special attention to the environmental

protection of all 150 hectares of the estate, composed of vineyards, woods and natural meadows. The vines can thus be admired among age-old oak woods, fruit trees and untamed grasslands teeming with wild animals. In fact the estate borders on the protected Roncolo Nature Park. Food also served by reservation. Hectares under vine: 50.

**Wines**: Reggiano Lambrusco Marchese Manodori, Graniers Vino Frizzante Bianco Secco, Rès Lambrusco Rifermentato IGP. Other products: Traditional Balsamic Vinegar of Reggio Emilia, balsamic dressings, nocino liqueur, grappa, honey.

**Azienda Agricola Rinaldini** – *Via Andrea Rivasi 27 - Loc. Calerno -* **Sant'Ilario d'Enza** *(RE)* - ℘ *0522 67 91 90 - www.rinaldinivini.it - info@rinaldinivini.it - Winery tours by reservation, closed Sun.* The vineyards are characterised by high vine density and low yields, and are tended with the utmost respect for nature. A private driveway through the regular rows of low vines takes you to the heart of the estate, where the 1884 farmhouse is located. Extended over the years, it has underground cellars and an old stable converted into a small enological museum, a tasting counter and a shop. Hectares under vine: 15.

**Wines**: Lambrusco Vecchio Moro, Lambrusco Pjcol Ross, Spumante Bianco Rinaldo, Vigna del Picchio IGP, Moro del Moro IGT. Other products: balsamic vinegar and grappa.

🍇 **Fattorie di Montechiaro** – *Via Tignano 30/A* - **Sasso Marconi** *(BO)* - ℘ *051 67 55 140 - www.fattoriedimontechiaro.it - info@montechiaro.it - Winery tours by reservation.* The winery, run by Carla Fini, has a scenic location. It makes Colli Piacentini DOC wines and table wines. The sunny Montechiaro vineyards yield fresh, fruity

© Szasz-Fabian Ilka Erika/Shutterstock

reds and whites. The grapes are harvested exclusively by hand at just the right degree of ripeness and are immediately vinified in the cellar, where the passion for wine is combined with the most modern technologies and cultured yeasts. The estate offers accommodation *(10 rooms, €80)* and restaurant service Fri. evening, Sat. and Sun. lunch and evening.
Hectares under vine: 10.
**Wines**: Cabernet Sauvignon, Pinot Nero, Pignoletto, Chardonnay. Other products: Pecorino di Montechiaro cheese, made from the milk of the estate's sheep.

⌂ **Casali Viticultori** *– Via delle Scuole 7 - Loc. Pratissolo -* **Scandiano** *(RE) - ☎ 0522 85 54 41 - www.casalivini.it - info@casalivini.it - Winery tours by reservation.* Up until the 20th c., the estate made wine strictly for the family, and it was only under Giuseppe Casali, grandfather of the current owner, that the activity became an actual business. Today as then, the domaine's philosophy is to create wines that are "structurally complete, true to their origins and gratifying on the palate". Accommodation on the Cavazzone estate ( *☎ 0522 85 81 00, www. cavazzone.it)* and at La Razza guest farm *(17 rooms, double from €78, ☎ 0522 59 93 42, www.larazza.it)*. Hectares under vine: 50.
**Wines**: Sanruffino Lambrusco Grasparossa, Albore Secco Bianco, Albore Dolce Bianco, Villa Jano Spumante Metodo Charmat, Rosa Casali Spumante Brut. Other products: Traditional Balsamic Vinegar of Reggio Emilia, Parmigiano Reggiano.

**Vigneto delle Terre Rosse** *– Via Predosa 83 -* **Zola Predosa** *(BO) - ☎ 051 75 58 45 - www.vignetoterrerosse.com - info@ vignetoterrerosse.com - Winery tours by reservation.* Enrico Vallania, physician by profession, vigneron and wine lover by vocation, but above all a scholar and keen researcher, re-established the winery in 1961, experimenting methods and technologies aimed at improving quality. Following his death in 1985, his wife Adriana and his children continued the business according to his philosophy. The vineyards are planted with Cabernet, Sauvignon, Riesling, Malvasia, Chardonnay, Sauvignon, Pinot Bianco, Pinot Nero and Merlot. The wines are made following the vocation of the terroir, limiting human intervention as far as possible. Hectares under vine: 20.
**Wines**: Cabernet Sauvignon, Chardonnay, Riesling Italico, Merlot, Malvasia, Viognier.

♀/ **Tenuta Santa Croce** *– Via Abè 33 -* **Monteveglio-Valsamoggia** *(BO) - ☎ 051 670 20 69 - www.tenutasantacroce.it - info@ tenutasantacroce.it - Winery tours and tasting by resevation (from €20).* Born of the Chiarli family's desire to expand their portfolio of DOC regional wines, in the early 1990s the family began collaborating with small, local production companies, mainly in and around the Colli Bolognesi area. After evaluating the potential of the area and its Pignoletto, a flavourful autochthonous grape with significant character, the family acquired Tenuta Santa Croce in Monteveglio. The challenge lay in honouring the peculiar characteristics of this local delight. The company headquarters houses all the winemaking sectors, from fermentation to aging and packaging. There is also a modern tasting room, set alongside an active dining room available for meals by appointment. Hectares under vine: 30.
**Wines**: Pignoletto, Barbera, Desimo, Rosso Bologna, Cabernet Riserva.

## FROM IMOLA TO CESENA

**Azienda Agricola Longanesi Daniele** *- Via Boncellino 114 -* **Bagnacavallo** *(RA) - ☎ 0545 64 224- www.longanesiburson.com - dlonganesi@email.it.* The fourth generation of Longanesi "Bursón" passionately continues to promote the vine named after its discoverer.
**Wines**: Bursón Etichetta Nera, Bursón Etichetta Blu, Rambëla, Anemo Passito, Decimello Passito. Other products: grappa.

**Azienda Ercolani** *– Via Albergone Vecchia 24 -* **Bagnacavallo** *(RA) - ☎ 0545 63 559 or ☎ 366 93 70 097 - www.aziendaercolani.it - info@aziendaercolani.it - Winery tours by reservation.* The winery's origins date back to 1929, when the 4 Ercolani brothers purchased the estate. It is part of an experimental programme of new varieties, conducted in conjunction with the Centro Nazionale Ricerche Produzioni Vegetali of Region of Emilia-Romagna. Back in 1976 the estate planted the native vine known as Bursón, which had been preserved and distributed by the Longanesi family. Hectares under vine: 22.
**Wines**: Ravenna Uva Longanesi IGP Zollanera, Passito Ravenna Bianco IGP Zolladoro, Ravenna Bianco Zollabianca.

🌳 **Fattoria Paradiso** *– Via Palmeggiana 285 -* **Bertinoro** *(FC) - ☎ 0543 44 50 44 - www.fattoriaparadiso.com - info@ fattoriaparadiso.com - Winery tours by reservation.* The farm dates back to at least the 15th c., while the villa and the adjoining land were purchased by the Pezzi family at the end of the 19th c. As well as making wine, the estate holds round tables, conferences, concerts and various types of events. The estate offers accommodation *(6 apts., €75)*. Restaurant service at Locanda Gradisca (300 m). Hectares under vine: 50.
**Wines**: Barbarossa Rosso Forlì IGT, Sangiovese Riserva Superiore Vigna delle Lepri, Mito Rosso Forlì IGT, Gradisca Albana Passito, Strabismo di Venere Bianco IGT.

Other products: oil, balsamic grape sauce and grappa.

**Terra di Brisighella** – Via Strada 2 - **Brisighella** (RA) - ☏ 0546 81 103 - www.brisighello.net - info@terradibrisighella.it - Winery tours by reservation. The Brisighella farm co-operative was founded by 16 winegrowers in far-off 1962. In 1971 the estate added an olive press and made its first oil. Currently 500 members contribute grapes and 300 members bring their olives, allowing the production of 100,000 hectolitres of wine and 60,000 litres of oil. The co-operative was founded to promote local products. The red varieties grown are Sangiovese, Merlot, Cabernet Sauvignon and Ciliegiolo, while the white ones include Albana di Romagna, Trebbiano, Pignoletto, Pinot Bianco, Chardonnay and Sauvignon. Tasting menu by reservation.
**Wines**: Sangiovese La Torre, Sangiovese Superiore Brisiglè, Trebbiano La Rocca, Albana Passito Ambra, Frizzante Picatrix Spumante Brut. Other products: olive oil, aqua vitae and nocino liqueur.

**Stefano Ferrucci** – Via Casolana 3045/2 - **Castel Bolognese** (RA) - ☏ 0546 65 10 68 - www.stefanoferrucci.it - info@stefanoferrucci.it - Winery tours by reservation. The winery was established in 1932 and has been distinguished in recent years by large investments in research and experimentation, with the aim of valorising the quality of the grapes and thus the wines. Legend tells that the winery was once a horse-changing station built by Gaius Gracchus in Roman times. Hectares under vine: 16.
**Wines**: Sangiovese di Romagna Superiore Domus Caia, Sangiovese di Romagna Superiore Centurione, Colli di Faenza Bianco Chiaro della Serra, Albana di Romagna Passito Domus Aurea, Mattinale Trebbiano.

**Villa Bagnolo** – Via Bagnolo 160 - **Castrocaro Terme** (FC) - ☏ 0543 76 90 47 - www.villabagnolo.it - info@villabagnolo.it - Winery tours by reservation. Traces of settlements dating as far back as the 4th and 3rd BC have been found along the road that leads to Villa Bagnolo, while the first written evidence dates from 1371. In 1997 the businessman Vito Ballarati purchased the estate, which comprises a church, the rectory and a farmhouse, and commenced large-scale renovation that has resulted in Villa Bagnolo's current appearance of an old fortress. At the same time, the surrounding land was annexed and the estate currently covers an area of 54 hectares, 15 of which are planted with Sangiovese, Cabernet Franc and Cabernet Sauvignon. Hectares under vine: 15.
**Wines**: Sangiovese di Romagna Superiore Sassetto, Sangiovese di Romagna Superiore

Sorgara, Sangiovese di Romagna Superiore Bagnolo, Rosso Forlì Alloro IGT.
Other products: acquavite di vinaccia.

**Fattoria Zerbina** – Via Vicchio 11 - Loc. Marzeno - **Faenza** (RA) - ☏ 0546 40 022 - www.zerbina.com - info@zerbina.com - Winery tours by reservation. The winery is renowned for its dessert wines from partially dried botrytised Albana di Romagna grapes. It was founded in 1966 by Vincenzo Geminiani, the grandfather of the current owner Cristina, who has been running it since 1987. It makes interesting wines from Albana grapes as well as Sangiovese and Trebbiano. Hectares under vine: 30.
**Wines**: Sangiovese Superiore Ceregio, Trebbiano Ceregio Bianco, Sangiovese Superiore Torre di Ceparano, Ravenna Rosso Marzieno IGT, Albana Passito Arrocco DOCG.
Other products: grappa.

**Poderi Morini** – Via Gesuita 4/B - San Biagio - **Faenza** (RA) - ☏ 0546 63 81 72 - www.poderimorini.com - info@poderimorini.com - Winery tours by reservation. This young winery's motto is "We give value to the Romagna we love". Founded in 1998 out of an idea by poultry farmer Natale Morini, the winery has made a name for itself due to the enthusiasm of Natale's son Alessandro and his wife Daniela, who have put body and soul into the production of quality wines, based on research into the local grape varieties and their valorisation. Hectares under vine: 40.
**Wines**: Sangiovese di Romagna Superiore Nonno Rico, Ravenna Rosso Nadél IGT, Ravenna Rosso Traicolli IGT, Rubacuori Passito Rosso da Uve Stramature, Albana di Romagna Passito Innamorato, Estroverso Spumante Brut.

🍇 **Trerè** – Via Casale 19 - **Faenza** (RA) - ☏ 0546 47 034 - www.morenatrere.com - trere@trere.com - Winery tours by reservation. The estate was founded in the early 1960s by Valerio Trerè, who started off producing the first 3 DOC wines of the zone: Albana, Trebbiano and Sangiovese. In 1976 his daughter Morena decided to join him and became so passionate about the world of winemaking that she took over the business. Accommodation available (10 rooms and 5 apts., doubles €68). Restaurant service Fri.-Sat. evening and Sun. Hectares under vine: 31.
**Wines**: VioLeo Sangiovese Superiore Riserva, Sangiovese Riserva Amarcord d'un ross, Arlùs Albana di Romagna Secco, Giòja Pagadebit di Romagna Frizzante. Other products: fruit jam, honey, grappa, oil, balsamic seasoning.

**Tre Monti** – Via Lola 3 - **Imola** (BO) - ☏ 0542 65 71 16 - www.tremonti.it - david@

*tremonti.it - Winery tours by reservation.*
The winery was founded in the early 1960s by Sergio Navacchia and his wife Thea. The early 1980s marked a turning point in the vineyard and in the cellar, due to cooperation with the leading names in the Italian world of wine and the desire for qualitative growth. Integrated pest management is used for all the vineyards, with green cover of rows and minimal use of synthetic chemical products. Cellar operations are reduced to a bare minimum, respecting the fruit, and the soil and climate conditions in which it grows. Hectares under vine: 55.

**Wines**: Albana di Romagna Secco Vigna Rocca, Trebbiano di Romagna Vigna Rio, Sangiovese di Romagna DOC Superiore, Sangiovese di Romagna Superiore DOC Thea, Albana Passito Thea, Boldo.

**Drei Donà - Tenuta La Palazza** – *Via del Tesoro 23* - **Massa di Vecchiazzano** *(FC), 4 km S of Forlì* - ✆ *0543 76 93 71 - www. dreidona.it - palazza@dreidona.it - Winery tours and tasting by reservation, closed Sun.* The estate has belonged to the Drei Donà counts since the beginning of the century and has always been committed to growing Sangiovese grapes. The current owner, Claudio Drei Donà, left his profession as a lawyer to dedicate himself to the winery full time. Today he is assisted by his son Enrico. Most of the vineyards are planted with Sangiovese, but Chardonnay and Sauvignon are also grown. Hectares under vine: 23.

**Wines**: Sangiovese Riserva Pruno, Sangiovese Notturno, Cabernet Sauvignon Magnificat, Chardonnay Il Tornese, Gran Riserva Graf Noir. Other products: olive oil and grappa.

**Castelluccio** – *Via Tramonto 15* - **Modigliana** *(FC), 11 km S of Brisighella* - ✆ *0546 94 24 86 - www.ronchidicastelluccio.it - info@ ronchidicastelluccio.it - Winery tours by reservation.* Castelluccio has a total area of approx. 50 hectares, 12 of which are vineyards, 2 olive groves and the rest farmland, woods and built-up areas. In 1975 several microzones, known as *ronchi* and particularly suitable for winegrowing, were found on the estate and planted with Sangiovese and Sauvignon Blanc. In 1999 the winery was taken over by Vittorio Fiore, together with his brothers Ermanno and GianMichele. The management is entrusted to enologist Claudio Fiore, assisted by his wife Veruska. Hectares under vine: 12.

**Wines**: Ronco dei Ciliegi IGT di Forlì Rosso, Ronco delle Ginestre IGT, Massicone IGT di Forlì rosso, Ronco del Re IGT di Forlì Bianco, Lunaria IGT di Forlì Bianco, Le More DOC Sangiovese di Romagna. Other products: grappa and olive oil.

### FERRARA

**Mattarelli** – *Via Marconi 35* - **Vigarano Pieve** *(FE), 11 km W of Ferrara* - ✆ *0532 43 123 - www.mattarelli-vini.it - info@ mattarelli-vini.it - Winery tours by reservation.* The winegrowing tradition has been in the Mattarelli family for 4 generations. Umberto, to whom the wine shop and the spirits range are dedicated, founded the business at the beginning of the 1950s. From a simple village wine bar, the estate's constant growth has allowed it to make a name for itself on the region's winegrowing scene. Hectares under vine: 15.

**Wines**: Fortana, Merlot, Sauvignon, Sangiovese, Trebbiano, Lambrusco.

## Where to stay

### BRISIGHELLA

**Relais Varnello** – *Borgo Rontana 34, 3 km W of Brisighella (RA)* - ✆ *338 54 98 373 - www.varnello.it - Closed Oct.-Mar. - 4 rooms and 2 suites, doubles from €90.* A small farmhouse located along the old Etruscan road, with comfortable modern rooms.

### CASTELVETRO DI MODENA

**Locanda del Feudo** – *Via Trasversale 2, Castelvetro di Modena (MO)* - ✆ *059 70 87 11 - www.locandadelfeudo.it - 6 rooms, doubles from €89.* A picturesque little place in the upper part of the town, with rooms and public areas that are a skilful blend of antique and modern. The restaurant serves local specialities and typical products.

### RIOLA

**Agriturismo La Fenice** – *Via Santa Lucia 29, Rocca di Roffeno, 18 km N of Riola di Vergato (BO)* - ✆ *051 91 92 72 - www. lafeniceagritur.it - Closed 1 month in winter - 9 rooms and 4 apts., doubles from €60.* A small group of 16th-c. farmhouses made from stone and wood.

### RIVERGARO

**Agriturismo Croara Vecchia** – *Loc. Croara Vecchia, Rivalta di Gazzola, 9.5 km S of Rivergaro (PC)* - ✆ *333 21 93 845- www. croaravecchia.it - Closed Nov.-Feb. - 15 rooms, doubles from €105.* This guest farm, with pretty bedrooms named after flowers, was a monastery until 1810.

### SALSOMAGGIORE TERME

**Agriturismo Antica Torre** – *Case Bussandri 197, Cangelasio, 3.5 km NW of Salsomaggiore (PR)* - ✆ *0524 57 54 25 - www.anticatorre.it - Closed Dec.-Feb. - 8 rooms, doubles from €120.* Set in the hills around Salsomaggiore, this 17th-c. rural complex boasts a 14th-c. tower.

# TUSCANY

The link between Tuscany and viticulture is very ancient and this region has always been extremely protective of its winemaking legacy: as early as 1716 Cosimo de' Medici heralded the concept of designated areas when he defined some of the highest-quality wine-producing zones. The region makes many wines that are famous around the world, such as the renowned Brunello di Montalcino, Chianti and the noble "Super Tuscans" produced in the area of Bolgheri from the international varieties Cabernet Franc, Cabernet Sauvignon and Merlot.

*Play of light and shade in the vineyards and "crete" of Siena*

## The terroir

Vines grow happily in all provinces in Tuscany and there are many appellations throughout the region. The most representative variety is unquestionably **Sangiovese**, a splendid vine whose grapes produce extraordinary wines. But there are other types too: the most common black grape varieties are Canaiolo Nero, Ciliegiolo and Aleatico, and among the whites, are Trebbiano Toscano, Vernaccia di San Gimignano, Malvasia Bianca, Ansonica and Vermentino. But over recent decades Tuscany has won itself fame above all for the wines it produces from **international varieties**, which here have found an ideal environment to grow. In consequence, the region has demonstrated that it can produce great wines from both its native species and Bordeaux vines.

Today winemaking in Tuscany is closely linked to appellations like **Brunello di Montalcino**, **Vino Nobile di Montepulciano**, **Chianti**, **Bolgheri**, **Carmignano**, **Morellino di Scansano** and many others. Whereas the region is normally associated with red wines, there are also excellent whites, such as **Vernaccia di San Gimignano**, **Bianco di Pitigliano**, **Ansonica Costa dell'Argentario**, and **Bianco dell'Empolese**, to mention just a few.

There are a number of fine sweet wines to boast too, starting with the extraordinary **Vin Santo** – perhaps *santo* (meaning "holy") because it was once used to celebrate mass, or perhaps "Xantos" because it was similar to the sweet wines of the Greek island of that name. Enjoyable when made from the sun-dried Trebbiano and Malvasia grapes, it becomes even more appealing in the "Occhio di Pernice" version made from Sangiovese, Malvasia Nera and Canaiolo grapes. Many appellations make a version of it, each with its own peculiarities. Another wine of the same type, one that should on no account be missed, is **Moscatello di Montalcino**.

## DOCG

Brunello di Montalcino
Carmignano
Chianti
Chianti Classico
Elba Aleatico Passito
   or Aleatico Passito dell'Elba
Montecucco Sangiovese
Morellino di Scansano
Rosso della Val di Cornia
   or Val di Cornia Rosso
Suvereto
Vernaccia di San Gimignano
Vino Nobile di Montepulciano

## DOC

Ansonica Costa dell'Argentario
Barco Reale di Carmignano
Bianco dell'Empolese
Bianco di Pitigliano
Bianco Pisano di San Torpé
Bolgheri and Bolgheri Sassicaia
Candia dei Colli Apuani
Capalbio
Colli dell'Etruria Centrale
Colli di Luni
Colline Lucchesi
Cortona
Elba
Grance Senesi
Maremma Toscana
Montecarlo
Montecucco
Monteregio di Massa Marittima
Montescudaio
Moscadello di Montalcino
Orcia
Parrina
Pomino
Rosso di Montalcino
Rosso di Montepulciano
San Gimignano
Sant'Antimo
Sovana
Terratico di Bibbona
Terre di Casole
Terre di Pisa
Val d'Arbia
Val d'Arno di Sopra
   or Valdarno di Sopra
Val di Cornia
Valdichiana Toscana
Valdinievole
Vin Santo del Chianti
Vin Santo del Chianti Classico
Vin Santo di Carmignano
Vin Santo di Montepulciano

## PRINCIPAL VARIETIES CULTIVATED

### WHITE GRAPES

Albana
Albarola
Ansonica
Biancame
Canaiolo Bianco
Chardonnay
Clairette
Durella
Grechetto
Greco
Livornese Bianca
Malvasia Bianca di Candia
Malvasia Bianca Lunga
Moscato Bianco
Müller Thurgau
Pinot Bianco
Riesling
Riesling italico
Roussane
Sauvignon
Semillon
Traminer Aromatico
Trebbiano Toscano
Verdea
Verdello
Verdicchio Bianco
Vermentino
Vernaccia di San Gimignano

### GREY GRAPES

Pinot Grigio

### BLACK GRAPES

Aleatico
Alicante
Alicante Bouschet
Ancellotta
Barbera
Barsaglina
Bonamico
Bracciola Nera
Cabernet Franc
Cabernet Sauvignon
Caloria
Canaiolo Nero
Canina Nera
Ciliegiolo
Colombana Nera
Colorino
Foglia Tonda
Gamay
Groppello Gentile
Groppello S. Stefano
Malvasia
Malvasia Nera
   di Brindisi
Malvasia Nera
   di Lecce
Mammolo
Mazzese
Merlot
Montepulciano
Pinot Nero
Pollera Nera
Prugnolo Gentile
Sangiovese
Schiava Gentile
Syrah
Teroldego
Vermentino Nero

# Itineraries

*Locations with a winery are indicated by the symbol ♥; for the addresses of the wineries, see p. 292.*

## 1. THE PROVINCE OF LUCCA

The province of Lucca is home to the appellations **Colline Lucchesi** and **Montecarlo**, which produce white, red and sweet wines from a wide assortment of grapes.

### Lucca★★

Once you enter Lucca's massive walls, you discover a welter of little streets clogged by bicycles, lacelike church façades, an ancient tower on which a tree grows, and a strange, hidden oval piazza that was once an amphitheatre. To see all this from above, take a pleasant walk along the top of the city walls. A free commune from the 12th c., Lucca's wealth and importance grew to the mid-14th c. as a result of the manufacture and trade of silk. Under the seigniory of *condottiero* Castruccio Castracani (1281-1328) the city reached the pinnacle of its splendour. From 1550, the city turned to agriculture, a shift that saw the return to an interest in architecture. Various country villas were built, a wall was constructed around the city centre, and most of the houses were rebuilt or renovated.

**The historic centre** – the streets and squares of the historic centre are a harmonious blend of Gothic and Renaissance architecture where the beauty of the past remains unaltered: ancient palaces, towers of the nobility, old shops, huge inlaid doors, carved coats of arms, gateways and wrought-iron balconies.

Your tour starts from the shady Piazza Napoleone, lined by the Palazzo della Provincia, which was built in the 16th c. by the Florentine architect Bartolomeo Ammannati.

Take Via Beccheria to Piazza San Michele. Built between the 12th and 14th c. over the old Roman forum, the white façade of the Church of **San Michele in Foro★★** dominates the square lined by ancient houses and Palazzo Pretorio. The façade is particularly tall as it was planned to be combined with a higher nave. It is in Pisan-Luccan style despite the renovation work carried out in the 19th c. The simplicity of the Romanesque interior contrasts with the elaborate exterior. A *Madonna* by Andrea della Robbia can be seen on the first altar in the right aisle. The right transept also has a beautiful and colourful painting by Filippino Lippi. Not far from the church is the house where **Giacomo Puccini** was born. It contains letters, a piano and sketches for various productions of the Maestro's operas. *Corte San Lorenzo 9. Open 10-19 (Nov.-Dec. 10-13 and 15-17, Jan.-Mar. 10-18, closed Tue., Oct. 10-18), ℘ 0583 58 40 28, www.puccinimuseum.it.*

The elegant **Via Fillungo★** is one of the prettiest streets in Lucca. The Romanesque and now deconsecrated Church of San Cristoforo stands at the start on the right. The light and dark lined marble façade has a rose window and a portal

with a superb architrave carved with floral motifs. The names of Luccans who fell in battle are carved on the walls of the simple, dignified interior illuminated by the pinkish light of the rose window.

Continuing, you will pass the civic Clock Tower (13th c.). If you have the legs to climb the 208 steps, you will be rewarded with a splendid **view**★★. *Open 9.30-19.30 (Mar. and Oct. 17.30, Apr.-May 18.30), closed Nov.-Feb.* ℘ *0583 48 090, www. lemuradilucca.it.*

The last section of Via Cesare Battisti is overlooked by the massive bell tower of **San Frediano**★. Rebuilt in the 12th c. before Pisa exerted its influence, it is an example of pure Luccan Romanesque. The bare façade is lined with white marble that was taken from the Roman amphitheatre. The high central part, which was renovated in the 13th c., is decorated with a mosaic of the *Ascen-*

*sion* executed by Luccan artists in Byzantine style. The aisles are lined with Renaissance and Baroque chapels and separated from the nave by ancient columns. A semicircular apse stands at the end. To the right of the entrance is a 13th-c. font carved with dynamic sculptures of the life of Moses. The Chapel of Sant'Agostino is lined with frescoes by Amico Aspertini from Ferrara, one of which refers to the transfer of the "Holy Face" (a wooden body from a crucifix) from Luni to Lucca.

*Return to Via Fillungo and take a vaulted alley on the right.*

The unusual **Piazza dell'Anfiteatro**★ is oblong in shape as it fills the space where the 2nd-c. Roman amphitheatre used to stand. The ancient building was gradually dismantled to provide materials during the Middle Ages for the construction of the city's churches and was then built

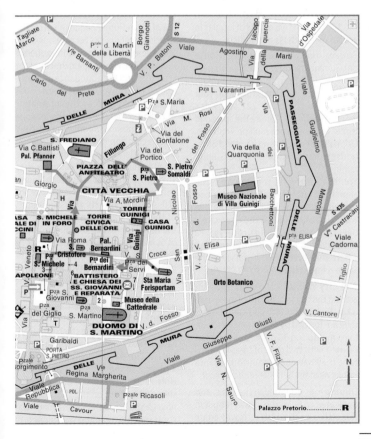

*Lucca duomo*

© FrankvandenBergh/iStock

over with houses. Close by, the small and irregularly shaped **Piazza San Pietro** is the setting for noble 16th-c. palaces and the two-coloured bell tower built from stone and brick for the Romanesque Church of **San Pietro Somaldi** (12th-c.). The church façade was completed in the 14th c. with two orders of loggias in accordance with Pisan tradition.

*Proceed along Via Guinigi.* The House dei Guinigi stands at no. 29, a compact group of buildings topped by a tower and crowned with trees (pluck up your courage to climb the 227 steps, it's worth the effort!). Admire the spread of three- and four-light mullion windows. Opposite, at nos. 20 and 22, stand other houses that belonged to the Guinigi family.

You then arrive at the Romanesque church of **Santa Maria Forisportam**, so named as it was built outside the Roman walls. To return to Piazza San Michele pass through Via Santa Croce, Piazza dei Servi and **Piazza dei Bernardini**, where the severe 16th-c. palace of the same name stands.

**The City Walls★** – the walls run right around the city for a length of more than 4 km. Built in the 16th and early 17th c., they are formed by 11 ramparts and curtains measuring 30 m deep at the base. Planted with two rows of trees last century, they have been transformed into public gardens, *www.lemuradilucca.it*.

**Duomo★★** – founded in the 6th c. and dedicated to St Martin, it was rebuilt in the 11th c. In the 13th c., it was again almost entirely rebuilt on the outside and then, in the 14th-15th c., on the inside too. Despite its asymmetry, the white and green marble façade gives an impression of strength and balance. The upper section, with three orders of columned loggias, was the first example of Pisan Romanesque in Lucca: this style is lighter than its Luccan equivalent, less severe, and adorned with exuberant imagination. Notice the richness of the sculpture and the abundance of marble inlays. The powerful but slender bell tower is lightened by the alternation of building materials and the increase in the number of openings as it rises. The decoration of the portal features slender pillars carved in primitive style, small arches, friezes and carved scenes.

The **Gothic interior** features an elegant triforium (gallery of arches above the aisles) that contrasts with the solidity of the pillars and round arches. Note the remarkable Romanesque sculpture of St Martin on the inside façade as he divides his cloak between the poor; its unadorned, classical style heralds that of Nicola Pisano. The elegant shrine that contains the **Holy Face** (the Volto Sacro) was built in the left aisle by Luccan artist Matteo Civitali (1436-1501). The story goes that after the climb to Calvary, Nicodemus carved the semblances of Christ. The Italian bishop Gualfredo, a pilgrim to the Holy Land, found the Holy Face and placed it on a crewless ship that arrived on the shore of Luni, near La Spezia. As the sacred image was contested between the worshippers of

## Ilaria or Caterina?

A recent study has raised doubts over both the name of the artist who carved the sarcophagus and the identity of the young girl represented on it. The sculptor of the tomb could have been a member of the French school and the girl is now thought to be Caterina Antelminelli, one of the four young girls who were betrothed to Paolo Guinigi but of whom three died before they reached a marriageable age. The first was Ilaria, the second Caterina.

Luni and Lucca, to resolve the dispute the bishop of Lucca had the idea of placing the carving on an ox-drawn, driverless cart. The oxen immediately followed the road to Lucca. The fame of the Holy Face was spread far and wide by the Luccan merchants, and even the kings of France sometimes swore an oath by "Saint Vaudeluc" (Santo Volto di Lucca). The large wooden sculpture of **Christ★** (12th c.) has been blackened by time but is clearly ori-ental in style. It is said to be a copy of the original at the base of the legend. One of the masterpieces of Italian funer-ary sculpture, made in 1406 by Jacopo della Quercia from Siena, is the **tomb of Ilaria del Carretto★★**, which can be seen in the sacristy. The wife of Paolo Guinigi, lord of Lucca in the early 15th c., the young woman is shown lying on a bed dressed in a long gown draped softly over her body. Lying at her feet is her dog, a symbol of faithfulness.

© kubais/Shutterstock

## THE TERROIR

**Area**: 22,987.44 km$^2$, of which approximately 60,262 hectares are planted to vine

**Production 2019**: 2,634,117 hectolitres of which 1,660,658 VQPRD

**Geography**: 66.5% hilly, 25% mountainous, 8.5% flat. Mixed soils, in part clayey and sandy; some areas of volcanic origin. A temperate climate, mild on the coast, fresher inland

## THE PROTECTION CONSORTIA

Consorzio del Vino Brunello di Montalcino – Via Boldrini 10, Montalcino (Siena), ℘ 0577 84 82 46, www.consorziobrunellodimontalcino.it

Consorzio di Tutela Vino Candia Colli Apuani – Largo Matteotti 22, Massa Carrara; ℘ 338 52 89 489, www.candiadeicolliapuani.it

Consorzio di Tutela Vini di Carmignano – www.consorziovinicarmignano.it

Consorzio Vino Chianti – ℘ 055 33 36 00, www.consorziovinochianti.it

Consorzio Vino Chianti Classico – ℘ 055 82 285, www.chianticlassico.com

Consorzio Chianti Colli Fiorentini – ℘ 055 49 35 338, www.chianti-collifiorentini.it

Consorzio Chianti Colli Senesi – ℘ 0577 43 186, www.consorziochianticollisenesi.it

Consorzio Vini Cortona – ℘ 0575 60 37 93, www.cortonavini.it

Consorzio di Tutela Vini dell'Elba – www.aleaticoelba.it

Consorzio Tutela Montecucco – ℘ 0564 99 04 24, www.consorziomontecucco.it

Consorzio Tutela Vino Montescudaio – ℘ 0586 65 16 31, www.consorziovinomontescudaiodoc.it

Consorzio Tutela Vino Morellino di Scansano – ℘ 0564 50 77 10, www.consorziomorellino.it

Consorzio del Vino d'Orcia – ℘ 0577 88 74 71, www.consorziovinoorcia.it

Consorzio della Denominazione San Gimignano – ℘ 0577 94 01 08, www.vernaccia.it

Consorzio Vini Valdichiana – ℘ 0575 27 229, www.vinivaldichianatoscana.it

Consorzio di Tutela Vini Val di Cornia – ℘ 0565 20 812

Consorzio del Vino Nobile di Montepulciano – ℘ 0578 75 78 12, www.consorziovinonobile.it

## The Villas in the province of Lucca

*Circular itinerary of 50 km starting from Lucca. Take the S 12 north, turn right in the direction of Marlia after 6 km, and cross over the railway line.*

**Villa Grabau** is today an elegant Neo-classical construction that originated in the first half of the 16th c. It stands at the centre of a particularly lovely vista. Fountains with bronze grotesques and white marble statues contribute to the beauty of the 9-hectare **park★★**, a botanic garden with a winter glasshouse and a 17th-18th c. lemonhouse. This latter construction has a very special architecture, with 7 doors with 7 oval openings in ashlar work. *Via di Matraia 269, S.Pancrazio, open Jul.-Aug. 10-13 and 14.30-18, Sept.-Nov. and Apr.-Jun. 10-13 and 14-18, Nov.-Easter only Sun. 11-13 and 14.30-17.30, ℘ 0583 40 60 98, www.villagrabau.it.*

**Villa Reale di Marlia** once belonged to Elisa Baciochi, the sister of Napo-leon, then to the Dukes of Parma, the Grand-Dukes of Tuscany, King Vittorio Emanuele II, Prince Carlo (the brother of the King of the Two Sicilies), and to the Counts Pecci-Blunt. One of the features of the magnificent 17th-c. **park★★** is an open-air "natural" theatre formed by yew bushes, statues, niches and stone seats. *Visits to the garden only: Mar.-Oct. 10-18; winter Sun. and public hols. only by appointment, ℘ 0583 30 108, www.parcovillareale.it.*

Passing through **Segromigno in Monte** ⛾, 4 km east of Marlia, you reach Villa Mansi, a 16th-c. construction with a façade adorned with statues, and surrounded by **gardens★** that are partly English and partly Italian in style. *Via delle Selvette 259, end of Oct.-Mar. Mon.-Wed. 11.30-15.30 Thu.-Sat. 14.30-15.30, closed Sun., ℘ 0583 92 02 34 or 347 75 29 340, www.villeepalazzilucchesi.it.*

A couple of km south, the 16th-c. **Villa Torrigiani★** stands at the end of a long avenue. In the 17th c. it was transformed

## WINE AND FOOD ROUTES

Strada dei Vini di Carmignano e dei Sapori Tipici Pratesi – ℘ 055 87 12 468, www.stradavinicarmignano.it

Strada dei Sapori del Casentino – ℘ 0575 50 22 31

Strada del Vino e dell'Olio Chianti Classico – ℘ 055 82 285, www.stradachianticlassico.it

Strada del Vino Colli di Candia e di Lunigiana – ℘ 338 88 53 067, www.stradadelvinoms.it

Strada del Vino Colli di Maremma – ℘ 0564 50 73 81, www.stradavinimaremma.it

Strada del Vino delle Colline Pisane – www.stradadelvinocollinepisane.it

Strada del Vino Costa degli Etruschi – ℘ 0565 74 97 05, www.lastradadelvino.com

Strada del Vino e dell'Olio Lucca, Montecarlo e Versilia – ℘ 338 22 11 779, www.stradavinoeoliolucca.it

Strada dell'Olio Monti Pisani – ℘ 050 78 46 847, www.stradadellolio.it

Strada del Marrone del Mugello di Marradi – ℘ 055 80 42 363, www.stradadelmarrone.it

Strada dell'Olio e del Vino del Montalbano – ℘ 327 35 94 603, www.stradadileonardo.org

Strada del Vino Montecucco e dei Sapori d'Amiata – ℘ 0564 99 46 30, www.stradadelvinomontecucco.it

Strada del Vino e dei Sapori Monteregio di Massa Marittima – ℘ 0566 90 27 56, www.stradavino.it

Strada del Vino di Montespertoli – www.chianti-montespertoli.it

Strada del Vino Orcia – ℘ 0577 88 74 71, www.stradavinorcia.com

Strada del Vino Terre d'Arezzo – ℘ 0575 29 40 66, www.stradadelvino.arezzo.it

Strada dei Sapori Valtiberina Toscana – ℘ 0575 74 05 36, www.valtiberinaintoscana.it

Strada del Vino Nobile di Montepulciano – ℘ 0578 71 74 84, www.stradavinonobile.it

Strada del Vino Vernaccia di San Gimignano – ℘ 0577 94 12 67, www.comune.sangimignano.si.it

Strade del Vino e dell'Olio, dei sapori di Toscana – ℘ 0571 60 60 48, www.stradevinoditoscana

into an opulent summer residence by Marquis Nicolao Santini, the ambassador of the Republic of Lucca to the Papal Court and to Louis XIV. A pleasant walk can be had in the gardens laid out by Le Nôtre with fountains, grottoes and nymphaea. *Via Gomberaio 3, open 10-13 and 14.30-17.30 (summer 10-13 and 14.30-18.30), closed Nov.-Feb., ℘ 0583 92 80 41 and 349 62 06 847, www.villeepalazzi lucchesi.it.*

Continue through **San Gennaro** ▼ to **Collodi**, which was also the pen-name of Carlo Lorenzini (1826-90), the "father" of Pinocchio. He chose Collodi as it was the name of his mother's village. **Villa Garzoni** was built by the lords of Collodi in the 18th c. in a splendid 17th-c. **garden★★** that was at one time famous throughout Europe. It was in the kitchen of the villa that Lorenzini, the cook's nephew, began to write the story of Pinocchio. Dedicated to the famous puppet is the **Pinocchio Park**, where you will find a maze and bronze sculptures created by famous artists, such as Emilio Greco and Venturino Venturi. *Open Mar.-Nov. 9-sunset, rest of the year Sat.-Sun. and public hols. 10-sunset, ℘ 0572 42 93 42, www.pinocchio.it.*

**Montecarlo**, which lies 7 km south of Collodi, lies at the centre of the **Montecarlo DOC** zone. The town stands in a panoramic position and has a pretty centre strung out around the castle. Several km before arriving at Montecarlo you will find the ancient Church of San Piero in Campo, documented as early as the 9th c., whose 12th-c façade is still intact.

## 2. THE HILLS OF PISA AND THE "ETRUSCAN COAST"

This area of Tuscany is the setting for various appellations, including **Chianti delle Colline Pisane**, **Colli dell'Etruria Centrale**, **Bianco Pisano di San Torpé**, **Bolgheri**, **Elba**, **Montescudaio**, **Terratico di Bibbona** and **Val di Cornia**. It is above all the home of the "**Super Tuscans**" that have made Tuscan wine famous throughout the world. These are wines made from Bordeaux varieties (Merlot, Cabernet Franc and Cabernet Sauvignon), which are aged in barrels and produced using techniques typical of Bordeaux. The first wine to be made in this manner was **Sassicaia** in Castagneto Carducci,

where rootlings of Cabernet Sauvignon were planted immediately after World War II. This was the start of what was to become a real revolution in Tuscan viticulture, which today has been followed by many producers in other areas.

On the **Isle of Elba** the vegetation is typically Mediterranean, with palms, eucalyptus, bamboo, cedar and magnolias, and the most common crops are olives, maize and grapes. The wines are scented and vigorous, like the white Moscato and red Aleatico. The **Elba DOC** zone produces reds, whites, rosés and sweet wines from Trebbiano, Ansonica, Sangiovese, Aleatico and Malvasia grapes. One of the leading winemaking centres on the island is **Capoliveri** ▼, a picturesque village from where the extraordinary **view★★** of the "Three Seas" can be had. These are the three gulfs: **Portoferraio** ▼, **Porto Azzurro** ▼ and Stella.

## The Hills of Pisa

*Itinerary of 85 km from Casciana Terme to Castellina Marittima.*

Set in a beautiful position in hilly countryside cultivated with vines, olive and peach trees, the town of **Casciana Terme**, which enjoys a balmy climate, offers a pleasant stay in which you can alternate spa treatments with visits to the nearby art cities. It is said that from her window in Casciana castle, every day Matilda of Canossa (1046-1115) saw a blackbird bathe its bent leg in the water of a stream, and that after a few days, the bird ceased to hop on one leg. Whether it is true or not, the spring has been famous since the time of Augustus Continue east to find three villages of winemaking tradition: **Terricciola** ▼, founded by the Etruscans at the confluence of several water courses, **Peccioli**, built around the remains of a castle, and **Ghizzano** ▼.

Heading north-west from Casciana Terme, in 2 km you arrive in **Casciana Alta**, where there is a fine polyptych by Lippo Memmi in the Church of San Niccolò. Now go west and then south through Santa Luce and you find a very pretty stretch of road as far as **Castellina Marittima** ▼, at one time famous for its alabaster quarries. The remains of walls and the medieval castle can still be seen.

## A small DOCG and a village with a famous name

**Carmignano DOCG** and **Barco Reale di Carmignano** are wines produced prevalently from Sangiovese, Canaiolo Nero, Cabernet Franc and Cabernet Sauvignon grapes in the hills around the municipalities of Carmignano and Poggio a Caiano, in the province of Prato. The area of production is very limited and the surface planted to vine measures a little less than 100 hectares spread over a hill zone at a height of between 250 and 400 m.

Ringed by vines and olive trees, **Carmignano** 🍷 is a village that has retained only a single tower of its medieval fort. But the real treasure of this place is in the Church of San Michele, where you can see the superb *Visitation* by Pontormo (ca. 1530). Expressed through the power of their mutual regard, the Madonna and Elisabeth convincingly communicate their deep love and reciprocal respect.

**Poggio a Caiano** is famous for its elegant villa and romantic intrigues: Paganini gave concerts there and it seems he may also have dallied with Napoleon's sister, and Vittorio Emanuele II took "la bella Rosina" there. But the most intriguing story connected with this villa built by Giuliano da Sangallo for Lorenzo de' Medici concerns Francesco I de' Medici and his second wife Bianca Cappello, who died there in 1587 within a day of one another, probably poisoned. *Open Jun.-Aug. 8.15-19.30 (Apr.-May and Sept. 18.30, Mar. and Oct. 17.30, rest of the year 16.30). Closed 2nd and 3rd Mon. of the month,* 📞 *055 87 70 12.*

At a distance of 18 km from Carmignano, close to the small town of **Vinci★** 🍷, Leonardo was born in 1452 on the slopes of Monte Albano in a landscape carpeted with vineyards and olive groves. The medieval centre of Vinci is built on a hill, on the top of which the pointed bell tower of the parish church stands out close to the castle. Built in the 11th c. for the counts Guidi, today the castle houses the **Leonardian Museum**, containing models and machines built from the artist's drawings. *Open 9.30-19 (Nov.-Feb. 18),* 📞 *0571 93 32 51, www.museoleonardiano.it.* Three km north, in the direction of Santa Lucia and Faltognano, the charming countryside of **Anchiano** provides the setting for Leonardo's presumed birthplace. *Open 10-19 (Nov.-Feb. 17),* 📞 *0571 93 32 48, www.museoleonardiano.it.*

## The "Etruscan Coast"

*Itinerary of approximately 120 km from Rosignano Marittimo to Piombino.*

This wide strip of land that runs along the coast between Livorno and Piombino will be of interest to lovers of nature, archaeology, literature and good food and wine. Since the 15th c. the Riviera degli Etruschi has been strongly linked with winemaking. The **Wine Route**, which runs from Rosignano Marittimo to Piombino, is 160 km long and can even be enjoyed by bike (especially the stretches between Bibbona, Bolgheri and Castagneto Carducci). The towns on the way are: Castellina Marittima, Riparbella, Cecina, **Montescudaio** 🍷, Guardistallo, **Casale Marittimo** 🍷, Bibbona, Bolgheri, Castagneto Carducci, Sassetta, Suvereto, Campiglia Marittima.

What remains of the medieval centre of **Rosignano Marittimo** can be seen in the upper part of the town. Here the castle has been turned into an archaeological museum that tells the history of the area from the Etruscan period to the Middle Ages. *Via del Castello 24.* Open 9-13 (10-13 Sun. and public hols.), in Sum. 10-13 and 17-20, closed Mon., 📞 0586 72 42 88. The industrial area of the town is called Rosignano Solvay after the Belgian chemist who invented a method for producing soda.

## Cecina

Cecina came into being in the mid-19th c. after the marshes of Maremma were drained. It is an agricultural and industrial town but has a seaside resort and pinewood close by at Marina di Cecina. The local archaeological museum recounts the history of the zone and exhibits Etruscan cups, decorated pottery from the Classical Greek and Hellenistic periods, urns from the 6th-c. BC, and funerary goods from the Roman imperial age. *For info.* 📞 *0586 61 12 66, www.museoarcheologicocecina.it.*

## Bolgheri and Castagneto Carducci

The Oratory of **San Guido** is the one referred to by Giosué Carducci in his poem *Davanti a San Guido*, and its avenue of cypresses still leads to **Bolgheri** 🍷, where the poet lived from 1838 to 1848.

Standing in a dominant position over a landscape of olive trees, **Castagneto Carducci** 🍷 was the ancient seigniory of the Counts della Gherardesca. The only remains of their castle are the ruins of Donoratico Tower. The town is very ancient but its fame is mostly literary: its name is derived from the Nobel Prize-winner poet who stayed there as a young man and sang the praises of this lovely strip of Tuscany. You can visit his house and the **Carducci Archive Museum** in the Municipal Palace. *10-13 and 16.30- 19.30 (mid-Oct.-mid-Jun. 10-13, Sat.-Sun. 15-18), closed Mon., 🖉 0565 76 50 32, www. carducciecastagneto.wordpress.com.* The town also attracts the followers of Bacchus as this is the area that produces **Sassicaia**, the first great Tuscan wine made using the methods of Bordeaux. Its quality was recognised with the appellation **Bolgheri Sassicaia DOC** in the 1990s.

**Suvereto** 🍷 is partly walled and medieval in appearance, and lies 11 km north-east of Castagneto Carducci. It huddles around the Aldobrandesca Fort and the 13th-c. Municipal Palace. Since 2011 Suvereto has been able to give its name to a DOCG wine, production of which falls exclusively within its municipal boundaries.

## Campiglia Marittima

Campiglia Marittima is situated in a lovely position on a hill 210 m above the sea. Ringed by walls, it was at one time unassailable. The centre clearly has a rich history, as attested by the Fort, Palazzo Pretorio and San Silvestro Castle. The central Piazza della Repubblica climbs to Palazzo Pretorio, which is decorated with the coats of arms of the "captains of the people" that lived there until 1406. Follow Via Cavour to Porta Fiorentina, where the four coats of arms record the rulers of Campiglia: the cross of Pisa, the lily of Florence, the greyhound of Campiglia and the stele of the Gherardesca family. Dating from the 12th-13th c., the Fort stands above Porta Fiorentina where there was once a fortress, probably built in the 8th c. If you continue down Via Roma you will come to Porta a Mare and Piazza della Vittoria, from where there is a **view** over the coast.

*Campiglia Marittima*

The **Church of San Giovanni** stands in the cemetery. Constructed in the 12th c., it has a cross plan in the form of the Greek letter *tau* and is carved with an odd inscription (*beneath the roof of the side chapel*) that reads both forwards and backwards, and was perhaps a magical formula against accidents:

SATOR
AREPO
TENET
OPERA
ROTAS

With its many archaeological and environmental resources, the southern tip of the **Etruscan Coast** is the zone of the Six Parks of Val di Cornia (Sterpaia and Rimigliano Coastal Parks, Archaeological Park of Baratti and Populonia, **San Silvestro Archaeomineral Park**, **Montioni Nature Park**, and Poggio Neri Forest Park). The 450 hectares of the San Silvestro Archaeological and Mineral Park on the hills to the north of Campiglia Marittima has paths that allow you to explore the mines and quarries that have been exploited here since the Etruscan age.

**Rocca San Silvestro** was a village built in the 10th c. dedicated to mining (copper, lead and silver) and metal-casting. *Parchi Val di Cornia, via Lerario 90, Piombino. For information 🖉 0565 22 64 45, www.parchivaldicornia.it.*

**San Vincenzo** is a well-known and well-equipped seaside resort, with a sandy beach 5 km long. Following the coastal road, you come to **Populonia★**.

**Baratti and Populonia Archaeological Park** encloses the necropolis of the Etruscan town Pupluna. Dominated by the acropolis, it dates from the Iron Age (9th-8th c. BC), when the Gulf of Baratti was the site of large necropolises and the local economy was based on smelting the iron and silver deposits mined on the Isle of Elba and in the hills around Campiglia. When exploitation of the iron deposits on Elba was increased in the 4th c., the necropolis became covered by slag, which was only removed last century. The earliest tombs were of the shaft, trench or chamber types, while the later ones were mound tombs influenced by the Orient. *For information* 𝄞 *0565 22 64 45, www.parchival-dicornia.it.*

## Piombino

Piombino tends to be dismissed as simply a port or industrial town but, in addition to its tourist interest, it has an Etruscan past to which a museum, Populonia and Baratti are testaments. Piazza Verdi is the point of departure for a walk in the town centre, where the Rivellino (1447, Piombino's ancient main gateway) and the 13th-c. Tower stand. The 15th-c. Municipal Palace faces onto Corso Vittorio Emanuele. Dating from 1377, the Cathedral of **Sant'Antimo** contains tombs of the Appiani family, once lords of Piombino, and a 15th-c. font. Next to the cathedral is a Renaissance cloister. At the end of Corso Vittorio Emanuele, there is a fine **view★** of the Tuscan archipelago from the prow-shaped Piazza Bovio. Leave the square on the right and head down to the port, where you will arrive at the Fonti dei Canali fountains attributed to the sculptor Nicola Pisano. The **citadel**, built between 1465 and 1470, features a marble water tank, in front of which stands the Renaissance Chapel of Sant'Anna built for the Appiani family. Inside there is an archaeological museum exhibiting finds from Baratti and Populonia.

Proceeding towards Via Leonardo da Vinci, you will see the bastions of the city walls. To the east of Piazza Verdi (*Piazza del Castello*) the Cassero (8th-16th c.) and Fortress built for Cosimo I de' Medici in 1552 are still visible.

There are frequent connections to the **Isle of Elba** from Piombino.

## 3. CHIANTI

Chianti is an area that lies between Florence and Siena. It is bounded to the east by the hills of Chianti that overlook the river Arno and stretches west and south into the Greve, Pesa, Elsa and Arbia valleys. Synonymous around the world with Tuscan wine, **Chianti** is produced in a large zone that spreads beyond its geographical boundaries: it incorporates Monte Albano to the south of Pistoia, the hills to the south of the province of Pisa, the upland area of Mugello, the slopes of Pratomagno along the Arno, the surrounds of Arezzo, the west bank of the Chiana valley, the area of Montepulciano, the southern part of the province of Siena around Montalcino, Montagnola to the west of Siena, and the area around San Gimignano. The Chianti appellation overlies the specific subzones of Colli Aretini, Colli Fiorentini, Colli Senesi, Colline Pisane, Montalbano, Montespertoli and Rufina, which correspond approximately to the geographic areas of the same names. The central production area, known as **Chianti Classico** (which represents the municipalities that founded the Chianti League in the 15th c.) coincides almost perfectly with the geographic territory from which it took its name. Classico wines are made following a different set of regulations from the "non-Classico" Chiantis. The grapes used to make Chianti are Sangiovese, Canaiolo Nero, Trebbiano Toscano and Malvasia Toscana.

However, Chianti is not only covered with vineyards. In spring especially, nature adorns this region of the countryside with a tapestry of colours and forms: the red of the poppies, the violet-blue of the irises, the silvery green of the olive trees, and the dark green of the chestnut, durmast and fir woods. Whenever the fancy takes you, halt the car, sit at a village table and order a *bruschetta* with a glass of Chianti.

The itineraries below each follow, to a greater or lesser extent, the **Via Chiantigiana** (SR 222).

## In the heart of the Chianti League

*Itinerary of approximately 150 km from Florence to Impruneta. Leave Florence on the Via Senese towards Galluzzo.*

## Certosa del Galluzzo★★

*The charterhouse stands on the right as you leave Galluzzo on the Siena road. Guided visits 10-11 and 15-17 (Sun. only aftern.), closed Mon.and public hols., ℘ 055 20 49 226, www.certosadifirenze. it.* Founded in the 14th c. by the Florentine banker Niccolò Acciaiuoli, the building was repeatedly transformed up to the 17th c. A monumental flight of steps leads to the monastic buildings and Palazzo Acciaiuoli, which is now a **picture gallery** decorated with frescoes by Pontormo (1523). Looking onto a large 16th-c. square is the church, which is divided into two parts to separate the Carthusians from the lay brothers. The monks' church dates from the 14th c., though the decoration and stalls are from the 16th. To reach the underground chapels where the Acciaiuoli family members are buried pass through the Gothic Chapel of Santa Maria *(on the right)*. To the left of the church, the parlour, where the monks had the right to talk for an hour a week, leads to the chapterhouse, the location of the magnificent tomb of Leonardo Buonafé sculpted by Francesco di Giuliano da Sangallo in 1550. Beneath the elegant arches the large Renaissance cloister is lined by 18 monks' cells *(one can be visited)*.

*Pass through Tavarnuzze and drive to Sant'Andrea in Percussina.* The road at first takes you through woods but then opens out progressively to allow sight of

## The Antinori family

The Antinori family has been making wine for over six hundred years, since Giovanni di Piero Antinori became part of the Arte Fiorentina dei Vinattieri in 1385. Throughout its long history, spanning 26 generations, the family has always managed the business personally, and with unwavering respect for tradition and the land. The two regions with which the Marchesi Antinori are associated are Tuscany and Umbria. Chianti Classico, in the heart of Tuscany, is the location of both the Tignanello estate, after which the famous wine is named, and the estate of Badia a Passignano, where the Sangiovese grapes produce the Chianti Classico Riserva of the same name. Guada al Tasso, near to Bolgheri on the coast of the Tyrrhenian Sea, is where Antinori makes Bolgheri Superiore. And finally in Umbria, close to the Tuscan border and only a few kilometres from Orvieto, stands the beautiful medieval fortress Castello della Sala, where Antinori produces great white wines. *The estates are open to the public. Direct sales of all the company's products are made at the Bottega di Passignano, Via Passignano 33, Loc.* **Badia a Passignano** 🍷, *Tavernelle Val di Pesa, ℘ 055 80 71 278 (see the list of addresses in the Notes). The registered office of Marchesi Antinori Srl is in Piazza Antinori 3a in Florence, ℘ 055 23 59 876, www.antinori.it, antinori@antinori.it.*

*Chianti vineyards*

the first vineyards. As you pass through **Sant'Andrea in Percussina** you will pass the Albergaccio di Machiavelli (*today a restaurant*) on the left. This is where Niccolò Machiavelli lived after being exiled from Florence when the Medici returned. He was punished for having served the Republic of Florence between the years 1498 and 1512, during the years the Medici were themselves in exile. It was here he wrote *The Prince* in 1513, and was obliged to wait until 1526, a year before his death, before being allowed to return to Florence.

## San Casciano in Val di Pesa ♟

Situated on a rise between the Greve and Pesa valleys, San Casciano still has some of the town walls it built between the 14th and 16th c. Leaving Piazza Orazio Pierozzi (*at the junction between Via Roma and Via IV Novembre*), take Via Morrochesi to the Church della Misericordia in Romanesque-Gothic style. Inside there are interesting Tuscan artworks from the 14th and 15th c. The **Museum of Sacred Art** can be seen in the Church of Santa Maria del Gesù on Via Roma (Tuscan paintings and sculptures, goldsmithery and altar furniture). A little further on there is the large public garden in Piazza della Repubblica and the remains of fortifications (a 14th-c. tower). The terrace gives a fine **view** over the Pesa valley. *Via Lucardesi, for information ✆ 055 82 56 385, www.chiantivaldarno.it.*

### The Chianti League

At the start of the 13th c. Florence created the **Lega del Chianti** (Chianti League), which was a military association with the aim of opposing Siena's territorial claims. The emblem of the league, whose members were the towns of Castellina, Gaiole and Radda, was a black cockerel, which today has been taken as the logo of the Chianti Classico winemaking consortium.

The league members, referred to as *terzieri*, were administered by a podestà, at first based in Castellina but from 1415 in Radda. In the mid-16th c., when the Republic of Siena was united with the Grand Duchy of Tuscany, the League was disbanded as there was no longer any reason for it to exist.

Follow the S 2 road into the Pesa valley for several kilometres. Before entering Sambuca, turn left to Badia a Passignano.

Founded in 1049, the splendid Vallumbrosan Abbey in **Badia a Passignano**★★ *Visits Sun. by appointment, ✆ 055 80 70 171 (After long restoration visible the fresco by Domenico Ghirlandaio)* stands on top of a gentle hill covered with vines and cypresses. Seen from afar, the embattled buildings, towers and few houses in the village suggest a fortified village rather than an abbey. You reach the Church of San Michele up a ramp lined by cypresses. The façade is topped by a marble statue of St Michael Archangel (13th c.). Inside there are 16th-c. paintings by Domenico Cresti, who was known as Passignano after his place of birth.

Return to the S 2, drive on through Sambuca and **Tavernelle**, after which you will see the hills of Florence to the right and the Pesa valley to the left.

## Barberino Val d'Elsa ♟

The upper fortified centre of Barberino still stands. Porta Senese, the only entrance to the town in the 13th-14th c. walls, leads to Barberino's high street, Via Francesco da Barberino. Here, immediately on the left, is a beautiful projecting house and a little further on Piazza Barberini. On the right in the square is Palazzo Pretorio, lined with coats of arms, and the rectilinear apse of the church beside it. Walk around the church to see the wonderful view over the Pesa valley from the top of the steps.

When you leave Barberino, leave the S 2 also and take the road to **Sant'Appiano**, from which you are given superb **views**★★ over the vineyards and olive groves. Constructed in the 10th and 11th c., the pre-Romanesque Church of **Sant'Appiano**★ has retained its original apse and a part of the left aisle. These were spared from the destruction wrought by the collapse of the bell tower in 1171. The rest was rebuilt at the end of the 12th c. Standing in front of the façade are 4 small pillars, the vestiges of an octagonal baptistery destroyed by an earthquake at the start of the 19th c. To the right of the church, a group of buildings rings a picturesque cloister from which you can access the **Antiquarium** situated at the rear

*Montefioralle, splendid examples of rural architecture*

of the site. *Open Sat. and Sun. 15-18.30, ℘ 055 80 52 290), www.chiantivaldarno.it.*

Continuing along the road, after passing through a winding, wooded stretch, you will see the village of **Linari** on a rise on the right. Close to the church is a small restored castle. *Take the S 429 in the direction of Castellina in Chianti.* As you climb into the hills of Chianti, the landscape begins to become harsher despite vines still covering much of the land. The road becomes particularly twisty when it reaches the crest of the massif; you then pass through woodlands that occasionally clear to allow glimpses of the hills beneath.

## Castellina in Chianti★ 🍷

Situated on the border between Florence and Siena in a strategic position between the Elsa, Pesa and Arbia valleys, Castellina in Chianti passed alternately between the two powers. Opposite the Neo-Romanesque Church del Santissimo Salvatore at the entrance to the village lies the odd **Via delle Volte★**: set against the walls, it allowed the fortifications to be toured on horseback. Leaving the street and returning down Via Ferruccio, you pass before the imposing Palazzo Ugolino (*no. 26*) built in the Renaissance era, which now accommodates good quality wine shops. Opposite, an alley takes you to the 15th-c. crenellated **fort** (*restored*). On the ground floor two display cases exhibit objects found in the Etruscan necropolis at Poggino a Fonteruoli (6th c. BC). The second floor offers views over the surrounding countryside.

**Radda in Chianti** 🍷 is a long medieval town that, with Castellina and Gaiole, was one of the three members of the ancient Chianti League, of which Radda became the chief town in 1415. It still has one side of its fortified walls and the 15th-c. Municipal Palace, which boasts a fresco by the Florentine school beneath a porch. The pretty fortified village of **Volpaia★** 6 km to the north is a good place to enjoy a fine meal

*Return to the S 222 and follow the upper Pesa valley and head for Panzano.*

The road winds and falls through the Pesa valley on its way to **Panzano**. Close to the village the landscape opens up and becomes more agreeable. Panzano can be seen from a distance on the left due to the elevated position of its church and bell tower.

## Greve in Chianti★

This large town stands in the bottom of the Greve valley. At its centre lies Piazza Matteotti, a gracious funnel-shaped plaza lined with irregular porticoes. At the narrow end of the piazza stands the small Church of Santa Croce, rebuilt last century. Its Renaissance interior includes a triptych of the *Madonna and Child with Saints* in the apse to the left of the choir, and, on the right wall, a small *Annunciation* by Bicci di Lorenzo.

Take a detour (*2 km west*) to the exquisitely pretty village of **Montefioralle★** to admire its circular street lined by medieval houses and towers (splendid examples of rural architecture) and the picturesque Gothic Church of Santo Stefano. Amerigo Vespucci was born in the house adorned with a V on the façade. The countryside between Greve and Strada is one of the most luxuriant in Chianti. This attractive route follows the crest of the hills and gives **broad views★★** over Chianti's vineyards.

An obligatory place of passage in the past to reach Chianti from Florence (from which its name is derived), **Strada in Chianti** has only retained the Romanesque Church of San Cristoforo of its historical buildings. The façade, adorned with a rose window, is preceded by a three-arch porch resting on two elegant columns.

*Pass through Ferrone to reach the Greve valley. A road lined by cypresses, firs and durmast leads to Impruneta (for approximately 500 m the road is not paved).*

### Impruneta ♟

This pleasant little town is known for its terracotta, and it is said that Brunelleschi demanded tiles from Impruneta to cover the duomo in Florence. The five arches of the Renaissance portico of the **Basilica of Santa Maria dell'Impruneta★** open onto the large central square. Only the 13th-c. bell tower remains from the Romanesque period. The interior has two kiosks designed by Michelozzo on either side of the choir. The one on the right is lined with glazed ceramics made by the Della Robbia family, while the one on the left houses the famous painting of the Madonna, thought to date to the 13th c. The building was seriously damaged by bombs in 1944 and rebuilt to match the parts unaffected. The **Treasure** of the basilica – resulting from centuries of worship of the Madonna and the generosity of great families of Florence, such as the Medici – comprises reliquaries, vestments, altar cloths, holy vessels, pieces of goldsmithery, numerous votive offerings and a fine collection of illuminated liturgical volumes. *(Open Sat. and Sun. 9-13 and 16-19, Nov.-Mar. 9-13 and 15-18, www.basilicaimpruneta.org)*

## From Siena to the mountains of Chianti

*Itinerary of 75 km from Siena to Castelnuovo Berardenga.*

Between Siena and Castellina the Via Chiantigiana (*the S 222*) passes through woodlands of small durmasts and firs, leaving little room for vines. The hills are fairly gentle as far as **Quercegrossa** and the road follows the rolling profile of the countryside, then slowly climbs, giving splendid **views★★** over the Staggia valley to the left.

Once past Castellina and Radda in Chianti (*see above*), the uniform rows of vines begin to alternate with dark patches of tree-lined hills, creating an admirably tended landscape.

### Badia Coltibuono★

This 11th-c. Vallumbrosan abbey was enlarged in both the 15th and 18th c. but abandoned by the monks after Napoleon suppressed the monasteries in his edict of 1810. It was then turned into a farm. The Romanesque church, crenellated bell tower and surrounding buildings give an idea of its previous splendour. From the apse there is a lovely **panorama★** of the Arno valley and the wooded heights of Pratomagno. *Guided visit of the cellars and Italian gardens Mar., Apr. and Oct. 14.30-17.30, May-Sept. 14.30-18.30 ℘ 0577 74 481, www.coltibuono.com.*

As far as Gaiole the road remains winding and the countryside wooded. **Gaiole in Chianti ♟** is an essentially modern town situated in a small valley surrounded by vine-clad hillocks.

*Follow the S 408 for 5 km, then turn left in the direction of Brolio Castle.*

You come to a farming area planted with vines and olives, overlooked by the enormous crenellated bulk of Brolio Castle.

Chianti fiasco

*Brolio Castle and its surroundings*

## Brolio Castle★★

*Drive for 1 km from the entrance to the castle gate. Open Apr.-Oct. 10-19 (7 Oct.-24 Oct. 10-18, 25 Oct.-8 Dec. 10-17) ℘ 0577 73 01, www.ricasoli.it.* Since the 11th c. this large embattled and still inhabited castle has belonged to the Ricasoli family. It was here that the illustrious Italian politician Bettino Ricasoli died in 1880. Dismantled in 1478, it was rebuilt in 1484 by the Florentines and greatly restored in the 19th c. in brick. The pentagonal fortified walls were probably the work of Giuliano da Sangallo when young. You can enter and make a tour of the castle wall by passing through the garden, and then following the patrol walkway. The Chapel of San Jacopo stands adjacent to the castle itself and is where the tombs of the Ricasoli family lie in the crypt. The south wall gives **magnificent views-★★★** over the Arbia valley to the towers of Siena and peak of Monte Amiata, and, low down to the west, the buildings of the castle winemaking buildings.

To go down into the valley, follow the unpaved road that curves widely through the vineyard with the castle on the right. Pass the farm buildings, take the S 484 right and continue past the property entrance.

The route remains relatively wooded until you come close to San Gusme, where the landscape opens up again.

## San Gusme ♆

Situated near the source of the river Ombrone, this small farming town is built entirely in stone and has conserved its medieval appearance unaltered with its walls, gates, narrow streets and occasional arch. The town enjoys views over the province of Siena to Monte Amiata, Radicofani fort on a flat-topped rise and, in the foreground, the gentle undulations of the grey hills of Siena known as the *crete senesi*.

## Castelnuovo Berardenga ♆

The southernmost town in Chianti, Castelnuovo Berardenga stands on a hill overlooking the upper Ombrone valley. As you turn around the town, you come to the majestic **Villa Chigi★** on the south side, built in the early 19th c. over medieval foundations. The villa has a lovely park with centuries-old trees. Next to a harmoniously proportioned square with a central fountain stands the Church of Santi Giusto e Clemente, with a Neoclassical porch and a small, free-standing bell tower. Inside is a work by Giovanni di Paolo, a *Madonna and Child with Angels* (1426). *For information and reservation ℘ 0577 35 13 03.*

As you leave Castelnuovo, marvellous **views★★** are to be had over the bare hills of the Sienese countryside. The famous battle won by the Ghibellines of Siena over the Guelphs of Florence on 4 September 1260 took place near **Montaperti** *(8 km west towards Siena)*.

## 4. SAN GIMIGNANO

This is the zone in which **Vernaccia di San Gimignano DOCG** is produced from the grape of the same name. This great white wine has a nose redolent of apples, bitter almond and flowers, and an almondy flavour with a bitter finish.

*Medieval town of San Gimignano*

## San Gimignano★★★ ▼

If you pass through Porta San Giovanni and head up to Piazza della Cisterna, you are likely to wonder if by some miracle you have been dropped into the Middle Ages. The 14 unadorned towers that characterise the skyline are what remain of the 70 the town once boasted. The solid **Porta San Giovanni** (13th c.), built with a turret and Sienese arch, lends its name to the street flanked by striking medieval houses. Before you arrive at the central square, note the remains of the Pisan Romanesque façade of the 13th-c. Church of San Francesco.

**Piazza della Cisterna★★** has an irregular plan, and herringbone brick paving as was customary in the Middle Ages. It is lined by plain 13th- and 14th-c. townhouses, some of which boast a tower. The square is named after the 13th-c. well that stands at its centre. On the south side of the square Casa Salvestrini (*occupied by a hotel*) dates from the 13th c. Palazzo Tortoli stands at the start of Via del Castello with two orders of twin Gothic windows (14th c.). The Devil's Tower is almost opposite. The north-west corner, which leads into Piazza del Duomo, is overlooked by the twin towers of the Ardinghelli family, the most powerful Guelph supporters in the town.

**Piazza del Duomo★★**, which lies next to Piazza della Cisterna, is framed by the austere façade of the collegiate church, ancient palaces and seven imposing towers.

**Basilica of Santa Maria Assunta★** – this 12th-c. Romanesque building was enlarged by Giuliano da Maiano, the presbytery in particular. The façade was notably restored in the 19th c. and the interior is completely lined with frescoes. The *Martyrdom of St Sebastian* (1465) by the Florentine artist Benozzo Gozzoli is in the lower section of the counter-façade; on either side there are two wooden statues by Jacopo della Quercia (1420). In the upper section, the *Universal Judgement* painted by Taddeo di Bartolo from Siena in 1393 runs over onto the first span of the nave. The left aisle has a cycle of colourful and dynamic **frescoes★** by Bartolo di Fredi (14th c.) that illustrates the Old Testament. The cycle of **frescoes★★** of the New Testament in the right aisle was executed around 1340 by Barna da Siena, who was employed in the workshop of Simone Martini. The artist succeeded in combining the elegant brushwork and chromatic delicacy typical of Sienese Gothic with a dramatic tension and humanity clearly deriving from Giotto. The **Chapel of Santa Fina** at the end of the right aisle is dedicated to the local saint, Serafina di Ciardi (d. 1254), and was painted by Giuliano da Maiano in 1468. The well-proportioned **altar★** is by Benedetto da Maiano and the **frescoes★** by Domenico Ghirlandaio (1475).

**Piazza Pecori** (*reached down a vaulted passage to the left of the Collegiate Church*) is a fascinatingly simple square by the Baptistery Loggia, part of a 14th-c. cloister in which Domenico Ghirlandaio painted the elegant fresco of the Annunciation in 1482.

Dating from the 13th-14th c., **Palazzo del Popolo**★ is dominated by the Torre Grossa. Inside there is a small two-level courtyard closed by a colonnade. An outside stairway leads to the **Civic Museum**★ (*Annunciation* by Filippino Lippi). The Council Room was where Dante gave an important speech in 1330 in favour of the Guelph league in Tuscany. One of the frescoes is a magnificent *Majesty* by Lippo Memmi (1317) that was restored around 1467 by Benozzo Gozzoli. Before visiting the second floor, a stairway on the right leads to the **Torre Grossa**, from where a marvellous **panorama**★★ is given of the town and surrounding countryside.

The 13th-c. **Palazzo del Podestà** in Piazza del Duomo is adorned with a large loggia surmounted by an arcade. Standing over them all is the Torre Rognosa (51 m) with the 13th-c. Palazzo Chigi and its tower beside it.

Walk down the pretty **Via San Matteo**, turn right into Via XX Settembre, and then left into Via delle Romite. The Romanesque-Gothic 12th-c. Church of **Sant'Agostino** has a sombre exterior. Inside the choir is covered by 17 **frescoes**★★ by Benozzo Gozzoli that illustrate scenes from the life of St Augustine. To the left of the entrance the Chapel of San Bartolo has a fine marble altar (1494) by Benedetto da Maiano.

## Certaldo★★

*13 km north*. You have the choice of visiting Certaldo Alto (Upper Certaldo) by funicular or *pedibus calcantibus* (on foot). Only a few minutes of effort are required, which are generously compensated by the red brick medieval town where Boccaccio was born. His house has been transformed into a museum (*open 9.30-13.30 and 14.30-19, Nov.-Mar. 16.30, closed Tue., ☎ 0571 66 42 08, www. casaboccaccio.it*). You can also visit the Church of San Jacopo where the writer was buried, and Palazzo Pretorio, which was rebuilt in the 16th c.

## San Vivaldo★

*17 km north-west*. A community of Franciscans settled here in 1500 to honour the body of St Vivaldo, who died here in 1320. In 15 years they built a monastery and a series of chapels (only 17 remain) that are miniature reproductions of the shrines of Jerusalem. The chapels of the

**Sacro Monte** have painted terracottas with almost life-size scenes from the Passion to Pentecost. *Open Nov.-Mar. 14-17, Apr.-Oct. 15-19, Sun. and holidays 10-19, ☎ 0571 69 92 67, www.sanvivaldo intoscana.com.*

# 5. THE PROVINCE OF AREZZO

The province of Arezzo has a wide range of wines, and the appellations **Cortona** and **Valdichiana**.

## Arezzo★★

An impression of strength and serenity is given of Arezzo in the frescoes by Piero della Francesca (1415-92), and which still comes to mind as you walk down from Piazza Grande, watch the medieval joust (the "Giostra del Saracino"), or remember Roberto Benigni on his bicycle in *Life is Beautiful*.

**Basilica of San Francesco** – this large 14th-c. Gothic building was constructed for the Franciscans to preach in. It was transformed in the 17th-18th c. but later returned to its original simplicity during careful restoration. In their capacity as Custodians of the Holy Land, the Franciscans used to worship the Holy Cross in particular and asked Piero della Francesca to decorate the choir of their church (the Bacci Chapel) with a cycle of **frescoes**★★★ dedicated to the Legend of the True Cross. Executed between 1452 and 1466, they are considered one of the greatest masterpieces of the Renaissance. *Via di San Francesco. Visits with obligatory reservation 9-19, Sat. 9-18 (17.30 in win.), Sun. 13-18 (17.30 in win.), ☎ 0575 35 27 27, www.pierodellafranc esca.it or www.museistaliarezzo.it.*

In **Piazza Grande**★ you can see medieval houses with crenellated towers, the Romanesque apse with arcades and loggias of Santa Maria della Pieve, the Palazzo del Tribunale (late 18th c.), the Palazzo della Fraternità dei Laici (Gothic in the lower section, Renaissance in the upper), and the Logge del Vasari (16th c.). Another bell tower, called the "Tower of the 100 Holes" due to the 40 twin-light windows included to lighten its appearance, stands over the Romanesque **Santa Maria della Pieve**★★, construction of which began in the mid 12th c. and continued till the 14th. It was remodelled in the 16th c., by Vasari in particular. The Pisan Romanesque façade

has a triple order of columns with differing decorative motifs. The high altar boasts an outstanding polyptych (1320) by Pietro Lorenzetti from Siena.

*Continue and take Via Ricasoli on the left.*

A number of old houses, palaces and Gothic towers line **Via dei Pileati**, which runs along the façade of Santa Maria della Pieve. On the corner close by stands the Palazzo Pretorio (14th-15th c.) decorated with coats of arms of the podestà.

The **Duomo** (1278–1511, the façade remodelled in Neo-Gothi style in the early 20th c.) has an elegant Romanesque-Gothic portal on the right from the early 14th c. The **artworks★** inside include a fine fresco of the Magdalene by Piero della Francesca.

*Continue down Via Ricasoli and turn right into Via Sasso Verde.*

The 13th-c. Church of **San Domenico** was built in Gothic style and restored in modern times. It has an asymmetric façade and several frescoes from the school of Arezzo and the Sienese school of Duccio. There is a superb **Crucifix★★** by Cimabue on the high altar.

## Valdarno, Val di Chiana and Cortona

*Itinerary of approximately 150 km from Arezzo to Castiglion Fiorentino.*

### Pieve di Gropina★

*Leave Arezzo to the north-west and pass through* **Castiglion Fibocchi** 🍷 *and* **San Giustino Valdarno** 🍷. *On the first slopes of the Pratomagno chain, at a height slightly above the Arno valley, stands the lovely Romanesque Church of San Pietro (12th c.) surrounded by a handful of houses that form the hamlet of Gropina.*

The elaborate **sculptural decoration★** inside is unequalled in the Casentino area. The capitals and pulpit of the right aisle are late 12th-c. in archaic Romanesque, whereas the capitals in the left aisle are later and perhaps by Emilian workshops. Indeed, until 1191 Gropina was under the authority of the Abbey of Nonantola, near Modena.

*Head for Terranuova and Montevarchi.*

Famous for its chicken market and wines from the Arezzo hills, the historic centre of **Montevarchi** is laid out on streets that follow the logic of the parallel arches at the sides of Via Roma. In Piazza Varchi (*in Via Roma*), the 18th-c. Collegiate Church of San Lorenzo holds the relic of the "Holy Milk" of the Madonna in the shrine on the high altar. Above it looms the dramatic sculpture of the *Madonna in Glory* by Giovanni Baratta.

Continue on the SR 69 south through Pergine Valdarno, then turn right towards **Civitella in Val di Chiana** ♟, which looks down on the Chiana valley from a dominant position, and is the home of the DOC wine of the same name.

*Continue south to Monte San Savino.*

## Monte San Savino★

This is birthplace of the sculptor and architect Andrea Contucci, called Sansovino (1470-1529). A medieval town probably of Etruscan origin, it is laid out about a long central street that at either end passes through the walls of the ancient Cassero Fort. When you enter Porta Fiorentina, you find yourself on Corso Antonio da Sangallo. An obelisk erected in 1644 stands in Piazza Gamurrini close to the gate. Next to the ancient castle built by the Sienese in 1383 is the modest 17th-c. Church of Santa Chiara, where there are two terracottas by Andrea Sansovino.

The lines of the majestic **Loggia dei Mercanti★**, attributed to Sansovino, are enhanced by the use of grey sandstone. Opposite the loggia is the **Municipal Palace★**, built in 1515 by the elder Sangallo.

The 14th-c. Church of **Sant'Agostino** (enlarged over later centuries) has an elegant Gothic portal and a rose window whose glasswork was designed by Guillaume de Marcillat. The interior has some early 15th-c. frescoes. A small cloister on the left of the church is lined by an open arcade designed by Sansovino, who was also responsible for the portal of the **Baptistery of San Giovanni**.

About 2 km east of Monte San Savino stands the Marian sanctuary of **Santa Maria delle Vertighe** of the 11th c.

Further west on the SS 73 is **Gargonza**, a silent and tiny village that has been turned into tourist accommodation. It is dominated by a massive tower and has a tiny 13th-c. church. Returning to Monte San Savino and continuing south you reach **Lucignano★**, a lovely town in the form of an ellipse. Set against the walls, the remains of the 14th-c. castle face the late 16th-c. Collegiate Church of San Michele, in which the monumental Baroque altar was designed by Andrea Pozzo. Passing the church on the left, you come to Piazza del Tribunale, at the end of which stands the Municipal Palace. Beside it, the Romanesque façade of the Church of San Francesco is built in alternating rows of black and white stone. Inside there are fine 14th-c. frescoes.

*Head east from Lucignano towards Foiano della Chiana and Cortona.*

## Cortona★★ ♟

Perched up high on the rocky slope of a hill overlooking the Chiana valley, close to Lake Trasimeno and at the southern tip of Tuscany, Cortona occupies a splendid natural terrace. Loved by artists since the 14th c., Cortona was the birth-place of Luca Signorelli (1450-1523), who was a precursor of Michelangelo in the sculptural plasticity of his paintings and his dramatic temperament, Pietro da Cortona (1596-1669), a painter, architect and master of Roman Baroque, and Gino Severini (1883-1969), a leading Futurist. Brother Elia, the first companion and disciple of St Francis, is buried in Cortona beneath the presbytery of the Church of San Francesco. The walk starts in **Piazza Garibaldi**, where there is a magnificent **view★★** over the Chiana valley as far as Montepulciano and Lake Trasimeno. Take Via Santa Margherita to the Church of San Domenico, an early 15th-c. Gothic building with a *Madonna and Child with Angels and Saints* by Luca Signorelli in the right apse, and a *Madonna and Child between two Dominicans* by Beato Angelico close to the left apse. Past the church there are more views of Lake Trasimeno.

Return to Piazza Garibaldi and take Via Nazionale, the only flat street in the town. Pretty little streets run off it, generally no more than flights of steps.

*Via Nazionale comes out into Piazza della Repubblica.*

The **Municipal Palace** (*www.comunedicortona.it*), built in the 13th c., was completed 200 years later with the clock tower and a flight of steps on Piazza della Repubblica. The Council Room overlooks Piazza Signorelli, onto which the building's original façade faced.

**Palazzo Pretorio★** was built in the 13th c. and later remodelled: the façade on Piazza Signorelli dates to the early 17th c. while the right side, adorned with the coats of arms of the various podestà, is Gothic. The building is the home of the **MAEC★** (Museum of the Etruscan Academy of Cortona), which unites Etruscan, Roman, Egyptian, medieval and Renaissance exhibits. MAEC - Museo dell'Accademia Etrusca e della Città di Cortona, *Piazza Signorelli 9. Open 10-19 (Nov.-Mar. 17, closed Mon.), ☎ 0575 63 04 15, www.cortonamaec.org.*

*Cortona, overlooking the Val di Chiana*

Bounded by the city's bastions, **Piazza del Duomo** gives views over the valley. The duomo is of Romanesque origin but was remodelled in the Renaissance. It has many 16th- and 17th-c. paintings and interesting furnishings.

Facing the duomo is the Church of Gesù; it has a lovely sculpted ceiling (1536), and the art collections of the **Diocesan museum★★** (works by Beato Angelico, Luca Signorelli and artists of the Sienese school). The lower church has 16th-c. frescoes and a beautiful polychrome terracotta *Pietà* from the same period. *Open 10-19 (Nov.-Mar. Fri.-Sun. 10-17, 25 Dec.-6 Jan. daily), ☎ 0575 62 810, www.cortonamia.com.*

*Return to Piazza Signorelli and walk down Via Berrettini.*

The tiny, narrow Church of San Cristoforo is thought to date from the late 12th c. *Take Via San Niccolò.* The 15th-c. Church of San Niccolò has two works by Luca Signorelli: a *Madonna and Child with Saints* (on the left as you enter), and a *Deposition* (on the high altar).

*Turn into Via Santa Margherita.*

The **Sanctuary of Santa Margherita** was built in the 19th c. in the upper section of the city. It incorporates the very unusual Gothic tomb (1362) of the saint (*to the left of the presbytery*), which features tall, pointed pediments. To the right of the presbytery is a lovely 13th-c. Christ. In the square below the sanctuary there are **views★★** over the city, the valley and Lake Trasimeno.

On the right in Via Santa Margherita there are mosaics by Severini of the stations on the Via Crucis.

### Sanctuary of Santa Maria delle Grazie al Calcinaio★★

*3 km south. Follow the signs towards Camucia. (For information on visits, ☎ 349 12 15 401, www.calcinaio.it)* Despite its very poor condition, this church built between 1485 and 1513 in the style of Brunelleschi by Francesco di Giorgio Martini has great architectural elegance and proportions. In the oculus of the façade the remarkable window (1516) by Guillaume de Marcillat is of the *Madonna della Misericordia*, whose figure can also be seen in a small 15th-c. fresco above the high altar.

### Eremo di Le Celle

*3.5 km north-east in the direction of Portole.* The drive to the hermitage is a pleasant one through the Chiana valley. After returning from Rome, where the pope had recognised his rule (1210), St Francis passed through Cortona and chose Le Celle for his first community. The place was ideal for its silence and simplicity, and he himself lived there after receiving the stigmata. Consisting of buildings that spill down the slope of Monte Egidio, the monastery (now occupied by the Capuchins) can be visited, including the cell behind the altar where Francis lived, and the oratory of his first companions. ☎ 0575 60 33 62.

*Take the SR 71 towards Arezzo.*

### Montecchio Vesponi Castle★

*For information on visits* ☎ *333 76 76 408, www.castellodimontecchio.it.* Standing directly above the road to Castiglion Fiorentino, the castle is striking for its crenellated walls, eight small towers and 30 m tall keep. Inside there used to be several houses, a church and municipal palace, but of which today there is no trace. This, the largest fortress in the Chiana valley, retained its military importance until the 17th c.

### Castiglion Fiorentino

The name may seem surprising, seeing that Florence is not close, but over its history the town bounced back and forth between Arezzo, Perugia and Florence, during which time it was also known as Castiglione Aretino and Castiglione Perugino. Its current name occurred when it passed definitively to Florence. The heart of the town is Piazza Municipio lined by the 16th-c. Municipal Palace, and a 16th-c. portico called the Logge del Vasari, not because it was designed by Giorgio Vasari but for its architectural style. The back wall is studded with coats of arms and opens through three loggias onto the Church of San Giuliano and the Chio valley. From here you can walk up to the Castle and the picture gallery in the **Chapel of Sant'Angelo**. *For information on visits* ☎ *0575 65 94 57, www.museicastiglionfiorentino.it.*

## 6. THE VINO NOBILE DI MONTEPULCIANO

The Vino Nobile di Montepulciano is produced in the municipality of Montepulciano in the province of Siena. It is made from Sangiovese grapes, locally called Prugnolo Gentile, to which a small percentage of Canaiolo Nero is sometimes added.

### Montepulciano★★ 🍷

Built on the crest of a tufa hill between two valleys, in a **panoramic★★** and beautiful setting, Montepulciano is an enchanting and typically Renaissance little town. On the Porta al Prato you will see the coat of arms of Tuscany and the Marzocco column with the lion of Florence on top. Pass through the gate into **Via Roma** which is lined by interesting palazzi and churches. The lovely Palazzo Avignonesi at no. 91 is late Renaissance

(16th c.) and attributed to Vignola, while the palazzo of the antiquarian Bucelli at no. 73 has fragments of Etruscan and Roman plaques in its basement. Further on you come to the Church of Sant'Agostino (restored) with a Renaissance façade by Michelozzo (15th c.). Facing it is the Pulcinella Tower, with an automaton that strikes the hours.

Turn left into Via di Voltaia nel Corso at the Logge del Mercato: Palazzo Cervini at no. 21 is by the elder Sangallo. With its ashlar work and curved and triangular gables, it is a fine example of Florentine Renaissance style. Next, follow Via dell'Opio nel Corso and Via Poliziano (the poet Angelo Poliziano lived at no. 1) to Piazza Grande. At the end of Via Poliziano the Church of Santa Maria dei Servi has a *Madonna and Child* by Duccio di Buoninsegna.

**Piazza Grande★★** represents the centre of the town. Irregular in shape, it is lined by palaces of different styles that together form an architectural whole. The **Municipal Palace★** is in Gothic but was remodelled in the 15th c. by Michelozzo; it is similar to the Palazzo Vecchio in Florence. The immense **view★★★** from the top of the tower ranges over all the town and surrounding area. On the other side of the square stands **Palazzo Contucci** *(for information,* ☎ *0578 75 70 06, www.contucci.it),* which was begun in 1519 by the same Sangallo but only completed in the 18th c. The façade of the **Duomo di Santa Maria** (16th-17th c.) still has a rough face as the marble lining has not yet been added.

Opposite the duomo and to the right is the majestic Renaissance **Palazzo Nobili-Tarugi★**, attributed to Antonio the Elder. To the left, note the opening above the central portal to allow sight of who is arriving. Palazzo del Capitano stands beside Palazzo Tarugi. In the same square admire the griffins and lions supporting the arms of the Medici above the town's original **well★**.

Continuing along the main street, you come to Piazza San Francesco, from where a view is given over the surrounding countryside and Church of San Biagio. From Via del Poggiolo turn right into Via dell'Erbe, which returns you to the Logge del Mercato.

Countryside around Pienza

© Giancarlo Malandra/Shutterstock

**Madonna di San Biagio★★** – *In the lower part of the town, 2 km south-west. Leave through Porta al Prato and take the road for Chianciano, then turn right. For information, ☏ 0578 28 63 00, www. tempiosanbiagio.it.* This exquisite church built in golden travertine is a masterpiece by Antonio da Sangallo the Elder. It stands in a lovely setting at the centre of a grassy embankment overlooking the valley. Built on a Greek cross plan, it is crowned by a dome, while the main façade is flanked by two separate bell towers aligned with the arms of the cross. One is unfinished, the other has the traditional three orders. The elegant palazzo, the **Canonica**, stands in front of the church, with a marvellous open gallery on two orders.

### Sinalunga

*20 km north. Take the SP 17, then go left on the SP 135 as far as Torrita di Siena. Next take the SS 326 right.* The ancient town of Sinalunga looks down on the once marshy and malaria infested Chiana valley. The town, which extends notably towards the plain, is famous for its wine and breeding of **Chianina cattle**. The vast Piazza Garibaldi is lined by three churches built in the 16th-18th c. One, the Collegiate Church of San Martino, was built at the end of the 16th c. Now go to Piazza XX Settembre (*to the right of San Martino*) and take Via Mazzini to the town centre. Palazzo Pretorio (remodelled in several stages) is embellished with the bearings of the magistrates and coat of arms of the Medici, to whom the town passed in 1533.

### Pienza★★

*14 km west of Montepulciano.* After completing several diplomatic missions, Enea Silvio Piccolomini (1405-64) was elected pope in 1458 and took the name Pius II. Shortly after ascending the papal throne he asked the Florentine architect Bernardo Rossellino (1409-64), a pupil of Leon Battista Alberti, to transform his place of birth, the village Corsignano, into a small town. The result is Pienza, named after its illustrious founder Pius. Like in a painting of an ideal city, Pienza is characterised by a seemingly unreal, clean definition of lines. **Piazza Pio II★★** lies at the heart of Pienza, where the town's major monuments stand along its longitudinal axis. The **cathedral★**, finished in 1462, has a lovely Renaissance façade though the interior is Gothicizing. It holds a superb *Assumption* by Vecchietta. A beautiful **view★** over the Orcia valley can be seen from behind the cathedral. Facing the cathedral is the Municipal Palace which opens into a loggia on the ground floor. The other sides of the square are faced onto by the Bishop's Palace (restored in the 15th c.) and Palazzo Piccolomini, in front of which stands a large well. The design of **Palazzo Piccolomini★★**, Rossellini's masterpiece, was strongly influenced by that of Palazzo Rucellai in Florence. The three façades that look onto the town are similar but the one that faces over the Orcia valley has three orders of loggias and one of the first hanging gardens. The inner courtyard owes its elegance to its very slender Corinthian columns. *Open 10-18.30* *(mid-Oct.-mid-Mar. 16.30), closed working Tue., 7 Jan.-14 Feb. and 16-30 Nov., ☎ 0577 28 63 00, palazzopiccolominipienza.it.*

# 7. BRUNELLO DI MONTALCINO

An emblem of Tuscan winemaking, Brunello di Montalcino is produced exclusively within the boundaries of the municipality of Montalcino in the province of Siena. It is made solely with **Sangiovese** grapes, which are locally referred to as "Brunello". An intense ruby red tending to garnet, the wine gives off a bouquet of scents that range from undergrowth to red jam, and from grass to spices. Lingering and intense, it matures extremely well and only gives its best after many years ageing.

## Montalcino★ 🍷

This little town on the side of the hill has retained a part of its 13th-c. walls and a magnificent **castle★★** *(open 9-20, in winter 18. ☎ 0577 84 92 11)*, built in 1361, with high walls, panoramic walkway, and five towers, one of which provided accommodation for the officers and shelter for the nobility in times of siege. The general public, on the other hand, was obliged to seek safety in the large open area between the walls. The 13th-c. **Municipal Palace★** stands in a dominant position on Piazza del Popolo and is flanked by an arched loggia from the 14th-15th c. and crowned by a tall bell tower. The Church of **Sant'Egidio** behind the palace has a trussed roof and three arches. There is a large 16th-c. shrine in gilded wood near to the entrance.

The Romanesque-Gothic Church of **Sant'Agostino** was built in the 14th-c. It has a rose window in the façade and an elegant marble portal. Inside there are 14th-c. frescoes by the Sienese school.

## Abbey of Sant'Antimo★★

*10 km south. Open 10-19 (Oct. 18, Nov.-Mar. 10.30-17). Church ceremonies sung in Gregorian chants. ☎ 0577 28 63 00, www.antimo.it.*

Standing alone in a pleasant hilly **landscape★** of olives and cypresses, the abbey was founded in the 9th c. It reached its apogee three centuries later and had a church built, a splendid example of Cistercian Romanesque architecture of Burgundian inspiration, as is attested by the ambulatory with the chapels arranged around it. The portico and pilasters of the bell tower and the various façades are, however, typically Lombard. The large interior is bare, and the aisles are separated from the nave by columns with alabaster capitals. There are wooden beams over the nave and cross vaults over the aisles. The monastic buildings have partly disappeared.

## San Quirico d'Orcia and the Orcia valley★

*Itinerary of 25 km from Montalcino to Castiglione d'Orcia.* By taking the Via Cassia and roads that follow the undulating hills, you come to the Orcia valley and the village of **San Quirico**, which has stood on a small rise on the Via Francigena for centuries. It is still ringed by its 12th-c. bastions and monumental gates. The very beautiful **collegiate church★★**

Abbey of Sant'Antimo

(12th-13th c.) has an elegant, plain façade that contrasts with the magnificence of the Romanesque portal. Two Gothic portals stand on the right side. In the left transept you can see a lovely retable painted by Sano di Pietro (15th c.).

Palazzo Chigi was built in the 16th c. so that the rear of the building closes off Piazza della Collegiata. Via Poliziano is a small medieval street that runs along the right side of Porta dei Cappuccini, the five-sided 13th-c. tower. From Palazzo Chigi take Via Dante Alighieri to the main square where the Church of the Madonna and 16th-c. park of the "Horti Leonini" are situated.

Leaving San Quirico in a southerly direction (*take the Via Cassia S 2 signposted to Rome*) you begin a slow descent into the **Orcia valley** where the gently rolling hills are framed by the dark lines of trees and copses, or punctuated by the occasional solitary cypress. In spring the entire landscape is impressed with an atmosphere of gaiety by a carpet of poppies and yellow and pink field flowers. The solid **Orcia Fort** stands on the nearest rise, while in the distance you can make out Monte Amiata and Radicofani Fort.

*Turn right towards Bagno Vignoni before the bridge over the river Orcia; the road climbs steeply through the valley and offers excellent views of the nearby fort.*

**Bagno Vignoni★** is a small town that has been visited since Roman times for its thermal waters. It stands around an ancient and remarkable steaming **pool** that also serves as a town square. The Portico of Santa Caterina along one side commemorates the fact that St Catherine is said to have visited the town at the end of her life.

Follow the steaming channels that flow down into the valley. An unusual sight is provided by the Mill Park, which recalls the era (until about 1950) when the mills of Bagno Vignoni were able to work all year round powered by the thermal water.

*Turn back on your steps and recross the bridge over the Orcia. Approximately 350 m away, take the road on the right for Castiglione.* An ancient feud of the Aldobrandeschi family, **Castiglione d'Orcia** passed into the hands of Siena at the start of the 14th c. The central Piazza

Vecchietta commemorates Lorenzo di Pietro, the painter known as Vecchietta, who is thought to have been born in Castiglione around 1412. The triangular, sloping piazza is paved with bricks and cobbles and has at its centre a travertine cistern built in the 17th c. Lower down, a *Madonna and Child* by Pietro Lorenzetti can be seen in the parish church. Standing at the top of the village, only a few traces remain of the Aldobrandeschi Fort. A flight of steps leads up to an expanse above the walls where you can see the remains of the castle and enjoy the magnificent panorama of Monte Amiata and the Orcia valley.

**Tentennano Fort★** stands on a rise that drops sheer onto the Via Francigena and the Orcia gullies. The site has been occupied since the 9th c. In addition to the wonderful views of the Orcia valley and Monte Amiata, the visit is also interesting as it is a good example of the layout of a medieval defensive construction. The pentagonal fortifications enclose a courtyard for military use, in which the massive five-sided tower stands. The various floors were supplied by a large cistern and an oven and are connected to one another by stairs and narrow corridors. *For information* 392 00 33 028.

**Rocca d'Orcia** is a medieval village that stands at the foot of Tentennano Fort, on which it depended. A large polygonal cistern topped by a well stands at the point where the picturesque and partially cobbled alleys join up.

## 8. MAREMMA

Maremma is a large region traditionally split into three areas: **Pisan Maremma**, which extends from the southern spurs of the hills of Livorno to San Vincenzo, **Grossetan Maremma**, which covers the province of Grosseto and is the largest of the three, and **Lazial Maremma**, which stretches from Tarquinia to Cerveteri. As well as running along the coast, Maremma extends inland as far as the western slopes of the Metalliferous Hills. The province of Grosseto is the most representative section of Maremma: it is formed by a plain that lies below sea level and undulates towards the interior. The hills are covered with olive trees and vines and the occasional Maremman farmhouse, and close to the sea take on intense and varied colours throughout the year. The coast is lined by pinewoods, which hem in the fine siliceous sand beaches.

The Maremma of the past was an unsavoury area, populated by brigands and infested by malaria, but the modern district is a welcoming corner of Tuscany that can be explored on foot or horseback. Its attractive countryside features villages built from tufa and offers the wine and food lover many delightful sorties. The most salient periods of Maremma's history revolve around the Etruscans, the Romans and huge drainage projects. The Etruscans, who founded Populonia, Roselle and Vetulonia, started the district's drainage works. The unstable Etruscan period was succeeded by the industriousness and relative peace of the Roman age, during which further but more ambitious hydraulic works were carried out. But with the fall of the Roman Empire the communication roads were left unused and the region suffered progressive decline. The marshes, which were left untended, permitted malaria to spread, and, with the raiding parties by pirates along the coast and the barbarian invasions, the Middle Ages was a dramatic time for Maremma until the 11th c. Relative peace returned under the rule of the Lombards and remained up until the era of the Aldobrandeschi. However, Maremma's fortunes continued to sway and malaria remained a constant threat. In 1826 the House of Habsburg-Lorraine, and in particular Leopold II, restarted drainage projects that were to continue even after Tuscany's joining of the Kingdom of Italy and throughout the Fascist period. Today agriculture, which provides Maremma's main income, is assured.

The zone includes the following appellations: **Sovana, Parrina, Morellino di Scansano, Monteregio di Massa Marittima, Montecucco, Capalbio, Bianco di Pitigliano** and **Ansonica Costa dell'Argentario**. Montecucco is a DOC zone situated between Maremma and the slopes of the spent volcano Monte Amiata, in an area bounded by the Ombrone and Orcia valleys. The river Orcia provides the boundary between the production areas of Montecucco and Brunello di Montalcino. The towns where winemaking is of greatest importance are **Cinigiano** ♟ and **Castel del Piano**.

## Countryside, pinewoods and sea to the north of Grosseto

*Itinerary of 160 km from Grosseto to Roccastrada. Leave Grosseto to the north-east along the S 223.*

**Roselle** is one of the most renowned towns in northern Etruria. It stands on a hill and was once separated from Vetulonia by Lake Prilius, a wide lagoon that has now been transformed into the farming plain called **Padule di Raspollino**. Excavations begun in 1942 and still in progress have revealed a cyclopean wall 3 km long composed of blocks of stone up to 2 m tall. On the north side this dates back to the 6th c. BC, and on the west side to the 2nd c. BC. Buildings from the

Maremma cows and the local cowboys

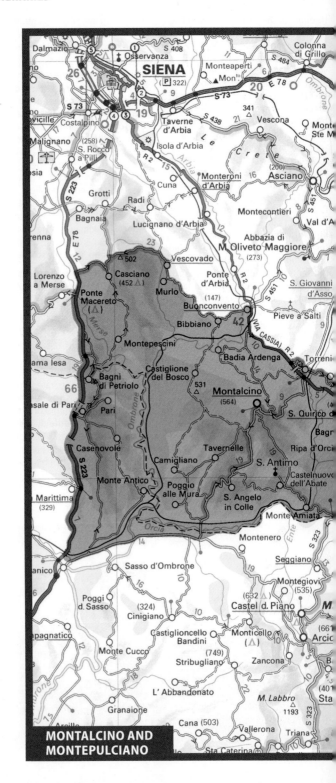

MONTALCINO AND
MONTEPULCIANO

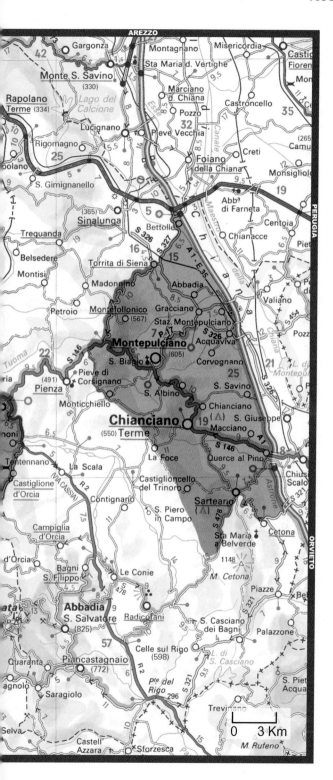

Roman age, such as the amphitheatre, the imperial forum, a villa with mosaic flooring, paved roads and the residential district from the end of the 6th c. can all be seen. *Via dei Ruderi, loc. Roselle. Open 8.15-16.45 (Mar.-Oct. 10.15-18.45), ℘ 0564 40 24 03 or 335 14 50361.*

*Cross the Via Aurelia and follow the signs to Buriano.* The road initially crosses flat countryside dominated by the hillside town of **Vetulonia★**, preceded by its ancient necropolis and excavation area. This was one of the most important towns in northern Etruria and still boasts its cyclopean walls (6th–5th-c. BC). Also visitable are the excavations of the Hellenistic and Etruscan-Roman city to the north-east of the town. *Open win. 8-17, sum. 10-19, closed Tue. and Fri. ℘ 0564 94 80 58.*

*Drive to the coast.*

## Castiglione della Pescaia ℘

Castiglione is a fishing port and seaside resort that looks like a canal port. It has a modern section by the sea, and a medieval centre ringed by walls on a rocky spur. The old town is characterised by steep streets paved with slabs, often covered by vaults, and lined by houses with grated windows and fortified doors. Views onto the canal port and the sandy beach can be had from the highest point, where there is also a small, 15th-c. castle with four-sided towers.

To the east is the Diaccia Botrona nature reserve, one of Italy's largest wetlands, which has a rare and particular ecosystem. Running south-east of Castiglione the road runs along the **Tombolo Pinewood**, a long stretch of umbrella pines.

As you head north, you come to **Scarlino**, where there is an important Etruscan necropolis (7th-6th c.) and a castle in the town centre. The area has lovely sandy beaches, such as Cala Violina and Cala Martina, and Mediterranean maquis.

A short journey (10 km) inland takes you to **Gavorrano ℘**, a small town in upper Grossetan Maremma, which gives lovely views. Mines and stone quarries from the past are today partly incorporated in Gavorrano Mineral and Nature Park, which also includes the lovely Rock Theatre, entirely cut out of the rock and used as a setting for shows and cultural events.

*Continue north to Massa Marittima.*

## Massa Marittima★★ ℘

The name Massa was a common term in the late Roman period, and is here associated with the misleading adjective Marittima. According to some this means the coastal area and its interior, while others consider it a synonym for Maremma. The beautiful **Piazza Garibaldi** is the setting for a harmonious set of medieval buildings: the Palazzo del Podestà, the crenellated Municipal Palace, and the **Duomo★★**. Probably constructed in the early 11th c. in Romanesque style, it was later remodelled by Giovanni Pisano in Gothic. The façade has such details as roaring lions, delicately carved capitals, and the architrave of the central portal carved with episodes of the life of St Cerbonius, the patron saint of the town. The **Palazzo del Podestà**, dating from 1230, was the seat of the municipality's highest magistrate, who held executive power. The building houses the **archaeological museum** and the splendid *Madonna in Majesty* by Ambrogio Lorenzetti (1285-1348 ca.).

Construction of Massa's town walls began in the early 13th c. The **Sienese Fortress** has five towers and was built in 1335. It divides the town in two parts that are connected by Silici Gate. The nearby Torre del Candeliere (Candlestick Tower) is all that remains of a fortress built in 1228, though it was reduced by a third from its original height by the Sienese. It is joined to the fortress by a flying arch with a span of 22 m.

Massa Marittima lies at the heart of the **Monteregio di Massa Marittima DOC** zone, where red, white, rosé wines and Vin Santo are made from Sangiovese, Trebbiano, Vermentino and Malvasia grapes.

About 26 km to the east of Massa Marittima, **Roccatederighi ℘** stands on a spur of Monte Sassoforte. Further east still, **Roccastrada ℘** has retained its medieval plan and offers fine views over the inland areas of Grosseto and Siena. In a cellar in Piazza dell'Orologio the **Vine and Wine Museum** describes winemaking in the area. *Piazza dell'Orologio. Open Mon.-Thu. and Sun. 9.30-13.30, Thu.-Sat. 16-20.30, closed Mon., ℘ 0564 56 33 76, www.stradavino.it.*

Argentario Promontory

© Hedda Gjerpen/iStock

## South of Grosseto: from the Uccellina mountains to Argentario

*Itinerary of approximately 250 km from Grosseto to Sorato. Take the Via Aurelia (SS 1) from Grosseto to the Alberese exit.* The countryside south of Grosseto becomes progressively more varied and more typical of Maremma.

### Maremma Regional Park★★

*Visitors Centre, Via del Bersagliere 7/9,* **Alberese** ☂, *℘ 0564 40 70 98, and Via Nizza 12,* **Talamone**, *℘ 0564 88 71 73, www.parco-maremma.it.*
The park is almost entirely occupied by the **Uccellina mountains** and covered for more than 4000 hectares by Mediterranean scrub. It runs parallel to the coast from Principina a Mare to Talamone. The very wide range of flora and fauna that lives in the park is affected by different climatic characteristics, which vary from continental to Mediterranean and, in some sections, even subdesertic. There are many traces of man's early settlements: from the Paleolithic to the Bronze Age to the Roman colonisation. It has been a hunting zone since antiquity due to the presence in Maremma of large mammals, even though the coastal areas, which were affected by malaria, discouraged long visits.

*From Alberese take the S 1 south.*

Fonteblanda, where you take the road to Talamone, is known for the **Osa Springs**. A typical fishing village, Fonteblanda stands beneath a 15th-c. fort. The Etruscan roots of **Talamone★** are mixed up with the legend describing its origin, according to which the hill on which it stands is the mound of Telamon, one of the Argonauts who sailed to Colchis with Jason to find the Golden Fleece.

*You are advised to reach Argentario via the strip of land called the Tombolo della Giannella, and to pass through Orbetello when you finish on the promontory.* The road follows the coastal pinewood as far as the lagoon zone.

### Argentario Promontory★

At one time an island, the small limestone massif of Monte Argentario is connected to the mainland by a large sandbar known as the **Tombolo della Feniglia★** and Tombolo della Giannella. A road offering wonderful views rings the perimeter of the promontory. Though it was once called the Promontorio Cosano (after the nearby town of Cosa), the name Argentario by which it is known today (argento = silver) either refers to the shiny surface of the rocks or the money-lending activity practised by its owners in the Roman period.

**Porto Santo Stefano★** is the peninsula's largest town and the port from which the boat leaves for Isola del Giglio. It is enchantingly situated on the side of the hill on either side of the castle built by the Spaniards in the 17th c. (fine **view★** of Talamone gulf and the port). *Leave Porto Santo Stefano northwards on the panoramic road.* Once past Punta Lividonia you will see the west coast of Isola del Giglio. *After the junction with the road to Porto Santo Stefano, the panoramic road begins to wind and descend without a guard rail. Drive with care.* The highest section of the road offers many beautiful **views★★** onto the rocky bays of the south-west shore, Isola Rossa and, to the left, the terraced fields and heights of Monte Argentario. A section of the road (*unpaved for more than 3 km*) looks down onto the wild Punta di Torre Ciana, the south shoreline, the Isolotto and Forte Stella. Next, the 16th-c. Spanish Fort comes into sight, and finally you reach **Porto Ercole★**. The tiny historic centre, which you reach through a medieval gate, is joined to the fort above by two parallel crenellated walls. Standing in Piazza Santa Barbara lined by the arcades of the former Governor's Palace (16th c.), you have a splendid view of the port, bay and two ancient Spanish forts on Monte Filippo.

The tour comes to an end as you skirt the east slope of Monte Argentario and the road squeezes between the outreaches of the mountain and the lagoon. Follow the edge of the water, then take the SS 440 in the direction of Orbetello. Situated on a thin strip of land in the middle of a lagoon (a nature reserve), **Orbetello** has fortifications that date from the rules of, first, the Sienese Republic, then of the Spanish, when it was the capital of the State of Presidi. The duomo was built over an ancient Etruscan-Roman temple and has a late Gothic façade.

The last stretch of this itinerary passes through the gentle, rolling countryside between Capalbio and Magliano planted with vines and olive trees.

### Ruins of Cosa★
*South of Orbetello, at the base of the southern sandbar, near Ansedonia. For information, ☏ 0564 88 14 21.* The ruins of the Roman colonia of Cosa (3rd c. BC – 4th c. AD) cover the top of a promontory that looks onto Orbetello lagoon. Excavations have unearthed two distinct sections: the acropolis was built with gigantic blocks of stone on the top of the hill, around an ancient temple and minor buildings; the town proper stood to the north. You can see the paved streets, the foundations of the forum, a number of water tanks and the residential district. The north gate, built with square blocks of stone, is the best preserved and its original structure is still standing.

The archaeological museum in **Ansedonia** displays some of the finds from the excavations and later eras. *Via Delle*

*Saturnia, synonymous with well-being*

© Shaiith/iStock

*Ginestre 35. Open Apr.-Oct. 10.15-18.30 (in win. 8.30-16.30) ☏ 0564 88 14 21.*

*Take the S 1 in the direction of Rome, then turn left onto the SP 63.*

### Capalbio★
You reach the medieval town closed inside its walls up on the hill through the Porta Senese and Porticina. The Church of San Nicola, in Romanesque style, is adorned with frescoes from the 14th c. (*chapels on the left*) and 15th c. (*chapels on the right*). The 12th-c. bell tower has twin-light windows. Close by stands the Aldobrandeschi Castle. Outside the walls, the Oratory della Providenza in Piazza Providenza has a 15th-c. fresco.

Contemporary art lovers will appreciate a visit to **Pescia Fiorentina**, 6 km east of Capalbio, where the **Tarot Gardens★** were created by Niki de Saint-Phalle with sculptures measuring 12-15 m in size, made from painted reinforced concrete and polyester, then lined with ceramic mosaics, Murano glass and mirrors. The figures represent the 22 principal cards in the Tarot pack. *Open Apr.-mid-Oct. 14.30-19.30, Nov.-Mar. first Sat. of the month 9-13, ☏ 0564 89 51 22, ilgiardinodeitarocchi.it.*

*Return to Capalbio and head north.*

You pass close to **Marsigliana**, through countryside of soft, changing colours, in the midst of which stand the ruins of the 12th-c. Church of **San Bruzio★**. Continue to **Magliano in Toscana 🍷**, set on a hill and ringed by 14th-c. and Renaissance walls. The main street, the ancient Via di Mezzo, is lined with the Church of San Giovanni Battista (Renaissance façade) and the Romanesque Church of San Martino.

Next, continue north to **Scansano**, the hometown of Morellino, where the Palazzo Pretorio houses an archaeological museum and the **Vine and Wine Museum** dedicated to the local DOC zones. *Piazza del Pretorio 4. For information on visits ℘ 0564 50 91 06, www.comune.scansano.gr.it.*

If you take the S 322 and then turn left, a drive of 30 km will bring you to **Saturnia**, the Etruscan town of *Aurinia*. The town, which was built on a travertine mass, is famous for its spa, where sulphurous water gushes out from its springs at 37 °C. To the left of the church, note the remains of the Sienese fort constructed in the 15th c. A few metres away, in Piazzale Bagno Secco on Via Italia, you can see the remains of what were once a Roman bath. Continuing on this street you reach the Roman Gate. Several necropolises can be visited in the area surrounding Saturnia, including Puntone burial ground (7th c. BC).

*Return to the S 322.*

Drive through **Montemerano★**, where the 15th-c. walls surround the interesting Church of San Giorgio, and head to **Manciano**, where a 15th-c. fort is surrounded by the historic centre of the town.

*Follow the pretty S 74.*

## Pitigliano★

This pleasant little town is another that stands on a volcanic spur of tufa amongst deep precipices where the Lente and Meleta torrents meet. Before entering the town it is worth stopping to view the small, attractive Church of the Madonna della Grazie. The last turns of the road reveal the grottoes dug out of the tufa by the Etruscans as tombs but which are now used as cellars or animal stalls. Interesting features of Pitigliano are the remains of the walls (the base was built by the Etruscans) and the aqueduct in the south part of the town, of which two large 16th-c. arches still stand. You have an excellent vista over the valley from Piazza della Repubblica. The medieval section of the town has not been altered, retaining its paved alleys connected by covered passageways, or by flights of steps lit by antique streetlights. The Renaissance façade and bell tower of the 12th-c. Church of **San Rocco** can be

admired in the lower part of the town. The left side is decorated with an 11th-c. low relief of a man with his hands in the jaws of two dragons.

The large square building of **Palazzo Orsini** dominates Pitigliano with its unaltered 14th-c. appearance. The **duomo** has an 18th-c. Baroque façade that forms a contrast with the heavy bell tower built in the Middle Ages. Close by, a travertine column from 1490 is topped by a bear, the symbol of the Orsini family.

*Take the SP 46, then turn left on the SP 22.*

## Sovana★ 🍷

You enter this secluded and lovely town up a street paved with bricks in herringbone fashion that seems magically to take you back in time. At the start of the long high street stand the ruins of the feudal castle. Further on, in an elegant little square, is the 12th-c. Church of **Santa Maria**. Striking features of the Romanesque interior are the refined 11th-c. ciborium and the 16th-c. frescoes. At the end of the street is the imposing Romanesque-Gothic **cathedral★**.

About 1.5 km to the west of Sovana (along the road to San Martino) is the local **Etruscan necropolis**. The limestone gullies on either side of the road contain tombs from between the 7th and 2nd c. BC. The most important (follow the signposts) can be reached along paths from the road or by following **cuts★** in the tufa walls. These represent a series of ancient Etruscan paths, some of which are several hundreds of metres in length and sometimes more than 30 m deep.

*Return to Sovana and continue on the SP 4.*

## Sorano★

Sorano is a very beautiful medieval town in its almost crib-like setting. It stands over the majestic **tufa ravines★** of the Lente torrent, where the natural caverns or grottoes dug by the Etruscans were used as places of burial. Dominated by the austere and semi-derelict 15th-c. fortress built by the Orsini, Sorano includes an upper section (18th c.) called the Masso Leopoldino built on a rock mass, from which magnificent views are to be had over the gullies below. The modern district has an elegant terraced park that looks onto the gullies, the town and the citadel.

# Addresses

## Tourist information

**Official Tourism Site of Tuscany** – www.turismo.intoscana.it

**Province of Arezzo** – Piazza della Libertà 3, Arezzo, ℘ 0575 40 19 45, www.arezzointuscany.it

**Coast of the Etruscans** – Piazza Barontini, 26, **Cecina** (SI), ℘ 0586 68 62 43, www.visitcostadeglietruschi.com

**Province of Lucca** – Piazzale Verdi, Lucca, ℘ 0583 58 31 50, www.luccaturismo.it and www.luccaitinera.it

**Maremma Tourist Office** – Corso Carducci 5, **Grosseto**, ℘ 0564 48 85 73, www.quimaremmatoscana.it

**Province of Pisa** –Piazza Duomo 7, Pisa, ℘ 050 55 01 00, www.turismo.pisa.it

**Siena and Val di Chiana Tourist Office** – Santa Maria della Scala/Palazzo Squarcialupi, Piazza Duomo 2, Siena, ℘ 0577 28 05 51, www.terresiena.it

Associazione Nazionale Città del Vino – Via Massetana Romana 58B, Siena, ℘0577 35 31 44, www.cittadelvino.it

## The wineries

*The addresses are listed in alphabetical order by location.*

### PROVINCE OF LUCCA

⌂ **Fattoria Sardi & Giustiniani** – *Via della Maulina 747* - **Monte San Quirico** *(LU), 3 km N of Lucca towards Camaiore* - ℘ *0583 34 12 30* - *www.fattoriasardi.com* - *fattoriasardi@ gmail.com* - *Winery tours by reservation.* Owned by the Sardi counts for over 200 years, the estate extends over 45 hectares, 19 of which planted to vine. Since 2002 it has been managed by Matteo Giustiniani, grandchild of Countess Maria Adele Sardi, and his Greek wife Mina. Numerous varieties are grown here: Sangiovese, Canaiolo, Merlot, Moscato, Muscat Hamburg, Chardonnay, Trebbiano Toscano, Ciliegiolo, Vermentino, Grechetto, Malvasia and Sauvignon. Accommodation available at the winery's guest farm (*7 apts.*). Hectares under vine: 18.

**Wines**: Toscana IGT Rosé, Toscana Rosato IGT Le Cicale, Vermentino, Sebastiano Merlot, Bianco, Vallebuia.

⌂ **Fattoria di Fubbiano** – *Via Tofori -* **San Gennaro** *(LU)* - ℘ *0583 97 80 11* - *www.fattoriadifubbiano.it* - *fubbiano@ fattoriadifubbiano.it* - *Winery tours and tasting by reservation.* The estate has 45 hectares of vineyards, olive groves and woods, about 20 of which under vine, and its annual production is approximately 100,000 bottles, mainly Colline Lucchesi DOC reds and whites. To safeguard the ecosystem, the winery uses only traditional natural products to protect the vines from disease. Accommodation available in estate-owned facilities (*4 apts. and 3 villas*). Hectares under vine: 20.

**Wines**: Rosso Colline Lucchesi, Schiller Vino Rosato, Vermentino Colline Lucchesi, San Gennaro Colline Lucchesi, I Pampini Rosso di Toscana IGT, Aleatico. Other products: olive oil.

⌂ **Colle di Bordocheo** - *Via di Piaggiori Basso 123* - **Segromigno in Monte -** **Capannori** *(LU)* - ℘ *0583 92 98 21* - *www.colledibordocheo.com* - *info@ colledibordocheo.com* - *Winery tours and tasting by reservation.* The Colle di Bordocheo estate boasts a typical Tuscan country atmosphere. It produces extra virgin olive oil and Colline Lucchesi DOC whites and reds made from Sangiovese, Canaiolo, Merlot, Ciliegiolo, Trebbiano, Malvasia, Greco, Grechetto, Vermentino and Chardonnay grapes. The guest farm has 4 charming apartments (*min. stay 3 days, 1 week in summer*). Hectares under vine: 10.

**Wines**: Bordocheo Bianco Colline Lucchesi, Bordocheo Rosso Colline Lucchesi, Picchio Rosso Colline Lucchesi, Bianco dell'Oca, Quinto, Sestilia Rosato. Other products: olive oil.

**Tenuta di Valgiano** – *Via di Valgiano 7 -* **Valgiano** *(LU), 3 km N of Segromigno* - ℘ *0583 40 22 71* - *www.valgiano.it* - *info@ valgiano.it* - *Winery tours by reservation.* The estate is set at an altitude of 250 metres, not far from the Tyrrhenian coast. As a result, it enjoys a Mediterranean climate and awash with sunlight, which ensures optimum phenolic maturation. The vineyards are managed with eco-friendly farming practices. Traditional cellar techniques are used, with minimal technological interference. The estate grows Sangiovese, Merlot, Syrah, Vermentino, Trebbiano and Malvasia grapes. Hectares under vine: 16.

**Wines**: Tenuta di Valgiano, Palistorti Rosso, Palistorti Bianco. Other products: olive oil and honey.

### CARMIGNANO

♞ **Artimino** – *Viale Papa Giovanni XXIII* - **Carmignano** *(PO)* - ℘ *055 87 51 41* - *www.artimino.com* - *info@artimino.com* - *Winery tours by reservation* (℘ *393 85 88 573*). Artimino is a complex and varied project of the Olmo Group that offers high-quality accommodation in Tuscan-style apartments in town, rooms at the Paggeria Medicea hotel (*37 rooms*) or villa Le Fagianaie. Gourmet menus are featured at the Biagio Pignatta restaurant; wines on sale and tastings at Artimino Wine Shop. Hectares under vine: 80.

**Wines**: Carmignano Riserva Grumarello, Barco Reale di Carmignano Rosato Vin Ruspo, Ser Biagio Barco Reale, Centocamini IGT, Vin Santo. Other products: olive oil.

↗ **Tenuta di Capezzana** – *Via Capezzana 100* - **Carmignano** *(PO)* - ☎ *055 87 06 005* - *www.capezzana.it* - *Winery tours by reservation.* The company philosophy is recapped by the words of the proprietor Ugo Contini Bonacossi: "Although the character of the wine and its terroir must not be lost, tradition is the result of countless improvements and innovations that have occurred through many generations over the centuries. Even today, we believe that we must continue to change to improve, as we have always done and as today's technology allows us to do". The estate offers guest accommodation (*La Fattoria di Capezzana, 8 rooms*). Hectares under vine: 90.

**Wines**: Barco Reale di Carmignano, Villa di Capezzana Carmignano, Ghiaie della Furba Rosso IGT, Trefiano Carmignano, Trebbiano Toscana IGT, Vin Santo. Other products: olive oil.

🍇 **Cantine Leonardo Da Vinci** – *Via Provinciale di Mercatale 291* - **Vinci** *(FI)* - ☎ *0571 18 26 823* - *www.cantineleonardo.it* - *enoteca@cantineleonardo.it* - *Winery tours by reservation, closed Sun.* The winery was established in 1961 through the efforts of 30 estates. The toponym Vinci seems to derive from vinco or vincastro, the willows whose branches were used to tied the vines. Wine shop Enoteca delle Vigne on the estate (*www.enotecadallevigne.com*). Accommodation at the Casale di Valle (*www.casaledivalle.com*). Hectares under vine: 750.

**Wines**: Leonardo Brunello di Montalcino, Chianti and Chianti Riserva Da Vinci, Sant'Ippolito IGT, Brunello and Rosso di Montalcino Da Vinci, Vin Santo Da Vinci.

## THE HILLS OF PISA AND THE ETRUSCAN COAST

**Tenuta San Guido** – *Loc. Le Capanne 27* - **Bolgheri** *(LI)* - ☎ *0565 76 20 03* - *www.tenutasanguido.com* - *info@tenutasanguido.com* - *Tenuta San Guido does not organize guided tours to the winery and the vines; no direct sales.* Sassicaia is unquestionably the best-known Super Tuscan and certain vintages, such as 1985, command astronomical prices in specialised auctions worldwide. It has

gradually climbed to the top of quality wine rankings and won the respect of even the most demanding consumers. The phenomenon of Super Tuscans arose thanks to the stubborn determination of Mario Incisa della Rocchetta, who decided to cultivate Cabernet Sauvignon in a gravelly area: hence the name Sassicaia, as *sassi* means stones. Hectares under vine: 90.

**Wines**: Bolgheri Sassicaia, Guidalberto Toscana IGT, Le Difese Toscana IGT.

**Tenuta dell'Ornellaia** – *Loc. Ornellaia 191- Fraz. Bolgheri* - **Castagneto Carducci** *(LI)* - ☎ *0565 71 82 42* - *www.ornellaia.com* - *hospitality@ornellaia.it* - *Winery tours and tasting by reservation.* The estate was founded by Marquis Lodovico Antinori in 1981, when he decided to grow Cabernet Franc, Merlot and Cabernet Sauvignon in an area of Tuscany that was still "wild". Since 2005 the estate has been owned by Marchesi de' Frescobaldi. Limited production, attention to detail, and the utmost care in the vineyard and cellar alike have made this a great winery. Ornellaia is now one of the most widely appreciated Super Tuscans in Italy and abroad. Hectares under vine: 100.

**Wines**: Toscana Bianco IGT Poggio alle Gazze, Toscana Rosso IGT Le Volte, Bolgheri Le Serre Nuove dell'Ornellana, Bolgheri Superiore Ornellaia, Ornus dell'Ornellaia Toscana Bianco IGT. Other products: olive oil and grappa.

**Michele Satta** – *Loc. Vigna al Cavaliere 61* - **Castagneto Carducci** *(LI)* - ☎ *0565 76 36 13* - *www.michelesatta.com* - *visite@ michelesatta.com* - *Winery tours and tasting by reservation (from €35).* By chance, Michele Satta had the opportunity to move from Varese to Castagneto Carducci in 1974, when he transferred from the Department of Agriculture in Milan to the one in Pisa and was hired by a Tuscan produce company as a student worker. He fell in love with the region – and its wine – as a result of this experience, and decided to work the land to make the sublime nectar of Bacchus. In 1988 he established the first part of his estate by purchasing a plot of land and building his wine cellar. Over the years, the winery has expanded and now has about 30 hectares planted with Sangiovese, Cabernet Sauvignon, Merlot and Syrah. Hectares under vine: 23.

**Wines**: Bolgheri Superiore I Castagni, Piastraia, Bolgheri Rosso, Costa di Giulia Bolgheri, Cavaliere IGT, Giovin Re IGT.

**Podere Grattamacco** – *Loc. Lungagnano 129*- **Castagneto Carducci** *(LI)* - ☎ *0565 76 50 69* - *www.collemassari.it* -*grattamacco@ collemassari.it*- *Winery tours by reservation* *(from €35)*. The winery was established in 1977 and is situated in the Bolgheri DOC area, the cradle of Cabernet Sauvignon in Italy. From its very first vintage – 1978 – this variety, blended with Sangiovese and Merlot, has yielded extraordinarily powerful and elegant wines. The estate covers an area of about 80 hectares, 28 of which planted to vine, 15 with olive groves and the remainder covered with woodlands. Hectares under vine: 28.

**Wines**: Grattamacco Bolgheri Vermentino, Bolgheri Rosso, L'Alberello Bolgheri Superiore, Grattamacco Bolgheri Rosso Superiore. Other products: olive oil and grappa.

**Castello del Terriccio** – *Loc. Terriccio - Castellina Marittima (PI) - 🕾 050 69 97 09 - www.terriccio.it - b.bertheau@terriccio.it - Winery tours by reservation.* The modern history of the Terriccio castle commenced with the period following WWI, when the Counts Serafini Ferri purchased the estate and undertook important renovation work. Until the 1970s the estate was better known for its cereal-growing business than its wines: in 1980 just 25 hectares were under vine, as opposed to 60 today, and now Lupicaia is one of the best-known Super Tuscans. Hectares under vine: 60.

**Wines**: Toscana Rosso IGT Lupicaia, Toscana Rosso IGT Castello del Terriccio, Toscana Rosso IGT Tassinaia, Toscana Bianco IGT Con Vento, Capannino Merlot. Other products: olive oil, spelt, barley.

**Tenuta Argentiera** – *Via Aurelia 412/A - Loc. I Pianali -* **Donoratico** *(LI), 4 km W of Castagneto Carducci - 🕾 0565 77 31 76 - www.argentiera.eu - info@argentiera.eu - Winery tours by reservation, 🕾 0565 77 45 81 enoteca@argentiera.eu.* The winery is part of the ancient Tenuta di Donoratico, an estate owned by the Serristoris, an influential Florentine family bound up with the local medieval history. During the Etruscan period, there were natural springs and silver mines here: hence the name Argentiera, as *argento* means silver. Today the estate is owned by the brothers Corrado and Marcello Fratini, and Stanislaus Turnauer. In all of the Bolgheri area, the Tenuta Argentiera is the one closest to the sea, and it is also the one at the highest altitude. Hectares under vine: 75.

**Wines**: Argentiera Bolgheri Superiore, Villa Donoratico Bolgheri Rosso, Poggio ai Ginepri Bolgheri Rosso. Other products: olive oil.

🏠 **Tenuta di Ghizzano** – *Via della Chiesa 4 -* **Ghizzano di Peccioli** *(PI) - 🕾 0587 63 00 96 - www.tenutadighizzano.com - info@ tenutadighizzano.com - Winery tours by*

*reservation.* The cellar, the winery and the oil mill are set around the tower that was built in 1370 by the Venerosi Pesciolini family. The estate now has about 350 hectares, 20 of which under vine, 20 planted with olive trees, 150 with cereals, and 150 covered with forests and poplar groves. The estate also has a guest farm and produces olive oil. Accommodation available at the estate *(6 apts.)*. Hectares under vine: 20.

**Wines**: Veneroso Rosso IGT, Nambrot Rosso IGT, Il Ghizzano Rosso IGT, Il Ghizzano Bianco IGT, San Germano Passito. Other products: olive oil and cereals.

🏠 **Fattoria Sorbaiano** – *Loc. Sorbaiano 39 -* **Montecatini Val di Cecina** *(PI), 22 km NE of Montescudaio - 🕾 0588 02 80 54 - www.fattoriasorbaiano.it - info@fattoria sorbaiano.it - Winery tours by reservation (from €15).* The farm is situated in an ancient medieval town on a hilltop overlooking the Val di Cecina. It was purchased by the current proprietors in the late 1950s. Of the farm's 270 hectares of land, 160 are planted with cereals, 70 are covered with woods, 15 with olive groves and 26 are under vine. The estate produces red and white Montescudaio DOC. The *vinsantaia* is picturesque: it is here that small casks of Montescudaio DOC Vin Santo, made in extremely small quantities using the ancient method of strainers and grapes dried on mats, are aged for 5 years. Accommodation available at the estate *(1 villa)*. Hectares under vine: 26.

**Wines**: Sorbaiano Bianco and Rosso, Vin Santo. Other products: olive oil.

🏠 **Fontemorsi** – *Via delle Colline -* **Montescudaio** *(PI) - 🕾 0583 34 90 25 - www.fontemorsi.it - info@fontemorsi.it - Winery tours and tasting by reservation.* The Fontemorsi estate covers 22 hectares, most of which under vine and the remainder planted with olive groves. Its wine production is tied to traditional local varieties – Sangiovese, Canaiolo and Malvasia Rossa – but it also caters to international tastes with Merlot and Cabernet. The estate has a country house in a splendid panoramic position that has been set up as a guest farm, and two shops in the historic district of Montescudaio with the Fontemorsi wine shop and, opening soon, a wine bar. Accommodation is available in apartments on the estate. Hectares under vine: 10.

**Wines**: Rosso Montescudaio Spazzavento, Montescudaio Toscana IGT Le Tinte, Toscana Rosso IGT Guadipiani, Toscana Rosso IGT Volterrano, Toscana IGT Tresassi Rosé and Bianco. Other products: olive oil.

🏠 **Fattoria Varramista** – *Via Ricavo - Loc. Varramista* - **Montopoli Val d'Arno** *(PI)* - ☎ *0571 44 711 - www.varramista.it -info@ varramista.it - Winery and vineyards tours by reservation.* The Tenuta di Varramista farmstead was donated by Gino di Neri Capponi (1350-1421) in commemoration of his victory as commander of the Florentine armies battling the city of Pisa in 1406. Varramista is famous, however, first and foremost for having been the residence of the Piaggio family, creators and builders of the legendary Vespa scooter. In 1990 Giovanni Alberto Agnelli, Enrico Piaggio's nephew, made Varramista his home residence and began reconverting the vineyards and organizing lodgings for visitors. Even back when Varramista was owned by Count Capponi, its vineyards produced an excellent sangiovese wine. But it was only during the 1990s, under Giovanni Alberto Agnelli's direction, that the entire production system was reviewed, renovated and modernized. Options for renting a suite *(12 flats, from €120)*. Hectares under vine: 15.

**Wines**: Varramista, Frasca, Monsonaccio, Sterpato, Ottopioppi. Other products: olive oil and grappa.

🍷 **Fattoria Santa Lucia** – *Via di San Gervasio 4* - **Pontedera** *(PI), 25 km E of Pisa* - ☎ *328 02 03 309 - www.fattoriasantalucia. it - cantina@fattoriasantalucia.it (winery tours), agriturismo@fattoriasantalucia.it (restaurant and guest farm) - Winery open Fri. 15-18 and Sat. 9-12.* The estate has 160 hectares, about 12 of which under vine and 3 with olive groves. The rest of the land is dotted with woods, a pond and a complex of rural buildings that have been converted into a guest farm *(7 rooms, 8 apts.)* and a restaurant *(Wed.-Sat. and Sun. lunch)*, where guests can try the estate's products along with typical local dishes and specialities. Hectares under vine: 12.

**Wines**: Chianti Santa Lucia, Sangiovese IGT, Gran Galateo, Ciliegiolo IGT cheRubino, Ciliegiolo IGT Ceragiolo, Bianco IGT Scassini. Other products: olive oil.

🍷 **Marchesi Ginori Lisci** – *Vicolo della Terrazza 6* - **Castello Ginori di Querceto Ponteginori** *(PI)* - ☎ *0588 37 472 - www.marchesiginorilisci.it - shop@ marchesiginorilisci.it - Winery tours and tasting by reservation.* Ginori di Querceto castle is an ancient fortified village dating back to around 1000 AD. In 1543 the Lisci di Volterra noble family moved into Querceto, and in 1786 the last descendant of the Lisci, Francesca, married Marquise Lorenzo Ginori. In 1814 Carlo Leopoldo Ginori inherited the property from his mother Francesca, and from that moment forward the castle and surrounding lands remained with the Ginori family, who adopted numerous innovations for cultivation, increasing harvests from the lands. During the 1900s Lorenzo and his son Leonardo developed agricultural efforts even further, helping make Querceto a famous agricultural model. Thanks to the hard work and commitment of current generations of descendants of the Ginori Lisci families, the property was progressively restored over recent years, while every effort was made to respect and maintain the original structure. Accommodation is available in apartments on the estate *(14 apts.)*; restaurant Locanda del Sole. Hectares under vine: 17.

**Wines**: Castello Ginori, Macchion del Lupo, Campordigno, Virgola, Bacio. Other products: olive oil and grappa.

🍷 **Azienda Agricola Bulichella** – *Loc. Bulichella 131-* **Suvereto** *(LI)* - ☎ *0565 82 98 92 - www.bulichella.it - info@bulichella.it - Winery tours and tasting by reservation, Mon.-Fri. 9-12 and 15-18.* Bulichella came into being in 1983, from the desire of four families to live together as an extended family and initiate farm production with respect for nature and the environment. This gave rise to organic farming. The real turning point towards high-quality, characteristic organic farming took place in the 1990s when the Miyakawa family – Japanese Hideyuki and Italian Maria Luisa Bassano along with their children – decided to invest in the Val di Cornia area and became the business's owners. The vineyards extend into a medium-textured soil and their management follows strict criteria, aimed at ensuring a high quality production in full respect of environmental balances. Bulichella offers accommodation *(14 rooms)* and a restaurant. Hectares under vine: 17.

**Wines**: Costa Toscana IGT Rosato Sol Sera, Vermentino Tuscanio, Syrah Hide and

Rosso Rubino, Suvereto DOCG Coldipietrerosse, Montecristo, Merlot Maria Shizuko and Sangiovese Tuscanio.

**Petra** – *Loc. San Lorenzo Alto 131 -* **Suvereto** *(LI) - ✆ 0565 84 53 08 - www.petrawine.it - info@petrawine.it - Winery tours by reservation (from €35), visit@petrawine.it.* The winery's stunning architecture, designed by Mario Botta, was inspired by the desire of owner Vittorio Moretti to create a place where wine is made and aged – but one that would also serve as a point for encounters, cultural exchanges and experiences, whilst conveying the company values. The estate boasts 300 hectares of vineyards, woods and olive groves. The name of the town is derived from *suvere*, which means cork forests. Hectares under vine: 93.
**Wines**: Toscana Rosso IGT Petra, Toscana Rosso IGT Quercegobbe, Toscana Rosso IGT Hebo, La Balena Viognier, L'Angelo di San Lorenzo Vino Dolce. Other products: olive oil.

**Tenuta Podernovo** – *Via Podernuovo 13* - **Terricciola** *(PI) - ✆ 0587 65 60 40 - www.tenutapodernovo.it - podernovo@tenutelunelli.it - Winery tours and tasting by reservation.* The estate, owned by the Lunelli family, has more than 80 hectares of land. The winery was created with an eye to respecting the environment and morphology of the area to the full, using local stone found in the nearby countryside and a colour scheme that takes up the surroundings. Accommodation available at Casale Podernovo, a complex of Tuscan-style rustic buildings from the late 18th c. (*✆ 0587 65 60 40, www.casalepodernovo.it, 12 apts from €210*). Hectares under vine: 25.
**Wines**: Costa Toscana IGT Teuto, Costa Toscana IGT Auritea, Rosso Toscana IGT Aliotto.

### ELBA ISLAND

**Fattoria delle Ripalte** – *Loc. Ripalte -* **Capoliveri** *- ✆ 0565 94 211 - www.fattoriadelleripalte.it - info@fattoriadelleripalte.it - Winery and vineyards tours with tasting by reservation (from €15).* The Fattoria delle Ripalte was built in 1896 by Count Tobler, a Swiss nobleman who had fallen in love with Italy and wanted to fulfil his great dream: growing grapes and making wine. After years of abandonment, in 2002 the owners decided to invest the winegrowing vocation of its land. No synthesised chemicals are used for phytosanitary treatments and the limited fertilising is organic. Accommodation available on the estate (*doubles from €78*). Restaurant service. Hectares under vine: 15.
**Wines**: Elba Aleatico, Brut Rosato delle Ripalte, Vermentino delle Ripalte. Other products: grappa.

© KHZ/Shutterstock

**Azienda Agricola Mola** – *Loc. Gelsarello 2* - **Porto Azzurro** *- ✆ 0565 95 81 51- www.tenutepavoletti.it - info@tenutepavoletti.it - Winery tours by reservation.* The estate produces whites, reds, rosés and dried-grape wines under the Elba DOC appellation. Great attention has always been paid to dried-grape wines, including Moscato and Aleatico. Since 1956 it has been owned by the Pavoletti family, who have been committed to quality tied above all to the island's most characteristic varieties. Hectares under vine: 12.
**Wines**: Elba Aleatico, Elba Ansonica, Elba Bianco Casa degli Ajali, Vermentino, Elba Rosso Gelsarello. Other products: olive oil.

**Acquabona** – *Loc. Acquabona 1 -* **Portoferraio** *- ✆ 0565 93 30 13 - www.acquabonaelba.it - info@acquabonaelba.it - Winery tours and tasting by reservation.* The estate dates back to the 18th c. and its 14 hectares under vine make it the largest winegrowing concern on the island. The winery, which has always been attentive to the environment, participates in the European Programme to reduce the use of phytosanitary products. Notable varieties here include Aleatico, Ansonica and Vermentino, but there are also vineyards with Cabernet Sauvignon, Sangiovese, Malvasia Bianca and Procanico. Hectares under vine: 16.5.
**Wines**: Elba Bianco, Ansonica dell'Elba, Elba Rosso, Elba Rosso Riserva Camillo Bianchi, Aleatico dell'Elba. Other products: wine jellies and grappa.

### CHIANTI

**Osteria di Passignano** – *Via Passignano 33 - Loc.* **Badia a Passignano - Tavarnelle Val di Pesa** *(FI) - ✆ 055 80 71 278 - www.osteriadipassignano.com - info@osteriadipassignano.com - Tours in the cellar in the abbey, by reservation. - The inn and shop are closed Sun.* The Abbey of

Passignano is a monastery that was built in 395 ad and was founded by the archbishop of Florence; Vallumbrosan monks still live here. The Antinori family (*see the inset on p. 271*) owns the vineyards around the abbey, whose grapes are used to make Classico Riserva di Badia a Passignano, aged in the cellars of the monastery. The Osteria and Bottega di Passignano – the inn and shop – were set up to allow visitors to taste and learn about the wines of the Antinori estates. The Bottega is the only shop with direct sales of all Antinori products.

**Ruffino** – *Via Poggio al Mandorlo 1 - Tenuta di Poggio Casciano -Loc. Quarate -* **Bagno a Ripoli** *(FI), 6 km E of Florence -* ✆ *055 64 99 712 - www.ruffino.com - hospitality@ ruffino.it - Winery tours and tasting by reservation.* Poggio Casciano is one of the 7 estates owned by Ruffino, the prestigious Tuscan winemakers established in 1877. The Ruffino estates include the area's main appellations, such as Chianti Classico, Montalcino and Montepulciano. Some of its labels have helped write the history of Italian enology, such as its Riserva Ducale and Chianti Ruffino, among the first wines to cross national borders in the early 20th c. Poggio Casciano is a stunning Renaissance villa with grounds of about 222 hectares; vineyards cover more than 70 hectares. The estate is surrounded by a vast hilly area with woods, meadows and ancient towns. Food and wine tasting available. Hectares under vine: 70.
**Wines**: Chianti Classico, Brunello di Montalcino, Nobile di Montepulciano, Toscana IGT. Other products: olive oil.

**Castello di Monsanto** – *Via Monsanto 8 -* **Barberino Val d'Elsa** *(FI) -* ✆ *055 80 59 000 - www.castellodimonsanto.it - monsanto@castellodimonsanto.it - Winery tours and tasting by reservation.* Everything started in 1962, the first vintage, but it was in 1968 that the winery's proprietors, the Bianchi family, decided to eliminate white grapes from the blend of their Chianti. A 250-metre tunnel connects the new winery to the old cellars of the castle built in 1740. The tunnel was built using medieval techniques and the materials of the era, making it an architectural masterpiece. Hectares under vine: 72.
**Wines**: Chianti Classico, Chianti Classico Riserva Il Poggio, Nemo IGT, Chardonnay Fabrizio Bianchi. Other products: olive oil.

🏠 **Castello di Fonterutoli-Marchesi Mazzei Spa Agricola** – *Via Ottone III di Sassonia 5 - Loc. Fonterutoli -* **Castellina in Chianti** *(SI) -* ✆ *0577 73 571- www.mazzei.it - mazzei@mazzei.it - Winery tours by reservation and tasting (from €25).* Today the estate has a total area of 650 hectares, 117 of which with specialised vineyards divided into 5 areas: Fonterutoli, Caggio, Siepi, Badiola and Belvedere. The land is characterised by disintegrating boulders and is thus very pebbly: tellingly, Fonterutoli wine is often referred as the "wine of stones". Hence the choice of winegrowing that respects the environment, with a yield of less than 4000 litres/hectare, guaranteeing consistently excellent quality and distinctive personality. Accommodation available on the estate (*15 rooms from €125 and apts. from €155*). Restaurant service available at Osteria di Fonterutoli ( ✆ *0577 74 11 25*) and bar La Società Orchestrale di Fonterutoli; the wine shop organises tours of the winery and wine tastings. Hectares under vine: 117.
**Wines**: Toscana IGT Siepi/Poggio Badiola/ Ser Lapo, Chianti Classico Gran Selezione Castello Fonterutoli, Chianti Classico Fonterutoli. Other products: olive oil, grappa and lavender.

🏠 **Fattoria La Castellina** – *Via Ferruccio 26 -* **Castellina in Chianti** *(SI) -* ✆ *0577 74 04 59 - www.lacastellina.it - info@lacastellina.it - Winery tours and tasting by reservation (from €18). Direct sale.* Castellina was once the property of Florence's noble Squarcialupi family. The first record of this noble and illustrious Italian family date to 1015 AD. The Squarcialupi were elected by the Florentine Republic as general commissaries for Castellina in Chianti. The company's historical headquarters is Palazzo Squarcialupi, the old residence of the Florentine noble family. The ground floor and underground level host the company's cantinas, shop and restaurant Taverna Squarcialupi. Today the upper floors, formerly a family residence, host the Palazzo Squarcialupi hotel. In 1989 the Bojola-Targioni family took over the company. Renovation of "La Ferrozzola", a historical hilltop residence surrounded by greenery where the company's farmworkers once lived has been turned into an agriturismo (4 flats with use of the kitchen and access to hotel services) near the town. Guests can stay overnight (*15 rooms from €120*) and dine in the restaurant. Hectares under vine: 30.
**Wines**: Chianti Classico, Chianti Classico Riserva, Vin Santo del Chianti Classico DOC, IGT Toscana Rosso/Bianco/Rosato. Other products: olive oil and grappa.

🏠 **Rocca delle Macie** – *Loc. Le Macìe 45 -* **Castellina in Chianti** *(SI) -* ✆ *0577 73 21 - www.roccadellemacie.com - info@ roccadellemacie.com - Winery tours by reservation* ✆ *0577 73 22 36 or enoteca@ roccadellemacie.com.* The winery was established in 1973, when Italo Zingarelli

decided to fulfil one of his dreams by purchasing the estate of Le Macìe, which had about 93 hectares – only 2 of which under vine. His children Fabio, Sandra and Sergio inherited his passion for these lands. In 1989, Sergio took over at the helm of the company, assisted by his wife Daniela. Today Rocca delle Macìe has about 500 hectares, over 200 of which covered with vineyards and 22 with olive groves, divided among its 6 estates:
Le Macìe, Sant'Alfonso, Fizzano and Le Tavolelle in the Chianti Classico zone, and Campomaccione and Casamaria in the Morellino di Scansano zone in the Maremma district. Hotel accommodation is available at Relais Riserva di Fizzano (*www.riservadifizzano.com, 19 apts. from €120*), with restaurant service. Hectares under vine: 31.

**Wines**: Chianti Classico Tenuta Sant'Alfonso, Toscana IGT Ser Gioveto, Rubizzo, Toscana IGT Sasyr, Morellino di Scansano Campo Maccione. Other products: grappa, honey and olive oil.

**Dievole** – *Loc. Dievole 6* - **Castelnuovo Berardenga** *(SI)* - *℘ 0577 32 26 32 - www.dievole.it - info@dievole.it - Vineyards tours and tastings by reservation (from €25).* Dievole is a small corner of the Tuscan region that has always been famous as a tiny terrestrial paradise. The roots of the name can be interpreted as "Dio vuole", or God wishes, and the first record to the term dates back to the 11th century. Eight centuries and countless generations later, another contract came to define Dievole: a marriage gift. Count Giulio Terrosi-Vagnoli gave the farmstead to his future wife, Ildegonda Camaiori, who became the noblewoman of Dievole. Beginning in the 1980s, the ancient winemaking knowledge inherent to Dievole came to fruition: 16 vineyards, reflecting the 16 different farms that the overall property was divided into. The company's objective is to recover the characteristics and flavours of historical autochthonous Tuscan vines, and transfer them to the drinking glass while fully respecting the authenticity of the terroir and identity of the varietal. The location includes a restaurant as well as lodgings (*28 rooms, from €250*). Barbecue on Friday evenings, and, by appointment, dinner in a historical cantina amidst the aging barrels Hectares under vine: 158.

**Wines**: Vigna di Sessina Chianti Classico Selezione, Novecento Chianti Classico Riserva, Chianti Classico, Bianco Le Due Arbie, Vin santo. Other products: olive oil and grappa.

**Fèlsina** – *Via del Chianti 101* - **Castelnuovo Berardenga** *(SI)* - *℘ 0577 35 51 17 - www.felsina.it - Winery tours by reservation,*

*0577 15 23 789.* Fèlsina is a modern winegrowing estate established with a sense of respect for the rural landscape that has long characterised the Chianti region. Its wines have long been among the most famous in the area, and top favourites in both Italy and abroad include Chianti Classico, Fontalloro (Sangiovese) and Maestro Raro (Cabernet Sauvignon). Hectares under vine: 95.

**Wines**: Chianti Classico Fèlsina Berardenga, Rancia Riserva Chianti Classico, Fontalloro IGT, Maestro Raro IGT. Other products: olive oil.

**San Felice** – *Loc. San Felice* - **Castelnuovo Berardenga** *(SI)* - *℘ 0577 39 911 - www.agricolasanfelice.it - info@sanfelice.com - Winery tours by reservation (℘ 0577 39 92 21).* An ancient town founded by the Etruscans, San Felice was a fief of the Sienese Cerretani family until the 19th c. It was then taken over by the Del Taja family, who managed the company until the first half of the 20th c., as they were among the founders of the Consorzio del Chianti Classico Gallo Nero. It was acquired by the Allianz Ras Group in 1978, under the leadership of Enzo Morganti, a man who had proven winemaking experience with Sangiovese. Morganti began to restructure the company, shifting from quantity-based production to one decidedly focused on quality. Accommodation and restaurant service available at Borgo San Felice Relais & Chateaux *(30 rooms and 30 suite)*. Hectares under vine: 147.

**Wines**: Chianti Classico Riserva Il Grigio, Vigorello Toscana IGT, Pugnitello Toscana IGT. Other products: olive oil.

**Frascole** – *Fraz. Frascole 27/a* - **Dicomano** *(FI), 36 km NE of Florence* - *℘ 055 83 86 340 - www.frascole.it - frascole@frascole.it - Winery tours and tasting by reservation.* The estate is spread out over nearly 100 hectares, part of which on the valley floor and planted with crops, whereas grapes and olives are grown on the hillsides. It was established thanks to the passion for agriculture that the Lippi family has handed down for generations. Podere Vico, the headquarters of the estate, is composed of a small group of medieval houses surrounded by vineyards and olive groves, and set in an important Etruscan archaeological area. Accommodation available on the Agriturismo *(5 apts. from €360/week)*. Hectares under vine: 15.

**Wines**: Chianti Rufina Frascole, Chianti Rufina Frascole Riserva, Limine IGT, InAlbis IGT, Vin Santo del Chianti Rufina. Other products: olive oil.

**Barone Ricasoli** – *Castello di Brolio* - **Gaiole in Chianti** *(SI)* - *℘ 0577 73 02 20 - www.ricasoli.it -shop@ricasoli.it - Winery* *tours by reservation.* Generations of Ricasolis have been frontrunners in history: for example, Bettino Ricasoli – "the iron baron" – served as prime minister in post-unification Italy. The family has always been devoted to the agricultural development of their lands and vineyards, producing renowned wines that were exported abroad as far back as the late 17th c. Accommodation available at Agriturismo L'Agresto. Restaurant at L'Osteria. Hectares under vine: 240. Wines: Casalferro Toscana IGT, Chianti Classico Brolio, Chianti Classico Riserva Rocca Guicciarda, Chianti Classico Castello di Brolio, Chardonnay Torricella Toscana IGT, Vin Santo. Other products: olive oil and grappa.

**Marchesi de' Frescobaldi** – *Via Santo Spirito 11-* **Firenze** - *℘ 055 27 141 - www. frescobaldi.it - info@frescobaldi.it - Winery tours by reservation.* The Frescobaldis are a Florentine family that has been making great Tuscan wines for 30 generations. They boast 700 years of winemaking tradition and today their empire covers 5000 hectares of land, over 1000 of which under vine. Their properties are divided into 9 estates in Tuscany, extending from Chianti to the Pomino DOC zone, from Montalcino to the Maremma district, and from the Mugello area to the province of Livorno. Hectares under vine: 1200. **Wines**: Nipozzano Riserva Chianti Rufina, Montesodi Toscana IGT, Mormoreto Toscana IGT, Santa Maria Morellino di Scansano, Campo ai Sassi Rosso Montalcino.

**Agricoltori del Chianti Geografico** – *Via Mulinaccio 10 -* **Gaiole In Chianti** *(SI) - ℘ 0577 98 82 62 - www.chiantigeografico.it - shop.gaiole@chiantigeografico.it - Winery tours by reservation.* This adventure started with 17 pioneers in 1961: nearly 60 years later, the association has more than 200 members. The key to its success is the unique bond between the territory and the individual members, and between them and their exclusive products. Furthermore, the Agricoltori del Geografico group assists each vigneron with expertise ranging from vineyard management to cellar work and on to marketing, guaranteeing results that enhance the uniqueness of each winemaking area. Hectares under vine: 550. Wines: Chianti Classico, Chianti Colli Senesi, Nobile di Montepulciano, Vernaccia di San Gimignano, Toscana IGT. Other products: olive oil and grappa.

⚘ **Badia a Coltibuono** – *Loc. Badia a Coltibuono -* **Gaiole in Chianti** *(SI) - ℘ 0577 74 481 - www.coltibuono.com - badia@ coltibuono.com - Winery tours and tasting (from €10) or with reservation (from €25).* Badia a Coltibuono, which means "abbey of the good harvest", was established in 1051 by Vallumbrosan monks, who began to build the monastery and simultaneously planted the area's vineyards. In 1846 it was purchased by the Florentine banker Michele Giuntini, the forefather of the current owners. With Piero Stucchi Prinetti at the helm, it developed into the successful winery it is today. His children Emanuela, Roberto, Paolo and Guido are continuing the work undertaken by their ancestors over a century ago. Accommodation and restaurant service available in estate-owned facilities *(rooms from €135, apts. from €210)*. Hectares under vine: 53. Wines: Chianti Classico Badia a Coltibuono, Chianti Classico Riserva Badia a Coltibuono, Chianti Classico Cultus Boni, Sangioveto di Toscana IGT, Vin Santo del Chianti Classico. Other products: olive oil.

⌂ **Capannelle** – *Loc. Capannelle 13 -* **Gaiole in Chianti** *(SI) - ℘ 0577 74 511 - www.capannelle.com - info@capannelle. com - Winery tours and tasting by reservation.* The history of the winery commenced in 1974, when the entrepreneur Raffaele Rossetti decided to purchase a 17th-c. farmhouse in Chianti. Today the estate has about 35 hectares, 16 of which under vine, and it produces about 80,000 bottles of wine annually. It is owned by James B. Sherwood, the founder and shareholder of the Orient-Express Hotels Group. Accommodation available at the luxury hotel annexed to the estate *(7 rooms)*. Hectares under vine: 16. **Wines**: Chardonnay IGT, Chianti Classico Riserva, Solare IGT, 50&50 IGT. Other products: olive oil and grappa.

© Ironi/Shutterstock

# ADDRESSES

⌂ **Tenuta di Nozzole** – *Via di Nozzole 12 - Passo dei Pecorai* - **Greve in Chianti** *(FI) - ☎ 055 85 98 11 - www.tenuteambrogio egiovannifolonari.com - folonari@tenute folonari.com - Winery tours and tasting by reservation.* The historic farm dates back to the 14th c. and was purchased by the Folonaris in 1971. The family has worked in the winemaking sector since the late 18th c. and as early as 1825 its philosophy was to develop, produce and distribute the finest Italian wines around the world. Tenuta di Nozzole has always been known for the quality of its wines and the famous Supertuscan Pareto is its flagship product. Accommodation available at the estate's guest farm *(9 room and 1 villa).* Hectares under vine: 90.
**Wines**: Toscana Rosso IGT Il Pareto, Chianti Classico Riserva La Forra, Chianti Classico Gran selezione Giovanni Folonari, Chianti Classico Nozzole, Chardonnay Toscana IGT Le Bruniche, Vin Santo. Other products: grappa and olive oil.

⌂ **Tenuta Vicchiomaggio** – *Via Vicchiomaggio 4* - **Greve in Chianti** *(FI) - ☎ 055 85 40 79 - www.vicchiomaggio.it - info@vicchiomaggio.it - Winery tours and tasting by reservation (from €15).* The castle of Vicchiomaggio is a magnificent historic residence with grounds of more than 130 hectares, and it is owned by John and Paola Matta. Wine has always been produced at the castle and the current owners have kept up this tradition. Different styles of wines are made here, varying from traditional to innovative. In order to achieve this, the land has been strictly classified according to variety and the exposure of the vineyards. The names of the specific vineyards are listed on all the labels. Accommodation is available at estate-owned facilities *(15 rooms, €160)* and meals are served at the castle restaurant. Hectares under vine: 34.
**Wines**: Chianti Classico San Jacopo di Vicchiomaggio, Chianti Classico Riserva Agostino Petri, Chianti Classico Riserva La Prima, Toscana IGT Ripa delle More, Toscana IGT FSM. Other products: olive oil and grappa.

⌂ **Castello di Ama** – *Loc. Ama* - **Lecchi in Chianti** *(SI) - ☎ 0577 74 60 69 - www. castellodiama.com - enoteca@castello diama.com - Winery tours and tasting by reservation. Wine shop at Villa Pianigiani 10-18.* The winery was established in 1972 and currently has a total area of about 250 hectares, 90 of which under vine and 40 planted with olive trees. Its annual production is approximately 300,000-350,000 bottles. The winery's iconic wine is "Castello di Ama", made by selecting the best clusters of Sangiovese grapes from the estate's finest vineyards. Also famous is L'Apparita – now a cult wine among connoisseurs – made from Merlot grapes; Castello di Ama's Vin Santo is also excellent. Accommodation available in 5 suites. Restaurant at Il Ristoro di Ama. Hectares under vine: 76.
**Wines**: Castello di Ama, Vigneto La Casuccia, Vigneto Bellavista, L'Apparita, Al Poggio, Vin Santo. Other products: olive oil, aqua vitae.

⌂ **Lanciola** – *Via Imprunetana 210 - **Impruneta** (FI) - ☎ 055 20 83 24 - www. lanciola.it - info@lanciola.it - Winery tours by reservation, closed Mon., Wed., Sun.* The estate has approximately 80 hectares of land, evenly divided between vineyards and olive groves. It boasts an ancient and illustrious history: during the Medici rule, it was owned by the noble Ricci family, which established it as an agricultural and winemaking concern. Today it is owned by the Guarnieri family. The Sangiovese, Cabernet Sauvignon, Chardonnay, Pinot Nero, Merlot, Syrah, Canaiolo and Colorino varieties are used. Its Chianti, Vin Santo and prized extra virgin olive oil are exceptional. The estate offers guest accommodation *(7 apts., from €100).* Restaurant service avaiable only by reservation. Hectares under vine: 40.
**Wines**: Chianti Colli Fiorentini, Chianti Classico Le Masse di Greve Riserva, Terricci, Riccionero, Vin Santo. Other products: olive oil, honey and grappa.

⌂ **I Veroni** – *Via Tifariti 5 - Pontassieve (FI) - ☎ 055 83 68 886 - www.iveroni.it - info@iveroni.it - Winery tours and tasting by reservation.* The history of this farmstead dates back to the end of the 1500s, when it was owned by the Gatteschi noble family, who built the first fermentation basins which can still be seen today, as well as the overall farm complex, at the beginning of the 12th century. The name was derived from *verone*, a Tuscan term used to indicate a terrace or loggia, and especially (within the agricultural sector) a small, covered terrace that was set at the end of a country house. The Veroni farmstead included numerous stone terraces, only one of which still exists today; they were most likely used to dry tobacco leaves cultivated along the banks of the Arno River. These terraces eventually lent their names to the entire complex, as well as the company and its wines. Overnight stays *(9 apts. from € 100. Minimum stay 3 nights).* Hectares under vine: 21.
**Wines**: Bianco di Toscana, Rosato di Toscana, Chianti Rufina, Chianti Rufina Riserva, Vin Santo. Other products: olive oil.

⌂ **Brancaia** – *Loc. Poppi* - **Radda in Chianti** *(SI) - ☎ 0577 74 20 07 - www.brancaia.com - degustazione@brancaia.it - Winery tours and tasting by reservation (from €40).* The winery has two estates – Brancaia and Poppi – and has been owned by a Swiss couple, Brigitte and Bruno Widmer, since 1981. The winery immediately gained a stellar reputation when its 1983 vintage won first prize in a major Chianti Classico tasting. In the years that followed, Brancaia reinforced its position, thanks also to the praise that was rightfully showered on its top wine, Brancaia Il Blu. Weekly accommodation available in apartments on the estate (*min. stay 1 week*). Hectares under vine: 80.
**Wines**: Rosso Toscana IGT Brancaia Il Blu, Chianti Classico Brancaia, Rosso Toscana IGT Brancaia Tre, Rosso Maremma Toscana IGT Ilatraia. Other products: grappa and olive oil.

⌂ **Castello d'Albola** – *Via Pian d'Albola 31* - **Radda in Chianti** *(SI) - ☎ 0577 73 80 19 - www.albola.it - accoglienza@albola.it - Winery tours at 12 and 17, in winter by reservation.* Owned by the Zonin family since the 1970s, Castello d'Albola boasts 900 hectares – 125 of which under vine – spread out in the historic holdings of Mondeggi, Selvole, Ellere, Bozzolo, Sant'Ilario, Casa Nova, Acciaiolo, Madonnino, Fagge, Montemaioni, Montevertine, Crognole and Vignale. Sunny and well-aspected, these lands have been ideal for winemaking for centuries, as indicated by documents that have been found. The estate's oldest buildings go back to the 12th c. Accommodation available in 2 villas. Hectares under vine: 125.
**Wines**: Chianti Classico, Chianti Classico Riserva, Acciaiolo, Vin Santo. Other products: grappa and olive oil.

⌂ **Castello di Volpaia** – *Loc. Volpaia* - **Radda in Chianti** *(SI) - ☎ 0577 73 80 66 - www.volpaia.it - info@volpaia.com - Winery tours by reservation (agriturismo@volpaia.com).* The Volpaia estate arose in the 11th c. as a fortified village through the efforts of the Della Volpaia family of Florence. Be sure to take the guided tour through the ancient cellars in the castle, going through the sacristy to the cellar of the Volpaia churches, now used to make and age wines. Castello della Volpaia also organises cookery courses. Accommodation available in villas, apts. or at La Locanda (*www.lalocanda.it, 7 rooms, doubles from €220*). Meals served at Osteria La Volpaia (*www.osteriavolpaia.it*). Hectares under vine: 47.
**Wines**: Chianti Classico Volpaia, Chianti Classico Riserva Coltassala, Balifico IGT, Vin Santo, Vermentino IGT Prelius. Other

products: olive oil and various types of vinegar (including aromatic versions).

⌂ **Colognole** – *Via del Palagio 15* - **Rufina** *(FI), 24 km NE of Florence - ☎ 055 83 19 677 - www.colognole.it - reception@colognole.it - Winery tours and tasting by reservation Wed. and Fri. at 17.30, ☎ 348 72 10 00, winetasting@colognole.it.* In the late 19th c., Count Venceslao Spalletti Trivelli and his wife purchased the Colognole farm, which until then had been owned by the noble Florentine family of Martini Bernardi. Since 1990 Countess Gabriella Spalletti Trivelli has overseen it, assisted by her sons Mario and Cesare. In addition to making wine, the family has also launched a hotel business and set up hunting grounds, which are important for maintaining the territory and environment. The estate offers restaurant service and accommodation at the Colognole B&B or in villas and apts. Hectares under vine: 27.
**Wines**: Chianti Rufina Colognole, Chianti Rufina Riserva del Don, Toscano IGT Sinopie. Other products: olive oil.

♀/ **Antica Fattoria Machiavelli** - *Via Scopeti 64 - Loc. Sant'Andrea in Percussina* - **San Casciano in Val di Pesa** *(FI) - ☎ 055 82 84 71 - www.villamachiavelli.it - info@villamachiavelli.it - Winery tours by reservation (from €23).* Antica Fattoria di Sant'Andrea in Percussina was founded in 1639. Niccolò Machiavelli chose this area that is now the Chianti Classico zone as his home as a Florentine exile and it was here that he wrote *The Prince*. Vermiglio, the forerunner of today's Chianti, was already being made in this area 5 centuries ago. The cellars under Machiavelli's house are the same Albergaccio wine cellars cited in a document dated 1498. Careful restoration work has recently recreated the original structure of the inn of "L'Albergaccio". The kitchen and rooms, mostly furnished with original furnishings from the villa museum, allow visitors to appreciate its ancient atmosphere. Meals served at the Albergaccio Machiavelli restaurant (*closed Mon.*). Hectares under vine: 27.
**Wines**: Chianti Classico Riserva Vigna di Fontalle, Chianti Classico Solatìo del Tani, Il Principe Toscana IGT.

⌂ **Le Corti** – *Via San Piero di Sotto 1* - **San Casciano in Val di Pesa** *(FI) - ☎ 055 82 93 01 - www.principecorsini.com - info@principecorsini.com - Winery tours by reservation, shop@principecorsini.com or ☎ 055 82 93 026.* The Corsini family's first purchases in San Casciano in Val di Pesa go back to 1427 and include the Palazzo delle Corti, and they were followed by others until the last half of the 19th c. Since 1992 Duccio Corsini and his wife Clotilde have devoted their every passion to the Fattoria

Le Corti, striving to establish a rapport with consumers and opening the doors of their villa for the "Alla Corte del Vino" event, an exhibition and market that, since 1997, has presented Tuscany's finest wines. They also promote "Giardini in Fiera", a fascinating international exhibition on gardens and landscaping that has been held at Villa Le Corti in the third week of September since 1994. The estate offers restaurant service and accommodation in B&B (*9 rooms from €100, apts. from €140*) or villas (*from €650 a week*). Hectares under vine: 49

**Wines**: Chianti Classico Don Tommaso, Chianti Classico Le Corti, Chianti Classico Riserva Cortevecchia, Vin Santo del Chianti Classico Sant'Andrea Corsini. Other products: olive oil and grappa.

**Massanera** – *Via Faltignano 68/76* - **San Casciano in Val di Pesa** *(FI), 6 km SW of the Florence Charterhouse* - ℘ *055 82 42 360* - *www.massanera.com* - *info@massanera. com* - *Winery tours and tasting, direct sale.* It seems likely that the name Massanera comes from the thick holm-oak forests that surrounded it in the Middle Ages. Established as a hunting lodge for Florentine noblemen, in the 18th c. it was transformed into a farming estate. The first holding was planted and two houses were built "as homes for farmers and to hold the harvest", as cited on the marble tablets on their walls. The estate has about 100 hectares, 30 of which covered with vineyards, olive groves and farm fields. Over 10 years ago, the ancient Cinta Senese pig was reintroduced here, and it now forages and breeds freely and undisturbed in the woods. Restaurant service and accommodation available in the guest farm (*3 apts., from €95*). Hectares under vine: 7.55.

**Wines**: Rosso Toscana IGT Prelato di Massanera, Rosso Toscana IGT Per Me, Chianti Classico Riserva Massanera, Chianti Classico Massanera, Toscana IGT Rosato di Camilla. Other products: olive oil, Cinta Senese charcuterie, Vin Santo, grappa, digestifs.

**Villa Mangiacane** – *Via Faltignano 4* - **San Casciano in Val di Pesa** *(FI)* - ℘ *055 82 90 123* - *www.mangiacane.com-reservation@mangiacane.com* - *Tours of the winery and villa by reservation, direct sales.* The estate has a little more than 40 hectares under vine, planted with Sangiovese, Canaiolo, Colorino and Merlot grapes. It produces outstanding traditional wines, such as Chianti Classico, as well as more modern ones like Toscana IGT, made from international varieties. The Mangiacane extra virgin olive oil is also excellent. Accommodation and restaurant service available at the luxurious and elegant Villa Mangiacane (*28 rooms, doubles from €195*). Hectares under vine: 43.

**Wines**: Chianti Classico Villa Mangiacane, Chianti Classico Riserva Villa Mangiacane, Toscana IGT Aleah, Toscana Rosso IGT Mhuri. Other products: olive oil and grappa.

**Villa S. Andrea** – *Via di Fabbrica 63 - Loc. Montefiridolfi* - **San Casciano in Val di Pesa** *(FI)* - ℘ *055 82 44 254* - *www.villasandrea. com* - *info@villas-andrea.it* - *Winery tours and tasting by reservation.* The winery owes its name to the nearby church dedicated to St Andrew, a lovely building dating back to the late 18th c. The other buildings and ancient cellars – carved into the hillside – descend from the highest point on the estate, following the lay of the land. Villa Sant'Andrea is part of the "Fabbrica - Santa Cristina" wildlife and hunting estate, and is set in striking untouched woodland with oaks, holm oaks, acacias and cypresses. Accommodation available in 12 apts. (*from €140*), 5 rooms (*from €110*) and 1 villa (*10 pers.*). Hectares under vine: 50.

**Wines**: Chianti Classico Villa S. Andrea, Chianti Classico Riserva Villa S. Andrea, Rosso di Toscana IGT Zobi, Chianti Classico Gran Selezione Montelodoli, Vin Santo del Chianti Classico.

**Tenuta di Arceno** – *Loc. Arceno* - **San Gusmè- Castelnuovo Berardenga** *(SI)* - ℘ *0577 35 93 46* - *www.tenuta diarceno.com* - *info@tenutadiarceno.com* - *Tasting room open Mon.-Fri., Sat. and Sun. by reservation.* According to the winery's philosophy, "To make wine, you simply need to listen to the message of the land. Everything you need to know is there, in the land and the vine". Consequently, the team working at Tenuta Arceno tried to understand the terroir of the various vineyards, identifying the most suitable areas for different types of grapes. The

© By Chan/Shutterstock

vineyards were then assessed individually, plot by plot, to allow the varieties to express themselves. Hectares under vine: 90.

**Wines**: Chianti Classico, Chianti Classico Riserva, Chianti Classico Strada al Sasso. Other products: olive oil.

⚐ **Fattoria Casalbosco** – *Via Montalese 117* - **Santomato** *(PT), 7 km E of Pistoia - ℘ 0573 47 99 47 - www.fattoriacasalbosco. com - info@fattoriacasalbosco.it - Winery tours by reservation*. The estate, established in 1960, has recently planted other varieties to add to its range of wines: Cabernet, Merlot, Sangiovese, Chardonnay and Syrah. Careful varietal selection and the decision to grow grapes only on the best plots of lands represent the key to its production. The wines are inspired by Tuscany's great winemaking traditions, but also pay tribute to the rest of the world by using international varieties. The elegant labels evoking the geometry of the Romanesque decorations of the Duomo in Pistoia and the Baptistery in Florence are striking. Accommodation available at Borgo Antico Fattoria Casalbosco *(apts. from €60)*. Hectares under vine: 45.

**Wines**: Chianti, Chianti Riserva DOCG, Terrecotte Merlot, Dorato, Vin Santo. Other products: olive oil.

⚐ **Donatella Cinelli Colombini - Fattoria del Colle** – *Loc. Il Colle* - **Trequanda** *(SI), 10 km SW of Sinalunga - ℘ 0577 66 21 08 - www.cinellicolombini.it - info@ cinellicolombini.it - Winery tours 9-13 and 14.30-18.30 by reservation*. Donatella Cinelli Colombini is from a family of producers of Brunello di Montalcino. In 1993 she founded the "Wine Tourism Movement" and invented "Open Wineries", the day devoted to wine tourism in Italy. After gaining 14 years of experience on the family estate, in 1998 she created her own, composed of Fattoria del Colle in Trequanda (with the Chianti cellar and guest farm) and Casato Prime Donne in Montalcino. Restaurant service and accommodation available at the Fattoria del Colle guest farm *(17 apts., rooms and 2 villas)*. Hectares under vine: 17.

**Wines**: Cenerentola Orcia Rosso, Il Drago e le Sette Colombe IGT, Chianti Superiore, IGT Rosato Rosa di Tetto. Other products: olive oil and grappa.

## SAN GIMIGNANO

**Castello di Montaùto** - *Loc. Montauto-* **San Gimignano** *(SI) - ℘ 0577 94 11 30 - www.castellodimontauto.it - info@ castellodimontauto.it - Winery tours by reservation, no direct sales*. Owned by the Cecchi family, which now has about 300 hectares of vineyards in the Chianti Classico zone, San Gimignano, Tuscan

Maremma district and Umbria, the estate of Castello di Montauto has an area of about 82 hectares, most of which under vine and with a few hectares of olive groves. The Vernaccia, Chardonnay, Sauvignon Blanc, Sangiovese, Cabernet Sauvignon and Colorino Toscano varieties are cultivated here. Some of the grapes are grown in an experimental vineyards, in collaboration with the Department of Agriculture of the University of Florence and the Vernaccia Consortium. San Gimignano's most interesting varieties of Vernaccia are grown in the vineyard and microvinification processes are applied to verify their respective qualitative potential. Hectares under vine: 48.

**Wines**: Vernaccia di San Gimignano DOCG, Castello di Montaùto Chianti DOCG.

⚐ **Cesani** – *Loc. Pancole 82/A* - **San Gimignano** *(SI) - ℘ 0577 95 50 84 - www.agriturismocesani.it - info@ agriturismocesani.it - Winery tours by reservation, closed Sun*. The Cesani family's estate was established in the early 1950s. Sangiovese and Vernaccia di San Gimignano are the main varieties grown here. The winery is well known, particularly for its reds, all of which made from Sangiovese. The estate also produces extra virgin olive oil and saffron. Accommodation available *(10 rooms, from €88, 1 apt. from €90)*. Hectares under vine: 20.

**Wines**: Vernaccia di San Gimignano, Chianti Colli Senesi, San Gimignano Rosso, Rosso IGT Luenzo. Other products: olive oil, saffron and wine gelly.

⚐ **Fattoria Poggio Alloro** – *Via S. Andrea 23* - *Loc. Ulignano* - **San Gimignano** *(SI) - ℘ 0577 95 01 53 - www.fattoriapoggio alloro.com - info@fattoriapoggioalloro.com - Farm tours and tasting by reservation, closed 24-26 Dec*. Fattoria Poggio Alloro has been owned since 1972 by Umberto, Amico and Bernardo Fioroni, who came from the Marches in 1955 to work as tenant farmers. The land is planted with vineyards, olive groves and cereals, and is also used to graze livestock. The know-how the Fioronis acquired in making and ageing wine inspired them to branch out in 1989, when they began to bottle and sell their products. The estate offers restaurant service and accommodation *(10 rooms and 1 apt.)*. Hectares under vine: 24.

**Wines**: Vernaccia di San Gimignano Le Mandorle, Chianti, Bianco di Toscana IGT, Rosso di Toscana IGT, Vin Santo. Other products: olive oil, saffron, honey, pasta, cantuccini biscuits, flour and cereals, Chianina beef, charcuterie.

⚐ **Mormoraia** – *Loc. Sant'Andrea 15* - **San Gimignano** *(SI) - ℘ 0577 94 00 96 - www.mormoraia.it - info@mormoraia.it -*

*Winery tours by reservation*. An ancient monastery in a splendid panoramic setting, with annexed grounds, houses the winery and elegant guest farm *(25 rooms from €190)* and restaurant Il Fienile. Hectares under vine: 30.

**Wines**: IGT Rosso Sangiovese Neitea, Syrah IGT Agrios, Vernaccia San Gimignano Riserva Antalis, Chianti Colli Senesi Haurio, Rosso IGT. Mytilus Other products: olive oil.

🍇 **Palagetto** – *Loc. Racciano 10 -* **San Gimignano** *(SI) -* ✆ *0577 94 30 90 - www. palagetto.it - tasting@palagetto.it - Winery tours by reservation (from €12).* Palagetto was the first estate acquired by Commendatore Luano Niccolai, the founder of Tenute Niccolai. Vineyards planted with Vernaccia, Chardonnay, Sauvignon, Vermentino, Sangiovese, Cabernet Sauvignon, Merlot and Syrah surround the modern fermentation cellar. The estate's oil mill also produces top-quality olive oil from classic Tuscan varieties such as Frantoio, Moraiolo, Leccino, Pendolino and Correggiolo. Accommodation available *(12 rooms and 4 apts., from €90)* and restaurant. Hectares under vine: 60.

**Wines**: Vernaccia di San Gimignano, Merlot Uno di Quattro, Chianti Colli Senesi, Brunello di Montalcino, Syrah Uno di Quattro. Other products: olive oil and grappa.

## PROVINCE OF AREZZO

**Tenuta Sette Ponti** –*Via Sette Ponti 71 -* **Castiglion Fibocchi** *(AR) -* ✆ *0575 47 78 57 - www.tenutasetteponti.it - tenutasetteponti@tenutasetteponti.it - Winery tours by reservation.* The Moretti family has owned the estate since the 1950s, when architect Alberto Moretti was attracted to the area by its rich game reserve and purchased the first 60 hectares from Princesses Margherita and Maria Cristina of Savoy-Aosta, the daughters of

Vittorio Emanuele III. The Morettis first planted vineyards in 1957, but it was not until 1997 that Alberto's son Antonio decided to oversee the vineyards and start bottling its wine on the estate. Hectares under vine: 54.

**Wines**: Chianti Vigna di Pallino, Toscana IGT Crognolo, Toscana IGT Oreno. The winery's estate Poggio al Lupo, in the Maremma district, produces Morellino di Scansano. Other products: olive oil.

🏠 **Camperchi** - *Via del Burrone 38 - Loc. Morcaggiolo -* **Civitella in Val di Chiana** *(AR) -* ✆ *0575 44 02 81 - www.camperchi. com - info@camperchi.com - Winery tours and tasting by reservation.* Camperchi is a very young winery: its first harvest was in 2006 and its first wines were released in 2008. Non-invasive techniques are used, with an eye to respecting the territory and the typicity of the varieties as much as possible. Camperchi welcomes connoisseurs of fine wine, who can stay at the estate's guest farm, which has four rural country houses renovated in a traditional Tuscan style *(4 farmhouses).* The estate also has stables. Hectares under vine: 24.

**Wines**: Camperchi Sangiovese, Camperchi Merlot, Anno "0". Other products: honey.

🍇 **Baracchi** – *Loc. San Martino a Bocena -* **Cortona** *(AR) -* ✆ *331 60 00 358 - www. baracchiwinery.com - info@baracchiwinery. com - Winery tours by reservation (from €25).* Riccardo Baracchi has been determined to continue the traditions of his family, which has grown grapes and made wine since 1860. Sangiovese, Syrah, Merlot, Cabernet and Trebbiano are grown on the estate. The elegant Relais Il Falconiere, which has always been owned by the family, is next to the winery. The estate's extra virgin olive oil is also outstanding. Accommodation and restaurant service available at Relais & Chateaux Il Falconiere *(22 rooms, from €240).* Hectares under vine: 30.

**Wines**: Ardito Toscana Rosso, Astore Trebbiano, Cortona Smeriglio Sangiovese, Cortona Smeriglio Merlot, Brut Trebbiano. Other products: olive oil.

🍇 **Il Borro** ¬ *Loc. Il Borro 1 -* **San Giustino Valdarno** *(AR) -* ✆ *055 97 70 53 - www. ilborro.it - winetour@ilborro.it - Winery tours and tasting by reservation.* Castello del Borro changed hands a number times over the years and was held by important nobles that helped write the history of Tuscany, such as the Pazzi and Medici Tornaquinci families. At the turn of the 20th c. it was purchased by Duke Amedeo of Aosta and in 1993 it was taken over by the Ferragamo family, who renovated it and launched two ambitious projects: winemaking and tourist accommodation in

© George5/Shutterstock

apartments in the medieval hamlet, in an independent farmhouse and luxury villas. Food also served. Hectares under vine: 45.

**Wines**: Il Borro Toscana Rosso IGT, Polissena Toscana Sangiovese IGT, Pian di Nova Toscana Rosso IGT, Lamelle Toscana Bianco IGT. Other products: olive oil and grappa.

## NOBILE DI MONTEPULCIANO

⚲ **Fattoria del Cerro** – *Via Grazianella 5-Fraz. Acquaviva* - **Montepulciano** *(SI) - ℘ 0578 76 77 22 - www.tenutedelcerro.it - info@tenutedelcerro.it - Winery tours and tasting by reservation*. Saiagricola purchased the estate in 1978. It produces a wide range of wines – Vino Nobile di Montepulciano, Rosso di Montepulciano, Chianti Colli Senesi, Chardonnay di Toscana, Merlot, Sangiovese, Trebbiano Toscano, Vin Santo and Vendemmia Tardiva – as well as olive oil, grappa and brandy. Villa Grazianella, a charming historic residence, is on the grounds of the estate *(11 rooms)*, and offers meals for hotel guests. Hectares under vine: 170.

**Wines**: Vino Nobile di Montepulciano Antica Chiusina, Vino Nobile di Montepulciano, Rosso di Montepulciano, Vin Santo di Montepulciano, Chianti Colli Senesi. Other products: olive oil, grappa and brandy.

**Cantina Fassati** – *Via di Graccianello 3/A* - **Gracciano di Montepulciano** *(SI) - ℘ 0578 70 87 08 - www.cantinafassati.it - info@cantinafassati.it - Winery tours and tasting by reservation*. Fassati was an old Chianti winery established in 1913 by the marquis after which it is named. In 1969 it was taken over by the Sparaco family, known for their passion for winegrowing and the owners of Fazi Battaglia, the Marches winery specialising in the production of local DOC labels. Since 1990 the new generation of Sparacos has been at the helm of the company, continuing the family vocation. Hectares under vine: 100.

**Wines**: Vino Nobile di Montepulciano Gersemi, Vino Nobile di Montepulciano Pasiteo, Rosso di Montepulciano Selciaia, Chianti Riserva Le Gaggiole, L'Augusto Vin Santo. Other products: grappa.

⚲ **Dei** – *Via Martiena 35* - **Montepulciano** *(SI) - ℘ 0578 71 68 78 - www.cantinedei.com - info@cantinedei.com - Winery tours by reservation*. In 1964 Alibrando Dei, the grandfather of Maria Caterina, the current owner who in 1991 gave up her stage career to devote herself entirely to her vineyards and land, acquired the first portion of what would become the Dei estate. Indeed, it was her grandfather who planted the vineyard that yields what is now the pride of the winery: Vino Nobile di Montepulciano Riserva Bossona. The new winery, realized completely in travertine, merges harmoniously with the gentle hill landscape. The estate offers guest accommodation in the apartments of the farmhouse. Hectares under vine: 50.

**Wines**: Rosso di Montepulciano, Vino Nobile di Montepulciano, Vino Nobile di Montepulciano Riserva Bossona, Sancta Catharina IGT, Bianco di Martiena IGT. Other products: olive oil and grappa.

**Fattoria della Talosa** – *Via Talosa 8* - **Montepulciano** *(SI) - ℘ 0578 75 79 29 - www.talosa.it - shop@talosa.it - Winery tours free 10.30-19 or by reservation*. Owned by the Roman entrepreneur Angelo Jacorossi since 1972, Talosa has 33 hectares of vineyards in one of the most charming parts of Montepulciano, at an altitude of 350-400 m, which are meticulously cultivated. The 16th-c. ageing cellar is fascinating, as it is in the historic district of Montepulciano in the vaults beneath two of the city's oldest palazzi, Tarugi and Sinatti. Hectares under vine: 33.

**Wines**: Vino Nobile di Montepulciano Filai Lunghi, Vino Nobile di Montepulciano Riserva, Rosso di Montepulciano, Chianti Colli Senesi, Toscana Rosso IGT Pietrose. Other products: olive oil and grappa.

**Icario** – *Via delle Pietrose 2* - **Montepulciano** *(SI) - ℘ 0578 75 88 45 - www.icario.it - info@icario.it - Winery tours Mon.-Fri. 10-13 and 14-18, Sat.-Sun. by appointment (reservation required at least 2 days in advance)*. The Cecchetti family purchased the original nucleus of the estate in 1998, later expanding to nearby plots. Today Icario boasts 22 hectares of vineyards and a new cellar, and in May 2015 the Rothenberger family took over the estate. Inside the winery, a space has been devoted to contemporary art, alternating group exhibitions with solo shows. The winery strives to introduce art lovers to the world of wine – and vice versa. Hectares under vine: 22.

**Wines**: Rosso Icario IGT, Vino Nobile di Montepulciano, Vino Nobile di Montepulciano Vitaroccia, Nysa Bianco IGT. Other products: grappa and olive oil.

⚲ **I Poderi di San Gallo** – *Via delle Colombelle 7* - **Montepulciano** *(SI) - ℘ 0578 75 83 30 or ℘ 339 77 69 444 - www.agriturismosangallo.com - info@agriturismo sangallo.com - Winery tours by reservation (from €25)*. The winery is composed of the Bertille and Casella estate, and has a total area of about 22 hectares, 15 of which under vine. It also has a centuries-old olive grove and a pond, where migratory herons are often seen. The old rural building was renovated to house the San Gallo guest farm *(6 apts., from €110)*. The vineyards are planted with Prugnolo Gentile, Mammolo,

Ciliegiolo, Colorino and Canaiolo. Hectares under vine: 15.

**Wines**: Vino Nobile di Montepulciano, Rosso di Montepulciano, Chianti Colli Senesi, L'Attesa IGT. Other products: olive oil.

**La Calonica** – *Via della Stella 27 - Fraz. di Valiano* - **Montepulciano** *(SI) - ℰ 0578 72 41 19 - www.lacalonica.com - info@ lacalonica.com - Winery tours by reservation.* The winery is composed of the "La Calonica" and "Capezzine Vecchie" estates. The winery has been owned by the Cattani family since 1973. Most of the vineyards are planted with Sangiovese di Montepulciano (Prugnolo Gentile), followed by Canaiolo Nero, Merlot, Cabernet Sauvignon, Sauvignon, Malvasia del Chianti and Grechetto. Hectares under vine: 45.

**Wines**: Vino Nobile di Montepulciano, Vino Nobile di Montepulciano Riserva San Venerio, Cortona Sangiovese Girifalco, Cortona Sauvignon Blanc Dongiovanni, Vin Santo di Montepulciano. Other products: olive oil and grappa.

♀/ **Palazzo Vecchio** – *Via Terrarossa 5 - Fraz. di Valiano* - **Montepulciano** *(SI) - ℰ 0578 72 41 70 - www.vinonobile.it - palazzovecchio@vinonobile.it - Winery tours by reservation.* In the 16th and 17th c. the current Palazzo Vecchio was owned by the Ospedale degli Innocenti of Florence and was inhabited by a confraternity of monks who farmed this land. After changing hands several times, in 1952 it was purchased by Count Riccardo Zorzi, who decided to devote himself to viticulture and winemaking. Today the estate is owned by Marco Sbernadori and Alessandra Zorzi.Restaurant La Dogana *(Closed Tue.)*
Hectares under vine: 28.

**Wines**: Vino Nobile di Montepulciano Terrarossa DOCG, Vino Nobile di Montepulciano Maestro DOCG, Rosso di Montepulciano Dogana DOC, Vino Cortona DOC, Vin Santo. Other products: olive oil.

**Poderi Boscarelli** – *Via di Montenero 24 - Fraz. Cervognano* - **Montepulciano** *(SI) - ℰ 0578 76 76 08 - www.poderiboscarelli. com - cantina@poderiboscarelli.com - Winery, vineyards tours and tasting by reservation (payment required).* In 1962 Egidio Corradi purchased 2 small estates in Cervognano di Montepulciano with the dream of establishing a winery that would focus above all on quality; his work was then taken over and continued by his daughter Paola and son-in-law Ippolito De Ferrari. Today it is run by Paola, assisted by her sons Luca and Nicolò, who pursue the goal of promoting Vino Nobile di Montepulciano through a constant quest for quality. Hectares under vine: 14.

**Wines**: Vino Nobile di Montepulciano DOCG, Riserva di Vino Nobile DOCG, Nobile di Montepulciano Nocio dei Boscarelli DOCG, Rosso di Montepulciano Prugnolo. Other products: grappa and olive oil.

**Poliziano** – *Via Fontago 1 -* **Montepulciano** *(SI) - ℰ 0578 73 81 71 - www.carlettipoliziano.com - info@ carlettipoliziano.com - Winery tours by reservation, closed Sun., booking@ carlettipoliziano.com.* The Poliziano estate, owned by the Carletti family since 1961, started out with just 22 hectares and has now grown to its current 120, all under vine. Its name is a tribute to the humanist and poet Angelo Ambrogini (1454-94), called Politian, who was born in Montepulciano. As a way to spread the culture of wine and give visitors a worthy welcome, the winery has built 3 tasting rooms run by specialised staff. Hectares under vine: 170.

**Wines**: Le Stanze del Poliziano, In Violas Nera Cortona, Rosso di Montepulciano, Vino Nobile di Montepulciano, Vino Nobile di Montepulciano Asinone. Other products: olive oil.

**Avignonesi** – *Fattoria Le Capezzine - Via Colonica 1* - **Valiano di Montepulciano** *(SI) - ℰ 0578 72 43 04 - www.avignonesi.it - info@avignonesi.it - Winery tours and tasting by reservation, closed Jan.-Feb.* Avignonesi is composed of 9 production units, for a total of 225 hectares, 157 of which under vine and 3 planted with olive trees. As part of its ongoing research, it set up the Vigna Tonda project, an experimental vineyard created to determine the extent to which wine quality is affected by vine density and the type of rootstock. Its Vin Santo and Vin Santo Occhio di Pernice are unanimously considered among the very best of their type. Hectares under vine: 157.

**Wines**: Chardonnay Il Marzocco, Vino Nobile di Montepulciano, Desiderio Merlot, Toscana IGT 50&50, Vin Santo di Montepulciano. Other products: olive oil, grappa and honey.

## BRUNELLO DI MONTALCINO

⌂ **Argiano** – *Loc. Sant'Angelo in Colle -* **Montalcino** *(SI) - ℰ 0577 84 40 37 - www.argiano.net - argiano@argiano.net - Winery tours by reservation.* It is said that scholars would come here to seek the *Ara Jani*, the legendary temple of the Roman god Janus, from which the winery's name is derived. The villa of Argiano, which was built during the Renaissance, has been owned by various noble Tuscan families over the centuries. In 1992 the villa was taken over by Countess Noemi Marone Cinzano, in 2013 the ownership was trasferred to a group of Brasilian entrepreneurs. Accommodation available at Arciano Dimore (*3 apts. and 3 rooms*). Hectares under vine: 50.

**Wines**: Rosso di Montalcino DOC, Brunello di Montalcino DOCG, Suolo IGT, Solengo IGT. Other products: olive oil and grappa.

**Azienda Agricola Cupano** – *Loc. Camigliano - Pod. Centine 31* - **Montalcino** (*SI*) - ✆ *0577 81 60 55 - www.cupano.it - cupano@cupano.it - Winery tours by reservation*. She's a photographer, journalist and art scholar, he's a director of photography: just over 10 years ago Ornella Tondini and Lionel Cousin opted for a brand-new lifestyle, and their passion for the land inspired them to purchase a winery in Tuscany. They make wines exclusively with natural yeasts, refusing to use cultured ones as they jeopardise the identity of the variety. Their wine reflects the full personality of the terroir and the variety from which it is made. Hectares under vine: 7.

**Wines**: Brunello di Montalcino DOCG, Rosso di Montalcino, Sant'Antimo Ombrone. Other products: olive oil.

**Camigliano** – *Via d'Ingresso 2 - Camigliano* - **Montalcino** (*SI*) - ✆ *0577 81 60 61 - www. camigliano.it - info@camigliano.it - Winery tours by reservation, closed Sat. and Sun. (from €18)*. The estate was purchased by the Ghezzi family in 1957 and now has 530 hectares, 93 of which under vine. The new cellar is entirely underground and annually produces approximately 330,000 bottles that are appreciated both in Italy and internationally. Today it is run by Gualtiero Ghezzi, who has lavished enormous efforts on increasing the quality of his wine even further. Hectares under vine: 93.

**Wines**: Brunello di Montalcino, Rosso di Montalcino, Vermentino IGT Gamal, Vermentino IGT Bianco delle Crete, Chianti Colli Senesi, Poderuccio IGT Toscana. Other products: olive oil and grappa.

© Wolfgang Amri/Shutterstock

⌂ **Caparzo** – *Strada Prov. del Brunello, km 1.700 - Loc. Caparzo* - **Montalcino** (*SI*) - ✆ *0577 84 83 90 - www.caparzo.com - caparzo@caparzo.com - Winery tours by reservation*. The vineyards, cellars and all the growing facilities were established in the late 1960s, with the progressive adaptation and constant renovation of the land and cellars. Even today, Caparzo continues to experiment with innovative training systems and, in particular, different clonal selections on its estate of 200 hectares, 90 of which under vine. Over the course of more than 30 years, Caparzo has grown, respecting the tradition of Brunello and of the different terroirs of this district, and it has brought out the best of its own wines with a spirit of creativity and innovation. Accommodation available at the estate's guest farm (*3 apts.*). Hectares under vine: 90.

**Wines**: Brunello di Montalcino Riserva, Rosso di Montalcino La Caduta, Moscadello di Montalcino. Other products: olive oli and grappa.

⌂ **Casato Prime Donne** – *Loc. Casato 17* - **Montalcino** (*SI*) - ✆ *0577 84 94 21 - www.cinellicolombini.it - casato@ cinellicolombini.it - Winery tours Mon.-Fri. 9-13 and 14-18, Sat. and Sun. by reservation*. The forebears of Donatella Cinelli Colombini already owned the estate in 1592. In more recent times it belonged to Donatella's grandmother and then her mother, who handed it down to her to continue the family tradition. It was the first winery in Italy to be staffed entirely by women. The International Casato Prime Donne Prize is awarded to those who promote the territory of Montalcino and its wine, and make them known; the main award goes to women who have valorised their gender in society and work. Accommodation available at Fattoria del Colle (*17 apts., 2 villas and rooms*, ✆ *0577 66 21 08*) and restaurant Osteria di Donatella. Hectares under vine: 18.

**Wines**: Brunello di Montalcino DOCG, Brunellodi Montalcino DOCG selezione Prime Donne, Brunello di Montalcino DOCG IOsonoDONATELLA, Vin Santo. Other products: olive oil.

⌂ **Castello Banfi** – *Castello di Poggio alle Mura* - **Montalcino** (*SI*) - ✆ *0577 84 01 11 - www.castellobanfi.com - banfi@banfi.it - Winery tours by reservation*, ✆ *0577 87 75 05 or 0577 87 75 14 - reservations@banfi.it, closed Sat. and Sun*. Established by Italian-American brothers, John and Harry Mariani, in 1978, it has now become one of the largest wineries in Italy. The estate is spread out over an area of 2830 hectares, approximately 850 of which under vine. In addition to the area's two traditional varieties, Sangiovese and Moscato, it also grows the most important international noble varieties: Pinot Grigio, Chardonnay, Sauvignon Blanc, Cabernet Sauvignon, Merlot and Syrah. Accommodation available at the Banfi castle (*14 rooms, from €500, closed Nov.-May*) and restaurant service at the Taverna Banfi or at the Sala dei Grappoli. Hectares under vine: 850.

**Wines**: Brunello di Montalcino, Rosso di Montalcino, Brunello di Montalcino DOCG Riserva Poggio all'Oro, Brunello di Montalcino Poggio alle Mura. Other products: prunes, olive oil and sauces.

**Castello Romitorio** – *Loc. Romitorio 279 -* **Montalcino** *(SI) -* ✆ *0577 84 72 12 - www.castelloromitorio.com - info@ castelloromitorio.com - Winery tours by reservation.* The castle is a massive and striking 14th-c. fortress. Since 1984 it has been owned by the contemporary artist Alessandro Chia, who has devoted a great deal of time to restoring the castle and reorganising the vineyards. The wine labels and the winery itself are adorned with some of his works, creating a fascinating blend of art and enology. The new cellars, with 3000 m² of floor space, and built in part underground at the foot of the castle, have been in operation since 2006. Hectares under vine: 29.

**Wines**: Brunello di Montalcino, Rosso di Montalcino, Toscana IGT Romito, Toscana IGT Romitòro, Chianti Colli Senesi. Other products: olive oil and grappa.

**Ciacci Piccolomini d'Aragona** – *Loc. Molinello - Castelnuovo dell'Abate -* **Montalcino** *(SI) -* ✆ *0577 83 56 16 - www.ciaccipiccolomini.com - visite@ ciaccipiccolomini.com - Winery tours by reservation.* The heart of the 17th-c. estate is its historic palazzo, dating to the same period. It was named Palazzo Ciacci Piccolomini in the early 20th c. and is now operated by the Bianchini family. The pride of the winery is its noble Brunello Pianrosso and Brunelllo Vigna di Pianrosso Riserva Santa Caterina d'Oro. Hectares under vine: 55,5.

**Wines**: Brunello di Montalcino DOCG, Brunello di Montalcino Vigna di Pianrosso Riserva, Rosso di Montalcino Rossofonte, Sant'Antimo DOC Fabius. Other products: olive oil, grappa and honey.

**Col'Orcia** – *Via Giuncheti -* **Montalcino** *(SI) -* ✆ *0577 80 891 - www.coldorcia.it - info@ coldorcia.it - Winery tours and tasting by reservation (from €15).* The estate is one of Montalcino's most historic wineries: in 1933 it presented 3 Brunello vintages at the 1st Italian Wine Show, held in Siena. Its origins go back to the first half of the 17th c., when the Della Ciaia family of noble Sienese knights acquired property in the area of

© Mars Evis/Shutterstock

Sant'Angelo in Colle and continued to expand it. In the second half of the 19th c. it was taken over by the Servadio family, followed by the Franceschi family. In 1973 Count Alberto Marone Cinzano acquired it with the aim of helping to develop and establish the reputation of Montalcino and its Brunello around the world. Edoardo Virano has been at the helm of the winery since 1977, and Count Francesco Marone Cinzano has been company chairman since 1992. Hectares under vine: 144.

**Wines**: Brunello di Montalcino Poggio al Vento, Brunello di Montalcino, Rosso di Montalcino Banditella, Sant'Antimo Cabernet Olmaia, Moscadello di Montalcino Pascena. Other products: olive oil and grappa.

🏠 **Fattoria dei Barbi** – *Loc. Podernovi 170 -* **Montalcino** *(SI) -* ✆ *0577 84 11 11 - www. fattoriadeibarbi.it - info@fattoriadeibarbi.it - Winery tours by reservation.* The Colombini family has owned land in Montalcino since 1352 and has held the Fattoria dei Barbi since 1790. Its first important award came in 1892: a silver medal from the Ministry of Agriculture. This was just the first in a long series of prizes won not only in Italy but also internationally. The estate is now run by Stefano Cinelli Colombini, who is descended from this family. He has safeguarded its age-old traditions whilst promoting major technological innovations. The vineyards cover nearly 100 hectares, representing about 20% of the entire estate. Annual production exceeds 800,000 bottles. 2 apts. avaible and food is served at Taverna dei Barbi (*closed Tue. evening and Wed.*). Hectares under vine: 97.

**Wines**: Brunello di Montalcino, Rosso di Montalcino, Brusco dei Barbi IGT, Birbone

Toscano IGT, Morellino di Scansano. Other products: charcuterie, cheese and olive oil.

**Fattoria Poggio di Sotto** – *Castelnuovo dell'Abate* - **Montalcino** *(SI)* - *☏ 0577 83 55 02 - www.collemassari.it - info@poggiodi sotto.it - Winery tours by reservation.* The winery was established following years of research into soil, exposure and microclimate. Owners Elisabeth and Piero Palmucci purchased their first vineyards, situated near the lovely Abbey of Sant'Antimo, in 1989. At the same time, they began to cooperate with the University of Milan to plant new vineyards with the most suitable Sangiovese clones. They rapidly achieved excellent results and Poggio di Sotto wines are now highly regarded. Hectares under vine: 20.
**Wines**: Rosso di Montalcino, Brunello di Montalcino, Brunello di Montalcino Riserva. Other products: olive oil and grappa.

**♨ Castello Di Velona Resort, Thermal Spa & Winery** – *Loc. La Velona* - **Montalcino** *(SI)* - *☏ 0577 83 57 00 - www.castellodivelonavini.it - reservation@ castellodivelona.it - Winery tours by reservation.* The heart of the winery is the 19th-c. farmhouse that has been exquisitely restored; the production and ageing cellars are on the ground floor. All of the estate-owned vineyards are planted with Sangiovese Grosso, the clone of this variety that is used to make Brunello.
In addition to its wines, be sure to try the estate's charcuterie and other products made from the Cinta Senese breed of pigs. Accommodation available *(46 rooms, from €315)* and 3 restaurants: Il Vignone, L'abbazia and Pool Bar. Hectares under vine: 5.
**Wines**: Brunello di Montalcino DOCG, Rosso di Montalcino DOC, Toscana IGT Dialogo. Other products: olive oil, Cinta Senese charcuterie and products.

**♨ Podere Piombaia** – *Loc. Crocina,1* - **Montalcino** *(SI)* - *☏ 0577 84 71 97 - www. piombaia.com - Piombaia@piombaia.com - Winery tours by reservation.* The Rossi-Cantini family has handed down the art of winemaking since the early 20th c. Today it vaunts an estate of about 210 hectares, growing grapes, olives and cereals. In addition to making wine, since 1995 the family has also been involved in the hospitality and restaurant trade, with the Piombaia guest farm, set in a traditional farmhouse *(7 apts., from €80)*, and the Osteria La Crocina, where guests can enjoy typical Tuscan dishes and products. Hectares under vine: 12.
**Wines**: Brunello di Montalcino, Rosso di Montalcino, Sant'Antimo DOC. Other products: olive oil, vinegar, grappa and brandy.

**♀/ Poggio Antico** – *Loc. Poggio Antico* - **Montalcino** *(SI)* - *☏ 0577 84 80 44 - www. poggioantico.com - mail@poggioantico.com - Winery tours and tasting by reservation (from €15)*. The development of Poggio Antico, which dates back to the 19th c., commenced around 1970, when the first vineyards were planted and work to build the cellar began. Since 1984 it has been owned by the Gloder family, in 2017 it was bought by the Belgian company Atlas Invest. The estate has approximately 200 hectares, covered with woods, vineyards, olive groves and farmland. Of the 33 hectares under vine, 30 are planted with Sangiovese and 3 with Cabernet Sauvignon. Meals served at the Poggio Antico restaurant. Hectares under vine: 33.
**Wines**: Riserva Brunello di Montalcino DOCG, Brunello di Montalcino DOCG Altero, Brunello di Montalcino DOCG, Rosso di Montalcino DOC, Toscana Rosso IGT Madre, IGT Lemartine. Other products: olive oil and grappa.

**Salvioni** – *P.zza Cavour 19* - **Montalcino** *(SI)* - *☏ 0577 84 84 99 - www.aziendasalvioni. com - info@aziendasalvioni.com - Winery tours by reservation.* Salvioni is one of the best-known producers of Brunello di Montalcino, and its wines are highly regarded in Italy and around the world. The philosophy of the winery, which is headed by Giulio Salvioni, is based on respect for tradition and terroir. Its production is very limited: its mere 4 hectares of vineyards are planted exclusively with the area's prime variety, Sangiovese da Brunello. Hectares under vine: 4.
**Wines**: Brunello di Montalcino DOCG, Rosso di Montalcino DOC. Other products: olive oil and grappa.

**⚲ Tenuta Friggiali** – *Strada Maremmana - Loc. Friggiali* - **Montalcino** - *☏ 0577 84 94 54 - www.tenutafriggialiepietranera.it, www. tenutedonnaolga.it - info@tenutafriggialie pietranera.it - Winery tours by reservation.* The Peluso Centolani family owns the estate named after it. In Montalcino it has two major production sites, Tenuta Friggiali, where the winery and offices are located, and Tenuta Pietranera, for a total of approximately 200 hectares with vineyards, olive groves, farmland and woods. Planted entirely with Sangiovese da Brunello, the vineyards are divided into 3 main sectors, each of which has a different name (Pietrafocaia, Maremmana, Poggiotondo), based on how they were traditionally known locally. The production of Donna Olga wines is personally overseen by Olga Peluso Centolani. Accommodation available at Relais Friggiali *(6 rooms and 2 apts., doubles from €110)*. Hectares under vine: 45.

## ADDRESSES

**Wines**: Brunello di Montalcino Tenuta Friggiali, Donna Olga Brunello di Montalcino, Rosso di Montalcino Tenuta Friggiali, Donna Olga Rosso di Montalcino. Other products: olive oil and grappa.

**Tenuta Greppo di Franco Biondi Santi** – *Villa Greppo 183* - **Montalcino** *(SI)* - *℘ 0577 84 80 23 - www.biondisanti.com - biondisanti@biondisanti.it - Winery tours by reservation (visite@biondisanti.it).* When it comes to Brunello, this is one of the greatest names, famed in Italy and around the world. It was Ferruccio Biondi Santi who revived the Greppo estate, planting Sangiovese Grosso that he had personally selected. In 1880 Ferruccio achieved the first satisfactory results, thanks also to the winemaking experience of his maternal grandfather, Clemente Santi. His son Tancredi, a farmer and enologist, continued his work equally successfully. Franco Biondi Santi, the current owner and Tancredi's son, has further developed the estate and winery. Hectares under vine: 25.

**Wines**: Rosso di Montalcino DOC, Brunello di Montalcino Annata, Brunello di Montalcino Riserva. Other products: olive oil.

⚲ **Tenuta Il Poggione** – *Loc. Sant'Angelo in Colle* - **Montalcino** *(SI)* - *℘ 0577 84 40 29 - www.tenutailpoggione.it - info@ilpoggione.it - Winery tours and tasting by reservation.* Long owned by the Franceschi family, more than a century later the work done by Lavinio is still a fundamental point of reference for his heirs, Leopoldo and Livia, who now run the estate with the very same commitment. With about 530 hectares – divided into 140 of vineyards and 50 of olive groves, as well as farmland

© LIUXIN/Shutterstock

and woods – Tenuta Il Poggione is one of the largest estates in the municipality of Montalcino. Accommodation available in 7 guest apartments on the estate. Hectares under vine: 140.

**Wines**: Brunello di Montalcino, Brunello di Montalcino Riserva Vigna Paganelli, Rosso di Montalcino Leopoldo Franceschi, Moscadello di Montalcino, Vin Santo Sant'Antimo. Other products: grappa and olive oil.

**Tenute Silvio Nardi** – *Casale del Bosco* - **Montalcino** *(SI)* - *℘ 0577 80 82 69 - www.tenutenardi.com - visite@tenutenardi.it - Winery tours by reservation, closed Sun., over Christmas and mid-Aug.* Silvio Nardi, father of the current owners, purchased the Casale del Bosco estate in 1950 – more out of passion than with an eye to reaping an income from it. The Umbrian family's main business was manufacturing agricultural machinery. Nevertheless, the winery released its first bottle of Brunello in 1958. Over the years, it has made numerous acquisitions, expanding the estate to its current 80 hectares of vineyards. In 1967 Nardi became one of the founders of the Brunello di Montalcino Wine Consortium. Hectares under vine: 80.

**Wines**: Brunello di Montalcino DOCG, Rosso di Montalcino DOC, Sant'Antimo Tùran, Moscadello, Vin Santo. Other products: olive oil and grappa.

### MAREMMA

**Poggio ArgentierA** – *Strada Banditella 2* - **Alberese** *(GR)* - *℘ 348 49 52 767 - www.poggioargentiera.com - Winery tours by reservation.* The estate was established in 1997 when Gianpaolo Paglia, a local agronomist, and Justine Keeling, an English marketing manager, purchased Podere Adua. A passion for the land inspired them to start producing Morellino di Scansano and, in a very short time, they achieved highly gratifying results that promptly attracted the attention of wine lovers and experts. Hectares under vine: 20.

**Wines**: Morellino di Scansano Ventoso, Morellino di Scansano BellamarsiliA, Syrah PodereAdua Toscana IGT, Vermentino Toscana IGT, Bucce Toscana IGT.

⚲ **Tenuta La Badiola-L'Andana** – *Loc. Badiola* - **Castiglione della Pescaia** *(GR)* - *℘ 0564 94 48 00 - www.acquagiustawine.it.* In the 19th c. the estate was owned by Grand Duke Leopold II, who undertook extensive reclamation work to rid the Maremma area of malaria. The names of the wine produced here – Acquagiusta and Acquadoro (perfect water and golden water) – evoke this work. The estate's 30 hectares produce 40,000 bottles of white, 20,000 of red and 15,000 of rosé. Two varieties, Vermentino and Viognier, are used for the whites; Cabernet, Merlot, Sangiovese and Syrah are used for the reds, whilst Alicante is used to make the rosé. Accommodation is available at L'Andana, which features a complete wellness centre (*www.andana.it, 20 rooms and 13 suites, doubles from €300*). Restaurant service at the Trattoria Enrico Bartolini (*only dinner*). Hectares under vine: 30.

**Wines**: Acquadoro, Acquagiusta Vermentino, Acquagiusta Rosato, Acquagiusta Rosso. Other products: olive oil.

**Castello Colle Massari** – *Loc. Poggi del Sasso* - **Cinigiano** *(GR)* - ℰ *0564 99 04 96 - www.collemassari.it - info@collemassari.it - Winery tours by reservation*. Indulging his passion for great wines, Claudio Tipa established the estate in 1998. Indeed, after years of working in the industrial sector, Tipa decided to make his dream come true: creating a French-style *domaine* in Italy, and getting his wife and sister involved in this adventure. Their first vintage was produced in 2000. The medieval castle is exceptionally beautiful and picturesque. Hectares under vine: 120.

**Wines**: Melacce Montecucco Vermentino, Gròttolo Montecucco Rosato, Colle Massari Montecucco Riserva, Rigoleto Montecucco Rosso, Poggio Lombrone Montecucco Sangiovese. Other products: olive oil and grappa.

⌂ **Castello di Vicarello** – *Loc. Vicarello 1 - Loc. Poggi del Sasso* - **Cinigiano** *(GR)* - ℰ *0564 99 07 18 - www.castellodivicarello.it - info@vicarello.it - Winery tours by reservation*. In 1993 Aurora Pagani and Carlo Baccheschi Berti, the owners of the Vicarello castle, decided to renovate and convert it into a winery and exclusive country residence. The wines are made from blends of Cabernet Sauvignon and Cabernet Franc ("Castello di Vicarello") and Merlot and Sangiovese ("Terre di Vico"). Accommodation and continental breakfast available in the castle's elegant and exclusive suites (*9 rooms, doubles from €500*). Hectares under vine: 7.

**Wines**: Castello di Vicarello, Terre di Vico, Merah. Other products: olive oil.

**Rocca di Frassinello** – *Loc. Giuncarico - Gavorrano* *(GR)* - ℰ *0566 88 400 - www.castellare.it - visite@roccadifrassinello.it - Winery tours by reservation (from €25)*. The estate is the outcome of a joint venture between Castellare di Castellina and Domaine Baron de Rothschild-Lafite, which decided to merge their different experiences: the former with the cultivation and vinification of Sangioveto, and the latter with traditional French varieties such as Cabernet, Merlot, Petit

Verdot and Syrah. The spectacular winery was designed by Renzo Piano. Hectares under vine: 90.

**Wines**: Poggio alla Guardia Vigne Alte, Le Sughere di Frassinello, Rocca di Frassinello.

⌂ **Fattoria Le Pupille** – *Piagge del Maiano 92/A* - **Grosseto** - ℰ *0564 40 95 17 - www.fattorialepupille.it - info@fattorialepupille.it - Winery tours by reservation 8.30-17.30, closed Sat., Sun. and public hols.* A small, linear farmhouse entirely surrounded by a 420-hectare property: this exclusive world was created by Elisabetta Geppetti in a little over twenty years, bringing to life a range of wines that express the values of a land that is perfect for winemaking. The vineyards run up and down low hills, between 200 and 280 metres above sea level, among terrain that can be quite different from one section to the next, though all rich in shells and relatively unfertile. Sangiovese is the primary vine. Every year Fattoria Le Pupille produces roughly 500,000 bottles, distributed in a capillary manner across Italy and abroad. Accommodation is available at guest house Fattoria Le Pupille. Hectares under vine: 60.

**Wines**: Poggio Argentato IGT Toscana Bianco, Morellino di Scansano DOCG, Riserva 2017 Morellino di Scansano Riserva DOCG, Saffredi IGT Maremma Toscana, SolAlto IGT Toscana Bianco. Other products: olive oil and grappa.

⌂ **La Fattoria di Magliano** – *Loc. Sterpeti 10* - **Magliano in Toscana** *(GR)* - ℰ *0564 59 30 40 - www.fattoriadimagliano.it - info@fattoriadimagliano.it - Winery tours by reservation*. Fattoria di Magliano stands in the middle of a sprawling farm estate near the Uccellina Nature Reserve. The cellar was completed in 2001, also the year it first produced wine. The estate currently makes Morellino di Scansano and several Maremma Toscana IGT wines. Vermentino, Sangiovese, Cabernet and Merlot grapes are grown here. Restaurant service (open on weekend only dinner or by reservation) and accommodation available at the estate (*13 rooms and 1 apt., doubles from €80*). Hectares under vine: 52.

**Wines**: Pagliatura, Heba, Poggio Bestiale, Sinarra, Perenzo.

⌂ **Fattoria La Maliosa** – *Loc. Podere Monte Cavallo - Manciano (GR)* - ℰ *327 18 60 416 - www.fattorialamaliosa.it - info@fattorialamaliosa.it - Winery tours by reservation Tue-Fri., closed Mon. and Jan.-Feb.* La Maliosa is the expression of a concept of natural agriculture developed by Antonella Manuli: a project based on quality, beauty and environmental wellbeing, cultivating the terrain while respecting the territory, its originality and establishing an intelligent collaboration with nature within an uncontaminated stretch of land. The decision to obtain biological and biodynamic certifications guarantees constant commitment over time. The company extends over roughly 160 hectares made up of semi-native terrain, vineyards, olive orchards and woods. The farm enjoys a partnership with Terme di Saturnia SPA Golf & Resort for both lodging (*124 rooms, double suites starting at €390, www.termedisaturnia.it, menu starting from € 40*) and for meals. Hectares under vine: 6.

**Wines**: Bianco IGT Toscano La Maliosa, Rosso IGT Toscano La Maliosa (both organic and biodynamic DEMETER). Other products: La Maliosa Extravirgin Olive Oil and biodynamic (DEMETER), Millefiori organic honey Fiore di Maremma.

⌂ **Marsiliana** – *Loc. Castello 1 -* **Marsiliana** *(GR), 20 km SW of Manciano - ☎ 0564 60 50 60 - www. tenutamarsiliana.it - marsiliana@ principecorsini.com - Winery tours by reservation, ☎ 0564 60 63 85 or silva@ principecorsini.com.* The noble Corsini family is one of the oldest in Tuscany. Today it still owns several large properties, including the Palazzo Corsini in Florence, with its world-renowned art collection, and the Tenuta Marsiliana in Maremma. The family's profound ties with Marsiliana go back to 1759, when Filippo Corsini, Duke of Casigliano and the first Prince of Sismano, took charge of the estate. In 1886 the family purchased the entire property from the newly established Italian state. Accommodation available in estate-owned apartments and villas. Hectares under vine: 20.

**Wines**: Maremma Toscana Rosso IGT Marsiliana, Costa Toscana IGT Birillo, Toscana IGT Vermentino.

⌂ **Moris Farms - Fattoria Poggetti** – *Loc. Cura Nuova -* **Massa Marittima** *(GR) - ☎ 0566 91 91 35 - www.morisfarms.com - info@morisfarms.com - Winery tours by reservation.* The Moris family left Spain 200 years ago and moved to the Maremma area of Tuscany. This marked the beginning of a great love for this land and its wine, a passion that is just as powerful today. It currently owns 476 hectares: 420 near Massa Marittima (Fattoria Poggetti), of which 37 hectares of vineyards in the Monteregio di Massa Marittima DOC zone and 56 in Poggio la Mozza, 33 of which under vine in the Morellino di Scansano DOCG zone. Accommodation available at the estate in several charming apartments. Hectares under vine: 70.

**Wines**: Avvoltore, Morellino di Scansano Riserva, Barbaspinosa Monteregio di Massa Marittima Bianco and Rosso, Vermentino. Other products: olive oil, grappa and dried-grape wine.

**Tenuta Poggio Verrano** – *Strada Prov.le 9 km 4 -* **Montiano** *(GR), 10 km NW of Magliano in Toscana - ☎ 0564 58 99 43 - www.poggioverrano.it - info@poggio verrano.it - Winery tours by reservation.* Founded by Francesco Bolla in 2000, the estate has 27 hectares of vineyards planted with Cabernet Sauvignon, Merlot, Alicante, Sangiovese and Cabernet Franc. Selective manual harvesting of the grapes is followed by fermentation at a controlled temperature and slow maceration in small vats. The winery was built entirely underground, using the principle of gravity flow. It has opted to produce unfiltered wine. Hectares under vine: 27.

**Wines**: Maremma Toscana Dròmos, Sangiovese Dròmos L'Altro, Sangiovese Vale.

**Tenuta Rocca di Montemassi** – *Strada Provinciale 91 - Loc. Pian del Bichi, Fraz. Montemassi -* **Roccastrada** *(GR) - ☎ 0564 57 97 00 - www.roccadimontemassi.it - info@roccadimontemassi.it - Winery tours Mon.-Sat.10-18 by reservation.* A fortified settlement thought to date back to the 10th c. overlooks the estate. The property is spread out over 430 hectares, 180 of which under vine. Architect Mirko Amatori, whose design philosophy is based on utter respect for the territory, built the winery to fit in perfectly with the landscape and surroundings. Indeed, he chose to maintain the area's rural appearance and safeguard the Tuscan landscape of Maremma by restoring existing buildings, which stand amidst maritime pines, olive trees and a small natural lake. The estate houses a museum of rural life, which bears witness to the oldest and most authentic traditions of the farming culture and population of Tuscany. Hectares under vine: 180.

**Wines**: Vermentino Calasole, Sangiovese Le Focaie, Maremma Toscana Sassabruna, Syrah Syrosa.

**Ampeleia** – *Loc. Meleta -***Roccatederighi** *(GR) - ☎ 0564 56 71 55 - www.ampeleia.it - info@ampeleia.it - Winery tours and tasting by reservation.* The estate was created through the targeted purchase of plots at different altitudes – some of which quite far apart – with the specific goal of creating broad variability in terms of altitude, soil and microclimate. Today its vineyards are set at 3 different altitudes, with 50 hectares of Cabernet Franc, Sangiovese and 5 other

Mediterranean varieties. The wine it produces expresses the biodiversity of this territory. Hectares under vine: 60.
**Wines**: IGT Costa Toscana Ampeleia, IGT Costa Toscana Kepos, IGT Costa Toscana Cabernet Franc.

**Sassotondo** – *Pian di Conati 52* - **Sovana** *(GR) -* ℘ *0564 61 42 18 - www.sassotondo.it - info@sassotondo.it - Winery tours by reservation.* The winery is run by the husband and wife team of Carla Benini and Edoardo Ventimiglia, who moved to Sovana in 1990 to get away from city life. They set out with very little: a 1-hectare vineyard, a tumbledown house, and 72 hectares of land that had been abandoned for years. With enormous effort and hard work, things gradually changed and they produced their first harvest in 1997. Today the winery continues to grow. Hectares under vine: 12.
**Wines**: Bianco di Pitigliano Isolina, Ciliegiolo Maremma Toscana DOC, Sovana Rosso Superiore Ombra Blu, Toscana IGT Franze, Ciliegiolo Maremma Toscana DOC San Lorenzo. Other products: olive oil.

# Where to stay

## BAGNO VIGNONI

**La Locanda del Loggiato** – *Piazza del Moretto 30, Bagno Vignoni (SI) -* ℘ *335 43 04 27 - www.loggiato.it - 9 rooms, doubles from €125.* The 15th-c. building in the centre of town is adjacent to a basin that was once a thermal pool.

## CAPALBIO

**Agriturismo Ghiaccio Bosco** – *Strada della Sgrilla 4, 4 km NE of Capalbio (GR) -* ℘ *0564 89 65 39 or 339 56 62 578- www. ghiacciobosco.com - 14 rooms, doubles from €80.* Set in grounds abounding in plants and flowers, the guest farm offers well-appointed rooms.

## CASTELLINA MARITTIMA

**Hotel - B&B Il Poggetto** – *Via dei Giardini 1, Castellina Marittima (PI) -* ℘ *050 69 52 05 or 348 92 85 231- www.ilpoggetto.it - 20 rooms, doubles from €75.* This family-run hotel set in the woods has simple uncluttered rooms.

## CASTELLINA IN CHIANTI

**Fattoria Tregole** – *Loc. Tregole 86, 6 km S of Castellina in Chianti (SI) -* ℘ *0577 74 09 91 - www.fattoria-tregole.com - Closed 15 Nov.-15 Mar. - 4 rooms, doubles from €140, 2 apts. from €240 (3 nights minimum).* The country house, with its elegant look created by lively and sunny colours, offers a breathtaking view, and fragrant, delicious homemade cakes for breakfast.

## MONTEPULCIANO

**Hotel Il Marzocco** – *Piazza Savonarola 18, Montepulciano (SI) -* ℘ *0578 75 72 62 - www.albergoilmarzocco.it - Closed 2 weeks in Nov. and 1 week in Feb. - 16 rooms, doubles from €95.* The hotel, which has a longstanding tradition, is in a historic palazzo inside the city walls.

## MONTE SAN SAVINO

**Castello di Gargonza** – *Loc. Gargonza, 7 km W of Monte San Savino (AR) -* ℘ *0575 84 70 21 - www.gargonza.it - Closed 10 Jan.-Feb. - 13 rooms, doubles from €150 and 8 apts.* The fortified medieval hamlet offers a truly uncommon atmosphere.

## SAN CASCIANO IN VAL DI PESA

**Agriturismo Salvadonica** – *Via Grevigiana 82, Mercatale, 3 km SE of San Casciano (FI) -* ℘ *055 82 18 039 - www.salvadonica.com - Closed 15 Nov.-15 Feb. - 16 rooms, doubles from €125.* The little hamlet surrounded by olive groves has been transformed into a guest farm that offers a peaceful oasis.

## SEGROMIGNO IN MONTE

**Fattoria Mansi Bernardini** – *Via di Valgiano 34, 3 km W of Segromigno (LU) -* ℘ *0583 92 17 21 - www.fattoriamansi bernardini.it - Closed Dec.- Apr. - 5 rooms and 7 apts., doubles from €140, 142 for apts.* Set against a charming backdrop of hills and vineyards, this large farm, which produces olive oil, offers its guests spacious and comfortable rooms.

## SUVERETO

**Agriturismo Bulichella** – *Loc. Bulichella 131, 1 km SE of Suvereto (LI) -* ℘ *0565 82 98 92 - www.bulichella.it - Closed Dec.- Jan. - 14 rooms and 4 apts., doubles from €85, €525 for apts. week.* In the verdant low hills rising from the Tuscan coast, this organic farm – nestling amidst vineyards and olive groves – offers guests comfortable and delightfully peaceful rooms.

© Boettcher & Petoe/Shutterstock

# UMBRIA

Umbria is a marvellously verdant region of mountains, hills, woods, lakes and rivers. Umbrian wines were renowned as early as the Middle Ages, and continue to be today. There is a great variety of native varieties, including Grechetto, Verdello, Drupeggio, Procanico, Verdicchio and Malvasia Bianca, among the white grapes, and Sagrantino, Sangiovese and Ciliegiolo for the blacks. Of these the Sagrantino has garnered the most attention from experts and wine lovers as it produces remarkable wines that age well. To complement the native vines, several varieties have been imported, such as Tocai, Traminer, Chardonnay, Riesling, Cabernet Sauvignon and Merlot.

© Gianni Fantauzzi/Shutterstock

*Vines growing within sight of Orvieto*

## The terroir

Although Umbria can boast many interesting wines, the most representative are Torgiano Rosso, Sagrantino and Orvieto. The first, which falls within the appellations **Torgiano Rosso DOC** and Torgiano Rosso Riserva DOCG, is made from Sangiovese and Lanaiolo grapes grown on the hills of Torgiano municipality in the province of Perugia. It is a full-bodied wine with intense fragrances of ripe fruit, jam and spices.

The second originates in the village of Montefalco in the same province. Its success is the consequence of the capacity of the native Sagrantino to produce wines

## PRINCIPAL VARIETIES CULTIVATED

### WHITE GRAPES

Biancame
Canaiolo Bianco
Chardonnay
Garganega
Grechetto
Malvasia Bianca di Candia
Malvasia Bianca Lunga
Moscato Bianco
Pecorino
Pinot Bianco
Riesling
Riesling Italico
Sauvignon
Tocai Friulano

Trebbiano Spoletino
Trebbiano Toscano
Verdello
Verdicchio Bianco
Vermentino
Vernaccia di San Gimignano

### GREY GRAPES

Pinot Grigio

### BLACK GRAPES

Aleatico
Alicante
Barbera

Cabernet Franc
Cabernet Sauvignon
Canaiolo Nero
Cesanese Comune
Ciliegiolo
Colorino
Dolcetto
Gamay
Merlot
Montepulciano
Pinot Nero
Sagrantino
Sangiovese
Vernaccia Nera

of surprising strength and density, suited to long maturation either in the barrel or the bottle. Two types of **Sagrantino di Montefalco DOCG** are produced: dry and passito (or dried-grape wine). Dry is the ideal accompaniment to heavy dishes like red meat and game; passito, which is made from slightly raisined grapes, is an excellent sipping wine.

**Orvieto** is an appellation shared between Umbria and Lazio (covering municipalities in the provinces of Terni and Viterbo). Orvieto wine is made from the following grapes: Procanico (a variety of Trebbiano Toscano that provides greater body, elegance and lifespan compared to traditional Trebbiano), Verdello, Grechetto, Canaiolo Bianco (also called Drupeggio) and Malvasia Toscana, and can be found in the versions *superiore*, dry, semi-dry, sweetish and sweet.

# Itineraries

*Locations with a winery are indicated by the symbol ♟; for the addresses of the wineries, see p. 326.*

## 1. COLLI ALTOTIBERINI AND TRASIMENO

The **Colli Altotiberini DOC** zone in the province of Perugia produces interesting white wines from Trebbiano and Malvasia grapes, and red and rosé wines from Sangiovese and Merlot. The range of wines from the **Colli del Trasimeno DOC** appellation is more varied: the whites are produced from Trebbiano, Grechetto, Chardonnay, Pinot Bianco, Pinot Grigio, Vermentino, Sauvignon and Riesling,

whereas the reds and rosés are based on Sangiovese, Ciliegiolo, Gamay, Merlot and Cabernet Sauvignon. Sparkling wines are also made from Grechetto and international white varieties, as well as a Vin Santo.

## Perugia★★

**Piazza IV Novembre★★**, the heart of the city, is one of the most beautiful in Italy. It is the setting for the most important monuments from the period of the medieval communes: Palazzo Priori, the Great Fountain (Fontana Maggiore) and the cathedral. Via **Maestà delle Volte★** at the far end of the square is a street of medieval houses and vaults constructed to support a building that no longer exists. The 13th-c. **Great Fountain★★** is celebrated for the harmony of its proportions and the beautiful panels sculpted by Nicola Pisano (lower basin) and his son Giovanni (upper basin). Some of the panels have been replaced by copies, and the originals can be seen in the National Gallery of Umbria.

The **cathedral★** is Gothic but the façade that faces Piazza Dante was added to with a Baroque portal. Inside, the chapel on the right has an interesting *Deposition* by Barocci (1567), while the chapel on the left guards the wedding ring supposedly worn by the Virgin. Both chapels have 16th-c. stalls inlaid with marquetry.

**Palazzo dei Priori★★** – begun in the 13th c. and enlarged in later centuries, the palace is a plain but striking building. The façade that faces the square is approached up a majestic flight of

## DOCG

Sagrantino di Montefalco
Torgiano Rosso Riserva

## DOC

Amelia
Assisi
Colli Altotiberini
Colli Amerini
Colli del Trasimeno *or* Trasimeno
Colli Martani
Colli Perugini
Lago di Corbara
Montefalco
Orvieto (with Lazio)
Rosso Orvietano
Spoleto
Todi
Torgiano

© kubais/Shutterstock

steps that leads to the pulpit reserved for discourses, whereas the façade on Corso Vannucci has a lovely 14th-c. portal. The rooms inside are decorated with superb 14th-c. frescoes or lined with boiserie. On the top floor of the palace, the **National Gallery of Umbria**★★ holds the country's most important collection of Umbrian art, which it follows from the 13th to late 18th c. *Corso Vannucci 19. Open 8.30-19.30, closed Mon. (summer 12-19.30), ℘ 075 57 21 009, www. gallerianazionaledellumbria.it.*

Standing beside Palazzo dei Priori, the **Collegio del Cambio**★ was constructed in the 15th c. to welcome money-changers; it has an audience room lined with **frescoes**★★ painted by Perugino and his pupils. The statue of Justice sculpted by Benedetto da Maiano (15th c.) is also remarkable.

*Corso Vannucci, 25. Open Mon.-Sat. 9-13 and 14.30-17.30, Sun. and public hols. 9-13, closed Mon. pm in Nov.-Mar., ℘ 075 57 28 599, www.collegiodelcambio.it.*

The main street in the historic centre is Corso Vannucci, which leads to Piazza Italia. The **Rocca Paolina**★ (Pauline Fort) represents the remains of the fort constructed on the orders of Pope Paul III in 1540. The huge walls, streets and wells in its interior dating from the 11th-16th c. are now oddly partnered by escalators to facilitate climbing and descending the hill it is built on. The district of San Pietro lies in a dominant position and offers a magnificent **view**★★ over the Tiber valley from the **Carducci Gardens**.

Returning to Piazza IV Novembre along Via Baglioni, you come to **Piazza Matteotti** lined by the Palazzo dell'Università

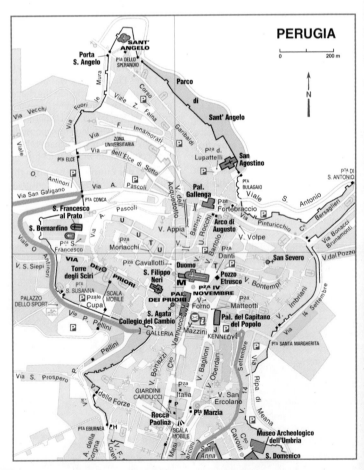

*Palazzo dei Priori*

Vecchia and the Palazzo del Capitano del Popolo. At the end of the square the **Via delle Volte della Pace★** is a picturesque medieval street formed by a long, 14th-c. Gothic portico that follows the course of the Etruscan walls.

Take **Via dei Priori★** from Piazza IV Novembre to the **Oratory of San Bernardino★★**. A jewel of Renaissance architecture (1461), it was designed by Agostino di Duccio, who succeeded in harmoniously blending the purity of its lines with the delicate decorative sculptures and polychrome marbles. Charming statues of music-playing angels stand in the piers.

To the south-west of the city centre stand the Church of **San Domenico★**, an imposing Gothic building whose interior was altered during the 17th c., the adjacent **National Archaeological Museum of Umbria★★** (*Piazza Giordano Bruno 10. Open 8.30-19.30, Mon. 10-19.30, ℘ 075 57 27 141, polomusealeumbria. beniculturali.it*) and, past Porto San Pietro at the end of Corso Cavour, the Church of **San Pietro★★**. Built at the end of the 10th c., the church was greatly remodelled during the Renaissance.

To the north of the city centre is the **Etruscan Arch★**, an impressive construction made from enormous blocks of stone. Past this you come to the majestic **Palazzo Gallenga**, which houses the city's university for foreign students. Proceeding along Corso Garibaldi you

come to the Church of **Sant'Angelo★**, built on a circular plan in the 5th-6th c. around 16 ancient columns.

## Trasimeno and the Tiber valley

*Itinerary of 126 km from Perugia to Città di Castello.*

Leave Perugia to the west, pass through **Corciano**, where there is an *Assumption* by Perugino in the Church of Santa Maria, then through Magione (15th-c. Castle dei Cavalieri di Malta) to reach the shores of Lake Trasimeno.

### Lake Trasimeno★

Trasimeno is the largest lake in the peninsular section of Italy. Settled by the Etruscans, the area was later developed by the Romans (they built an underground emissary from the lake to prevent flooding). The lake has 3 islands: **Maggiore** (the most interesting from an artistic standpoint), **Minore** and **Polvese**. The gentle countryside, with its olive groves and vineyards, combines harmoniously with the medieval architecture of the surrounding villages.

When you arrive at Monte del Lago, tour the lake in a clockwise direction as far as Panicarola, where you turn off left to visit **Panicale ♟**. This medieval village looks onto the lake from a hilltop. The *Martyrdom of St Sebastian* by Perugino can be seen in the Church of San Sebastiano. Return to Panicarola and continue round the lake to **Castiglione del Lago★ ♟**, a delightful walled town that gives marvellous views over the lake. The historic centre comprises the elegant 16th-c. Palazzo della Corgna, which is joined by a covered passageway to the medieval Rocca del Leone. *Open Mar. 10-18, Apr.-Sept. 9.30-19, Nov.-Feb. 10-17, ℘ 075 95 10 99, www.palazzodellacorgna.it.*

Continue your tour of the lake to **Passignano sul Trasimeno** to admire the walled historic centre. A few km further on, take a left to **Castel Rigone**, which stands in a panoramic position; visit the Sanctuary of the Madonna dei Miracoli built in Renaissance style.

### The Tiber valley

Continue in the same direction for about 20 km cross-country to **Umbertide**, then another 20 km north along the E 45 to **Città di Castello**. The town's most important monuments are grouped in Piazza Matteotti and Piazza Gabriotti: the Palazzo del Podestà, the Gothic Palazzo dei Priori, and the duomo (of Romanesque origin, later remodelled).

A little to the east, the 15th-c. Palazzo Albizzini holds the **Burri Collection** donated by artist Alberto Burri to his hometown. One section of the collection is housed in a former tobacco-drying building (*Via Pierucci*). *Open 10-13 and 14.30-18.30 (Sat., Sun. and public hols. 10.30-18.30), in Oct.-May 9-12.30 and 14.30-18, closed working Mon., ℘ 075 85 54 649, www.fondazioneburri.org.*

Standing opposite Palazzo Albizzini, Palazzo Vitelli a Sant'Egidio was built in the 16th c. and faces onto a beautiful garden.

In the southern part of the historic centre, the Palazzo Vitelli alla Cannoniera, on whose design Giorgio Vasari worked, houses an **art gallery★** with many important works, such as the *Gonfalon of the Santissima Trinità* by Raphael. *Open 10-13 and 14.30-18.30 (Nov.-Mar. 15-18), closed Mon., ℘ 075 85 54 202.*

## 2. THE UMBRA VALLEY, TODI AND MONTEFALCO

*Circular itinerary of approximately 270 km starting from Assisi.*

The bed of the former Lake Tiberino, which lay between Terni and Sansepolcro, is today filled by a pleasant vista of vines and olive trees, with the occasional stone-built village, monastery or church. Hillside towns from where the countryside can

### THE TERROIR

**Area:** 8,464.22 km², of which approximately 12,300 hectares are planted to vine

**Production 2019:** 629,104 hectolitres, of which approximately 307,232 VQPRD

**Geography:** 30% mountainous and 70% hilly. The soil is a mixture of clay and limestone, with the presence of marl, tufa and volcanic residues. The climate is sub-Mediterranean: the winters are not excessively cold and the summers are hot, breezy and dry

### THE PROTECTION CONSORTIA

Consorzio Tutela Vini Montefalco – ℘ 0742 37 95 90, www.consorziomontefalco.it

Consorzio Tutela Vini di Orvieto – ℘ 0763 34 37 90, www.consorziovinidiorvieto.it

Consorzio Tutela Colli del Trasimeno – www.trasimenodoc.it

Consorzio Tutela DOC Colli Martani – ℘ 075 62 11 682, www.stradadeivinidelcantico.it

Consorzio Tutela dei Vini di Torgiano – ℘ 075 98 86 634, www.consorziotutelavinitorgiano.it

Consorzio Tutela Vini Colli Amerini – c/o Cantina Colli Amerini, Zona industriale Fornole, Amelia (TR), ℘ 0744 98 97 21

### WINE AND FOOD ROUTES

Strada del Vino Colli del Trasimeno – ℘ 333 98 54 593, www.stradadelvinotrasimeno.it

Strada dei Vini del Cantico – ℘ 075 62 11 682, www.stradadeivinidelcantico.it

Strada del Sagrantino – ℘ 0742 37 84 90, www.stradadelsagrantino.it

Strada dei Vini Etrusco Romana – ℘ 0763 34 19 11, www.stradadeivinietruscoromana.com

Strada dell'Olio DOP Umbria – ℘ 0742 33 22 69, www.stradaoliodopumbria.it

*Assisi seen as you arrive from the plain*

be admired are Assisi, Spello, Montefalco and Trevi. With regard to winemaking this zone comprises many appellations, such as **Sagrantino di Montefalco DOCG** and **Torgiano Rosso Riserva DOCG**, and the DOC zones **Assisi**, **Colli Martani**, **Colli Perugini** and **Montefalco**. Between them, these produce a broad selection of white, red, rosé, sparkling and sweet wines made from local and international varieties. In addition to the two great reds, **Grechetto di Todi DOC** is also representative of the area. It is a white wine made from Grechetto grapes and has intense scents of pale flowers, ripe peaches and apricots.

## Assisi★★★

As you approach Assisi from the plain, the sight of the tall, stately arcades of the basilica suddenly appears. Next you see the earth-coloured stone houses perched on the slopes of Monte Subasio.

**Basilica of San Francesco★★★** – consecrated in 1253, the basilica is formed by two churches, one constructed above the other, that together rest on huge arches. Built shortly after the death of St Francis, the basilica was designed by Brother Elia. The dark, austere interior of the **Lower Church** has a long narthex and is entirely covered by 13th- and 14th-c. **frescoes★★★**. The first chapel on the left is decorated with frescoes by Simone Martini of the life of St Martin. They are remarkable for the refinement of their design, harmony of composition and vivid colours. Above the pulpit is the *Coronation of the Virgin* by Maso, a disci-

ple of Giotto. The vault over the choir is adorned with scenes of the *Triumph of St Francis* and the virtues he practised, painted by another of Giotto's pupils. The vault of the left transept is decorated with scenes of the Passion, which are attributed to the school of Pietro Lorenzetti. The wall frescoes, which are by the same Sienese master, are striking in their dramatic power. A majestic composition by Cimabue, the *Madonna with Four Angels and St Francis*, can be seen in the right transept.

Pass through the right cloister to see the basilica's treasure and to visit the Perkins Collection (paintings, 14th-16th c.). Next, go down to the crypt to see the simple but beautiful **tomb of St Francis**, which lies at the centre of the cross.

In net contrast with the simple volumes of the **Lower Church**, the soaring nave of the **Upper Church** is a perfect Gothic structure, bathed with light thanks to the tall windows in the walls. The apse and transept are decorated with frescoes (sadly deteriorated) by Cimabue and his school. The master himself painted a *Crucifixion* in the left transept of tragic intensity.

Between 1296 and 1304 **Giotto** and his assistants painted a cycle of 28 **frescoes★★★** of the life of St Francis. The clarity and uncluttered definition of each scene, and the tendency towards realism of these paintings, opened a new direction in Italian figurative art that was to achieve its culmination in the Renaissance two centuries later.

**Via San Francesco**★ is a picturesque street lined by medieval and Renaissance houses. The **Oratory dei Pellegrini** at no. 13/a is decorated with 15th-c. frescoes. *Open 10-12 and 16-18, closed Sun., ✆ 075 81 22 67, www.assisinforma.it.*

**Piazza del Comune**★ occupies the area of the ancient Roman forum where the Temple of Minerva (1st-c. BC, today a church) used to stand. On its left is the Palazzo del Capitano del Popolo (13th c.).

Follow Via San Rufino on the left of Piazza del Comune to the **duomo**★. Dating to the 12th c., the building has one of the most beautiful Romanesque **façades**★★ in Umbria owing to the harmony of its decoration, portals and rose windows. Laid out in a single space, the interior was renovated in 1571. As you enter, note the font on the right where St Francis, St Clare and Emperor Frederick II were baptised.

Preceded by a terrace giving a superb view of the Umbrian countryside, the Church of **Santa Chiara**★★ was built between 1257 and 1265 with a Gothic structure similar to the Upper Church in the Basilica. There are numerous works of art, in particular 14th-c. Giottoesque frescoes of the life of St Clare. In the Church of San Giorgio next door, on the right of the nave is the Byzantine cross from the Church of San Damiano which, according to legend, was responsible for St Francis' conversion. The tomb of St Clare lies in the crypt.

Standing beside the city walls, the **Rocca Maggiore**★★★ (Great Fort) is a very fine example of 14th-c. military architecture and offers marvellous **views**★★★ over the city and surroundings.

### Eremo delle Carceri★★

*4 km east.* This hermitage has an impressively atmospheric and physical setting in an ilex wood. Founded by St Bernardino (1380-1444), this was the voluntary spiritual "prison" where Francis and his followers retreated to search for spiritual purity. A series of narrow passages lead to Francis's grotto and the ancient refectory. The hillside is an integral part of the structure of the hermitage.

### Convent of San Damiano★

*2 km south from Porta Nuova. Open 10-12 and 14-18 (in win. 14-16.30), ✆ 075 81 22 73.* Isolated amongst cypresses and olive trees, the convent and adjacent church are part of the story of St Francis. It was here that Francis was called to his vocation and composed the *Cantico delle Creature*. It is also linked to St Clare, who died here in 1253. The humble, plain interior is a fine example of a 13th-c. Franciscan convent.

### Basilica of Santa Maria degli Angeli★

*5 km south-west in the plain.* The basilica was constructed in the 16th c. around the **Porziuncola** (the small Church of Santa Maria degli Angeli), the name of which was taken from the land (*small portion*) where the church was first built before the year 1000. This was where Francis consecrated Clare as a "bride of Christ". A fresco (1393) above the altar illustrates episodes from his life. Francis died on 3 October 1226 in the nearby Chapel del Transito. There is an enamelled terracotta polyptych in the crypt by Andrea della Robbia (*ca.* 1490). Next to the church is the rose garden in which Francis rolled to evade the temptation to give up his life of poverty, and the cave where he prayed. Doves have always nested in the hands of the statue of the saint in the corridor to the rose garden.

*Continue south.*

### Spello★

Spello is a town of medieval appearance but with gates and bastions that testify to its Roman past. The Via Consolare leads into the ancient town through the Consular Gate. The Baglioni Chapel in the Church of **Santa Maria Maggiore**★ has superb frescoes by Pinturicchio of the Sibyls and episodes from the life of

*Courtyard of an ancient palazzo, Spello*

© Claudio Giovanni Colombo/Shutterstock

Jesus. Frescoes by Perugino can be seen on either side of the high altar.

The nearby Church of Sant'Andrea (1025) has a painting by Pinturicchio and a 14th-c. cross by the Umbrian school.

Piazza della Repubblica is closed on one side by the old Municipal Palace (13th-c.). Beyond the square, Via Giulia leads to the monastery of Vallegloria built in the 14th c. but remodelled at later dates. Take Via dell'Arco Romano to the site of the ancient acropolis, now occupied by the 16th-c. castle, from which there are attractive views of the hills.

## Foligno 🍷

The ancient heart of what is today a prevalently modern town is Piazza della Repubblica. This is the setting for Palazzo Trinci and the façade of the left transept of the **duomo**, which is adorned with a magnificent, geometrically decorated portal in Lombard style. The main façade and interior were remodelled in the last 200 years. Embellished by a fine Gothic stairway, the 14th-c. **Palazzo Trinci** was built by the lords of the town and decorated with frescoes boasting almost perfect perspective. The paintings in the Room of the Liberal Arts and Planets are attributed to Gentile da Fabriano and depict the arts of the Trivium (Grammar, Rhetoric and Dialectics) and the Quadrivium (Arithmetic, Geometry, Music and Astronomy). The hours of the day are represented in relation to the planets and the age of man. *Piazza della Repubblica 6. Open 10-13 and 15-19, closed Mon.,* ✆ *0742 33 05 84.*

Take Via Gramsci from Piazza della Repubblica. Once past the Church of San Domenico you come to the ancient Church of Santa Maria Infraportas on the edge of the historic centre (12th-c. frescoes in the apse, and 16th-c. on the walls).

The **Abbey of Sassovivo** is 6 km east of Foligno. It was founded by the Benedictines in the 11th c. and had sections rebuilt at later times.

## Trevi★

Several km after Foligno, take the left turn to Trevi. This small town winds around the hill all the way up to the centre at the top. The 13th-c. Municipal Palace stands in Piazza Mazzini. Sections of the Church of Sant'Emiliano, for example, the apses, were constructed in the 12th c. Opposite the church is the **Palazzo Lucarini Contemporary**, which exhibits artworks by contemporary artists, *via Beato Placido Riccardi, Fri.-Sun. 15.30 -18.30,* ✆ *0742 38 10 21, www.palazzolucarini.it.*

The small Piazza della Rocca lies beside the duomo. The 14th-c. Church of San Francesco and annexed convent are home to various museums: a collection of art, the **Olive Museum** and the museum of the local area. *Open Nov.-Mar. Fri.-Sun. (Oct. Thu.-Sun.) 10.30-13 and 14.30-17, Apr.-Jul. and Sept. 10.30-13 and 14.30-18, closed Mon., Aug. open daily 10.30-13 and 15-19,* ✆ *0742 38 16 28.*

## Fonti del Clitunno★

These springs, which rise in a setting of thick vegetation, were sacred to the Romans, who used to purify animals here prior to their sacrifice. At a distance of 1 km (at a lower level than the road) stands the small **Temple of Clitumnus★★**, originally a pagan temple but later converted into an early Christian church.

*Continue on the SS 3.*

## Spoleto★

Like many cities in Umbria, Spoleto is a harmonious combination of sedateness and mellowness. An ancient Roman municipium, then the seat of an important Lombard dukedom from the 6th-8th c., its buildings are ranged across the slopes of a hill crowned by the Rocca dei Papi (Popes' Stronghold) and each year hosts the *Festival of the Two Worlds.*

From the remains of the Roman theatre in Piazza della Libertà, head upwards towards Spoleto's historic heart. Pass by **Druso's Arch**, erected in 23 AD in honour of Tiberius's son, and now flanked by the Romanesque Church of Sant'Ansano. You come to Piazza del Mercato and the **Town Hall** (14th c. but with 18th-c. modifications) that incorporates the remains of a Roman house and holds the town's picture gallery. *For informations* ✆ *0743 45 940.*

Pass the bishop's palace and Romanesque Church of Sant'Eufemia and enter the splendid Piazza del **Duomo★★**. The church has a fine Renaissance portico, a rose window and a 13th-c. mosaic. Inside there is a 12th-c. altar cross, several frescoes by Pinturicchio (*1st chapel on the right*), the tomb of Fra Filippo Lippi (*right transept*) and apsidal frescoes by Lippi and others that recount the *Life of the Virgin*. In the scene of the *Dormition*,

*Façade of Spoleto duomo*

Lippi portrayed himself on the right in the habit of a Dominican monk.

A pleasant walk around the 14th-c. fort takes you to the 13th-c. **Tower Bridge★★**, 80 m high by 230 long, that runs over a Roman aqueduct. The Popes' Fort is the home of the National Museum of the Dukedom of Spoleto and displays statues, paintings and funerary goods that illustrate the history of the dukedom. *Open 9.30-19.30 (Mon. 9.30-13), in win. 9.30-18.30 (closed Mon.) ℘ 0743 22 30 55, www.spoletocard.it.*

Three important churches are located a little out of the historic centre. The first is **San Salvatore★** (*to the north of the centre*), one of the earliest churches in Italy. It was constructed in the 4th c. by monks from the Orient and modified in the 9th c. **San Gregorio Maggiore★** (*north-west*) is a Romanesque church of the 12th c. To the left of the entrance porch, the walls of the baptistery (14th c.) are lined with frescoes. The bell tower is built from blocks taken from ancient buildings. **San Domenico** (*west*) is a beautiful 13th-c. church with walls built from alternating rows of white and pink stone. A canvas by Lanfranco and 14th- and 15th-c. frescoes can be seen inside.

## Monteluco★

A pretty, winding **road★** leads to Monteluco (850 m), a place dedicated to an ancient cult and today a retreat from the summer heat. At the bottom of the hill

the Church of **San Pietro** has a lovely and interesting Romanesque **façade★** with carved reliefs. In the town itself you can visit the 15th-c. monastery of San Francesco.

Return to Spoleto and head west along the SP 418 to **Acquasparta**, an ancient spa town in a lovely position. One of its finest buildings is the elegant Palazzo Cesi, which has an outstanding wooden ceiling.

*Follow the S 3 bis to Todi.*

## Todi★★ ☙

Todi is the lovely city of the Franciscan friar Jacopone. It stands on a hill inside the three concentric circles of walls: Etruscan (Porta Marzia), Roman and medieval. Its extraordinary charm, beauty and atmosphere fascinate at first sight. The enchanting **Piazza del Popolo★★** is ringed by buildings that illustrate the enterprising spirit of the communes in the Middle Ages. The 13th-c. Palazzo dei Priori (originally the seat of the podestà) has a single trapezoidal tower constructed in the 14th c. The Palazzo del Capitano, of the same era, has mullion windows and massive pillars with round arches. Joined to Palazzo del Capitano and also supported on huge arches, Palazzo del Popolo is one of Italy's oldest municipal buildings. It houses the Lapidarium, picture gallery and Etruscan and Roman Museum. *For information on visits ℘ 075 89 44 148, www.coopculture.it.*

A fine **view★★** is given from nearby **Piazza Garibaldi**.

The early 12th-c. **duomo★** stands at the top of a majestic flight of steps. Its white and pink marble façade is embellished with a large rose window and the apse is Romanesque. Inside, the capitals are Gothic, the font Renaissance and the lovely inlaid stalls are 16th-c.

Crossing back over Piazza del Popolo, you come to the Church of **San Fortunato★★**, which unites elements of Gothic and Renaissance architecture. The portal is elaborately decorated, and inside you can see the tomb of Jacopone and a fresco by Masolino (1432, *4th chapel on the right*). The Roman water tank nearby is known as "St Cassian's prison" because it was here that the saint was supposed to have been incarcerated in the 2nd c. The remains of the 12th-c. Rocca (fort) stand to the right of San Fortunato.

## Santa Maria della Consolazione★

*1 km west on the road to Orvieto*. This Renaissance church was built in yellowish stone by various architects from a design said to be by Bramante. Built to a Greek cross plan, the church has four polygonal apses and pillars with composite capitals. The decoration of the dome is 16th-c.

Go back to the SP 382 and then take the SP 414 to **Massa Martana** (*15 km west*) and **Giano dell'Umbria** 🍷. The latter is a medieval walled village near the Abbey of San Felice, a monastery founded by the Benedictines (11th-12th c.).

*Continue to Montefalco.*

## Montefalco★ 🍷

Perched up on a hill like an eagle's nest, as its name suggests, this enchanting town in Sagrantino is ringed first by 14th-c. walls, then by vineyards and olive groves. Its panoramic position has earned it the nickname the *"ringhiera dell'Umbria"* (the balustrade of Umbria) and, indeed, a street named Via Ringhiera Umbra leads to a point from where there is a splendid and very wide **panorama★★★**.

The deconsecrated Church of San Francesco provides an attractive setting for the **St Francis Museum★**, which is frescoed with stories of the saint and St Jerome painted in the 16th c. by Benozzo Gozzoli. There is also a *Nativity* by Perugino and an impressive *Crucifix* by the Maestro of Santa Chiara (late 13th-early 14th c.). *Via Ringhiera Umbra 6. Open daily Apr.,* May, Sept., Oct. 10.30-18, Jun.-Aug. 10.30-19, rest of the year 10.30-13 and 14.30-17, closed Mon. and Tue., ☎ 0742 37 95 98, www.museodimontefalco.it.

The tympan of the portal and various niches inside the Renaissance Church of **Santa Illuminata** were painted by Francesco Melanzio, who was active in Montefalco in the 15th and 16th c.

The Gothic **Sant'Agostino** is adorned with frescoes by the Umbrian school of the 14th, 15th and 16th c.

Preceded by a small 14th-c. cloister, the Church of **San Fortunato** (*1 km south*) has a tympan with a fine **fresco★** by Benozzo Gozzoli of the *Madonna, St Francis and St Bernardino*. The fresco of *St Fortunatus* on the right altar is by the same artist.

*Proceed north for 7 km.*

## Bevagna★

Bevagna is a typically medieval town once divided into four districts. Called *Mevania* in the Roman age, it has several examples of buildings mostly from the 2nd c. AD: the ambulatory of the Roman theatre, a temple, baths, and lovely mosaics featuring sea creatures (behind the door of a house on the right as you walk down from Piazza Garibaldi). **Piazza Silvestri** is a typical medieval square lined by the churches of San Michele (late 11th c.) and San Silvestro (late 12th c., note the epigraph on the façade), and by the 13th-c. Palazzo dei Consoli, which is home to the elegant Teatro Torti.

Leave Bevagna to the south-west and go cross-country to **Gualdo Cattaneo** 🍷, then right on the SP 415 as far as the E 45. Head north to **Deruta**, where ceramics have been a vocation since the Renaissance. The history of pottery in the town is illustrated in the **Regional Ceramics Museum** in the former Convent of San Francesco in Largo San Francesco. *For information on visits* ☎ 075 97 11 000, www.museoceramicadideruta.it.

**Torgiano** 🍷, the home of the DOC wine of that name, lies 8 km to the north. A visit well worth the trouble is to the **Lungarotti Wine Museum** in the 17th-c. Palazzo Graziani-Baglioni. *Corso Vittorio Emanuele II 31. For information on visits* ☎ 075 98 80 200, www.lungarotti.it.

A further 6 km east takes you to **Bettona**, set amongst olive trees. The town was founded by the Etruscans and still retains some of its Etruscan and medieval walls.

## 3. ORVIETANO AND COLLI AMERINI

The province of Terni boasts 5 appellations: **Colli Amerini**, **Lago di Corbara**, **Orvieto**, **Orvieto Classico** and **Rosso Orvietano**. The zone's wines employ many types of grapes, both local and international. The best known wine is undoubtedly **Orvieto Bianco**, but the reds are of no less interest.

### Orvieto★★ ♀

Orvieto stands on a volcanic tufa elevation in an ideal position for the colours on the sumptuous façade of its cathedral to be rendered more intense by the sun. The town produces an excellent refreshing and palatable white wine, and has a surprising underground labyrinth of tunnels cut in the soft rock.

**Cathedral★★★** – The building stands at the centre of a peaceful and majestic piazza beside the severe architecture of the **Palazzo dei Papi★**. It was built in tufa at the end of the 13th c. and is a perfect example of the transition from Romanesque to Gothic. Begun in 1290, a hundred or so architects, sculptors, painters and mosaicists worked on it up to its completion in 1600. It has the most colourful and daring **façade★★★** in Italian Gothic architecture. The verticality of its lines is emphasised by the slenderness of its pointed gables and the upward thrust of its counterforts, which are composed of small panels of coloured marble crowned by pinnacles. However, what makes the cathedral so extraordinary is the richness of its decoration: sculptures in the lower section and polychrome mosaics and marbles in the upper. The original design, which was created around 1320 by Lorenzo Maitani from Siena, was continued by Andrea Pisano, Andrea Orcagna and Sanmicheli. It was Maitani who devised the magnificent low reliefs that adorn the pillars. The mosaic on the central, triangular gable is of the *Coronation of Mary* (late 18th c.). The bronze doors are by the 20th-c. sculptor from Sicily, Emilio Greco.

The interior is built in alternate layers of white and black stone. The floor rises towards the choir, squeezing the perspective, while alabaster windows provide a warm light. The cathedral contains extraordinary works of art, such as the *Madonna Enthroned with Child* (1425) by Gentile da Fabriano, the *Madonna della Misericordia* (1320) by Lippo Memmi, and the famous cycle of frescoes by Beato Angelico and Luca Signorelli in the Chapel of the Madonna di San Brizio. *Open 9.30-13 and 14.30-sunset, Sun. only pm. Closed during celebrations, www.opsm.it.*

Under the monumental organ (16th c.) in the left arm of the transept stands the entrance to the chapel where the corporal of the miracle of Bolsena is stored. A shrine holds the **reliquary★★★**, a begemmed and enamelled masterpiece of medieval goldsmithery (1338).

**Orvieto Underground★** – *Piazza Duomo 23. Guided visits only. For information, ℘ 0763 34 06 88 - 339 73 32 764, www.orvietounderground.it.* Orvieto rests on volcanic rock: tufa and pozzolana. It will help to understand the history and structure of Orvieto if you "go down to the cellar". Many of the caverns were excavated in the Etruscan era as cellars. During the visit to the grottoes (over a thousand have been recorded), you will see medieval vaults lined with burial niches, the foundations and bulk

---

### The frescoes by Luca Signorelli

The Chapel of San Brizio is decorated with a disturbing scenario, featuring monsters, the torture of the damned, cadaverous demons, and monstrosities in every detail. From the left, the first fresco is the *Sermon and Deeds of the Antichrist*, in which the Antichrist, with a devil as an advisor, presents himself in the semblance of Jesus. Signorelli portrayed himself as the noble dark figure on the extreme left. Next comes the *Coronation of the Chosen Ones*, then on the left on the altar wall, the *Blessed Consigned to Paradise*, and on the right, *The Damned Consigned to Hell*, where the river Acheron flows. On the right wall, there are the two scenes, *Hell* and the *Resurrection of the Dead*. On the entrance wall is the *End of the World*. In this last fresco, the sun and moon have lost all trace of familiarity, the world is shaken by an earthquake, and a sibyl, prophet and demons are portrayed.

© David Morgan/iStock

*Façade of Orvieto duomo*

of a 14th-c. mill for processing olive oil, and wells dug in the 6th c. BC.

Not far from the cathedral, the Church of **San Bernardino** is an attractive and richly decorated Baroque building built on an elliptical plan.

Follow Via Duomo to meet **Corso Cavour**, which is lined with medieval and 16th-c. houses and runs through the length of the city centre. Continue to Piazza del Popolo. Built in volcanic tufa in Romanesque-Gothic, the **Palazzo del Popolo★** has a large balcony, elegant windows and an odd volute embattlement.

To the west of the square, the silent and tranquil **Old District★** has retained its medieval buildings. At the far western end stands the Church of **San Giovenale**, with an apse frescoed in the 13th-15th c. Standing over the ancient forum, **Piazza della Repubblica** is overlooked by the Church of Sant'Andrea, with its curious, twelve-sided Romanesque bell tower.

**Pozzo della Cava** – *Via della Cava 28. Open 9-20, closed Mon.,* ☎ *0763 34 23 73, www.pozzodellacava.it.* This is a walk that is named after a well 36 m deep dug in the tufa in the 16th c. for Pope Clement VII. During the tour, you will see the kiln of a medieval pottery workshop, a room used to make wine in the Middle Ages, and several ancient tombs.

**Pozzo di S. Patrizio★★** – *open 9-sunset (Nov.-Feb. 10-sunset),* ☎ *0763 34 37 68.* At the eastern end of the city, this well was dug for Pope Clement VII to provide Orvieto with water in case of siege. It was designed by Antonio da Sangallo the Younger. The very pure well water lies at a depth of 62 m. To reach it there are two superimposed spiral staircases that never meet and are lit by 72 windows.

## Colli Amerini between Orvieto and Narni

*Itinerary of approximately 90 km.*

Lying 13 km to the west of Orvieto, Lake Corbara is a reservoir created to power a hydroelectric plant. The north shore of the lake marks the start of the **Tiber River Park**, which stretches as far as Todi.

*Take the S 205 Amerina, which offers pretty views.*

Pass through **Baschi** 🍷, **Montecchio** 🍷 and **Lugnano in Teverina** (note the remarkable Romanesque Church of Santa Maria Assunta). Shortly before Lugnano there is a right turn to **Alviano**, a village in a lovely position close to which you can visit Alviano oasis, a marsh in the Tiber River Park.

Continue along the S 205 to **Amelia**, whose walls date back to the 3rd c. BC. The Church of San Francesco in the centre has architectural elements built in the 13th c. The duomo was originally Romanesque but was rebuilt in the 17th c.

A short distance away you come to **Narni** 🍷, a town that stands on a rise over the Nera valley. You reach the historic centre from a 15th-c. fortified gate. Via Garibaldi opens out into the long and narrow **Piazza dei Priori★** where you can see a 14th-c. loggia, a tall tower, the Palazzo del Podestà (13th-16th c.) with Romanesque low reliefs, and an elegant fountain reminiscent of the Great Fountain in Perugia. A little further on stands the 12th c. duomo embellished by a Renaissance portico. The Bridge of Augustus, one of whose massive arches still stands entire, was built over the river Nera down in the valley.

# Addresses

## Tourist information

**Regione Umbria** – www.regione.umbria.it

**Assisi Tourist Office** – Piazza del Comune, Assisi, ☎ 075 81 38 680, www.visit-assisi.it

**Foligno Tourist Office** – Corso Cavour 126, Foligno, ☎ 0742 35 44 59, www.comune. foligno.pg.it

**Orvieto Tourist Office** – Piazza Duomo 24, Orvieto, ☎ 0763 34 17 72, www.comune. orvieto.tr.it

**Perugia Tourist Office** – Loggia dei Lanari, Piazza Matteotti 18, Perugia, ☎ 075 57 36 458, turismo.comune.perugia.it

**Spoleto Tourist Office** – Piazza della Libertà 7, Spoleto, ☎ 0743 21 86 20, www.comune.spoleto.pg.it

**Lake Trasimeno Tourist Office** – Piazza Gramsci 1, **Castiglione del Lago**, ☎ 075 96 58 293, www.lagotrasimeno.net

## The wineries

*The addresses are listed in alphabetical order by location.*

**Lamborghini** – *Loc. Soderi 1 -* **Panicale** *(PG) -* ☎ *075 83 50 029 - www.tenutalamborghini.it - wine@ tenutalamborghini.com - Winery tours by reservation.* The estate was purchased in the early 1970s by Ferruccio Lamborghini, who had abandoned the automotive industry and decided to return to his roots: agriculture. It has an area of 100 hectares, and includes a golf course, a guest farm and vineyards. Different varieties – both red and white grapes – were initially planted. In addition to the classic Sangiovese and Ciliegiolo, he also planted varieties that were more unusual at the time: Merlot and Cabernet Sauvignon. In the mid-1990s Patrizia Lamborghini also joined the management, and since then most of the vineyards have been replanted, eliminating the white varieties and focusing on Sangiovese and Merlot. The estate has a restaurant and accommodation (*12 apts.*). Hectares under vine: 32.
**Wines:** Campoleone, Trescone, Torami, Era.

### THE UMBRIAN VALLEY, TODI AND MONTEFALCO

**Tenuta San Lorenzo** – *Via San Lorenzo Vecchio 30 -* **Foligno** *(PG) -* ☎ *0742 22 553 - www.tenutasanlorenzo.it - info@tenuta sanlorenzo.it - Winery tours and tasting by reservation.* An agricultural estate going back to the 10th c., today it has 400 hectares of vineyards, olive groves, woods, meadows and pastures, part of which enclosed to form a hunting reserve where fallow deer and hares live wild. A space is also allocated to training hunting dogs. The centre of the estate is a tiny hamlet with an ancient monastery founded in the 14th c., a consecrated chapel and a charming cloister. Hectares under vine: 30.
**Wines:** San Lorenzo Rosso, Sagrantino di Montefalco, Silence Wine Assisi Merlot, Bio 2016 IGP Umbria Bianco, Celos Pinot Nero. Other products: olive oil.

**Moretti Omero** – *Via S. Sabino 19 -* **Giano dell'Umbria** *(PG) -* ☎ *0742 90 426 - www.morettiomero.it - info@moretti omero.it - Winery tours and tasting by reservation.* The winery, established after World War II, now practises organic agriculture and cultivates olives, grapes and mycorrhized plants for truffles. The grandparents' house has been turned into a guest farm with rooms that take up the colours and names of the wines and oil produced here (*3 rooms and 1 apt.*). Hectares under vine: 14.
**Wines:** Grechetto, Sagrantino, Passito. Other products: olive oil and grappa.

**Còlpetrone** – *Via Ponte La Mandria 8 - Loc. Marcellano -* **Gualdo Cattaneo** *(PG) -* ☎ *0742 99 827 - www.tenutedelcerro.it - colpetrone@tenutedelcerro.it - Winery tours by reservation.* Còlpetrone was taken over by Saiagricola in 1995. It was expanded from the original 4.5 hectares to the current estate of 140. Alongside the development of vineyards, the new centre of Còlpetrone was also established, with a total area of about 3200 m², built in the typical local style. There are also plans to restore the adjacent church of Santa Maria del Fico, built in 1275, which was known to pilgrims travelling on the Via Franchigena. Hectares under vine: 63.
**Wines:** Montefalco Sagrantino Sacer, Montefalco Sagrantino, Montefalco Rosso, Montefalco Sagrantino Passito.

**Castello di Monte Vibiano Vecchio** – *Loc. Monte Vibiano Vecchio di Mercatello -* **Marsciano** *(PG), 20 km SW of Perugia -* ☎ *075 87 83 001 - www.montevibiano.it - info@montevibiano.it - Winery tours and tasting by reservation (from €25).* This marvellous estate is spread out over hundreds of hectares (300 cultivated and 400 wooded) dominated by the lovely old castle. The farmland around the structure is owned by the Fasola family, whose finest

products are oil and wine. The oldest walls of the castle date back to the pre-Christian era, but most of the complex was restored in the 16th c. Hectares under vine: 40.
**Wines**: Maria Camilla Bianco Umbria, San Giovanni Colli Perugini Rosso, L'Andrea Colli Perugini Rosso. Other products: olive oil, grappa, balsamic condiment, cosmetics.

⌂ **Antonelli San Marco** – *Loc. San Marco 60* - **Montefalco** *(PG)* - ☎ *0742 37 91 58* - *www.antonellisanmarco.it* - *info@antonelli sanmarco.it* - *Winery tours and tasting Mon.- Sat. 9-12 and 15-18, Sun. 10-12.30 and 15- 18.30 by reservation*. The origins of the estate are extremely ancient, and medieval documents refer to "San Marco de Corticellis" as a Lombard court. The Bishop of Spoleto owned the estate from the 13th to the 19th c., and in 1881 it was purchased by Francesco Antonelli, a Spoleto lawyer. He promptly began to grow grapes, but bottling did not commence until 1979. Accommodation available at the Casale Satriano holiday farm (*www.satriano.it, 6 apts. and 1 room, min. stay 2 days, from €60*). Hectares under vine: 40.
**Wines**: Montefalco Rosso, Montefalco Rosso Riserva, Sagrantino Montefalco, Sagrantino Montefalco Passito, Montefalco Grechetto. Other products: grappa, olive oil, emmer wheat, emmer wheat pasta and chickpeas.

**Arnaldo Caprai** – *Loc. Torre* - **Montefalco** *(PG)*- ☎ *0742 37 88 02* - *www.arnaldocaprai.it* - *info@arnaldocaprai.it* - *Winery tours and tasting by reservation, tour@arnaldocaprai.it*. In 1971 the textile industrialist Arnaldo Caprai purchased 45 hectares in Montefalco to fulfil his dream of owning an estate and making wine. In 1988 his son Marco took over and started collaborating with research institutes, modernising the company, making acquisitions and conducting experiments. The results were evident immediately and Caprai became one of the region's most famous wineries. Hectares under vine: 136.
**Wines**: Sagrantino di Montefalco 25 Anni, Sagrantino di Montefalco Collepiano, Rosso di Montefalco Montefalco Rosso, Rosso dell'Umbria Rosso Outsider, Grechetto dei Colli Martani Grecante. Other products: grappa, olive oil and beer.

⌂ **Rocca di Fabbri** – *Loc. Fabbri* - **Montefalco** *(PG)* - ☎ *0742 39 93 79* - *www. roccadifabbri.com* - *info@roccadifabbri.com* - *Winery tours by reservation*. The winery was conceived and established by the Umbrian businessman and antiquarian Pietro Vitali, who purchased property in the heart of the Montefalco area so he could replant vines and make wines whose fragrance would evoke this land. Restoration of the 14th-c. stronghold led to the establishment of the

© Alistair Scott/Shutterstock

Rocca di Fabbri winery, which began production in 1984. Accommodation available at the lovely Subretia Residenze di Campagna (*18 apts. from €160, 2 nights minimum*). Hectares under vine: 60.
**Wines**: Rosso di Montefalco, Sagrantino di Montefalco, Sagrantino Passito di Montefalco, Faroaldo IGT, Grechetto. Other products: grappa and olive oil.

⌂ **Cantina Roccafiore** – *Fraz. Chioano Loc. Collina 110/A* – **Todi** *(PG)* - ☎ *075 89 42 746* - *www.roccafiorewines.com* - *info@roccafiore wines.com* - *Winery tours Mon.-Sat. 9.30- 13.30 and 14.30-18.30 by reservation (from €18)*. Roccafiore is a company made up of people, a microcosm that still treasures the awareness that mankind plays a central role. These are the people who make wine, along with tradition, technology and innovation. The company was among the first in Italy to use solar power, building a facility that, in addition to providing power for the company, has allowed a significant reduction in emissions. This sensitivity for nature can also be found in the company's choices in other areas, for example its use of lighter bottles, using biofuels to power its agricultural machinery and a reduction in water consumption. The company's mission is biological and eco-sustainable winemaking. Vineyard safaris, picnics and cooking classes available by request. Roccafiore is also a resort (*13 rooms, from €130*), wellness centre and restaurant. Hectares under vine: 15.
**Wines**: Bianco Fiordaliso, Rosso Melograno, Fiorfiore, Rosato Roccafiore, Il Roccafiore, Prova d'Autore, Collina D'Oro. Other products: olive oil.

⌂ **Cantina Todini** – *Loc. Collevalenza* - **Todi** *(PG)* - ☎ *075 88 71 22* - *www.weare todini.com* - *cantina@wearetodini.com* - *Winery tours and tasting by reservation*. The estate, which has 300 hectares of farmland and vineyards, uses techniques with low environmental impact and has merged agricultural activities with tourism. It is no accident that the estate has its own wildlife park and represents a spectacular attraction for wine buffs and nature lovers alike. It also has a relais with a restaurant (*www.relaistodini.it, 8 rooms and 4 suites, from €130*). Hectares under vine: 70.

**Wines**: Grechetto di Todi Bianco del Cavaliere, Sangiovese di Todi, Rosso IGT Umbria Nero della Cervara, Grechetto di Todi, Rosso IGT Umbria Marte. Other products: olive oil, honey.

🏠 **Lungarotti** – *Via Lungarotti 2 -* **Torgiano** *(PG)* - ☏ *075 98 86 61 - www. lungarotti.it - lungarotti@lungarotti.it - Winery tours by reservation (from €18).* Founded in the 1960s by Giorgio Lungarotti, the winery is now run by his daughters Chiara and Teresa, whereas Maria Grazia Lungarotti oversees the Foundation. The winery's objectives are high-quality wines, environmental protection, accommodation and the promotion of tourism. Although its staff numbers over 100 people, it is still clearly a family business. The family also owns the exclusive luxury hotel Le Tre Vaselle, housed in an 18th-c. building inside the medieval walls of Torgiano (*Via Garibaldi 48, ☏ 075 98 80 447, www.3vaselle.it, 52 rooms*) and the Poggio alle Vigne guest farm (*Via del Colle 46, Montespinello Brufa, 4 km E of Torgiano, ☏ 075 98 29 94, www. poggioallevigne.com, apts. from €510/ week*). Hectares under vine: 250.

**Wines**: Torre di Giano, Rubesco, Rubesco Riserva Vigna Monticchio, San Giorgio and Vin Santo. Other products: olive oil, grappa.

### ORVIETO AND THE COLLI AMERINI

🏠 **Tenuta Vitalonga** – *Loc. Montiano -* **Ficulle** *(TR), 20 km N of Orvieto -* ☏ *0763 83 67 22 - www.vitalonga.it - info@vita longa.it - Winery tours by reservation.* Luigi Maravalle purchased the estate in the 1950s to make high-quality red wine and oil for his family. His son Fabio and wife Gigliola then modernised the winery and renovated the vineyards. Today it is run by his grandchildren and is one of Umbria's most interesting wineries. In addition to winemaking, it has also set up accommodation that beautifully meets the needs of wine tourists (*5 rooms from €120, min. stay 3 nights*). Restaurant Osteria Vialonga service with tastings of wine and typical products. Hectares under vine: 19.

**Wines**: Terra di Confine, Elcione, Phiculle. Other products: olive oil.

**Falesco** – *Loc. San Pietro -* **Montecchio** *(TR) -* ☏ *0744 95 56 - www.famigliacotarella.it - info@famigliacottarella.it - Winery tours by*

reservation, closed Sat. and Sun. (☏ *0744 95 56 16*). The winery was established in 1979 by two brothers, Riccardo and Renzo Cotarella, who decided to devote their energies to reviving the area's ancient varieties and finding the ideal vinegrowing areas. The ancient and rarest local white varieties – including Roscetto – survived here. Falesco has recently enriched its assets with the purchase of the Marciliano estate. Hectares under vine: 260.

**Wines**: Ferentano, Montiano, Marciliano, Trentanni, Vitiano. Other products: grappa.

🏠 **Castello di Corbara** – *Loc. Corbara 7 -* **Orvieto** *(TR) -* ☏ *0763 30 40 35 - www.castellodicorbara.it - info@ castellodicorbara.it - Winery tours by reservation.* For over 30 years the winery has had approximately 100 hectares of vineyards. As far as reds are concerned, it has focused on Merlot, Cabernet Sauvignon, Cabernet Franc, Sangiovese and Montepulciano (of which it has identified a historic clone, probably dating back to 1897, on the estate); its whites include an interesting Grechetto clone found on the estate. The estate has a restaurant and accommodation. Hectares under vine: 100.

**Wines**: Orvieto Classico Sup. Castello di Corbara, Grechetto Umbria IGT Castello di Corbara, Orzalume Grechetto, Lago di Corbara Cabernet Sauvignon, Lago di Corbara Merlot De Coronis.

🏠 **Barberani** – *Corso Cavour 167 -* **Orvieto** *(TR) -* ☏ *0763 34 18 20 - www. barberani.com - info@barberani.com - Winery tours Mon.-Fri. 8-13 and 14-17.* The estate is spread over an area of over 100 hectares, 55 of which under vine. It also cultivates olives and other crops. The microclimate benefits from the nearby

lake, which acts as a heat regulator, preventing sudden temperature swings. The main production is Orvieto Classico, dry, medium dry and sweet, with various selections. The estate grows Chardonnay, Sauvignon, Sémillon, Riesling Renano, Moscato, Cabernet Sauvignon, Cabernet Franc and Pinot Nero, as well as the traditional local grapes. Accommodation available in the guest farm (*☎ 0763 34 18 20, agriturismo@barberani.it, 10 rooms*). Hectares under vine: 55.
**Wines**: Orvieto Classico Castagnolo, Calcaia Muffa Nobile, Grechetto Umbria IGT, Moscato Passito, Umbria IGT Rosso Polvento, Umbria IGT Rosato Amore.

⌂ **Decugnano dei Barbi** – *Loc. Fossatello 50* - **Orvieto** *(TR)* - *☎ 0763 30 82 55* - *www.decugnanodeibarbi.com* - *info@ decugnano.it* - *Winery tours and tasting by reservation, visit@decugnano.it*. Decugnano dei Barbi boasts a stunning location: the view of the Umbrian countryside is surreally beautiful, with the Orvieto cliff in the background. Visitors can also tour the fascinating tufa grottoes, where the winery makes its spumante and ages its finest reds. Claudio Barbi purchased the estate in 1973. He produced his first bottles in 1978 and in 1981 the winery brought out Italy's first wine made from botrytised grapes, in the style of the famous French Sauternes. Weekly accommodation available at Villa Barbi - Luxury Wine Resort (*prices on request*). Hectares under vine: 32.
**Wines**: Orvieto Classico Sup. Decugnano dei Barbi Bianco, Umbria IGT Decugnano Bianco Maris, Decugnano dei Barbi Rosso IGT, Orvieto Classico Villa Barbi Bianco, Decugnano Brut Metodo Classico.

⌂ **Palazzone** – *Loc. Rocca Ripesena 68* - **Orvieto** *(TR)* - *☎ 0763 34 49 21* - *www.palazzone.com* - *info@palazzone.com* - *Winery tours by reservation*. In 1969 Angelo Dubini and his wife Maria purchased the Palazzone estate and undertook intensive restructuring and organisation work. In order to make high-quality wine, they painstakingly planted 24 hectares of vineyards. Now managed by their children Giovanni and Lodovico, Palazzone has become one of Umbria's most important wineries. Following years of restoration work, the estate's historic *palazzo* has now opened its doors to guests. Accommodation at Locanda Palazzone (*www.locandapalazzone.com, 5 rooms, 2 apts.*), with wine bar and evening meals for hotel guests. Hectares under vine: 24.
**Wines**: Orvieto Classico Sup. Campo del Guardiano, Orvieto Classico Sup. Terre Vineate, Grechetto Umbria IGT, Armaleo Umbria Rosso IGT, Muffa Nobile Orvieto Classico Sup. Other products: olive oil.

⌂ **Castello delle Regine** – *Strada Ortana 2/v* - **San Liberato di Narni** *(TR), 13 km SW of Narni* - *☎ 0744 70 20 05* - *www.castello delleregine.it* - *info@castellodelleregine.com* - *Winery tours by reservation*. The estate covers approximately 400 hectares, 75 of which under vine, set around the stronghold of Castelluccio Amerino, which overlooks the valley "delle regine" ("of the queens"). Its current owner, the attorney Paolo Nodari, has rebuilt it and revived its age-old winegrowing tradition. Success was in the wings and the winery soon gained the attention of wine professionals. Restaurant service at the Pordenovo (*closed Sun. evening and Mon.*) and accommodation at the Country House, offering apartments with private pools and a tennis court (*18 apts.*). Hectares under vine: 75.
**Wines**: Merlot, Selezione del Fondatore, Princeps, Rosso di Podernovo, Bianco delle Regine. Other products: olive oil.

## Where to stay

### ORVIETO

**Agriturismo Borgo San Faustino e Relais del Borgo** – *Borgo San Faustino 11/12, Morrano, 15 km N of Orvieto* - *☎ 0763 21 53 03* - *www.borgosanfaustino.it* - *21 rooms, doubles from €120*. A hamlet in the traditional style of Umbrian homes, combining the amenities of a hotel with the features of a holiday farm.

### PERUGIA

**Agriturismo San Felicissimo** – *Strada Poggio Pelliccione 2, 5 km NE of Perugia* - *☎ 345 97 73 266* - *www.sanfelicissimo.com* - *10 rooms, doubles from €85*. A small guest farm just out of town but surrounded by hills and olive groves.

### SPELLO

**Agriturismo Le Due Torri** – *Via Torre Quadrano 1, Loc. Limiti, 4.5 km W of Spello* - *☎ 335 77 83 400* - *www.agriturismoledue torri.com* - *Closed mid-Jan.- Easter* - *6 apts. and 4 rooms, double from €90, apts. from €120*. In the shade of a medieval watchtower, the farmhouse offers well-appointed rooms and is surrounded by greenery.

### UMBERTIDE

**La Locanda del Capitano** – *Via Roma 7, Montone (PG), 10 km N of Umbertide* - *☎ 075 93 06 521* - *www.ilcapitano.com* - *Closed 10 Jan.-15 Feb.* - *10 rooms, doubles from €95*. This ancient building that was once the home of the *condottiere* Fortebraccio offers the timeless charm of a medieval village but with modern amenities. The restaurant serves traditional dishes interpreted with a personal touch.

# THE MARCHES

The revival and enhancement in the quality of native grape varieties is the goal that the Marches is working towards and there is no shortage of results. One obvious example is that the region's wines are no longer represented by Verdicchio alone. Since 2004 the surge in new appellations – Vernaccia di Serrapetrona DOCG, Conero DOCG, Offida DOCG, Terreni di Sanseverino DOC, Pergola DOC and San Ginesio DOC – has demonstrated the dynamic changes the local wine industry is experiencing. The discovery near Ascoli Piceno of fossilised remains of *Vitis vinifera*, dating from the Iron Age, are a clear indication of the long history viticulture has in the region, which, thanks to its soil composition and the mildness of the climate, offers ideal conditions for winemaking.

*Gentle hills around Jesi*

## The terroir

Despite the presence of international grape varieties like Chardonnay, Pinot Bianco and Pinot Nero, it is the native cultivars that triumph in the Marches. **Verdicchio** has always been the standard bearer for the region, which acquires unique qualities near Matelica and in the zone of Castelli di Jesi thanks to the very special characteristics of the soil and climate. Here Verdicchio grapes create white wines with a greenish tinge (whence its name), with scents of acacia flowers, hawthorn, peach, apple and citrus fruits. Known and appreciated abroad, Verdicchio is refreshing and zesty in the mouth, with an aftertaste reminiscent of almonds.

Among the other representative varieties, those increasingly making a name for themselves are Vernaccia Nera and Lacrima. The first is used to make **Vernaccia di Serrapetrona DOCG**, a dry or sweet red sparkling wine. The second lends its name to **Lacrima di Morro d'Alba DOC**

and produces red wines with an unmistakable smell of raspberries, myrtles, redcurrants, and other soft fruit.

The northernmost province is Pesaro, where the designated zones of **Colli Pesaresi, Bianchello del Metauro** and **Pergola** are situated. This last appellation was created in 2005 and produces red, novello and dried-grape wines in the municipality of the same name and its neighbouring zones. In the provinces of Ancona and Macerata lie the appellations **Verdicchio dei Castelli di Jesi**, **Esino**, **Conero**, **Rosso Conero** and **Lacrima di Morro d'Alba**. In Macerata there are **Colli Maceratesi**, **Verdicchio di Matelica**, **San Ginesio** and **Terreni di Sanseverino**; and further south in the province of Ascoli Piceno lie **Offida**, **Falerio dei Colli Ascolani** and **Rosso Piceno** (which is the largest designated zone in the region and extends into the provinces of Macerata and Ancona, even though it gives best results in Ascoli).

# Itineraries

*Locations with a winery are indicated by the symbol ▼; for the addresses of the wineries, see p. 340.*

*for the addresses of the wineries, see p. 340.*

## 1. COLLI PESARESI

*Itinerary of approximately 90 km from Pesaro to Fano.*

The province of Pesaro is home to the appellations **Colli Pesaresi**, **Bianchello del Metauro** and **Pergola**. Sangiovese is the preferred variety in Colli Pesaresi, whereas Bianchello del Metauro is a white wine made from Biancame grapes. Aleatico grapes are more common in Pergola DOC, where red, rosé and novello wines are produced.

### Pesaro★

Located on the Adriatic coast at the mouth of the Foglia valley, this popular seaside resort was the birthplace of **Gioacchino Rossini**, whose house (*Via Rossini 34*) has been turned into a museum. *For information on visits ☎ 0721 38 73 57, www.pesarocultura.it.* **Piazza del Popolo** features a fountain with tritons and seahorses and is the setting for the imposing **Ducal Palace** built in the 15th c. for a member of the Sforza family.

The façade of the palace features an arched gallery, crenellations on its crown, and an upper storey with windows decorated with festoons and putti in the 17th c.

The deconsecrated Church of San Domenico stands beside the central Post Office building. All that remains of it is the 14th-c. façade (*in Via Branca*) and the portal framed by sculptures and spiral columns.

On Corso XI Settembre behind the Ducal Palace, the Church of Sant'Agostino has a

### DOCG
Castelli di Jesi Verdicchio Riserva
Conero
Offida
Verdicchio di Matelica Riserva
Vernaccia di Serrapetrona

### DOC
Bianchello del Metauro
Colli Maceratesi
Colli Pesaresi
Esino
Falerio
I Terreni di Sanseverino
Lacrima di Morro
    *or* Lacrima di Morro d'Alba
Pergola
Rosso Conero
Rosso Piceno
San Ginesio
Serrapetrona
Terre di Offida
Verdicchio dei Castelli di Jesi
Verdicchio di Matelica

## PRINCIPAL VARIETIES CULTIVATED

### WHITE GRAPES
Albana
Biancame
Bombino Bianco
Chardonnay
Fiano
Grechetto
Incrocio Bruni 54
Maceratino
Malvasia Bianca di Candia
Malvasia Bianca Lunga
Manzoni Bianco
Montonico Bianco
Mostosa
Passerina
Pecorino
Pinot Bianco
Riesling
Riesling Italico
Sauvignon
Tocai Friulano
Trebbiano Toscano
Verdicchio Bianco
Vermentino

### GREY GRAPES
Pinot Grigio

### BLACK GRAPES
Aleatico
Alicante
Barbera
Cabernet Franc
Cabernet Sauvignon
Canaiolo Nero
Carignano
Ciliegiolo
Gaglioppo
Lacrima
Maiolica
Merlot
Montepulciano
Pinot Nero
Rebo
Sangiovese
Vernaccia Nera

*Piazza del Popolo, Pesaro*

beautiful portal in Gothic-Venetian style and, inside, elegantly inlaid Renaissance stalls in the choir.

Behind the cathedral and Rossini's house stands the **Rocca Costanza**, a 15th-c. defensive construction built by Luciano Laurana for Costanzo Sforza.

**Civic Museums★** – *Piazza Toschi Mosca 29. Open 10-13 and 16.30-19.30, Oct.-May 10-13 and 15.30-18.30 (Fri.-Sun.), closed Mon., ☎ 0721 38 75 41, www.pesaro musei.it*. The picture gallery has panels by Giovanni Bellini, one of which is the magnificent *Pesaro Altarpiece* (1475). The **Ceramics Museum★★** mostly gives examples of local earthenware (Casteldurante, Pesaro, Urbino) but also displays pieces from Umbria (Gubbio, Deruta) and Abruzzo (Castelli).

### The panoramic road to Gabicce★

*15 km north-west of Pesaro.* Lined on either side by juniper, agaves, cypresses and umbrella pines, the road winds through the hills above Pesaro offering splendid views of the city. It passes through the walled town of **Fioren-zuola di Focara** and **Castel di Mezzo**, then slowly descends towards **Gabicce Mare**. As it wanders from hill to hill, the road offers superb vistas of countryside and the sea, and in the distance on the left it is possible to make out Gradara Fort.

### Gradara

Gradara is a more or less intact medieval village, ringed by walls and gates with machicolations for dropping rocks or boiling oil onto unwanted visitors. The **Fort★** was built on a square plan with corner towers and is a fine example of 13th and 14th-c. military architecture. This was where Gianni Malatesta surprised and killed his wife Francesca da Rimini with his brother Paolo Malatesta, who were supposedly enflamed by passion after reading the story of Lancelot and Guinevere. The episode inspired one of the best known passages in Dante's *Divine Comedy*, in which the two lovers are described as inseparable even in death. *Open 8.30-18.30, closed Mon. pm, ☎ 0541 96 41 15, www.gradara.org.*

### Metauro Valley

Continue inland towards **Tavullia**, Sant'Angelo in Lizzola, and **Montecicca-rdo**. The road climbs giving good views as far as **Mombaroccio**, an ancient walled village. From here you enter the **Metauro valley**, down one side of which pass the ancient Via Flaminia and a new highway. Once past **Cartoceto** you cross the river Metauro and arrive at **Montemaggiore al Metauro**, another town with a walled medieval centre.

*Return to the coast.*

### Fano

A very lively and popular seaside resort, Fano was a Roman colony and from the 13th to 15th c. a feud of the Malatesta family from Rimini. The Augustan Arch (1st c. AD) gives its name to **Via Arco di**

**Augusto★**, which passes through the town centre and leads to the sea. The medieval cathedral of Fano was remodelled but still has some original features and interesting works of art.

Take Corso Matteotti on the right to **Piazza XX Settembre**. The square is the setting for a 16th-c. fountain of the goddess Fortuna standing on a globe, her cloak flying in the wind. Facing down on it are the 13th-c. Palazzo del Podestà, and the very beautiful Renaissance **Corte Malatestiana★**, composed of a palace and courtyard-garden, and containing the Civic Museum. *For information,* ☏ *0721 88 78 45.*

Not far away, beneath the portico of the deconsecrated Church of San Francesco, are the elegant 15th-c. **Malatestian Arches**. The Church of Santa Maria Nuova (16th-18th c.) has works by the painter Perugino, which are notable for the elegance of their design and softness of colour.

Standing close to the railway lines is the **Malatestian Fort**, built around 1450 by Sigismondo Pandolfo Malatesta.

About 5 km south-west of Fano stands the belvedere of the **Hermitage of Monte Giove**, which gives views right across the Metauro valley.

## 2. THE PROVINCE OF ANCONA

The area that straddles the border between the provinces of Ancona and Macerata is home to white Verdicchio wine in **Castelli di Jesi DOC** and interesting reds like **Conero DOCG** and **Rosso Conero DOC** made from Montepulciano grapes, Esino DOC from Sangiovese grapes, and **Lacrima di Morro d'Alba DOC** from Lacrima grapes.

### The Verdicchio zone

*Itinerary of approximately 150 km from Senigallia to Jesi.*

The trip starts in **Senigallia**, a busy seaside town with several interesting monuments, such as the Rovere Castle, built towards the end of the 15th c. for Giovanni della Rovere. From here you go inland as far as Arcevia to explore the Misa valley, then return to the coast along the river Esino.

**Ostra** is an attractive walled town that looks down on the Misa valley. It was founded by refugees from Ostra Antica, a town destroyed by the Goths in the 5th c. A similar fate befell **Ostra Vetere** 🍷 *(12 km west)*, which stands on a terraced hill slope between the Misa and Névola valleys.

## THE TERROIR

**Area**: 9,401.38 km$^2$, of which approximately 15,972 hectares are planted to vine

**Production 2019**: 932,070 hectolitres of which 342,322 VQPRD

**Geography**: clayey soil. Temperate climate, colder inland, milder on the coast

## THE PROTECTION CONSORTIA

Istituto Marchigiano di Tutela Vini – ☏ 0731 21 48 27, www.imtdoc.it

Consorzio Vini Piceni – ☏ 342 91 19 547, www.consorziovinipiceni.com

Consorzio Tutela Rosso Conero – ☏ 071 93 31 879, www.parks.it/parco.conero/prodotti.tipici/rossoconero

## WINE AND FOOD ROUTES

Strada del Vino Verdicchio di Matelica – ☏ 0737 78 18 11
Strada del Rosso Conero – www.rossoconero.info
Strada del vino Serrapetrona della Vernaccia ed i sapori dei Sibillini – ☏ 0733 90 83 21

*Rolling hills and varying colours of Verdicchio*

Leave Ostra and pass through Belvedere Ostrense to reach **Morro d'Alba** 🍷, the homeland of the Lacrima cultivar. Morro is an ancient town whose walls have an internal walkway called "La Scarpa".

*Return to the S 360 and continue in the direction of Arcevia.*

A short detour left takes you to **Serra de' Conti**, where there is another well preserved city wall, and **Montecarotto** 🍷, which stands between the Misa and Esino valleys.

Further down the S 360 you come to **Arcevia**, a town founded in the Middle Ages that overlooks the river valley from a rock spur. The 17th-c. Church of San Medardo holds paintings by Luca Signorelli and Giovanni della Robbia.

*Turn left towards Genga.*

Created by a branch of the Sentino torrent, the **Frasassi Grottoes**★★ are an immense underground chain of caves. The largest is the Grotto of the Wind, which has 7 chambers that feature stalagmites, stalactites and various concretions of diverse colours. *Opening times vary during the year. For information 🕿 0732 97 21 66 or 800 16 62 50, www. frasassi.com.*

*Follow the S 76 towards Jesi for 20 or so km.*

Set among the Verdicchio lined slopes, **Maiolati Spontini** 🍷 was the birthplace of musician Gaspare Spontini in 1774. In addition to the fine Verdicchio wine it produces, the village is worth a visit for its walls. **Cupramontana** 🍷 dominates the surrounding hills and is the home of

the unusual **Wine Label Museum**. You can visit it in the 18th-c. Palazzo Leoni in Via Leopardi 58. *Corso Leopardi 58, open 10.30-12.30 and 16.30-19.30 (Sun.) 🕿 0731 78 01 99, www.museiingrotta.it.*

A further 8 km south-east along a very pretty road, you come to **Stàffolo** 🍷, a walled town high above the Esino and Musone valleys. Visit the **Art of Wine Museum** at number 31 Via Marconi. *Sept.-Jun. Fri.-Sat. 18-2, Sun. and holidays 11-13 and 18-2, Jul. and Aug. Tue.-Sat. 18-2, Sun. and public hols. 11-13 and 18-2, for informations 🕿 338 13 50 308.*

*Continue to Jesi on the panoramic S 502.*

## Jesi★

The Roman city of *Aesis* became a rich free commune in the 12th c. that enjoyed the protection of Emperor Frederick II, who was born in the city in 1194. Jesi later passed to the Papal States, to which it remained attached until the Union of Italy. Reminders of its past are its medieval and Renaissance city centre, splendid **city walls**★ (13th-16th c.), gateways and large towers. The city theatre is dedicated to the local composer Giovan Battista Pergolesi (1710-36). The high street, Corso Matteotti, is lined with fine palaces and churches.

The **Municipal Picture Gallery**★ has an admirable collection of Rococo paintings filled with allegories and symbolism. The collection also has a large number of works by the Venetian painter Lorenzo Lotto, including one of his masterpieces, the *Santa Lucia Altarpiece. Via XV Settembre 10. Open 10-13 and 16-19* (in sum. 10-19), closed Mon., ✆ 0731 53 83 42/34143.

**Palazzo della Signoria★** was designed in the late 15th c. by the Sienese architect Giorgio Martini, a pupil of Brunelleschi. This imposing building has an elegant façade decorated with a stone kiosk.

The **Regional Wine Cellar** of the Marches is housed in Palazzo Balleani, between Piazza Federico II and Palazzo della Signoria (*see the Addresses*).

## Ancona and Cònero

*Itinerary of 70 km from Ancona to Offagna.*

### Ancona★

The city stands on an elbow-shaped promontory after which it was named (in Greek *ankon* = elbow). The most interesting buildings and monuments are to be found in the northern part of the city, behind the port. To the south stretches the splendid Riviera del Conero, one of the most beautiful and dramatic parts of the Adriatic coastline.

The **cathedral★** is dedicated to St Cyriac, the patron saint of Ancona and a 4th-c. Christian martyr. It was constructed in Romanesque style with elements from Byzantine (the Greek cross plan) and Lombard architecture (pilasters and small external wall arches). The façade is preceded by a majestic Gothic porch made from pink stone that rests on lions.

*Take Via Pizzecolli.* Built in the 15th c., the Church of San Francesco delle Scale has a splendid Gothic-Venetian portal and is a masterpiece by Giorgio Orsini. *At the bottom of the street turn right towards the port.* **Santa Maria della Piazza★** is a small, 10th-c. Romanesque church with an interesting 13th-c. façade adorned with a sculpted frieze. It was built over two early Christian sanctuaries (5th and 6th c.) and retains their mosaic floors. Not far away is the **Loggia dei Mercanti★**, built in the 15th c. by Giorgio Orsini with a fine Gothic-Venetian façade.

*Return north along the coast.*

**Trajan's Arch** was constructed to celebrate the emperor who had reorganised the port in 115 AD.

### The Conero Riviera★

*Leave Ancona on the "Strada del Monte" (Mountain Road) for Portonovo.* This winding road takes you to Marcelli, offering marvellous views over the coastline and hills inland. The area you pass through has been designated the **Monte Conero Regional Park**.

**Portonovo★** is a picturesque village perched high up on the rocky coastline on the Conero massif. The small fort there (which has been turned into a hotel) was built in 1808 by Eugène de Beauharnais to help protect the coast from the British navy. A small private road leads through the wood to the enchanting Church of **Santa Maria★** built by the Benedictines in the 11th c. *Open Sat. and Sun.* A short distance on you come to the **Abbey of San Pietro**, also founded by the Benedictines, which enjoys magnificent views over the sea and inland countryside.

The Mountain Road continues south for 30 or so km visiting pleasant holiday villages such as the medieval **Sirolo**, and **Numana** ♟. This small town is split in two halves: the upper half is the administrative centre, with the Town Hall in

*Conero Riviera*

*Lush vines in the province of Ancona*

Piazza del Santuario, and is connected to the lower half by the Castarella, a stepped alley that goes down to the sea. From the port boats are available to take you to delightful hidden bays.

*Shortly before Porto Recanati leave the coast road and turn inland towards Loreto.*

### Loreto★

The small town of Loreto has been built up around its famous sanctuary, which is a constant place of pilgrimage. The town has kept its beautiful ancient centre encircled by 16th-c. brick walls. The legend says that angels miraculously transported the house of Mary of Nazareth here and placed it down in a laurel wood (*loreto* in Italian), which gave the town its name. Indeed, three walls of the House of Nazareth were transported here in 1294 by the Angelus, that at that time was the ruling family of the Despotate of Epirus in Greece. The **Piazza della Madonna★** is flanked by the uncompleted but elegant portico of the Palazzo Apostolico. This building houses the **Picture Gallery**, including a remarkable collection of paintings by Lorenzo Lotto. *Open 10-13 and 15-18, ℘ 071 97 47 198, www.santuarioloreto.it.*

**Sanctuary of the Santa Casa★★** – *Open 6.15-19.30 (Oct.-Mar. 19); the Santa Casa is closed from 12.30 to 14.30, ℘ 071 97 47 198, www.santuarioloreto.it.* Famous architects, painters and sculptors have contributed to the development of the sanctuary, which was begun in 1468 and completed in the 18th c. Giuliano da Sangallo and Bramante designed and built the side chapels, while Vanvitelli built the domed bell tower. Walk around the church to admire the three-part apse and Sangallo's elegant cupola. At the far end of the right aisle the dome of the Sacristy of San Marco was frescoed by Melozzo da Forlì in 1477 with daring foreshortened views of angels carrying the instruments of the Passion. A basin designed by Benedetto da Maiano and frescoes by Luca Signorelli can be seen in the Sacristy of San Giovanni. In the 16th c. Antonio Sansovino, among others, sumptuously decorated the Santa Casa with sculpted marble, and there is a fine cycle of paintings by Pomarancio (1610) in a stairwell that looks onto the left transept.

*Continue on the SS 77 for another 7 km.*

### Recanati

Built on top of a hill, the town of Recanati is famous for having been the birthplace of the poet **Giacomo Leopardi** (1798-1837), whose life and work Palazzo Leopardi celebrates. *Spring-sum. 9-19, fall-win. 9-17, closed working Mon., ℘ 071 75 73 380, www.giacomoleopardi.it.* The **Civic Museum** can be found in the Villa Colloredo Mels (*Via Gregorio XII*). It has various departments (archaeological, medieval, Renaissance, 17th-18th c., Leopardian, and modern and contemporary art) and exhibits several works by Lorenzo Lotto, including an *Annunciation*. *Open 10-13 and 15-18, closed Mon. (in sum. Mon.-Sun. 10-19), ℘ 071 75 70 410, www.villacolloredomels.it.*

Return towards Loreto and take the road to **Castelfidardo** 🍸, a town that is known for its accordions and a historic battle during the Risorgimento. From here continue to Osimo.

## Osimo 🍸

The historic centre of Osimo is ringed by Roman and medieval walls and crossed internally by Via Matteotti and Via Mazzini. Sights to see are the magnificent Baroque interior of the Church of San Marco and Piazza Dante, lined by 17th- and 18th-century palaces, including the imposing **Palazzo Campana**. This building holds the civic museum and its collections of paintings, sculptures and archaeology. *Piazza Dante 5, open Fri. and Sat. 17.30-19.30, Sun. and public hols. 10-12.30 and 17.30-19.30; on all other days it is open by appointment, 𝒫 071 72 31 773.* Pass by the 14th-c. Sanctuary of San Giuseppe da Copertino remodelled in the 18th c., and continue to Piazza del Comune. This is lined by some lovely buildings, including the Town Hall (16th-17th c.) and a 13th-c. tower. The duomo was founded in the early Christian era but was later restored (12th-14th c.). Inside, note the raised presbytery and fine 4th-c. stone slabs and sarcophaguses in the crypt.

About 8 km to the north, **Offagna** is the site of a 15th-c. castle that gives good views over the surrounding countryside.

## 3. THE PROVINCE OF MACERATA

### Colli Maceratesi, Matelica and Serrapetrona

*Itinerary of 140 km from Macerata to Matelica.*

Three longer established appellations lie in the province of Macerata: **Colli Maceratesi**, **Vernaccia di Serrapetrona** and **Verdicchio di Matelica**. The first produces **white wines** from Maceratino grapes (which are also known as Ribona or Montecchio) and **reds** from Sangiovese, **Vernaccia di Serrapetrona**; the second makes sparkling scented reds from Vernaccia Nera and **Verdicchio di Matelica**; and the third is of course famous for its elegant Verdicchio. More recently created are the designated zones **Terreni di Sanseverino** (red and dried-grape wines from Vernaccia Nera)

and **San Ginesio** (still and sparkling dry and sweet red wines, mainly produced from Sangiovese grapes).

Leave Macerata on a pretty road in the direction of the **Convent of Forano**. The original core of the convent, which St Francis visited, dates to the 13th c. A few km to the west **Appignano** 🍸 has a medieval centre enclosed by walls. A further 9 km takes you to **Treia**, a pretty town of ancient appearance strung out along a ridge. After crossing the S 361 you come to the Church of **Santa Maria di Rambona** (*7 km south of Treia*). This was founded in the 8th c. on the site of a pagan temple dedicated to the goddess Bona, and restored in the 11th c.

*Continue to Tolentino.*

## Tolentino 🍸

Tolentino is famous for the **Basilica of San Nicola**★★. The saint was an Augustinian monk capable of performing miracles who died in Tolentino in 1305 and was buried in the crypt of the sanctuary. The composite appearance of the building reflects the different stages of its construction, which lasted from the 14th to the 18th c. The 15th c. portal in the 14th-c. façade was designed by the Florentine architect Nanni di Bartolo, a follower of Donatello. The interior abounds with decorative work in marble, stucco and gold, and boasts a superb lacunar ceiling. The **Chapel of San Nicola** (*right transept*) is covered with very fine 14th-c. frescoes painted by an anonymous master from Rimini. *For information, 𝒫 0733 97 63 11, www.sannicoladatolentino.it.*

As you leave Tolentino in a southerly direction, a short detour to the left through Urbisaglia will take you to the Cistercian abbey of **Chiaravalle di Fiastra**.

About 20 km from Tolentino, **San Ginesio** dominates the Adriatic coast and mountainous interior from high on a hill. The Romanesque collegiate church in Piazza Gentilini has an attractive 15th-c. façade and frescoes by Salimbeni painted in International Gothic style. The town is also the home of the recently created San Ginesio DOC zone.

Now head north through Caldarola and **Serrapetrona** 🍸, where you can taste the excellent **Vernaccia DOCG** and admire the parish church's many fine works of art.

## San Severino Marche

The medieval and Renaissance layout of the town developed around the elliptical Piazza del Popolo. There is a marvellous **view**★ of the town and surrounding mountains from the top of the hill on which the Old Duomo stands (*take Via Pitturetta*). The **picture gallery** in Palazzo Tacchi-Venturi (*no. 39 Via Salimbeni*) has interesting works from the local school: Lorenzo Salimbeni and his brother Jacopo revolutionised 15th-c. pictorial language with a style in which the heavy hand of Courtly Gothic was lightened in pictures of dynamic immediacy. The collection also includes a very fine polyptych by Vittore Crivelli and the delicate *Madonna della Pace* by Pinturicchio (1454-1513). *Oct.-Jun. Tue.-Fri. 9-13, Sat.-Sun. 9-13 (Sun. 10) and 15-18, Jul.-Sept. 9-13 (Sun. 10) and 15-19, ☏ 0733 63 80 95.* Turn left at the bottom of Via Salimbeni to reach the 11th-c. Church of San Lorenzo in Dolìolo. It has interesting architecture and a lovely crypt covered with frescoes attributed to the Salimbeni brothers and their school. The appellation **I Terreni di Sanseverino DOC** has recently been established in the zone of San Severino.

From San Severino, pass through Castelraimondo to reach **Matelica** ♟, which lies on a spur in hilly countryside on the course of the river Esino. The town's most important buildings stand in the central Piazza Mattei.

## 4. THE PROVINCE OF ASCOLI PICENO

### Offida, Falerio and Rosso Piceno

*Itinerary of 90 km from Ascoli Piceno to Fermo.*

The province of Ascoli Piceno encompasses the DOC zones **Offida**, Falerio and Rosso Piceno. In the first, most of the vines grown are the two very interesting local varieties **Passerina** and **Pecorino**, which are also represented in **Falerio DOC**. In contrast, it is Sangiovese and Montepulciano that are used to produce the excellent red wines of **Rosso Piceno**.

### Ascoli Piceno★★ ♟

Ascoli Piceno is known as "little Siena" due to the uniformity and grace of its travertine medieval and Renaissance buildings and towers. The delightful city is centred on **Piazza del Popolo★★**, one of Italy's most beautiful squares. It is paved with large slabs, lined by elegant porticoes and faced onto by impressive Gothic and Renaissance palaces. The Palazzo dei Capitani del Popolo was built in the 13th c. but gets its current appearance from restoration work in the 16th c. It has a very fine porticoed internal courtyard (16th c.). The Church of **San Francesco** (13th-16th c.) features characteristics of Lombard architecture. On the right side of the church stands a lovely 16th-c. portal crowned by a monument in honour of Pope Julius II, and the Loggia dei Mercanti, an elegant 16th-c. construction with capitals of Tuscan derivation. On the left is the Large Cloister (16th-17th c.), where a fruit and vegetable market is held, and the 14th-c. Small Cloister (*entrance in Via Ceci*). Another feature of the church is the twin bell towers in the apsidal section.

*With the church behind you, cross the square to Via XX Settembre and turn left.*

Constructed during the 12th c., the **Duomo** has a large Renaissance façade designed by Cola dell'Amatrice. The fine late-Renaissance Porta della Musa is on the left. In the right aisle, the Chapel del Sacramento holds a magnificent polyptych by Carlo Crivelli in which the Late Gothic grace of the *Madonna and Child* contrasts with the dramatic nature of the *Pietà*, itself a reference to Mantegna. *Open 8-12 and 15-19, ☏ 0736 25 99 01.* The 11th-c. **Baptistery** stands to the left of the Duomo. This lovely square building has an octagonal tympan made less heavy by elegant arched three-light blind windows. At number 24 Via Bonaparte, **Palazzo Bonaparte** offers one of the best examples of residential Renaissance architecture.

**Corso Mazzini★** is Ascoli's high street. It is lined with palaces of different epochs and displays maxims written in Latin and the vernacular. At number 24, Palazzo Malaspina (16th c.) has an unusual loggia with columns made to resemble tree trunks. On the corner of Via delle Torri there is the Renaissance Church of Sant'Agostino, which contains a fresco by Cola dell'Amatrice and a *Madonna dell'Umiltà* (14th c.) by the school of Fabriano. The street is named after the many towers that used to stand here, of which a fine example is given by the twin 12th-c. towers. At the bottom of the street is the 14th-c. Church of San Pietro Martire.

An instance of Romanesque architecture, the Church of **Santi Vincenzo e Anastasio★**, founded in the early Christian era, has a 14th-c. façade divided into 64 panels covered by frescoes. The simple yet beautiful interior includes a 6th-c. crypt with the remains of 14th-c. frescoes.

The **Solestà Roman bridge★** is an ambitious construction due to its single span over 25 m high. It was built during the reign of Augustus and has been embellished by a 14th-c. gateway. Shortly after the bridge is an impressive public washhouse constructed in the 16th c.

**Via dei Soderini** was the city's most important street during the Middle Ages, as the many palaces, towers and picturesque cross-streets indicate. The most interesting building is Palazzetto Longobardo (11th-12th c.). This stands beside the Torre degli Ercolani (over 40 m tall), whose entrance has a typical Ascolan architrave with a triangle cut out above it to lighten the load.

*Take the SP 235 (Via Salaria) towards the coast and turn left onto the SP 43.*

## Offida

The lovely ancient town of Offida lies between the Tronto and Tesino valleys. It has a splendid 15th-c. Municipal Palace (that incorporates a 19th-c. theatre) on a triangular plaza. At the edge of the historic centre is the 14th-c. Church of Santa Maria della Rocca, adorned with ancient frescoes. Offida is a leading producer of **Rosso Piceno** wine and was awarded the **Offida DOC** designation in 2001.

The **Regional Wine Cellar of the Marches** is located in the lovely rooms of the former Convent of San Francesco. *Open 10.30-13 and 15.30-19 (Sat.-Sun. 20), ✆ 073 66 18 023.*

The town of **Ripatransone** 🍷 stands 13 km north-east on a hill looking down onto the Tesino and Menocchia valleys. It is typically medieval with its ancient walls and alleys.

As you continue north, pass through **Monterubbiano**, a pleasant town over the Aso valley, but make a short detour to visit **Montefiore dell'Aso**, a gracious town where, in the **San Francesco Museum**, you can see one of the masterpieces painted by Carlo Crivelli, a **polyptych★★** illuminated with gold, with six panels of saints. His depiction of Mary Magdalene is one of Crivelli's greatest works: the saint is shown dressed in sumptuous gold brocade and silk and wearing a scarlet mantle, a symbol of the Passion of Christ. She steps lightly forward, holding an ointment vase in her hand. *For information on visits ✆ 0734 93 87 43 or 328 17 75 908.*

## Fermo★

Yet another very lovely town in a fine hillside position overlooking the countryside and sea. At its centre is the elegant **Piazza del Popolo★** ringed by 16th-c. loggias, porticoes and palaces. Note the Palazzo dei Priori (15th-16th c.) whose façade features a statue of Pope Sixtus V, formerly the bishop of Fermo. Other buildings in the square are the Palazzo degli Studi, which was once a university and is now the Town Library, and on the other side the Palazzo Apostolico.

On Via degli Aceti are the **Roman cisterns**, an extraordinary engineering work of the 1st c. AD, composed of 30 communicating chambers with a total surface area of 2000 square metres. They were used to supply water to the city and port. *For information on visits ✆ 0734 21 71 40.*

Piazza del Popolo marks the start of **Corso Cefalonia**, the main street in the historic centre. It is lined by Renaissance palaces, such as Palazzo Azzolino and Palazzo Vitali Rosati, and the 13th-c. Torre Matteucci.

The wide esplanade of Piazza del Duomo gives a great **view★★** of the surrounding countryside, the Apennines, the sea and the Conero promontory. The **Duomo★** was built in the 13th c. in Romanesque-Gothic style with a majestic façade and a finely sculpted portal in white Istrian stone. The sarcophagus of Giovanni Visconti, lord of the city in the 14th c., stands in the atrium, which was part of the ancient church that preceded the duomo on this spot. The 18th-c. interior has a lovely Byzantine icon and a 5th-c. mosaic in which the peacock drinking from a vase symbolises the resurrection of Christ. *Open 10-13 and 15.30-18, ✆ 0734 22 87 29.*

# Addresses

## Tourist information

**Marche Regional Tourist Office** –
Via Gentile da Fabriano 9, **Ancona**,
✆ 071 80 62 431 or 800 22 21 11
www.turismo.marche.it

**Ancona Tourist Office** – Banchina N. Sauro
50, Ancona, ✆ 071 20 76 431,
www.turismo.marche.it

**Ascoli Piceno Tourist Office** – Piazza Arringo
7, Ascoli Piceno, ✆ 0736 29 83 34

**Province of Macerata** – Corso della
Repubblica 32, Macerata, ✆ 0733 23 48 07,
www.turismo.provinciamc.it

**Province of Pesaro Urbino** – Viale Trieste
164, Pesaro, ✆ 0721 69 341 or 800 56 38 00,
www.turismo.pesarourbino.it

## Regional wine cellars

**Marche Regional Wine Cellar of Jesi** –
Palazzo Balleani, Via Federico Conti 5, Jesi,
✆ 0731 21 33 86

**Marche Regional Wine Cellar of Offida** –
Former Monastery of San Francesco, Via
Garibaldi 75, Offida, ✆ 0736 88 00 05, www.
vineamarche.it

## The wineries

*The addresses are listed in alphabetical order
by location.*

### COLLI PESARESI

**Fattoria Mancini** – *Strada dei Colli 35 -
**Pesaro** (PU) - ✆ 0721 51 828 - www.fattor
iamancini.com - info@fattoriamancini.com.*
The grapes for the estate's elegant, well-
structured wines grow on the Pesaro hills, a
few hundred metres from the sea and the
Monte San Bartolo Nature Park. The
principal variety grown by Mancini is Pinot
Nero, which is used to make red and white
wines, but it also grows Sangiovese,
Ancellotta and Albanella. Hectares under
vine: 20.
**Wines**: Colli Pesaresi Focara Pinot Noir Rive,
Colli Pesaresi Sangiovese, Colli Pesaresi
Roncaglia, Impero Blanc de Pinot Noir.

### PROVINCE OF ANCONA

♀ **Moroder** – *Via Montacuto 121 - **Ancona**
- ✆ 071 89 82 32 -www.moroder.wine - mail@
moroder.wine - Winery tours by reservation
(from €15).* The winery founded by Serenella
and Alessandro Moroder makes wines for
laying down, which are aged in a
picturesque 18th-c. grotto that was
originally a snow house, dug out of the clay
beneath the cellar. Today the Moroders

have diversified business, not only
producing excellent wines, but tending
olive groves, distilling grappa, and growing
small amounts of cereals and legumes
destined for sale and for the restaurant of
their guest farm. Hectares under vine: 28.
**Wines**: Conero Riserva Dorico, Rosso Conero
Aiòn, Rosa di Montacuto, Oro Passito. Other
products: olive oil, truffes.

**Azienda Santa Barbara** – *Borgo Mazzini 35
- **Barbara** (AN), 5 km N of Serra de' Conti -
✆ 071 96 74 249 - www.vinisanta
barbara.it - info@vinisantabarbara.it -
Winery tours Mon.-Fri.8-12 and 14-18 by
reservation.* The aim of the winery is to
revive the native grape varieties Verdicchio
and Montepulciano, and to make original
international-style wines with great
personality. Consequently, it also grows
Cabernet Sauvignon, Merlot and Syrah. In a
short space of time the winery has risen to
prominence and won several awards.
Hectares under vine: 45.
**Wines**: Verdicchio dei Castelli di Jesi Classico
Le Vaglie, Verdicchio dei Castelli di Jesi
Riserva Stefano Antonucci, Marche Rosso
IGT Stefano Antonucci, Marche Rosso IGT
Pathos, Rosso Piceno Il Maschio da Monte.
Other products: olive oil, grappa.

**Garofoli** – *Via C. Marx 123 - **Castelfidardo**
(AN) - ✆ 071 78 20 162 - www.garofolivini.it
- info@garofolivini.it - Winery tours Mon.-Fri.
by reservation, wineshop@garofolivini.it.* The
origins of Casa Vinicola Garofoli go back to
the late 19th c., for Antonio Garofoli was
already making and selling local wines in
1871. His son Gioacchino followed in his
father's footsteps, founding the company
with his own name in 1901. The winery has
grown constantly ever since and today it is a
joint-stock company owned by the Garofoli
family and headed by brothers Carlo and
Gianfranco. Hectares under vine: 50.
**Wines**: Verdicchio dei Castelli di Jesi Classico
Superiore Podium, Verdicchio dei Castelli di
Jesi Classico Riserva Serra Fiorese, Conero
Riserva Grosso Agontano, Brut Riserva
Metodo Classico. Other products: olive oil,
grappa.

**Colonnara** – *Via Mandriole 6 -
**Cupramontana** (AN) - ✆ 0731 78 02 73 -
www.colonnara.it - info@colonnara.it -
Winery tours by reservation.* Colonnara was
founded in 1959 by 19 growers. Today the
co-operative has more than 110 members. It
uses innovative technologies and eco-
friendly farming methods, but without
abandoning its origins associated with the
country tradition. Hectares under vine: 120.
**Wines**: Verdicchio dei Castelli di Jesi Classico
Superiore Cuprese, Falerio Pecorino,

Tornamagno Marche Rosso IGT, Lacrima di Morro d'Alba, Verdicchio Colonnara Brut Metodo Classico. Other products: grappa, dried-grape wine, honey, olive oil.

**La Distesa** – *Via Romita 28 -* **Cupramontana** *(AN) - ℘ 0731 78 12 30 - www.ladistesa.it - info@ladistesa.it - Winery tours and tasting by reservation.* The estate's aim is to make wines that respect the terroir and the grape varieties, with their own personality rather than standardised aromas. Production follows the rhythms of nature and the seasons. The winery uses organic farming methods, characterised by low yields per vine, attentive selection of the grapes, harvesting by hand using cases, and painstaking care at every stage in the cellar. Guest farm accommodation available with restaurant service *(only w.e.)* for guests *(4 apts.)* and private swimming pool. Hectares under vine: 7.
**Wines**: Verdicchio, Marche Bianco IGT, Marche Rosso IGT. Other products: olive oil.

**Vallerosa Bonci** – *Via Torre 15/17 -* **Cupramontana** *(AN) - ℘ 0731 78 91 29 - www.vallerosa-bonci.com - info@vallerosa-bonci.com - Winery tours 9-13 and 14-18, Sat. 9-13 by reservation only (from €15).* The Bonci family have been winegrowers for 4 generations. Indeed, the winery was founded by Domenico Bonci in the early 20th c. and currently boasts a 50-hectare estate, with 26 hectares of vineyards dedicated to the production of Verdicchio dei Castelli di Jesi Classico and Rosso Piceno DOC wines. Hectares under vine: 26.
**Wines**: Verdicchio dei Castelli di Jesi Classico Superiore San Michele, Verdicchio dei Castelli di Jesi Classico Riserva Pietrone, Verdicchio dei Castelli di Jesi PassitoPietrone, Verdicchio dei Castelli di Jesi Spumante Metodo Classico Millesimato Caterina. Other products: grappa.

**Fattorie Mancini** – *Via Santa Lucia 7 - Moie di **Maiolati Spontini** (AN) - ℘ 0731 70 29 75 - www.manciniwines.it - mancini@manciniwines.it - Winery tours by reservation.* The winery continues a family tradition dating back to the 1960s. The third generation is now active in the business, with owner Benito Mancini supported by his 3 children. Close to the winery is a completely renovated country house used to display the products, welcome guests and house tastings, because the Mancinis dedicate great attention to hospitality *(villavallugola.it)*. Hectares under vine: 30.
**Wines**: Verdicchio dei Castelli di Jesi Classico Ghibellino, Verdicchio dei Castelli di Jesi Classico Santa Lucia, Verdicchio dei Castelli di Jesi Classico Riserva, Spumante Brut Mancini, Rosso Piceno Panicale. Other products: Verdicchio dried-grape wine and grappa.

**Monte Schiavo** – *Via Vivaio -* **Maiolati Spontini** *(AN) - ℘ 0731 70 03 85 - www.monteschiavo.com - info@monteschiavo.it - Wine shop open 8.30-12.30 and 14.30-18.30, closed Sat. and Sun.* Monte Schiavo belongs to the Pieralsi Group, which has always been engaged in the development of the agro-industrial sector. It is a dynamic modern winery that uses production processes in line with the very latest international standards, and its has a customer service policy based on a wide range of select products able to satisfy all requirements. Hectares under vine: 115.
**Wines**: Verdicchio dei Castelli di Jesi, Rosso Conero, Rosso Piceno, Lacrima di Morro d'Alba. Other products: olive oil.

**Terre Cortesi Moncaro** – *Via Piandole 7/a -* **Montecarotto** *(AN) - ℘ 0731 89 245 - www.moncaro.com - ecommerce@moncaro.com - Winery tours by reservation.* The Società Cooperativa was founded in 1964 by a group of growers who wished to showcase their production and that of the entire area. In 1987 the co-operative winery changed its name to MONCARO (short for Montecarotto) and in 1995, following the takeover of the Cantina del Conero, it became Terre Cortesi, alluding to the various *Terre* ("lands"), each with their own *Corte* ("courtyard"). Accommodation available and restaurant *(www.erard.it)* Hectares under vine: 60.
**Wines**: Verdicchio Classico Superiore Verde Cà Ruptae, Verdicchio Classico Riserva Vigna Novali, Verdicchio Passito Tordiruta, Rosso Conero Vigneti del Parco. Other products: beer, wild cherries wine and chocolate.

**Marotti Campi** – *Via Sant'Amico 14 -* **Morro d'Alba** *(AN) - ℘ 0731 61 80 27 - www.marotticampi.it - wine@marotticampi.net - Wine tasting by reservation.* The Marotti Campi family have owned land around Morro d'Alba for more than a century, and over the years they have made the transition from sharecroppers to farmers concentrating mainly on winegrowing. The winery is housed in an austere 19th-c. aristocratic villa on the hill of Sant'Amico. The Vigna Sant'Amico Country House, a renovated farmhouse standing above the vineyards, was inaugurated in 2006 *(www.vignasantamico.it, 9 apts., €620/week, min. stay 2 nights)* and has a swimming pool for guests. Hectares under vine: 53.
**Wines**: Lacrima di Morro d'Alba Orgiolo, Verdicchio dei Castelli di Jesi Classico Albiano.

**Stefano Mancinelli** – *Via Roma 62 -* **Morro d'Alba** *(AN) - ℘ 0731 63 021 - www.mancinellivini.it - info@mancinellivini.it - Winery tours and tasting by reservation,*

*closed Sun.* "Each wine must have the flavour and aroma of the grapes from which it is made": this is the production philosophy of the 52-hectare estate, half of which covered with vineyards for the production of Lacrima di Morro d'Alba and Verdicchio dei Castelli di Jesi Classico DOC wines. The complex also includes a modern oil mill, which allows the immediate pressing of the harvested olives and the production of extra virgin olive oil, and a distillery – the region's first – which makes Lacrima and Verdicchio grappa. Accommodation available *(5 apts.).* Hectares under vine: 25.
**Wines**: Lacrima di Morro d'Alba, Verdicchio dei Castelli di Jesi (Classico, Superiore, Passito). Other products: grappa, olive oil and condiments.

**Conte Leopardi Dittajuti** – *Via Marina II 24* - **Numana** *(AN)* - ✆ *071 73 90 116* - *www.conteleopardi.com* - *info@ conteleopardi.com* - *Winery tours and tasting by reservation.* The estate's history is associated with that of the Leopardi counts, a family that boasts ancient origins. Indeed, they appear to have come to Italy from Byzantium with the Teutonic Knights around the middle of the 4th c. Its vineyards are divided into two distinct areas, known as Podere del Coppo and Podere degli Svarchi, in the municipality of Numana. The chief grape variety is Montepulciano, while the most important of the whites is Sauvignon, introduced to the estate in 1972. Hectares under vine: 45.
**Wines**: Rosso Conero Pigmento Riserva, Rosso Conero Fructus, Casirano Rosso Conero, Verdicchio dei Castelli di Jesi Castelverde, Calcare Marche Sauvignon IGT. Other products: olive oil.

**Fattoria Le Terrazze** – *Via Musone 4* - **Numana** *(AN)* - ✆ *071 73 90 352* - *www. fattorialeterrazze.it* - *info@ fattorialeterrazze.it* - *Winery tours by reservation.* La Fattoria Le Terrazze has belonged to the Terni family since 1882, the year in which the current winery was built. Today it is run by Antonio and Georgina. The estate's most representative wines include Rosso Conero, in the normal and Sassi Neri vineyard selection versions, as well as Visions of J in the best vintages. These DOC wines are flanked by Chaos (a blend of Montepulciano, Syrah and Merlot) and Chardonnay Le Cave, as well as a Classic Method sparkler called Donna Giulia. Hectares under vine: 21.
**Wines**: Rosso Conero, Sassi Neri, Praeludium, Pinkfluid, Le Cave, Donna Giulia. Other products: olive oil.

⌂ **Umani Ronchi** – *Via Adriatica 12* - **Osimo** *(AN)* - ✆ *071 71 08 019* - *www. umanironchi.com* - *wine@umanironchi.it* - *Winery tours and tasting by reservation.* Umani Ronchi has belonged to the Bianchi-Bernetti family for over 50 years. It was founded in 1957 by Gino Umani Ronchi, but the arrival of Roberto Bianchi and his son-in-law Massimo Bernetti marked a turning point for the winery in terms of the development of sales and production. Today Massimo's son Michele also works for the family business. The winery's success is the result of its patient, far-sighted and constant investment in the traditional wines of the area. Accommodation available *(Grand Hotel Palace or in Villa Bianchi Country House).* Hectares under vine: 210.
**Wines**: Pelago, Cùmaro, Plenio, Casal di Serra, Vigor. Other products: olive oil.

**Villa Bucci** – *Via Cona 30* - **Ostra Vetere** *(AN)* - ✆ *071 96 41 79* - *www.villabucci.com* - *bucciwines@villabucci.com.* The Bucci family have been farmers for 3 centuries. The farm currently has an area of 350 hectares and grows maize, durum wheat, sugar beets, sorghum and sunflowers. In addition to the olive groves, which yield excellent oil, it also has 25 hectares of Verdicchio dei Castelli di Jesi vineyards in the Classico DOC zone and 6 hectares of Montepulciano and Sangiovese red grape varieties that are comprised in the Rosso Piceno DOC. In recent years the estate has adopted 100% organic growing techniques in the vineyards and olive groves. Hectares under vine: 31.
**Wines**: Verdicchio dei Castelli di Jesi Classico Riserva Villa Bucci, Verdicchio dei Castelli di Jesi Classico Superiore Bucci, Rosso Piceno Tenuta Pongelli, Rosso Piceno Villa Bucci. Other products: olive oil and grappa.

⚇ **Brunori Mario & Giorgio** – *Tenuta San Nicolò, via San Nicolò 4* - **San Paolo di Jesi** *(AN)* - *www.brunori.it* - *info@brunori.it* - *Winery tours by reservation.* The Tenuta San Nicolò farm, located in the heart of the Verdicchio dei Castelli di Jesi Classico area, was founded in 1956 by Mario Brunori together with his son Giorgio. Today the company is run by Brunori's grandchildren Carlo and Cristina. Both sommeliers, Carlo and Cristina personally oversee the entire production cycle, from vine cultivation to sales, carefully calibrating tradition and experimentation. The company's Verdicchio dei Castelli di Jesi DOC Classico Superiore San Nicolò wine has been earning accolades since the 1970s, when it was first celebrated by Italian food and wine expert Luigi Veronelli. Another crown jewel of the company is its biological Fonteascosa Marche Bianco IGT wine, born of collaboration with the lively Belgian owner of La Battinebbia, who breathed new life into a vineyard that had been almost forgotten… Tastings available in the company wine bar (*Enoteca Brunori, Viale della Vittoria 103, Jesi, ☎ 0731 20 72 13*), where wine enthusiasts are welcomed warmly by Simonetta Battistelli, Carlo's wife. Hectares under vine: 6.5.

**Wines**: Verdicchio Le gemme/San Nicolò/Brut, Fonteascosa, Lacrima di Morro d'Alba Alborada/Roccolo, Rosso Conero Barco, Rosso Piceno Torquìs. Other products: olive oil and grappa.

**Fattoria Coroncino** – *C.da Coroncino 7 - **Staffolo** (AN) - ☎ 0731 77 94 94 - www.coroncino.it - info@coroncino.it.* Luca Canestrari's Fattoria Coroncino is a young, family-run estate that still uses artisanal methods for the fermentation and bottling of its wines. During the 1970s the Canestrari family moved to the area from Rome and in the space of just a few years they assimilated the passion for the land and the skill to work it from the local growers. Hectares under vine: 9.5.

**Wines**: Verdicchio dei Castelli di Jesi Classico Superiore Il Bacco/Il Coroncino/Gaiospino and Stracacio, Ganzerello Marche Rosso IGT Sangiovese.

## PROVINCE OF MACERATA

**⌂ Villa Forano** – *C.da Forano 43 - **Appignano** (MC) - ☎ 0733 57 102 - www.fattoriaforano.it - info@fattoriaforano.it - Winery tours with food and tasting by reservation (☎ 347 30 05 307).* La Fattoria di Forano is one of the Lucangeli group of agribusinesses. The vineyards (*20 hectares*) have been planted on the best winegrowing land of the entire 190-hectare estate. The cellars are housed in an old rural building, partly below ground level and protected by thick brick walls. An old grotto houses the bottles from the best vintages and a tunnel connects the winery to the underground barrique cellar. The recently restored old barrel cellar is flanked by two other cellars used for fermentation and the serving of unbottled wines. Accommodation at Forano guest farm, consisting of four 19th-c. farmhouses on the estate (*doubles from €60*). Hectares under vine: 20.

**Wines**: Colli Maceratesi Bianco Le Piagge, Colli Maceratesi Bianco Monteferro, Occhio di Gallo IGT Rosato, Colli Maceratesi Rosso Montelipa, Rosso Piceno Bulciano. Other products: aqua vitae.

**La Monacesca** – *C.da Monacesca - **Matelica** (MC) - ☎ 0733 67 26 41 - www.monacesca.it - info@monacesca.it. Winery tours by reservation.* The winery was founded in 1966 by Casimiro Cigola, who had previously worked in the footwear sector. Current annual production is

around 160,000 bottles made with painstaking care and attention. The name is derived from the fact that several Benedictine monks fled Lombard persecution in northern Italy and settled in the area around 900 AD. Hectares under vine: 27.

**Wines**: Verdicchio di Matelica, Verdicchio di Matelica Riserva Mirum, Marche Chardonnay IGT Ecclesia, Marche Rosso IGT Camerte.

**Alberto Quacquarini** – *Via Colli 12 - **Serrapetrona** (MC) - ☎ 0733 90 81 80 - www.quacquarini.it - info@quacquarini.it - Winery tours by reservation.* The winery was founded by Alberto Quacquarini. His passion is expressed in his entrepreneurial courage and his unwavering belief in his land at a time when many were emigrating. Alberto and his wife Francesca have transferred the love for their job and their land to their children, who now make their own precious contribution to the winery. Quacquarini also produces excellent confectionery. Hectares under vine: 35.

**Wines**: Vernaccia di Serrapetrona sweet/dry, Vino Petronio IGT Marche Rosso, Vino Colli della Serra IGT Marche Rosso, Vino Serrapetrona. Other products: grappa.

**⌂ Colli di Serrapetrona** – *Via Colli 7/8 - **Serrapetrona** (MC) - ☎ 0733 90 83 29 - www.tenutacollidiserrapetrona.it - info@tenutacollidiserrapetrona.it - Winery tours and tasting by reservation (☎ 339 70 25 513, one week in advance).* The winery is committed to promoting the area and the Vernaccia Nera grape variety, and thus dedicates great attention to historical research and reviving traditions. The guiding light in this quest is enologist Federico Giotti. Accommodation and restaurant available on the estate. Hectares under vine: 20.

**Wines**: unbianco, Blink, Collequanto, Robbione, Sommo, Il Borgiano, Vernaccianera.

**Il Pollenza** – *Via Casone 4 - **Tolentino** (MC) - ☎ 0733 96 19 89 - www.ilpollenza.it - lacantina@ilpollenza.it - Winery tours by reservation.* Pursuing his love of wine, Count Aldo Brachetti Peretti, chairman and managing director of the API oil group, decided to convert part of the family estate, purchased over 20 years ago, into vineyards. The land around the stunning 16th-c. building designed by Sangallo has thus been planted with rooted Cabernet Franc, Cabernet Sauvignon, Pinot Nero, Merlot, Petit Verdot, Gewürztraminer, Syrah, Trebbiano and Sangiovese. Hectares under vine: 70.

**Wines**: Il Pollenza, Cosmino, Porpora, Brianello, Didi, Pius IX.

## ADDRESSES

### PROVINCE OF ASCOLI PICENO

**Velenosi** – *Via dei Biancospini 11* - **Ascoli Piceno** - ☏ *0736 34 12 18* - *www.velenosi vini.com* - *info@velenosivini.com* - Velenosi was founded in 1984 and boasts cutting-edge cellar and production techniques that have allowed it to achieve excellent results, particularly with Rosso Piceno Superiore and the sparkling wines. Hectares under vine: 105.

**Wines**: Rosso Piceno Superiore Roggio del Filare, Falerio Vigna Solaria, Offida Rosso Ludi, Rosso Piceno Superiore Brecciarolo, Offida Pecorino. Other products: olive oil.

☘ **Oasi degli Angeli** – *C.da Sant'Egidio 50* - **Cupra Marittima** *(AP), 11 km E of Ripatransone* - ☏ *0735 77 85 69* - *www. kurni.it* - *info@kurni.it* - *Winery tours by reservation, closed during harvest*. The estate comprises approximately 16 hectares of old Montepulciano vines grown using biodynamic methods, from which it makes a single wine, Kurni. It is an impressive wine – complex, rich and layered – that is unfiltered and undergoes long ageing in oak. A real gem for connoisseurs. Accommodation in the guest farm (*3 rooms, €65*), with restaurant service Sat. and Sun. by reservation. Hectares under vine: 16.

**Wines**: Marche Rosso IGT Kurni. Other products: olive oil.

**Le Caniette** – *C.da Canali 23* - **Ripatransone** *(AP)* - ☏ *0735 92 00* - *www. lecaniette.it* - *info@lecaniette.it* - *Winery tours by reservation, closed Sat.-Sun.* In the local dialect Le Caniette means "young reed beds", as the area in the municipality of Ripatransone where the winery is situated is known. The Vagnoni family have been growing grapes here for around 4 centuries. Today the estate is run by Giovanni and Luigi Vagnoni, who have successfully combined tradition with modern technologies. The estate is particularly renowned for its Rosso Piceno wines. Hectares under vine: 16.

**Wines**: Passerina Lucrezia, Pecorino Veronica, Rosso Piceno Rossobello.

⌂ **Tenuta Cocci Grifoni** – *C.da Messieri 12* - **San Savino di Ripatransone** *(AP)* - ☏ *0735 90 143* - *www.tenutacoccigrifoni.it* - *info@tenutacoccigrifoni.it* - *Winery tours and tasting by reservation, closed Sat. pm and Sun.* The noble Grifoni family has Umbro-Tuscan origins and the Cocci belonged to the landed middle class of the southern Marches: the 2 families merged at the end of the 19th c. The estate grew cereals until after WW II, but at the beginning of the 1960s it started to cultivate vines. Today Cocci Grifoni is a winery that uses cutting-edge technologies and is committed to promoting the wines and vines of the region, particularly Pecorino and Passerina. Accommodation is available in 2 apartments on the estate. Hectares under vine: 45.

**Wines**: Offida Pecorino Colle Vecchio, Passerina Spumante Brut Tarà, Passerina San Basso, Rosso Piceno Superiore Vigna Messieri, Offida Rosso Il Grifone. Other products: olive oil, chickpeas and legumes. **Fattoria Dezi** – *C.da Fontemaggio 14* - **Servigliano Fermo** *(AP), 27 km W of Fermo* - ☏ *0734 71 00 90* - *info@ fattoriadezi.com* - *Winery tours by reservation*. The estate is located in an excellent position in the hills just below the Apennines, in a fascinating archaeological area. Hectares under vine: 15.

**Wines**: Regina del Bosco, Solo, Dezio, Solagne, Servigliano. Other products: olive oil.

## Where to stay

### RIPATRANSONE

**Il Corbezzolo** – *Via Sant'Egidio 25, Ripatransone (AP)* - ☏ *0735 99006* - *www. hotel-corbezzolo.com* - *18 rooms, doubles from €49.* Set in a quiet spot in the countryside with superb view of the valley and the Adriatic Sea, this hotel offers comfortable rooms, a swimming pool area and abundant breakfast.

### PESARO

**Locanda di Villa Torraccia** – *Strada Torraccia 3,5 km W of Pesaro* - ☏ *072 12 18 52 or 335 52 31 810* - *www.villatorraccia.it* - *Closed Christmas hols.* - *5 suites from €100.* Housed in a small medieval tower surrounded by age-old trees, Locanda di Villa Torraccia offers stunning suites for a romantic stay.

### SAN SEVERINO MARCHE

**Locanda Salimbeni** – *Loc. Valle Dei Grilli 8 - SP 361, 4 km W of San Severino (MC)* - ☏ *0733 63 40 47* - *www.locandasalimbeni. it* - *8 rooms. doubles from €65.* Named after the Salimbeni brothers, who rank among the greatest artists of the 15th c., the inn evokes art on its walls and the Marches region in its cuisine. The rooms are furnished in period style with wrought-iron beds.

### SENIGALLIA

**B&B Il Papavero** – *SP Arceviese 98, Bettolelle, 8.5 km SW of Senigallia (AN)* - ☏ *071 66 09 440* - *www.agrituristil papavero.it* - *3 rooms, doubles from €80.* Nestling among the hills, this farmhouse has been converted into a guest farm with rooms furnished in a simple country style.

# ABRUZZO AND MOLISE

Regions where nature is unspoilt and at times spectacular, Abruzzo and Molise have always been rural areas given over to agriculture and stock-raising. It is no surprise then that the origin of their link with viticulture is lost in the mists of time. What captures the wine-lover's attention, however, is their recent dedication to quality, which has resulted in the establishment of new appellations. Until 1982, Molise did not have a single DOC zone, whereas today it has four; and in Abruzzo it was not until 2003 that the region could boast a DOCG zone. Another development is that over recent years there has been a progressive diminution in the sale of loose table wine, and a substantial increase in the sale of hectolitres of VQPRD wine. The estates are for the most part small to medium-sized and family-run, with the exception of the cooperative wine associations.

*Hills in Montepulciano*

## Abruzzo

The wine of Abruzzo is made pre-dominantly from two grape varieties: **Montepulciano** for the reds and **Trebbiano d'Abruzzo** (elsewhere known as Bombino Bianco) for the whites.

### DOCG
Montepulciano d'Abruzzo
   Colline Teramane

### DOC
Abruzzo
Cerasuolo d'Abruzzo
Controguerra
Montepulciano d'Abruzzo
Ortona
Terre Tollesi *or* Tullum
Trebbiano d'Abruzzo
Villamagna

Added to these are Trebbiano Toscano, Sangiovese, Malvasia and a series of native species, such as Passerina, Monsonico, Pecorino and Cococciola. Cultivation of international varieties is limited. Trebbiano and Montepulciano are so representative of the territory that the two principal DOC zones and the only DOCG are named after them. To a great extent the appellations Trebbiano d'Abruzzo and Montepulciano d'Abruzzo overlap, covering hills and uplands that rise to an altitude 600 m.

The appellation **Montepulciano d'Abruzzo Colline Teramane** lies across a series of municipalities in the province of Teramo, in hills up to 450 m in height. In addition to the district in which they are made, aspects that distinguish Montepulciano d'Abruzzo DOC from Colline Teramane DOCG are the prolonged maturation required and the greater percentage of Montepulciano grapes. The grapes used to produce Trebbiano

## PRINCIPAL VARIETIES CULTIVATED

### WHITE GRAPES

Biancame
Bombino Bianco
Chardonnay
Cococciola
Falanghina
Garganega
Grechetto
Greco Bianco
Malvasia Bianca
    di Candia
Malvasia Bianca Lunga
Manzoni Bianco
Montonico Bianco
Moscato Bianco
Mostosa
Passerina

Pecorino
Pinot Bianco
Regina
Regina dei Vigneti
Riesling
Riesling Italico
Sauvignon
Sylvaner
Tocai Friulano
Traminer Aromatico
Trebbiano Toscano
Veltliner
Verdicchio Bianco
Vermentino

### GREY GRAPES

Pinot Grigio

### BLACK GRAPES

Aglianico
Barbera
Cabernet Franc
Cabernet Sauvignon
Canaiolo Nero
Ciliegiolo
Dolcetto
Gaglioppo
Maiolica
Malbech
Merlot
Montepulciano
Pinot nero
Sangiovese
Syrah

---

d'Abruzzo DOC are, naturally, Trebbiano d'Abruzzo, but also Trebbiano Toscano. The appellation **Controguerra** is a small area in the province of Teramo on Abruzzo's northern border with the Marches. Controguerra makes a wide variety of wines: whites, reds, sparkling and sweet, produced from both local and international varieties.

*Locations with a winery are indicated by the symbol ♥; for the addresses of the wineries, see p. 352.*

## 1. THE PROVINCE OF TERAMO

The siliceous, clayey and ferrous soils of this province ensure high quality wines. The various labels of **Montepulciano d'Abruzzo** have great character, body and mellowness, with a pleasant hint of tannin. They are intensely ruby-red, have a complex and persistent aroma of red fruits and spices, and are dry and warm in the mouth. Wines like the **Colline Teramane DOCG** are even more powerful and structured. The various **Cerasuolo del Montepulciano d'Abruzzo DOC** are surprisingly full-bodied for a rosé, while the wines from the designated zones **Controguerra** and **Trebbiano d'Abruzzo** have great personality.

## From Teramo to Vomano

*Itinerary of 120 km from Teramo to San Clemente al Vomano.*

Leave from **Teramo**, which has a lovely medieval cathedral in the middle of the old city, and take the panoramic S 81 in the direction of Civitella del Tronto. A small detour leads to **Campli**, set high on a hill. It has many ancient buildings, such as the churches of Santa Maria in Platea and San Francesco, and in particular the Scala Santa (Holy Stairway), whose 28 wooden steps were climbed by wrongdoers on their knees to absolve them of their sins and allow them to obtain full indulgence.

Return to the S 81 and pass through **Campovalano**, near which you can visit the Benedictine Church of San Pietro.

### Civitella del Tronto★

This delightful little town is perched in a splendid **position★★** on a travertine hill at an altitude of 645 m. Its twisting and picturesque alleyways are lined with lovely civil and religious buildings from the 16th and 17th c. The town is dominated by the 16th-c. **Fortress★**, the last Bourbon stronghold to capitulate to the combined troops of Sardinia and Piedmont in 1861. *Open 10-20 in Jun.-Aug., 10-19 in Apr.-May and Sept.,*

*Mar. and Oct. 10-17 (Sat.-Sun. 18), rest of the year 10-16 (Sat.-Sun. 17), ☎ 320 84 24 540, www.fortezzadicivitella.it.*

Now head down to the coast through **Torano Nuovo** 🍷 and **Controguerra** 🍷. The latter stands on a rise and is dominated by a tower and the Ducal Palace. A farm with vines at 26 Via San Giuseppe is home to the **Farming Culture Museum** (*open 9-19, ☎ 0861 85 66 30*). One of the eight Abruzzese DOC zones is named after this town.

Having passed through **Colonnella**, which also stands in a lovely panoramic position, you arrive on the coast. Follow the shoreline to **Roseto degli Abruzzi** 🍷 and **Pineto** 🍷, two of the most popular seaside resorts on the Abruzzo coast.

*Head inland.*

## Atri 🍷

Atri stands in a fine position on a hill overlooking the Adriatic, with a picturesque historic centre constructed during the medieval, Renaissance and Baroque ages. The gem in the city's crown is its **cathedral★**. Constructed in the 13th-14th c. over the remains of a Roman building, it is a good example of Romanesque-Gothic, with a series of sculpted portals that became the model for later Abruzzese architecture. Admire the **frescoes★★** in the apse by the local painter Andrea de Litio (1450-73). The remains of Roman baths and mosaic floors from the 3rd c. AD can be seen beneath the presbytery. Pass through the cloister next door to reach the Roman cistern and Chapterhouse Museum, where there is a lovely collection of local ceramics. The remains of the ancient Roman city can be seen in the square.

Driving 2 km north-west on the SS 353 takes you to the **Calanques Nature Reserve★**. The calanques, or ravines, were created by the washing away of an ancient plateau. Suggestive of Dantesque pits of hell, what is striking about them is the series of ledges that have been formed over hundreds of metres and the lack of vegetation, which, combined with the paleness of the sediments, are evocative of a lunar landscape.

## 2. THE REALM OF TREBBIANO

Coinciding with the appellations Montepulciano d'Abruzzo and **Trebbiano d'Abruzzo**, the Trebbiano area focuses particularly on the production of the latter type of wine. Trebbiano d'Abruzzo is by no means a simple, refreshing and easily drinkable white but a complex, structured wine with a surprising capacity for ageing, though of course there are simpler versions with a fruity and flowery bouquet that should be drunk young.

In the province of Pescara **Montepulciano** has two sub-zones: **Terre dei Vestini** (inland and coastal hills) and **Casauria** or **Terre di Casauria**, the wines of which are both subject to maturation of at least 18 months.

*Calanques Nature Reserve, Atri*

© Claudio Giovanni Colombo/iStock

*Abbey of San Clemente, Casauria*

## The Pescara valley and Chietino interior

*Circular itinerary of approximately 300 km from Pescara.*

### Pescara

The regional capital and largest city in Abruzzo (approximately 120,000 people), Pescara is a modern and pleasant place that draws many visitors in summer to its beaches and littoral. The city was built up along the two banks of the port-canal framed all round by hills that step down to the sea. The oldest part of the city is the location for the Bourbon fortress that today houses the interesting **Museum of the People of Abruzzo** (*Via delle Caserme 24, open 10-13, Sat. 10-13 and 16.30-19.30, Sun. 16.30-19.30, ℘ 085 45 10 026, www.gentidabruzzo.it*), the house where **Gabriele d'Annunzio** was born (*Corso Manthonè 116, open 8.30-19.30, ℘ 085 60 391, www.casa-dannunzio.beniculturali.it*) and the **Dannunzian Pinewood★** nature reserve, which covers an area of 3000 hectares.

In the hilly area along the river Tavo to the west of Pescara, pass through **Spoltore** 🍷 to reach **Loreto Aprutino** 🍷, where you can admire the lovely Church of Santa Maria del Piano. It was founded in the early Middle Ages but was rebuilt on several occasions though it still retains its excellent Renaissance frescoes.

A drive of 30 km on panoramic roads will take you to Chieti.

### Chieti

Constructed at the top of a hill of olive groves and ringed by massive mountains, Chieti's position has earned it the name "terrace of Abruzzo". The city's main street, Corso Marrucino, is lined by elegant porticoes. The main tourist attraction is the **Villa Frigerj National Archaeological Museum★★** (*Via G. Costanzi 2, open Tue.-Sat. 9-20, closed Mon., ℘ 0871 40 43 92*). Surrounded by the **gardens★** of the Neoclassical Municipal Villa, the museum displays archaeological objects discovered in Abruzzo, including the famous **Capestrano Warrior★★** (6th c. BC). This statue has become a symbol of the region, and is the most important remnant of the civilisation of the Piceni peoples. This magical and disturbing figure was made to protect a royal grave, as the inscription on the right pillar attests. It has been interpreted as "Aninis made this lovely statue for the king Naevius Pompuledius".

Chieti also has a number of Roman remains, all from the 1st c. AD. Three temples were discovered in 1935 near Corso Marrucino, close to the remains of the theatre that held 5000 spectators. And the baths lie in the east side of the city, outside the ancient centre.

Take Via Tiburtina Valeria (the S 5) inland to Popoli. The occasional detour will allow you to explore the winemaking towns of **Rosciano** 🍷 and **Alanno** 🍷.

## San Clemente a Casauria★★

About two thirds of the way to Popoli, a site on the route that should not on any account be missed is the abbey founded in 871 on the orders of the Holy Roman Emperor Louis II. It was destroyed by the Saracens but rebuilt in the 12th c. by Cistercian monks in a transitional style between Romanesque and Gothic. It has a distinctive façade, with a deep, three-arch porch that rests on beautiful capitals. The main portal is characterised by exceptional sculptural decoration and a bronze door cast in 1191 showing images of the castles owned by the abbey. The atmosphere inside is one of the mystical solemnity so loved by St Bernard and the Cistercians. The monumental paschal candelabrum and superb 12th-c. pulpit are two of the greatest examples of Abruzzese Romanesque. The high altar is composed of a 5th-c. Christian sarcophagus, topped by a finely carved Romanesque ciborium. The crypt (9th c.) has cross vaults resting on ancient columns, and is one of the few surviving sections of the original abbey. *Open 9-13.30, closed Mon., ℘ 085 88 85 162, www.sanclemente acasauria.beniculturali.it.*

Before reaching Popoli, a viticultural visit could be paid to the village of **Bolognano** 🍷.

## Popoli 🍷

This elegant little town is gathered around Piazza Matteotti, which is lined on the left by the Church of San Francesco, with Gothic façade and Baroque crown, and on the right by the impressive flight of steps that leads to the 18th-c. Church of the Santissima Trinità. Next to the square is the **Ducal Tavern★** (14th c.), a graceful Gothic building adorned with low reliefs and coats of arms that was used in the past as a post station and to store tithes.

About 20 km north on the pretty S 153 you come to Ofena 🍷, in a lovely setting of vineyards, almond and olive groves, and perched villages. The town has a pretty historic centre.

*Return to Popoli.* Drive 7 km south to the town of **Corfinio** to see the Basilica of **San Pelino★**. This ancient episcopal seat was built between the 9th and 12th c.

*Return towards Chieti on the S 5.* Two more visits of major spiritual and artistic importance on the route are **Manoppello**, where the "Veronica Veil" displayed during Roman Jubilees is conserved in the Shrine of the Holy Face, and a short distance on, the Church of **Santa Maria Arabona** at Manoppello Scalo, built in beautiful Cistercian architecture of the 13th c.

## THE TERROIR

**Area of Abruzzo:** 10,831.50 km$^2$, of which approximately 32,685 hectares are planted to vine; 65% mountainous, the rest prevalently hilly

**Area of Molise:** 4,460.44 km$^2$, of which approximately 5,593 hectares are planted to vine; 55% mountainous, the rest hilly

**Production 2019 Abruzzo**: 2,944,657 hectolitres, of which 845,117 VQPRD

**Production 2019 Molise**: 450,634 hectolitres, of which 25,142 VQPRD

**Geography**: the soil is a mixture of clay, limestone and sand, with some chalky areas. The climate is mild on the Adriatic coast, the interior is continental, breezy and averagely rainy

## THE PROTECTION CONSORTIA

Consorzio Tutela Vini d'Abruzzo – ℘ 085 90 59 679, www.vinidabruzzo.it

Consorzio di Tutela Colline Teramane DOCG – ℘ 085 80 71 699, www.collineteramane.com

Consorzio per la Valorizzazione dei Vini DOC Molise – ℘ 0874 47 12 94 www.consorziovinimolise.it

## WINE AND FOOD ROUTES

Strade del Vino d'Abruzzo – www.vinidabruzzo.it
Strada del Vino del Molise – c/o Regione Molise, ℘ 0874 42 91, www.regione.molise.it

*Land in Molise shaped by the wind, a factor that affects the growth of the vines*

From Manoppello a series of twisting but panoramic roads takes you to **Guardiagrele**, a charming village on a spur of the east side of Monte Maiella. It is famous for its bell foundries and jewellers, one of whom was Nicola da Guardiagrele, who worked with Ghiberti in Florence. The Church of Santa Maria Maggiore is a beautiful building constructed between the 11th and 13th c.

From Guardiagrele, take the S 84 to **Lanciano** in the hills close to the coast. As you descend towards the sea you reach the panoramic site of the Abbey of **San Giovanni in Venere** with views★ over the Adriatic. Founded in the 8th c. on the site of a temple dedicated to Venus, it was remodelled in the 13th c. The Portal of the Moon on the façade is adorned with reliefs of sacred and profane subjects. The interior shows the austere influence of the Cistercians and features a raised presbytery and aisles. The crypt is decorated with frescoes painted between the 12th and 15th c. *Guided tour by reservation only,* ✆ *0872 60 132.*

As you drive up the coast back towards Pescara, you pass through **Ortona** 🍷, a seaside resort that boasts a Spanish fort and superb cathedral, and is the home of the Regional Wine Cellar of Abruzzo (*see the list of addresses*). Inland from Ortona and **Francavilla al Mare** stretches an agricultural area where there are several villages known for winemaking, such as **Crecchio**, **Canosa Sannita**, **Tollo** 🍷, **Miglianico** and **Villamagna**.

# Molise

Molise has always been an agricultural and stock-raising region, so viticulture has never been very important. The area planted to vine and the quantity of wine produced remain limited but fortunately change for the better is beginning to get underway. Similarly, the emphasis placed on greater quality is reflected in the increase in DOC wines as opposed to the production of undesignated wine as a whole.

The future of winemaking appears rosy if the region's great potential is taken into consideration. There are four appellations: **Biferno**, **Molise**, **Pentro** and **Tintilia**, which together produce various types of white, red, rosé, sparkling and sweet wines from traditional and international grape varieties.

In Molise the most common grape types are, among the blacks, Montepulciano, Sangiovese and Aglianico; and among the whites, Trebbiano Toscano, Bombino Bianco and Malvasia di Candia. Worthy of note among the red wines is the original **Tintilia**, made from Bovale grapes.

## DOC
Biferno
Molise *or* del Molise
Pentro *or* Pentro d'Isernia
Tintilia Molise

## PRINCIPAL VARIETIES CULTIVATED

### WHITE GRAPES

Bombino Bianco
Chardonnay
Falanghina
Garganega
Greco
Malvasia Bianca Lunga
Manzoni Bianco
Moscato Bianco
Pinot Bianco
Riesling
Riesling Italico

Sauvignon
Sylvaner Verde
Traminer Aromatico
Trebbiano Toscano
Veltliner

### GREY GRAPES

Pinot Grigio

### BLACK GRAPES

Aglianico
Bovale Grande
Barbera
Cabernet Franc
Cabernet Sauvignon
Ciliegiolo
Montepulciano
Pinot Nero
Sangiovese

Various international varieties have recently been introduced, including Sauvignon, Pinot Bianco, Cabernet and Chardonnay, which are producing interesting results.

## ALONG THE BIFERNO VALLEY

*Itinerary of 40 km from Termoli to Larino.*

**Termoli**, Molise's only port and the departure point for the Tremiti Islands, has a fine 13th-c. castle that was built as part of the fortifications ordered by Emperor Frederick II to defend the port. Set among the narrow, winding streets of the old centre is the **cathedral★** (12th c.), one of the most important examples of Molisan Romanesque architecture. The façade is enlivened with pilasters and blind arches set with blind twin-light windows. The motif of the arches continues on the right side and apse (13th c.). The mosaics in the flooring of the crypt are from the 10th-11th c.

A distance of 15 km to the south-west of **Campomarino** 🍷 you come to **Guglionesi**, which overlooks the sea and hills and has several lovely religious buildings in its upper section, for example, the churches of Santa Maria Maggiore (18th c.) with a Romanesque crypt, and San Nicola di Bari (12th c.).

Once through the town, turn left to **Larino** 🍷, where remnants of the town's Roman past can be seen to the west on the San Leonardo plain. In Larino itself, the beautiful 14th-c. **cathedral★** has traces of frescoes.

*Old town of Termoli from the harbour*

# Addresses

## Tourist Information

**Region of Abruzzo** – Corso Vittorio Emanuele II, 301- Pescara, **Pescara**, ☏ 085 42 90 02 12, toll-free number 800 50 25 20, www.abruzzoturismo.it

**Province of Teramo** – Via Guglielmo Oberdan 16, ☏ 0861 24 42 22, www.provincia.teramo.it

**Termoli Tourist Office** – Piazza Melchiorre Bega 42, ☏ 0875 70 39 13, www.termoli.net

## Regional Wine Cellars

**Abruzzo Regional Wine Cellar** – Palazzo Corvo, Corso Matteotti 1, **Ortona** (CH), ☏ 085 90 64 024

## The Wineries

*The addresses are listed in alphabetical order by location.*

**PROVINCE OF TERAMO**

**Villa Medoro** – *C.da Medoro 1 -* **Atri** *(TE) - ☏ 085 87 08 139 - www.villamedoro.it - info@villamedoro.it - Winery tours by reservation.* The estate has been producing wine since the 1970s, but it was in 1997 with the arrival of the third generation that it decided to focus on quality wines. Its annual output of 300,000 bottles is produced in accordance with local tradition, striving to raise appreciation of the native grape varieties and making careful use of modern techniques. Hectares under vine: 98.
**Wines**: Montepulciano d'Abruzzo Villamedoro, Cerasuolo Villamedoro, Trebbiano Villamedoro, IGT Bianco Montonico, Pecorino, Passerina, Chimera. Other products: olive oil.

**Illuminati** – *C.da San Biagio 18 -* **Controguerra** *(TE) - ☏ 0861 80 80 08 - www.illuminativini.com - info@illuminativini.it - Winery tours by reservation.* Around 1890 Nicola Illuminati started making wine and founded a winery called "Fattoria Nicò". His nephew Dino and the subsequent generations inherited his passion and continue to run the business, which produces excellent red, white, rosé, dessert and sparkling wines. Hectares under vine: 130.
**Wines**: Riparosso, Zanna, Ilico, Pieluni, Lumen, Costalupo, Nicolino.

**Fattoria Nicodemi** – *C.da Veniglio -* **Notaresco** *(TE), 15 km W of Roseto - ☏ 085 89 54 93 - www.nicodemi.com - info@nicodemi.com - Winery tours by reservation.* Nicodemi's winning hunch was to reinterpret the winemaking tradition with a modern slant. In 1970 Bruno Nicodemi launched a program to transform the family's farmland and decided to promote the Montepulciano and Trebbiano d'Abruzzo native vines. In 2000 the management of the winery passed to his children, who continue to follow the course mapped out by their father. Hectares under vine: 30.
**Wines**: Montepulciano d'Abruzzo Riserva Neromoro, Montepulciano d'Abruzzo Notàri, Trebbiano d'Abruzzo Notàri, Trebbiano d'Abruzzo Le Murate. Other products: olive oil

⌂ **Barba** – *Strada Rotabile to Casoli - Fraz. Scerne -* **Pineto** *(TE) - ☏ 085 94 61 020 - www.fratellibarba.it - cantina@fratellibarba.it - Winery tours by reservation, closed Sun.* Over the years generations of the Barba family have succeeded one another in the management of the estate, and at the end of the 1950s Cavaliere Luigi Barba was the first to take over the direct running of the winery, which his descendants continue to lead with success. Accommodation available at the guest farm *(closed Nov.-Mar., 6 apts., from €60)*. Hectares under vine: 68.
**Wines**: Montepulciano d'Abruzzo Collemorino, Trebbiano d'Abruzzo Collemorino, Montepulciano d'Abruzzo Vignafranca, Trebbiano d'Abruzzo di Mare, Bianco IGT Vignafranca. Other products: olive oil and honey.

**Orlandi Contucci Ponno** – *Loc. Piana degli Ulivi 1 -* **Roseto degli Abruzzi** *(TE) - ☏ 085 89 44 049 - www.orlandicontucciponno.it - info@orlandicontucci.com - Winery tours by reservation.* Since its beginnings at the turn of the last century, when it was purchased by the current owners, the estate has always made wine. The winery has attempted to reappraise several original Montepulciano d'Abruzzo clones, selecting them according to their characteristics in relation to the soil and microclimate. The results are evident in the glass. Hectares under vine: 27.
**Wines**: Trebbiano, Montepulciano, Cerasuolo d'Abruzzo, Montepulciano Colline Teramane La Regia Specula, Ghiaiolo Sauvignon Colli Aprutini IGT.

⌂ **Emidio Pepe** – *Via Chiesi 10 -* **Torano Nuovo** *(TE) - ☏ 0861 85 64 93 - www.emidiopepe.com - info@emidiopepe.com - Winery tours by reservation, closed Sun.*

The art of winemaking has been handed down from father to son through 4 generations at Azienda Pepe. The business was founded in 1899 by Emidio Pepe; his son Giuseppe sold unbottled wine, but the winery started to sell bottled Montepulciano d'Abruzzo under the management of his grandson Emidio. Today Emidio's daughters Daniela and Sofia continue to make wine using the fermentation methods adopted by their father 50 years ago. Accommodation and restaurant available at the estate's guest farm (*7 double rooms and 2 apts.*). The estate also has a wine and olive oil museum. Hectares under vine: 15.
**Wines**: Montepulciano d'Abruzzo, Trebbiano d'Abruzzo, Pecorino, Cerasuolo. Other products: olive oil.

## THE REALM OF TREBBIANO

**Podere Castorani** – *Via Castorani 5 -* **Alanno** *(PE) -* 🖊 *346 63 55 635 - www. poderecastorani.it - info@castorani.it - Winery tours by reservation.* Podere Castorani's origins can be traced back to 1793. However, the estate was abandoned during the 1960s until a group of friends revived it and put it on the road to success. Organic farming methods are employed throughout, without the use of chemical pesticides or fertilisers. Hectares under vine: 30.
**Wines**: Montepulciano d'Abruzzo, Trebbiano d'Abruzzo, Cerasuolo Montepulciano d'Abruzzo, Pecorino Colline Pescaresi IGT, Rosso Colline Pescaresi IGT. Other products: grappa.

**Zaccagnini** – *C.da Pozzo -* **Bolognano** *(PE) -* 🖊 *085 88 80 195 - www.cantinazaccagnini. it - info@cantinazaccagnini.it - Winery tours by reservation, closed Sat. and Sun.*
The winery was founded as a family-run business in 1978 with the name Fattoria Zaccagnini. It has an annual production of around 3,000,000 bottles. Both traditional and local grape varieties are grown on the estate. Zaccagnini is distinguished by the marriage between art and wine, which is immediately apparent from a glance at the winery's architecture. Hectares under vine: 300.
**Wines**: Montepulciano San Clemente, Abruzzo Bianco San Clemente, Mont. d'Abruzzo Kasaura, Plaisir Bianco. Other products: olive oil, grappa, preserves.

**Valentini** – *Via del Baio 2 -* **Loreto Aprutino** *(PE) -* 🖊 *085 82 91 138 - Winery closed to the public and no direct sales.*
The winery produces unforgettable wines, capable of ageing very well. An example is its excellent Trebbiano d'Abruzzo, an authentic white for laying down and well worth the wait, because it acquires inebriating aromas over the years. While its Trebbiano is striking for its cellarability, Valentini's Montepulciano and Cerasuolo are equally big on texture and character. Hectares under vine: 70.
**Wines**: Trebbiano d'Abruzzo, Montepulciano d'Abruzzo Cerasuolo, Montepulciano d'Abruzzo. Other products: olive oil.

⌂ **Cantine Luigi Cataldi Madonna** – *Loc. Piano -* **Ofena** *(AQ) -* 🖊 *0862 95 42 52 - www.cataldimadonna.com - info@ cataldimadonna.com - Winery tours by reservation.* The winery was founded back in 1920 and is currently run by Luigi Cataldi Madonna. Ofena lies in a basin traditionally known as the "oven of Abruzzo" due to its sun-drenched position and considerable temperature differences. These characteristics give it enormous potential for winegrowing. The grape varieties grown are Montepulciano, Trebbiano d'Abruzzo, Pecorino and Cabernet Sauvignon. Accommodation available at La Cataldina guest farm. Hectares under vine: 31,4.
**Wines**: Tonì, Malandrino, Supergiulia, Giulia, Trebbiano, Cerasuolo d'Abruzzo.

**Il Feuduccio di S. Maria d'Orni**– *Loc. Feuduccio 2 -* **Orsogna** *(CH), 7 km NE of Guardiagrele -* 🖊 *0871 89 16 46 - www. ilfeuduccio.it - info@ilfeuduccio.it - Winery tours and tasting by reservation.* Gaetano Lamaletto, an Italian immigrant in Venezuela, had always longed to return to his homeland to commence the production of quality wine. He returned to Italy 40 years later a successful businessman and made his dream come true by founding the Feuduccio di Santa Maria d'Orni with his daughter, son-in-law and their children. The winery is located in the splendid setting of the Annunziata Territorial Park. Hectares under vine: 54.
**Wines**: Pecorino Colline Teatine Bianco IGT Yare, Montepulciano d'Abruzzo Feuduccio, Montepulciano d'Abruzzo Ursonia, Montepulciano d'Abruzzo Margae, Colline Teatine Rosso IGT Passito. Other products: olive oil.

🍃 **Agriverde** – *Via Stortini 32 - Loc. Villa Caldari -* **Ortona** *(CH) -* 🖊 *085 90 32 101 - www.agriverde.it - cantina@agriverde.it - Winery tours by reservation.* The winery's mission is to produce quality wines while respecting nature and man. Consequently, the grapes are grown using organic and natural methods, adopting innovative eco-friendly farming processes. The use of natural yeast is a further step towards the enhancement of the terroir and its products, to the great benefit of the character and personality of the wines. Restaurant and accommodation at the

Villa Fania organic guest farm (*6 rooms*). Hectares under vine: 65.

**Wines**: Montepulciano, Trebbiano, Pecorino, Passerina, Cerasuolo. Other products: olive oil and vinegar.

**Dora Sarchese** – *C.da Caldari Stazione 65 - **Ortona** (CH) - ℘ 085 90 31 249 - dorasarchesevignai.wix.com/dorasarchese - sarchese.dora@tin.it - Winery tours by reservation, closed Sat. pm and Sun.* The estate is run with great commitment by Dora and her children, with the precious aid of her son-in-law Maurizio. Although the estate's flagship products are its wines, it also produces other specialities, such as olive oil, jams, sauces, preserves in oil, condiments and pâtés. This wide range can fully satisfy even the most demanding gourmets. Hectares under vine: 18.

**Wines**: Trebbiano d'Abruzzo Mimì, Pecorino Dorad'oro, Spumante Esmery's. Other products: olive oil, tomato sauce, jams.

**Valle Reale** – *Loc. San Calisto - **Popoli** (PE) - ℘ 085 98 71 039 - www.vallereale.it - info@vallereale.it - Winery tours by reservation.* The vineyards of Villa Reale grow in very poor soil, close to the Gran Sasso and Majella massifs, at a high altitude that causes great temperature differences between day and night and summer and winter, when it is extremely cold. The area's distinctive features are reflected in the wines, which are characterised by an elegant nose and complex aromas. The Pizzolo family, who own the winery, are working in conjunction with the Faculty of Agriculture of the University of Milan to select the best plants for this environment and thus the best ones for obtaining a wine that reflects both the grape variety and the terroir. Hectares under vine: 46.

**Wines**: Trebbiano d'Abruzzo Vigna di Capestrano, Cerasuolo d'Abruzzo Vigneto Sant'Eusanio, Montepulciano d'Abruzzo Vigneto Sant'Eusanio, Trebbiano d'Abruzzo DOC Vigneto di Popoli, Montepulciano d'Abruzzo San Calisto.

**Marramiero** – *C.da Sant'Andrea 1 - **Rosciano** (PE) - ℘ 085 85 05 766 - www.marramiero.it - info@marramiero.it - Winery tours by reservation, closed Sat. pm and Sun.* The Marramiero family have been growing grapes since the beginning of the 20th c., but it was not until the 1990s, under the management of Dante Marramiero, that the estate started to make its own wine. Today his children Enrico and Patrizia are following in his footsteps. The winery produces 3 different types of Trebbiano d'Abruzzo and Montepulciano d'Abruzzo, all of which are very high quality. Hectares under vine: 50.

**Wines**: Trebbiano d'Abruzzo Anima, Trebbiano d'Abruzzo Altare, Montepulciano d'Abruzzo Incanto, Inferi and Dante Marramiero. Other products: olive oil.

⌂ **Masciarelli** – *Via Gamberale 1 - **San Martino sulla Marrucina** (CH), 5 km N of Guardiagrele - ℘ 0871 85 241 - www.masciarelli.it - info@masciarelli.it - Winery tours by reservation, closed Sat. and Sun.* Abruzzo owes much to winegrower Gianni Masciarelli, who died in 2008. He always believed in his land and its products, and he helped make the region's wines known throughout Italy and the world. His venture in the world of wine commenced in 1981 and in the space of just a few years he had created a large business. It is now his wife, Marina Cvetic, who continues the family business with the same dedication. Accommodation available at Castello di Semivicoli ( ℘0871 89 00 45, www.castellodisemivicoli.com). Hectares under vine: 273.

**Wines**: Villa Gemma Bianco, Villa Gemma Cerasuolo, Villa Gemma Montepulciano d'Abruzzo, Montepulciano d'Abruzzo Marina Cvetic, Trebbiano d'Abruzzo Marina Cvetic. Other products: olive oil and grappa.

**Fattoria La Valentina** – *Via Torretta 52 - **Spoltore** (PE) - ℘ 085 44 78 158 - www.lavalentina.it - lavalentina@fattorialavalentina.it - Winery tours by reservation.* Fattoria La Valentina was founded in 1990. Its chief objective is to promote the Abruzzo DOC wines while respecting biological equilibrium through the sparing use of chemicals and technology and with as little intervention as possible in natural processes. The

© Carole Castelli/Shutterstock

winery's philosophy is to focus on quality and pay maximum attention to environmental problems. Hectares under vine: 30.

**Wines**: Montepulciano d'Abruzzo Bellevedere, Montepulciano d'Abruzzo Binomio, Montepulciano d'Abruzzo Spelt, Montepulciano d'Abruzzo La Valentina, Montepulciano d'Abruzzo Cerasuolo La Valentina.

**Cantina Tollo** – *Viale Garibaldi 68* - **Tollo** *(CH)* - ☎ *0871 96 251 - www.cantinatollo.it - info@cantinatollo.it - Winery tours by reservation.* Cantina Tollo was founded in 1960 with the aim of raising appreciation of the local winegrowing tradition. The first big step came in 1962, when the cellar started making wine. Bottling was introduced 10 years later, as was the brand name and a new identity with which to present itself to the consumer. In 1960 the co-operative winery counted 19 members; today it has 1200 and occupies an important market position. Hectares under vine: 3000.

**Wines**: Cagiòlo, Hedòs, Pecorino, Mo Montepulciano, Cococciola Abruzzo DOP.

## MOLISE

🏠 **Cantine Borgo di Colloredo** – *Via Colloredo 15* - **Campomarino** *(CB)* - ☎ *0875 57 453 - www.borgodicolloredo.com - Winery tours by reservation.* The winery's current owners, brothers Enrico and Pasquale Di Giulio, are the third generation of a family of winegrowers. Enrico is an enologist and Pasquale works in the vineyard to protect the vines with integrated pest-management systems to respect the environment. Tradition and technology are the cornerstones of the winery, which conceives its cellars as a place open for tours and tastings to anyone eager to learn more about the world of wine. Accommodation and meals at Masseria le Piane (*4 rooms*). Hectares under vine: 80.

**Wines**: Gironia Biferno Rosso, Gironia Biferno Bianco, Gironia Biferno Rosato, Molise Falanghina, Molise Rosso.

**Di Majo Norante** – *C.da Ramitello - Via Colle Savino 6* - **Campomarino** *(CB)* - ☎ *0875 57 208 - www.dimajonorante.com - vini@dimajonorante.it - Winery tours by reservation.* The estate has been producing wine since the 19th c. "New wines from old vines" is the motto that underpins the production of the winery, which has always been engaged in promoting and reviving local grape varieties in danger of extinction. The result is wines packed with personality, which express the terroir. Don't miss a tour of the old barrel cellar housed in a 17th-c. stone granary. Hectares under vine: 85.

**Wines**: Ramì Bianco Falanghina del Molise, Ramitello Rosso, Molì Bianco, Rosso and Rosato, Greco, Moscato Apianae.

🏠 **Angelo d'Uva** – *C.da Ricupo 13* - **Larino** *(CB)* - ☎ *0874 82 23 20 - www.cantineduva.it - angelo@cantineduva.com - Winery tours by reservation, enrica@cantineduva.com.* The D'Uva family have long been dedicated to vine growing. Furthermore, they have strong bonds with the area, showing great commitment and dedication in promoting its distinctive winegrowing features, products, and historical and artistic aspects. The names of its wines underscore this quest. The handsome cellar is designed like an ancient temple, topped by imposing roof trusses. Accommodation and meals available at I Dolci Grappoli guest farm (*13 rooms*). Hectares under vine: 15.

**Wines**: Rosso del Molise Console Vibio, Trebbiano del Molise Kantharos, Rosso del Molise Ricupo, Trebbiano delle Terre degli Osci IGT Keres. Other products: grappa.

# Where to stay

## CIVITELLA DEL TRONTO

**Zunica 1880** – *Piazza Filippi Pepe 14, Civitella del Tronto (TE)* - ☎ *086 19 13 19 - www.hotelzunica.it - 17 rooms, doubles from €90.* An elegant place with typical regional cuisine situated in the upper part of town. Simple comfortable rooms.

## GUARDIAGRELE

**Villa Maiella** – *Via Sette Dolori 30, 1.5 km SW of Guardiagrele (CH)* - ☎ *0871 80 93 19 - www.villamaiella.it - 14 rooms, doubles from €90.* The creative flair and experience of the young owners of this hotel on the edge of the Majella Park are renowned. The comfortable, well-lit rooms have been fitted with the latest equipment.

## LORETO APRUTINO

**Agriturismo le Magnolie** – *C.da Fiorano 83, 5 km W of Loreto Aprutino (PE)* - ☎ *085 82 89 534 - www.lemagnolie.com - Closed Dec.-Feb. - 2 rooms and 10 apts., doubles rooms from €85, apts. from €150.* This 17th-c. cottage is located in the centre of a great estate that grows fruit and vegetables, and produces olive oil.

## GUGLIONESI

**RiBo** – *C.da Malecoste 7, 5.5 km NE of Guglionesi (CB)* - ☎ *0875 68 06 55 - www.ribomolise.it - 9 rooms, doubles from €85.* Guglionesi is situated in the heart of the countryside, not far from the sea. Its great position and the quest for quality are also evident in the food.

# LAZIO

Lazio is one of Italy's top wine-producing regions. The zones that are most suited to viticulture are the hills of volcanic origin, whose soil, composed of lava and tufa, provides high-quality nourishment to the vines. Back in the times of the Romans the Castelli Romani hill area was already used to grow grapes, and the wines they produced were sought after in the banquets and festivities of Rome's leading citizens. White wines are more prevalent but there are also interesting reds, like those made from Cesanese grapes.

*Countryside between Rieti and Terni*

## The terroir

Historically a **white wine producer**, most of Lazio's viticulture is concentrated in the Castelli Romani and the provinces of Viterbo, Frosinone and Latina. The most commonly grown white-skinned grapes are Trebbiano, Malvasia, Bellone, Bombino Bianco, Grechetto and Moscato di Terracina. The most widespread black-skinned grapes, on the other hand, are **Cesanese**, Ciliegiolo, Sangiovese, Montepulciano, Cabernet and Merlot. Today Lazio can boast 27 DOC zones of which one, Moscato di Terracina, was only recently established.

Though white wines predominate, it should be pointed out that very enjoyable and well structured red wines are made from the **Cesanese** variety in the area that straddles the border between the provinces of Frosinone and Roma. And a DOCG zone has recently been defined for just this cultivar: **Cesanese del Piglio** or **Piglio DOCG**.

The **Colli della Sabina** wines are produced in **Rieti** in tandem with other municipalities around Rome.

## Itineraries

*Locations with a winery are indicated by the symbol ♟; for the addresses of the wineries, see p. 371.*

### 1. THE PROVINCE OF ROMA

A very productive area enologically, the province of Roma is home to many appellations: Cerveteri, Tarquinia, Bianco Capena, Aprilia, **Castelli Romani**, Colli Albani, Colli Lanuvini, **Frascati** (with the two 2011 DOCGs **Cannellino di Frascati** and **Frascati Superiore**), Genazzano, Marino, Montecompatri Colonna, Zagarolo, **Cesanese di Olevano Romano**, Cesanese di Affile and Cesanese di Nettuno.

### Castelli Romani and Colli Albani★★

*Itinerary of 90 km from Frascati to Marino.*

The Castelli lie in the region of the **Alban Hills**, a circular mountainous chain of quiescent volcanoes whose perimeter formed the ancient crest of an immense crater. The interior of the crater is in turn dotted with secondary craters in which lakes formed. The hilltops are covered with grassland and chestnut groves whereas the slopes are generally used to cultivate vines and olive trees. In the beds of the dried-up lakes the volcanic terrain is ideal for growing high-quality firstlings, such as the strawberries from Nemi.

The Alban Hills were the site of the country houses of Cicero and the emperors Tiberius, Nero and Galba. During the Middle Ages 13 villages were transformed into *"castelli"* (a sort of stronghold) by a number of noble families, who took refuge there during Rome's anarchic period. These *castelli* were Albano, Ariccia, Castel Gandolfo, Colonna, Frascati, Genzano, Grottaferrata, Marino, Nemi, Montecompatri, Monte Porzio Catone, Rocca di Papa and Rocca Priora. From the 17th c. on, the Alban Hills lost their defensive nature and were visited for purposes of relaxation and pleasure, and to escape the city. Splendid residences were built, which are still a feature of the Alban countryside.

## Frascati ♛

Famous for its white wine and superb Tuscolana Villas built in the 16th and 17th c., the town of Frascati has sweeping views over the countryside as far as Rome and onto Villa Aldobrandini. To the right of the villa lies the Municipal Park that was once part of the land belonging to Villa Torlonia (destroyed). The Aldobrandini Stables at 6 Piazza Marconi have been transformed into a versatile space by architect Massimiliano Fuksas that now houses temporary exhibitions and the **Tuscolano Museum** (archaeological finds and models of the Tuscolana Villas). *Open 9-18 (Sat. and Sun. 19), closed Mon.,* ☏ *06 94 17 196.* **Villa Aldobrandini★** was constructed at the end of the 16th c. It has a lovely park featuring terraces, avenues, grottoes and fountains (*for visits contact the Tourist Office at 5 Piazza Marconi,* ☏ *06 94 18 44 09*).

*Take the road that leads to the Tuscolana Villas and Monte Porzio Catone.*

The road offers views of **Monte Porzio Catone**, where the **Wine Museum** can be visited. *Open Fri.-Sun. 9-13 and 15-19,* ☏ *06 89 68 65 03, www.monteporzio catonemusei.it.*

You next come to **Rocca Priora**, perched on the northern edge of the largest crater in the Alban Hills at an altitude of 768 m.

*Drive down to Via Latina (S 215).*
*After about 4 km turn right to Tuscolo (Tusculum). A winding road climbs up to the ruins.*

## Tusculum

Founded in the 9th c. BC, in the Roman era Tusculum became an exclusive holiday resort for city dwellers, as is demonstrated by the remains of a 2nd-c. amphitheatre (able to seat 3000 spectators) and the ruins of Tiberius's villa. It was also the birthplace of Cato the Censor (243-149 BC). During the Middle Ages Tusculum became the feud of

## DOCG

Cannellino di Frascati
Cesanese del Piglio *or* Piglio
Frascati Superiore

## DOC

Aleatico di Gradoli
Aprilia
Atina
Bianco Capena
Castelli Romani
Cerveteri
Cesanese di Affile *or* Affile
Cesanese di Olevano Romano
  *or* Olevano Romano
Circeo
Colli Albani

Colli della Sabina
Colli Etruschi Viterbesi *or* Tuscia
Colli Lanuvini
Cori
Est! Est!! Est!!! di Montefiascone
Frascati
Genazzano
Marino
Montecompatri Colonna
Nettuno
Orvieto (with Umbria)
Roma
Tarquinia
Terracina *or* Moscato di Terracina
Velletri
Vignanello
Zagarolo

the Conti family (known as the Counts of Tuscolo), who were so powerful they rivalled Rome, however, in 1191 the city's army destroyed the town and overthrew its dynastic ruling family. Amongst the ruins are the remains of a small theatre and a cistern.

*Return to the Via Latina and turn right. When you arrive in* **Grottaferrata** 🍷 *walk down the central Corso del Popolo.*

## Grottaferrata Abbey★

In 1004 a community of Greek monks from Rossano Calabro under the guidance of St Nilus the Younger founded a monastery on the ruins of an ancient Roman villa that may have belonged to Cicero.

The abbey, which received the protection of princes and popes, continues today in the Byzantine rite. The construction, which appears like a fort ringed by bastions and dikes, was commissioned from Giuliano da Sangallo in the 15th c. by Cardinal Giuliano della Rovere (the future pope Julius II).

Passing through the entrance you find yourself in a lovely courtyard with the Church of Santa Maria on one side and a portico designed by Sangallo. The museum in the rooms that belonged to the commendatory cardinals exhibits Roman and Greek objects and frescoes from the church.

**Santa Maria di Grottaferrata★** – *2nd courtyard.* Pass by the beautiful 12th-c. bell tower and through the entrance porch to the narthex where the 10th-c. font can be seen on the left. The lovely 11th-c. portal is decorated with images of animals and plants and still has its original carved wooden doors. Above it is an 11th-c. mosaic. The interior of the church was remodelled in the 18th c. The triumphal arch is lined with a large Pentecostal mosaic from the late 12th c. The right aisle gives entry to the Chapel of San Nilo e San Bartolomeo, which is decorated with a 17th-c. lacunar ceiling and frescoes of the lives of the two saints (1608) painted by Domenichino. The *Crypta Ferrata* is a room in the ancient Roman villa that was transformed into a place of Christian worship in the 5th c. from which the village and church took their names.

*When you leave the abbey, drive down Viale San Nilo on the left. At the traffic light turn right into Via Roma and follow the directions to Rocca di Papa.*

## Rocca di Papa

**Magnificently situated★**, Rocca di Papa is spread in a fan-shape across the slopes of Monte Cavo. Surrounded by countryside rich with game, the town is famous for its rabbit and hare dishes *"alla cacciatora"*.

## PRINCIPAL VARIETIES CULTIVATED

### WHITE GRAPES
Bellone
Bombino Bianco
Canaiolo Bianco
Chardonnay
Falanghina
Grechetto
Greco
Greco Bianco
Malvasia Bianca di Candia
Malvasia Bianca Lunga
Malvasia del Lazio
Manzoni Bianco
Moscato Bianco
Moscato di Terracina
Mostosa
Passerina
Pecorino
Pinot Bianco
Riesling

Riesling Italico
Sauvignon
Tocai Friulano
Trebbiano di Soave
Trebbiano Giallo
Trebbiano Toscano
Verdello
Verdicchio Bianco
Vernaccia di San Gimignano

### GREY GRAPES
Pinot Grigio

### BLACK GRAPES
Abbuoto
Aleatico
Alicante
Barbera
Bombino Nero
Cabernet Franc

Cabernet Sauvignon
Canaiolo Nero
Carignano
Cesanese Comune
Cesanese di Affile
Ciliegiolo
Grechetto Rosso
Greco Nero
Merlot
Montepulciano
Nero Buono
Olivella Nera
Petit Verdot
Pinot Nero
Primitivo
Sangiovese
Sciascinoso
Syrah

*Lake Nemi*

*Reach the S 217 and turn left towards Velletri.*

The beautiful **Via dei Laghi**★ passes through woods of oak and chestnut trees. After 3.5 km, turn right to Nemi.

## Nemi

Nemi (from the Latin word *nemus*, meaning wood) stands in an amphitheatre on the rocky slopes of a volcanic crater in an enchanting **position**★★. The crater is now filled with a lake that lies about 200 m below the town. All that remains of Nemi's architectural heritage is a single tower of the old Ruspoli Castle. The town is famous for its delicious wild strawberries, which are celebrated in the Sagra delle Fragole (Strawberry Fair) in June.

## Lake Nemi

The road down to the lake passes through open countryside. The lake is known as "Diana's mirror" as the sacred wood, which stands close to the temple dedicated to the goddess, is reflected in its water.

## Roman Ship Museum

*Via del Tempio di Diana 13, open 9-19, ℰ 06 93 98 040, www.polomuseale-lazio.beniculturali.it.* Between 1929 and 1931 the level of the lake was lowered by 9 m to allow two luxurious boats from the reign of Caligula (37-41 AD) to be removed from the water. They were used in ceremonies held in honour of the goddess Diana. The museum was built in 1935 to hold the remains of the boats but these were both destroyed in 1944 by a fire. Today the museum holds reconstructions of the boats on a 1:5 scale. The museum also displays part of the ancient Roman road that led to the Temple of Diana.

*Follow the S 7 to Velletri passing through Genzano di Roma.*

## Velletri

The largest city in the Castelli Romani was founded before the 6th c. BC. It was visited by Augustus, who spent his childhood here as his family were from the area. Lying on the south slope of the crater in the Alban Hills and surrounded by vineyards, the town has retained its medieval centre. This stretches from Piazza Cairoli (site of the 14th-c. Trivio Tower) to Piazza del Comune, the site of the stern palazzo designed by Vignola in the 16th c. (which houses the Civic Archaeological Museum) and the Church of Santa Maria del Sangue. The square gives fine, wide-ranging views over the **countryside**★.

*Take the S 7 Via Appia to Ariccia.*

## Ariccia

The Via Appia passes through the impressive **Piazza di Corte**★★ designed by Bernini. On the left stands the palace that belonged to the Chigi family of bankers originally from Siena, who became the owners of this area in the 17th c. On the right is the Church of Santa Maria dell'Assunzione (also by Bernini), which is embraced by two

© Romaoso/iStock

elegant lateral porches. In addition to its Baroque monuments, Ariccia is known for its traditional dish of whole roasted pig, which is celebrated at the Sagra della Porchetta (Roasted Pig Fair) on the first Sunday of September.

**Palazzo Chigi★** – *Guided tours only, closed Mon., ℘ 06 93 30 053, www. palazzochigiariccia.it.* Built in the 16th c., the palace owes its current appearance to Carlo Fontana, who redesigned it in the 18th c. Its attractive interior, featuring leather wall hangings, Baroque furniture and a series of beautiful paintings, was used by Luchino Visconti to film some of the interior scenes in his film *The Leopard*, as the photographs in the rooms show. The outstanding pieces in the collections are the 17th-c. Pharmacy designed by Fontana, and Bernini's sanguine drawing of *St Joseph and the Child*. A large park of 28 hectares lies behind the palace.

Continuing along the S 7 towards Albano you pass over the monumental Ariccia Bridge, built originally by Pope Pius IX in 1854.

## Albano Laziale★

This town stands on the land of the famous Alba Longa, which was destroyed by the Romans in the 7th c. BC.

During the republican and imperial ages the area became a retreat from Rome for important individuals, while the large military camp built in 192 BC, the *Castra Albana*, which housed 6000 of Septimus Severus's legionaries, gave a large boost to the town.

**Tomb of the Horatii and Curatii★** – *As you arrive from Ariccia, at the start of Borgo Garibaldi on the edge of the town, turn left into the road going downhill.* This tomb built of huge blocks of peperino stone dates from the republican period. To the right of Borgo Garibaldi stands Villa Ferraioli (19th c.), where you can visit the **Albano Civic Museum**. It contains archaeological remains from prehistory to the Middle Ages. *Viale Risorgimento 3, open 9-13 (Mon. and Thu. also 15.30-18.30), Sat. 9-14 ℘ 06 93 23 490, www.museicivicialbano.it.*

The Romanesque Church of San Pietro stands on the left of Corso Matteotti (*the continuation of Borgo Garibaldi*). On the right, behind the Town Hall, lie the remains of **Porta Pretoria★**, the principal entrance to the military camp built by Septimius Severus. The gateway was discovered after wartime bombardments in 1944.

## THE TERROIR

**Area:** 17,231.72 km², of which 20,349 hectares are planted to vine

**Production 2019:** 1,439,970 hectolitres, of which approximately 719,968 VQPRD

**Geography:** 54% hilly, 26% mountainous, 20% flat. The soil is sandy, marly, calcareous and partly of volcanic origin. A temperate climate

## THE PROTECTION CONSORTIA

Consorzio Tutela Denominazione Frascati – ℘ 06 94 01 52 12, www.consorziofrascati.it

## WINE AND FOOD ROUTES

Strada dei Vini dei Castelli Romani – www.stradadeivinideicastelliromani.it

Strada del Vino del Cesanese DOC e dell'Olio Rosciola – ℘ 0775 50 15 78, www.lastradadelvinocesanese.it

Strada dell'Olio e dei prodotti tipici della Sabina – ℘ 06 69 79 24 01, www.stradadelloliodellasabina.com

© Francesco Dazzi/Shutterstock

*Castel Gandolfo*

*Walk down Via Saffi behind the gate.* A street on the left leads to the Church of Santa Maria della Rotonda. This was created out of the nymphaeum of a 1st-c. AD villa and given a bell tower in the 13th c. Further down Via Saffi you come to the huge five-aisle water **cistern★** built by Septimius Severus for his legions and still used today to supply water to Albano. For visits to the cistern, ask in the Civic Museum.

Return to Corso Matteotti and walk down to Piazza Mazzini. Here lies the vast **public garden★** that incorporates the ruins of a villa said to have belonged to Pompey (1st c. BC).

*Continue to Castel Gandolfo.*

## Castel Gandolfo★

Set on a rise on the edge of the same crater as Albano, and also overlooking the same lake, Castel Gandolfo is the pope's summer residence. As you walk down Corso della Repubblica, you come to the gracious **Piazza della Liberta★**, at the centre of which stands a lovely fountain designed by Bernini. This architect also designed the Church of San Tommaso da Villanova (*on the right*), featuring a large dome. The square is closed off solidly by the **Papal Palace** (*closed to the public*). The Holy See became the owner of Castello Gandolfo at the end of the 16th c. and in 1628 Urban VIII had a palace designed and constructed by Maderno on the site of Domitian's villa (emperor 81-96 AD). The Roman remains lie within the palace's large park, which

stretches as far as Albano Laziale. Since the papacy of Pius XI the palace has included the astronomic observatory known as the Specola Vaticana.

To the right of the Church of San Tommaso an alley leads to a panoramic lookout point over **Lake Albano**. This can be reached by a road that leaves the town just outside of the historic centre.

### Marino

Built on a ridge that slopes down towards the Roman countryside on the outside of the crater, Marino is known for its **white wine**. Historically the town has been ruled over by the following families: the Conti of Tuscolo, the Frangipane, the Orsini and the Colonna. A fountain in Piazza Matteotti is in the form of four Turkish slaves tied to a column to commemorate the victory of Marcantonio Colonna over the Ottoman navy at Lepanto in 1571. Continue down the main street to the square lined by the 17th-c. Church of San Barnaba. Shortly after on the left you find Palazzo Colonna, designed by Antonio da Sangallo the Younger, which faces onto Piazza della Repubblica.

## The Prenestini Mountains

*Itinerary of 35 km from Palestrina to Olèvano Romano.*

### Palestrina★

Palestrina is an elegant town of medieval appearance perched on the Prenestini mountains. It enjoys extraordinary **views** but above all boasts the ruins of the magnificent Temple of the Dea Fortuna. This construction is a jewel of Hellenistic mosaic art that in itself is worthy of a visit. Due to its strategic position due to the passage of goods and transhumant flocks, many attempts were made to conquer the town over the centuries. Subjected by the Romans in the 4th c. BC, it became a place of relaxation for emperors and patricians. During the imperial age, both Tiberius and Hadrian had a residence built there.

**Palazzo Barberini★** – *Piazza della Cortina*. The Colonna family were the first to build over the sanctuary dedicated to the Dea Fortuna in the 11th c. Remodelled in the 15th, their palace passed to the Barberini in 1630, who altered it to its current appearance. The semicircular form is the result of keeping the structure of the sanctuary's ancient open gallery (the remains of the columns are visible inside) and the cavea of the theatre. Several rooms inside are decorated with high-quality frescoes painted by artists in the Zuccari circle. The front terrace gives fine **views★** over the town and valley. Today the palace houses the Archaeological Museum, which has some exceptional pieces. One is the splendid **Nile mosaic★★**, an extraordinary geographical map of Egypt depicted during the annual flooding of the Nile. It was made by artists from Alexandria in the 2nd c. AD but it was taken to pieces and recomposed wrongly in the 17th c. The large model of the Sanctuary della Fortuna Primigenia provides a preparation for the visit to the archaeological zone.

**Sanctuary della Fortuna Primigenia★** – This magnificent sanctuary dates from the 2nd and 1st c. BC. It covered almost the entire area occupied by the town today and stood on a series of 6 terraces connected by ramps and flights of steps. The upper terrace, called the Terrace della Cortina, was a vast plaza closed on three sides by an open gallery and crowned by a cavea enclosed by a colonnade (incorporated today in the Palazzo Barberini). Above this stood the circular temple. The goddess Fortuna was an oracular divinity associated, naturally, with fortune but also fertility. This dual aspect of her nature was reflected in the layout of the sanctuary, which had two separate places of worship: the east part of the Terrace of Hemicycles was where the goddess was worshiped for her powers related to fertility, while the faithful had to climb to the circular sanctuary (visible on the second floor of the museum) to invoke the oracle.

Lying 9 km to the south, **Valmontone** is the setting for the 17th-c. Palazzo Doria, a superb building with its original frescoes, and the coeval Collegiate Church dell'Assunta.

Another ancient town on the slopes of the Prenestini mountains is **Genazzano**, which has also managed to keep its constructions from the Middle Ages and Renaissance. Genazzano was a feud of the Colonna, who, from their castle, controlled the transits between Rome and Naples. The most important buildings were constructed along Corso Vannuttelli, such as the Church of San

Nicòla, the Colonna Castle, and Casa Apolloni, a Gothic house where Pope Martin V was born. The Sanctuary of the Madonna del Buon Consiglio was founded in the Middle Ages but later remodelled. It is visited by pilgrims who come to view the fresco of the Madonna del Buon Consiglio.

On the slopes of Monte Celeste 12 km north-east, **Olèvano Romano** was built on the foundations of ancient cyclopean walls and is dominated by the 13th-c. Colonna Castle.

## 2. CERVETERI DOC
## From Cerveteri to Tarquinia
*Itinerary of 60 km.*

Cerveteri appellation touches on the municipalities of Cerveteri, Ladispoli, Santa Marinella, Civitavecchia, Rome, Allumiere and Tolfa in the province of Roma, and that of Tarquinia in the province of Viterbo. White, red and rosé wines are produced from Trebbiano Toscano, Giallo, Malvasia Bianca and Lazio varieties for the whites, and Sangiovese, Montepulciano and Cesanese for the reds and rosés.

When you arrive in Cerveteri from Rome, you pass through the village of **Torrimpietra** ♈, which is famous for the model estate founded by Luigi Albertini (journalist and politician) in 1925.

### Cerveteri★★ ♈
The powerful Etruscan city of Cerveteri was built on a rise to the east of the modern town. Its period of greatest splendour was achieved in the 7th-6th c. BC due to its busy cultural and religious activities. The superb **Banditaccia necropolis** (some of the materials of which are exhibited in the Villa Giulia Etruscan museum in Rome) is like a real town: it has a main street lined on each side by tombs (mostly mound tombs dating from the 7th c. BC) arranged serenely yet mysteriously in a setting of natural vegetation. The primary interest of the tombs at Cerveteri is architectural as, with respect to those at Tarquinia, they have little pictorial decoration. One of the most interesting is the **Tomb of the Reliefs★★**, which features polychrome stuccoes and paintings that illustrate many aspects of daily life. The necropolis lies 2 km north of the town. *Open 8.30-1 h before sunset, closed Mon., ☎ 06 99 40 001.*

*Continue north along the Via Aurelia.*

### Civitavecchia
During Trajan's reign, Centumcellae became Rome's leading port. Today, under the name of Civitavecchia, it provides the mainland's sea connections with Sardinia. The port is defended by the Michelangelo fort, a solid Renaissance construction begun by Bramante, continued by the younger Sangallo and Bernini, and completed by Michelangelo in 1557. **Trajan's Baths** (or the Taurin Baths, 3 km north-east) consist of two sets of buildings: the first (on the west side) date to the republican era and the second, better preserved, were built by Hadrian, Trajan's successor. *Open 9.30-13.30, ☎ 327 26 99 665, prolococivitavecchia.com.*

### Tarquinia★
Ringed by a crown of medieval walls and towers, Tarquinia stands on a rocky rise facing the sea, in a landscape of olive groves and fields of barley and wheat. The historic centre of the town is strung out along Corso Vittorio Emanuele, onto which the two principal squares face: Piazza Cavour, where the **Palazzo Vitelleschi★** (15th c.) stands, and, further up, Piazza Matteotti, the setting for the Town Hall. The **National Museum of Tarquinia★** in Palazzo Vitelleschi has a notable collection of Etruscan works: 6th-c. sarcophaguses, ceramics, furnishings, Attic vases and **frescoes★★** removed from certain tombs. The pride of the museum is the **winged horses ★★★** made of terracotta, which have become the symbol of Tarquinia. *Open 8.30-19.30, closed Mon., ☎ 0766 85 60 36, www.tarquinia-cerveteri.it.*

The small **medieval district★** lies on the north side of the Corso, and features such fine buildings as the Palazzo dei Priori and the Church of San Martino. The fortified citadel that protected the ancient city lay in the north-west section of the walls. It is an attractive medieval corner of the town, beyond which you will find the Church of **Santa Maria in Castello★**. Built in the 12th-13th c., it has an elegant entrance with Cosmatesque decorations and a majestic interior, including a Cosmatesque pavement.

## Monterozzi Necropolis★★

*4 km south-east of Tarquinia. Open 8.30--1 h before sunset, closed Mon., ✆ 0766 85 63 08.* Covering an area 5 km long by 1 km wide, the necropolis contains about 600 tombs dug between the 6th and 1st c. BC. No architecture is visible from the outside (unlike Cerveteri) but the walls of the funeral chambers are decorated with superb, colourful and dynamic **paintings★★★**. The paintings often recreate the deceased's earthly existence and are therefore of extreme interest to scholars of the Etruscan civilisation.

## 3. FROM VITERBO TO LAKE BOLSENA

*Itinerary of 150 km.*

In the province of Viterbo the most renowned wines are the white Orvieto (an appellation that lies partly in Umbria), **Est! Est!! Est!!! di Montefiascone** and **Aleatico di Gradoli**, but there are many more designated zones, including Vignanello, Colli Etruschi Viterbesi and – in the province of Roma – Cerveteri and Tarquinia. Deserving of special mention is **Aleatico di Gradoli**, a red liqueur wine with a powerful fruity nose that recalls the port made from the Aleatico grape.

## Viterbo★

The ancient city walls (which partly collapsed in January 1997) still ring the lovely historic centre of the chief town of Roman Tuscia. Squares, palaces, churches and fountains are all demonstrative of the city's important past, which from the 13th to 15th c. was a papal seat and the setting for a number of conclaves.

The focus of the city's religious buildings is **Piazza San Lorenzo★★**, the site of the ancient Etruscan acropolis. The cathedral (12th c.) has a fine 14th-c. bell tower and some excellent works of art, including the panel of the *Madonna della Carbonara* (12th c.). On the right, the elegant **Papal Palace★★** was constructed in the 13th c. It is one of the most interesting examples of medieval civil architecture in Lazio. A number of conclaves were held here, including the important one of 1271 that 33 months later led to the election of Gregory X as pope. Excellent views are to be had from the loggia.

Continue past the Piazza della Morte towards the district of **San Pellegrino★★**, a 13th-c. quarter set out along the length of Via San Pellegrino. It features tiny squares, towers, alleyways, arches and old houses in a timeless setting.

Return to Piazza della Morte and turn right into Via San Lorenzo, which connects the religious quarter of the city to the political centre in Piazza del Plebiscito. Roughly halfway along the street, on the right hand side, you will see the Romanesque Church of Santa Maria Nuova, which still has the pulpit, to the left of the façade, from which Thomas Aquinas preached. Inside, the church has a superb wooden ceiling and a unique *San Salvatore Triptych* on leather (13th c.) and frescoes by local artists from the 14th to 16th c. The exquisite Lombard cloister is reached from the left side of the church.

**Piazza del Plebiscito★** is lined by the Palazzo del Podestà (medieval but later rebuilt), the Clock Tower, the Palazzo dei Priori (15th c.) and the Palazzo della Prefettura. The symbol of the city, a lion, stands at the foot of the Clock Tower. Views over the Faul valley are given from the courtyard of Palazzo dei Priori.

## Vignanello

Vignanello is where Ottavia Orsini built the **Ruspoli Castle** in 1610, with its superb **Italian garden★** laid out in flowerbeds lined with geometric and alphabetic motifs of boxwood. *Open Sat.-Sun. and public hols. 10-13 and 15-18 (14.30-17 in win.), ✆ 0761 75 53 38, www.castelloruspoli.com.*

The municipality lies at the centre of the **Vignanello DOC** wine zone, which produces white, red, rosé and Greco versions. The appellation covers a series of municipalities in the Monte Cimino hills in the province of Viterbo.

## Lake Vico★

*Entrance to the Reserve on Via Cimina.* This enchanting lake of volcanic origin fills a crater in the Cimini mountains. Its banks are lined with woods of beech, chestnut, oak and hazel trees, and are an integral part of the Lake Vico Nature Reserve.

## Palazzo Farnese in Caprarola★★

*Caprarola lies on the eastern edge of Lake Vico Reserve. For information on visits ✆ 0761 64 60 52.* This imposing

*Lake Bolsena*

building dominates the little town of Caprarola. It was constructed in the late 16th c. by Cardinal Alessandro Farnese from a design by Vignola. It is pentagonal in plan around a circular courtyard. The magnificent **spiral staircase★★** is decorated with grotesques and landscapes painted by Antonio Tempesta. The rooms are embellished with sumptuous and highly refined frescoes by the Mannerist school of Taddeo and Federico Zuccari and Bertoja, but the two most outstanding are the Room of the Deeds of the Farnese and the Map Room. A huge **park** with terraces and fountains lies behind the palace.

## Lake Bolsena★

Bolsena is Italy's largest volcanic lake, and its water level is continually altered by telluric tremors. Set in a hollow in the Volsini mountains, it has a beautiful lakeside promenade, particularly on the west bank. There is a great deal of aquatic wildlife, eels especially. Excursions to the two islands of Bisentina and Martana (themselves probably residues of volcanic craters) leave from Bolsena and the elegant little port of Capricciolo.

## Montefiascone

The vineyards around Montefiascone produce the acclaimed wine *Est! Est!! Est!!!*. The town has a fine view over the lake at its height of 560 m. The panoramic Rocca dei Papi (Popes' Fort, founded in the 12th c. and remodelled in the 16th) stands in the upper part of the town, its garden looking towards

the Duomo's cupola built in the 17th c. by Carlo Fontana. In the lower section, the unusual Romanesque Church of **San Flavio★** is formed by two superposed buildings; its façade has a Renaissance loggia from which the popes used to bless the faithful.

Inside, 14th-c. frescoes illustrate the brevity of life and the vanity of existence (*Legend of the Three Dead and Three Live Men*), and the tombstone of Giovanni Fugger is conserved in the third chapel on the left.

## Bolsena

The ancient Etruscan town of *Volsinii* has become the lake's main tourist destination. Centred on Piazza Matteotti, the town castle and its dark medieval houses are set out on a small rise behind the square. There is a good view of the buildings from the ancient Via Cassia (SS 2). The **Basilica of Santa Cristina★** is dedicated to the martyr from Bolsena who died during the persecution of Christians carried out by Emperor Diocletian. The building dates to the 11th c. but the light façade is Renaissance and the columns inside are Roman. The floor of the Chapel of the Miracle, reached from the left aisle, is marked with the blood of the Host. You can see the altar of the miracle and statue of St Cristina (carved by Buglioni in the 15th c.) in the grotto and the extended network of catacombs dug in the 3rd and 4th c. *Guided visits to the catacombs 10-12 and 16-18, (10-12 and 15.30-17 in win.), ℘ 0761 79 90 67, www. basilicasantacristina.it.*

## Est! Est!! Est!!!

During a trip to Rome, the German bishop Johannes Fugger, a lover of good wine, sent his servant on ahead to scout the villages for inns that served the best wine. When he found one he was supposed to write "Est" (*Vinum est bonum*). on the door in chalk. When Fugger arrived in Montefiascone, he found Est! Est!! Est!!! written on one door.

### Civita di Bagnoregio★

The "Dying Village" stands on a tufa hill in a state of continual erosion. An earthquake separated it on a permanent basis from nearby Bagnoregio in 1784 and began the continual flow of its inhabitants away from the village. The pedestrian bridge leads to the medieval Porta Santa Maria which constitutes the entrance to the attractive centre. There is a fine **view★** of the ravines that surround the village from the end of the main street.

**Gradoli** is a medieval village on the north-west side of the lake. The **Palazzo Farnese** there was built by Antonio da Sangallo the Younger and contains a museum dedicated to clothes worn in the times of the Farnese family. *For information,* 📞 *0761 45 60 82.* Don't forget to taste a glass of **Aleatico di Gradoli**, a liqueur wine similar to port.

## 4. THE PROVINCES OF LATINA AND FROSINONE

Latina produces the DOC wines **Cori**, **Circeo**, **Velletri**, **Moscato di Terracina** and, with the province of Roma, also Aprilia and Castelli Romani. The **Moscato di Terracina DOC** zone was established in 2007 and lies in the municipalities of Monte San Biagio, Terracina and Sonnino, where the Moscato di Terracina cultivar produces dry, sweetish, dried-grape wine and sparkling wines.

The province of Frosinone makes wines that go under the names of Genazzano, **Cesanese del Piglio**, Affile and **Atina**.

### From Terracina to Cori along the coast

*Itinerary of 180 km from Terracina to Sermoneta.*

### Terracina★

Terracina lies in a pleasant position at the foot of the Ausoni mountains that separate the Pontine plain from the Fondi plain. Even during the Roman age the town was a place for city-dwellers to retire to for relaxation. The lovely Piazza del Municipio lies over the old Roman forum and has maintained its shape. Looking onto it is the **duomo★**, consecrated in 1075. The ancient columns of its porch support a 12th-c. mosaic frieze. The bell tower is in Romanesque-Gothic style. Principal features of the interior are a Cosmatesque pulpit and paschal candelabrum (13th c.).

Also facing onto the square is the 14th-c. Palazzo Venditti (*to the right of the duomo*) and the ruins of the Roman theatre. Pass under the arch beneath Palazzo Venditti to see the remains of the Capitolium (1st c. BC), a temple dedicated to the Capitoline Triad (Jove, Juno and Minerva).

The **Temple of Jove Anxur** was built in the 1st c. BC on top of Monte Sant'Angelo (3 km east of the historic centre). All that is left today is the base and a cryptoportico but there are superb **views★★** over the town, canals, port, Monte Circeo, Agro Pontino, the plain, the Fondi lakes, and along the coast as far as Gaeta.

*Continue along the coast to San Felice Circeo.*

### Circeo National Park★

*For information on visits: Visitors Centre, Via C. Alberto 188, Sabaudia,* 📞 *0773 51 13 85, www.parcocirceo.it.* The park lies in a narrow coastal strip between Anzio and Terracina that incorporates the Circeo promontory, part of the old Pontine marshes, dunes, coastal lakes and Zannone Island. Two of the most beautiful places in the park are **Monte Circeo**, the legendary refuge of the sorceress Circe, who helped Ulysses and his men on his travels, and **Lake Sabaudia**, which you can reach by taking the bridge to **Sabaudia★**, a holiday resort built in the 1930s on Rationalist principles. The tower of the Town Hall is built from an interesting mix of materials. From the top there is an extraordinary **panorama★**. Another building of architectural relevance is the Post Office, designed by Mazzoni, the colours of which (blue and red) are those of the House of Savoy after which the town is named.

From San Felice Circeo a **pretty road** flanked by luxurious villas, flowers and Mediterranean vegetation takes you to Torre Cervia. This park is part of the UNESCO Biosphere Reserve.

From Sabaudia the route can deviate inland to visit **Fossanova Abbey★★** (*20 km*). Situated in a solitary place, as the Cistercian rule prescribed, this is the oldest abbey of this order in Italy. The monks settled here in 1133 and began to build the church 30 years later. The buildings were set out in a manner functional to the activities of the community, which was divided into professed monks, who lived in seclusion, and lay brothers, who did the manual work. Consecrated in 1208 the church has elements typical of Cistercian architecture, such as the Latin cross plan, flat apse and octagonal crossing tower. The soaring, luminous and sober interior has aisles with ribbed vaulting. The Gothic chapterhouse is joined to the elegant **cloister**.

Visit the guesthouse, which stands slightly away from the main buildings, to see the room in which St Thomas Aquinas died on 7 March 1274.

From Sabaudia follow the coast for about 40 km to arrive at the pleasant seaside resorts of **Nettuno** and **Anzio**. It was on the beaches of Anzio that the Allied troops landed on 22 January 1944. The town has created an archaeological zone around Nero's villa and the so-called Nero's Grottoes, which were in fact Roman storerooms.

## Cori

To reach Cori leave Nettuno inland and pass through **Le Ferriere** 🍷 and Cisterna di Latina. Cori stands on the Lepine mountains ringed by cyclopean walls, part of which date to the 5th c. BC. Medieval houses line Via del Porticato in the lower part of the town, called Cori a Valle, whereas the upper section, Cori a Monte, is the site of the Temple of Hercules (1st c. BC). On a clear day the view from the temple reaches as far as the Pontine islands and Circeo National Park.

## Lepine Mountains

The partly medieval **Norma** lies 13 km south-east of Cori. Just 1 km away lie the ruins of **Norba**, a city founded by the Latins, with cyclopean walls dating from the 4th c. BC. It is an attractive ghost town abandoned in the 17th c. because of malaria (it stands beside a lake). Its ruins are part of the **Ninfa naturalistic oasis**.

The **Abbey of Valvisciolo** was founded in the 8th c. but was rebuilt by the Cistercians in the 14th c.

*For information on visits 𝄞 0773 30 013.*

Surrounded by turreted walls 3 km to the south **Sermoneta** is watched over by the stern-looking Caetani Castle, built by Pope Alexander VI at the start of the 16th c.

*Circeo coast*

## Ciociarìa

*Itinerary of 95 km from Anagni to Piglio.*

The route passes through the hills and perched villages and towns of Ciociarìa, which runs along the Sacco valley and between the Ernici mountains to the north and Ausoni mountains to the south. The name is taken from *ciocie*, the local word for the traditional footwear consisting of a thick leather sole and bands that wrap around the calf.

## Anagni★ 🍷

Standing on a rock spur looking over the hills and fertile valleys of Ciociarìa, Anagni is a medieval looking town whose history is indissolubly linked to the popes who were born there and made it their official residence. These included Boniface VIII (Benedetto Caetani, 1235-1303).

The imposing **cathedral★★** stands on the site of the acropolis founded by the Ernici, an Italic people who lived in the Sacco valley before the Romans. Built in Romanesque style in the 11th and 12th c., it was remodelled with Gothic elements a century later. Note the three Romanesque apses with Lombard arches and pilasters, the statue of Boniface VIII (14th c.) above the loggia on the left side, and the solid bell tower standing separate from the body of the church. The 13th-c. floor inside is **Cosmatesque★** in style. Close to the presbytery, the ciborium, the bishop's throne and the paschal candelabrum

were made by Pietro Vassalletto (1263). The Caetani Chapel stands at the end of the left aisle.

Also featuring a fine Cosmatesque floor, the **crypt★★★** is adorned with magnificent 13th-c. frescoes of biblical and cosmological scenes painted by three Benedictine artists. Next to the crypt the Chapel of Thomas Becket was built over an ancient Mithraeum (a sanctuary dedicated to the god Mithra). *Open 9-13 and 15-19 (15-18 in win.), 🕿 0775 72 83 74, www.cattedraledianagni.it.*

The **medieval district★** begins from the beautiful Piazza della Cattedrale and lies on either side of Via Vittorio Emanuele. On the left stands the Palazzo di Bonifacio VIII. Its façade has two overlaid loggias, one with an immense round arch, the other with twin-light windows. The

palace is said to have been where Boniface VIII received a slap in the face (more moral than material) from the emissaries of Philip the Fair, king of France, who came to Anagni in 1303 to persuade the pope to revoke his excommunication of the French king and to convince him to abdicate. The citizens of Anagni rose up against this sacrilege and Boniface returned to Rome under the protection of the Orsini.

Continuing along Via Vittorio Emanuele, a large vault on the right forms the base for the Town Hall (12th-13th c.), the façade of which features the elegant Loggetta del Banditore.

Further down Via Vittorio Emanuele you come to **Piazza Cavour**, which looks onto the Parco della Rimembranza.

*Head south-east on the SS 6 (Via Casilina).*

## Ferentino

Like many other towns in Ciociarìa, Ferentino is set on a hill. Right on the top of the ancient acropolis stands the town's lovely Romanesque duomo (12th c.), whose flooring, paschal candle and bishop's throne are all Cosmatesque in style. Behind the duomo stands the bishop's palace. As you come down the hill on Via Don Morosini, on the left you will note the impressive archways of the market that dated from the age of the Roman republic.

In the lower part of the town, the lovely Gothic Church of Santa Maria Maggiore (12th-13th c.) can be seen near the south side of the city walls.

*Continue on the SS 6. Shortly before Frosinone, take the SS 214 in the direction of Sora and turn off to visit Casamari Abbey.*

## Casamari Abbey★★

*Open 9-12 and 15-18, 🕿 0775 28 23 71, www.casamari.it.* The abbey was founded by the Benedictines in the 11th c. but during the following century it passed to the Cistercians, who enlarged it on the model of Fossanova and the principles of austerity set down by St Bernard. The courtyard in front of the church is reached from a porch crowned by a twin-light loggia. The façade is very simple: it has a lovely rounded portal, a richly decorated tympan, and a deep porch set with arches. The interior is simple but beautiful and

*Casamari abbey church portal*

raked by warm light. The huge pillars support very high ogival vaults and, as is typical of Cistercian architecture, the church is built on a Latin cross with a flat, shallow apse.

To reach the **cloister**, leave through the right transept of the church. The cloister features twin columns and gives onto the chapterhouse. On the other side of the cloister you can see the ancient *dispensarium*, which now functions as a refectory.

*Return to the SS 214 and continue. Leave at Il Giglio and follow the signs to Véroli.*

## Véroli

Veroli is a delightful village founded in ancient times on a rise roughly 600 m high. The churches and aristocratic houses in the centre provide a testimony of its importance (it used to be the seat of the bishop) during the Middle Ages and Renaissance. Close to the cathedral the courtyard of the medieval Casa Reali displays the *fasti verolani*, a Roman calendar from the Augustan age of which only the first three months have survived.

*Follow the signposts to Alatri.*

## Alatri★

Founded by the Ernici, Alatri still has some of its cyclopean walls (6th-5th c. BC). The lower part has steep steps and streets lined by late medieval houses, one of which is the impressive, austere, 13th-c. Palazzo Gottifredo (*on Corso Cavour*). As you wander down Corso Vittorio Emanuele, turn right into Via Regina Margherita to see the 14th-c. Church of San Francesco and Church of **Santa Maria Maggiore★**, which stands in Alatri's main square. Constructed in the 12th-13th c. in Romanesque-Gothic style, it features a large rose window and a separate bell tower. There are some interesting wooden sculptures from the 12th to 15th c. inside (*1st chapel on the left*).

From Via Matteotti and Via del Duomo climb up to the trapezoidal **acropolis★**, from where you can continue to the magnificent Porta Maggiore. The architrave of this gateway is made from a monolith 5 m long. Continue to the duomo (11th c. but greatly remodelled) and a public park that offers superb **views★★** over Alatri and the Frosinone valley. Take Via di Porta Civita down the hill through the winding streets of the medieval district and reach the 13th-c. Church of San Silvestro, which retains frescoes painted between the 13th and 16th c.

*Return to the S 155 and follow the signs to Fiuggi.*

## Fiuggi

Called Anticoli until 1911, this famed spa was visited by Boniface VIII and Michelangelo. The town is composed of the ancient Fiuggi Città, uphill, and the more recent Fiuggi Fonte, downhill. Its water is low in mineral content and is particularly suitable for sufferers of renal calculosis.

*Abbey of Montecassino courtyard*

© ROMAOSLO/iStock

Back on the S 155, pass through **Acuto** to reach **Piglio**, the home of **Cesanese del Piglio DOCG**. The remains of the Orsini Castle can be seen in its ancient centre.

## Montecassino★★ and the Atina DOC zone

*Open 8.45-19 (9-17 in win., booking recommended), ℘ 0776 31 15 29, www.abbazia montecassino.org.* The white, square bulk of this famous abbey, one of the cradles of Western monasticism, dominates the surrounding countryside from 500 m up on Monte Cassino. The abbey was founded in 529 by St Benedict, and it was here that he drew up the Order's Rule founded on study and manual work, to which he added the virtues of chastity, poverty and obedience. The abbey enjoyed its greatest splendour in the 11th and 12th c., when it was one of Europe's most important centres of art and culture and the diffusion of Western monasticism. It has been destroyed on several occasions but it was reconstructed in accordance with its ancient design after the ruinous Battle of Cassino in 1944. After you enter the abbey site, you walk through three cloisters in line. The middle cloister, from where there are good views of the Cassino plain, gives access to the elegant Renaissance-style Cloister of the Benefactors. The bare façade of the basilica gives no hint of the magnificence of the interior, which was rebuilt on 17th-c. lines, using marble, stucco, mosaics and gilt to create a sumptuous ensemble. The choir has splendid walnut stalls made in the 17th c. and the sepulchre that holds the remains of St Benedict and St Scholastica. The crypt is decorated with frescoes from the Benedictine school of art in Beuron, Germany, painted in 1913.

The area to the north of Cassino is the production zone of **Atina DOC** wines, which are mostly reds made from Cabernet Sauvignon.

### A tragic event

Monte Cassino was the setting for one of the most terrible battles of World War II, one that cost the lives of thousands of men and featured intensive bombing of one of the greatest centres of Christianity. After Naples had been taken by the Allies in 1944, the Germans turned Cassino into their main stronghold on the road to Rome. On 17 May the Allies launched the decisive attack. After a bitter fight the following day, the Germans abandoned Cassino and the Allies regrouped and opened the road to Rome. The **Historiale di Cassino★** tells the story with documentation and audiovisual and animated presentations of those tragic days. *Via San Marco 23, closed at the time of writing, for information contact ℘389 60 91 18, museohistorialecassino@gmail.com.*

# Addresses

## Tourist information

**Park of the Castelli Romani** – Ente Parco, Villa Barattolo, Via Cesare Battisti 5, **Rocca di Papa** (RM), ℘ 06 94 79 931, www.parcocastelliromani.it

**Province of Frosinone** – Via Francesco Veccia 23, Frosinone, ℘ 0775 85 14 04

**Province of Latina** – Piazza del Popolo 16, Latina, ℘ 0773 48 06 72, www.latinaturismo.it

**Rome Tourist Office** – ℘ 06 06 08, www.060608.it

**Province of Viterbo** – Via Saffi 49, Viterbo, ℘ 0761 31 32 36, www.provincia.viterbo. gov.it/turismo

**Regione Lazio** – www.visitlazio.com

## The wineries

*The addresses are listed in alphabetical order by location.*

**PROVINCE OF ROME**

♈/ **Principe Pallavicini** – Via Roma 121 - **Colonna** (RM) - ℘ 06 94 38 816 or 800 97 31 25 - www.principepallavicini.com - info@ www.principepallavicini.com - Winery tours and tasting by reservation 9-16.30. This complex business encompasses several winegrowing estates and has been part of the SAITA SpA company since 1939. Several varieties are grown here, including Trebbiano Toscano, Malvasia del Lazio, Malvasia di Candia, Chardonnay, Sauvignon, Greco, Grechetto and Bonvino for the whites, and Sangiovese, Cesanese, Merlot, Cabernet Sauvignon, Montepulciano, Ciliegiolo and Petit Verdot for the reds. Restaurant service at Osteria della Colonna. Hectares under vine: 84

**Wines**: Frascati, Frascati Poggio Verde, Casa Romana, Stillato. Other products: olive oil.

**Azienda Agricola Casale Marchese** – Via di Vermicino 68 - **Frascati** (RM) - ℘ 06 94 08 932 - www.casalemarchese.it - info@ casalemarchese.it - Winery tours and tasting by reservation. Casale Marchese stands above two ancient Roman cisterns, and was first mentioned in an official proclamation from Pope Boniface VIII on 12 May 1301 as part of the Annibaldi family's feudal estate. Casale became the residence of the famous musician Marquise Emilio de' Cavalieri (1550-1602). Starting in the 1800s, it became the property of the Carletti family. The property has been mentioned in many different official documents, for example in the Pontifical cadastre of 1860, and described by poets

and literary figures including Clara Wells, who featured it in one of her books in 1878. Casale, as it appears today, dates back to the 18th century. The palazzo has been divided into two parts: the Carletti family lives in one wing, while the other section is devoted to wine production. The company also owns a modern olive oil mill. Hectares under vine: 50.

**Wines**: Frascati Superiore DOCG, Clemens IGT, Rosso Eminenza IGT, Cortesia IGT, Marchese de' Cavalieri IGT. Other products: olive oil and grappa.

♈ **Azienda Agricola L'Olivella** – Via Colle Pisano 5 - **Frascati** (RM) - ℘ 06 94 25 656 - www.olivella.it - info@olivella.it - Wine and food tasting by reservation. Olivella was founded in 1986 through the joint efforts of an excellent winegrower from Puglia, Umberto Notarnicola, and a Piedmont enologist, Bruno Violo. Since 2003 it has applied organic agricultural methods. In addition to making high-quality wines, it also produces an outstanding extra virgin olive oil and has paralleled its agricultural activities with a guest farm, which offers meals (*by reservation*) and accommodation. Hectares under vine: 12.

**Wines**: Pivot, IGT Lazio Bianco Tre Grome, IGT Lazio Bianco Bombino, Bianco Racemo, IGT Lazio Rosso Quaranta/Sessanta, Cesanese IGT Lazio Rosso Maggiore. Other products: olive oil.

**Castel de Paolis** – Via Val de Polis - **Grottaferrata** (RM) - ℘ 06 94 13 648 - www.casteldepaolis.it - info@casteldepaolis. it - Winery tours and tasting by reservation (payment required). The wines are the outcome of a long programme of research and experimentation, and the cellar boasts state-of-the-art equipment. Its wines are highly regarded in Italy and internationally. Hectares under vine: 14.

**Wines**: Frascati Sup., I Quattro Mori, Donna Adriana, Muffa Nobile.

**La Luna del Casale** – Via Fontana Parata 11 - **Lanuvio** (RM) - ℘ 06 87 80 14 61 - www. lalunadelcasale.it - info@lalunadelcasale.it - Winery tours by reservation. La Luna del Casale is a family-owned and -run company in which each member makes his or her own contribution to achieving an excellent final product. An avant-garde, highly technological cantina, a close working relationship with an expert oenologist and especially a territory – the Colli Lanuvini – that is perfect for winemaking and which the company supports with natural processes, paying close attention to biological practices and low yields, all permit this cantina to create wines with extraordinary personality. Today these wines bear the names of the owner's children. Visitors can enjoy gourmet catering. Hectares under vine: 12. **Wines**: Lunario, Sara, Alessandro, Meridies, Spumante Brut. Other products: olive oil.

**Colle Picchioni -** *Via Colle Picchione 46 -* **Frattocchie di Marino** *(RM) - ℘ 333 19 63 261 - www.collepicchioni.it - info@ collepicchioni.it - Winery tours by reservation, closed Sun.* In the late 1970s and early 1980s Paola Di Mauro decided to abandon his career to devote himself passionately to the production of wine. He began to experiment and study enology books and pore over enology books, becoming well versed in winemaking techniques and methods. Since 1985 his son Armando has been running the cellar and during this period Colle Picchioni has expanded, going from a production of 10,000 bottles to approximately 100,000. Hectares under vine: 12.
**Wines**: Mèva Bianco and Rosso, Donna Paola, Le Vignole, Perlaia, Il Vassallo.

**Fontana Candida** *– Via Fontana Candida 11 -* **Monteporzio Catone** *(RM) - ℘ 06 94 01 881 - www.cantinefontanacandida.it - fontanacandida@giv.it - Winery tours by reservation.* The Fontana Candida winery, which continues what was long a family-run business, became a corporation in 1958. It is situated on the knoll of Fontana Candida, in a farmhouse built over the area where there was once an impressive Roman villa that may have belonged to the poet Horace. Hectares under vine: 25.
**Wines**: Frascati Superiore Luna Mater, Frascati Superiore Vigneto Santa Teresa, Frascati DOC, Sìroe Rosso del Lazio IGT, Kron Rosso del Lazio IGT.

### THE CERVETERI AREA

**Azienda Vinicola Casale Cento Corvi** *– Via Aurelia Km 45,5 -* **Cerveteri** *(RM) - ℘ 06 99 03 902 - www.casalecentocorvi.it - giorgia@casalecentocorvi.it- Winery tours by reservation (from €20).* In 2001 Collacciani, well-aware of the historical and gastronomic patrimony of Cerveteri, founded this small company with the aim of promoting the area's longstanding traditions. Right from the beginning, the project for creating a company moved in parallel with an even more ambitious goal: to recover il Giacché, or Ciambrusca, an autochthonous vine that, according to legend, was already growing in Cerveteri during the Etruscan period. For the moment the company only produces 3,000 bottles (plus another 1,000 of passito), since the vine gives a low quantity yield but boasts extraordinary organoleptic qualities. Hectares under vine: 16.
**Wines**: Giacchè, Malvasia, Trebbiano Lo Scrodato, Rosé. Other products: olive oil.

**Cantina Cerveteri** *– Via Aurelia Km 42.7 -* **Cerveteri** *(RM) - ℘ 06 99 44 420 - www. cantinacerveteri.it - direzione@cantina cerveteri.it.* Cantina Cerveteri is a cooperative of approximately 750 winegrowers and it is a major presence on the Lazio wine scene. Established in 1961, in just a few years it has created a quality label, making inroads on the national and international wine market.
**Wines**: Cerveteri Rosso Viniae Grande, Merlot Menade, Cerveteri Bianco Viniae Grande. Other products: olive oil.

🍴 **Cantina Castello di Torre in Pietra** *– Via di Torrimpietra 247 -* **Torrimpietra** *(RM) - ℘ 06 61 69 70 70 - www.castelloditorre inpietra.it - cantina@castelloditorreinpietra. com - Winery tours or food and tasting by reservation.* The winery is part of the old estate of Torre in Pietra, which extended over a vast territory straddling Via Aurelia. The cellar is now set in a picturesque medieval hamlet by the tower after which the winery is named. Carved out of the tufa hillside behind the castle, the cellar was used as far back as the 15th c. to store wine at the perfect temperature. Restaurant Osteria Elefante. Hectares under vine: 52.
**Wines**: IGT Bianco Chardonnay, IGT Rosso Terre di Breccia, IGT Rosso Syrah, Elephas Bianco, Elephas Rosso. Other products: honey, olive oil, Merlot grappa and spelt pasta.

### FROM VITERBO TO LAKE BOLSENA

**Paolo e Noemia d'Amico** *– Loc. Palombaro, Fraz. Vaiano -* **Castiglione in Teverina** *(VT) - ℘ 0761 94 80 34 - www. paoloenoemiadamico.it - info@damico wines.it - Winery tours 10-17 by reservation, closed Jan. and Aug.* Paolo, the scion of a family of shipowners, and Noemia, who is Portuguese Brazilian, decided to devote themselves to farming and wine. The winery was launched in the late 1980s with a Chardonnay vineyard, to which they added vineyards planted with Grechetto, Malvasia, Procanico, Pinot Nero, Cabernet Sauvignon and Merlot. Food also served by reservation. Hectares under vine: 25.
**Wines**: Chardonnay Falesia, Chardonnay Calanchi di Vaiano, Orvieto Noe, Merlot Villa Tirrena, Seiano Bianco.

🍷 **Mottura Sergio** *– Loc. Poggio della Costa 1 -* **Civitella d'Agliano** *(VT) - ℘ 0761 91 45 33 - www.sergiomottura.com - vini@ sergiomottura.com - Winery tours and tasting by reservation (tana@sergiomottura. com).* The Mottura estate, which has been in the family since 1933, covers 130 hectares. The Motturas have safeguarded the area's rich natural heritage as much as possible, and the vineyards have been planted according to the standards of the Italian Association for Organic Agriculture.

Accommodation available at La Tana dell'Istrice (*Piazza Unità d'Italia 12, ℘ 0761 91 45 33, 11 rooms*), with breakfast and evening restaurant service. Hectares under vine: 36.

**Wines**: Orvieto Secco, Grechetto Poggio della Costa, Grechetto Latour a Civitella, Grechetto Muffo, Lazio Rosso Magone.

## PROVINCES OF LATINA AND FROSINONE

**Casale della Ioria** – *Strada provinciale Anagni-Paliano* - **Anagni** (FR) - ℘ 0775 56 031 - www.casaledellaioria.com - info@casaledellaioria.com - *Winery tours by reservation.* The estate is surrounded by woods and the winery logo depicts the enormous old holm oak in front of the farmhouse. A native red variety, Cesanese, and Passerina, a typical white variety, have always been grown here. Hectares under vine: 38.

**Wines**: Torre del Piano, Colle Bianco, Olivella. Other products: olive oil.

**Corte dei Papi** – *Loc. Colletonno* - **Anagni** (FR) - ℘ 0775 76 92 71 - www.cortedeipapi.it - info@cortedeipapi.it - *Winery tours by reservation.* The logo takes up the symbolism and precise workmanship of the 12th-c. flooring of Anagni cathedral. The Colletonno estate covers an area of approximately 190 hectares and the name of the winery is inspired by that of one of the area's three hills, Colle Rotondo, called "Colletonno" in the local dialect. Approximately 25 hectares planted to vine, mainly with Cesanese and, to a lesser extent, Sangiovese. Selections from old and historic vineyards have been preferred for these varieties. Hectares under vine: 25.

**Wines**: IGP Lazio Quattro Profeti, Cesanese del Piglio Colle Ticchio, Cesanese del Piglio San Magno.

**Casale del Giglio** – *Strada Cisterna Nettuno km 13* - **Le Ferriere** (LT) - ℘ 06 92 90 25 30 - www.casaledelgiglio.it - info@casaledelgiglio.it - *Winery tours by reservation, closed Sun. (from €15).* Casale del Giglio was founded by Berardino Santarelli in 1967. His son Antonio was convinced - even as a boy - that the reclaimed lands of the Pontine Marshes represented a virgin area ideal for experimenting in winegrowing. The fact that the area had no enological past stimulated his creativity and he called in ampelographers and university researchers. In 1985 he launched a project to plant nearly 60 different experimental varieties on his estate. The results of these experiments rapidly made the winery one of the most famous and recognised in the region. Hectares under vine: 160.

**Wines**: Satrico, Antinoo, Shiraz, Petit Verdot, Mater Matuta. Other products: olive oil and grappa.

🍇 **Vigneti Massimi Berucci** – *Via Maggiore 121* - **Piglio** (FR) - ℘ 338 95 17 909 - www.anticacasamassimi.it - mberucci@yahoo.it - *Wine tasting by reservation.* Casa Massimi has roots that stretch back into the medieval period. The 1,000 m$^2$ house boasts nine levels and various different environments. Cesanese del Piglio is the emblematic vine of the company's production, although they also cultivate Passerina grapes with excellent results. The company's olive oil, jellies and jams are also worth mentioning. Restaurant dining (by appointment) or lodging in the agriturismo (*4 rooms, €70*) are both available to visitors. Hectares under vine: 26.

**Wines**: L' Onda Cesanese del Piglio DOCG Superiore, Vino Bianco Passerina del Frusinate IGT, Rosso del Frusinate IGT.

## Where to stay

### ATINA

**Villa Il Noce** – *Via Antica 1, Picinisco, 6 km NE of Atina* - ℘393 94 68 514 - www.villailnoce.com - *5 rooms, doubles from €60.* In the valley at the foot of this town, the villa offers a relaxing milieu boasting a large and well-tended garden with a swimming pool.

### BAGNOREGIO

**Romantica Pucci** - *Piazza Cavour 1, Bagnoregio (VT)* - ℘ 0761 79 21 21 - www.hotelromanticapucci.it - *Closed Feb. - 5 rooms, doubles €80.* The hotel, with tastefully furnished rooms, is situated in a 14th-c. palazzo. The kitchen serves simple home-style dishes.

### BRACCIANO

**Villa Clementina** – *Traversa Quarto del Lago 12/14, Bracciano (RM)* - ℘ 06 99 86 268 - www.vclementina.com - *Closed Jan.-Feb. - 7 rooms, doubles €160.* A quiet location, a beautifully manicured garden, a swimming pool, a wellness centre and a tennis court make this the perfect location for an utterly relaxing stay.

### FRASCATI

**Hotel Colonna** – *Piazza del Gesù 12, Frascati (RM)* - ℘ 06 94 01 80 88 - www.hotelcolonna.it - *20 rooms, doubles from €110.* This recently built hotel with modern amenities is in the town's historic district.

### TARQUINIA

**Locanda di Mirandolina** – *Via del Pozzo Bianco 40/42, Tuscania (VT)* - ℘ 0761 43 65 95 - www.mirandolina.it - *5 rooms, doubles from €69.* This B&B is in the heart of the ancient medieval *borgo* of Tuscania. The façade is covered with jasmine. Excellent regional specialities.

# CAMPANIA

The beauty of the Campanian countryside is such that it can bewitch the soul. In addition, its cuisine makes it one of the most interesting regions of Italy to explore. The predominant varieties of grape in Campania are native to the area: Aglianico, Greco, Fiano, Coda di Volpe, Piedirosso (or Per'e Palummo), Asprinio, Biancolella and Forastera, which produce a vast range of whites and reds, all of great character.

*Village of Ravello with terraced vineyards*

## The terroir

Campania boasts 4 DOCG and 14 DOC zones. The long-standing Taurasi DOCG was joined by Fiano di Avellino and Greco di Tufo and in 2011 by Aglianico del Taburno.

Three DOCGs are situated in the province of **Avellino**. **Taurasi** is a great red wine made from Aglianico grapes that ages well. It is full-bodied, warm and pleasingly tannic. **Fiano di Avellino** is a white wine produced from the grape of the same name, with intense fruity and flowery scents and unique character, just like the **Greco di Tufo**. In addition to its grapes of the same name, this latter wine requires a certain though reduced percentage of Coda di Volpe. The versions produced are brut and extra brut classical method sparkling wines.

Whereas the above three vines are the most common in the province of Avellino, around Benevento the most representative varieties are **Aglianico**, **Piedirosso**, **Sciascinoso** and **Falanghina**.

In the **province of Caserta**, the white **Asprinio** grape is grown successfully. Its name comes from its characteristic acidity, which makes it ideal for use in sparkling wines, along with Falanghina, Aglianico, Piedirosso and Primitivo.

Around **Naples** there is a wider range of grape varieties cultivated, including Biancolella and Forastera, while in the province of **Salerno** there are excellent wines based on Moscato Bianco and Barbera in addition to traditional cultivars.

## Itineraries

*Locations with a winery are indicated by the symbol ♀; for the addresses of the wineries, see p. 392.*

### 1. THE PROVINCE OF AVELLINO

A wine zone of great depth and variety, in Avellino wines are produced under the appellations **Taurasi DOCG**, **Fiano di Avellino DOCG**, **Greco di Tufo DOCG** and **Irpinia DOC**. Irpinia produces a broad range of wines from Greco, Fiano, Aglianico, Falanghina, Piedirosso, Sciascinoso and Coda di Volpe grapes.

### Avellino ♀

Avellino is the chief city in Irpinia, a green and mountainous area on the eastern border of Campania. The city was founded in ancient times but was heavily damaged by bombing raids in 1943 and the dreadful earthquake of 1980, of which this area still shows the wounds. It stands in the green basin of the river Sabato and is overlooked by the Sanctuary of Montevergine. Between 1589 and 1844 it was a feud of the Caracciolo family, who encouraged strong architectural development under the direction of Cosimo Fanzago, the leading figure in Neapolitan Baroque.

Traces of the medieval and Baroque city remain between Piazza Amendola and Piazza Castello. Palazzo Caracciolo, the 18th-c. residence of the princely family, faces onto the modern Piazza della Libertà.

Designed in Baroque style by Cosimo Fanzago, **Piazza Amendola** is the setting for some of Avellino's most important monuments: the 17th-c. clock tower, the Customs Palace founded in the Middle Ages but remodelled by Fanzago, the obelisk dedicated to Charles II Bourbon, and several fine town-houses that belonged to the nobility.

A small street adjacent to the tower leads to underground passages built by the Lombards that connect the old town to the ancient castle, now in ruins.

On Corso Umberto I you can admire Fanzago's Bellerofonte Fountain and the Church of Santa Maria di Costantinopoli. The **Duomo** was founded in the 12th c. and was where Roger II was invested with the Kingdom of Sicily. The bell tower was constructed using materials from Roman buildings. The duomo holds a tabernacle by Giovanni da Nola and a fine wooden choir. The crypt retains elements of the original ancient building.

### Sanctuary of Montevergine★

*To reach the sanctuary from Mercogliano, either take the panoramic road by car (14 km) or the funicular railway. For information on visits ✆ 0825 72 924, www.santuariodimontevergine.com.*

---

### DOCG

Aglianico del Taburno
Fiano di Avellino
Greco di Tufo
Taurasi

### DOC

Aversa
Campi Flegrei
Capri
Castel San Lorenzo
Cilento
Costa d'Amalfi
Falanghina del Sannio
Falerno del Massico
Galluccio
Irpinia
Ischia
Penisola Sorrentina
Sannio
Vesuvio

---

## PRINCIPAL VARIETIES CULTIVATED

### WHITE GRAPES

Asprinio Bianco
Bellone
Biancolella
Bombino Bianco
Chardonnay
Coda di Volpe
Falanghina
Fiano
Forastera
Greco
Guarnaccia
Malvasia Bianca di Candia
Montonico Bianco
Moscato Bianco

Pinot Bianco
Riesling
Riesling Italico
San Lunardo
Sylvaner Verde
Traminer Aromatico
Trebbiano Toscano
Veltliner
Verdeca

### GREY GRAPES

Pinot Grigio

### BLACK GRAPES

Aleatico
Aglianico
Barbera
Cabernet Franc
Cabernet Sauvignon
Greco Nero
Lambrusco Maestri
Ciliegiolo
Malvasia
Merlot
Montepulciano
Pinot Nero
Piedirosso
Primitivo
Sciascinoso
Sangiovese
Uva di Troia

## 90 terrible seconds…

were all that it took to rob thousands of people of their lives and devastate Irpinia and Basilicata. At 7.34pm on 23 November 1980 a single tremor measuring 6.8 on the Richter scale killed 3000 people and destroyed the municipalities of Sant'Angelo dei Lombardi, Lioni, Torella dei Lombardi, Conza della Campania and Teora, in addition to razing entire parts of Avellino to the ground.

The abbey was founded in the 12th c. by Guglielmo da Vercelli, the patron saint of Irpinia. It is a place of pilgrimage and stands in a setting of beech and chestnut trees in a **spectacular site★★** at an altitude of 1270 m above the Avellino plain. The abbey buildings were renovated in the 17th and 20th c. Of its many important artworks, the old church, which is a 17th-c. reconstruction of the medieval church, contains a magnificent Baroque high altar and a 13th-c. baldachin in cosmatesque style. The new church was consecrated in 1961 and holds the venerated *Black Madonna of Montevergine*, a panel in Byzantine style dating from the late 14th c.

## Irpinia

*Itinerary of 120 km to the east of Avellino.*

This green, mountainous and well-watered zone is where three DOCG zones are situated. The area offers plenty of opportunities for excursions in the countryside and partly falls within the boundaries of the **Picentini Regional Park**. This is a vast forest that straddles the provinces of Avellino and Salerno and is where South Italy's largest reservoir of drinking water (the Serino Channel) is located.

Leaving eastwards from Avellino, make a stop at **Atripalda** 🍷, the city of Abellinum founded by Sulla in 80 BC. The Church of Sant'Ippolisto contains Roman and medieval remains and the crypt in which the Avellinese martyrs, persecuted by Diocletian, are buried. Next, drive through **Sorbo Serpico** 🍷, **Montemarano** 🍷, Castelfranci and Nusco, then turn right onto the S 368 to reach **Bagnoli Irpino**, a pleasant mountain town (654 m) set among walnut, chestnut and beech trees, where there is an admirable parish church. From here a popular excursion is to visit Lake Laceno. Return to the S 7 and before Lioni take a left to Sant'Angelo dei Lombardi, one of the villages most seriously damaged by the 1980 earthquake. Along the way you come to the **Abbey of San Guglielmo al Goleto★**, which, like Montevergine, was founded by Guglielmo da Vercelli in the 12th c. The Febbronia Tower is a notable Romanesque construction that made use of low reliefs taken from a Roman mausoleum. The heart of the complex is formed by the two superposed medieval churches that mark the passage from Romanesque art (in the lower church) to Gothic (upper). The upper church is also known as the **Chapel of San Luca** as it was built to hold the relics of St Luke. The abbey is the site of the remains of the church built by Domenico Vaccaro in the 18th c. *For information on visits ✆ 0827 24 432, www.goleto.it.*

Return to Avellino through the wine zone that passes through the municipalities of Gesualdo, Mirabella Eclano, **Sant'Angelo all'Esca** 🍷, **Taurasi** 🍷, Lapio and Montefalcione. Taurasi lends its name to the eponymous DOCG.

If you leave Avellino northwards through Montefredane, you come to **Prata di Principato Ultra**. In the modern Church dell'Annunziata, just outside the town, there are traces of the original church, one of the most ancient monuments in Irpinia (6th c.), and the remains of the early Christian catacombs (3rd-4th c.) to the left of the church.

The surrounding zone has several other winemaking towns, including Altavilla Irpina, Tufo and **Montefusco** 🍷.

## 2. THE PROVINCE OF BENEVENTO

The province of Benevento is the home of **Sannio** and **Falanghina del Sannio** DOC zones.

### Benevento★

Ancient Maleventum, which was renamed Beneventum by the Romans after they defeated Pyrrhus, still bears the marks of World War II, though a walk through the historic centre reveals an illustrious past. In August and September the city hosts the Benevento Città Spettacolo, a series of shows and cultural events in various parts of the city.

Starting your tour in Piazza Duomo, the bulk of the cathedral was seriously damaged by Allied bombardments in 1943 (only the façade and bell tower, both built in the 13th c., remain of the original construction). Skirt the right side of the duomo (*Via Carlo Torre*) and walk to Via Port'Arsa. Built in the 2nd c. AD by Emperor Hadrian and enlarged by Caracalla, the **Roman theatre**★ is one of the biggest to have survived. In summer it is used for performances of opera, dance and theatre.

*Entrance in Via Port'Arsa, to the left of the Church of Santa Maria della Verità. Open 9-1 h before sunset, ℘ 0824 47 213.*

Return to Piazza Duomo and take **Corso Garibaldi**, onto which the city's most important buildings face. Don't miss the obelisk that stood in front of the Roman city's Temple of Isis (88 AD).

*From Corso Garibaldi turn left into Via Traiano.*

**Trajan's Arch**★★, called "Porta Aurea", was erected in 114 AD to commemorate the emperor who had made Benevento an obligatory point of passage on the way to Puglia. It is the best conserved triumphal arch in Italy. The reliefs carved in honour of the emperor are of high artistic value: they show scenes and engineering works representing peace on the side that faces the city, and scenes of war and rural life on the side that faces the countryside.

Erected in the 8th c. and rebuilt in the 17th, the interior of the Church of **Santa Sofia**★ has a surprising and daring hexagonal plan at its centre enclosed within a complex ten-sided structure. The apse contains fragments of 8th-c. frescoes. *Open 8-12 and 16-19 (16.30-20 in sum.), ℘ 0824 21 206, www.santasofiabenevento.it.* Next to the **cloister**★ (12th c.), with its arches in Moorish style, **Sannio Museum**★ has large archaeological collections and a set of 17th- and 18th-c. paintings by the Neapolitan school. *Open 9-19, closed Mon., ℘ 0824 77 47 63, www.museodelsannio.it.*

Constructed in the 14th c. over the ruins of a Lombard fort, the imposing bulk of **Benevento Castle** (Rocca dei Rettori) stands in Piazza IV Novembre, at the end of Corso Garibaldi.

## Sannio

*Itinerary of 70 km from Benevento to Guardia Sanframondi.*

Sannio is a region of hills, woods and villages that have succeeded in maintaining their beautiful medieval centres. Lying off the major tourist routes, this itinerary will introduce you to the authentic Cam-

## THE TERROIR

**Area**: 13,670.60 km$^2$, of which approximately 25,617 hectares are planted to vine

**Production 2019**: 1,406,349 hectolitres, of which 251,828 VQPRD

**Geography**: 34.5% mountainous, 51% hilly, 14.5% flat. The soil is calcareous and clayey, in part of volcanic origin. The climate is mild, Mediterranean on the coast and continental inland

## THE PROTECTION CONSORTIA

Consorzio Tutela Vini dei Campi Flegrei, Ischia e Capri – consorziocfic@gmail.com

Consorzio Tutela Vini d'Irpinia – ℘ 3420494288, www.consorziovinidirpinia.it

Samnium Consorzio Tutela Vini DOC e IGT di Benevento – ℘ 0824 18 15 763, www.sanniodop.it

## WINE AND FOOD ROUTES

Strade del Vino Campi Flegrei – (Coldiretti) 081 563 60 60, consorziocfic@gmail.com

Strade dei Vini e dei Sapori d'Irpinia – ℘ 348 74 66 963

Strade del Vino in Terra di Lavoro – ℘ 0823 925313

Strada dei Vini e dei Prodotti Tipici Terre dei Sanniti – ℘ 0824 86 58 65

Strada dei Vini e dei Sapori dell'Isola d'Ischia – www.stradadelvino.ischia.it, stradadelvino@ischia.it

pania. Part of this region falls within the **Matese Regional Park**, which extends across parts of the provinces of Caserta and Benevento. *For information on the park and its activities, ℘ 0823 78 69 42, www.parcoregionaledelmatese.it.*

Leave Benevento in a north-easterly direction and pass **Torrecuso** 🍷, Paupisi, **Solopaca**, the spa town of **Telese** (near to which lie the ruins of the Roman *colonia* of Telesia), and **Castelvenere** 🍷. You then come to **Cerreto Sannita**, celebrated for its handmade ceramics and fabrics; the centre of the town was rebuilt in the 17th c. after a ruinous earthquake. Not far away the houses of **Cusano Mutri** cling to the sides of Monte Mutria. The panoramic road climbs to the pass of Santa Crocella (1219 m), which marks the border between Campania and Molise.

Return to Cerreto Sannita and head for **Guardia Sanframondi** 🍷, a characteristic town overlooking the valley. The Church dell'Annunziata has a lovely Baroque interior with a gilded lacunar ceiling and a statue of Our Lady of the Assumption wearing 18th-c. dress.

### The Caudina Valley

*45 km from Benevento to Sant'Agata de' Goti.*

Leave Benevento south-west on the SS 7 Via Appia that runs alongside the Caudina valley. The municipalities of **Arpaia** and **Forchia** were the setting for the battle in which the Romans were humiliated by the Samnites in 321 BC and forced to sign a dishonourable peace treaty.

Pass through the hillside town of **Montesarchio**, with its 15th-c. castle, and reach **Sant'Agata de' Goti** 🍷. Standing on a rocky spur over the river Isclero, the town (first Samnite, then Roman) was named after the presence of the Goths here in the 6th c. AD. Among the town's interesting buildings are the Church dell'Annunziata (13th c.), which contains a remarkable 15th-c. *Last Judgement* and frescoes in the apse. Other interesting religious buildings line the central Via Roma.

## 3. THE PROVINCE OF CASERTA

The province of Caserta produces some interesting wines in its three DOC zones: **Galluccio**, **Falerno del Massico** and, shared with municipalities in the province of Naples, **Asprinio di Aversa**. The wines are in white and sparkling versions and the grapes used are from vines that "climb" up the poplar trees to a height of 15 m, which is a characteristic form of cultivation in the zone.

### Terra di Lavoro

*Itinerary of 100 km from Caserta to the Garigliano plain.*

### Royal Palace of Caserta★★

*Via Douhet 22. Visits to the apartments 8.30-19.30, park and gardens 8.30-1 h before sunset, the English garden closes 1 h before the last entrance to the park, closed Tue., ℘ 0823 44 80 84, www.reggiadicaserta.beniculturali.it.*

In 1752 Charles VII of Naples ordered his architect Luigi Vanvitelli to design and

Majestic park of the Royal Palace of Caserta

build a new palace based on a rigorously geometric plan. Whereas the purity of the lines seems almost to anticipate Neoclassical style, the dramatic manner in which the spaces are distributed is still typically Rococo.

The building is a grandiose rectangular block (249x190 m) with four internal courtyards interconnected by a magnificent **vestibule★**. The façade seen by the arriving visitor has a columned avant-corps and a double row of windows over an ashlar base. The principal façade, which looks onto the garden, takes up the motif but enhances it with pilasters beside each window. The magnificent **main stairway★★**, Vanvitelli's masterpiece, leads to the Palatine Chapel and the royal apartments furnished in Neoclassical style. The Eighteenth-Century Apartment is particularly interesting for its vaults frescoed with the Four Seasons and superb canvases of port views. The elegant Queen's Apartment is furnished in frivolous *rocaille* taste: two of the most unusual pieces are the lamp decorated with small tomatoes and the cage-clock containing a stuffed bird. A fine 18th-c. **Neapolitan manger scene★** can be seen in the Elliptical Room. The elegant Court theatre, completed in 1769, is an exact scaled down version of the San Carlo in Naples.

The lovely rooms of the 18th-c. apartments contain a permanent exhibition of contemporary art called **Terrae Motus**, containing installations executed after the earthquake of 1980.

**The Park** – the enormous park represents the ideal of the Baroque garden, in which infinite space is arranged around a central axis (the canal).

The fountains and fishponds are fed by the Caroline Aqueduct, a colossal engineering work 40 km long built by Vanvitelli. It carries the water across 5 mountains and 3 valleys. The most notable sculptural group with a mythological theme is Diana and Actaeon at the foot of the **Great Cascade★★** (78 m high), in which Actaeon (as a deer) is assailed by Diana's hunting dogs.

To the right of the cascade is the picturesque **English garden★★** created for Maria Carolina of Austria.

*Leave Caserta northwards on the SS 87 to Santo Iorio.*

## Basilica of Sant'Angelo in Formis★★

*Open 9-12.30 and 15-18 (Sat.-Sun. 9-17), ℘ 0823 96 08 17.* The basilica is one of the most beautiful medieval constructions in Campania. Built in the 11th c. for Desiderio, abbot of Montecassino, the basilica has a fairly basic plan but one of the richest pictorial cycles of Romanesque painting. The interior is entirely covered with frescoes by the local school in which the clear Byzantinizing influence, which was given by the Greek painters who worked at Montecassino, is moderated by the well-defined use of colour and dynamism typical of the local artistic tradition. In the apse, where Desiderio is seen offering the church to God, the abbot's square halo signifies that at the moment the fresco was painted he was still alive.

## Santa Maria Capua Vetere

This is the famous Roman city of Capua, to which Hannibal's army withdrew and where they supposedly lived in such luxury that they lost their chance to defeat the Romans. Famous for its bronze vases and black-paint ceramics, Capua was one of the most opulent cities in the Roman empire. After the devastation wrought by the Saracens in the 9th c., its inhabitants moved to a bend on the river Volturno where they founded the modern Capua. The **amphitheatre★** (restored in the 2nd c. AD) is the largest in the Roman world after the Colosseum and was the home of the gladiatorial school where the revolt led by Spartacus broke out in 73 BC. The **Gladiators Museum** is sited near the amphitheatre. *Open 9-1 h before sunset, closed Mon., ℘ 0823 84 42 06 / 18 31 093.*

The **Mithraeum** (2nd c. AD) is an underground rectangular room decorated with a rare **fresco★** of the Persian god Mitra sacrificing a bull.

## Capua

The lovely Piazza dei Giudici is the setting for the Baroque Church of Sant'Eligio, a Gothic arch crowned by a loggia, and the 14th-c. Municipal Palace. The nearby Church dell'Annunziata (16th c.) has a lovely dome raised on a drum and, inside, an exceptionally well crafted wooden choir and ceilings. Constructed in the 9th c. but several times destroyed and rebuilt, the **Duomo** has a beautiful bell tower that incorporates ancient fragments at the base. The atrium contains some lovely Corinthian columns (3rd c.), while inside the church, the 13th-c. paschal candelabrum, an *Assumption* by Francesco Solimena (1657-1747) and an 18th-c. sculpture of the *Dead Christ* in the crypt are all worth seeking out. *Open 8-11.30 and 17-20.*

An interesting set of churches founded by the Lombards stands to the north-east of the Duomo: San Giovanni a Corte, San Salvatore Maggiore a Corte, San Michele a Corte, and San Marcello.

*Continue on the S 7.*

## Sessa Aurunca

Founded in the 4th c. BC by the Aurunci people, the town has interesting buildings from the Middle Ages and Baroque period. The Romanesque **Duomo★** is a 12th-c. construction with a simply decorated pale stone façade featuring construction materials taken from Roman buildings. The sumptuously Baroque interior contrasts strongly with the plain columns. The flooring has traces of 12th-c. mosaics but the pride of the duomo is the ensemble formed by the pulpit and paschal candelabrum, which are lined with mosaics and adorned with tiny sculptures.

A panoramic road takes you through Roccamonfina to the Sanctuary of **Santa Maria dei Làttani**. This shrine was built in the Middle Ages to hold an 11th-c. statue of the Virgin that is supposedly endowed with the power to give women male children.

Further north is **Galluccio** ♟, a farming town on Garigliano plain.

Driving west from Sessa Aurunca and passing through **Cellole** ♟, you reach the Domitian Shoreline, a popular section of the Tyrrhenian coast named after the Roman Via Domitiana that ran from Rome to Pozzuoli.

## From Caserta to Sannio

*Itinerary of 40 km from Caserta to Castel Campagnano.*

**Caserta Vecchia★** (*north-east of Caserta*) offers the unusual sight of gracious alleyways running between walls of dark tufa. The impressive 12th-c. **cathedral** combines elements of Pugliese, Lombard and Sicilian Arab architecture, and inside has a very fine 13th-c. pulpit. *For information, ☏ 0823 37 13 18.*

Continue northwards. After Castel Morrone you climb to **Caiazzo** set in a landscape of woods and olive groves. The town's main street is lined with ancient houses and overlooked by a Lombard castle.

When you reach Ruviano, turn right towards **Castel Campagnano** ♟.

## 4. THE GULF OF NAPLES AND ISCHIA

The **Campi Flegrei DOC** zone lies in the municipalities of Procida, Pozzuoli, Basoli, Monte di Procida, **Quarto** ♟, Marano, Napoli and the island of Procida, and it produces the following wine types: white, red, Piedirosso (dry and passito) and Falanghina (still and sparkling). To the south of the city of Naples lie the designated zones of **Vesuvio** (whites, rosés, reds) and **Lacryma Christi del Vesuvio** (whites, natural sparkling, rosés, reds, liqueur wines). **Ischia** produces a range of prestigious wines: whites (still and sparkling), reds, Biancolella, Forastera and Piedirosso (dry and passito).

## Campi Flegrei★★

*Itinerary of 30 km from Pozzuoli to Arco Felice.*

The area that stretches along the Pozzuoli Gulf from Capo Posillipo to Cumae was given the name Campi Flegrei (Phlegraean Fields, "burning fields") in antiquity to describe the volcanic activity here. Hot water springs, fumaroles, gases and sulphurous vapours gush up from underground, and the ancient volcanic craters (about 20) are today filled with water. The ground is affected by bradyseism (the gradual rising and falling of part of the Earth's surface). Roman patricians and emperors greatly appreciated the beauty of this area and there are many archaeological remains of their villas.

## Pozzuoli★★

The fall of the Roman empire in 476 and the repeated bradyseismic phenomena that affect the city were the main reasons for its decline, which became an easy target for Saracen and barbarian raids. The city began to re-establish itself from the 13th c., but this was interrupted by volcanic activity in 1538 that

*Sulphurous Campi Flegrei*

caused the creation of the Monte Nuovo. Development was restarted under the Spanish viceroy Pedro of Toledo. The name Pozzuoli gave rise to the word pozzolana, signifying siliceous rock of eruptive origin that is used to make several types of cement. **Rione Terra**, the acropolis of the Greek city inhabited for more than 2000 years, was abandoned during the 1970s owing to bradyseism. A project is currently underway to turn it into a sort of open-air museum. Currently there is an underground archaeological route that follows the course of the ancient decumanus (east-west street) and cardus (north-south) with the remains of shops, taverns and storerooms. *Open Sat.- Sun. and public hols. only on reservation (9-12 and 13.30-16.30), ℘ 081 19 93 62 86 or 081 19 93 62 87, www.comune.pozzuoli.na.it.*

This is the site of the **Temple of Augustus★**, which dates from the first years of the empire and was transformed into a church in the 11th c. In 1964 a fire revealed the Roman structure of the building: a magnificent marble colonnade topped by a large trabeation.

**Flavian amphitheatre★★** – *Via. Terracciano 75. Open 9-1 h before sunset, closed Tue., ℘ 081 52 66 007.* Begun during the reign of Nero and completed by Vespasian (69-79 AD), this is the third largest amphitheatre in the Roman world after those of Rome and Capua, and was able to seat 40,000 spectators. Built of brick and stone, it was the centre of social life in Puteoli. The galleries on the outside of the building were filled with places

of worship and professional associations. The amphitheatre is in excellent state: note in particular the enclosures, entrances and **underground★★** corridors and rooms, which illustrate how the amphitheatre functioned "behind the scenes".

**Macellum (Temple of Serapis)★** – *Set slightly back on Via Roma. For information on visits check www.pafleg.it.* Situated close to the sea, the ancient *macellum* (food market) was a large porticoed area lined by shops. The main entrance was connected to the wharfs of the port where the goods were unloaded. An apse in the far wall contained the statue of the god Serapis (*now in Naples Archaeological Museum*) who was the protector of tradesmen. When the statue was found in the 18th c., it was believed the area was a religious area dedicated to the god. Corrosion of the lower 5.7 m of the columns supporting the central pavilion shows that in certain eras the *macellum* was below sea level, a clear example of bradyseism.

### Solfatara Volcano★★

*Via Solfatara 161. Open 8.30-19 (16.30 Nov.-Mar.), ℘ 081 52 62 341, www.solfatara.it.* The *Sulpha Terra* ("land of sulphur") is the vast crater of an ancient volcano formed 4000 years ago. Though it is now extinct, volcanic phenomena continue to exist inside it, such as miniature volcanoes that spew mud, jets of boiling sand, and fumaroles of sulphur dioxide, leaving a strong smell and yellowish deposits. The soil is warm on the surface and gives a hollow sound when stamped on.

The patches of Mediterranean flora (heather, arbutus and myrtle) contrast strongly with the harshness of the landscape. From the Roman era to the 19th c. the sulphurous gases were used for therapeutic purposes and were certainly at the origin of less polite names associated with Pozzuoli. The beauty of this extraordinary place is such that the ancient Greeks referred to it as the entrance to the Underworld, and called it the "Forum of Hephaestus", the god of fire.

*Continue along the coast.*

## Lake Lucrino and Monte Nuovo

In the Roman age Lake Lucrino was larger and separated from the sea by a string of dunes. Famous since antiquity as a place of leisure and worldly delights, the lake was used to farm oysters and fish for sea bass, and its banks were lined with luxurious villas owned by such leading figures as Sulla and Cicero. On the inland side of the lake stands **Monte Nuovo** (130 m), Europe's youngest volcano, which was formed on 29-30 September 1538. This geological event reduced the size of Lake Lucrino, isolated Lake Averno from the sea, and altered the original morphology of this stretch of coastline.

Before reaching Baia, you will see the remains of **Nero's Stoves**, an ancient spa that exploited the steam from a fumarole.

## Baia★

Legend says that the town was founded in honour of Baios, the helmsman on Ulysses' ship, who died and was buried here (two sculptures of Baios and Ulysses were found in 1969 at Punta Epitaffio and are now in Baia Castle archaeological museum (*via Castello 39, open 9-14, closed Mon.* ☏ *081 52 33 797, www.pafleg.it*). In the Roman age, Baia (the ancient port of Cumae) was a fashionable seaside resort and spa equipped with the largest hydrotherapy facilities in the empire. Huge villas were built by emperors and patricians but have disappeared under the sea owing to bradyseism. Between the 1st and 3rd c. emperors competed to endow the imperial palace complex with the most impressive embellishments and enlargements.

**Archaeological Park★★** – *Via Sella di Baia 22. Open 9-1 h before sunset, closed Mon.,* ☏ *081 86 87 592.* The most important remains of the ancient imperial site are the baths, which date to different periods. Ranged across the hill overlooking the sea are the Baths of Venus, Sosandra and Mercury. The dome of the latter is more than 20 m in diameter and still standing. The archaeological zone also includes the remains of the imperial palace and a late Republican villa.

**Underwater Park of Baia★** – *Dives, snorkelling and glass-bottom boat rides are organised. For information* ☏ *081 52 32 739, www.parcoarcheologicosommersodibaia.it.* To explore Baia's extraordinary archaeological heritage, which extends more than 400 m into the sea, an underwater park has been created. The site is occupied by the ancient Lacus Baianus (Lake Baianus), baths, the villa and porticoed gardens that belonged to Lucius Calpurnius Piso, a villa with a porch and mosaic flooring, and the imperial nymphaeum close to Punta Epitaffio on the north side of the bay.

## Bacoli

The **Cento Camerelle★** (*Via Cento Camerelle in the upper part of the town, to the right of the church*) is a gigantic water tank that belonged to a private villa. It is split on two levels: the upper floor (1st c. AD) is a huge structure in four sections supported by immense arches; the lower level is older and includes tunnels that open out directly over the sea. The famous **Piscina Mirabilis★** (*entrance on Via Ambrogio Greco, from the left of the church take Via Piscina Mirabile and straight on*) is another immense cistern which stored water carried by aqueduct from the Serinus springs. The water was used to supply the Roman fleet that anchored in the port of Misenum. The immense cistern measures 70 m long, by 25 wide and 15 deep. It is divided into 5 sections and has vaults supported by 48 pillars. The effects of the light are very impressive. *Visits to Cento Camerelle and Piscina Mirabilis are open only on reservation, visit www.pafleg.it or contact pa-fleg.comunicazione@beniculturali.it.*

## Miseno

Miseno is the name of a lake, a port, a village, a promontory and a cape. To the ancients, **Lake Misenum** was on a par with the river Styx, over which the ferry-man Charon rowed the souls of the dead. Under Emperor Augustus Misenum was connected by a canal to the port of Misenum, which was used as a base by the Roman fleet and functioned as the principal military port throughout the imperial age. The modern village lies below Monte Miseno, at the feet of which the ancient hero Misenus, the trumpeter of Aeneas, is said to have been buried. The slopes of the mount were lined with magnificent villas, including the one in which Emperor Tiberius was suffocated to death in 37 AD. A detour up **Monte di Procida** offers superb **views** over the promontory, the isle of Procida and Ischia in the background.

## Lake Fusaro

A small island at the centre of the lagoon is where Carlo Vanvitelli built an elegant **hunting lodge** in 1782 for Ferdinand IV Bourbon. Its Rococo forms seem to emerge directly from the water. *For information ℘ 379 10 30 885, www. prolococittadibacoli.it.*

On one side of the lake Monte Cuma (80 m) interrupts the flatness of the coastline.

## Cuma★★

Founded in 730 BC in an excellent natural position on the sea, but protected by Monte Grillo, Cumae developed into an important cultural and commercial centre whose influence spread around all of the Gulf of Naples. Despite alternating fortunes, the importance of the city was maintained during the Roman period even though a certain decline set in that favoured the rise of Pozzuoli. Contested by the Byzantines and Lombards, the city was devastated by the Saracens in 915 and became a hide-out for marauders. It became so dangerous that in 1207 the duchy of Naples decided to destroy the city entirely.

**Excavations at Cumae★★** – *Via Acropoli 1, open 9-1 h before sunset, ℘ 081 80 40 430, www.pafleg.it.* The ruins of the ancient city lie in an area not far from the sea. The acropolis was built on a hill of lava and tufa of volcanic origin, set in an isolated spot and preceded by an avenue lined with laurels. On the left was the famous **Sibyl's Grotto★**, one of the most venerated places in the ancient world. According to Virgil this was where the priestess of Apollo, who guided Aeneas on his descent into the Underworld, transcribed the oracles of the god into obscure hexameters on palm leaves. The long gallery (100 m) was created in two stages between the 4th c. BC and the Augustan age and was in reality a service portico with a defensive function for the port below. It was used during the Paleochristian era as a burial place.

Climb up to the Sacred Way to visit a lookout point that gives a lovely **view★** of the sea, then continue to the vestiges of the Temple of Apollo that was later turned into a Christian church. The Temple of Jove, which stood further on, was transformed in the same way.

The lower section of ancient Cumae contained the remains of an amphitheatre, a Capitoline temple and the city baths.

## Arco Felice★

If you take the small road in the direction of Naples you can admire this arch built over the ancient Via Domitiana.

## Lake Avernus★

*The lake lies below the road from Cumae to Naples, approximately 1 km after Arco Felice. A visit at dusk is particularly atmospheric.* Dark and silent, Lake Avernus lies in a volcanic crater whose sides are covered with woodland. Its sense of mystery was even greater in antiquity as the birds that flew over it were swallowed up, asphyxiated by the gases it exudes. This fact prompted its Greek name, *aornos* ("without birds"). The Romans considered it one of the entrances to the World of the Dead (Avernus), which Aeneas took when guided by the Cumaean Sibyl. An underground military gallery 1 km long, known as **Cocceius' Grotto** after its Roman builder, connected Cumae to Lake Avernus and, via Lake Lucrinus, to the Portus Julius on the Gulf of Pozzuoli.

## Vesuvius★★★

With Etna, Vesuvius is one of the few volcanoes still active in Europe, even though there have been no eruptions since 1944. It has two summits: to the north Monte Somma (1132 m), and to the south Vesuvius itself (1227 m). With time the volcanic materials that were hurled down its lower slopes have turned into very fertile soil now used to grow fruit and grapes: this is the region where **Lacryma Christi** ("Tears

*Vesuvius and the ruins of Pompeii*

of Christ") is made. "God, recognising the Gulf of Naples as a strip of heaven taken by Lucifer, wept and there, where His divine tears fell, the Lacryma Christi vine sprang up". This ancient legend is referred to by Curzio Malaparte in his novel *The Skin*. The DOC zone covers 15 municipalities on the slopes of Vesuvius, where native cultivars such as Caprettone and Falanghina have always been grown.

**Vesuvius National Park** was established in 1995 and has been included by UNESCO in its network of Biosphere Reserves. The park covers 8480 hectares and its purpose is to protect a unique area that is home to a rich flora (more than 1000 plant species) and fauna (including a large range of butterflies and birds). The human element is also a facet to be developed, in particular the protection and conservation of traditional manual activities, such as leather-working, and the carving of coral and lava stone. *For more information: Ente Parco Nazionale del Vesuvio, Palazzo Mediceo, via Palazzo del Principe, Ottaviano, ℘ 081 86 53 911, www.parco nazionaledelvesuvio.it.*

The beauty of Vesuvius and its surroundings is such that emperors, kings and aristocrats of all levels have "defied" the mountain and built a hundred or so villas and gardens on its sides. And still today much less grand examples of unauthorised building take place along this stretch of coast, which unsurprisingly is referred to as **Miglio d'Oro** ("Golden Mile").

**Visit to the crater** – *You can reach the top on either the west slope, the easier climb, starting from Ercolano or Torre del Greco, or the more difficult south slope from Torre Annunziata and passing through Boscotrecase. A guide is obligatory if you wish to approach the rim of the crater, ℘ 081 23 95 653, www.parco nazionaledelvesuvio.it.* A road in good condition takes you through lava flows to a crossroads where you turn left (car park several km ahead). Leave the car and start climbing up an easy but very beautiful path through an oppressive landscape of ashes and lapillus. The **view★★★** from the top stretches across all of the Gulf of Naples, the islands, the Sorrentina peninsula to the south, and Capo Miseno and the Gulf of Gaeta to the north.

## Ischia★★★

Ischia is known as the Green Island because of its thick and abundant vegetation. It is the largest island in the Gulf of Naples and was the first settlement to be built by Greek colonists in this zone. The extraordinary light renders even more beautiful the island's different vistas: jagged coastlines and pine woods, multicoloured ports and cubical houses, slopes covered in olive trees and vines, and villages in which white houses have their stairs outdoors, are covered with gaily coloured climbing plants, and sometimes crowned by a dome. Created by an undersea volcanic eruption in the Tertiary era, Ischia's soil is mostly composed of lava, and its thermal waters have many different beneficial properties.

The narrow road that winds through the vineyards gives marvellous views over the coast and sea.

### Ischia★

The town is split into two sections: **Ischia Porto**, formed since the 18th c., and **Ischia Ponte**, which originated with the Angevin town that grew up around the castle. Most of the boats arriving from Naples berth in Ischia Porto. Corso Vittorio Colonna (just known as the **Corso** locally) is lined by bars, restaurants and shops, and connects the two parts of the town. The "Ponte" in question is the causeway built by the Spaniards to join the coast to the rocky island. The Corso is where you will find the 18th-c. Church of San Pietro, with its fine Baroque façade. Just in front of Ischia Ponte lies the lively Fishermen's Beach seen in hundreds of paintings and postcards. Ischia Ponte is the site of the Cathedral dell'Assunta, founded in the Middle Ages but rebuilt in the Baroque era. The bell tower was originally a guard-tower.

The elegant Spanish bridge connects Ischia Porto to the **Aragonese castle★★** built on the rocky islet. Its appearance as a fortified citadel dates back to the 15th c. Its walls enclose several churches. The Cathedral dell'Assunta built in the 14th c. was destroyed by the cannon fire from the English in 1809, though the crypt still retains traces of Giottoesque frescoes, and the 18th-c. Church dell'Immacolata was built to serve the Convent of Poor Clares next door. The abbesses were buried in a graveyard below the church. Higher up the hill stands the Church of San Pietro a Pantaniello and the Bourbon prison. There is an **Arms Museum** inside the castle. *Open 9-sunset,* ℘ *081 99 28 34, www. castelloaragonese.it.*

A lookout tower close to **Serrara Fontana** offers a splendid and perpendicular **view★★** down onto Sant'Angelo, with its beach and peninsula.

### Sant'Angelo★★

Sant'Angelo is the most exclusive town on the island. Its houses step down the hillside to cluster at the bottom around the tiny port. Following the paths or taking water taxis, you can reach some of the island's most beautiful beaches, like **Maronti Beach★**, which is about 2 km long and has interesting thermal phenomena, and the **Sorgeto**, where the water is heated by underwater thermal springs. The island's oldest thermal facilities, **Cavascura Baths**, lie at the end of Maronti Beach. The spring rises about 300 m from the beach and you can find it by following a hot rivulet that opens in the tufa walls of the hill. *Can be reached via water taxi. Open mid-Apr.- mid-Oct. For information* ℘ *081 99 92 42, www. cavascura.it/terme.*

Closed off at one end by the majestic Punta Imperatore, **Citara Beach★** is the site of the Poseidon Gardens, a thermal complex with hot water pools, flowers and statues.

### Forìo★ ⚲

This stretch of the coast was particularly exposed to attack by the Saracens, as the many lookout towers suggest. Piazza del

*Ischia Ponte*

Municipio at the centre of the town is a tropical garden overlooked by two churches. An attractive square is Piazza del Soccorso, lined by the church of the same name, which gives splendid views. The ancient Church of San Vito offers yet more wonderful views in the upper part of the town.

Even higher up you can visit the exotic **La Mortella Gardens★** in Villa Walton, a setting for classical music concerts. *Open Apr.-Oct. Tue., Thu., Sat. and Sun. 9-19 ℘ 081 98 62 20, www.lamortella.org.*

## Lacco Ameno★

This was the site of the first Greek settlement on Ischia. The acropolis stands on the promontory of Monte Vico and the necropolis lies in the bay of San Montano, while the zone where the ceramic vases were made, for which the island was famous, has been built over by the modern town. During the early Christian era a community developed around the relics of St Restituta. The church dedicated to this saint has resulted from the rebuilding of two churches of different ages, beneath which the remains of a Paleochristian basilica (4th-5th c.) and a necropolis were found. The ruins of the buildings where the vases were fired have also been discovered and now hold a very pleasant little archaeological museum. *Archaeological area of Santa Restituta, Piazza Santa Restituta, open 9.30-12.30 and 16-18 (Jun.-Aug. 17-19), closed Sun. afternoon, ℘ 081 98 01 61.*

Lacco Ameno is home to the famous Regina Isabella Spa that was frequented by the jet-set during the 1950s and 60s. Its symbol is a tufa rock that erupted from Monte Epomeo and is commonly known as "the mushroom".

The 18th-c. **Villa Arbusto** (the summer residence of Angelo Rizzoli) contains an interesting archaeological museum displaying finds from Ischia's ancient settlements, including the famous **Nestor's Cup★**. One part of the residence is devoted to the years when Angelo Rizzoli made Ischia one of the favourite destinations of the international in-crowd. *Corso Rizzoli 210 (Open Apr-Oct. 9-19, Nov.-Mar. 9-17, closed 25 Dec., ℘ 081 99 61 03, ℘ 081 33 30 288, www.pithecusae.it).*

The tour of the island concludes at **Casamicciola Terme**, an important spa facility, that was destroyed by the 1883 earthquake but has since been rebuilt. Villa Ibsen stands a little outside the town, and was where the playwright wrote *Peer Gynt*.

# 5. THE SORRENTO PENINSULA AND AMALFI COAST

Split between the provinces of Napoli and Salerno, this area includes the **Penisola Sorrentina**, **Capri** and **Costa d'Amalfi** DOC zones (with Furore, Ravello and Tramonti subzones). The red and white wines of Capri, produced in limited quantities, are very ancient and have been appreciated since the times of Tiberius. They are obtained from vinification of local grapes, such as Falanghina, Greco and Biancolella for the white, and Piedirosso for the red.

## The Sorrento peninsula★★

*Itinerary of 30 km from Vico Equense to the Hills of San Pietro.*

In a distance of just 30 km you will discover lush citrus orchards, tiny coves, steep cliffs and Saracen towers that gaze unceasingly out at the horizon. The beauty of art and nature is echoed by the stirring local cuisine, which celebrates the vitality of Mediterranean nature. The peninsula formed by the Monti Lattari separates the gulfs of Naples and Salerno: the northern coast, which runs from Sorrento to Castellammare di Stabia, is gentler, while its northern equivalent is more eroded and jagged, and less suited to human habitation.

### Vico Equense★

This little coastal resort stands in a picturesque position on a rocky promontory. It has a pretty **historic centre★**, with a rare example of Gothic architecture in its cathedral. An Angevin castle faces out to sea surrounded by beautiful grounds.

### Sorrento★★

Overlooking a wide and very lovely bay, Sorrento has been a famous resort since antiquity, its villas and palaces hidden among wonderfully blooming gardens. The town and surrounding countryside is dotted with groves of oranges and lemons (small and thin-skinned), their savours and scents important ingredients in the local pas-

*Positano and a view of the Amalfi coastline*

try shops. Via San Cesareo (the ancient Roman decumanus) leads to the Sedile Dominova, the town hall in the Angevin epoch: it has a loggia crowned with a dome and is decorated with 17th-c. majolicas and frescoes.

Take Via San Giuliani to reach the Baroque Church of San Francesco: it is topped by a bulb-shaped bell tower and has an enchanting 13th-c. **cloister★** in which the capitals decorated with plant motifs support crossed arches in Sicilian-Arab style.

The nearby gardens in Villa Comunale provide a magnificent **view★** of the Gulf of Naples.

*Leave Sorrento west on the S 145 and turn right onto the road for Massa Lubrense.* This little winding road takes you around the peninsula, and allows you to admire the hills lined with olive, orange and lemon trees, and vines that snake up trellises featuring strange, house-like stacks of straw mats that are used to protect the plants from the winter mists.

**Massa Lubrense** is a small town founded in ancient times that was at one time the home of the sirens of Ulysses. Today it is a seaside resort, and has a delightful fishing port at Marina della Lobra. After **Sant'Agata sui Due Golfi**, built on a crest over the gulfs of Naples and Salerno, the steep descent to Colli di San Pietro is spectacular.

From here you can return to Sorrento on the S 163, admiring the **views★★** over the Gulf of Naples, or continue towards Positano.

## The Amalfi coast★★★

*Itinerary of 50 km from Positano to Vietri sul Mare.*

Adorned with cypresses, citrus groves, vineyards, almond trees and bougainvilleas, the natural beauty of one of the world's most famous coastlines is displayed at every turn along an extraordinary panoramic road. The history of this area includes its period as a successful marine republic struggling for supremacy of the seas against the Republic of Venice, and the myth of the Dolce Vita in the 1950s and 60s.

### Positano★★

Positano is an ancient sailors' village, whose Moorish, cubic white houses get lost among the colours of the gardens and terraces that descend to the sea. Loved by artists and intellectuals (Picasso, Cocteau, Steinbeck and Moravia; and Nureyev bought a house on an island in the Li Galli archipelago), Positano is one of the most popular towns on the Amalfi coast. It was the home of Moda Positano in the 1950s, a clothes fashion typified by bright colours and light materials. Equally famous are its sandals, which were a fashion staple of the beautiful people.

A Black Madonna can be seen in the Church of Santa Maria Assunta in Piazza Flavio Gioia. Built in the 13th c. and remodelled in Baroque, the church is topped by a tiled dome.

**Vettica Maggiore** is an elegant tourist resort with houses spilling down its

© Agustavop/iStock

slopes. The church square offers a fine **view**★★ of the coast and sea.

Moorish in appearance and scattered across the hillside, **Praiano**★ hides the lovely **Marina di Praia**★, a tiny beach surrounded by houses and fishing boats. You can reach the port down a path that passes in front of the Asciola Tower built at the time of the Saracen raids.

## Furore Gorge★★ ♀

The ancient *Terra Furoris*, where the Romans hid out when fleeing from the barbarians, is the largest ravine in the coastline. Its name comes from the deep, dark cut in the steeply falling cliffs and the violence of the sea on days of rough weather. Despite the natural difficulties of the site, a fishing village has been created at the mouth of a torrent, houses cling to the slopes, and brightly coloured boats are drawn up out of the water. When the actress Anna Magnani came here with Roberto Rossellini in 1948 to film *L'Amore*, she wanted to buy a fisherman's house. To explore the village, take the path down one side of the gorge. In addition to the standard sights, you can see the **Muri d'autore**, outdoor paintings and sculptures by contemporary artists that reflect on the history of the local area.

## Grotta dello Smeraldo (Emerald Grotto)★★

*Reached via a lift from the road, 9.30-16, closed public hols., ℘ 089 87 11 07, www. amalfitouristoffice.it.* The water in this sea grotto is of an extraordinary transparency. It is illuminated by reflected sunlight that confers an astonishing and dazzling emerald colour upon it. The bottom of the grotto, which seems very close despite being 10 m deep, has not always been covered by the sea, as is shown by the stalagmites that emerge from the water. The fact that the sea now enters the grotto is due to bradyseism.

## Amalfi★★

The tall white houses of Amalfi are piled high on the slopes of a deep ravine looking onto an intensely blue sea, where they enjoy a very mild climate. Starting from Piazza Duomo, the picturesque **historic centre**, featuring flower-lined balconies and niches, is formed by Via Genova, Via Capuano (its continuation) and **Via dei Mercanti**★ (parallel on the right). The Moorish town plan is composed of alleys, flights of steps and vaulted passageways that open into small squares with a fountain at their centre.

**Duomo of Sant'Andrea**★ – founded in the 9th c., enlarged in the 10th-13th c., and several times remodelled with a clear oriental influence. The 19th-c. façade stands at the top of a wide flight of steps and replicates the forms and coloured geometric motifs of the original. The bell tower (12th-13th c.) on the left is decorated with majolica tiles. A wide atrium leads to a lovely **bronze door**★ (11th c.) that came from Constantinople. The Baroque interior contains two 12th-c. ambons decorated with mosaics and two coeval candelabra. The **Cloister of**

*Amalfi coast from the gardens of Villa Rufolo, Ravello*

© Alfio Ferlito/Shutterstock

© bluejayphoto/iStock

*Atrani*

Paradise★★ built in 1268 blends the simplicity of Romanesque with the imaginative aspects of Arabian architecture. Several sarcophaguses are conserved in the galleries.

The Diocesan Museum can be visited in the **Basilica del Crocifisso**, the former 9th-c. cathedral. Once incorporated in the main building and transformed into Baroque style, it has been returned to its original Romanesque forms (note the women's gallery with single- and twin-light openings, and the chapels with traces of frescoes). The crypt holds the relics of St Andrew, which were brought from Constantinople to Amalfi in 1206. *Visits to the Cloister of Paradise and Diocesan Museum 9-19, in win. 10-13 and 14.30-16.30,* ℘ *089 87 13 24.*

**Valle dei Mulini★** – from Piazza Duomo take Via Genova and Via Capuano and pass between the rock walls of the Dragone torrent. Here you will see the old paper mills that were powered by the many small waterfalls. The history of Amalfi paper is recounted in the **Paper Museum** in one of the old mills. *Open 10-18.30, closed Sun. (Nov.-Jan. 10-16, closed Mon.),* ℘ *089 83 04 561, www. museodellacarta.it.*

## Atrani★

Atrani lies at the mouth of the Dragone valley. It is a gracious fishing village built in the local architecture. There are two ancient churches: Santa Maria Maddalena and San Salvatore de Bireto. Founded in the 10th c., the latter has rich decorations and a bronze door seemingly inspired by the one in Amalfi's cathedral. The name of the church comes from the fact that it was here that the doges of Amalfi were elected and "crowned" with the placing of the special beret (the *bireto*) on their head.

Fine views of the coast and village roofs are given from the road above the village. A splendid hairpin road snakes along the narrow Dragone valley to Ravello.

## Ravello★★★ 🍷

Suspended between the sky and the sea, Ravello has an unforgettable **setting★★★**. With its alleys, flights of steps and vaulted passageways that seem to cling to the hill slopes, the aristocratic composure of Ravello has been a magnet over the centuries to artists, musicians and writers.

**Villa Rufolo★★★** – *Piazza Duomo. Open 9-21 (18 in win.),* ℘ *089 85 76 21, www. villarufolo.it.* Built in the 13th c. by the Rufolo family mentioned by Boccaccio in the *Decameron*, the villa was used as a residence by many popes, Charles of Anjou and, in 1880, Richard Wagner, who was looking for inspiration for *Parsifal*. You arrive down a lovely tree-lined avenue, pass the Gothic tower and enter the Moorish courtyard with arcades in Sicilian-Norman style. This used to be a cloister in the 11th c. A massive tower overlooks the luxuriant gardens and terraced architecture of the elegant villa. The **panorama★★★** takes in the jagged mountains as far as Capo d'Orso, Maiori Bay and the Gulf of Salerno. In the foreground you see the domes of the Church dell'Annunziata. In summer the gardens are the setting for **concerts** against the extraordinary backdrop of the trees, flowers and sea. *For information, Società dei Concerti di Ravello,* 💶 *089 842 40 82, www.ravelloarts.org.*

**Duomo** – the duomo was founded in 1086 and transformed in the 18th c. It has a 13th-c. bell tower and a superb **bronze door★** from the 12th c. The two magnificent marble **ambons★★** in the nave were carved in the 12th-13th c. A small museum in the crypt holds fragments of sculptures, mosaics and reliquaries.

Via San Giovanni del Toro leads to a lovely small 11th-c. church. Note the splendid **belvedere★★** on the right.

**Villa Cimbrone★★** – *Open 9-sunset,* 💶 *089 85 74 59.* An enchanting **alleyway★** leads from Piazza Vescovado to the villa, passing beneath the Gothic porch of the Convent of San Francesco. Built in eclectic style at the start of the 19th c., with references to Villa Rufolo and the convent, Villa Cimbrone is a tribute to the history of Ravello. An elegant cloister and lovely room with ogival vaults lie on the left at the entrance to the villa. A large avenue passes through splendid gardens to the belvedere on the bust-lined terrace. The dizzying **view★★★** before you, of terraced fields, Maiori, Capo d'Orso and the Gulf of Salerno, is one you will not forget.

**Minori** is one of the few settlements on this stretch of the coast that existed in Roman times, as the remains of a magnificent **villa** from the 1st c. BC attests. It was equipped with its own thermal baths and pool. During the era of the Amalfi marine republic the town had an important dockyard.

Pass the ancient fishing village of **Maiori**, which was completely reconstructed after the terrible flood of 1954, and reach the church dug out of the rock called **Santa Maria de Olearia★**. This ancient abbey was founded in 973 and contains Byzantine frescoes from the 11th c., including *Three Figures with a Halo* in the crypt, and in the upper chapel, various scenes from the life of Jesus. *Open Wed. and Sat. 15.30-18.30, Sun. 10-13,* 💶 *089 87 74 52.*

Formed of bizarrely jagged rocks, **Capo d'Orso★** is an interesting lookout point on **Maiori Bay★**.

In ancient times **Cetara** was renowned for its *cetarie*, tunny pools in which the fish were bred and worked. A local speciality today is *colatura di alici*, a sauce made by pressing anchovies: an updated and "domesticated" version of the famous Roman *garum*.

### Vietri sul Mare

Stepped on terraces up the hillside at the end of the Amalfi Coast, Vietri sul Mare offers magnificent **views★★**. The town is celebrated for its traditional handmade **pottery** in an explosion of Mediterranean colours. In **Raito**, 3 km before Vietri, the tower in the grounds of Villa Guariglia has a small **museum of Vietrese pottery**. *Villa Guariglia - Via Nuova Raito, Raito di Vietri sul Mare, open Jun.-Sept. 9-18 (9.30-15 in win.), closed Mon.,* 💶 *089 21 18 35.*

### Abbey of the Santissima Trinità★

*5 km north of Vietri sul Mare. Open 8.30-12,* 💶 *089 46 39 22 or 347 19 46 957, www. badiadicava.it.* During the Middle Ages this 11th-c. Benedictine abbey was one of the most powerful in southern Italy. The church was rebuilt in the 18th c. in the original style, and boasts a lovely pulpit and paschal candelabrum. A visit here also takes in the rooms of the monastery, the 13th-c. cloister, the Lombard cemetery and a small museum.

## 6. CILENTO

Cilento (in the province of Salerno) is where Castel San Lorenzo and **Cilento DOC** zones are located. The local vines were introduced to the Greek colonies of Elea and Paestum by settlers and find the clayey-calcareous soil and climate ideally suited to their requirements. The vines produce few bunches but the wines are of excellent quality. The **Castel San Lorenzo**, which is produced in eight municipalities in the Calore valley, is vinified in white, rosé, red, Barbera (aged in oak barrels) and Moscato versions.

### Cilento and Vallo di Diano National Park★★

*Circular itinerary of 240 km starting from Agropoli.*

Lying a few kilometres away from the crowds on the Amalfi Coast is the start of the vast horizons and peaceful beaches of Cilento. In strident contrast with the other parts of Campania, this is a region of open spaces, isolated towns and empty roads; it is an invitation to discover hidden treasures. It encompasses Italy's largest Carthusian monastery, changing landscapes, fields of broom, beech forests, and deep ravines inhabited by numerous species of birds. The Cilento National Park is part of UNESCO's Biosphere Reserve and a Mediterranean park par excellence. For thousands of years the area has been a meeting place between nature and civilisation, and a junction of different traditions ranging from the Apennines to the great cultures of the Mediterranean.

The town of **Agropoli** 🍷 is dominated by a lovely castle. At its centre is the Church of Santa Maria di Costantinopoli dedicated to a holy image of the Virgin found in the sea, claimed to have originated in Constantinople. To the south of the town lies the lovely beach of Trentova, squeezed between the sea and the mountains.

Continue south to visit **Santa Maria di Castellabate**, the small town of San Marco and **Punta Licosa**, a nature park covered by Mediterranean scrub. Ernest Hemingway was a habitual visitor to **Acciaroli**.

As you follow the SS 267, you pass close to the ruins of **Velia★**, originally the Greek city of Elea founded in 535 BC. It was famous for its philosophy school, which flourished in the 6th and 5th c. BC.

*Continue on the SS 447.*

## Capo Palinuro★★

The name of the headland refers to Aeneas's mythical helmsman, who was lulled to sleep by the gods, fell into the sea, and was buried on the promontory. Boat excursions leave from the port of Palinuro to the **Blue Grotto★** and other grottoes along this coastline. In spring you can see the Palinuro primrose, the symbol of Cilento Park.

*Take the SS 562 north-east, then the SS 447 (passing through Poderia and heading for Policastro Busentino), then the SS 517 and SS 19.*

## Certosa di San Lorenzo in Padula★

*Open 9-19, closed Tue., ☎ 0975 77 745.* Certosa di San Lorenzo was founded in 1306 and is one of the largest architectural complexes in southern Italy. Given its size, construction of the monastery went on for several centuries and the current appearance of the buildings is mostly Baroque. A superb 14th-c. cedar portal in the Cloister della Foresteria leads to the magnificent Baroque church, where there are two 16th-c. choirs and the remarkable high altar lined with majolica tiles. The monks' cells ring the enormous cloister (104x149 m). If you walk down the portico on the left you come to a majestic and dramatic 18th-c. staircase inspired by the architecture of Vanvitelli.

*Continue on the SS 19 in a north-westerly direction.*

## Pertosa Grottoes★

*Only guided visits, ☎ 0975 39 70 37, www. grottedipertosa-auletta.it.* The natural amphitheatre in the Alburni mountains provides the setting for the grottoes, which you reach via a small lake formed by an underground river. Strung out for about 2.5 km, the grottoes were inhabited during the Neolithic period. They feature beautiful stalagmites and stalactites, mostly made of sodium carbonate. The most interesting cave is the "Sala delle Spugne" (Sponge Room).

Head for Polla and San Rufo, then take the SS 166 that climbs to the Passo della Sentinella (932 m) through an enchanting **landscape★** turned yellow by flowering broom in early spring. A brief detour takes you to **Roscigno Vecchia**, a ghost village abandoned in the early 20th c. due to repeated earth slips. Restoration projects in course allow you to appreciate the rural architecture of the village, which features stone buildings, wrought-iron balconies and an 18th-c. church. *For information ☎ 0828 96 33 77, www. roscignovecchia.it.*

*Follow the SR 488 north to Castelcivita.*

## Castelcivita Grottoes★

*For information on visits, ☎ 0828 77 23 97, www.grottedicastelcivita.com.* These caves stretch for 5 km at the feet of the Alburni mountains. Formed by an underground river roughly 50,000 years ago, they were inhabited during the early Paleolithic era, as is attested by fragments of bone and worked stone discovered during exploration. The guided visits show you about 1.2 km of caves and their interesting geological formations, one of which is the Cathedral, a hall 28 m high high filled with stalagmites and stalactites. In summer you can explore 3 km of caves.

# Addresses

## Tourist information

**Region of Campania** – www.regione.campania.it

**Campania ArteCard** – www.campaniartecard.it

**Province of Avellino** – Corso Vittorio Emanuele II, 42, Avellino, ✆ 0825 74 731, www.eptavellino.it

**Province of Benevento** – Via Sala 31, Benevento, ✆ 0824 31 99 11, www.eptbenevento.it

**Province of Caserta** – Viale Douhet, 2/a, Palazzo Reale, Caserta, ✆ 0823 55 00 11, www.eptcaserta.it

**Province of Naples** – Piazza dei Martiri 58, Naples, ✆ 081 41 07 211, www.eptnapoli.info

**Province of Salerno** – Piazza Velia 15, Salerno, ✆ 089 23 04 11, www.eptsalerno.it

**National Park of Cilento and Vallo di Diano** – Via Montesani, **Vallo della Lucania** (SA), ✆ 097 47 19 92 00, www.cilentoediano.it

## The wineries

*The addresses are listed in alphabetical order by location.*

### LA PROVINCIA DI AVELLINO

🍸 **Mastroberardino** – *Via Manfredi 75/81 - Atripalda (AV) -* ✆ *0825 61 41 11 - www. mastroberardino.com -pr@mastroberardino. com - Winery tours by reservation.* The Mastroberardino family has been producing wine for 10 generations and has always had a strong bond with the territory, origins, cultural setting, and natural and social environment of their land. Consequently, it has made a profound commitment to defending and valorising native varieties (Fiano, Greco and Aglianico) and the local viticultural tradition. Accommodation available at the Radici Resort, with a 9-hole golf course (*www.radiciresort.com, 12 rooms*) and restaurant service at Morabianca. Hectares under vine: 340.

**Wines**: Taurasi Radici, Taurasi Naturalis Historia, Fiano di Avellino Radici, Greco di Tufo Novaserra, Falanghina Irpinia Morabianca. Other products: grappa and olive oil.

**Terredora** – *Via Serra 2- Montefusco (AV) -* ✆ *0825 96 82 15 - www.terredora.com - info@terredora.it - Winery tours by reservation.* Terredora has been a leading player on Campania's winemaking scene since 1978. The 150 hectares of vineyards owned by Terredora make it one of the region's most important winegrowing concerns. Terredora pays close attention to the best cultivation techniques, constantly seeking the perfect balance with the environment. The winery's crus are a must. Hectares under vine: 150.

**Wines**: Campania IGT Terredora, Greco di Tufo Terre degli Angeli, Falanghina Campania IGT, Taurasi Riserva CampoRe, Lacryma Christi del Vesuvio. Other products: grappa and olive oil.

**Salvatore Molettieri** – *C.da Musanni 19/B - Montemarano (AV) -* ✆ *0827 63 722 - www.salvatoremolettieri.com - info@ salvatoremolettieri.com - Winery tours by reservation.* The estate boasts a winemaking tradition that has been handed down from father to son. The estate's vineyards – "Cinque Querce", "Ischia Piana" and "Alopecis" – cover approximately 11 hectares and yield outstanding Taurasi DOCG and Irpinia IGT. They are situated in areas that have historically been considered among the finest for winegrowing. Hectares under vine: 13.

**Wines**: Aglianico, Taurasi, Taurasi Riserva, Fiano di Avellino, Greco di Tufo. Other products: grappa.

🍸 **Tenuta Cavalier Pepe** – *Via Francesco de Sanctis - Sant'Angelo all'Esca (AV) -* ✆ *0827 73 766 - www.tenutapepe.it - info@tenutacavalierpepe.it - Winery tours by reservation.* The winery, which is expertly run by Angelo Pepe and his daughter Milena, has always been involved in a constant quest for quality. Native varieties reign supreme: Aglianico, Greco, Fiano and Coda di Volpe are expertly fermented to bring out their full personality and extraordinary typicity. Restaurant service available at La Collina (*www.lacollina ristorante.it*), accommodation at B&B L'Antica Fattoria. Hectares under vine: 55.

**Wines**: Irpinia Coda di Volpe Bianco di Bellona, Fiano di Avellino Brancato, Greco di Tufo Nestor, Irpinia Aglianico Terra del Varo, Taurasi Opera Mia. Other products: olive oil and flavoured wine.

🍸 **Feudi di San Gregorio** – *Loc. Cerza Grossa - Sorbo Serpico (AV) -* ✆ *0825 98 66 83 - www.feudi.it - info@feudi.it - Winery tours by reservation (from €20).* The winery has devoted enormous energy to research and experimentation in both the vineyard and the cellar, on a level unique to the Irpinia area. Over the years, it has monitored all of its sites, evaluating various aspects of the terroir and microclimate. Specialists continue to conduct trials involving microvinification. Meals served at the Marennà restaurant (*closed Sun. pm and Tue.*). Hectares under vine: 250.

**Wines**: Irpinia Bianco DOC Campanaro, Greco di Tufo Cutizzi, Fiano di Avellino Pietracalda, Irpinia Aglianico Serpico, Taurasi Riserva Piano di Montevergine, Dubl Greco Metodo Classico.

♀/ **Caggiano** – *C.da Sala 4* - **Taurasi** *(AV)* - ℰ *0827 74 723 - www.cantinecaggiano.it - visite@cantinecaggiano.it - Winery tours by reservation (ℰ 328 83 10 782)*. A tour of the winery, which reflects the concepts of Antonio Caggiano and was built according to modern technical criteria and a classic taste, is a must. Visitors enter through rooms that convey the atmosphere of a mysterious underground world, with walls built from massive boulders, arches and vaulted ceilings: a fascinating experience. Meals served at the Salae Domini guest farm. Hectares under vine: 23.

**Wines**: Taurasi Vigna Macchia dei Goti, Irpinia Aglianico Salae Domini, Fiano di Avellino Béchar, Greco di Tufo Devon. Other products: grappa.

### PROVINCE OF BENEVENTO

**Antica Masseria Venditti** – *Via Sannitica 120/122* - **Castelvenere** *(BN)* - ℰ *0824 94 03 06 - www.venditti.it - masseria@venditti.it - Guided tours of the winery and tasting by reservation*. The winery was named after the family residence built in 1595, seemingly over the foundations of a Benedictine monastery where wine has always been made. The headquarters is referred to as the "island of the culture of wine", reflecting Castelvenere's philosophy. Moreover, all of its wines are certified as organic. Every area of the winery is designed specifically with wine tourists in mind. The teaching vineyard, a late-16th-c. press and the artwork by Lorenza, Nicola Venditti's wife, are noteworthy. Hectares under vine: 11.

**Wines**: Falanghina Vandari, Barbera Barbetta, Aglianico Marraioli, Bianco Bacalat, Rosso Bosco Caldaia. Other products: olive oil, grappa, saba vinegar.

♣ **Cantina SimoneGiacomo** – *Via Curtole* - **Castelvenere** *(BN)* - ℰ *320 776 1 637 - www.simonegiacomo.it or www.facebook. com/cantinasimonegiacomo - info@simone giacomo.it - Guided tours of the winery and tasting by reservation Mon.-Fri. 9-13, 15-18*. At the slopes of the Matese and Taurno parks, Cantina SimoneGiacomo produces

organic wines since 2016. The estate grows various types of autochthonous vines; grapes are hand-picked and put in partially open crates avoiding the hot hours of the day; a first sorting is done in the vineyard, then they are transported to the cellar and immediately processed. Hectares under vine: 8.

**Wines**: Sannio Barbera DOP Camaiola, Falanghina del Sannio DOP Silvana Benevento Bianco IGP Bianco, Benevento Rosato IGP Rosalba and Barberosa, Benevento Aglianico IGP Aglianico, Benevento Rosso IGP without added sulphites. Other products: olive oil.

**La Guardiense** – *Loc. S. Lucia* - **Guardia Sanframondi** *(BN)* - ℰ *0824 86 40 34 - www.laguardiense.it - puntovendita@ laguardiense.it - Winery tours by reservation*. La Guardiense is one of Italy's largest farming co-operatives. Founded by 33 members in 1960, today it is a modern and dynamic concern with over 1000 winemakers who cultivate about 1500 hectares of vineyards. Its annual production is approximately 240,000 hectolitres/year. Hectares under vine: 1500.

**Wines**: Falanghina, Fiano, Greco, Aglianico, Coda di Volpe, Piedirosso, Rosso Riserva.

♣ **Mustilli** – *Via Caudina 10* - **Sant'Agata de' Goti** *(BN)* - ℰ *0823 71 81 42 - mustilli. com - info@mustilli.com - Winery tours by reservation*. The Mustilli family settled in Sant'Agata de' Goti in the early 1600s. Even then, the cellars carved into the tufa 15 metres below the family palazzo were used to age prestigious wines. Today's winery was established in 1960 by Leonardo and Marilì Mustilli, and the main varieties used here are Greco, Falanghina, Piedirosso and Aglianico. The estate offers restaurant service and accommodation (*6 rooms, €100*). Hectares under vine: 35.

**Wines**: Vigna Segreta Falanghina Sant'Agata, Greco Sannio, Piedirosso Sannio, Aglianico Sannio.

**Fattoria La Rivolta** – *C.da Rivolta* - **Torrecuso** *(BN)* - ℰ *0824 87 29 21 - www. fattorialarivolta.com - info@fattoriala rivolta.com - Guided tours of the winery by reservation*. The Cotroneo family, which owns the winery, has long been involved in various professional and business sectors. The farm was established in the early 20th c., but Paolo established Fattoria La Rivolta in 1997. It has always focused on high-quality cultivation and winemaking. The winery released its first bottles in 2001 and since then its success has continued to grow. Hectares under vine: 31.

**Wines**: Beneventano IGT Sogno di Rivolta, Taburno Falanghina, Aglianico del Taburno Terra di Rivolta, Fiano Coda di Volpe. Other products: olive oil, grappa.

# ADDRESSES

## PROVINCE OF CASERTA

🍇 **Fattoria Selvanova** – Via Selvanova - Squille - **Castel Campagnano** (CE) - 📞 342 12 40 071 - www.selvanova.com - contatti@selvanova.com - Winery tours by reservation. The winery's heart and soul is Antonio Buono, a geologist who, in 1995, fell in love with the hill of Selvanova – abandoned at the time – and decided to devote his energy to rejuvenating the area's landscape and agriculture. Aglianico is the main variety grown here, but other less-known native varieties such as Pallagrello white and red are also fundamental. Organic farming methods are applied here. The estate offers accommodation (4 rooms, €70, min. stay 2 days), with restaurant service. Hectares under vine: 12.

**Wines**: Aglianico Vignantica, Pallagrello Bianco Acquavigna, Cabernet Sauvignon Sopralago, Aglianico Silicata, Aglianico Selvanova. Other products: grappa, olive oil, pâté.

**Terre del Principe** – Via Municipio 4 - **Castel Campagnano** (CE) - 📞 0823 86 71 26 - www.terredelprincipe.com - info@terredelprincipe.com - Winery and vineyards tours with tasting by reservation. In 2003 the love for winegrowing inspired Peppe Mancini to abandon his career as a lawyer to become a vigneron, a passion that also inspired the journalist and writer Manuela Piancastelli to make the same choice. They can be credited with inclusion of the Pallagrello Bianco, Pallagrello Nero and Casavecchia varieties in the national catalogue of wine grapes. Hectares under vine: 11.

**Wines**: IGT Terre Del Volturno Pallagrello Bianco Fontanavigna, Pallagrello Bianco Le Sèrole, Pallagrello Nero Ambruco, Castello delle Femmine Casavecchia Centomoggia. Other products: olive oil and grappa.

🍇 **Villa Matilde** – S.S. Domitiana 18 - **Cellole** (CE) - 📞 0823 93 20 88 - www.villamatilde.it - info@villamatilde.it - Winery and vineyards tours with food and tasting by reservation. In the 1970s Francesco Paolo Avallone replanted the ancient varieties once used to make Falerno, a local wine famous in Roman times, and he established the Villa Matilde winery, which is now run by his children Maria Ida and Salvatore. Respect for the environment, the quest for quality and harmony, and the convergence of tradition and innovation are the cornerstones of Villa Matilde's philosophy. Accommodation available in B&B Locanda del Falerno (double rooms from €60), with restaurant service (reservation required). Hectares under vine: 110.

**Wines**: Falerno del Massico Rosso Villa Camarato, Cecubo IGT, Falerno del Massico Bianco Vigna Caracci, Falanghina di Roccamorfina, Falanghina Passito Eleusi. Other products: olive oil.

🍇 **Telaro** – Via Cinque Pietre 2 - C.da Calabritto - **Galluccio** (CE) - 📞 0823 92 58 41 - www.vinitelaro.it - info@vinitelaro.it - Winery tours by reservation. Telaro wines are made at the Cooperativa Lavoro e Salute, established in 1987 when the Telaro brothers and other young vintners decided to devote their energy to organic farming. The estate has a regional experimental plot where over 80 different varieties are cultivated and studied. Accommodation and meals available at the guest farm on the slopes of the volcano, dotted with vineyards (6 apts.). Hectares under vine: 35.

**Wines**: Ara Mundi Aglianico Riserva DOC, Bariletta IGT, Bella Femmena Aglianico Rosé IGT, Calivierno Aglianico IGT, Ciesco Rosso Aglianico IGT, Cinque Pietre Passito di Falanghina IGT, Femmena Falanghina IGT, Fonte Caja Falanghina IGT, Le Cinque Pietre Fiano and Greco IGT, Ripa Bianca Falanghina DOC, Tefrite Falanghina Brut. Other products: grappa, olive oil.

**Tenuta Spada** – SP 14 Sessa - Mignano - **Galluccio** (CE) - 📞 0823 92 57 09 - www.tenutaspada.it - info@tenutaspada.it - Winery tours by reservation. The Spada family has owned the estate since 1973. The vineyards enjoy an exceptional climate thanks to the mild sea breezes from the nearby Tyrrhenian. A manor built in the early 20th c., which also has a barrique cellar, was restructured on the estate to accommodate wine tourists. Hectares under vine: 25.

**Wines**: Aglianico Roccamonfina Gladius, Falanghina FiorFlòres, Falanghina Gallìcius, Greco Gallìcius, Aglianico Rosso Gallìcius.

## THE GULF OF NAPLES

🍇 **Azienda Agricola Sorrentino** – Via Fruscio 2 - **Boscotrecase** (NA) - 📞 081 858 49 63 - www.sorrentinovini.com - info@sorrentinovini.com - Winery and vineyards tours with tasting by reservation. The Sorrentino agricultural company was established in the foothills of Mount Vesuvius in 1989, born of the passion for winemaking that is part of the Sorrentino family's DNA. Thirty hectares of vineyards, surrounded by olive orchards, form the perfect arena in which to apply winemaking experience the family has earned since the 1800s. Amid the wild natural landscape that populates this volcanic soil, the company boasts a historical farmstead from which visitors can appreciate the beauty of the Sorrentina peninsula and the island of

Capri. Overnight stays at Vesuvio Inn (*www.vesuvioinn.it, rooms and apts. from €88*) and restaurant (*menu starting from €25*) are available to visitors. Hectares under vine: 35.

**Wines**: Spumante del Vesuvio Lacryma Christi, Vesuvio Piedirosso Rosato Dòrè, Lacryma Christi Bianco. Other products: marmelade, olive oil, preserves of piennolo del Vesuvio dop tomatos.

**Cantine degli Astroni** – *Via Sartania 48 - **Napoli** (NA) - 𝒫 081 58 84 182 - www.cantineastroni.com - info@cantine astroni.com - Winery and vineyards tours with tasting by reservation (from €20).* The company was established along the external slopes of the Astroni crater, between Naples and Pozzuoli, which was once a hunting reserve for the Borboni family and is today a WWF Italia nature preserve. The cantina is committed to safeguarding and championing the grand winemaking traditions passed down over generations in this area. Over the past several years, the company has initiated a project to promote the territory through art, communications and education. Teaching routes, guided tastings and visits, wine and food events, exhibitions and thematic lessons are just a few of the activities the company has promoted and realized within its cantina, and form a key part of its wine tourism and cultural offerings. Hectares under vine: 12.

**Wines**: Falanghina Campi Flegrei Colle Imperatrice, Falanghina Campi Flegrei Cru Vigna Astroni, Falanghina Campania Strione, Piedirosso Campi Flegrei Colle Rotondella, Riserva di Piedirosso Campi Flegrei Tenuta Camaldoli.

**Cantina del Vesuvio** – *Via Panoramica 65 - **Trecase** (NA) - 𝒫 081 536 90 41 - www.cantinadelvesuvio.it - info@cantinadel vesuvio.it - Winery tours and tasting by reservation, Mon.-Sun. 11.-16.* In 1948 – just as Italy was recovering from World War II – Giovanni Russo founded his small family winery on the volcanic slopes of Mount Vesuvius, only 5 minutes from Pompei and 40 from Naples. Cantina del Vesuvio produces wines from Caprettone, Piedirosso, Aglianico, and Falanghina grapes, using both traditional and organic agricultural methods. Traditional cooking classes available. Hectares under vine: 16.

**Wines**: Vesuvio Lacryma Christi Bianco DOC, Rosé Vesuvio Lacryma Christi DOC, Vesuvio Lacryma Christi Rosso DOC, Vesuvio Lacryma Christi Superiore DOC Bianco and Rosso, Passito bianco Pompeiano IGT, Vesuvio Lacryma Christi Rosa DOC Etichetta nera, Extradry Capafresca "Spumante Rosé".Other products: olive oil.

## ISCHIA

**D'Ambra Vini** – *Via Mario d'Ambra 16 - **Forio** - Isola di Ischia (NA) - 𝒫 081 90 72 46 - www.dambravini.com - info@dambravini. com - Winery tours by reservation.* The winery was founded in 1888 by Francesco D'Ambra, known as Don Ciccio, who was born into a family of local vignerons. Even as a very young man, he worked in the wine trade. The estate, now run by his grandson Andrea, is an icon of Ischian wine. Hectares under vine: 14.

**Wines**: Ischia Biancolella, Ischia Forastera, Ischia Per'e Palummo, Ischia Bianco, Ischia Frassitelli.

**Cenatiempo Vini d'Ischia** – *Via Cossa 84 - **Serrara Fontana** - Isola di Ischia (Na) - 𝒫 081 98 11 07 - www.cenatiempovini dischia.it - info@vinicenatiempo.it - Winery tours and tasting by reservation.* A family-run business, with cellar dating back to the 1600s. The founder Francesco Cenatiempo started making wine in 1945, in 2019 Pasquale Cenatiempo and Federica Predoni's deep golden yellow Ischia DOC Kalimera 2017 wins the Decanter World Wine Awards. The Cenatiempo wines are the expression of the volcanic and sea nature of Ischia. Hectares under vine: 6.

**Wines**: Ischia DOC Bianco Superiore Lefkòs, Ischia DOC Bianco Forastera, Biancolella and Kalimera, Campania IGT Falanghina GranTifeo Bianco, Rosso and Rosé, Campania IGT Rosato, Epomeo IGT Rosso Màvros, Ischia DOC Rosso, Per' 'e Palummo.

## THE SORRENTO PENINSULA AND AMALFI COAST

🍇 **Marisa Cuomo "Gran Furor Divina Costiera"** – *Via G.B. Lama 16/18 - **Furore** (SA) - 𝒫 089 83 03 48 - www.marisa cuomo.com - info@marisacuomo.com - Winery tours and tasting by reservation (reservation@marisacuomo.com or 𝒫 333 43 13 667).* Viticulture on the Amalfi Coast can be described as nothing short of heroic, because the land on which grapes are grown is wrested from the rocky cliffs through inventive tillage and terracing. It is here that the Marisa Cuomo cellar makes its wines from local varieties such as Coda di Volpe, Bianca Zita, San Nicola, Ripoli, Ginistrella, Per'e Palummo, Serpentaria, Tintore and Taralluzzo. Restaurant service and accommodation available at the Hotel Baccofurore (𝒫 089 83 03 60, www.baccofurore.it). Hectares under vine: 10.

**Wines**: Furore Bianco Fiorduva, Furore Rosso Riserva, Costa d'Amalfi Rosato, Furore Bianco, Furore Rosso, Ravello Rosso Riserva, Ravello Bianco, Costa d'Amalfi Rosso, Costa d'Amalfi Bianco.

## ADDRESSES

**Ettore Sammarco** – *Via Civita 9 -* **Ravello** *(SA) - ℘ 089 87 27 74 - www.ettoresammarco.it - info@ettoresammarco.it - Winery tours by reservation.* Ettore Sammarco, who defines himself as a "wine artisan", established the eponymous winery in 1962. His son Bartolo oversees production and vinification, whereas his two daughters handle management and sales. The winery also has a state-of-the-art liqueur factory that makes the Amalfi Coast's typical spirits, such as limoncello, liqueurs made from wild strawberries, mandarin oranges and wild fennel, and lemon cream and strawberry cream, all of which are marketed with the Melodie d'Amalfi label. Hectares under vine: 10.
**Wines**: Costa d'Amalfi Ravello Bianco Selva delle Monache, Costa d'Amalfi Ravello Rosato Selva delle Monache, Costa d'Amalfi Ravello Bianco Vigna Grotta Piana, Costa d'Amalfi Bianco Terre Saracene, Costa D'Amalfi Rosso Terre Saracene. Other products: grappa and liquors.

🍷 **Montevetrano** – *Via Nido -* **San Cipriano Picentino** *(SA), 20 km NE of Vietri sul Mare - ℘ 089 88 22 85 - www.montevetrano.it - info@montevetrano.it - Winery and vineyards tours with tasting by reservation.* Montevetrano was established thanks to the enthusiasm of a group of friends who share a great passion for wine. The estate was original owned by the Bourbons; purchased by the Imparatos in the 1940s, until 1985 it produced fruit, hazelnuts, wine and oil strictly for the family's own use. Accommodation (*doubles from €135, min. stay 2 days*) and restaurant service at La Vecchia Quercia (*www.lavecchiaquercia.it*). Hectares under vine: 5.
**Wines**: Colli di Salerno Rosso Montevetrano, Core Rosso, Core Bianco. Other products: jams and preserves.

### CILENTO

**Viticoltori De Conciliis** – *Loc. Querce 1 - Prignano Cilento (SA), 10 km E of* **Agropoli** *- ℘ 0974 83 10 90 - www.viticoltorideconciliis.it - info@viticoltorideconciliis.it - Winery tours by reservation.* This important winemaking concern in Campania is managed by the De Conciliis family with great passion and dedication. The estate chiefly grows the region's traditional native varieties such as Aglianico, Fiano and Primitivo, making wines with great personality, a seductive palate and enticing aromas. Hectares under vine: 20.
**Wines**: Aglianico Donnaluna, Fiano Donnaluna, Aglianico Naima, Vino Spumante Selim, Fiano Perella. Other products: grappa and olive oil.

## Where to stay

### ATRIPALDA

**Civita** – *Via Manfredi 124, Atripalda (AV) - ℘ 0825 61 04 71 - www.hotelcivita.it - 29 rooms, doubles from €95.* The hotel has elegant but cosy common areas with modern furnishings.

### CASTIGLIONE DI RAVELLO

**Villa San Michele** – *Via Carusiello 2, 5km/3mi S of Ravello - ℘089 87 22 37 - www.hotel-villasanmichele.it. Closed Dec.-Feb. - 12 rooms.* Situated at the top of the cliff-face, the hotel boasts fine views over the Gulf and the Capo d'Orso. Delightful setting with its luscious garden and the steps down to the beach.

### CELLOLE

**Della Baia** – *Via dell'Erica, Baia Domizia (CE), 5 km W of Cellole - ℘ 0823 72 13 44 - www.hoteldellabaia.it - Closed Oct.-mid-May - 50 rooms, doubles from €130.* The delightful and well-tended garden stretches down to the beach.

### FURORE

**Agriturismo Sant'Alfonso** – *Via S. Alfonso 6, Furore (SA) - ℘ 089 83 05 15 - www.agriturismosantalfonso.it - 8 rooms, doubles from €100.* Set amidst the typical terraces of the coast, this 19th-c. monastery still has its original chapel, ceramics, frescoes and a wood-burning oven. The kitchen offers seasonal dishes and the estate's own wines.

### ISCHIA

**Il Giardino del Nonno** – *Via Fondolillo 9, Sant'Angelo d'Ischia - ℘ 081 99 98 33- www.ilgiardinodelnonno.it. - 6 rooms, doubles from €170.* This charming guestfarm is set in an enchanting scenery offering stunning view of the sea. Half board available. It also offers two outdoor thermal swimming pools with hydromassage.

### MASSA LUBRENSE

**Piccolo Paradiso** – *Piazza Madonna della Lobra 5, Marina della Lobra, 2 km W of Massa Lubrense (NA) - ℘ 081 87 89 240 - www.piccolo-paradiso.com - Closed 15 Nov.-15 Mar. - 54 rooms, doubles from €80.* In the small coastal town, this seafront hotel has a lovely swimming pool on a broad terrace.

### VELIA

**Agriturismo i Moresani** – *Loc. Moresani Casal Velino (SA), 6 km N of Velia - ℘ 0974 90 20 86 - www.agriturismoimoresani.com - Closed 10 Jan.-Feb. - 9 rooms and 5 apts., doubles from €50.* Set just above the town, the guest farm is an oasis of peace and quiet surrounded by olive groves. It has simple but tastefully furnished rooms. The kitchen offers genuine dishes made using outstanding local products.

# BASILICATA

The name Basilicata has Byzantine origins: it is derived from the word *basilikos*, the governor who ruled the area in the 9th and 10th centuries AD. The region is also referred to as Lucania, in honour of the Liky people who lived here in 1300–1200 BC. From an enological standpoint, this is a very exciting period for Basilicata. Terre dell'Alta Val d'Agri, Matera and Grottino di Roccanova recently attained the DOC status, respectively in 2003, 2005 and 2009, and in 2010 celebrated its first DOCG, Aglianico del Vulture Superiore. Vineyards flourish at the foot of Monte Vulture, with its fertile tufaceous soil, but today the area is not the only one under vine, as viticulture has also carved out increasingly important spaces in other parts of Basilicata. Aglianico, the variety emblematic of the region, yields austere, full-bodied reds with intense aromas of blackberries, cherries and raspberries: these wines are eminently cellarable.

*Lucania is providing new resources to viticulture*

## The terroir

When it comes to Basilicata, the motto "a terroir, a variety, a wine" couldn't be more apropos: **Aglianico** is the standard-bearer of Lucanian enology and has given great impetus to the region's reputation in the wine world. Today it is one of the most widely esteemed varieties and Aglianico del Vulture, made from grapes grown in the volcanic soil around the cone of Monte Vulture, in the province of Potenza, is rightfully one of Italy's best-known reds. The ancient Greeks introduced the variety to the region in the 8th c. BC, when they brought in the bush or gobelet vine-training system that is still widely used. Consequently, it should come as no surprise that the name of this variety derives from the word Ellenikon, which became Hellenico, Hellanico and, ultimately, Aglianico. In addition to Aglianico, the varieties cultivated here are Fiano, Bombino Bianco, Asprinio, Moscato Bianco and Trebbiano Toscano among the whites, and Aleatico, Aglianicone, Ciliegiolo, Bombino Nero, Malvasia Nera di Basilicata and Sangiovese among the reds.

The **Val d'Agri**, in the area of the municipalities of Moliterno, Grumento and Viggiano, boasts a unique microclimate that has contributed to the success of its wines. Reds and rosés are produced

---

**DOCG**
Aglianico del
   Vulture Superiore

**DOC**
Aglianico del Vulture
Grottino di Roccanova
Matera
Terre dell'Alta Val d'Agri

© Shebeko/Shutterstock

here, mainly from Merlot, Cabernet and Malvasia Nera di Basilicata grapes.

**Matera DOC** encompasses a large range of reds, rosés, whites and sparkling wines. Specifically, Matera Rosso is made from Sangiovese, Aglianico and Primitivo; Matera Primitivo from the eponymous variety; Matera Moro from Cabernet Sauvignon, Primitivo and Merlot; Matera Greco from Greco Bianco; and Matera Bianco from Malvasia Bianca di Basilicata and Greco Bianco, which are also used to make the sparkling Matera Spumante.

The cultivation of table grapes flourishes in the **Basento valley** in the municipalities of Tricarico and Metaponto, also in the province of Matera.

# Itineraries

*Locations with a winery are indicated by the symbol ♀; for the addresses of the wineries, see p. 401.*

## 1. VENOSA AND MONTE VULTURE

*Circular itinerary of approximately 90 km starting from Venosa.*

### Venosa

Lying at the eastern edge of Monte Vulture, in a basin that was once covered by a prehistoric lake, is the ancient city of Venosa, the birthplace of the Latin poet Horace (65-8 BC). The **castle** was built by Pirro del Balzo in 1470 and houses a fascinating archaeological museum. *Piazza Castello, open 9-20, closed Tue. am, ℘ 0972 36 095.*

The **Abbey of the Santissima Trinità★** is an exceptional complex set in an archaeological area with the Chiesa Vecchia (*open to visitors*), the ruins of the Roman baths and the Chiesa Incompiuta (11th c.), which was roofless from the very beginning. The Chiesa Vecchia, which has a few extant frescoes, was built by the Benedictines over another Early Christian church before the arrival of the Normans, who buried Robert Guiscard (1085) and his wife Alberada here. A small epigraphic museum is annexed to it. The Roman amphitheatre is across the street. *For information on opening times ℘ 0972 34 211.*

*From Venosa, take the S 168 west to Melfi, and turn right at the junction with the S 93.*

## THE TERROIR
**Area**: 10,073.11 km², of which approximately 2006 hectares are planted to vine

**Production 2019**: 90,671 hectolitres, of which 32,026 VQPRD

**Geography**: 47% mountainous, 45% hilly and 8% flat. The soil is tufaceous and clayey. The climate is mild and Mediterranean on the coast and continental inland

## THE PROTECTION CONSORTIA
Consorzio Tutela Vino Aglianico del Vulture DOC – ℘ 0835 24 46 51, www.aglianicodelvulture.net/consorzio

Consorzio Tutela e valorizzazione Terre dell'Alta Val d'Agri – www.terredellaltavaldagri.it

Consorzio Tutela Vini DOC Matera – www.vinomateradoc.it

## PRINCIPAL VARIETIES CULTIVATED

### WHITE GRAPES
Asprinio Bianco
Bombino Bianco
Chardonnay
Fiano
Garganega
Greco Bianco
Malvasia Bianca di Basilicata
Manzoni Bianco
Moscato Bianco
Pinot Bianco
Riesling Italico

Traminer Aromatico
Trebbiano Toscano
Verdeca

### GREY GRAPES
Pinot Grigio

### BLACK GRAPES
Aglianico
Aglianicone
Aleatico

Barbera
Bombino Nero
Cabernet Franc
Cabernet Sauvignon
Ciliegiolo
Malvasia Nera
   di Basilicata
Merlot
Montepulciano
Pinot Nero
Primitivo
Sangiovese

**Lavello** ♟, established over various settlements from the Neolithic period and the Iron Age, has maintained its medieval quarter and the Swabian castle, which was restructured in the 18th c. *Go back to the S 93 and head towards Rapolla.*

### The Vulture Area★

A prehistoric volcano that has long been extinct – covered with woods, and culminating with Monte Vulture (1326 m) and Monte San Michele (1262 m) – offers its crater to the lakes of Monticchio and its fertile lava soil to the area's renowned vineyards.

Set on the northern slopes of Monte Vulture, **Rapolla** is one of the area's main winemaking towns. The town's old Byzantine-Norman cathedral, Santa Lucia, is far more interesting than the newer one.

*Go north on the panoramic S 303.*

**Melfi** is dominated by the majestic castle built by the Normans and restructured extensively over the centuries. Its walls have seen great historic events, such as 4 papal councils, the coronations of kings, and imperial sojourns, such as that of Frederick II. The cathedral, also built under the Normans, was restructured in a Baroque style. The bell tower was built in the 12th c.

Continue on the S 401. The **Lakes of Monticchio** occupy the double crater of the ancient volcano and house the remains of the Benedictine abbey of Sant'Ippolito e San Michele. The cableway offers a 10-minute ride to the top of

Monte Vulture, which affords a splendid and sweeping **panorama★**.

From **Rionero in Vulture** ♟, a winemaking town set between two hills, the 6-km scenic route leads to the hilltop.

Continuing north, you go through **Barile** ♟, a centre of Albanian culture and traditions due to various waves of immigration, including those that followed the Ottoman conquest of 1464. Wineries carved out of tufa are situated near the town and have often been used for film sets.

### 2. MATERA★★ ♟

Anyone arriving at the Sassi for the first time is astonished by this indescribable sight. It is a city like so many others – modern, bustling and seemingly in the plains – but then you suddenly descend into a narrow valley dotted with stairways, doors, windows and balconies. The unique lay of the land has been exploited since antiquity, and the tufa was carved to create homes for humans and animals. It was a village of farmers and shepherds until the Middle Ages, when it was fortified by the Lombards. The fortified city was erected along the hilltop of Colle della Civita, while farmhouses clung to the sides of the ravine, in the areas now called **Sasso Caveoso** and **Sasso Barisano**. Matera was conquered by the Normans in 1042, but the most significant "invasions" were the ones that aroused far less fear: those of the monks who arrived from the 8th to the 12th c.

*Matera*

and carved churches and monasteries out of rock. The deterioration of the Sassi became evident in the 20th c. and Carlo Levi (1902-75) described this dramatic situation in his book *Christ Stopped at Eboli*. This raised civil awareness and evacuation commenced in 1954. Today, the Sassi, which UNESCO declared a World Heritage site in 1993, are flourishing once more. Their abandonment was captured on film by Pier Paolo Pasolini (1922-75), who made *The Gospel According to St Matthew* in 1964 using the abandoned Sassi as a backdrop: the perfect setting for a timeless story. More recently (2004), Mel Gibson filmed *The Passion of Christ* using the Sassi as his set.

From an enological standpoint, this is the area of **Matera DOC**, which is produced in various municipalities using Aglianico, Sangiovese, Primitivo, Greco and Malvasia di Basilicata in the red, white and sparkling versions.

The two main cave-dwelling areas can be seen on both sides of the cliff with the duomo. They are composed of small whitewashed dwellings set on top of one another so that the roofs serve as roads. The differences in level, roads and stairways thus create an extraordinary jumble. The **Strada dei Sassi★★** is the scenic route that skirts the wild gorge and circles around the cliff with the duomo. On the rock face across from it there are numerous natural and manmade caves. The **duomo★★**, built in the Apulian Romanesque style (13th c.), has a tripartite façade with a single portal, and boasts a lovely rose window and loggia; there are 2 ornate portals on the right side. The interior, restructured in the 17th and 18th c., houses a Byzantine Madonna from the 12th-13th c., a 16th-c. Neapolitan Nativity scene and, in the choir, beautiful carved stalls from the 15th c.; the **Chapel of the Annunziata★** has Renaissance decorations.

**San Giovanni Battista★** is a small but starkly beautiful church that was built in the Apulian Romanesque style in 1233. Slender columns with zoomorphic figures rise alongside the rose window. Be sure to see the 2 elephants set on brackets below the gable of the apse, and the richly decorated window further down. At the **Church of San Pietro Caveoso** (*for information on visit ℘ 0835 33 40 33, www.sassiweb.it*), you can tour several **cliff churches**, some of which frescoed, situated along a short but picturesque route through town. They are Santa Lucia alle Malve (11th c., frescoes from the 12th to the 17th c.), Convicinio di Sant'Antonio (15th-c. frescoes), Madonna de Idris (frescoes from the 15th to the 17th c.), San Giovanni in Monterrone (frescoes from the 12th to the 18th c.) and Santa Maria de Armenis (11th c.).

On the other side of the stream, the rock face is carved at several points. The area covered with cliff churches can be difficult to access, but affords a lovely **view★★** of Matera. *Follow the road to Altamura for 4 km and then the one for Laterza-Taranto; take the road to the right marked "chiese rupestri".*

# Addresses

## Tourist information

**Region of Basilicata** – www.regione.basilicata.it, www.basilicataturistica.it and www.aptbasilicata.it

**Matera Tourist Office**– Proloco, Via Ridola 60, www.prolocomatera2019.it, ☏ 329 19 54 667 or ☏ 328 93 33 548

**Sassi di Matera Tours** – www.sassiweb.it, www.infosassidimatera.com

## The wineries

*The addresses are listed in alphabetical order by location.*

### VENOSA AND THE VULTURE

**Elena Fucci** – *C.da Solagna del Titolo -* **Barile** *(PZ) -* ☏ *320 48 79 945 - www.elenafuccivini.com - info@elenafuccivini.com - Winery and vineyards tours with tasting, light buffet, lunch or dinner by reservation.* First established in 2000 with vineyards acquired during the 1960s by the founder's grandfather Generoso, this company sits on the highest part of farmlands located in Contrada Solagna del Titolo. The company and its cantina overlook the vineyards, which stretch out along the foothills of Monte Vulture at roughly 600 metres above sea level. The decision to promote a single label, the "Titolo", was motivated by the production capabilities of these vines and the high quality of the fruit they produce. Work in these vineyards requires true gardening skills, and the vines are nursed carefully. Respect for nature and its cycles, no use of chemicals or chemical products, even the vines are tied using natural gorse left out to dry during the summer months. Hectares under vine: 6.
**Wines**: Aglianico del Vulture DOC Titolo.

© Khz/Shutterstock

**Macarico** – *Via Roma, 159 -* **Rionero in Vulture** *(PZ) -* ☏ *0972 72 36 89 - www.macaricovini.it - info@macaricovini.it - Winery tours by reservation.* The winery is situated in two fascinating caves carved out of the tufa in the 16th c. It employs a vinification process based on respect for the fruit and the use of healthy grapes, natural yeasts, spontaneous fermentation and no filtering. It produces two sumptuous monovarietal Aglianico del Vulture wines. Hectares under vine: 5.
**Wines**: Basilicata IGT Bianco Xjnestra, Nido d'Amore, Rosé Ripa delle Rose and Rosso del Vulcano, Aglianico del Vulture DOC Macarico and Macarì, Spumante Serra delle More and Serra del Giglio.

**Paternoster** – *C.da Valle del Titolo -* **Barile** *(PZ) -* ☏ *0972 77 02 24 - www.paternostervini.it and www.facebook.com/paternostervini - info@paternostervini.it - Winery tours by reservation.* The Paternoster family has been making wine since the turn of the 20th c. Grandfather Anselmo, who learned the noble art of vine dressing from his father, decided in 1925 – the date is proudly listed over the entrance to the winery – that he would sell some of his bottles of Aglianico, produced until then strictly for the family. This launched a business that is now run by the third generation. Hectares under vine: 20.
**Wines**: Aglianico del Vulture DOC Calibro, Don Anselmo, Rotondo, Synthesi, Giuv Bio, IGT Basilicata Rosso Barigliott, IGT Basilicata Bianco Biancorte and Klīno, IGT Basilicata Rosato Retabli, Aglianico Basilicata IGT Sorso, Basilicata IGT Falanghina Vulcanico, Spumante L'antico, Assensi and Il Moscato. Other products: grappa.

⚲ **Bisceglia** – *C.da Finocchiaro -* **Lavello** *(PZ) -* ☏ *0972 87 70 33 - www.vinibisceglia.it - info@vulcanoevini.com - Winery tours and tasting by reservation (Vulcano Wines, ☏ 0972 88 687, from €10).* This innovative winery boasts a modern architectural structure that also hosts the "Territorio" photography exhibition, a collection of pictures linking viticulture with the territory, people, history and landscape. In addition to excellent wines, the estate also produces organic extra virgin olive oil. Across from the winery there is a large archaeological complex (4th-7th c. AD) that was probably an ancient smithy. On the western side there are holes that housed two *pithoi*, containers that were coated with mortar and used to ferment high-quality wine. Hectares under vine: 40.

## ADDRESSES

**Wines**: Merlot and Chardonnay Bosco delle Rose, Aglianico del Vulture DOC Gudarrà, Gudarrà Riserva, Tréje, Terra di Vulcano Primitivo Basilicata IGT, Aglianico Del Vulture DOC, Syrah Basilicata IGT, Merlot Basilicata IGT and Falanghina Beneventano IGT. Other products: olive oil and grappa.

**Cantine del Notaio** – *Via Roma 159 -* **Rionero in Vulture** *(PZ) - ℘ 0972 72 36 89 - www.cantinedelnotaio.it - info@cantinedel notaio.it - Winery tours and tasting by reservation.* Gerardo Giuratrabocchetti's love for grapes and wine goes back to his childhood, when he would watch his grandfather work in the vineyard. He inherited those vineyards and has made the most of them, so that today Cantine del Notaio is renowned among connoisseurs. The name of the winery is a tribute to Gerardo's father, who was a notary public. Hectares under vine: 26.
**Wines**: Basilicata IGT Rosso L'atto, Aglianico del Vulture DOC Rosso Il Sigillo, La Firma, Il Repertorio, Il Lascito and Il Patto, Vino Frizzante Il Protesto, Basilicata IGT Bianco Secco La Parcella and Il Patto, Basilicata IGT "Rossato" Il Patto. Other products: grappa and olive oil.

**D'Angelo** – *Via Padre Pio 8 -* **Rionero in Vulture** *(PZ) - ℘ 0972 72 15 17 - www.dangelowine.com - dangelowine@tiscali.it - Winery tours by reservation.* The family business – now in its third generation of vintners – is owned by Donato and Lucio D'Angelo, whose efforts to improve the quality of their products starts with their work in the vineyard. The area's unique climate and volcanic soil, the position of the vineyards and significant day-night temperature swings allow the D'Angelos to make complex wines with good structure, and intense and persistent aromas. Hectares under vine: 35.
**Wines**: Aglianico del Vulture Tecum, Caselle, Valle del Noce and Canneto, Basilicata IGT Rosso Serra delle Querce, Brigante Lucano, Vendemmia Tardiva and Sacra Vite, Basilicata IGT Bianco Villa dei Pini, Spumante Aglianico, Moscato. Other products: grappa.

### MATERA

🏠 **Masseria Cardillo** – *SS 407 Basentana km 96 -* **Bernalda** *(MT), 40 km S of Matera - ℘ 0835 74 89 92 - www.masseriacardillo.it - info@masseriacardillo.it.* Just a few kilometres from the coast and the beach of Metaponto, the winery – housed in a lovely 19th-c. farmhouse – produces wines that express the finest of the area. It also offers accommodation in elegant and well-appointed rooms *(10 rooms, doubles €120).* Hectares under vine: 21.
**Wines**: Basilicata IGT Rosso Vigna Giadì, Tittà and Vigna del Borgo, Basilicata IGT

Rosato Bacche Rosa, Basilicata IGT Bianco L'ovo di Elena and Burla, Matera Primitivo DOC Baruch, Aglianico del Vulture DOC Rubra, Matera Moro DOC Malandrina. Other products: olive oil.

**Dragone Vini** – *Piazza degli Olmi 66 - Loc. Pietrapenta -* **Matera** *- ℘ 0835 38 51 49 or 328 10 40 972- www.dragonevini.it - info@dragonevini.com - Winery tours and tasting by reservation.* The family has been making wine for over 100 years and its first label was sold in 1955. The winery now produces over 7000 hectolitres of wine. Be sure to try its classic method sparkling wine.
**Wines:** Basilicata IGT Rosso Fiaschetto Rosso, Matera DOP Rosso Pietrapenta and Primitivo Opus 199, Basilicata IGP Bianco Pietrapenta, Spumante Brut Cento Santi, Ego Sum, Vincent. Other products: grappa and olive oil.

## Where to stay

### RIONERO IN VULTURE

**Borgo Villa Maria** – *Località Monticchio Laghi, 13 km NW of Rionero in Vulture (PZ) - ℘ 0972 73 13 02 or 347 34 03 205 - www.cantucciodelvulture.it - 32 rooms., doubles from €80.* Completely surrounded by natural countryside, a few steps from the lake, this hotel boasts a warm atmosphere. Rooms are simple, rustic and pleasant. It also offers a restaurant service *(Ristorante Bramea, ℘ 0972 73 13 02)* and a swimming pool.

### MATERA

**Locanda di San Martino** – *Via Fiorentini 71 - ℘ 0835 25 66 00 - www.locandadisanmartino.it - 40 rooms, doubles from €160.* In the heart of the famous historic town of Matera, a fascinating venue with cave dwellings on 4 floors and with independent entrances. Traditional and elegant décor.

# CALABRIA

A combination of almost nothing but mountains and coastline, Calabria is a region of enormous beauty that greatly repays the effort invested to explore its geography and gastronomy. Called Enotria by the ancient Greeks due to its thriving viticulture, today Calabria cultivates an abundance of varieties. The most common black grapes are Gaglioppo, Magliocco, Marsigliana, Nerello Mascalese, Prunesta, Sangiovese and Alicante, and among the whites Greco Bianco, Mantonico, Pecorello and Guardavalle. The local varieties are of course joined by international cultivars, in particular, Cabernet, Merlot, Syrah, Chardonnay and Sauvignon. Grapes are also grown high on the Sila plateau, allowing Calabria to claim the record for the highest vineyards in Europe.

© Brytta/iStock

*Byzantine church called the Cattolica, Stilo*

## The terroir

Despite a glorious past, the image today of Calabria's winemaking industry has deteriorated due to the excessive division of the vineyards into small plots and the production of wine in bulk. Happily the situation is changing thanks to a reappraisal of the value of local varieties and the improved quality of the grapes and production methods. New growing and cellar techniques are being introduced to replace obsolete methods.

In recent years there has been a great deal of experimentation and forgotten cultivars have been rediscovered. In consequence, a wine with very ancient origins has been recreated: the **Moscato di Saracena**, produced in the municipality of the same name in the province of Cosenza. This wine was referred to in 16th-c. writings, a period when it was much appreciated at the papal court. It is made from a particular variety of Moscato that was perhaps introduced by the Saracens. The town of Saracena is the only location where it achieves interesting levels of quality. The must obtained with selected, sun-dried Moscatello grapes is combined with concentrated must from Guarnaccia, Malvasia and Odoacra grapes (Odoacra is a particularly scented local cultivar). The resulting mixture is then left to ferment in wooden barrels and only after several rackings is the wine bottled. The final product is amber in colour, highly scented with notes of resin, exotic fruit, almonds, honey and dry figs, and has a pleasantly bitterish finish.

**DOC**
Bivongi
Cirò
Greco di Bianco
Lamezia
Melissa
Sant'Anna di Isola Capo Rizzuto
Savuto
Scavigna
Terre di Cosenza

In general the path of experimentation and an emphasis on quality is bringing new life to the existing appellations. This is the case, for example, with **Greco di Bianco**, one of Italy's best and rarest sweet wines.

# Itineraries

*Locations with a winery are indicated by the symbol ▼; for the addresses of the wineries, see p. 407.*

## 1. POLLINO NATIONAL PARK AND THE "CEDAR COAST"

The designated areas of **Pollino** and **Verbicaro** are situated in the north-west corner of Calabria. The first produces a red wine, the second whites, rosés and reds from Gaglioppo, Greco Nero, Malvasia Bianca, Montonico Bianco and Guarnaccia Bianca grapes.

Inhabited since ancient times, **Castrovillari** is composed of a new section and the Civita, the historic centre that lies between the castle and the Basilica of Santa Maria di Castello. The basilica was built in the 12th c. but later remodelled in Baroque style. The castle was constructed by the Spanish at the end of the 15th c.

The area around Castrovillari has several interesting winemaking towns, such as

**Saracena** ▼ (*12 km south*), home of the renowned Moscato di Saracena (*see above*) and **Frascineto** (*8 km north-east*), a town with an Albanian origin that looks over the Sibari plain.

## Pollino National Park

An area of almost 200,000 hectares falling in Calabria and Basilicata was designated as Pollino National Park in 1992. It is in great part mountainous, with peaks reaching over 2000 m (Serra Dolcedorme, Monte Pollino, Serra del Prete, Serra delle Ciavole and Serra di Crispo). The symbol of the park is the Loricate pine. *Pollino National Park info point, Monumental Complex of Santa Maria della Consolazione, Rotonda (PZ), 9-13, ℰ 0973 66 93 35, parcopollino.gov.it.*

## Verbicaro and the Riviera dei Cedri

*57 km west of Castrovillari.*
Verbicaro still has sections of its ancient walls in the Bonifanti district, the oldest part of the city. From here you reach the Tyrrhenian Sea, where three seaside resorts can be visited: **Scalea** (*20 km north-west*), set out on terraces on Scalea promontory, and with its historic centre still laid out on its original plan, **Praia a Mare** (*13 km north of Scalea*), set amongst plantations of cedars, and

© Norman Pogson/Shutterstock

## PRINCIPAL VARIETIES CULTIVATED

**WHITE GRAPES**
Ansonica
Chardonnay
Greco Bianco
Guardavalle
Guarnaccia
Malvasia Bianca
Manzoni Bianco
Montonico Bianco
Moscato Bianco
Pinot Bianco
Riesling Italico
Sauvignon

Semillon
Traminer Aromatico
Trebbiano Toscano

**GREY GRAPES**
Pinot Grigio

**BLACK GRAPES**
Aglianico
Calabrese
Barbera
Cabernet Franc
Cabernet Sauvignon

Castiglione
Gaglioppo
Greco Nero
Magliocco Canino
Malvasia Nera di Brindisi
Marsigliana Nera
Merlot
Nerello Cappuccio
Nerello Mascalese
Nocera
Pecorello
Prunesta
Sangiovese

## Two small DOC zones in the province of Reggio Calabria

**Bivongi** is the chief town of the DOC zone of the same name, which produces white, red and rosé wines. Very close by is the town of **Stilo**, the birthplace of the Renaissance philosopher Tommaso Campanella (1568-1639). Built 400 m up on the slopes of a mountain, it was a site of Basilian hermitages and monasteries. Right at the top of the town stands the Byzantine church called the **Cattolica★★**. Constructed in the 10th c. on a square plan, the brick church has five cylindrical domes lined with terracotta tiles. Inside, the Greek cross is formed by nine squares covered by domes and barrel vaults. The mosaics were once splendid but sadly are now very damaged.

Rebuilt after the 1783 earthquake, **Bianco** retains traces of its past in the ruins of Bianco Vecchio, a town at 260 m altitude just inland from the coast. This is the zone that produces the renowned **Greco di Bianco DOC**, a sweet white wine made almost exclusively from Greco Bianco grapes. In addition to its DOC zones, the province boasts several IGT wines: Arghillà, Costa Viola, Locride, Palizzi, Scilla and Pellaro.

**Diamante** (*16 km south of Scalea*), also surrounded by cedars.

## 2. FROM COSENZA TO LAMEZIA TERME

*Itinerary of 75 km along the very winding but panoramic S 19 and S 109.*

This route partly skirts the Crati valley and follows the S 19 and S 109 roads, several sections of which offer superb views of the countryside. You also pass through the **Donnici**, **Savuto**, **Scavigna** and **Lamezia** designated zones. These produce white, red and rosé wines from Montonico Bianco (also called Mantonico), Greco Bianco, Malvasia Bianca, Guarnaccia, Pecorello, Nerello Cappuccio, Gaglioppo (also called Magliocco or Mantonico Nero) and Greco Nero grapes. Scavigna Bianco also requires proportions of Trebbiano Toscano and Chardonnay.

A little off the route, 30 or so km north of Cosenza, you can find the white, red and rosé versions of **San Vito di Luzzi**. Close to **Luzzi** 🍷 stand the remains of the Benedictine **Sambucina Abbey**, which, until the 16th c., was an important centre of art and culture.

## Cosenza

The modern city has been built at a lower level than the old city, in which the streets and palaces reflect the wealth of the periods of Angevin and Aragonese rule, when Cosenza was considered the artistic and religious capital of Calabria. Following recent restoration, the **Duomo** (12th-13th c.) has been returned to its original condition. Inside is the **mausoleum★** of Isabella of Aragon, who

died in Cosenza during her return from Tunis with the body of her father-in-law, St Louis, the king of France.

Leaving Cosenza in a southerly direction on the road to Dipignano, at **Laurigliano** you come to the Sanctuary of the Madonna della Catena, from where there is a lovely view.

*Continue on the S 19 and then the S 109.*

### Lamezia Terme 🍷

This municipality was created in 1968 when Nicastro, Sambiase and Sant'Eufemia Lamezia were unified. The chief town is **Nicastro**, where there is a majestic Baroque cathedral. The old section of the town, the quarter called San Teodoro, is the site of a Norman castle from where superb views are offered. **Sambiase** is a well-known wine town, which is followed by Terme Caronte, a spa town that was known to the Romans.

## 3. THE IONIC COAST FROM CIRÒ TO CAPO RIZZUTO

*Itinerary of 70 km.*

This stretch of the coast is where the appellations **Cirò**, **Melissa** and **Sant'Anna di Isola Capo Rizzuto** are situated. Melissa produces white wines (using mostly Greco Bianco grapes) and reds (mostly Gaglioppo and Greco Nero); Cirò makes white, red, and rosé wines from Greco Bianco and Gaglioppo grapes. Sant'Anna di Isola Capo Rizzuto makes a red wine produced principally from Gaglioppo grapes.

Lying among the pines and eucalyptuses a few km north of **Cirò Marina** 🍷, Punta Alice is the site of the Doric temple dedi-

## THE TERROIR

**Area:** 15,221.61 km², of which approximately 8,831 hectares are planted to vine

**Production 2019:** 475,666 hectolitres, of which 39,915 VQPRD

**Geography:** 9% flat, 49% hilly, 42% mountainous. The soil is generally not very firm, in part calcareous and clayey, in part of alluvial origin. The climate is Mediterranean but continental on the highest ground

## THE PROTECTION CONSORTIA AND WINE AND FOOD ROUTES

Consorzio di Tutela e Valorizzazione del Vino DOC Cirò e Melissa – ✆ 0962 35 599

Strada dei Sapori del Poro – ✆ 0963 59 27 39

Strada del Vino e dei Sapori del Pollino - Castrovillari – ✆ 0981 38 035, www.vinopollino.com

Strada del Vino e dei Sapori della Sibaritide – ✆ 0981 94 48 89

Strada dei Sapori del Medio Tirreno Cosentino

Strada del Vino e dei Sapori del Brutium – ✆ 0984 26 133

Strada dei Sapori Silani – ✆ 0984 57 80 31

Strada del Vino dei Saperi e dei Sapori – ✆ 0962 86 58 01

Strada del Bosco e del Vino – ✆ 0968 66 23 80

Strada del Vino e dei Sapori Lamezia – ✆ 0968 20 72 47

Strada dei Sapori Cassiodorei – ✆ 0961 91 08 43

Strada dei Vini e dei Sapori della Locride – ✆ 0964 20 146

cated to Apollo Aleos (5th c. BC). Inland 6 km stands **Cirò** 🍷, a perched town of narrow alleyways founded in ancient times. It is ringed by walls and centred around Carafa Castle, where a music festival is held each summer. The name Cirò is linked to the wine, which has been known since the 18th c.

Proceeding south for a few km, you reach **Melissa**, and then drive along a panoramic road to **Strongoli** 🍷, where excellent views are given from the top of the castle.

## Crotone

Crotone was a colony of Magna Grecia founded in 710 BC. In antiquity the city was celebrated for its wealth, the beauty of its women and the feats of its athletes, like Milo of Croton, as praised in the poetry of Virgil. Around 532 BC, Pythagoras founded a secret society in the city dedicated to mathematics, but it became too powerful, was banned, and forced to move to Metapontus.

Today the city is a flourishing maritime port. It has a large and interesting **archaeological museum** (*Via Risorgimento 121, open 9-19, closed Mon.,* ✆ *0962 23 082*) and the castle built in the 16th c. on the orders of Don Pedro, the Spanish viceroy in Naples. The venerated image of the Black Madonna of Capo Colonna is conserved in a 19th-c. chapel in the duomo. Legend says the statue was brought from the East in the first centuries after Christ.

## Capo Colonna

The place used to be called Capo Lacinio in honour of the Temple of Hera Lacinia that stood here, one of the most famous temples in Magna Grecia. Today only one of the Doric temple's original 48 columns remains. The cape's golden age was the 5th c. BC, but 300 years later it began to decline. It was raided by pirates and used as a quarry by the Aragonese in the 16th c. to build the fortifications at Crotone. Capo Colonna received its coup de grace in 1683 when it was struck by an earthquake. It was in these parts in 1964 that Pierpaolo Pasolini filmed some scenes for his *Gospel According to St Matthew*. Elsewhere on the cape stand a lighthouse, a 16th-c. tower and the Church of the Madonna di Capo Colonna, which once guarded the Black Madonna now in Crotone's duomo.

The road cuts inland for the last stretch of the journey before meeting the sea again at **Capo Rizzuto**. The cape marks the start of Squillace Gulf, which stretches down to Monasterace.

# Addresses

## Tourist information

**Region of Calabria** – portale.regione.
calabria.it and turismo.regione.calabria.it

**Cosenza Tourist Office** – Piazza XI
Settembre, Cosenza, ✆ 328 17 54 422
www.cosenzaturismo.it

**Crotone Tourist Office** – Proloco, Via Molo
Sanità 2 (Lega Navale), ✆ 329 81 54 963
prolococrotone.it

## The wineries

*The addresses are listed in alphabetical order
by location.*

**POLLINO NATIONAL PARK AND
THE COAST**

**Cantine Viola** – *Via Roma 18 -* **Saracena**
*(CS) -* ✆ *340 36 74 357 - www.cantineviola.it
- info@cantineviola.it - Winery tours by
reservation.* Luigi Viola, a retired
schoolteacher with a longstanding passion
for nature and farming, decided to devote
his energies full-time to recovering,
improving and making people aware of
Moscato di Saracena, which was on the
verge of extinction. In his work, he is
supported by his entire family: his wife
Margherita and their three children
Roberto, Alessandro and Claudio. Hectares
under vine: 2.
**Wines**: Moscato Passito di Saracena, Rosso
Viola, Bianco Margherita. Other products:
grappa.

**FROM COSENZA TO LAMEZIA TERME**

🍴 **Serracavallo** – *Via Piave 51 - C.da
Serracavallo -* **Bisignano** *(CS), 15 km N of
Luzzi -* ✆ *0984 21 144 - www.viniserracavallo.
com - demetriostancati@virgilio.it - Winery
tours by reservation.* The winery is especially
well aspected, as its microclimate, altitude
and soil are ideal for wine-growing.
Constant breezes mean mild temperatures,
yet the area also enjoys the significant day-
night temperature swings that help bring
out the full bouquet of the wines.
Traditional grapes such as Magliocco and
Greco are grown alongside international
varieties like Cabernet Sauvignon, Merlot
and Riesling. Food also served by
reservation. Hectares under vine: 30.
**Wines**: Calabria IGP Bianco Besidiae and
Petramola, Terre di Cosenza DOP Rosso
Sette Chiese, Terraccia, Quattro Lustri and
Vigna Savuco, Calabria IGP Rosato Filì and
Don Filì, Spumante Alta Quota. Other
products: olive oil and grappa.

**Cantine Lento** – *Via del Progresso 1 -*
**Amato**, *Lamezia Terme (CZ) -* ✆ *0968 99
30 31 - www.cantinelento.it - info@
cantinelento.it - Winery tours by reservation.*
From generation to generation, with every
bottle it produces the Lento family has
strived to convey a heritage of traditions,
experience and knowledge tied to the
territory. This is the spirit that inspires their
work as winemakers, and it is a life and work
philosophy that has proved successful.
Hectares under vine: 70.
**Wines**: Federico II, Lamezia Rosso Riserva,
Greco, Contessa Emburga, Dragone.

**Statti** – *C.da Lenti -* **Lamezia Terme** *(CZ) -*
✆ *0968 45 61 38 - www.statti.com - info@
statti.com - Winery tours Mon.-Fri. by
reservation (marketing@statti.com,* ✆ *329
00 82 285).* Alberto and Antonio Statti have
long been committed to demonstrating
the international importance of wines
made from traditional varieties. They have
pursued this goal with great commitment
and their efforts have been rewarded. The
area where the vineyards are situation is
called Setteventi – seven winds – due to
the strong sea breezes. It enjoys an ideal
microclimate that prevents the formation of
moulds and fungal diseases. As a result, the
vineyards can be managed using integrated
systems with a low environmental impact.
Hectares under vine: 100.
**Wines**: Calabria IGT Rosso Cauro, I Gelsi
and Gaglioppo, Calabria IGT Bianco I Gelsi,
Bluette, Mantonico and Greco, Calabria IGT
Rosato Greco Nero and I Gelsi, Lamézia DOC
Rosso and Bianco, Lamezia Riserva DOC
Batasarro, Spumante Ferdinando 1938 Brut
and Rosé, Passito Nosside. Other products:
olive oil.

© Senai Aksoy/Shutterstock

## ADDRESSES

### THE IONIAN COAST

**Fattoria San Francesco** – *Loc. Quattromani - Cirò (KR) - ☎ 0962 32 228 - www.fattoria sanfrancesco.it - info@fattoriasanfrancesco.it - Winery tours by reservation.* During the 16th c. the estate included a monastery surrounded by vineyards and olive groves. Today those vineyards produce the estate's wines and the old monastery is now the Casale San Francesco, an agricultural centre and the home of the Siciliani family, who have managed the estate for generations. In 2013 it was taken over by Iuzzolini family, which continues with this philosophy. As a tribute to the family's winemaking tradition, the Sicilianis' noble coat of arms has been adopted as the winery's logo. Hectares under vine: 50.

**Wines:** Cirò Bianco, Cirò Rosato, Cirò Rosso, Cirò Rosso Classico Ronco dei Quattroventi, Spumante Brut Cardonna.

**Santa Venere** – *Tenuta Voltagrande - SP 04 km 10 - Cirò (KR) - ☎ 0962 38 519 - www. santavenere.com - info@santavenere.com - Winery tours by reservation.* The estate, named for the stream that crosses it, has been in the Scala family since the 17th c. One of the winery's goals is to valorise Gaglioppo and native varieties that now risk extinction. The winery uses organic methods, fully respecting the land and its biodiversity. Hectares under vine: 25.

**Wines:** Santa Venere Cirò Rosso, Bianco and Rosato, Cirò DOP Rosso Riserva Federico Scala, Calabria IGP Rosso Vurgadà and Speziale, Marsigliana Nera and Scassabarile, Calabria IGP Bianco Vescovado, Sp1 Bianco and Rosé, Frankye Go Bianco and Rosé, Passito VoltaGrande. Other products: olive oil.

**Librandi** – *SS 106, C.da San Gennaro - Cirò Marina (KR) - ☎ 0962 31 518 - www.librandi. it - librandi@librandi.it - Winery tours and tasting by reservation.* The Librandis have cultivated grapes for 4 generations, but it was not until the 1950s that they decided to bottle wine. Antonio and Nicodemo Librandi have always been committed to valorising Calabrian viticulture and can be credited with demonstrating to other local wineries that success lies in combining tradition and innovation. Hectares under vine: 232.

**Wines:** Cirò DOC Rosso Duca Sanfelice, Segno Librandi, DOC Melissa Rosso and Bianco Asylia, Calabria IGT Rosso Magno Megonio and Gravello, Calabria IGT Bianco Efeso and Critone, Cirò DOC Bianco Segno Librandi, IGT Calabria Rosé Terre Lontane, Cirò DOC Rosé Segno Librandi. Other products: olive oil and grappa.

**☆ Azienda Agricola Ceraudo** – *C.da Dattilo - Strongoli (KR) - ☎ 0962 86 56 13 or 329 41 88 323- www.ceraudo.it - info@ dattilo.it - Winery tours and tasting by reservation, closed Sun.* The estate extends over 60 hectares, 38 of which with olive groves, 20 under vine and the rest covered with citrus trees. Since 1992 it has used organic farming methods, achieving excellent results not only in terms of quantity but also in the quality of its products. Tellingly, it is considered a regional model for organic agriculture. The estate has a restaurant (*www.dattilo.it*) and accommodation (*10 apts., from €100*). Hectares under vine: 20.

**Wines:** Val di Neto IGT Rosso Petraro, Nanà and Dattilo, Val di Neto IGT Rosé Grayasusi, Val di Neto IGT Bianco Imyr, Petelia and Grisara, Doro bè. Other products: grappa.

## Where to stay

### CASTROVILLARI

**Agriturismo la Locanda del Parco** – *C.da Mazzicanino 12, Morano Calabro, 7 km N of Castrovillari (CS) - ☎ 0981 31 304 or 389 07 46 648 - www.lalocandadelparco.it - 7 rooms, from €60.* The little villa, set in the countryside and ringed by the mountains of the Pollino National Park, is an elegant and cosy centre for equestrian tourism and offers cooking classes.

### CROTONE

**B&B Elisa** – *Via Interna Marina 19 - ☎ 327 65 18 962 - www.bebelisa.it or www. facebook.com/ElisBeB - 4 rooms, doubles from €60.* This simple and comfortable B&B is very close to the beach. Wifi and air conditioning in every room.

### LAMEZIA TERME

**Agriturismo Le Carolee** – *C.da Gabella 1, Pianopoli, 12 km E of Lamezia Terme - ☎ 0968 35 076 - www.lecarolee.it - 8 rooms, from €90, 1 apt. from €800/week.* The 19th-c. fortified manor is set in a splendid and peaceful position surrounded by olive trees.

© Ironi/Shutterstock

# PUGLIA

Continuous trading relationships with different civilisations, particularly from the Middle East, ensured that this region accumulated a substrate of different customs, cultures and traditions, resulting in a set of unique characteristics. And in its viticulture, too, Puglia was different, cultivating a huge range of grape varieties, many of which were clearly from the East, such as Aleatico, Malvasia, Uva di Troia and Moscato, but prevalently cultivars representative of the region itself, like Negroamaro, Primitivo, Notar Domenico, Susumaniello, Ottavianello, Bianco d'Alessano, Pampanuto and Impigno. Today, after years in which quantity was always considered more important than quality, things are seen differently and Puglian wine is undergoing consistent improvement.

*A group of Trulli, typical stone houses in Puglia*

© kamillok/Fotolia.com

## The terroir

In terms of the quantity of wine Puglia produces, it is one of the top regions in Italy, but in terms of image it has to cope with the fact that for a long time its wines were considered second class, and indeed much of its must and wines has not been bottled in the region but sold to strengthen the structure and colour of wines of other regions or countries. However, efforts to upgrade Puglia's winemaking have brought some very interesting results.

Black grapes predominate. **Negroamaro** is the most common, followed by **Primitivo**, a close relation of the Californian Zinfandel. It seems that the name Primitivo might be derived from the vine's tendency to ripen early.

These two varieties and **Malvasia Nera** represent a good part of the production in the provinces of Lecce and Taranto in south Puglia, whereas the centre tends to be planted with the white grape varieties **Verdeca** and **Bianco d'Alessano**. In the north **Bombino Bianco**, **Trebbiano Toscano**, **Uva di Troia**, **Sangiovese** and **Montepulciano** prevail. And then there is Aleatico, grown in the zone named after it, **Aleatico di Puglia**, which is used to make a red dessert wine also produced in Riserva and Liquoroso versions.

There are 4 DOCG and 28 DOC zones spread across four macro areas: the province of Foggia (also known as Daunia), the province of Bari, and the two areas of Salento and Taranto.

Puglia is one of Italy's leading regions for the production of **rosé** wines, with that of Salento being especially renowned.

## Itineraries

*Locations with a winery are indicated by the symbol ♟; for the addresses of the wineries, see p. 422.*

## PRINCIPAL VARIETIES CULTIVATED

### WHITE GRAPES

Asprinio Bianco
Bianco d'Alessano
Bombino Bianco
Chardonnay
Cococciola
Falanghina
Fiano
Francavidda
Garganega
Greco
Greco Bianco
Grillo
Impigno
Malvasia Bianca di Candia
Malvasia Bianca Lunga
Malvasia Bianca
Manzoni Bianco
Montonico Bianco
Moscatello Selvatico
Moscato Bianco

Mostosa
Pampanuto
Pinot Bianco
Riesling
Riesling Italico
Sauvignon
Semillon
Sylvaner Verde
Traminer Aromatico
Trebbiano Giallo
Trebbiano Romagnolo
Trebbiano Toscano
Verdeca
Vermentino

### BLACK GRAPES

Aleatico
Aglianico
Barbera
Cabernet Franc
Cabernet Sauvignon

Ancellota
Bombino Nero
Ciliegiolo
Lambrusco Maestri
Lacrima
Malbech
Merlot
Montepulciano
Pinot Nero
Malvasia Nera di Brindisi
Sangiovese
Malvasia Nera di Lecce
Negroamaro
Notar Domenico
Ottavianello
Piedirosso
Primitivo
Susumaniello
Troia
Uva di Troia

## 1. DAUNIA

### From San Severo to Cerignola

*Itinerary of 100 km.*

The term Daunia (after the people that inhabited the area) represents the province of **Foggia** where wines are produced under the names **Cacc'e Mmitte di Lucera**, **San Severo**, **Orta Nova**, **Rosso di Cerignola** and **Rosso Barletta**, the last jointly with the province of Bari. These are all red DOC wines with the exception of San Severo, where whites and rosés are also made, and Orta Nova which also produces rosés.

**Cacc'e Mmitte di Lucera** is a ruby-red table wine made from Uva di Troia, Montepulciano, Sangiovese and Malvasia Nera di Brindisi. Its odd name derives from the fact that in the past the wine was made in *palmenti*, farms equipped with wine tanks owned by the farm-owner that were made available by the day. At the end of the day's work the winemaker took the must to his own cellar and left the *palmente* free for someone else. This procedure led to the name "Cacc'e Mmitte", which literally means "take and put".

### San Severo 🍷

Earthquakes have ensured that few of the ancient buildings and monuments have survived in this town. Today a leader in wine and cereal production, in the 15th and 16th c. San Severo used to be the seat of the governor of the Provincia della Capitanata and the Contado del Molise. The cathedral of Santa Maria Assunta was rebuilt in Baroque style erasing all trace of the previous Romanesque place of worship (11th c.). Better conserved is the Church of San Severino, the right side of which incorporates the old, 12th-c. Romanesque façade.

*Head south on the SP 109.*

### Lucera 🍷

An important city during the time of the Roman empire, Lucera was consigned by Frederick II, duke of Swabia and Holy Roman Emperor, to the Saracens of Sicily, but these were then chased out by Charles of Anjou. The town still has its imposing **fort★** (900 m perimeter) built in the 13th c. by the Angevins, which gives a good **view★** over the Tavoliere plain. The 14th-c. Duomo stands on an attractive square at the centre of the town. The lovely church in Romanesque style close by is dedicated to St Francis of Assisi but is also linked to the name of St Francis Fasani (lived in the 18th c.) who instigated its restoration.

A short distance from the centre, the **Roman amphitheatre★** built during the reign of Augustus is still well conserved.

*Continue south.*

## Troia

This flourishing farming town stands on a hill overlooking the Tavoliere plain. It boasts a fine **cathedral★** in Pugliese Romanesque begun in the 11th c. and completed 200 years later. The façade features tall blind arches and a very lovely rose window. The superb 12th-c. bronze door was made in Byzantine style.

*Continue towards Giardinetto and at the junction with the S 110 turn left in the direction of Castelluccio and Orta Nova.*

Once one of Frederick II's favourite hunting areas, the region of **Orta Nova** is today the chief town in the DOC zone of the same name. Here red and rosé wines are made mostly from Sangiovese grapes.

## Cerignola

The tall-standing olive tree, **Bella della Daunia**, for which Cerignola is famous, was developed in the countryside around the town. Nothing remains of the old centre of Cerignola, which was destroyed in the earthquake of 1731. The modern duomo, construction of which was begun in the 19th c., keeps the painting on panel of the *Madonna di Ripalta* (13th c., the town's patron saint) for half of the year. For the other six months it is kept in the Sanctuary of the Madonna di Ripalta 10 km south of the town. The zone's agricultural life from the past and present is celebrated in the **Polo Museale Civico Città di Cerignola** – **Corn Museum** and **Ethnographic collections** – (*ex Opera Pia Monte Fornari, Piano delle Fosse; for information Pro Loco Cerignola ☎388 93 04 884*) and in the **Ethnographic collections**. The latter is also interesting for its section on religious traditions.

## 2. THE PROVINCE OF BARI

The province of Bari is the location of the appellations **Rosso Barletta** (shared with the province of Foggia), **Moscato di Trani** (an extraordinary sweet wine also produced as a fortified wine), **Rosso Canosa**, **Castel del Monte**, **Gravina** and **Gioia del Colle**.

Locorotondo DOC is shared between the provinces of Bari and Brindisi, while **Martina Franca**, also a white DOC zone, spreads into the provinces of Brindisi and Taranto.

## From Canosa di Puglia to Castel del Monte

*Itinerary of 155 km.*

### Canosa di Puglia ♀

This ancient Greek and later Roman city became famous for its ceramic vases. Its 11th-c. Romanesque **cathedral** has clear Byzantine influences and was restored in

| DOCG | |
| --- | --- |
| Primitivo di Manduria Dolce Naturale | Gravina |
| Castel del Monte Bombino Nero | Leverano |
| Castel del Monte Nero di Troia Riserva | Lizzano |
| Castel del Monte Rosso Riserva | Locorotondo |
| | Martina Franca *or* Martina |
| **DOC** | Matino |
| Aleatico di Puglia | Moscato di Trani |
| Alezio | Nardò |
| Barletta | Negroamaro di Terra d'Otranto |
| Brindisi | Orta Nova |
| Cacc'e Mmitte di Lucera | Ostuni |
| Castel del Monte | Primitivo di Manduria |
| Colline Joniche Tarantine | Rosso Canosa |
| Copertino | Rosso di Cerignola |
| Galatina | Salice Salentino |
| Gioia del Colle | San Severo |
| | Squinzano |
| | Tavoliere delle Puglie *or* Tavoliere |
| | Terra d'Otranto |

## THE TERROIR

**Area**: 19,540.9 km², of which approximately 87,790 hectares are planted to vine

**Production 2019**: 10,584,617 hectolitres of which 648,652 VQPRD

**Geography**: 1.5% mountainous, 45.5% hilly, 53% flat. The soil is partly calcareous and tufaceous, partly clayey and sandy. The climate is Mediterranean and breezy

## THE PROTECTION CONSORTIA

Consorzio Daunia Verde – ✆ 0881 31 18 31, consorziodauniaverde.it

Consorzio Movimento Turismo del Vino Puglia– ✆ 080 52 33 038, www.mtvpuglia.it

Consorzio Tutela del Vino Primitivo di Manduria – ✆ 099 97 96 696, www.consorziotutelaprimitivo.com

Consorzio Tutela e Valorizzazione DOC Leverano – ✆ 0832 92 50 53

Consorzio Tutela Vini DOC Brindisi e DOC Squinzano – ✆ 0831 65 27 49, www.vinibrindisisquinzanodoc.it

Consorzio Tutela Vini DOC Castel del Monte – ✆ 080 89 83 010, www.pugliasveva.it, facebook.com/consorziodoccasteldelmonte

Consorzio Tutela Vini Salice Salentino – www.consorziosalicesalentino.it

Consorzio Tutela Vino DOC Locorotondo – ✆ 080 43 11 298 / 080 4311644

Consorzio per la Tutela del Vino DOC Rosso Barletta – ✆ 0883 51 06 81

Consorzio Tutela Vino DOC Rosso Canosa – ✆ 0883 66 14 10

Consorzio Tutela Vino Gravina DOC – ✆ 080 32 65 865, www.gravinadop.it

Consorzio Tutela Vino Moscato di Trani – ✆ 0883 40 33 62 or 349 08 51 639

## WINE AND FOOD ROUTES

Associazione Strada degli Antichi Vini Rossi – ✆ 0883 61 02 10/06

Strada Appia dei Vini DOC Brindisi-Ostuni – ✆ 347 87 75 848

Strada dei Vini DOC Castel del Monte – ✆ 329 68 89 389, www.stradavinicasteldelmonte.it

Strada dei Vini DOC Locorotondo e Martina Franca – ✆ 080 43 11 644,

Strada dei Vini DOC Primitivo di Manduria e Lizzano – ✆ 099 95 52 013,

Strada del Vino Vigna del Sole – ✆ 0832 68 24 16

Strada dell'Olio Extravergine Castel del Monte – ✆ 0883 55 10 51, www.stradaoliocasteldelmonte.it

Strade del vino di Puglia – ✆ 0883 33 43 76 or 393 93 72 503, www.lestradedelvinopuglia.it

the 17th c. following damage caused by an earthquake. Note the bishop's throne (11th c.) and the tomb of Bohemund (d. 1111), the son of Robert Guiscard. This unusual cubical mausoleum is crowned by a dome. Its beautiful bronze door is decorated with figures damascened with silver.

Other places to visit in Canosa are the three **Lagrasta** underground burial chambers built in the 4th c. BC (*Via Cadorna 2*), and the remains of the early Christian Basilica of San Leucio (*to the right of the road to Andria*) built over an earlier Roman temple. *Visits to the burial chambers 9-13 and 15-19, ℘ 333 88 56 300, www.canusium.it.*

*Drive to Barletta.*

## Barletta★

During the 12th and 13th c. Barletta was a very important city. It was the base for the Crusaders on their departure for the Holy Land and chosen as a seat for many military and hospitaller orders of knights. Today it is a farming and commercial town with a lovely historic centre of medieval civil and religious buildings. The symbol of the town is a statue that probably dates from the 4th c.: it is a **colossal figure★** (4.5 m tall) of an Eastern Roman emperor, thought to be Valentinian II. The statue is of interest in that it is an example of the transition from Roman art to early Christian art. Standing behind the statue is the **Basilica del San Sepolcro** (12th-14th c.) that contains a relic of the Holy Cross. The base of the reliquary is lined with enamels from Limoges. The beautiful **castle★** is an impressive construction built by Frederick II to guard the port. It was greatly modified during later periods, particularly under Charles V in the 16th c. It was to Charles that the unusual shape of the four corner bastions is owed: they are in the form of an arrowhead and each contains two casemates, one above the other.

From the castle garden you can see the cathedral, built partly in Romanesque style (12th c.) and partly in Gothic (14th c., the apse).

The ground floor of Palazzo di Don Diego de Mendoza (14th c.) in Via Cialdini is where the **Disfida** (Challenge of Barletta) was made by an Italian knight following an insult made by a Frenchman, Charles

*Trani cathedral*

de la Motte (*Open 10-14 and 16-20, www.centrostoricobarletta.it*). The challenge was a chivalrous tournament between 13 French and 13 Italian knights (the latter led by Ettore Fieramosca). The Italians won and in consequence the French left the district. The 17th-c. Palazzo della Marra with a Baroque façade contains the splendid **De Nittis picture gallery★★**, donated by Léontine Lucie Gruvelle, wife of the painter Giuseppe de Nittis, to the town of his birth. *Via Cialdini 74. Open 10-20 (9-19 in win.), closed Mon., ℘ 0883 53 83 72, www.barlettamusei.it.*

*Proceed along the coast.*

## Trani★

Trani is an important wine market with a port where every evening the fishing boats unload their catch and the fish market is held. The symbol of the city is its Romanesque **cathedral★★★**. Dedicated to St Nicholas the Pilgrim, a humble Greek shepherd who is supposed to have arrived in Trani on the back of a dolphin, it was built between the 11th and 13th c. The bell tower stands on the right. The fine bronze door was cast around 1180. The nave and aisles are slightly raised over a couple of immense crypts: the lower of the two contains a veritable forest of ancient columns.

The **public gardens★** to the east of the port offer views over the old city and its tall cathedral. The castle beside the sea was built by the Swabian duke Frederick II.

*Castel del Monte*

The road that leads to Bari passes through several pleasant little coastal towns that were obliged to build fortifications due to the constant threats from the sea, starting with the attacks of the Saracens in the early Middle Ages and lasting till the invasions of the Turks at the end of the 15th c. The picturesque fishing port **Bisceglie** has a medieval cathedral with a lovely central portal that rests on two lions; **Molfetta** has a white limestone cathedral built in Pugliese Romanesque that looks out to sea; and **Giovinazzo** is another fishing port with its own small 12th-c. cathedral.

Return in the direction of Molfetta and turn left towards **Corato**, another olive oil and wine town, where the Church of San Vito (11th-12th c.) is an interesting building of Byzantine derivation with a central dome.

In the countryside to the north-west of Corato, on the road to Andria, a simple building constructed at the end of the 16th-c. commemorates the **Challenge of Barletta** and indicates the place where the famous tournament was held on 13 February 1503.

## Andria ♟

Frederick II had his second and third wives – Yolande of Jerusalem (d. 1288) and Isabella of England (d. 1241) – buried in the **Duomo** here. Little remains of the original construction as it was almost completely rebuilt at the end of the 15th c. and several times modified since. The bell tower, whose solid architecture is lightened by openings and a spire, was constructed between the 12th and 14th c. Inside the cathedral, the arch that separates the nave from the presbytery is 15th c. The crypt, which belonged to the church that was replaced by the duomo, contains two tombs that have always been considered the resting places of Frederick's two wives.

## Castel del Monte★★★ ♟

*Open Apr.-Sept. 10.15-19.45, rest of the year 9-18.30, ℘ 0883 56 99 97 or ℘ 388 30 26 000, www.casteldelmonte.beniculturali.it. The last stretch of road is closed to traffic so leave your car in the car-park.*

The road from Andria is straight and passes among olive trees and old farms. The view as you arrive at Castel del Monte is surprising: the golden limestone castle stands on top of a rise on the Murgia plateau and is a perfect blend of power and refinement. Before entering, you are recommended to walk around it to admire the exterior. Frederick had it built in 1240. Structurally it is the exception to the approximately 200 castles the emperor had built as the others were all square. Castel del Monte is octagonal, with 8 corner towers 24 m high and themselves octagonal. The triumphal archway portal leads to the inner courtyard, onto which 8 trapezoidal rooms with ogival vaults open. On the upper floor 8 identical rooms are illuminated by richly decorated windows. The water conveyance system is very sophisticated: the rainwater falling on the roof flowed into the tower cisterns and

## The castles of Frederick II

A versatile and cultured man, the Holy Roman Emperor Frederick II (1194-1250) built numerous castles and forts in Puglia, the designs of which he oversaw personally. The basic model was square, which was derived from the ancient Roman castrum, but also a reference to numerical symbology, which in the Middle Ages was thought to be almost magical. The square and circle were considered symbols of the two vital forces: Earth and Heaven, man and God. The highest expression of this practical yet also magical synthesis was achieved in the octagonal plan of the Castel del Monte. The octagon was thought of as a combination of the square and circle, and thus united the divine and the human. Eight is the number that recurs almost obsessively in this construction: it has 8 sides, 8 corner towers, and 8 rooms on each floor.
Other castles built in Puglia by Frederick are those in Bari, Barletta, Brindisi, Castel del Monte, Gioia del Colle, Manfredonia (built by Frederick's son, Manfredi) and Trani.

was then conveyed through lead pipes to each of the rooms.

## 3. THE PROVINCES OF BRINDISI, TARANTO AND LECCE

The area of Puglia that straddles the provinces of Brindisi, Lecce and Taranto contains many DOC zones: in Brindisi **Ostuni**, **Brindisi**, **Salice Salentino** (with the province of Lecce) and **Locorotondo** (with the province of Bari); in Taranto **Primitivo di Manduria**, **Lizzano**, **Colline Joniche Tarantine** and **Martina Franca** (with the province of Bari); in Lecce **Leverano**, **Copertino**, **Nardò**, **Alezio**, **Matino**, **Squinzano**, **Salice Salentino** and **Galatina**. The range produced encompasses white, red, rosé and sweet wines.

### The trulli area in Brindisi

*Itinerary of 120 km from Alberobello to San Donaci.*

A landscape of olive trees and low walls is dotted increasingly with *trulli* as you draw closer to Ostuni. *Trulli* are plastered buildings with a square or circular base, and conical roofs topped by *chiancarelle* (tiles made from local grey limestone). The differently shaped spires on the roofs are derived from either ancient pagan cults or, in the cases of crosses, Christianity. Magical and religious symbols often appear, sometimes on the roofs. In Puglia there are no ancient *trulli* (the oldest has the date 1559 carved on it) because they were not considered buildings to be conserved: if they were in poor condition they were destroyed and rebuilt. The name *trullo* only appeared in the Italian language in the last 100 years.

### Alberobello★★★

Alberobello has a large district of *trulli* (numbering roughly 1400) on a hill on the south side of the town. This is known as the Monumental Zone and is divided into the following sections: Rione Monti, which has a great number of *trulli* and is very touristic, and Aia Piccola, where there are fewer *trulli* but more linked to the local inhabitants' everyday life. The Church of **Sant'Antonio**, built in the form of a *trullo*, stands on the top of Rione Monti (*access from Via Monte Sant'Angelo*).

The **Territory Museum** (*in the modern district of the town in Piazza XXVII Maggio*) is housed in a large 18th-c. trullo. *Guided visits 10-13 and 15.30-19, closed Mon., ℘ 380 41 11 273.*

Close to the main church in Piazza Sacramento is the **Trullo Sovrano★**, which dates from the 17th c. and has two floors (in local dialect the house on the first floor is called *subbrane*, from which the name *sovrano*, or "sovereign", is taken). To begin with this

*The "trulli" of Alberobello*

© PixAchi/Shutterstock

was a religious building but it was turned into a patrician's residence. The interior is still furnished with the belongings of the family that lived here.

*Open Apr.-Oct. 10-13.15, 15.30-19, rest of the year 10-13.15, 15.30-18, ☏ 080 43 26 030, www.trullosovrano.eu.*

*Take the S 172 to Locorotondo.*

## Locorotondo★

The name Locorotondo means "round place" and is linked to the fact that the town was constructed on a hill all around which concentric rings of roads were built. The historic centre includes the Neoclassical Church of San Giorgio and the Church of Santa Maria la Greca embellished by a fine Gothic rose window. The Town Hall offers a lovely view over the town and plain beyond.

The road from Locorotondo to Martina Franca passes through the **Itria valley★★**, a huge fertile plain covered by vineyards and olive groves and *trulli*.

## Martina Franca★

This white little town is built on a hill in Murgia. The walled old city stands on the top, a mixture of Baroque and Rococo buildings. The lovely Piazza Roma is the setting for the **Ducal Palace** (1668), whose *piano nobile* is decorated with 18th-c. frescoes. *For information on visit ☏ 080 48 05 702.* Follow Corso Vittorio Emanuele to Piazza Plebiscito, where the square is dominated by the white façade of the Church of San Martino. The adjacent Piazza Maria Immacolata has an attractive ringed portico, and **Via Cavour★** is lined on either side by Baroque palaces. The Baroque façade of the Church of San Domenico can be seen in Via Principe Umberto.

*Return to Locorotondo and head east.*

A fine lookout point over the Itria valley is the Town Hall in **Cisternino** (*10 km east*). An oriental atmosphere is created in the historic centre by the twisting alleys and the low houses with outdoor stairways.

## Ostuni★

This gem of a town on the edge of the Murgia area is dazzlingly white under the summer sun; its huddle of small, lime-washed houses is threaded with alleyways that lead to small squares and courtyards. The old city is set inside walls built by the Spanish. The **cathedral**, constructed at the end of the 15th c. with

elements of Romanesque and Gothic styles, stands at the top of a tiny sloping square. The crown of the façade is formed by the interplay of concave lines (at the centre) and convex (at the sides) emphasised by small decorative arches. The middle is embellished with a very beautiful rose window whose decoration symbolises the passing of time: there are 24 outer arches to represent the hours, 12 inner ones for the months, while Christ at the centre is ringed by 7 angel heads representing the days of the week. On the road to Brindisi you pass through **Carovigno**, where you can admire its fine medieval centre and a 12th-c. castle restored 200 years ago. At the centre of **San Vito dei Normanni** is a Norman tower that is part of the castle built by Bohemund d'Altavilla in the 12th c. Do not neglect to visit the Church of Santa Maria della Vittoria, which was built in the 16th c. to celebrate the defeat of the Turks at the battle of Lepanto in 1571.

## Brindisi ♟

Brindisi was founded at the end of a deep inlet between two bays, the Seno di Ponente on the north-west side, and the Seno di Levante to the east. This port has long been a bridge with the East and at the centre of the routes that the Greeks, first, and then the Romans took in their travels to the south-east Mediterranean. Over the centuries many other cultures came to the area and left their marks on the city.

The city's importance was increased by the Roman emperor Trajan from 109 AD when he replaced the old Via Appia with a new road, the Via Traiana, which reached Brindisi directly from Benevento. Like Barletta, after the Norman conquest of southern Italy, the city became a setting-off point for the crusaders to the Holy Land, in particular the during the Sixth Crusade led by Frederick II in 1228.

The main gateway to the city was Porta Mesagne, built in the 13th c. Guarding the Seno di Ponente is the castle built by Frederick in 1227 that today is one of the homes of the Italian navy. A marble column close to the port was probably raised by the Romans to mark the end of the Via Appia. It was one of a pair, but the other was taken to Lecce at some time since 1528.

*Ostuni with its white houses*

**Piazza Duomo** is the setting for the Romanesque duomo, the Portico dei Cavalieri Templari (14th c.) and the Loggia Balsamo (14th c.). The duomo was rebuilt in the 18th c. though the remains of the ancient mosaic floor were retained in the new building. **The Archaeological Museum** (also on the square) has a collection of Attic, Apulian and Messapican vases, the two latter peoples being indigenous to Puglia. *Open 8-17, closed Sat.-Sun.,* ✆ *0831 54 42 57.*

Brindisi's historic centre has many churches. **San Giovanni al Sepolcro** is a Templar church built in the 11th c. with a porch supported by columns resting on lions. The Church of **San Benedetto** (11th c.) has a very simple interior; its nave is covered by ribbed cross-vaults and is lined with columns with Corinthian and zoomorphic capitals. The Romanesque Church of **Santa Lucia** has 13th-c. frescoes and was constructed over an ancient Basilian church. Its 12th-c. frescoes, some of which are well conserved, include a fine *Madonna and Child* and, to its right, the *Maddalena Mirrofora* (the Magdalene with Myrrh), which supports a small shrine containing two ampoules.

Not far from the airport, 5 km to the north, is a splendid example of Romanesque-Gothic architecture: the Church of **Santa Maria del Casale**, built by Philip of Anjou and his wife Catherine of Flanders in the 14th c. The interior has an interesting cycle of frescoes in Byzantine style. On the counter-façade note the *Last Judgement* and, in the right aisle, the *Tree of the Cross.*

Due to its strategic position on the old Oria-Brindisi road, **Mesagne**, 14 km south-west of Brindisi, was destroyed and rebuilt several times. Its castle was also rebuilt and today it houses an archaeological museum. One side of the fort guards the Church of Sant'Anna (1690), a good example of Pugliese Baroque.

In **Latiano** ☙ *(8 km south-west)* the Boschetto della Marangiosa is a beautiful wooded area covered with typical Mediterranean vegetation.

Drive for 16 km in a straight line across the Salentino plain (also called Tavoliere di Lecce) to **San Dònaci** ☙, the last town in the province of Brindisi. It is an important winemaking centre, as is **Cellino San Marco** ☙, a few km to the north-east.

## Taranto and the Tarantino ravines

*Itinerary of 50 km from Taranto to Castellaneta.*

### Taranto★

Anyone arriving in Taranto along the coast from the west is struck by the city's immense industrial zone and huge port, which was turned from a commercial concern into a military port during the Napoleonic era. At first glance the old city on the sea seems a bit dilapidated. Once on the revolving bridge, however, your gaze is drawn by the noble Aragonese castle and, on the other side of the canal that joins the Mar Grande to the Mar Piccolo, by the elegance of the palaces and seafront. Taranto was the most important city in Magna Grecia and of very ancient and legendary origin. The myth goes that it was named by Taras, the son of the Greek sea god Poseidon, though at a more mundane level it is believed that it was founded in 706 BC by Spartan colonists. The city's past is narrated in the marvellous MARTA, the city's completely revamped archaeological museum.

**MARTA – National Archaeological Museum of Taranto★★★** – *Via Cavour 10. Open Tue.-Sat. 8.30-19.30, Sun. and public hols. 9-13, 15.30-19.30* ✆ *099 45 32 112, www.museotaranto.beniculturali.it.* This completely renovated and refitted museum recounts the history of the region of Taranto and Magna Grecia. Among its many objects on display, special mention must be given to the bronze statue of Zeus (6th c. BC), the superb collection of ceramics, and above all the outstanding collection of gold jewellery dating from the Hellenistic era (4th-3rd c. BC).

Marvellous views of the inland bay (the Mare Piccolo) and port can be seen from the **Villa Peripato municipal gardens★**, planted with lush, exotic vegetation.

The **Vittorio Emanuele Seafront★** is an attractive promenade by the sea lined with palms and oleanders.

The **old city★** was built on an island connected to the mainland by two bridges, one of which is a revolving bridge. The **Aragonese castle** at the eastern end is today the premises of the Italian navy command. Constructed during the 11th and 12th c. but largely rebuilt (the façade is Baroque), the **Duomo** boasts ancient columns with Romanesque and Byzantine capitals, a 17th-c. ceiling, and the 18th-c. Chapel of San Cataldo lined with polychrome marbles and decorated with statues.

The Church of San Domenico Maggiore was founded in the 14th c. but was rebuilt to a great extent in the Baroque age.

*Follow the SS 7 north-west for 14 km.*

## Massafra★ and the ravine★

Massafra has an extraordinary number of **rock churches** (hermits' cells, crypts, grottoes) hidden in the ravine that surrounds the town. The Old Bridge, which joins Massafra's two centres, offers a magnificent view over the ravine in which the cell-cenoby of Santa Marina is hidden. It consists of a crypt (12th-13th c.) and a residence. Another visit not to be missed is to the crypt of Sant'Antonio Abate near the hospital. This dates from the 10th-11th c. and is decorated with frescoes from the 12th-18th c. In the direction of the cemetery you will find the crypt of San Leonardo, which was opened in the 13th or 14th c., also decorated with a cycle of frescoes. The crypt of Candelora, which has been damaged by rockfalls, has the plan of a basilica, elegant capitals, and frescoes from the 13th-14th c.

The rock church in the best condition is the Church-crypt of San Marco.

*For guided visits (recommended) to the rock churches, ask at the Nuova Hellas Tourist Office,* ✆ *099 88 04 695, www. massafraturismo.it.*

Just 2 km north-east of Massafra stands the 18th-c. **Sanctuary of the Madonna della Scala** where the legendary icon of the Madonna della Cerva is conserved (12th-14th c.). The crypt, which probably dates from the 8th c., is thought to be the earliest example of religious practice on the site. The troglodytic village of hundreds of rock caves in the wall of the ravine can be reached from in front of the sanctuary. Another rock village definitely deserving of a visit is **Petruscio** on the road to Mòttola. This series of caves was formed in the 9th c. with crypt-churches that date from the 13th c. Next comes **Mòttola★**, another town surrounded by ravines cut with grottoes inhabited in the Middle Ages.

The ravine that surrounds **Castellaneta** ♟ on three sides is the largest in the Ionian arc, and was chosen as a settlement in the 10th c. during the period of raids by Saracen pirates. In addition to its superb natural setting, the town has been made famous as the birthplace of Rodolfo Pietro Filiberto Raffaello Guglielmi, better known as the star of the silent screen **Rudolf Valentino** (1895-1926), to whom the town has dedicated a museum.

# Salento

*Itinerary of approximately 200 km from Taranto to Lecce.*

The tour around the Salento peninsula begins in Taranto, heads to Gallipoli and then cuts across inland to Lecce. Those who prefer to take the coast road on this last stretch will be dazzled by the pastel-coloured sea, which changes hues with every variation in the light. However, taking the inland road gives you the chance to visit winemaking towns like **Carosino** and **San Marzano di San Giuseppe** (where the language spoken is based on the dialect of the Albanian community that moved here over past centuries), the rock sanctuary of the Madonna delle Grazie, and Sava and Lizzano. This is the zone where Primitivo di Manduria DOC is produced, a red wine made from Primitivo grapes, to which a special museum is dedicated: the **Primitivo a Manduria Wine Museum** (*Consorzio Produttori Vini di Manduria, Via Massimo 19, Manduria, Open 9-13, 16-19, closed Sun. pm, ℘ 099 973 53 32, www.museodelprimitivo.it*).

## Manduria 🍷

The rather austere lines of the 18th-c. Palazzo Imperiali are tempered by its elegant portal and Baroque balcony in the town's main square. Take Via Mercanti to reach the Duomo, dedicated to St Gregory the Great. Only the bell tower reflects the church's medieval origins as the rest was renovated in Renaissance and Baroque styles. The archaeological park of the Messapican walls is home to the symbol of Manduria: the town's **three rings of walls★** (5th-2nd c. BC), which at their longest measure 5 km in perimeter and allowed the town to successfully defend itself against the expansionistic designs of its rival, Taranto.

Continue eastwards from Manduria through San Pancrazio Salentino and **Guagnano** 🍷 to arrive at **Salice Salentino** 🍷, the chief town of the DOC zone of that name, which produces white, rosé and red versions of the wine from the native Negroamaro grapes.

Two towns 13 km further south give their names to DOC wines: one is **Leverano** 🍷, the other **Copertino**. The latter is also known for its 16th-c. castle, one of those in best condition in the Salento region. The cathedral della Vergine delle Nevi was founded in 1088,

renovated between the 12th and 16th c. and transformed in the 18th c. It has an attractive Renaissance portal on one side and a Baroque bell tower. Further along the coast you come to **Porto Cesàreo**, built on a superb spot on the coast, with a natural port that looks onto the Isola Grande. An ancient section that extends into the sea is where you can see the Cesàrea Tower and the Marine Biology Station with an annexed museum. Since 1997 the sea around Porto Cesàreo has been protected by a park of approximately 170 square kilometres as the sea bed is sub-tropical in nature and inhabited by creatures typical of warm seas.

## Nardò★

The Baroque arches, balconies, loggias and decorated portals testify to the artistic, cultural and architectural vitality of Nardò, which rivalled Lecce in the 17th and 18th c. This is the home of **Nardò DOC** wine and the ancient and famous Cellina di Nardò olive trees, one of the most representative varieties of Salento. One of the entrances to the historic centre, which in some points is still closed off by low towers, is Largo Osanna. The centre of the town is **Piazza Salandra**, with the 18th-c. spire of the Immacolata at the centre. Facing onto the square are the Church del Trifone (18th c.), the Sedile with the statue of St Gregory Armenian (patron saint of the town), and the Palazzo di Città (19th c.). Take Via De Pandi and Via Amendola to reach Piazza Cesare Battisti to see the 18th-c. Acquaviva Castle, today the Town Hall. The 18th-c. façade of the cathedral conceals the building's early origin: the first construction here was built by Byzantine monks, but this was superseded in 1080 by the present building, though it has been remodelled several times. The third chapel on the left contains a very beautiful black crucifix made from cedar (13th c.).

*Continue along the coast.*

## Gallìpoli★

"Kalé pólis" ('beautiful city') is how the Greeks named what is today Gallipoli, one of the most glamorous towns in the Salento area. The multi-coloured houses aligned like a city wall seem almost to float on the water and the Riviera offers pleasant promenades as far as the rear of the castle. The tip of the peninsula is where the **Borgo** was built, the town constructed in the 18th-19th c. and divided into two parts (called Scirocco and Tramontana) by the central Corso Roma. The castle was built by the Angevins to defend the port, which today is filled with fishing vessels. It is square in plan with round corner towers. A ravelin built in 1522 extends into the sea as a preliminary defensive system.

Once you cross the bridge you find yourself in **Città**, the ancient nucleus of the town, where the narrow streets twist and turn around the central Via De Pace. The cathedral dedicated to Sant'Agata is the only example of Leccese Baroque architecture in the town. Once you leave the centre and reach the Church of San Francesco d'Assisi (18th c.), you find yourself on the Riviera, which runs alongside the inner side of the walls and gives pleasant views of the sea.

The area to the east of Gallipoli is the production zone of two DOC wines based mainly on Negroamaro grapes: **Matino** and **Alezio**, the second also available as a rosé.

*Return towards Nardò and take the S 101 towards Lecce.*

The centre of **Galàtone** has maintained several Baroque buildings, including the Church del **Crocifisso della Pietà**, a masterpiece by Giuseppe Zimbalo, the genius of Leccese Baroque. Built at the end of the 17th c., it has a monumental façade punctuated by statues and pilasters with Corinthian capitals. The gilt and stucco interior is magnificent. Facing it is the Palazzo Marchesale (16th c.).

Before reaching Galatina you could make a detour to visit Cutrofiano 🍷.

## Galatina★

Galatina is an art city and home to the delightful Galatina DOC wine, a blend of Negroamaro and Malvasia grapes. The town was greatly appreciated by the princes Orsini del Balzo, who decided to have their residence here and also constructed the splendid Basilica of **Santa Caterina d'Alessandria★★**. This was built in 1384 in Romanesque-Gothic from a design by Raimondello Orsini del Balzo, who had the works begun after his return from the Holy Land and a visit to St Catherine's monastery and church at the foot of Mount Sinai. The façade is in Pugliese Romanesque. The interior contains a marvellous set of frescoes by 15th-c. artists from the Marches and Emilia in which the female figures often have the features of Marie d'Enghien, the wife of Raimondello. A cloister on the left side of the church is decorated with 18th-c. frescoes.

Continue left to reach Corso Vittorio Emanuele, and left again to reach the Church of Santi Pietro e Paolo. Probably begun in the second half of the 14th c., it was rebuilt in the 1700s. The church is known for its rites celebrated on 29 June with a procession accompanied by tambourines.

**Soleto** (*4.5 km north-east*) was for centuries an Italo-Greek cultural and religious town, of which traces remain in the local dialect called *grìko*, spoken most of all by the elderly. Architecturally, the town prides itself on the very fine late Gothic bell tower, 45 m tall and dated to the late 14th c.

*Gallipoli, Consuma beach with the ancient nucleus of the town*

## Lecce★★★ 🍷

The "Florence of the Baroque" and "Athens of Puglia" is a triumph of ornate Baroque architecture. This partly due to the architects but mostly to the many anonymous stonemasons in the 17th and 18th c. who understood the extraordinary potential of the local limestone. Lecce, the chief town of the Salento peninsula, is an open-air museum, but it is by wandering among the bars, shops and craftsmen's workshops that you will discover the town's real nature.

The historic centre was once enclosed by a **castle** (built by Charles V over an earlier Angevin fort) and a 16th-c. city wall but little of this remains. Today the centre is bounded by a ring of avenues. The heart of the city is the busy **Piazza Sant'Oronzo**, where the statue of Lecce's patron saint (St Orontius) has been placed on a column. This was one of the two Roman columns that marked the end of the Via Appia in Brindisi but it was brought to Lecce after it fell in 1528.

The square is also the setting for the deconsecrated church of San Marco (built by a Venetian colony) and the ancient Palazzo del Seggio (late 16th c.) called the "Sedile". A section of the city's Roman amphitheatre (2nd c.) has been excavated to the south of the square.

**Santa Croce★★** – The basilica was designed by several architects during the 16th and 17th c. and is the most representative example of Leccese Baroque. The façade is very elaborate but not overly heavy. The richly decorated upper register is almost undoubtedly by one of the inventive Zimbalo family of artists who worked right across the Salento area. The soaring and luminous interior is characterised by a simplicity of architecture suggestive of Florentine Renaissance style but it also possesses an abundance of Baroque ornamentation.

Next to the church is the **Palazzo del Governo**, which was once a convent belonging to the Celestine order.

Completely ringed by a uniform set of Baroque buildings and heralded by an archway that faces onto Corso Vittorio Emanuele, **Piazza del Duomo★★** is one of the best known squares in southern Italy. The left side is lined by the bell tower designed by Giuseppe Zimbalo (1617-1710), followed by the Duomo renovated

*Baroque architecture of Lecce*

© Valeria/Shutterstock

by the same architect, the 17th-c. Palazzo Vescovile and the Palazzo del Seminario. This last building was constructed in 1709 with a sumptuously decorated well in the inner courtyard. The façade of the duomo that appears first is in fact the left side of the building. It has an imposing entrance and an arch above containing the statue of St Orontius. The main façade is more sobre. The crypt (rebuilt in the 16th c. over the existing medieval building) is supported by 92 columns with capitals of zoomorphic figures.

Giuseppe Zimbalo's last work, the **Church del Rosario★** (also known as the Church of San Giovanni Battista) has an over-decorated but handsome façade. The **interior★** has Baroque altars with lovely 17th-c. altarpieces.

Many elegant buildings flank **Via Palmieri**, such as Palazzo Marese and Palazzo Palmieri (close to Piazzetta Falconieri). At the end of the street, Porta Napoli (or the Triumphal Arch) was constructed in the 16th c. in honour of Charles V.

On the right of the road to Brindisi, 14 km from Lecce, you will see the Church of **Santa Maria di Cerrate★** standing solitary in the countryside. This charming 12th c. Benedictine abbey has a refined portal and is closed on the left side by a porch with beautiful historiated capitals (13th c.). Only some of the frescoes that probably once covered the entire interior of the church are still extant.

The wine produced in this part of the country is the red **Squinzano**, made for the most part from Negroamaro grapes.

# Addresses

## Tourist information

**Region of Puglia** – www.viaggiareinpuglia.it
**Agenzia Puglia Promozione** – Piazza Moro 33/A, Bari, ✆ 080 52 42 361, www.agenziapugliapromozione.it
**Tourist Office Brindisi** – Via Duomo 20, ✆ 0831 22 97 84
**Tourist Office Lecce Castello Carlo V** – Via XXV Luglio, ✆ 0832 24 65 17
**Tourist Office Foggia** - Via Scillitani 2
**Tourist Office Taranto** – Piazza Castello, Galleria Comunale, ✆ 334 28 44 098
**Puglia Wine Tourism Movement** – Via Sangiorgi 15, **Bari**, ✆ 080 52 33 038, www.mtvpuglia.it

## The wineries

*The addresses are listed in alphabetical order by location.*

### DAUNIA

**Alberto Longo** – SP Lucera 5, km 4 - **Lucera** (Fg) - ✆ 0881 53 90 57 - www.albertolongo.it - info@albertolongo.it - Winery tours by reservation. The winery is located in a 19th-c. farmhouse, the Fattoria Cavalli. The vineyards are divided between the Fattoria Cavalli and the Masseria Cementano. Montepulciano, Bombino Bianco, Nero di Troia, Falanghina, Chardonnay, Negroamaro, Merlot, Syrah, Cabernet Franc and Sauvignon grapes are grown here, and the cellar produces wines that are representative of the terroir. Hectares under vine: 35.
**Wines**: Cacc' e Mmitte di Lucera, IGT Puglia Rosso Le Cruste, Primitivo, 4.7.7. Syrah, Montepeloso Aglianico and Capoposto, IGT Puglia Bianco Passito Il Va Puglia Bianco Le Fossette and Le Valli, IGT scello and Suyan, IGT Puglia Rosato Donnadele. Other products: olive oil.

**Paolo Petrilli** – C.da Motta della Regina - **Lucera** (Fg) - ✆ 0881 52 39 80 - www.paolo petrilli.it - lamotticella@libero.it - Winery tours by reservation. The winery is set in an old fortified masseria or farmstead documented as early as the year 1000. Acquired by Paolo Petrilli during the last century, today the estate grows grapes as well as vegetables, olives and cereals. It produces typical local wines such as Cacc' e Mmitte and Nero di Troia. Hectares under vine: 11.
**Wines**: Cacc' e Mmitte Agramante, Ferraù IGT, Nero di Troia Il Guerro, Fortuita IGT. Other products: tomato purée, pasta.

**D'Alfonso Del Sordo** – Ss 89, km 5 - C.da Sant'Antonino - **San Severo** (Fg) - ✆ 0882 22 14 44 - www.dalfonsodelsordo.it - info@dalfonsodelsordo.it. The history of the estate goes back to the mid-19th c. when Baron Antonio del Sordo decided to plant vineyards on part of his property in San Severo and Lucera; during this same period the vigneron Ludovico d'Alfonso was making wine in the cellar of his home. In the early 20th c. Antonio's son Giovanni del Sordo adopted Ludovico's son Felice D'Alfonso. The D'Alfonso del Sordo family was thus formed and the eponymous farming estate was established in the latter part of the 20th c. Hectares under vine: 90.
**Wines**: IGT Puglia Rosso Casteldrione and Montero, IGT Puglia Bianco Pepito's and Catapanus, IGP Puglia Bianco Dammisole and Cortecampana, S. Severo DOC Arignano, IGP Puglia Rosso Dammitempo and Guado San Leo, IGP Puglia Rosato Dammirose

**D'Araprì** – Via Zannotti 30 - **San Severo** (Fg) - ✆ 0882 22 76 43 - www.darapri.it - info@darapri.it - Winery tours by reservation. D'Araprì was established in 1979 when three friends and jazz musicians with a passion for wine – Girolamo d'Amico, Louis Rapini and Ulrico Priore, whose surnames were combined to create the name of the cellar – decided to make sparkling wine in San Severo. Today the winery is the only one in Puglia (and one of the few in southern Italy) to produce exclusively Classic Method sparkling wine. Hectares under vine: 7.
**Wines**: Brut, Pas Dosé, Rosé, Sansevieria, Gran Cuvée, La Dama Forestiera, RN.

**L'Antica Cantina** – Cantina Sociale San Severo - Via San Bernardino 94 - **San Severo** (Fg) - ✆ 0882 22 11 25 - www.anticacantina.it - info@anticacantina.it - Winery tours by reservation. The winery, established in 1933, makes wines that have gained national and international recognition, and it has been rewarded for valorising local varieties, considered the historical heritage of a land and its people. Hectares under vine: 1000.
**Wines**: San Severo "1933" and Castrum Bianco, Rosato and Rosso; Nero di Troia, Falanghina, Primitivo and Bombino Nobiles; Bombino, Daunia Falanghina, Daunia Merlot, Daunia Pinot and Uva di Troia Capitolo. Other products: olive oil.

### THE PROVINCE OF BARI

**Rivera** – SP 231, km 60.5 - **Andria** (Bt) - ✆ 0883 56 95 01 - www.rivera.it - info@rivera.it - Winery tours by reservation. In the early 20th c. Giuseppe De Corato acquired the enormous Rivera estate and decided to plant vineyards and olive groves. In the 1950s his son Sebastiano established the winery with the specific aim of promoting and spreading the high-quality winemaking potential of the Castel del Monte area. He thus restructured the cellar, replanted the vineyards and built a bottling plant. Over the years, Sebastiano – assisted by his son Carlo – planted international varieties such as Sauvignon and Chardonnay alongside native grapes such as Bombino Nero, Nero di Troia, Montepulciano and Aglianico. Hectares under vine: 75.

**Wines**: Primitivo di Manduria DOC Triusco, Castel del Monte Nero di Troia Puer Apuliae and Violante, Bombino Bianco Marese, Salento IGT Primitivo, Castel del Monte DOC Bianco Fedora, Locorotondo DOC, IGT Puglia Furfante Frizzante Bianco and Rosé, Castel del Monte Bombino Nero Pungirosa, IGT Puglia Fiano Scariazzo, Castel del Monte Chardonnay Preludio N.1, Castel del Monte DOC Sauvignon Terre al Monte. Other products: olive oil and grappa.

**Agricola Marmo** – *Via Saffo 5* - **Andria** *(Bt)* - *℘0883 26 24 89 - www.agricolamarmo.com - prodotti@agricolamarmo.com - Winery tours by reservation.* Azienda Agricola Marmo was born in 1999 in Contrada Cocevola along the itinerary that connects Andria to Castel del Monte. The vinicultural project is projected on the production of "Vandalo", Nero di Troia, a structured wine that became DOCG "Nero di Troia Castel del Monte" in 2010. Hectares under vine: 7.

**Wines**: Castel del Monte Nero di Troia DOC Vandalo, Castel del Monte Rosso and Rosato Cocevola. Other products: taralli and olive oil.

**Ognissole** – *SP 143, km 3 - C.da Cefalicchio* - **Canosa di Puglia** *(Bt)* - *℘ 0825 98 66 86 - www.ognissole.it - info@ognissole.it - Winery tours and tasting by reservation.* The former Cefalicchio company, today Ognissole, is managed by Luca D'Attoma, an affirmed oenologist and biodynamics-expert. The main business is conducted at the Cefalicchio estate, between Canosa di Puglia and Castel del Monte. There is also another estate exclusively dedicated to organic Primitivo (14 hectares), about 100 km South, on the Gioia del Colle plateau. The estate offers restaurant service and accommodation ( *℘ 0883 19 78 671, www.aziendaagricolacefalicchio.it*). Hectares under vine: 27.

**Wines**: Castel del Monte DOP Bianco Pietraia, Rosso Brecciato and Rosé Pontelama, Primitivo di Gioia del Colle DOC, Puglia Bianco IGP Jalal, Castel del Monte Rosso DOP Nero di Troia Romanico.

**Torrevento** – *SP 234, km 10.6 - Loc. Castel del Monte, Corato (Ba)* - *℘ 080 89 80 923 - www.torrevento.it - accoglienza@torrevento.it - Winery tours by reservation.* After changing hands a number of times, in 1948 an enchanting 18th-c. monastery and its land were purchased by the Liantonio brothers, who started a winegrowing business and established Torrevento. The outline of the stunning octagonal castle nearby has been adopted as the winery's logo. Hectares under vine: 400.

**Wines**: Salice Salentino Rosso Riserva DOC Sine Nomine, Castel del Monte DOCG Rosso Vigna Pedale, Ottagono and Rosé Veritas, Castel del Monte DOC Bianco Pezzapiana, Rosé Primaronda, Rosso Bolonero, Puglia Bianco IGT Torre del Falco Fiano, É Arte, Matervitae Falanghina and Matervitae Verdeca, Puglia Rosso IGT Torre del Falco, Kebir, Since 1913 Primitivo, Ghenos Primitivo di Manduria, É Arte Nero di Troia, Matervitae Negroamaro and Matervitae Primitivo, Puglia Bianco IGT Bacca Rara, Moscato di Trani DOC Dulcis in fundo, Maremosso Bianco and Rosé. Other products: pasta, olive oil.

## THE PROVINCE OF BRINDISI

**Tenute Rubino** – *Via Fermi 50* - **Brindisi** - *℘ 0831 57 19 55 - www.tenuterubino.com - info@tenuterubino.com - Winery bars Mon.-Fri. 9-16 by reservation (visite@tenuterubino.it).* In the 1980s Tommaso Rubino decided to change métier and devote his energies to the Salento terroir. The outcome is a flourishing farming and winegrowing business that has rapidly risen to the highest levels. Tommaso's son Luigi has followed in his footsteps. Tenute Rubino also has a fascinating wine bar on the magnificent Brindisi waterfront (*www. vinotecanumeroprimo.it*). Hectares under vine: 200.

**Wines**: Salento IGT Bianco Giancòla, Marmorelle and Rosato, Susumaniello Torre Testa and Vermentino Libens, Salento IGT Rosso Visellio, Marmorelle, Torre Testa and Oltremé, Brindisi DOC Rosso Jaddico, Salento Primitivo IGT Punta Aquila, Negroamaro DOC Miraglio. Other products: olive oil.

**Azienda Vinicola Al Bano** – *C.da Bosco 12* - **Cellino San Marco** *(BR)* - *℘ 0831 61 92 11 - www.vinicolacarrisi.com - aziendavinicola@albanocarrisi.com - Winery tours and tasting by reservation.* A passion for wine inspired one of Italy's best-known singers to establish a high-quality winegrowing business that is now one of the most famous in the region. Respect for the terroir and local traditions underpins the philosophy of this winery, which grows traditional varieties using organic farming methods. Restaurant service and accommodation available (*www.tenute albano.com*). Hectares under vine: 65.

**Wines**: IGP Salento Rosso Platone, Taras, Bacchus, Nostalgia, Don Carmelo and Il Basiliano, IGP Salento Rosé Romina, Don Carmelo and Mediterraneo, IGP Salento Bianco Don Carmelo and Felicità, DOP Salice Salentino. Other products: grappa, olive oil.

**Masseria Li Veli** – *SP Cellino-Campi* - **Cellino San Marco** *(BR)* - *℘ 0831 61 82 59 - www.liveli.it - info@liveli.it - Winery tours by reservation.* In 1999 the Falvo family purchased the Masseria Li Veli, which was long owned by Antonio de Viti de Marco, a nobleman from Lecce and a farseeing farming entrepreneur who understood the potential of the area and transformed the estate into an efficient wine-growing business. Hectares under vine: 33.

**Wines**: Salento IGT Bianco Fiano and Askos verdeca, Salento IGT Rosé Primerose and Askos Susumaniello, Salento IGT Rosso Primonero, Orion, Passamante, Susumaniello, Primitivo and Malvasia Askos, Salice Salentino DOC Garrisa, Salice Salentino DOC Riserva Pezzo Morgana and "Mlv" Masseria Li Veli.

**Candido** – *Via Diaz 46 -* **San Donaci** *(BR) -* ℘ *0831 63 56 74 -www.candidovini.it - candido@candidowines.it - Winery tours by reservation.* The estate mainly produces reds, but its whites and rosés are also delightful. The area's typical Mediterranean climate, with significant day-night temperature swings, plays a key role in the ideal maturation of the grapes. Indeed, it is this microclimate that gives the grapes intense aromas and great personality. Hectares under vine: 140.

**Wines**: IGT Salento Cappello Di Prete, Duca D'Aragona, Salice Salentino DOC Rosè Le Pozzelle, Primitivo di Manduria Rosso DOC Cassio Dione, Primitivo Salento Rosso Devinis, Salice Salentino Rosso DOC Immensum, La Carta, Salice Salentino Fiano Tenuta Marini, Chardonnay Salento Luminosìa, Salento Passito Paule Calle.

**Masseria Altemura** – *SP 69 Mesagne -* **Torre Santa Susanna** *(BR) -* ℘ *0831 74 04 85 - www.masseriaaltemura.it - info@ masseriaaltemura.it - Food and wine tasting by reservation.* While it's true that the etymology of "Salento" contains the strength of images like the Sun, salt and soil, the project put in motion by this Masseria does everything possible to exalt these concepts. The farmstead is set at the heart of the Salento peninsula, equidistant from the Ionic and Adriatic seas, drawing benefits from the windy currents of one, more open to the Mediterranean, as well as the salinity of the other. The 1676 cantina was designed to preserve the sobriety, attraction and characteristics of Pugliese architecture. The choice of natural materials was based on the desire to avoid altering the landscape and quality of the wine produced there. Hectares cultivated: 130.

**Wines**: Puglia IGT Petravia and Aglianico, Primitivo di Manduria DOC Altemura, Salento IGT Sasseo, Falanghina, Negroamaro, Fiano and Negroamaro Rosato Zìnzula, Apulo Rosso, Apulo Bianco. Other products: olive oil.

## TARANTO AND THE TARANTINO RAVINES

⌂ **Perrini** – *Masseria Carabella -* **Castellaneta** *(TA) -* ℘*328 81 48 068 - www. perrini.it - perrini@perrini.it - Winery tours by reservation.* The Perrini family have grown grapes and made wine for generations; the Masseria Carabella, built in 1809, is the winery's historic headquarters. Tonia, Mila and Vito Francesco Perrini have used organic farming methods since 1993.

Accommodation available on the estate (*www.masseriacarabella.blogspot.it*). Hectares under vine: 50.

**Wines**: Negroamaro, Primitivo, Cuvée, Barriquè, Salento Rosso, Mater Christy, Rosso Naturale and Mila, Prymus, Primitivo gallo, Primitivo Selezione Decanter, Salento Rosso Senza Solfiti, Bianco Salento, Mila, Fiano and Naturale, Negroamaro Rosè. Other products: olive oil, vinegar, marmalade, capers.

## SALENTO

⌂ **L'Astore Masseria** – *Via di Vittorio 1 -* **Cutrofiano** *(LE) -* ℘ *0836 54 20 20 - www. lastoremasseria.it - info@lastoremasseria.it - Winery tours by reservation.* The winery has been run by the Benegiamo – Di Summa family since the 1930s. It initially produced enormous quantities of wine that it sold in northern Italy and on foreign markets. Production was interrupted in the 1970s and 1980s, but in the late 1990s Achille Benegiamo and his children decided to resume winemaking, focusing on quality. Near the picturesque 18th-c. oil mill there is a Salento-style ageing cellar built with Lecce stone and featuring star vaults, making the winery especially appealing.

Accommodation available on the estate (*3 rooms*).Hectares under vine: 20.

**Wines**: Massaro Rosa, Filimei, L'Astore, Jèma, Krita. Other products: olive oil.

♀/ **Cantele** – *SP 365 Km 1 -* **Guagnano** *(LE) -* ℘ *0832 70 50 10 - www.cantele.it - cantele@ cantele.it - Winery tours by reservation, closed Sat. pm and Sun.* The history of the Cantele winery goes back to the 1950s with the grandparents of the current owners. Cantele also has a food-lab and restaurant, iSensi, a vivid expression of Puglia's gastronomic legacy. Hectares under vine: 50.

**Wines**: Salice Salentino DOC, Salento IGT Negroamaro, Fanòi Negroamaro, Fanòi Primitivo, Amativo, Teresa Manara, Varius, Primitivo, Le Passanti, Teresa Manara, Alticelli, Chardonnay, Negroamaro Rosato, Rohesia and Rohesia Brut, Puglia IGT Verdeca.

**Vigneti Reale** – *Via E. Reale 55 -* **Lecce** *(LE) -* ℘ *0832 24 84 33 - www.vignetireale.it - vignetireale@vignetireale.it - Winery tours by reservation.* The Reale family started in 1921 to grow grapes and sell both wine and grapes to third parties. Nevertheless, its chief business had always been tobacco, initially as dealers for the government monopoly and then as processors. After a period devoted to the production of blending wine, now the estate focuses on top quality. The logo depicts the family villa, built in the early 20th c. Hectares under vine: 85.

**Wines**: Salento IGP Malvasia Bianca, Rosata and Nera, Salento IGP Chardonnay Blasi, Negroamaro Norie, Primitivo Rudiae, Salice Salentino DOP Santa Croce, Primitivo di Manduria Gloria. Other products: olive oil.

**Conti Zecca** – *Via Cesarea* - **Leverano** *(LE)* - ☎ *0832 92 56 13* - *www.contizecca.it* - *enoteca@contizecca.it* - *Winery tours and tasting by reservation, closed Sun.* It was in the 1580 that a noble family of Neapolitan counts, the Zeccas, decided to move to Puglia and establish a farming estate. In 1935 Count Alcibiade decided to use the grapes grown on the estate to make wine. His descendants, Counts Alcibiade, Francesco, Luciano and Mario Zecca, have continued his work with great passion. Hectares under vine: 320.

**Wines**: Salento IGP Rosso Rodinò, Nero, Rifugio and Terra, Salento IGP Bianco Luna, Sole, Calavento, Mendola and Agapò, Leverano Riserva DOP Liranu, Salento IGP Rosé Venus.

**Attanasio** – *Via per Oria 13* - **Manduria** *(TA)* - ☎ *099 97 37 121* - *www.primitivo-attanasio. com* - *info@primitivo-attanasio.com* - *Winery tours by reservation.* Giuseppe Attanasio has passionately continued the traditions of a typical Salento family of vignerons. The picturesque cellar in a late-19th-c. palazzo with enormous star vaults merits a visit. The winery works exclusively with Primitivo grapes, which are harvested using traditional methods. Giuseppe personally oversees the work in the vineyards and every phase in the cellar, from fermentation to bottling. Hectares under vine: 6.

**Wines**: Primitivo di Manduria DOCG Dolce Naturale, DOP and DOP Secco, Salento IGP Rosé Primitivo.

**Felline** – *Via S. Stasi I* - **Manduria** *(TA)* - ☎ *099 97 11 660* - *www.agricolafelline.it* - *info@agricolafelline.it* - *Winery tours and tasting by reservation.* The winery has always been committed to valorising the "vineyard of Puglia", i.e. the research and vinification. Here the *racemi* – the second fruits that some varieties develop in large quantities and mature about 20 days after the harvest of the primary clusters – are harvested and vinified later, and offer an opportunity to improve the results of the first vinification. Hectares under vine: 120.

**Wines**: DOP Dunico, Giravolta, Primitivo di Manduria and Zinfandel, Puglia IGP Rosso Alberello, Fellone, Malvasia Nera, Puglia IGP Bianco Fiano, Verdeca and Vermentino.

⚲ **Leone de Castris** – *Via de Castris 26* - **Salice Salentino** *(LE)* - ☎ *0832 73 11 12* - *www.leonedecastris.com* - *marketing@ leonedecastris.com* - *Winery tours Mon.-Fri. 9-16.30 by reservation.* Salice Salentino has been home to this ancient winery for over 300 years. Duke Oronzo Arcangelo Maria Francesco, Earl of Lemos, established the winery in 1665. Nevertheless, regular bottling commenced in 1925. Five Roses, the first rosé to be bottled and sold in Italy, goes back to 1943. The name is tied to the fact that there is a district in the fief of Salice Salentino called "Cinque Rose" – five roses – because the Leone de Castris family astonishingly bore five children for generations. The estate also has a wine museum and a winebar. Accommodation available (*24 rooms*). Hectares under vine: 300.

**Wines**: Salento IGT Per lui Rosso, Primitivo, Susumaniello, Donna Lisa Malvasia Bianca, Angiò Fiano, Imago Chardonnay, Vigna Case Alte Sauvignon, Messapia Verdeca, Aleikos Aleatico, Marlisa Negroamaro, Villa Larena Primitivo, Elo Veni Negroamaro, Villa Santera Primitivo, Il Lemos Shiraz, Maiana Rosso and Rosato, Five Roses, Five Roses Anniversario, 50° Vendemmia, Copertino DOC, Locorotondo DOC. Other products: grappa, olive oil.

## Where to stay

### ALBEROBELLO

**Fascino Antico** – *SS 172, km 36 Alberobello (BA)* - ☎ *329 09 42 119* - *www.fascinoantico trulli.com* - *4 trulli from €110.* A small hamlet of trulli, some of which with a kitchenette.

### CANOSA DI PUGLIA

**Biomasseria Lama di Luna** – *Loc. Montegrosso, 10 km SE of Canosa (BA)* - ☎ *0883 56 95 05* - *www.lamadiluna.com* - *11 rooms, doubles from €170.* The 19th-c. farmhouse has been restructured based on the principles of bioarchitecture and feng shui, for a fascinating blend of regional traditions and Japanese philosophy.

### LUCERA

**B&B Le foglie di Acanto** – *Via L. Frattarolo 3* - ☎ *340 36 52 912* - *www.lefogliediacanto.it* - *4 doubles from €95.* In the centre of Lucera, it offers elegant accommodation. It also hosts exhibitions and art workshops.

### MOTTOLA

**Masseria Cassiere** – *C.da Matine 180, San Basilio Mottola (TA), 10 km NW of Mottola* - ☎ *349 32 69 302* - *www.masseriacassiere.it* - *4 rooms and 3 apts, doubles from €60.* The lovely farmhouse hosts the Fondazione Murgia delle Gravine, a library on the history and environment of Terra delle Gravine; open for consultation on request. The rooms are charming and comfortable.

### UGENTO

**Vivosa Apulia Resort** – *Via Vicinale Fontanelle, Marina di Ugento (LE), 7 km SW of Ugento, south of Gallipoli* - ☎ *0833 93 10 02* - *www.vivosaresort.com* - *doubles from €200.* The enormous complex has a private beach and a wellness centre with a fitness area.

# SICILY

Trinacria – the queen of the Mediterranean – was invaded time and again over the centuries by various peoples: the Phoenicians, the Greeks, the Romans, the Byzantines, the Normans and the Arabs. Consequently, the island has a particularly varied cultural heritage. In recent years, the region's wine production has attracted enormous attention, thanks to the prudent redevelopment of viticulture and the excellent results achieved with the cultivation of international varieties.

© Domenico Pellegriti/iStock

*Sicilian vineyards*

## The terroir

Sicily boasts an extraordinary heritage of grape varieties: among the **whites** Catarrato, Carricante, Inzolia, Grillo, Grecanico, Minnella Bianca, Malvasia delle Lipari, Zibibbo (or Moscato d'Alessandria) are native to the island, as are Frappato, Nero d'Avola, Perticone, Calabrese, Nerello Mascalese, Pignatello, Gaglioppo and Nocera among the **reds**. Nevertheless, **international varieties** – Cabernet, Merlot, Syrah, Chardonnay and Sauvignon – are also grown here successfully, yielding exceptional wines. For centuries, Sicily has been associated with **sweet wines**. Moscato di Noto, Moscato di Siracusa, Passito di Pantelleria and Malvasia delle Lipari are distinguished by their seductive and fruity bouquets, whereas **Marsala**, the Italian fortified wine that has made history, deserves special mention.
**Cerasuolo di Vittoria**, a red made from Frappato and Calabrese grapes, has recently been granted DOCG status. Its name is derived from its cerise colour. A wine with ancient origins, it offers aromas of morello cherries, black cherries,

cinnamon, cocoa and liquorice. Sicily's 23 appellations are spread out over various provinces, making most of the island quite intriguing in terms of winemaking. In most cases, the appellations produce their various types of wine from an array of varieties.

## Itineraries

*Locations with a winery are indicated by the symbol ♆; for the addresses of the wineries, see p. 447.*

### 1. MOUNT ETNA★★★

The DOC is named after the volcano and the appellation envisages the production of whites from Carricante, Catarrato and Minnella grapes, as well as reds and rosés from Nerello Mascalese and Nerello Cappuccio.

Capped with snow in winter, Mount Etna – still active – is one of the most important volcanoes in Europe. Its height is constantly altered by eruptions and its current altitude is approximately 3323 m, making it the tallest peak in Sicily. Mount Etna is also one of the island's top tourist attractions, not only because of the breathtaking spectacle of its volcanic activity, but also because visitors can enjoy hiking, fascinating artistic and cultural points of interest, and a wealth of fine food and wine, notably Etna wine, Bronte pistachios, orange-blossom honey from Zafferana Etnea, Maletto strawberries, and granita, which is delicious with fragrant warm brioches. Mount Etna can be explored from the south or north slope. The two routes offer different but equally fascinating vistas: the route that leads to the Rifugio Sapienza on the south slope is bleak, black and desert-like, whereas the stretch that goes to Piano Provenzana on the north side is verdant, with a lovely larch forest. A good starting point for either slope is the charming town of **Zafferana Etnea**, which has numerous tourist facilities; situated at an altitude of 600 m, it offers enchanting views of the coast from Acireale to Taormina. The best time for a hike on the volcano is at the height of summer, when all roads are accessible; the best time of day is the early morning.

The mountain, which rises like an enormous black cone, is visible for a radius of 250 km. Numerous groves of oranges, mandarin oranges, lemons, olives, agaves, prickly pears, bananas, eucalyptuses, palms, maritime pines and vines – used to make excellent Etna red, rosé and

## DOCG
Cerasuolo di Vittoria

## DOC
Alcamo
Contea di Sclafani
Contessa Entellina
Delia Nivolelli
Eloro
Erice
Etna
Faro
Malvasia delle Lipari

Mamertino *or* Mamertino di Milazzo
Marsala
Menfi
Monreale
Noto
Moscato di Pantelleria,
    Passito di Pantelleria *and* Pantelleria
Riesi
Salaparuta
Sambuca di Sicilia
Santa Margherita di Belice
Sciacca
Siracusa
Vittoria

## PRINCIPAL VARIETIES CULTIVATED

### WHITE GRAPES
Albanello
Ansonica
Carricante
Catarrato Bianco Comune
Catarrato Bianco Lucido
Chardonnay
Damaschino
Greganico Dorato
Grillo
Malvasia Bianca
Malvasia di Lipari
Manzoni Bianco
Minnella Bianca
Montonico Bianco
Moscato Bianco
Moscato Giallo

Müller Thurgau
Pinot Bianco
Sauvignon
Semillon
Trebbiano Toscano
Vermentino
Vernaccia di San Gimignano
Viognier

### BLACK GRAPES
Aglianico
Alicante
Barbera
Cabernet Franc
Cabernet Sauvignon
Calabrese
Catanese Nero

Ciliegiolo
Corinto Nero
Frappato
Gaglioppo
Merlot
Montepulciano
Nerello Cappuccio
Nerello Mascalese
Nocera
Perricone
Petit Verdot
Pinot Nero
Sangiovese
Syrah
Tempranillo
Tannat

white wine – thrive around its extremely fertile base. Hazels, almonds, pistachios and chestnuts grow above an altitude of 500 m, and higher up there are oaks, beeches, birches and pines, especially in the area around Linguaglossa. At these altitudes, the landscape is also characterised by Mount Etna broom.

The desert zone commences above an altitude of 2100 m, with Astragalus aetnensis (known locally as *spinosanto*), a small thorny bush that is often found near colourful endemic varieties of violets, groundsels and other flowers that populate the slopes of the secondary craters. At the highest points, snow and extended periods of hot lava flows prevent any type of macroscopic vegetation from growing: this area is known as a volcanic desert.

## From the coast to the southern slope

*Itinerary of 16 km from Aci Sant'Antonio to Nicolosi.*

Going through **Aci Sant'Antonio**, whose main city monuments are in Piazza Maggiore, you come to **Viagrande** ♟, which is paved with enormous slabs of lava stone. The façade of the 18th-c. mother church is distinguished by the same dark stone, which underscores the vertical lines, portals and windows.

The toponym **Trecastagni** seems to refer to the three saints (three *casti agni*, or lambs) venerated here: Alphius, Philadelphius and Cirinus. You can walk down Via Vittorio Emanuele, lined with lovely palazzi, to the mother church of

## THE TERROIR
**Area**: 25,832.55 km², of which approximately 118,731 hectares are planted to vine

**Production 2019**: 4,924,333 hectolitres of which 1,219,412 VQPRD

**Geography**: 24.5% mountainous, 61.5% hilly, 14% flat. Mixed soil, clayey sandstone, volcanic and calcareous. Mediterranean climate

## THE PROTECTION CONSORTIA
Consorzio Tutela Vino Cerasuolo di Vittoria – ℘ 334 3421136, www.cerasuolovittoria.eu

Consorzio Tutela dei Vini Etna – ℘ 333 86 21 113, www.etnadoc.com

Consorzio Volontario per la Tutela del Vino Marsala – ℘ 0923 95 32 55, www.consorziovinomarsala.it

Consorzio Tutela Vini dell'isola di Pantelleria – ℘ 0923 95 35 64, www.consorziopantelleria.it

## WINE AND FOOD ROUTES
Federazione delle Strade Vini e Sapori di Sicilia – ℘ 095 94 02 17, federazionestradedelvinodisicilia.it

Strada del Vino Alcamo DOC – ℘ 0924 25 008

Strada del Vino dei Castelli Nisseni – ℘ 0934 92 93 08

Strada del Cerasuolo di Vittoria, dal Barocco al Liberty – ℘ 338 31 61 251, www.stradadelvinocerasuolodivittoria.it

Strada del Vino Erice DOC – ℘ 0923 81 17 00, www.stradadelvinoericedoc.it

Strada dei Vini dell'Etna – ℘ 349 92 44 672 info@stradadelvinodelletna.it, www.stradadelvinodelletna.it

Strada del Vino di Marsala Terre d'Occidente – ℘ 0923 71 58 33

Strada del Vino di Messina – ℘ 090 92 21 555, www.stradadelvinomessina.it

Strada del Vino DOC Monreale – ℘ 091 84 63 512

Strada del Vino Terre Sicane – ℘ 0925 94 31 39 / 94 02 17, www.stradadelvinoterresicane.it

Strada del Vino Val di Mazara – ℘ 0923 94 06 07, www.stradadelvinovaldimazara.it

Strada del Vino e dei Sapori del Val di Noto – ℘ 0931 16 28 713, www.stradadelvaldinoto.svweb.it

*Vineyards on Mount Etna*

San Nicola, which has a steep staircase in front of it. Above, a terrace offers a beautiful view of the valley.

In **Pedara**, Piazza Don Diego is dominated by the Duomo, which has a unique spire covered with brightly coloured ceramic tiles. From here you come to **Nicolosi**, the starting point for a lovely winding road to Rifugio Sapienza.

## The north-east slope

*Itinerary of 50 km from Linguaglossa to Milo.*

**Linguaglossa** 🍷 (literally, tongue-tongue, as it combines the Latin *lingua* and the Greek *glossa*) is in a "hot" position on the slopes of Mount Etna. The main square is dominated by the mother church built in lava stone and sandstone. In Piazza Annunziata the local tourist office has an interesting **ethnographic museum of Mount Etna**. *Open 9-12.30 and 16-19 (15.30-18.30 winter), Sun. 9.30-12.30* 📞 *095 64 30 94.*

The lovely and scenic★ road, flanked by a beautiful larch forest (which was affected by the 2002 eruption) leads to **Piano Provenzana**, from which the Mareneve road can be taken, skirting the summit from the east side. There are numerous small farming towns on the lower eastern slopes of Mount Etna, and they exploit the fertile volcanic soil to cultivate grapes and citrus fruit.

In **Fornazzo,** just before the road linking Linguaglossa and Zafferana Etnea,

you can see the astonishing lava flow of 1979, which spared the little **Chapel of Sacro Cuore**, although it penetrated part of its interior.

**Sant'Alfio** has a monumental 17th-c. mother church that was restructured in the 19th c., with a singular belfry façade made of lava stone. The terrace in front of the church affords a splendid **view★** of the Ionian coast. The town's main attraction is the **hundred-horse chestnut★** (*on the provincial road for Linguaglossa*), a majestic tree that is over 2000 years old and whose trunk, composed of 3 different shoots, has a circumference of 60 m. Its name derives from a legend according to which a certain Queen Joan (Joan of Aragon or Joan of Anjou) found shelter here on a stormy night with her retinue of 100 knights.

*Go back towards Fornazzo and turn left to Milo.*

The small farming town of **Milo** owes its survival to the blind and unpredictable path of lava, which has always spared it. Numerous times its flow has come very close, but then diverted its course.

## The Circumetnea

*Itinerary of 130 km from Misterbianco to Riposto.*

The road that circles Mount Etna offers ever-changing views of the volcano and goes through several fascinating towns. As an alternative to driving, you can take the Circumetnea railway.

## Caltanissetta 🍷

Set on an upland 568 m high in the centre of Sicily, Caltanissetta enjoys a vast panorama of low hills and shallow valleys in an area of sulphur and rock salt mines. At the heart of the city's historic centre lies **Piazza Garibaldi**, at the point where the two main streets (Corso Umberto and Corso Vittorio Emanuele) meet. The square is lined by the City Hall (a former Carmelitan convent), the Baroque façade of the Church of San Sebastiano – characterised by the contrast of dark red plaster and tufa stone – and the cathedral. Constructed in the late 16th c., the cathedral has an interior of a theatrical nature, in which frescoes by the Flemish painter Guglielmo Borremans (1720) alternate with stuccowork.

The province of Caltanissetta is the area of production for Cerasuolo di Vittoria DOCG and Vittoria DOC (shared with the provinces of Catania and Ragusa), and also **Riesi**, the only DOC zone that falls entirely within the province, and which produces red, white, rosé, sparkling and sweet wines.

In **Misterbianco** the impressive 18th-c. Church of Santa Maria delle Grazie has a lovely façade that rises above the houses and is visible from a distance. Inside, the right apse has a Virgin and Child attributed to Antonello Gagini.

*Continue on the SS 121.*

In **Paternò**, the castle with a square plan was built in 1072 by Roger II, and religious centres rise around it: the mother church (founded by the Normans but restructured in the 14th c.) and the Church of San Francesco. The layout of the town, at the foot of the cliff, goes back to the 17th c.

*From the SS 121, turn right (7 km).*

The centre of **Santa Maria di Licodia** is composed of Piazza Umberto, set in an elevated position and bounded by the former Benedictine monastery (now the town hall) and the Church of the Crocifisso. Along the left side of the church there is a beautiful bell tower (12th-14th c.) decorated with two-colour bands.

*Continue to **Adrano**.* This is one of Mount Etna's oldest towns. Its earliest traces go back to the Neolithic period, and the remains of Cyclopean walls, built with enormous squared blocks of lava stone, are still visible. The castle in Piazza Umberto was built by the Normans and restructured during the Swabian period. The square extends eastward to the delightful gardens of the Villa Comunale, with the impressive façade of the church and monastery of Santa Lucia overlooking it. The church's two-tone façade goes back to the 18th c.

Take the SS 284 for **Bronte**, which is famous for its pistachios. *From Bronte,* follow the signs for "Castello di Nelson", which is just before the entrance to the village of Maniace.

### Abbey of Maniace (Nelson's Castle)★

*Closed for renovation at time of writing.*
℘ 095 69 00 18 or 095 69 08 23.

The Benedictine abbey was founded in the 12th c. and in 1799 Ferdinand III gave the structure – along with the title of Duke of Bronte – to the English admiral Horatio Nelson for his help in suppressing the anti-Bourbon uprisings in Naples. The admiral never visited it, but his descendants lived there until 1981 and transformed the "Ducea" into a lavish private residence. The abbey church has a Byzantine icon that, according to the local population, is the original one brought back by the Byzantine *condottiere* Giorgio Maniace, who crushed the Arab forces here in 1040. The manor, surrounded by a 4-hectare park and a lovely garden, still has several exquisitely furnished rooms.

*Continue on the SS 284.*

### Randazzo★

The "black city" is an excellent epithet for Randazzo, due to all the lava stone used to pave its roads, line the arches of doors and windows, and build monuments in the beautiful city centre, whose main thoroughfare is Corso Umberto. The Aragonese court chose the town as its summer residence. The Church of Santa Maria, commenced in the 13th c., has been restructured several times; the neo-Gothic façade and bell tower go back to the 19th c.

*Turn right into Piazza Roma.*

Lining **Piazza San Nicolò** are the late 16th-c. church by the same name, the Palazzo Clarentano (1508) and the little Church of Santa Maria della Volta (14th c.). The picturesque **Via degli Archi** opens up to the right of the building.

*Take Via Duca degli Abruzzi, which merges into Corso Umberto.*

The arch on the right marks the ancient entrance to the Royal Palace, which was destroyed by the 1693 earthquake; all that remains is part of the façade. You then come to the Church of San Martino, founded in the 13th c. and rebuilt in the 17th c., which has an exquisite **bell tower★** (13th-14th c.); the interior houses two works depicting the Virgin by the Gagini school, and a polyptych attributed to Antonello de Saliba, a pupil of Antonello da Messina. The remains of the Swabian castle, a tower incorporated into the medieval citadel and then transformed into a prison in the 16th c., stand opposite the church.

*Continue on the SS 120 and after about 15 km turn left for* **Castiglione di Sicilia** ▼. The ancient Castel Leone clings to an astonishing rocky spur in a magnificent position offering a fantastic **view★★** of Mount Etna and the town. The main monuments are grouped in the upper part of town. The 18th-c. Church of Sant'Antonio is flanked by a bell tower with structural elements made of lava stone. The bell tower of the Church of San Pietro has preserved the structure of the original Norman church with small suspended arches. The Church of Santa Maria della Catena, preceded by a staircase, has a lovely portal with twisted columns.

*Return to the Circumetnea and continue to the coast; take the SS 114 towards Catania for 10 km.*

Going through **Giarre**, which boasts fine shops and elegant homes along Via Callipoli, you come to **Riposto**. The town was developed by a colony from Messina (which brought in the cult of the Virgin of the Letter) and in the 19th c. it became an important trade centre for the exportation of wine. There are numerous remains of 19th-c. industrial buildings. The charming **Sanctuary of the Madonna della Lettera**, overlooking the sea, was built in 1710, although a religious building probably already existed here during the Norman period.

## 2. MESSINA AND THE EOLIE ISLANDS

The 2 DOC zones in the province of Messina are concentrated in the northeast corner. The **Faro DOC** zone covers the far end of the island and refers to a red wine produced mainly from Nerello grapes. **Mamertino di Milazzo DOC** or **Mamertino** is a wine with an extremely old history that is thought to have been produced as early as the Roman period; it is made in the Milazzo hinterland in both the white and red versions. The **Malvasia delle Lipari DOC** indicates one of Italy's most famous dried-grape wines, made by letting the grapes dry on the vine before the harvest. This sweet, aromatic and amber-coloured nectar is ideal as a dessert wine. Various types of Malvasia can be found on the market: the DOC wine, produced only in the islands, must list the entire appellation of *Malvasia delle Lipari* on the label.

### From Messina to Milazzo
*Itinerary of 40 km.*

### Messina★
The monuments that survived the terrible earthquake of 1908 and bombing during World War II dot the area behind the central part of the harbour. The **Duomo**, which was almost entirely rebuilt, has maintained the lines of its original Norman style (12th c.); the exquisitely sculpted central portal is from the 15th-c. Rising to the left of the cathedral is a 60-metre tall campanile with an **astronomical clock★★**, made in Strasbourg in 1933, which is said to be the biggest in the world.

*Take Via Cesare Battisti, setting out from the right side of the Duomo.* Built in 1100 during the Norman era, the Church of the **Santissima Annunziata dei Catalani** has a distinctive apse in a composite Norman style that merges Romanesque input (blind arcades on slender columns), Arab influences (geometric motifs made using polychrome stones) and Byzantine elements (the dome set on a drum).

North of the city, at the end of Viale della Libertà, the **Regional Museum★★** (*open 9-19, Sun. and public hols. 9-13, closed*

Mon., 𝒞 090 36 12 92) has a number of fascinating works, including the *Polyptych of St Gregory* (1473) by Antonello da Messina and two paintings by Caravaggio, *Adoration of the Shepherds* and *The Raising of Lazarus*.

## Milazzo

*40 km west of Messina.* Ancient Mylae is the natural gateway to the Eolie Islands, which are visible in the background and are just a few miles away. The town is situated at the beginning of the peninsula jutting into the Tyrrhenian. Its modern and industrial appearance conceals significant historical and artistic traces. The oldest part is the medieval district, rising to the north on the hill with the castle, whereas the 18th-c. lower part, on level ground, extends to the south along the eastern coast.

**The citadel and castle★** – *Open 9-18.30, closed Mon., 𝒞 090 92 21 291 or 320 79 47 874.* Beyond the Spanish walls there is an enormous open space with the Duomo Vecchio (1608), an example of Sicilian Mannerism, on the left. The Aragonese walls (15th c.) are characterised by 5 frustum-shaped towers; 2 of them, set close together, conceal a beautiful gate with a lancet arch, surmounted by the crest of the Spanish monarchs, Ferdinand and Isabella. The castle, which was built by Frederick II and has later additions, is inside the walls. The far end of the castle affords a stunning view of the Eolie Islands (from the left: Vulcano, Lipari, Panarea and, on especially clear days, Stromboli) and the Bay of Tono.

**The upper town** – the oldest part of Milazzo encircles the fortified citadel, which overlooks the medieval quarters extending down the hillside below it. The old town has numerous religious edifices, such as the Sanctuary of San Francesco di Paola, the 18th-c. reconstruction of the church founded by St Francis of Paola when he stayed in the city (1464). A little further ahead is the Palazzo dei Viceré, built in the 16th c. but embellished in the 18th c. with lovely balconies set on Baroque brackets. Further up and across the street is the 18th-c. façade of the Church of the Santissimo Salvatore, by Giovan Battista Vaccarini. Continuing along Via San Domenico, to the right is the Church of the Madonna del Rosario, which housed the Court of the Inquisition until 1782. On the left, the Salita Castello climbs to the impressive Spanish walls, the outermost and most important of the 3 rings of walls encircling the castle.

**The lower town** – this is the newer section, which was built in the 18th c. when the populace decided to abandon the upper town and settle in a level area closer to the sea. The hub of the lower town is Piazza Caio Duilio, next to which a small fish market is held every morning.

## The Cape of Milazzo★

Taking the lovely Lungomare Garibaldi along the seafront and crossing the fishing village of Vaccarella, you come to a picturesque **panoramic road★** that runs east of the promontory of Milazzo. At the Cape of Milazzo, an enchanting

*Capo di Milazzo*

spectacle★★ of colours unfolds: deep green, dotted with the burnt browns of the Mediterranean maquis covering the rocky spur, meets the dazzling blue of the sea. To the west, the coast opens up into a lovely stretch of sand and the coastal road running parallel to the sea leads to Grotta di Polifemo, where the mythical episode of Ulysses' encounter with the Cyclops Polyphemus supposedly occurred.

### The Eolie Islands★★★

These seven sisters dot the blue waters in front of the north-east coast of Sicily. The clear, warm sea – which is the colour of cobalt that turns crystalline closer to shore – and the rocky coast, the ideal environment for aquatic fauna (such as sea anemones, sponges, mussels, algae, crustaceans and molluscs), make it a paradise for sea lovers as well as enthusiasts of diving and underwater fishing. Of the islands comprising the archipelago, **Filicudi** and **Alicudi**, the two most distant ones, are wild and rugged, **Salina** is remote and solitary, and **Lipari**★★ and **Panarea** have long been famed by droves of tourists. **Vulcano** and **Stromboli**, with their pulsating volcanic hearts, never fail to arouse astonishment and fear with the fiery lapilli they spew into the sky.

### 3. THE BAROQUE TOWNS OF THE VAL DI NOTO

The south-east part of Sicily is known for the appellations **Moscato di Siracusa**, **Noto**, **Eloro**, **Cerasuolo di Vittoria** – the island's only DOCG – and **Vittoria**. The most representative varieties here are Calabrese (or Nero d'Avola), Ansonica, Frappato and Pignatello, which are used predominantly to make reds and rosés.

### Siracusa★★★ ♟

The seaside city, which extends into the sea with the island of Ortigia, is set along a graceful bay. Its name promptly evokes its Greek past, its tyrants, and its rivalry with Athens and Carthage, and the city still has numerous traces of its history. In the narrow streets of **Ortigia**, time instead seems poised between the Middle Ages and the Baroque, in a delightfully folksy atmosphere with stunning views and ancient palazzi that are gradually being restored to their for-

mer splendour. **Acradina**, the modern and commercial part crossed by Corso Gelone, extends behind Ortigia. Northwest of Acradina is **Neapolis**, the "new" area with the archaeological zone, and east of this is the **Tyche** quarter, an old residential district. **Epipoli** (the "city that lies above") dominates the entire city and is protected by the Eurialo Castle, set in a strategic elevated position. The celebrated mathematician **Archimedes**, who was born here in 287 BC, discovered – as he was taking a bath – the principle named in his honour. Ecstatic over his discovery, he leapt from his tub and ran through the streets naked crying *"Eureka"* (I have found!). When the city was besieged by the Romans, he invented a set of mirrors and lenses to burn their fleet, but when the enemy invaded the city he was killed by a soldier who surprised him as he pored over his calculations.

**Ortigia**★★★ – the island has a wealth of lovely medieval and Baroque palazzi. The latter edifices, which are quite numerous in **Via della Maestranza**★, dot the cool and narrow streets that beckon visitors to enjoy a stroll. **Piazza Duomo**★★ is especially lovely, with palaces that have elegant balconies and the monumental façade of the **Duomo**★★, built in the 7th c. over the foundation of a Doric temple dedicated to Athena. The Porta Marina, whose linearity is broken up by a lovely shrine in the Catalan style, is the city gate that leads to the Adorno promenade created on the walls in the 19th c. Beyond them, there is a view of the enormous expanse of the Porto Grande, which was once the theatre of impressive battles. The **Spring of Arethusa**★ is the legendary cradle of the city: the nymph Arethusa, pursued by the river god Alpheus, sought refuge on the island, where Artemis turned her into a spring. Despite its vicinity to the sea, the water of the spring – enclosed by a tall wall – is fresh.

The impressive **Maniace Castle**★, a sandstone fortress built by Frederick II of Swabia in the first half of the 13th c., rises on the far end of Ortigia.

**Neapolis Archaeological Park**★★★ – *Entrance from Via Rizzo or Via Paradiso. Open 9-18,* ✆ *0931 66 206.* On its grounds there is a **Greek theatre**★★★ from the 5th c. BC, which was one of the largest in antiquity. Opening up behind it is the Via dei Sepolcri – the path of the tombs – that was carved out of rock. The **Latomia del Paradiso**★★ is an ancient quarry, some of whose vaults collapsed following the earthquake of 1693. A lovely orange grove has been created over the rubble.

The **Orecchio di Dionisio**★★★ is a manmade cave whose cavity is shaped like an ear (*orecchio*). The painter Caravaggio gave it this name in 1608, in remembrance of a legend according to which an extraordinary echo allowed the tyrant Dionysius the Elder to hear what the prisoners held inside were saying.

The park tour ends with the Ara di Ierone II, an immense altar that is about 200 m long and was used for public sacrifices, and the Roman amphitheatre (Imperial era), part of which is carved out of rock.

**Paolo Orsi Regional Archaeological Museum**★★ – *Viale Teocrito 66, open 9-19 (Sun. and public hols. 9-14), closed Mon.,* ℘ *0931 48 95 14.* Situated in the park of the **Villa Landolina**, it commemorates the history of Sicily, from the prehistoric era to the temples of the colonies of Syracuse (7th c. BC).

**Catacombs of San Giovanni**★★ –*Open 9.30-12.30 and 14.30-17.30, closed Mon.,* ℘ *0931 64 694.* In Italy, Siracusa is second only to Rome in its number of cata-

combs. Unlike the Roman catacombs however, which were carved from fragile tuff, the ones here were hollowed out from solid limestone, permitting larger cavities that could hold up to 7 tombs.

## Spring of Cyane★★
*8 km to the south-east. For reservations* ℘ *0931 44 58 92.*

You go up the **River Ciane**★★, which is densely populated with papyruses

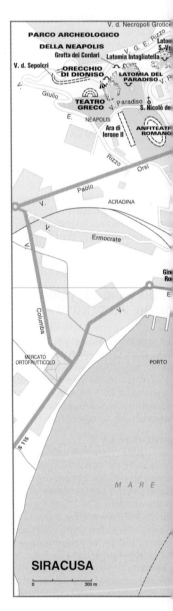

*Orecchio di Dionisio, Siracusa*

© Slalomgigante/iStock

making this area unique in Italy. It was here that the nymph Cyane was turned into a spring for trying to prevent Pluto from abducting Proserpina.

*Take the SS 115.*

## Avola

*25 km south-west of Siracusa.*

This Baroque city is the homeland of the delicious pizzuta almond (so named because of its pointed shape),

which plays a leading role in Sicilian confectionery, and of **Nero d'Avola**. One of Sicily's finest red varieties, Nero d'Avola is used mainly in blends to produce the island's best-known reds, giving them a typical aroma of plums and marasca cherries. As a monovarietal, it has shown itself to be a great red wine with an intense and balanced palate, and it is ideal for long ageing.

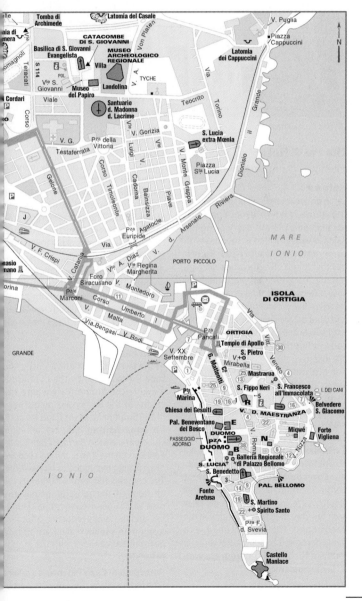

*Majestic Noto cathedral*

## The Val di Noto

*Itinerary of 120 km from Noto to Vittoria.*

### Noto★★

Set in an area where olive and almond trees thrive, Noto is a Baroque gem that sits high on a plateau overlooking the Asinaro valley, which is covered with citrus groves. Its beauty – so harmonious that it looks like theatrical scenery – stems from the tragic earthquake of 1693, after which Noto was rebuilt with stately palazzi constructed using soft and compact local sandstone, which has gradually acquired a magnificent golden and rosy hue that the sunset illuminates like magic.

The historic district revolves around Corso Vittorio Emanuele, which runs through three squares dominated by the façades of churches built in a majestic yet delicate Baroque style: San Francesco all'Immacolata, the **Cathedral★★** in the charming **Piazza Municipio★**, and **San Domenico★**. **Via Corrado Nicolaci★**, to the right before San Domenico, slopes downhill slightly, offering an enchanting view with the Church of Montevergine in the background. The street is lined with finely decorated buildings, notably the **Palazzo Nicolaci di Villadorata** with its lavish **balconies★★**.

*Head towards the coast.*

### Eloro

The town, which was probably founded around the 7th c. BC by the Syracusans, is set in a splendid **position★** on a low hill overlooking the sea, close to the mouth of the Tellaro. The archaeological area has the remains of a sanctuary, theatre, temple and segments of the town walls.

Take the SP 19. You go through the **Vendicari Nature Reserve**, a narrow and swampy stretch of coast in which the presence of large lagoons with a high level of salinity have helped create a singular ecosystem that attracts numerous migratory birds.

### Cape Passero

At the far south-east end of Sicily, the cape is dominated by the lighthouse marking the promontory where the waters of the Ionian Sea meet those of the Strait of Sicily. At Cape Passero, the **tuna-fishing** industry, which is still owned by the Baron of Belmonte, flourished in the 20th c. and still used the drop-fishing technique as late as 1994. The complex has a tuna cannery, now abandoned, the house of the *rais* (the man who supervised the tuna slaughter), and the family residence, affording a splendid **view★★** over an infinite horizon that changes with the moods of the sea.

**Portopalo di Capo Passero** is a quaint little fishing village. The hub of this activity is naturally the port, which comes to life every day between noon and 2 pm, when the fishing boats come in and buyers crowd the docks.

*Go north-west to Ispica.*

# Ispica ♥

The heart of the town centre is Piazza Regina Margherita, with the mother church, San Bartolomeo and the Palazzo Bruno (1910), with its distinctive corner tower. Behind the church, Corso Umberto – lined with lovely palazzi – leads to the city's Art Nouveau treasure, the Palazzo Bruno di Belmonte (the town hall), designed by Ernesto Basile. Nearby there is a lovely covered market that has been set up as a space for events organised by the municipal government. Piazza Regina Margherita and Via XX Settembre lead to Santa Maria Maggiore, in front of which there is an elegant semicircular loggia that creates a beautiful atmosphere. The interior has a beautiful series of Rococo frescoes. On the opposite side, Corso Garibaldi leads to the elegant Church of the Annunziata, whose interior is decorated with exquisite 18th-c. stucco-work depicting biblical scenes.

Set between the municipalities of Ispica and Modica, the **Cava d'Ispica** – the Ispica quarry – is a 13-km-long gash dotted with cave dwellings, small sanctuaries and necropolises. The first human settlements in this area go back to the Neolithic period. The quarry has 2 sectors: the first, between Modica and Ispica, is composed of an enclosed area that is easy to visit, and an area further north that is more difficult to access. Consequently, guided tours are advised for this portion. The second sector, called **Parco della Forza** *(Closed at the time of writing ✆ 0932 95 26 08)*, is in Ispica and tours have been set up for it.

# Modica★

Modica before and after the 1693 earthquake, Modica before and after the 1902 flood: the city was devastated twice, and twice it changed its appearance. Modica is divided into 2 parts: the upper town dominated by the castle, and the lower town, enclosed by hills and set along two main arteries, Via Marchesa Tedeschi and Corso Umberto, which converge to form a Y. Since the 19th c. the upper and lower towns have been connected by the extraordinary and striking flight of steps (completed in 1818) that goes from **San Giorgio★★** to Corso Umberto. Any tour of the city must start from this breathtaking Baroque monument. The steps – nearly 300 – pay tribute to the elegant façade, and form a picturesque and dramatic **complex★★**. The façade culminating in a soaring tower, characterised by the convex central portion that creates an elegant sense of movement, rises to 3 levels. You descend to **Corso Umberto I**, lined with lovely 18th-c. palazzi and religious buildings. San Domenico and the Town Hall stand at the intersection with the other arm of the Y (Via Marchesa Tedeschi). The Baroque Church of Il Carmine, which has preserved the portal and the exquisite rose window of the original Chiaramonte layout, is at the end of the Corso.

# Ragusa★★

This city, part of which was reconstructed following the 1693 earthquake, is set on a spur surrounded by profound and steep gorges. It has 2 distinct urban areas: the actual city of **Ragusa** and **Ibla**, an enchanting nucleus with a medieval layout but a Baroque appearance that owes its extraordinary charm to the convergence of rich Baroque ornamentation and the welter of narrow medieval streets that cross at several points.

The tour starts with the long staircase of Santa Maria delle Scale, which winds its way from the new town to the heart of Ibla: the beginning of the climb affords a breathtaking **view★★** of the city. In Ibla, the statue of St Francis of Paul on the corner of the Palazzo Cosentini, which has lovely **balconies★★**, marks the start of the climb known as the Salita Commendatore *(on the right)*. This is one of the town's most intimate corners, characterised by a series of staircases that intersect to form a virtual maze. Some of Ibla's most fascinating buildings are tucked away here. The Church of **Santa Maria dell'Itria**, with lovely floral ceramic panels from Caltagirone that adorn the upper part of the bell tower, conceals chapels framed by lovely columns, none of which are alike. Just past this is the **Palazzo Nicastro★★** (1760), with a beautiful balcony jutting over its majestic portal. The descent on

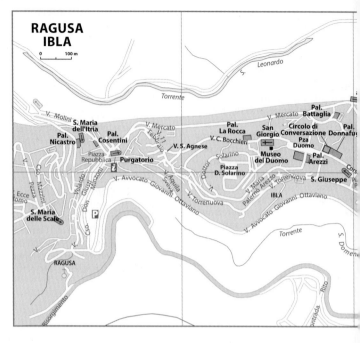

# RAGUSA IBLA

the left leads to the convex façade of the Church of the Purgatorio, preceded by a staircase.

The **Palazzo La Rocca** is a Baroque edifice that has maintained parts of the previous medieval structure. The entrance, marked by a striking double staircase, leads to the *piano nobile*, where the tourist office is located.

The 6 **balconies★★** adorning the façade are decorated with portraits of figures who actually lived during the era, includ-

ing flautists, lutists, and trumpeters, and a mother nursing her child.

From a distance, the most striking element of the **Duomo of San Giorgio★★** is the large Neoclassical dome illuminated by blue windows, but in the square it is the magnificent steep staircase that attracts your attention and trains your gaze towards the stunning pink façade. Elegant and harmonious, it is composed of a slightly convex central body with three orders of columns

*Ragusa Ibla with the dome of Santa Maria dell'Itria*

The map shows: San Francesco all' Immacolata, V. Giardino, Peschiera, ...agata, Pza G.B. Marini, Giardino Ibleo, S. Vincenzo Ferreri, S. Giacomo, Aprile, Pza G.B. Odierna, Sant'Agata ai Cappuccini, 25, ...azza ...ola, San Giorgio Vecchio, Modica, V. Avvocato Giovanni Ottaviano, V.le Margherita, Santissimo Trovato, ico

and is lined with beautiful palazzi, such as the Art Nouveau Palazzo Carfì-Manfré (*no. 71*) and the Venetian-Gothic Palazzo Traìna (*nos. 108-16*). Via Cavour leads to the mother church (1695) dedicated to John the Baptist.

# 4. THE PALERMO HINTERLAND AND LE MADONIE

## The Palermo hinterland

*Itinerary of approximately 100 km from Monreale to Bagheria.*

The province of Palermo counts several appellations – **Contea di Sclafani, Monreale, Alcamo** (with the province of Trapani) and **Contessa Entellina** – which encompass a wide range of whites, reds and rosés made from native and international varieties.

This itinerary through archaeology, art and nature crosses a breathtaking verdant countryside, parts of which look alpine. The first part of the route offers splendid views of the gulf.

### Duomo of Monreale★★★

*Treasure in the Chapel of the Santissimo Crocifisso and terraces 9.30-12.30 (public hols. 8.30-9.30) and 15-16.30. For reservation ☏ 327 35 10 886, www.monreale duomo.it.* The church, built by William II in the 12th c., is a marvellous blend of two styles: the Arab (decoration of the apses) and the Norman (towers and structure). The exquisite **bronze portal★★★** by Bonanno Pisano (1185) stands out beneath the portico. Inside, the rich series of **mosaics★★★**, aglitter in gold, overwhelms the senses. Whilst the colours are more muted than those of the Palatine Chapel in Palermo, these works are nevertheless more personalised and expressive. Completed at the turn of the 13th c. by Venetian and Sicilian craftsmen, they illustrate the Old and New Testaments. The cathedral hosts the tombs of William I and William II, and – in an altar – the heart of St Louis, who died in Tunis in 1270 when his brother Charles I reigned in Sicily.

Don't miss the **climb to the terraces**, which afford magnificent **views★★★** of the cloister and the Conca d'Oro.

**Cloister★★★** – This masterpiece merging Western tradition with the Islamic love for decoration offers unique views

and two wings surmounted by volutes. A delicate sculpted decoration adorns the portal and cornice. The figure of St George astride a horse and armed with a lance, with which he spears the dragon, is depicted on the façade and in the middle of the beautiful railing that closes the staircase. The building was erected in the 18th c.

Nearby, the Church of **San Giuseppe★** closely resembles San Giorgio, making it likely that it was designed by the same architect.

## Vittoria

Going through Comiso you come to the clean and orderly town of Vittoria, with straight roads set at right angles, many of which boast striking Art Nouveau residences. Vittoria is the capital city of Sicily's only DOCG, **Cerasuolo di Vittoria**, whose territory also extends into the provinces of Catania and Caltanissetta. Made from **Frappato** and **Nero d'Avola**, it is a versatile and very drinkable wine. **Vittoria DOC**, in the red and white versions, is also produced in the same area. The centre revolves around Piazza del Popolo, with Santa Maria delle Grazie, which has an elegant curvilinear façade, and the Neoclassical municipal theatre. Via Cancellieri extends from the square

*Mosaics of the Christ Pantocrator in the central apse*

of the abbey complex. The capitals of the columns are extraordinary, and striking in their variety and imaginative execution.

*Take the SS 186.*

After Pioppo and the junction for San Giuseppe Jato there is an enchanting **panorama★** of Palermo and the sea. *Take the road for Piana degli Albanesi.* This road, which has splendid views of the valley, climbs to **Portella della Ginestra**, where a memorial commemorates the massacre by Salvatore Giuliano, and descends to Piana degli Albanesi and **Santa Cristina Gela** 🍷. **Piana degli Albanesi** is a centre of Albanian culture that has kept these traditions alive, especially during the celebration of the Epiphany and Easter, when typical costumes embroidered in gold and silver are worn and people crowd the main street, Corso Giorgio Kastriota, with the churches of Santa Maria Odigitria, San Giorgio and San Demetrio, the mother church. Signs of the Albanian culture are visible everywhere and are evident in the local dialect, celebrations in the Graeco-Byzantine rite, and the dual names on street signs and roads. Even the city itself is also known by its Albanian name, Hora.

*From Piana degli Albanesi take the road for Ficuzza.* The road winds its way uphill and affords beautiful views of the city and the manmade **lake of Piana degli Albanesi**, surrounded by greenery, which offers the best vista of the Basilian monastery situated above the town of Piana.

## The Royal Palace and Forest of Ficuzza

*For information on hours* 📞 *091 62 74 111 or 320 47 785 23.* The little town of Ficuzza is set around the square in front of the hunting lodge built by the Bourbon monarch Ferdinand III in the early 19th c. Behind the edifice, which boasts elegant Neoclassical lines, is the impressive limestone wall of the **Busambra Fortress** (1613 m), which dominates the **Forest** of Ficuzza, once the royal game preserve.

*From Ficuzza go back to the state road, and head to Godrano and Cefalà Diana.*

## Cefalà Diana

The village is famous above all for its Arab baths, Sicily's only example of a spa building dating back to the 10th c. In town, it is worth taking a look at the 13th-c. **castle**, of which a stout square tower and the ruins of the outer walls are all that remain. The **baths** (*located 1 km north of the village, for information on* 📞 *091 70 71 425*) are 1 km north of town, inside a fascinating restored baglio that cannot be dated accurately but was undoubtedly built before 1570.

*Go back to the state road and continue to the junction with the SS 121. Follow the signs for Palermo and Bagheria.*

## Bagheria

This is the city of splendid **Baroque villas★** (there are more than 20) that evoke the glory and grandeur of Palermo's aristocracy, which built lavish summer residences here in the 17th and 18th c. The **Villa Palagonia★** (1715) is the most famous residence in Bagheria, although its decorative and structural oddities horrified Goethe. *Entrance at the back, open 9-13 and 16-19 (Nov.-Mar. 15.15-17.30),* 𝄐 *091 93 20 88, www.villapalagonia.it.*

## Cefalù and Le Madonie

*Circular itinerary of 180 km from Cefalù.*

### Cefalù★★

This enchanting fishing village has become a favourite tourist destination, thanks not only to its cathedral but also its marvellous natural landscape. The golden stonework of the **Duomo★★** (*Piazza Duomo, for information* 𝄐 *0921 92 20 21, cattedraledicefalu.com*) seems to blend into the colour of the cliffs. The cathedral, built by King Roger II between 1131 and 1240, is an example of the Norman style, with a tall apse flanked by two apsidioles, and a façade framed by square towers. **Inside**, the columns are crowned with splendid **capitals★★** in the Sicilian-Norman style.

The presbytery is covered with exquisite **mosaics★★** with a gold ground and a surprisingly variable palette, which are an extraordinary expression of Byzantine art. The angels depicted on the vault and the prophets on the side walls of the choir are from the 13th c.

**Corso Ruggero**, the main road in Cefalù, is lined with all kinds of shops and, like the ancient Roman cardo, it cuts the city in half from north to south. The two areas that are thus created are different in layout: to the west is the medieval quarter, which is a labyrinth of terraced alleys, arches and narrow openings, whereas to the east lies a uniform grid of perpendicular streets. The **Osterio Magno★** was the celebrated residence of King Roger and it later belonged to the Ventimiglia family. The picturesque Via **Mandralisca** is home to the eponymous **museum** (*Via Mandralisca 13, open 9-19,* 𝄐 *0921 42 15 47, www.fondazionemandralisca.it*), with the splendid **Portrait of a Man★** painted by Antonello da Messina around 1470.

### Le Madonie★★

The gentle relief of Le Madonie, which dominates the coast between Cefalù and Castel di Tusa, becomes rugged on the northern slopes, with Piano Battaglia and Battaglietta, Pizzo Carbonara (1979 m, the tallest peak) and the Serre di Quecella, whose dolomitic appearance has earned them the title of "the Alps of Sicily". The route winds its way along breath-taking **panoramic roads★★** that, depending on which direction you are travelling, offer extremely varied vistas. From Cefalù, take the coast road offering a view of the sighting tower on the east promontory. Just past it, take the road to the right for **Castelbuono** 🍷, a charming village that grew up in the 14th c. around the castle of the Ventimiglia family. Piazza Margherita, with the Madrice Vecchia (14th c.) and the old Banca di Corte, form the centre of town. The Church of San Francesco houses the Ventimiglia Mausoleum, an octagonal building from the late Middle Ages, that is accessed from

*Cefalù*

the church via a Renaissance portal.

From Castelbuono the panoramic road continues to **Geraci Siculo**, the upper part of which has maintained its medieval appearance with a maze of cobblestone streets. All that remain of the castle (*accessible from a street on the right at the entrance to town*), built by the Marquises Ventimiglia, are a few ruins and the little Church of Sant'Anna, the family chapel. From here there is a beautiful **panorama★** of the surroundings. The Gothic mother church is in the centre of town.

The road from Geraci to Petralia offers breathtaking mountain **views★**, and the plateau with Enna and Mount Etna is clearly visible. At an altitude of 1147 m, **Petralia Soprana** is the highest municipality in Le Madonie and it dominates the entire countryside, offering unforgettable vistas. The centre of town is Piazza del Popolo, where the town hall is located. There is also an ancient Dominican monastery that has preserved its original Gothic forms with lancet arches. A panoramic point behind the Church of Santa Maria di Loreto, which occupies the site of an ancient Saracen fortress, offers an incredible **view★★★** that stretches as far as Mount Etna.

*Follow the signs for Polizzi Generosa.* Set in a beautiful **position★** on a limestone spur, **Polizzi Generosa** overlooks the northern and southern sides of the Imera Valley. The visit starts in the square with the ruins of the castle, the town's highest point (917 m). The Palazzo Notarbartolo (16th c.), with the **Madonita Environmental Museum**, is also in the square. *For information ✆ 329 22 50 048, www.mam.pa.it* Descending along Via Roma you come to the Palazzo Gagliardo (16th-17th c.) and, across from it, the mother church that has a 19th-c. appearance but has maintained several elements of the building from the 14th-15th c. (the portico and a Gothic arch). From Piazza Umberto I and Via Garibaldi you come to Piazza XXVII Maggio, with a stunning **view★★★** – a virtual amphitheatre – of the tallest peaks of Le Madonie.

*Continue towards the coast on the SS 643 for about 15 km; at the junction turn left to go to Caltavuturo and Sclafani Bagni.* A picturesque and incredibly varied **land-**

**scape★** unfolds along this route: barren stretches alternate with verdant slopes and sudden steep limestone faces. Set in a beautiful **position★** high on the end of a rocky spur, **Sclafani Bagni** has maintained its medieval appearance. The entry is marked by the gate of Porta Soprana, with a lancet arch surmounted by the Sclafani crest. The structure on the left was probably a defensive tower. Beyond that is the mother church with a lovely Gothic portal (15th c.) adorning its façade. The ruins of a 14th-c. fortification, of which a tower remains, are in an elevated position to the right of the church. From here there is an enchanting **view★★** of the peaks of Le Madonie, the sea by Himera and Caltavuturo.

*Go back to the SS 643 and continue to* **Collesano**. The historic centre of this little resort town has maintained its original urban fabric. The most interesting monument is the **mother church★**, preceded by a dramatic staircase. The church holds notable sculptures and paintings, above all by Gaspare Vazzano, called Zoppo di Gangi (1550-1630).

## 5. ALCAMO

The Alcamo DOC encompasses a broad range – white, rosé, red, sparkling and late-harvest wines – produced in the territory of Alcamo and other municipalities, including Calatafimi, Castellammare del Golfo, Balestrate, Camporeale and **Partinico ♟**.

### Alcamo

Its name calls to mind the 13th-c. poet Cielo d'Alcamo, author of the famous *Rosa fresca aulentissima*, one of the first literary works in the vernacular. Nevertheless, a simple look at the landscape, covered in vineyards, will unquestionably suffice to evoke sensations that, although less poetic, are equally delightful: the wine that is produced here and is named after the town. Its churches boast works by Gagini (16th c.) and Serpotta, one of the leading Baroque artists. They can be seen in Sant'Oliva, San Francesco d'Assisi, San Salvatore and the magnificent Basilica of **San Maria Assunta**, which also has a beautiful 15th-c. chapel. The **Castle of the Counts of Modica** overlooks Piazza della Repubblica, which has been laid out as a garden. Built in the 14th c., it has a rhomboid plan, with two square towers and two cylindrical ones. The north side has Gothic-style double lancet windows. The Regional Winery of Sicily and a wine museum are being set up inside.

*From Calatafimi (16 km south-west of Alcamo) you can go to Segesta, which is just 4 km away.*

## Segesta★★★

*Open Apr.–Sept. 9-19.30, Oct. and Mar. 9-18.30, Nov.–Feb. 9-17. A shuttle bus goes to the theatre, ℘ 0924 95 23 56.* Set in a splendid position amidst rolling hills of ochre and brownish red that create a delightful contrast with the infinite shades of green, the archaeological park is dominated by the striking temple that stands out as a solitary presence against a hillock surrounded by a deep narrow valley. It is a pure and elegant Doric structure (430 BC) girded by a peristyle of 36 columns carved from golden limestone. A magnificent **view★★** of it can be enjoyed from the little road (*2 km, there is also a shuttle bus*) that climbs to the theatre.

Built during the Greek era, the **theatre★** is composed of a semicircle (diameter 63 m) and is set on a rocky slope. The tiers face the hills, behind which the Gulf of Castellammare is visible on the right.

## 6. SCIACCA AND ENVIRONS

All of provincial DOC zones – **Sciacca**, **Santa Margherita Belice**, **Sambuca di Sicilia** and **Menfi** (with the province of Trapani) – are concentrated in the north-west corner of the province of Agrigento, bordering with the provinces of Trapani and Palermo, and they include whites, reds and rosés.

*Circular itinerary of 115 km.*

### Sciacca★

The Arabic-looking town of Sciacca, which is entirely white, is an important spa. It is also known for its pottery, which can be purchased at the town's numerous crafts shops. Rising on the slope of Mount Kronio, it is divided into three parts: north of Via Licata is the labyrinth of alleys of the medieval quarter of Terravecchia; the town's most important monuments are between Via Licata and Piazza Scandaliato; and the port area extends below the square. The perfect centre of town is represented by **Piazza Scandaliato**, a large panoramic terrace with a beautiful view of the sea and the colourful port, packed with fishing boats. The piazza is bounded to the west by the 18th-c. Church of San Domenico and, on the long side, by the former Jesuit College (which has a charming 17th-c. courtyard), which is now the town hall. Just beyond this is Piazza del Duomo; the cathedral was built by the Normans and reconstructed in the 17th c. At the end of Viale della Vittoria, in an elevated position, is **Santa Maria delle Giummare** (in Via Valverde), founded by the Normans but rebuilt in the 16th c. Turning right, further ahead are the remains of the **Cas-**

*Temple of Segesta (430BC)*

© Lolari/shutterstock.

tle of the **Counts Luna**, erected in the late 14th c. and rebuilt in the 16th c., but almost entirely destroyed in the 19th c. The outside walls and an impressive cylindrical tower still stand.

The road in front of the castle descends to the beautiful Norman Church of **San Nicolò la Latina**.

The 13th-c. Church of **Santa Margherita** was restructured in the late 16th c. Its façade has a beautiful Catalan Gothic portal, although the most famous element is the Gothic Renaissance portal on the left by Francesco Laurana.

*Take the beautiful panoramic road to* **Menfi** ♟ *and then turn off for Portella Misilbesi and Sambuca di Sicilia (SS 188).* The road skirts **Lake Arancio**, a reservoir that is very important because of the presence of storks. LIPU (the Italian League for Bird Protection) has transformed it into a nature reserve. Stretched across a gentle slope, **Sambuca di Sicilia** boasts noble palazzi that line Corso Umberto I in the centre of town. A staircase at the end of it leads to a panoramic terrace, and the mother church rises behind it.

*From Sambuca, follow the signs for Scavi di Monte Adranone and then continue to Contessa Entellina and Bisacquino.* The road crosses over into the province of Palermo and the Contessa Entellina DOC zone, going through **charming countryside★** in which rolling hills alternate with steeper ones. **Bisacquino**, the birthplace of film director Frank Capra (1897-1991), who made *It's a Wonderful Life*, is a town set gently

across the slopes of Mount Triona. Its intricate urban fabric, reflecting Arabic influence, includes an 18th-c. mother church whose impressive cupola dominates the cityscape. Going through **Chiusa Sclafani**, whose historic district has maintained its medieval layout and is set around a Benedictine abbey, and **Giuliana**, an Arab-Norman town with the castle of Frederick II dominating the Sosio river valley, you come to **Caltabellotta**. The city enjoys a breathtaking **position★★** at an altitude of about 900 m. The chapel, the hermitage of San Pellegrino and the ruins of the Norman castle – which seem to blend into the landscape – are at the summit. The old Arab-Norman mother church and the Church del Salvatore, with a beautiful late-Gothic portal, still stand at the foot of the castle.

## 7. THE PROVINCE OF TRAPANI: SALT AND MARSALA

### From Erice to Marsala

*Itinerary of 50 km.*

The province of Trapani boasts a wealth of appellations, wine types and grape varieties. The best-known wine here is **Marsala**, but other highly regarded appellations are **Alcamo** (with the province of Palermo), **Delia Nivolelli**, made in the municipalities of Mazara del Vallo, Marsala, Petrosino and Salemi, **Menfi** (with the province of Agrigento), **Salaparuta**, a small DOC zone centred around the area of Salaparuta, and **Erice**.

© Steve Geer/iStock

*Salt pans on the Trapani coast*

*Castle of Venus, Erice*

### Erice★★★

An unforgettable setting at an altitude of 751 m on Mount Erice and crowned by a plateau overlooking the sea, combined with a medieval atmosphere, fresh air, the lovely pine forests surrounding the town, a peaceful ambience and local crafts make Erice a destination not to be missed. Defended by bastions and city **walls★** (the north-east portion goes back to the Punic period), Erice is a maze of narrow cobblestone streets, with openings so narrow that you must walk through them in single file. Built by the Normans in the 12th c. over the area of the temple dedicated to Venus, the **Castle of Venus** sits atop a solitary cliff at the end of Mount Erice. There are exceptional **views★★** from here and from the nearby **Balio gardens**, and on clear days you can even see the Tunisian coast. The **mother church★**, built in the 14th c. using stones from the temple of Venus, has a portico that was added in the 15th c. and it is flanked by a square bell tower with merlons (13th c.).

### The salt road★

The coast road that links Trapani and Marsala is lined with salt pans that create a striking **vista★★**: the expanses of water divided by slender strips of land form an irregular and colourful mosaic. At certain points the silhouette of a windmill emerges in the middle, evoking an era in which this was the chief means of pumping water and grinding salt. The spectacle is even more astonishing in summer, when the salt is gathered, as the rosy hues of the water in the different basins become more intense (the different degrees of salinity determine the colour) and the innermost pools – completely dried up at this point – glitter in the sun.

Exploitation of the coastal area between Trapani and Marsala goes back to the Phoenicians, who realised that the conditions here were extremely favourable and created pools to extract salt, which they then exported around the Mediterranean.

In Nubia there is a small but interesting **Salt Museum**, in which the exhibition of work implements and explanatory panels illustrates this ancient trade. *For information Saline Culcasi, Via Chiusa, open 9.30-18, ℘ 320 6635818, www. salineculcasi.it.* Near Mozia you can visit a renovated **windmill**. *Oct.-Dec. 9.30-17; Mar.-Sept. 9-20.30. If there is enough wind, the windmill operates in summer. For information, Saline Ettore e Infersa ℘ 0923 73 30 03, www.salineettorein-fersa.com.*

### Island of Mozia★★

*Leave the car at the landing.* The ancient Phoenician colony was founded in the 8th c. BC on one of the four islands in the Stagnone Lagoon. Destroyed by the Syracusans and soon forgotten, the little island was rediscovered in the late 19th c. by Joseph Whitaker, an English nobleman with a passion for archaeology whose family had settled in Sicily and started a thriving business to export Marsala wine. The family home is on the island and has now been transformed into a **museum** with artefacts found on the island, including the superb **Motya Ephebe★★**, a noble figure with a proud bearing and a long pleated gown that unquestionably shows Greek influence. *Museum open 9.30-18.30 in summer, 9-15 in winter. For information on connections to the island ℘ 0923 71 25 98.* A trail can be taken around the island to discover the remains of the Phoenician city (*it is best followed anti-clockwise*).

### Marsala★ ♟

How many things are evoked by just one name! It reflects one of the key moments in Italian history but also a heady nectar, a place telling a story that starts with "once upon a time there was an English merchant..." and ends by bringing the name of this city to tables around the world. With its potpourri of people (there are many Tunisians), its port and alleys, Marsala has a distinctively North African atmosphere. Set at the western end of Sicily – closer to Africa than it is to the rest of Europe – the town boasts a historic district set around Cape Lilibeo (or Boeo), behind the seafront promenade of Boeo and Piazza Vittoria, with a labyrinth of streets that can be covered only on foot.

The heart of the city revolves around **Piazza della Repubblica**, bounded by the Palazzo Senatorio, called the Loggia, which was completed in the 18th c., and the mother church built by the Normans but reconstructed in the 18th c., which has an impressive tufa façade. Piazza della Repubblica faces Corso XI Maggio, the ancient decumanus maximus of the Roman city, which is lined with beautiful palazzi. Perpendicular to it and heading south is **Via Garibaldi**, closed by the gate of Porta Garibaldi and flanked by the town hall, once the Spanish military quarters. The fish market is held every morning behind the town hall.

Near the sea (*Lungomare Boeo*), the **Baglio Anselmi Archaeological Museum**, housed in an old wine cellar, has the wreck of a **Punic warship★** that was found near Mozia. *Open Tue.-Sat. 9-19.30, Sun. and public hols. 9-13.30, closed Mon. ℘ 0923 95 25 35.*

## The story of Marsala

A storm off the Sicilian coast in 1770 obliged an English ship to stop off in the port of Marsala. The merchant John Woodhouse disembarked and took his first sip of Marsala wine in an inn. Accustomed to the fortified wines of Spain and Portugal, he immediately noticed the similarity and was induced to send a large quantity of the wine back home to test the market. The response was positive and Woodhouse set up his first production establishment. Soon after, another English trader came to Marsala, Ben Ingham, a connoisseur of fortified wines, who improved the quality of the wine through better grape selection. His company passed to his nephews, the Whitakers. In 1833 **Vincenzo Florio**, a tradesman from Calabria who had settled in Palermo, bought the land between the two largest Marsala producers and began production, restricting further the variety of grapes that could be used. At the end of the century other companies were founded, such as Pellegrino in 1880. At the start of the 20th c. Florio bought up both the Ingham-Whitaker and Woodhouse companies but kept their trademarks. With time Florio too was absorbed but the company's products and trademarks have all been kept.

Marsala DOC is limited to the province of Trapani and a small part of the provinces of Agrigento and Palermo. The wine is made from very sweet grapes which, once pressed, are allowed to ferment and caramelise, or are added to with ethyl alcohol to give different types of Marsala. Depending on the quantity of sugars, three types of Marsala can be obtained: dry, semi-dry and sweet. The years the wine is left to age determines how it is marketed: Marsala Fine (1 year), Superiore (2 years), Superiore Riserva (4 years), Vergine (5 years) and Vergine Riserva (10 years). It can be drunk as an aperitif (if dry) or as a dessert wine, but never at a temperature greater than 10° (if dry) or 18° (if sweet).

© Kim D. Lyman/Shutterstock

# Addresses

## Tourist information

**Region of Sicily** – www.visitsicily.info

**Cefalù and Le Madonie Tourist Office** – Corso Ruggero 77, Cefalù, ℘ 0921 42 10 50 or 0921 42 14 58

**The Eolie Islands Tourist Office** – Via Maurolico 17, Lipari (ME), ℘ 090 98 80 095

**Pro LocoErice** – Via Castello di Venere, Erice (TP), ℘ 329 06 58 244, www.prolocoerice.it

**Etna Tourist Office** – South Etna: Via Martiri d'Ungheria 36/38, Nicolosi (CT), ℘ 095 91 15 05; North Etna: Piazza Annunziata, Linguaglossa (CT), ℘ 095 64 36 77

**Messina Tourist Office** – Via dei Mille 270, Messina, ℘ 090 29 35 292

**Palermo and Monreale Tourism** – Via Notarbartolo 9, Palermo, ℘ 091 70 78 035

**Sciacca Tourist Office** – Corso Vittorio Emanuele 84, Sciacca (TP), ℘ 0925 22 744

**Siracusa Tourist Office** – Via Maestranza 33 and Via Duca Degli Abruzzi 4, Siracusa, ℘ 0931 46 42 55 and 0931 17 56 232

## The wineries

*The addresses are listed in alphabetical order by location.*

### MOUNT ETNA

**Cottanera** – *SP 89 - C.da Iannazzo* - **Castiglione di Sicilia** *(CT)* - ℘ *391 39 39 072 - www.cottanera.it - staff@cottanera.it - Winery and vineyards tours with tasting by reservation.* The winery was founded in the 1960s by Francesco Cambria, father of the current owners, Guglielmo and Enzo. In the 1990s the two brothers began to renew the winery with a project that focused on valorising Mount Etna's viticultural heritage. Today Guglielmo's children pursue this goal with the selfsame dedication and passion. Hectares under vine: 65.

**Wines**: Etna Rosso DOC Riserva Contrada Zottorinoto, Barbazzale, Contrada Feudo di Mezzo and Contrada Diciassettesalme, Sicilia DOC L'Ardenza, Sicilia DOC Syrah Sole di Sesta, Etna Bianco DOC Bianco, Contrada Calderara, Barbazzale Bianco Sicilia DOC, Etna Rosato Cottanera, Etna DOC Spumante.

**Tenuta di Fessina** – *Via Nazionale SS 120, 22 - C.da Rovittello* - **Castiglione di Sicilia** *(CT)* - ℘ *0942 39 53 00 - www.tenutadifessina. com - fessina@tenutadifessina.com - Winery and vineyards tours, food and wine tasting by reservation.* Tenuta di Fessina is an emotional experience, born of Silvia Maestrelli's love for this land and its sharp contrasts. In 2007, in collaboration with oenologist Federico Curtaz (Gaja's agronomist for over two

decades), Maestrelli acquired an established vineyard of Nerello Mascalese dating back to the previous century. At the centre of the vineyard stood an 18th-c volcanic stone millstone, along with its original *chianca* – a torque used to press grapes – still intact. The vineyards are situated between two semicircles of volcanic stone, like traditional French clos, creating a unique microclimate. Accommodation available on the estate (*7 rooms, hospitality@tenutadifessina.com*). Hectares under vine: 10.

**Wines**: Etna Rosso DOC Il Musmeci Rosso Riserva, Il Musmeci Rosso Riserva Roberto Silva, Erse and Erse Contrada Moscamento 1911, Etna Bianco DOC A' Puddara and Erse, Etna Rosato DOC Erse and Il Musmeci Contrada Caselle, Sicilia DOC Laeneo. Other products: olive oil.

**Murgo** – *Via Zafferana 13* - **Santa Venerina** *(CT), 7 km SW of Giarre* - ℘ *095 95 05 20 - www.murgo.it - info@murgo.it - Winery and vineyards tours with wine tasting by reservation.* The careful selection of grapes and ongoing experimentation has allowed the winery to achieve excellent quality. These wines from the slopes of Mount Etna show a powerful bond with the terroir. The estate also produces olive oil, preserves, marmalades and honey. In addition to making wine, the estate offers accommodation and serves food at the Tenuta San Michele guest farm (*10 rooms, tenutasanmichele.it*), with swimming pool available. Hectares under vine: 25.

**Wines**: Etna Rosso DOC Tenuta San Michele and Etna Rosso, Etna Bianco DOC Tenuta San Michele and Etna Bianco, Etna Rosato DOC, IGT Terre Siciliane Lapilli Rosso and Bianco, Arbiato. Other products: olive oil.

**Vinicola Benanti** – *Via Garibaldi 361* - **Viagrande** *(CT)* - ℘ *095 789 09 28 - www. vinicolabenanti.it - info@benanti.it - Winery tours and wine tasting by reservation.* The Benanti family's estate boasts a tradition going back to the late 19th c. and the grandfather of the current proprietor. The winery's success is the merit of a selection of the finest plots and the clones of the most suitable local varieties, coupled with modern techniques. At Benanti, the goal is to make wines with an old-fashioned taste and packed with personality: wines that fully express the terroir. Restaurant service by reservation. Hectares under vine: 37 on Mount Etna and 27 in Siracusa.

**Wines**: Etna Bianco Superiore Pietramarina, Etna Rosso Serra della Contessa, Rosso Sicilia IGT Majora, Nero d'Avola Drappo, Moscato di Noto Passito Il Musico. Other products: olive oil and grappa.

# ADDRESSES

## THE BAROQUE TOWNS OF VAL DI NOTO

⌂ **Riofavara** – *Cda. Favara* - **Ispica** *(RG)*
- ☏ *0932 70 51 30* - *www.riofavara.it* - *info@ riofavara.it* - *Winery tours by reservation, hospitality@riofavara.it*. In 1994 Massimo and Marianta Padova began to modernise the estate with an eye to achieving outstanding quality. Investments were made in the vineyard and cellar alike, high-density and low-yield varieties were planted, and the harvests became very selective. The results were noticeable within just a few years and today Riofavara is renowned for its excellent wines. The estate also organises itineraries to allow visitors to discover Eloro and Moscato di Noto, both of which are DOC. Accommodation available at the estate (*3 rooms*). Hectares under vine: 16.
**Wines**: Sicilia DOP Sciavè, Spaccaforno, IGP Terre Siciliane Bianco Marzaiolo, IGP Terre Siciliane Rosso San Basilio, Moscato DOP Mizzica and Notissimo.

**Pupillo** – *Contr. La Targia* - **Siracusa**
- ☏ *0931 49 40 29* - *cantinepupillo.it* - *info@ solacium.it* - *Winery tours and tasting by reservation (from €10)*. Baron Antonino Pupillo founded the winery in 1908. The pride of the winery is its Moscato di Siracusa Solacium and the Pupillo family can be credited with valorising this sweet wine, which attained DOC status in 1973. Nino, the founder's descendant, has been faithful to old traditions and has given the vineyards new impetus, achieving significant results. Hectares under vine: 24.
**Wines**: Moscato di Siracusa DOC Cyane and Pollio, Siracusa DOC Passito Solacium, Sicilia DOC Bianco Targetta, Sicilia DOC Rosso Re Federico and Baronessa di Canseria, Sicilia DOC Vignazza delle Monache Rosé, Spumante Podere 27.

## THE PALERMO HINTERLAND AND LE MADONIE

⌂ **Abbazia Santa Anastasia** – *C.da Santa Anastasia* - **Castelbuono** *(PA)* - ☏ *0921 67 19 59* - *www.abbaziasantanastasia.com* - *winery@abbaziasantanastasia.com* - *Winery tours by reservation*. The winery is considered one of the most illustrious names in Sicilian enology. Founded by Count Ruggero d'Altavilla in 1100, the Abbey of Santa Anastasia became a cultural, farming and labour hub for the mountain population of Le Madonie. Abandoned for centuries, in 1980 Francesco Lena decided to reclaim the land to establish a winery. Organic and biodynamic farming techniques are applied since 2004. Meals and accommodation available at the Relais ( ☏ *0921 67 22 33, 28 rooms*), created inside a 12th-c. Benedictine abbey. Hectares under vine: 65.
**Wines**: IGP Terre Siciliane Rosso Syrah, Passomaggio, Nero d'Avola and Merlot, IGP Sicilia Rosso Litra, Cabernet Sauvignon Biodinamico and Montenero, IGP Terre

Siciliane Bianco Grillo, Chardonnay mosso, Chardonnay Biodinamico, Sinestesia, Zurrica, Traminer and Chardonnay Viognier, IGP Terre Siciliane Rosato Cannemasche

**Corvo - Duca Salaparuta** – *Via Nazionale SS 113* - **Casteldaccia** *(PA)*, *4 km SE of Bagheria* - ☏ *091 94 52 01* - *www.duca.it* - *info@duca.it* - *Winery tours by reservation*. Corvo wines strive to be a clear expression of their terroir. They are made exclusively with the island's best native varieties, such as Inzolia and Nero d'Avola, selected from the best-suited areas for each wine based on climate and quality. Hectares under vine: 137.
**Wines**: IGT Terre Siciliane Corvo Rosso, Bianco, Rosa, Glicine and Glicine Rosso, IGT Terre Siciliane Irmàna Floris, Grillo and Nero d'Avola e Frappato, IGT Terre Siciliane Duetto Frappato-Syrah and Duetto Insolia-Chardonnay.

⌂ **Baglio di Pianetto** – *Via Francia* - **Santa Cristina Gela** *(PA)* - ☏ *091 85 70 002* - *www.bagliodipianetto.com* - *info@bagliodi pianetto.com* - *Winery tours and wine tasting by reservation*. Count Paolo Marzotto established the business in 1997 with the goal of producing fine wine, in keeping with the values that have always distinguished the Marzotto family. The Count's profound ties to Sicily go back to his 1952 victory when he raced with Ferrari in this region, which he especially admires for its bond with history and tradition. Accommodation available at Agrirelais Baglio di Pianetto (*13 rooms, doubles from €135*), with restaurant service by reservation. Hectares under vine: 158.
**Wines**: Sicilia DOC Cembali Riserva, Viognier, Insolia, Catarratto, Nero D'Avola, Syrah, Frappato, Timeo, Ficiligno and Ramione, IGT Terre Siciliane Shymer, Syraco, Natyr Insolia, Natyr Petit Verdot, Moscato Ra'is Essenza, Rosé Baiasyra, Viafrancia DOC Bianco and Rosso, DOC Murriali. Other products: olive oil.

## ALCAMO

**Cusumano** – *C.da San Carlo* - *SS 113 Km 307* - **Partinico** *(PA)* - ☏ *091 89 03 456* - *www.cusumano.it* - *info@cusumano.it*.
One of Sicily's most prestigious wineries, it has vineyards in various parts of the island. Hectares under vine: 450.
**Wines**: Sicilia DOC Angimbé, Shamaris, Jalé, Cubìa, Benuara, Disueri, Sàgana, Nero d'Avola Noà, Lucido, IGT Terre Siciliane Syrah, Merlot, Insolia, Ramusa, I Trubi and Marena, IGT Sicilia Moscato dello Zucco.

## SCIACCA AND ENVIRONS

⌂ **Lanzara** – *Cda San Vincenzo* - **Menfi** *(AG)* - ☏ *0925 75 065* - *www.bagliosanvincenzo.it* - *info@bagliosanvincenzo.net* - *Winery tours by reservation*. The winery boasts an area of 2000 m² and it fully respects the style of the baglio, inspired by the age-old tradition of these places. This creates a magical atmosphere, above all in the underground portion and the tufa tunnels used to age the wines. Restaurant, accommodation (*12 rooms, from €100*) and swimming pool available. Hectares under vine: 52.

**Wines**: Cabernet Sauvignon, Merlot, Nero d'Avola, Syrah, Terre dell'Istrice, Cromazio, Serico, Chardonnay, Elitre "Grillo 100%", Ipsas, San Vincenzo Bianco.

🌱 **Planeta** – *C.da Dispensa* - **Menfi** *(AG)* - ℰ *0925 19 55 460* - *www.planeta.it* - *wine tour@planeta.it* - *Winery tours by reservation but no direct sales.* Planeta's estate is actually composed of five different areas from west to east (Menfi, Vittoria, Noto, Etna and Capo Milazzo) with the idea of producing each wine in its territory. These areas are the island's hottest and driest areas, but the similarities end here, as they are very different in terms of soil, grape varieties, altitude, winds and more. Indeed, the grapes grown in these areas offer the unique typicity that is one of the hallmarks of Planeta wines. Accomodation available at the resort in Menfi (*7 rooms, www.planeta estate.it*). Hectares under vine: 390.

**Wines**: Sicilia Menfi DOC Cometa, Burdese, Sito dell'Ulmo, Maroccoli, Chardonnay, DOCG Cerasuolo di Vittoria Classico Dorilli, Vittoria DOC Frappato, DOC Noto Santa Cecilia, Allemanda, Controdanza, Mamertino, La Segreta Bianco and Rosso, Nocera, Moscato di Noto, Passito di Noto, Eruzione 1614 Carricante. Other products: olive oil.

### PROVINCE OF TRAPANI

**Cantine Rallo** – *Via Vincenzo Florio 2 -* **Marsala** *(TP)* - ℰ *0923 72 16 33* - *www. cantinerallo.it* - *Winery tours by reservation.* Diego Rallo founded the winery in 1860, and in 1996 it was taken over by the Vesco family, which helped relaunch the business. "Genuine rational passion" is the byword that distinguishes the winery's work and the way it interprets the world of Vesco wines. Hectares under vine: 75.

**Wines**: Sicilia DOP Beleda, Rujari, Lacuba, Lazisa, Bianco Maggiore, Evrò, Al Qasar, Il Manto, La Clarissa, IGT Terre Siciliane AV01, Marsala DOC Soleras and Mille, DOP Passito di Pantelleria. Other products: olive oil.

**Carlo Pellegrino** – *Via del Fante 39* - **Marsala** *(TP)* - ℰ *0923 71 99 11* - *www.carlo pellegrino.it* - *info@carlopellegrino.it* - *Winery tours by reservation.* Established in 1880 through the entrepreneurial spirit of a family of notaries with a passion for viticulture, the Pellegrino estate has made a name for itself as one of the most important cellars for the production of Marsala. Pellegrino is composed of several estates situated in the best winegrowing areas of western Sicily. Hectares under vine: 157.

**Wines**: IGT Gibelè, Rinazzo Gazzerotta, Kelbi Catarratto, Il Salinaro Grillo, Materico,

Biosfera, Cent'Are, Single Variety Tareni, Marsala Superiore Anita Garibaldi, Uncle Joseph, Horatio, Soleras, Riserva Bip Benjamin, Marsala Vergine and Old John.

**Donnafugata** – *Via Lipari 18* - **Marsala** *(TP)* - ℰ *0923 72 42 63* - *www.donnafugata.it* - *visitare@donnafugata.it* - *Winery tours by reservation.* Donnafugata is owned by the Rallo family, which has always believed in the oenological potential of its land and has 150 years of experience in making fine wine. Giacomo and his wife Gabriella established it in 1983 and although the winery itself was new, it could trace its pedigree back to the historic family cellars in Marsala and the vineyards in Contessa Entellina. Today Donnafugata is one of Sicily's best-known wineries. Hectares under vine: 260 in Contessa Entellina and 68 in Pantelleria.

**Wines**: Sicilia DOC Rosso Mille e Una Notte, Angheli, Sedàra and Sherazade, Etna Rosso DOC Fragore and Sul Vulcano, Cerasuolo di Vittoria DOCG Floramundi, Vittoria DOC Bell'Assai, Terre Siciliane IGT Rosso Tancredi, Contessa Entellina DOC Chardonnay Sicilia Chiarandà and La Fuga, Etna Bianco DOC Sul Vulcano, Sicilia DOC Bianco Vigna di Gabri, Anthìlia, Damarino Zibibbo Lighea, Grillo SurSur, Lucido Prio, Rosato Lumera, Passito di Pantelleria DOC Ben Ryé, Moscato di Pantelleria DOC Kabir.

**Florio - Duca di Salaparuta** – *Via Vincenzo Florio 1* - **Marsala** *(TP)* - ℰ *0923 78 11 11* - *www.duca.it* - *hospitality@duca.it* - *Winery tours by reservation.* In 1832 Vincenzo Florio built the cellars of this historic Marsala winery from tufa in the typical English style of the era. They were destroyed during WW II, but in 1980 they were restored to their former splendour. Walking through the aisles of this veritable temple of Marsala and fortified wines means embarking on a journey back through time: a sensation well worth experiencing.

**Wines**: Marsalas (Baglio Florio, Donna Franca, Terre Arse, Targa Riserva 1840, VecchioFlorio dry and sweet, Riserva Aegusa, Florio's Historic Reserves), fortified wines (Morsi di Luce, Ambar, Oxydia, Zighidì, Grecale, Zibibbo, Pantelleria), Passito di Pantelleria, Malvasia delle Lipari, Spumante Florio. Other products: Amaro della Compagnia.

**Marco De Bartoli** – *C.da Fornara Samperi 292* - **Marsala** *(TP) and C.da Bukkuram 9* **Pantelleria** *(TP)* - ℰ *0923 96 20 93 and 0923 91 83 44* - *www.marcodebartoli.com* - *info@ marcodebartoli.com* - *Winery tours and tasting Mon.-Fri. by reservation.* De Bartoli is an icon of Marsala and of Sicilian wines in general. In the 1970s he succeeded his mother at the Baglio Samperi and invented his personal vision of Marsala, furnishing the space with a collection of vintage cars, another of his great passions. In addition to

# ADDRESSES

Marsala, his Passito di Pantelleria Bukkuram is not to be missed. Hectares under vine: 10 in Marsala and 7 in Pantelleria.

**Wines**: Marsala Vecchio Samperi, Superiore Oro DOC, Vergine Riserva 1988, Superore Oro DOC Vigna La Miccia and Vecchio Samperi Quarantennale, Grillo Sicilia DOC Integer, Grappoli del Grillo, Vignaverde, Terre Siciliane IGP Sole e Vento, Lucido, Rosso Di Marco, Zibibbo Pietranera and Integer, Passito di Pantelleria DOC Bukkuram Padre Della Vigna and Sole D'Agosto.

## CALTANISSETTA

**Feudo Principi di Butera** – *C.da Deliella - Butera (CL) - ☎ 0934 34 77 26 - www.feudo butera.it – info@feudobutera.it - Winery tours by reservation*. Feudo Principi di Butera is an island within an island; an extraordinary vineyard kissed by sea breezes. It extends across the ancient lands of Feudo Deliella, which includes 320 hectares, creating an exclusive terroir with a hot, arid climate that optimizes the perfect maturation of the grapes, as well as sea breezes that benefit the vines and an enveloping, penetrating sunlight typical of this corner of the planet. Hectares under vine: 180.

**Wines**: Sicilia DOC Deliella, Amìra, Merlot, Grillo, Syrah, Cabernet Sauvignon, Insolia, Serò and Chardonnay, Terre Siciliane IGT Symposio, Surya. Other products: olive oil.

🏠 **Masseria del Feudo** – *C.da Grottarossa 115 - Caltanissetta - ☎ 0934 83 08 85 - www.masseriadelfeudo.it - info@masseria delfeudo.it - Winery tours by reservation*. Masseria del Feudo was established by Francesco and Carolina Cucurullo who, after intense research and tours of winemaking estates, decided to create their own winery. The project is part of a more sweeping plan to valorise 4 areas of production: vineyards, orchards, olive groves and livestock. The structure is designed with wine tourism in mind, in order to welcome visitors who want to learn more about these sectors. Accommodation available at the estate (6 rooms, €70). Hectares under vine: 12.

**Wines**: Sicilia DOC Haermosa, Grillo, Inzolia, Nero d'Avola, Rosso delle Rose, Syrah and Nero d'Avola DOC Riserva. Other products: olive oil, plums, apricots, lemons, oranges and tangerines.

# Where to stay

## MILAZZO

**Hotel Thomas** – *Via Sfameni 98, Torregrotta (ME), 12 km S of Milazzo - ☎ 090 99 82 273, www.hotelristorantethomas.net - 18 rooms, doubles from €60*. The hotel, on the road to the sea, offers excellent value for money. Classic seafood restaurant and a simple family atmosphere.

## MODICA

**Casa Talía** – *Via Exaudinos 1/9 - ☎ 0932 75 20 75 - www.casatalia.it - 10 rooms and various apts., doubles from €160*. Rooms inspired by Mediterranean countries in an utterly charming historical setting. The roof garden and view are unforgettable.

## PETRALIA SOTTANA

**Agriturismo Monaco di Mezzo** – *C.da Monaco di Mezzo, 6.5 km S of Petralia Sottana (PA) - ☎ 0934 67 39 49 - www.monacodimezzo.com - 5 rooms and 6 apts., doubles from €90*. The restructured old farmhouse offers various well-appointed apartments with a kitchen. Guests can admire the landscape as well as the lounge by the swimming pool. The restaurant serves traditional dishes.

## PIANA DEGLI ALBANESI

**Masseria Rossella** – *C.da Rossella 12, km SE of Piana degli Albanesi (PA) - ☎ 366 46 93 129 - www.masseria-rossella.com - Closed Jan.-Feb. - 11 rooms, doubles from €80*. This peaceful farmhouse is set in the countryside and the rooms open onto a large courtyard with two enormous mulberry trees. The simple rooms have wrought-iron beds. Traditional home-style cooking.

## RANDAZZO

**Agriturismo L'Antica Vigna** – *C.da Montelaguardia, 3 km E of Randazzo (CT) - ☎ 349 40 22 902 - www.anticavigna.it - 12 rooms and 2 apts., doubles from €70*. In the enchanting setting of the Mount Etna Nature Park, this guest farm offers an extraordinary taste of an idyllic family atmosphere amidst vineyards and olive groves.

## SCIACCA

**Locanda al Moro** – *Via Liguori 44 - Sciacca (AG) - ☎ 092 58 67 56 - www.almoro.com - 5 rooms, doubles from €70*. This delightful B&B, which has charming and comfortable rooms, is situated in the historic district.

## SIRACUSA

**Agriturismo La Perciata** – *Via Spinagallo 77 - 10 km SW of Siracusa - ☎ 0931 71 73 66 - www.perciata.it - 12 rooms, doubles from €75, apt. from €145*. The house has an intensely Mediterranean air and is set in the countryside. This top-level guest farm offers plenty of amenities and services, for an utterly relaxing holiday.

## TRAPANI

**Ai Lumi** – *Corso V. Emanuele 71 - ☎ 0923 54 09 22 - www.ailumi.it - 5 rooms, doubles from €75*. On the 1st floor of the 18C Palazzo Ferro, this guesthouse is right in the historic centre. Some rooms have a corner kitchen, but you might as well eat in the restaurant of the same name just downstairs, which is very popular for its generous portions.

# SARDINIA

Sardinia has always been open to commercial and cultural exchange: in consequence, having also been conquered by the Phoenicians, Romans, Spanish and Piedmontese, the island has been strongly marked by the passage of other peoples of the Mediterranean, even in its viticulture. The range of native varieties is enormous and includes Bovale, Cannonau, Carignano, Monica, Girò, Cagnulari, Pascale, Nuragus, Nasco, Seminano, which, with others like Vermentino, Moscato, Malvasia and Vernaccia, are used to produce the region's most important wines. However, despite this wide assortment, the cultivars that are most representative of Sardinia are essentially two: Vermentino and Cannonau.

*Wild coastline of the island of San Pietro*

## The terroir

Sardinian wines are generally of good quality, well structured, fairly alcoholic, full flavoured and complex in terms of taste and smell. The inherent interest of the production zone is heightened by its varied character. Appreciation of the native varieties has always been broad and the island's traditional wines have never been forgotten or neglected.

The region's only DOCG wine is **Vermentino di Gallura**, which is produced in twenty or so municipalities in the province of Sassari and two in the province of Nuoro using the grapes of the same name. These, it appears, were brought to Sardinia by the Spanish during their rule over the island. The wine is straw-coloured with green highlights and in the mouth generally gives a delicate finish suggestive of almonds. Though it reaches its highest quality in Gallura, Vermentino is also produced with success in other parts of the island under the appellation **Vermentino di Sardegna**.

Then there are 4 DOC wines that are produced in either all or nearly all of the region's winemaking areas: they are **Cannonau di Sardegna**, **Semidano di Sardegna**, **Moscato di Sardegna** and **Monica di Sardegna**, all made from grapes of the same names.

Whereas Vermentino is the island's leading white wine, **Cannonau** is its equivalent among the reds. This is a wine of great character, also made from a cultivar that originated in Spain. It is intensely ruby-red, with a lingering bouquet of fruits – plums and blackberries in particular. It is also produced as a rosé and liqueur wine.

There are many DOC wines limited to specific zones, for example, among the whites, **Nuragus di Cagliari**, and the reds, **Monica di Cagliari**, **Campidano di Terralba**, **Carignano del Sulcis** and **Mandrolisai**.

There is also an extensive choice of sweet and sipping wines, such as **Nasco di Cagliari**, **Girò di Cagliari**, **Malvasia**

Sherri R. Camp/Shutterstock

## DOCG
Vermentino di Gallura
  *or* Sardegna Vermentino di Gallura

## DOC
Alghero
Arborea
Campidano di Terralba *or* Terralba
Cannonau di Sardegna
Carignano del Sulcis
Girò di Cagliari
Malvasia di Bosa

Malvasia di Cagliari
Mandrolisai
Monica di Cagliari
Monica di Sardegna
Moscato di Cagliari
Moscato di Sardegna
Moscato di Sorso-Sennori
Nasco di Cagliari
Nuragus di Cagliari
Sardegna Semidano
Vermentino di Sardegna
Vernaccia di Oristano

## PRINCIPAL VARIETIES CULTIVATED

### WHITE GRAPES
Albaranzeuli Bianco
Ansonica
Arneis
Arvesiniadu
Biancolella
Chardonnay
Clairette
Cortese
Falanghina
Fiano
Forastera
Garganega
Greco
Malvasia Bianca di Candia
Malvasia di Sardegna
Malvasia Istriana
Manzoni Bianco
Müller Thurgau
Nasco
Nuragus
Pinot Bianco
Retagliando Bianco
Riesling
Riesling Italico
Sauvignon
Semidano
Semillon

Sylvaner Verde
Tocai Friulano
Torbato
Traminer Aromatico
Trebbiano Romagnolo
Trebbiano Toscano
Verdicchio Bianco
Verduzzo Friulano
Vermentino
Vernaccia di Oristano
Vernaccia di San Gimignano

### GREY GRAPES
Pinot Grigio

### BLACK GRAPES
Aglianico
Albaranzeuli Nero
Aleatico
Alicante Bouschet
Ancellotta
Barbera
Barbera Sarda
Bombino Nero
Bovale
Bovale Grande
Cabernet Franc
Cabernet Sauvignon

Caddiu
Cagnulari
Calabrese
Canaiolo Nero
Cannonau
Caricagiola
Carignano
Croatina
Dolcetto
Gaglioppo
Girò
Greco Nero
Malbech
Malvasia
Marzemino
Merlot
Monica
Montepulciano
Nebbiolo
Nieddera
Nieddu Mannu
Pascale
Pinot Nero
Primitivo
Refosco dal
  Peduncolo Rosso
Sangiovese
Syrah
Teroldego

di Bosa, **Malvasia di Cagliari**, **Moscato di Sorso-Sennori**, **Moscato di Cagliari** and **Vernaccia di Oristano**. Produced in limited quantities, they are all truly memorable.

# Itineraries

*Locations with a winery are indicated by the symbol ♀; for the addresses of the wineries, see p. 461.*

## 1. THE PROVINCE OF CAGLIARI

Cagliari is the province with the greatest number of local DOC wines: the appellations under which they go are **Campidano di Terralba** (a red wine made from Bovale grapes), **Carignano del Sulcis** and, in common with several municipalities in the province of Oristano, **Girò di Cagliari**, **Malvasia di Cagliari**, **Monica di Cagliari**, **Moscato di Cagliari**, **Nasco di Cagliari** and **Nuragus di Cagliari**.

## Cagliari★★

The Carthaginian city of Karalis was made into a Roman city and today has developed into the regional capital. Its more recent history is still visible in the ancient centre ringed by walls built by the Pisans in the 13th c. The Umberto I terrace gives views of the city, port and gulf.

**The Castello district** – the upper part of the city was fortified in the Middle Ages by the Pisans. Known as the Castello (Castle), it encompasses the **Santa Maria cathedral★★**, which was built in the 13th c. in Pisan style but remodelled in the 17th c. The building contains two magnificent **pulpits★★** from the 12th c., with superb carved panels of scenes of the life of Christ. A small door in the choir leads to the Sanctuary, where the remains of 292 Christian martyrs are held in urns along the walls. A chapel on the right contains the tomb of Marie Josephine of Savoy, wife of the future Louis XVIII of France and sister of the king of Sardinia.

Dating from the early 14th c. the **Elephant Tower** and **St Pancras Tower★** are the remains of the Pisan fortifications. Close by the first, the **St Remy Bastion** at the south tip of the fortified city is a 19th-c. lookout point connected with Piazza Costituzione in the lower section of the city.

The north part of Castello is where the **Roman amphitheatre** was built in the 2nd c. AD. This is Sardinia's largest and most important Roman building. *Winter 09-17, summer 10-19, for information ℘ 366 25 62 826.* Close to the amphitheatre lies the **botanical garden**, where you can admire Mediterranean and tropical vegetation, aromatic flowerbeds for the blind, and archaeological remains.

**The lower city** – this is composed of the Marina district at the foot of the Castle, the Stampace district to the west, and Villanova to the east. The Church of Sant'Eulalia in Marina contains traces of ancient Roman roads. Piazza Yenne is joined to Piazza Costituzione by the

*Santa Maria cathedral, Cagliari*

shopping street Via Manno. When visiting Villanova be sure to see the Basilica of **San Saturnino★**, one of the oldest Christian buildings in Sardinia. Built in the 5th and 6th c. on the site of an earlier Christian necropolis, it was restored in the 11th and 12th c. *Piazza San Cosimo, open Thu.-Sat. 9-13, closed Mon.-Wed. and Sun., ☎ 070 66 24 96.*

## From Cagliari to the South Coast

*Circular itinerary of 220 km from Cagliari.*

The Poetto is Cagliari's main beach and lies on the Gulf of Quartu south-east of the city. Just inland lies the **Molentargius-Saline Regional Park**, one of the island's most important wetlands. This zone dedicated to wildlife also incorporates ancient salt-works.

Driving north from here, you come to **Dolianova**, where you can visit the Romanesque Church of San Pantaleo, built in the 11th-12th c. Inside are traces of original frescoes and an early Christian font. About 2 km to the west, the 12th-c. Church of Santa Maria di Sibiola is situated in **Serdiana ☕**.

If you continue west, you will find the Church of **San Gemiliano** (13th c.), which stands alone on a rise.

Driving north-west you come to **San Sperate**, a typical Sardinian village decorated with murals, and **Assemini**, where the Church of San Giovanni (10th-11th c.) was built in Byzantine style on the plan of a Greek cross.

A little to the west **Uta** has the interesting Romanesque Church of Santa Maria, built in the early decades of the 12th c. Continuing in a westerly direction towards Silìqua and then heading south, you skirt the ruins of the 16th-c. castle of **Acquafredda**, which stands in a spectacular position on top of a rugged hill. Further down the SS 293, stop off at **Santadi ☕** to visit the ruins of the Phoenician-Punic fort of Pani Loriga (8th c. BC) and, 5 km south of this town, the grottoes of Is Zuddas in Monte Meana in the hamlet of Su Benatzu.

After Teulada you take the twisting, panoramic road to the **South Coast**, which offers splendid views over unspoilt **countryside★**, small bays and limestone cliffs. At the eastern tip of the coast, by Chia Tower, lie the ruins of the Phoenician city of Bithia.

Follow the coast road through **Santa Margherita di Pula ☕** and **Pula**, near which you can visit the archaeological area of Nora. This was a trading port for the Phoenicians (9th c. BC), a Punic city, then a Roman city, and was only abandoned in the Middle Ages.

The lovely coast road follows the west shoreline of the **Gulf of Angels** as far as Cagliari, skirting the Stagno di Cagliari, a wetland complex.

## Sulcis and the Island of Sant'Antioco★★

Sulcis is the south-west corner of Sardinia. It lies between Capo Teulada and

## THE TERROIR

**Area**: 24,099.45 km$^2$, of which approximately 26,619 hectares are planted to vine

**Production 2019**: 626,223 hectolitres of which 423,008 VQPRD

**Geography**: the soil is principally granitic with limestone deposits. The climate is Mediterranean and breezy

## THE PROTECTION CONSORTIA AND WINE AND FOOD ROUTES

Consorzio Tutela Vini di Alghero e di Sorso-Sennori DOC – ☎ 079 99 77 00

Consorzio Tutela del Cannonau di Sardegna DOC – ☎ 0784 24 25 00, www.ctvsardegna.com

Consorzio Tutela Vini di Sardegna DOC, Cagliari DOC, Carignano del Sulcis DOC – ☎ 070 56 02 24

Consorzio Tutela del Vermentino di Gallura DOCG – ☎ 0789 26 096 or 328 67 62 960

Strada del Vino Cannonau – ☎ 377 97 56 512, www.stradadelvinocannonau.it

Strada della Malvasia di Bosa – ☎ 0785 37 70 43

Strade dei vini della Sardegna – www.lestradedelvino.com

Strada del Vermentino di Gallura DOCG – www.stradavermentinogallura.it

© ROBERT67/iStock

*Sant'Antioco*

Portoscudo and includes the islands of Sant'Antioco and San Pietro. A bare and desolate area, with the occasional herd of sheep, in antiquity Sulcis was used for mining purposes.

### Sant'Antioco★

This, the largest of the Sardinian islands, is of volcanic origin. A road links the island's main town (Sant'Antioco) to the mainland. The **archaeological area** encloses the ancient city of Sulci, which was founded by the Phoenicians in the 8th c. BC, after which the area is named. The visit includes several sites: the Ferruccio Barreca Archaeological Museum, which has a fine collection of objects; the Phoenician-Punic **tophet★**, a place where it used to be thought the eldest male child was sacrificed, but which now is considered simply a cemetery for children who died either during childbirth or very young; and the ethnographic museum, underground village and Savoyard fort. *Open 9-19,* ℘ *0781 82 105.*

### San Pietro

The island was populated in 1738 at the wish of Carlo Emanuele III with a colony of prisoners from Tunisia. This past is conserved in the local language and traditions. The island is mountainous, with a rocky coastline on the west side and sandy beaches on the east. The only inhabited centre is Carloforte.

Traces of a fortified Phoenician-Punic settlement built around 750 BC but abandoned about 110 BC can be seen on **Monte Sirai**, 4 km north-west of Carbonia.

## 2. ORISTANO AND ITS SURROUNDING AREA

Besides the designated zones that it shares with the province of Cagliari, the province of Oristano prides itself on the following appellations: **Arborea**, wines made from Trebbiano and Sangiovese grapes, **Vernaccia di Oristano**, a wine that in its liqueur version resembles sherry, and, in common with the province of Nuoro, **Mandrolisai**, which is made in red and rosé versions. The municipality of **Tresnuraghes** is where **Malvasia di Bosa** is made, though it is also produced in six municipalities in Nuoro.

### Oristano

Oristano is an ancient, proud city that was founded by the inhabitants of nearby Tharros. It lies close by the lovely Punic-Roman archaeological ruins left by its founders, and also near the unspoilt Sinis peninsula where the wetland areas provide a natural habitat to many species of birds.

**Piazza Roma** is a large esplanade, the site of the crenellated Tower of San Cristoforo, and originally part of the bastion built in 1291. It marks the start of **Corso Umberto**, the city's high street. Rebuilt in the 19th c., the Church of **San Francesco** contains interesting works of art, for example, a wooden Christ (School of the Rhine, 14th c.), a fragment of the polyptych *St Francis Receiving the Stigmata* by Pietro Cavaro, a Sardinian painter in the 16th c., and a statue of St Basil by Nino Pisano (14th c.).

### Basilica of Santa Giusta★

The basilica is situated 3 km south of the city. It was built between 1135 and 1145 in the hamlet of Santa Giusta, where the houses are grouped on the bank of a coastal lake. The building has the sobriety and elegance typical of Sardinian churches, in which Pisan and Lombard influences are blended. The bases and capitals of the columns inside are made from materials taken from Roman and medieval buildings. The chapels in the right aisle and the bell tower are modern constructions. A crypt lies beneath the raised choir.

### The area around Oristano

**Cabras** ⚑ lies 8 km to the north of Oristano. It is a fishing village on the banks of the Stagno Cabras, which is fed by freshwater and saltwater sources and provides a habitat for birds.

San Giovanni di Sinis and Tharros are situated on **Capo San Marco** at the top of Oristano Gulf. With its solid low structure, small domes and barrel roof **San Giovanni di Sinis** seems to be an ancient Greek church. It is thought to date to the 5th c. and its central dome is certainly from that period, but the rest was restored in the 11th c.

**Tharros★** was founded by the Phoenicians in the 8th-7th c. BC on the narrow Sinis peninsula at the top of Oristano Gulf. It turned into an important port on the route between Marseilles and Carthage before it was conquered by the Romans in the 3rd c. BC. Around 1000 it was suddenly abandoned by its inhabitants, who settled in Oristano, and was subsequently covered by sand; the archaeological zone lies near a hill crowned by the Spanish tower of San Giovanni. It is possible to make out the skeleton of the Punic city, the drainage systems, the cisterns and baths, the residential quarters, the Punic temple with Doric half-columns, and, on the hill, the tophet. The two white attractive columns that stand alone are reconstructions built in the 1960s. *Open Apr., May and Oct. 9-18, Nov.-Mar. 9-17, Aug. 9-20, rest of the year 9-19, ☎ 0783 37 00 19.*

## 3. THE PROVINCE OF SASSARI

The treasures of the west side of the province of Sassari are the **Moscato di Sorso-Sennori** and **Alghero**. The tallest is an extraordinary and rare sweet wine, whereas the second is a DOC zone that produces white, red and rosé wines from Chardonnay, Sauvignon, Torbato, Vermentino, Cabernet, Cagnulari and Sangiovese grapes.

## From Alghero to Capo Caccia

*Itinerary of 30 km.*

### Alghero★ ⚑

The origin is unknown of this lovely small port ringed by walls and set amidst olive trees, eucalyptuses and umbrella pines. The narrow streets of the old city are squeezed tightly inside the fortifications. The **cathedral** (*Via Roma*) has a fine portal and bell tower in Catalan Gothic. The Church of **San Francesco** (14th-15th c.) boasts a lovely Gothic interior and a wonderful **cloister** built in golden tufa.

*Promenade of Alghero*

© Gabriele Matrinti/iStock

The fishing port, from where coral is still fished, lies at the foot of the fortifications. Boats leave from here to take trippers to **Neptune's Grotto**.

## Porto Conte and Capo Caccia

*Leave Alghero in a northerly direction on the SP 42, then head left on the SP 44.* The road that tours Capo Caccia offers magnificent **views★★** of the rocky coastline. Along the way (on the SS 127bis) you pass the **Palmavera nuraghe★** (*nuraghi* are prehistoric tower-like constructions found in Sardinia) surrounded by the remains of a prehistoric village of about 50 huts. The nuraghe is made from white limestone and has two towers and two entrances. *Open Apr. and Oct. 9-18, Nov.-Mar. 10-14, rest of the year 9-19, ℘ 329 43 85 947.*

**Neptune's Grotto★★★** – *27 km west of Alghero, also reached by boat. (For information ℘ 079 97 90 54)* This deep cave has been carved out by the sea at **Capo Caccia**. It is reached down 654 steps cut out of the cliff. Attractions in the grotto are "Lake Lamarmora", huge concretions like the "Great Organ", and delicate features like the luminous threads that decorate the "Christmas tree".

## Towards the Gulf of Asinara: from Alghero to Porto Torres

*Itinerary of 120 km.*

The **necropolis of Anghelu Ruju** is formed of 38 underground tombs cut out of the rock around 3000 BC. The complex lies 16 km north of Alghero. *Open Apr. and Oct. 9-18, Nov.-Mar. 10-14, rest of the year 9-19, ℘ 329 43 85 947.*

*At the junction with the S 291 turn right in the direction of Sassari.*

## Sassari

Sardinia's second largest city is divided into two contrasting sections: its spacious modern districts and the medieval centre huddled around the Duomo. Dedicated to St Nicholas of Bari, the duomo combines elements from different epochs and styles: a 13th-c. bell tower with a crown added in the 17th c., a façade in ornate Spanish Plateresque style (late 17th c.), and a Gothic interior.

*Leave Sassari south-west in the direction of Cagliari and Olbia.*

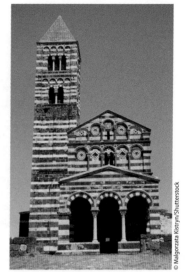

*Santissima Trinità di Saccargia*

## Santissima Trinità di Saccargia★★

Arriving from Sassari, this abbey-church of a Camaldolese convent suddenly appears in the middle of a bare landscape. It was built in the 12th c. with alternating rows of black and white stone in the Pisan style. The façade porch dates from the 13th c. and there is a hint of Romanesque in the interior. In the apse the faintly Byzantine frescoes (13th c.) illustrate scenes from the Passion. The Madonna and apostles are seen in the upper register and Christ among angels and archangels in the basin.

On the way back to Sassari, it is worth the trouble to make a detour to **Osilo** along a pleasant panoramic road. This perched town stands beneath the remains of the Malaspina Castle.

Twenty km further on in this panorama of rocks and woods, you come to **Sènnori** ☗. The village is set in an amphitheatre on a hill and surrounded by olive trees and vineyards. A further 10 km takes you to **Sorso**, which is the other municipality to share the appellation Moscato di Sorso-Sennori DOC.

## Porto Torres

After reaching the sea at Marina di Sorso, a left turn will take you along the coast the 14 km to Porto Torres, situated at the end of a wide bay. Founded by

*Red rocky bay near Sassari*

© F. Fuxa/Shutterstock

Caesar, it was particularly important during the Roman age, as remains close to the station testify. The Church of **San Gavino★** was built at the end of the 11th c. by the Pisans (characteristics of their architecture are the blind arches on the left side), but shortly afterwards it was modified and enlarged by Lombard masters. The church is a fine example of medieval Sardinian art. A 15th-c. portal in Catalan Gothic stands between the small arches. Down in the large crypt you can see the relics of St Gavin and a beautiful Roman **sarcophagus★** adorned with sculptures of the Muses.

## 4. THE COSTA SMERALDA AND GALLURA

*Itinerary of 150 km from Arzachena to Tempio Pausania.*

Gallura is the north-eastern tip of Sardinia. Its interior, which is dominated by Monte Limbara (1359 m), features granitic highlands, cork oaks and grottoes. The Emerald Coast, better known as the **Costa Smeralda★★★**, has been shaped by the wind. It is wild in appearance and the scrub-covered hills run right down into the green, transparent sea. Once this area was only used by shepherds and farmers but, since 1962 when the Aga Khan decided to build a tourist paradise here, it has been a destination of the jet-set. The most upmarket towns are Porto Cervo, Cala di Volpe and Baia Sardinia. From a winemaking standpoint, this is the realm of **Vermentino di Gallura DOCG** and **Moscato di Sardegna Spu-**mante sottozona Tempio Pausania**. Mention has been made of the first in the introduction; the second is a sweet, aromatic, light, white wine with a fine foam.

### Arzachena ♞ and the archaeological sites

The fame of this small town, which was once a farming and stock-breeding village, is owed to a bizarre rock eroded to the shape of a mushroom, to its proximity to the Costa Smeralda, and to local archaeological finds. *From Arzachena head towards Luogosanto. After about 7 km turn right.* The **Tomb of the Giants of Li Golghi★** dates to a period between 1800 and 1200 BC and was covered by an ellipsoidal mound 27 m long. *Return to the crossroads and follow the signs to the* **Li Muri Necropolis**. This burial place dates to 3500-2700 BC and consists of a central dolmen (the grave) surrounded by five concentric circles of standing stones that supported the covering mound.

**San Pantaleo** lies about 10 km southeast of Arzachena in a landscape of granite rocks. *Return to Arzachena and head north.* A pretty road takes you to **Palau**, near where you will find the famous rock of Capo d'Orso ("bear's head").

Continue west on the S 133 and S 133bis, pass through the seaside town of Porto Pozzo and arrive in **Santa Teresa Gallura**, a well-known tourist resort 5 km from **Capo Testa**. The cape is a spectacular spur of rock that extends into the sea and has been used since antiquity as a granite quarry.

Next, follow the west coast of Gallura through the pleasant villages of Vignola Mare, Costa Paradiso, Isola Rossa, Trinità d'Agultu and **Badesi** 🍷.

Heading inland into a dramatic landscape of eroded granite boulders, you come to **Àggius**, situated 514 m above sea level on Monte della Croce.

## Tempio Pausania

Tempio Pausania is a town that stands surrounded by vineyards and cork plantations with Monte Limbara as a backdrop. The centre of life here is Via Roma, which connects Piazza Gallura to Piazza d'Italia. Between the two is Piazza San Pietro, where the 15th-c. cathedral (retouched in the 18th c.) stands. Tempio is a source of mineral water, and a fountain on Viale Fonte Nuova gushes a constant stream of it. The renowned Rinaggiu springs rise in a small wood close by. Take the road for Olbia and turn right after Telti to visit **Monti** 🍷, a winemaking town ringed by cork plantations.

## 5. THE PROVINCES OF NUORO AND OGLIASTRA

The province of Nuoro is where the red wine **Mandrolisai DOC** is produced from Bovale, Cannonau and Monica grapes, and **Malvasia di Bosa** in dry, sweet and liqueur versions.

## From Nuoro to Arbatax

*Itinerary of approximately 150 km.*

### Nuoro

The home town of Grazia Deledda (Nobel Prize for Literature, 1926) stands at the foot of Monte Ortobene on the edge of Barbagia and the Gennargentu mountains. It retains many of its traditions, as can be seen in the **Museum of Sardinian Life and Popular Traditions** (*Via Mereu 56, open 16 Mar.-Sept. 10-13 and 15-20, rest of the year 10-13 and 15-19, closed Mon., ☎ 0784 24 29 00, www.isre-sardegna.it*), which presents a collection of traditional costumes from all over the island. For superb views over the local area from the top of **Monte Ortobene★**, take Via Monte Ortobene (*a turn-off on the SP 45*).

Drive through **Oliena★**, a winemaking town that has been famous for centuries for its Cannonau di Sardegna, and continue east to Dorgali. About 6 km after Oliena take the turn-off to the right to the karstic springs of **Su Gologone★**. These arise from a crack in the rock of a particularly craggy slope in the Supramonte mountain chain.

## Dorgali

Dorgali is a town of handcrafts and winemaking set on the hill above the seaside village of Cala Gonone. Its high street, Via Lamarmora, provides an enjoyable stroll among shops selling local products, including carpets made using a particular knot. On the road that leads to the S 129 you can visit the nuraghic village of **Serra Orios★**, and if you continue towards Lula, you come to the Tomb of the Giants **Sa Ena 'e Thomes**.

Approximately 10 km east of Dorgali a twisting **road★★** descends towards the small port of Cala Gonone from where tourist boats leave on outings. The transparent water of **Cala Luna** is lined by a white sandy beach and a backdrop of oleanders. The **Grotto of the Sea Ox** (Bue Marino) is dedicated to the monk seal, which inhabited this part of the world until the end of the 1970s. *For information on visits ☎ 0784 96 243.*

### Ispinigòli Grotto★★

*7 km north-west of Dorgali, on the SS 125. For information on visits ☎ 0784 92 72 00.* Your gaze is immediately attracted by

*Ancient nuraghe*

© Dirk Ercken/iStock

*Medieval town of Bosa*

© Lalocracio/iStock

the enormous stalagmite that seems to hold up the ceiling. At 38 m in height, it is the second tallest in the world (the first is in New Mexico). The grotto has reached a fossil stage, meaning that it no longer drips the water necessary for new concretions to grow. The Phoenician jewellery and human bones found here suggest the place was used for sacrificial purposes but it may also have been a burial place used by the Nuragics.

### Road from Dorgali to Arbatax★★★

The SS 125 from Dorgali to Arbatax is a magnificent road that skirts beautiful ravines as it enters deeper into the extraordinary landscape of the Barbagia region of Sardinia. A yellow sign at Lotzorai indicates the turn-off for the **Domus de janas**. The archaeological zone encloses ten or so rather perturbing stone constructions. When you reach the highest point on the road (*alt. ca 1000 m*), stop and admire the scenery. In summer the mountains are dotted with the strongly smelling yellow flowers of broom.

**Tortolì** is the principal town of the wild region of **Ogliastra**, which is characterised by rocky mountains like truncated cones called "*Tacchi*". By the coast farmers practise agriculture but inland it is stock-breeding. The action of the sea smoothes the rocks, particularly at Gairo, where the stones are called "*coccorocci*".

**Arbatax★** is the port close to Tortolì. The town's most noted feature is the red porphyry rocks close to the port.

The view of the bay, which is closed off by mountains, is very beautiful. Cala Moresca is a smaller version.

Continuing south you arrive at **Cardedu** 🍷, **Jerzu** and **Osini**, winemaking towns set among the tacchi of Ogliastra.

### Mandrolisai

Barbagia Mandrolisai is an upland of green hills planted to vine that lies west of the Gennargentu mountains between Sòrgono and Làconi. It is here that red and rosé Mandrolisai wines are made from local grapes. The zone falls mostly in the province of Nuoro but partially crosses the boundary into Oristano.

### Malvasia di Bosa

The westernmost tip of the province of Nuoro is the production zone of the highly thought of Malvasia wine named after the medieval town of **Bosa★**. Bosa is situated on the river Temo beneath the looming presence of Serravalle Castle. This was constructed in the 12th c. and enlarged two hundred years later. The Church of Nostra Signora de Regnos Altos in Piazza d'Armi has remarkable 14th-c. frescoes. The town's main street is Corso Vittorio Emanuele, lined by 18th- and 19th-c. houses. The characteristic district of Sas Conzas on the other side of the river is the historic tanning centre and has been declared a national monument.

The Church of **San Pietro** (11th-12th c.) 2 km to the south-west reflects the architecture of the Cistercians, to whom the church was entrusted.

# Addresses

## Tourist information

**Region of Sardinia** – Viale Trieste 105, Cagliari, www.sardegnaturismo.it

**Cagliari Tourist Office** – Palazzo Civico, Via Roma 145, Cagliari, ℘ 070 67 77 397 and 338 64 98 498, www.cagliariturismo.it

**Nuoro Tourist Office** – Piazza Italia 8, Nuoro, ℘ 0784 44 18 23

**Oristano Tourist Office** – Piazza Eleonora 18, Oristano, ℘ 0783 36 83 210, www.gooristano.com

**Sassari Tourist Office** – Palazzo di Città, Via Satta 13, Sassari, ℘ 079 20 08 072, www.turismosassari.it

**Tempio Pausania Tourist Office** – Piazza Gallura 3, Tempio Pausania, ℘ 079 67 99 99, www.visit-tempio.it

## Regional wine cellars

**Sardinia Regional Wine Cellar** – Wine Museum, Via Casu 5, Berchidda (SS), ℘ 079 70 52 68, www.muvisardegna.it

## The wineries

*The addresses are listed in alphabetical order by location.*

**THE PROVINCE OF CAGLIARI AND SOUTHERN SARDINIA**

**Cantina di Santadi** – *Via Cagliari 78 -* **Santadi** *(VS) -* ℘ *0781 95 01 27 - cantina disantadi.it - info@cantinadisantadi.it - Winery tours by reservation in the website.* This co-operative winery was founded in 1960 to promote the local wines and particularly Carignano, the most characteristic grape variety of the area, but without neglecting the region's other traditional cultivars. The winery's philosophy marries the even broader concept of protecting the local heritage of traditions, culture, flavours, style and history. Hectares under vine: 550.
**Wines**: Valli di Porto Pino IGT Villa di Chiesa, Shardana and Araja, Carignano del Sulcis DOC Grotta Rossa, Riserva Rocca Rubia and Rosato Tre Torri, Carignano del Sulcis Superiore DOC Terre Brune, Passito Latinia, Festa Norìa, Cannonau di Sardegna DOC Noras, Monica di Sardegna DOC Antigua, Vermentino di Sardegna DOC Cala Silente and Villa Solais, Nuragus di Cagliari DOC Pedraia. Other products: grappa.

**Antonella Corda** – *Loc. Pranu Raimondo, Strada Statale 466 km 6,8 -* **Serdiana** *(CA)*
*-* ℘ *070 79 66 300 - www.antonellacorda.it - info@antonellacorda.it. - Winery tours Mon.-Sat. by reservation.* This "boutique winery" was founded in 2010, when Antonella inherited the wine-making family tradition. Thanks to her expertise in the field, she created in Serdiana, the homeland of her mother Maria Argiolas, a farm capable of producing high quality wines using organic fertilizers, integrated pest control actions and sustainable irrigation systems. The estate consulting oenologist is Luca D'Attoma, one of the most influential wine expert in Italy and abroad. Hectares under vine: 15.
**Wines**: Vermentino di Sardegna DOC, Nuragus di Cagliari DOC, Cannonau di Sardegna DOC, IGT Isola dei Nuraghi Ziru

**Argiolas** – *Via Roma 28/30 -* **Serdiana** *(CA) -* ℘ *070 74 06 06 - www.argiolas.it - info@ argiolas. - Winery tours and tasting by reservation (www.visitargiolas.it).* The first member of the family to grow vines was Francesco Argiolas in 1918, but the adventure in the world of wine commenced with his son Antonio in the 1930s. Three generations of the family currently work in the winery. The philosophy of this estate is inspired by the assumption that good wine is not the result of technique alone, but a combination of factors, in which the passion for this job and the care of the vineyard and the grapes play a fundamental role. Cooking classes held in the tasting room of the Argiolas vinery. Hectares under vine: 230.
**Wines**: Cannonau di Sardegna DOC Costera and Riserva Senes, Carignano del Sulcis DOC Cardanera, Riserva Is Solinas, Monica di Sardegna DOC Perdera, Superiore Iselis Monica, Nasco di Cagliari DOC Iselis Nasco, Nuragus di Cagliari DOC S'Elegas, Vermentino di Sardegna DOC Costamolino, Is Argiolas and DOC Merì, IGT Isola dei Nuraghi Bianco Angialis and Cerdeña, Novello Alasi, Rosato Serra Lori, Rosso Antonio Argiolas, Korem and Turriga, Brut Tagliamare. Other products: olive oil, must and grappa.

**ORISTANO AND ITS SURROUNDING AREA**

**Attilio Contini** – *Via Genova 48/50 -* **Cabras** *(OR) -* ℘ *0783 29 08 06 - www. vinicontini.com - info@vinicontini.com - Winery tours by reservation (2 days in advance).* Founded in 1898 by Salvatore Contini, this is one of Sardinia's oldest wineries. His son Attilio, father of the current owners, capably continued in his

# ADDRESSES

footsteps, renovating and extending the winery and increasing the area of vineyards in the best winegrowing areas. The top of the winery's range is its Vernaccia di Oristano. Hectares under vine: 150.

**Wines**: Vernaccia di Oristano DOC, Componidori, Riserva and Antico Gregori cuvée, IGT Tharros Rosso Maluentu, Rosato I Giganti, Bianco I Giganti and Karmis, IGT Isola dei Nuraghi Rosso Barrile and I Giganti, Cannonau di Sardegna DOC Sartiglia, Tonaghe, Mamaioa and Riserva 'Inu, IGT Valle del Tirso Rosato Nieddera, Vermentino di Sardegna DOC Tyrsos, Mamaioa and Pariglia, Vermentino di Gallura DOCG Elibaria, Bianco dolce Pontis, Attilio Rosé, Attilio Brut. Other products: grappa.

### THE PROVINCE OF SASSARI

**Tenute Sella&Mosca** – *Loc. I Piani* - **Alghero** *(SS)* - ☏ *079 99 77 00 - www.sellaemosca.com - anna.cadeddu@ sellaemosca.com - Winery tours Mon.-Fri. by reservation.* The greatest strengths of this winery are its close bond to tradition and its ability to satisfy the ever-changing tastes of consumers with a broad, varied range featuring red, white, dessert and sparkling wines, in both complex and easy-drinking styles. The most popular include Marchese di Villamarina, Tanca Farrà and Anghelu Ruju fortified wines. Hectares under vine: 520.

**Wines**: Alghero Bianco DOC Parallelo 41, Cabernet Riserva DOC Marchese di Villamarina, Alghero Liquoroso Riserva DOC Anghelu Ruju, Alghero Rosato DOC Anemone, Alghero Rosso DOC Tanca Farrà, Vittorio 90, Alghero Torbato DOC Catore, Terre Bianche Cuvée 161, Alghero Torbato Spumante Brut Metodo Classico DOC Oscarì, Alghero Torbato SPUMANTE DOC Torbato Brut, Cannonau di Sardegna Mustazzo, Cannonau di Sardegna DOC, Cannonau di Sardegna DOC Riserva Dimonios, Carignano del Sulcis DOC Riserva Terre Rare Riserva, Vermentino di Gallura Superiore DOCG Monteoro, Vermentino di Sardegna DOC Ambat and Cala Reale, Passito DOC Monteluce.

♟ **Dettori** – *Loc. Badde Nigolosu - SP 21 km 10* - **Sennori** *(SS)* - ☏ *079 51 55 11 - www. tenutedettori.it - info@tenutedettori.it - Winery tours by reservation (kentannos@ tenutedettori.it).* Alessandro Dettori likes to call himself a "wine artisan", which evokes the amount of care and passion he applies to his work in the vineyard and the cellar. All the processes are carried out by hand by the family, according to the traditional farming techniques used before the advent of chemicals and mechanisation. Consequently, the focus is on maintaining natural balances. Farm restaurant Kent'Annos (*www.kentannos.it*) available. Hectares under vine: 33.

**Wines**: Romangia IGT Rosso Tenores, Tuderi, Dettori, Ottomarzo, Chimbanta and Chimbanta & Battoro, Romangia IGT Bianco Dettori and Passito Moscadeddu. Other products: bread, preserves in oil, confectionery, charcuterie, cheeses.

### THE COSTA SMERALDA AND GALLURA

**Capichera** – *Strada per Sant'Antonio di Gallura km 4* - **Arzachena** *(OT)* - ☏ *0789 80 800 - www.capichera.it - info@capichera.it - Winery tours Mon.-Fri. 8.30-13, 14-17.30 by reservation* Capichera's history dates back to the early 1920s, when the current owners' grandfather inherited an estate of over 50 hectares. New Vermentino vines were planted in the 1970s and a modern winery was built. The first wine with the Capichera label was sold during the following decade. Today the original 10 hectares of vineyards have become 60 and new vineyards are being planted. Hectares under vine: 60.

**Wines**: Vermentino di Sardegna DOC Lintòri, IGT Isola dei Nuraghi Bianco Capichera, VT and Santigaìni, IGT Isola dei Nuraghi Rosso Liànti, Assajé, Mantènghia and Albóri di Làmpata, IGT Isola dei Nuraghi Rosé També, Vermentino di Gallura DOCG Vign'angena.

**Cantina Li Seddi** – *Via Mare 29* - **Badesi** *(OT)* - ☏ *0796 83 052 - www.cantinaliseddi.it - amministrazione@cantinaliseddi.it - Winery tours by reservation.* This family-run business was founded in the 1960s by the paternal grandparents of the current owners. At the time it comprised 8 hectares of vineyard and 5 hectares of farmland. The wine was sold unbottled. The winery embarked on a new path in 2002, focusing its efforts on quality, and it is now acknowledged as one of the best wineries in Sardinia. The estate offers guest accommodation. Hectares under vine: 8.

**Wines**: Vermentino di Gallura Superiore DOCG Li Pastini and Lagrimedda, Cannonau di Sardegna DOC Maistrali Riserva, Rosamarina Rosato and Lichittu Passito, IGT Isola dei Nuraghi Petra Ruja and Lu Ghiali.

**Pedra Majore** – *Via Roma 106* - **Monti** *(OT)* - ☏ *0789 43 185 - www.pedramajore.it/web. tiscali.it/pedramajore - info@pedramajore.it - Winery tours by reservation., closed Sat. and Sun.* The cantina is run by by the Isoni brothers, Salvator Paolo and Giovanni, and their sister Lucia, the third generation in a long family tradition of winemaking. They produce organic wines, taking advantage of local vines and Sardinian winemaking traditions in general. Be sure to try the company's Vermentini. Hectares under vine: 18.

**Wines**: Vermentino di Gallura DOCG Superiore Hysony, Vermentino di Gallura

DOCG I Graniti and Le Conche, Colli del Limbara IGT Rosso Murighessa, Colli del Limbara IGT Roccas Rosé, Mirju Passito Bianco.

## THE PROVINCES OF NUORO AND OGLIASTRA

**Alberto Loi** – *Offices Viale Trieste 61, Cagliari (CA) - Winery SS 125 km 124.1 -* **Cardedu** *(NU) - ✆ 070 24 08 66 - www. albertoloi.it - Winery tours by reservation (min. 10 days in advance).* The winery was established in the 1950s and is run by the founder's children. Cannonau is the grape with which it is most closely associated, but it also grows other native varieties and several hectares are destined for recently introduced cultivars. The winery is built on several levels. The central structure is the oldest and was built from granite quarried on the estate. Hectares under vine: 52.
**Wines**: Cannonau di Sardegna DOC Jerzu Al and Sa Mola, Cannonau di Sardegna DOC Jerzu Riserva Alberto Loi Riserva and Cardedo, Cannonau di Sardegna DOC Jerzu Riserva, Cannonau di Sardegna DOC Jerzu Rosé Rosemonti, Cannonau di Sardegna DOC Jerzu, IGT Isola dei Nuraghi Astangia, Isola dei Nuraghi IGT Leila, Loi Corona, Nànà and Tuvara, Monica di Sardegna DOC Nibaru, Vermentino di Sardegna DOC Theria.

**Perda Rubia** – *Offices Via Asproni 29 - Nuoro - Winery ex SS 125, km 121.6 -* **Cardedu** *(OG) - ✆ 0784 32 832 - www.tenuteperdarubia. com -info@tenuteperdarubia.com - Winery tours by reservation.* Founded in 1949, Perda Rubia specialises in the production of Cannonau di Sardegna, offering wines characterised by the strong, rounded palate of the quintessential Sardinian red grape variety. Its wines are produced exclusively *in purezza* (varietal)from "the juice of healthy grape berries", without filtration or artificial stabilisation. Hectares under vine: 20.
**Wines**: Cannonau di Sardegna DOC Riserva Perda Rubia, Cannonau di Sardegna DOC Naniha. Other products: olive oil.

## Where to stay

### AGGIUS

**Agriturismo il Muto di Gallura** – *Strada Provinciale 27, Loc. Fraiga, 1 km S of Aggius (OT) - ✆ 079 62 05 59 - www.mutodigallura. com - 16 rooms, doubles from €110.* Set among cork oaks, this farmhouse with hunting reserve is named after a romantic bandit and it is for guests who are not interested in the amenities of a hotel. Rooms are in stone cottages called *stazzi*. It offers horseback tours in "beautiful" countryside. The dining room is characterised by lots of wood and serves typical local specialities, from wild boar to Gallura-style soup.

### BAIA SARDINIA

**Hotel Villa Gemella** – *Loc. Baia Sardinia, Arzachena (OT) - ✆ 0789 99 303. www. hotelvillagemella.com - 25 rooms.* One of the main attractions of this hotel is the lovely flower-filled garden, which is a great spot for relaxation. There is also a swimming pool… not to mention the sea (the Bay of Sardinia) nearby. The rooms, which are light and airy, have been tastefully furnished; some have a terrace

### BOSA

**Hotel Al Gabbiano** – *Viale Mediterraneo 5, Bosa Marina (OR) - ✆ 0785 37 41 23 - www. hotelalgabbiano.it - 30 rooms, doubles from €100.* Hotel Al Gabbiano is a beach-front small family-run hotel housed in a villa, with wooden furniture and simple, comfortable rooms. The kitchen offers home cooking with regional flavours.

### OLIENA

**Locanda tipica-ristorante Sa Corte** – *Via Nuoro 138, Oliena (NU) - ✆ 347 26 33 784 or 0784 18 76 131- www.sacorte.it - Closed 10 Jan.-15 Feb. - 6 rooms, doubles from €75.* This country establishment presents the Nuoro gourmet tradition at its best, with delicious pasta, excellent meat and fragrant Sardinian wines. Pleasant, well furnished rooms.

### PULA

**Villa Alberta** – *Via Segni 76, Pula (CA) - ✆ 070 92 45 447 - www.villa-alberta.com - 4 rooms, doubles from €65.* Characterised by simplicity, the whole family welcomes guests with the sincere warmth of Sardinian hospitality in this little white house built in the early 1970s.

### SANT'ANTIOCO

**Hotel Ristorante Moderno** – *Via Nazionale 82, Sant'Antioco (CI) - ✆ 0781 83 105 - www.hotel-moderno-sant-antioco.it - 16 rooms, doubles from €70.* Beyond the small hotel's lobby lies Ristorante Da Achille (*Jun.-Sept., ✆ 375 58 400 87, www.ristorante daachille.it*), an original restaurant run by a skilled chef, who offers traditional gourmet delights and Sardinian specialities.

### TORTOLÌ

**Il Vecchio Mulino** – *Via Parigi, Loc. Porto Frailis, Arbatax, Tortolì (OG) - ✆ 0782 66 40 41 - www.hotelilvecchiomulino.it - 24 rooms, doubles from €60.* This building with a traditional atmosphere houses elegant rooms decorated with warm colours, rooms with exposed beams and marble bathrooms. Beautiful terrace and garden. Sailing trips on the Orisei Gulf available.

*Ascona, Lake Maggiore*
© Xantana/iStock

# Canton Ticino

# CANTON TICINO

Canton Ticino in Switzerland has strong links with Italy, starting with their common language and a passion for wine. The canton lies in a critical location touched upon by a variety of physical landscapes: those of the Alps, Lakes Maggiore and Lugano, woodlands and the plain. The canton enjoys a continental climate but is also affected by the proximity of the Mediterranean. The human presence has created everything from villages founded in ancient times to large modern cities. The winemaking districts are divided between Sopraceneri (Bellinzona, Blenio, Riviera, Leventina, Locarno, Vallemaggia) and Sottoceneri (Lugano and Mendrisio). The most common variety of grape is Merlot, which alone covers more than 80% of the land planted to vine and is vinified almost exclusively pure.

© Avner Richard/Shutterstock

*Vineyards in the Swiss sunshine*

## The terroir

The vineyards for the most part occupy hillside terraces. Today there are more than 200 wineries in operation in Canton Ticino, almost all of which are small to medium-sized. For many producers winemaking is more of a hobby than a business.

On average approximately 6000 tonnes of grapes are harvested each year, which are turned into 4 million litres (about 5.3 million bottles) of wine. Though **Merlot** provides the great bulk of the territory's grape harvest, other cultivars give pleasing results: **Gamaret**, a precocious red grape variety with excellent qualities of adaptation that creates tannic wines with good body and fine ageing capabilities; **Carminoir**, another red grape variety, a bit of a late ripener that produces structured wines of strong colour and interesting acidity; and **Doral**, a white grape cultivar that gives fine, scented, elegant wines.

**Merlot del Ticino** is a ruby-red wine with a fruity, flowery and slightly spicy nose. In the mouth it is velvety, refreshing and of medium body. When Merlot is vinified without maceration of the skins, **Bianco di Merlot** is produced, which now represents 16% of overall production in Ticino and is the region's most common white wine.

Ticino white wines are generally the colour of pale straw, light in body, scented and best drunk young.

The most interesting aspects of Ticino viticulture are the commitment of the local producers to researching the best growing and production techniques, and their study of the peculiarities of the terrain and the vines grown. The result of this constant effort and dedication is twofold: first, wines of excellent quality, and second, the fact that today Ticino is the fourth most important wine-producing area in Switzerland after Vallese, Vaud and Geneva.

To mark the centenary of the presence of Merlot in Ticino, many events were held in 2006 to celebrate what has become the "Ticino variety" par excellence. It was also a moment for reflection on what has been accomplished so far and on the plans for the future, of which two objectives are to achieve yet higher quality and to harmonise production more carefully with the characteristics of the land.

The **Canton Ticino Wine Routes** (5 itineraries that take in wineries, and places of geographical, cultural and historic interest) explore the following winemaking districts:

**Mendrisiotto**: from Mendriso to Chiasso
**Locarnese**: from Tenero to Ascona
**Bellinzonese**: from Camorino to Bodio
**Malcantone**: from Lamone to Termine
**Piano di Magadino and Valle di Blenio**: from Gudo to Dongio.

# Itineraries

*Sites with a winery are indicated by the symbol ♀; for the addresses of the wineries, see p. 477.*

## 1. LUGANO AND SURROUNDING AREA

### Lugano★★ ♀

Lugano is the southernmost city in Ticino, situated in the wedge that points down towards Como. Its name comes from the lake on which it lies, though this is also known as Lake Ceresio. Since the second half of the 19th c., Lugano has benefited from its beautiful physical setting on a dark, still bay between two wood-lined mountains (Monte Brè and Monte San Salvatore). Lugano's attractions appeal to all tastes, with its pedestrian areas, small squares, luxury shops in the centre, boutiques and quiet walks in the surrounding countryside.

**Piazza della Riforma★** is very lively thanks to its bars and, in July, the concerts given as part of its summer jazz festival. It is the setting for the city's striking Municipal Palace (1844). Interesting streets to wander through are Via Petrarca and Via Soave, and the narrow Via Pessina lined by small food shops and inviting shop windows.

In **Piazza Cioccaro** (cable railway), the Baroque **Palazzo Riva★** (1671) hides an internal courtyard with a surprising wall decorated with a trompe-l'œil painting (*Via Soave 9*).

*Take the steeply sloping Via della Cattedrale.* Roman in origin, the **Cathedral of San Lorenzo** has an elegant façade with three portals decorated with lovely Renaissance motifs. The Chapel of Nostra Signora delle Grazie in the right aisle is a fine example of Baroque decoration. Views of the lake and Lugano can be had from the square.

*Return to Piazza Cioccaro and turn right into Via Pessina, then into* **Via Nassa**. With its porticoes and shops, this is the main street in the historic centre. It is named after the basket net used by fishermen who used to repair their boats and nets under the porticoes. In

## PRINCIPAL VARIETIES CULTIVATED

### WHITE GRAPES
Chardonnay
Chasselas
Doral
Kerner
Müller Thurgau
Pinot Bianco
Pinot Grigio
Sauvignon Blanc
Semillon

### BLACK GRAPES
Ancellotta
Bondola
Cabernet Franc
Cabernet Sauvignon
Carminoir
Diolinoir
Gamaret
Merlot
Pinot Nero

© Razvan Chirnoaga/Shutterstock

Piazzetta San Carlo note the sculpture of Salvador Dalí entitled *The Nobility of Time*. Palazzo Vanoni (*Via Nassa 66*) used to be the seat of the bishopric, as the papal coats of arms on the façade indicate.

**Church of Santa Maria degli Angeli★★** – Construction of this convent church began in 1499, which has three splendid **frescoes★★** by Bernardino Luini (1480-1532 ca). The most notable decorates the separating wall in the choir: representing the Passion, it is striking for the extraordinary expressiveness of the Crucifixion scene.

*Return to the centre along the shaded lakeside promenade. After Piazza*

Harvested grapes

*Manzoni, turn left into Via Albrizzi to reach Via Canova.*

After passing the Canton Museum of Art, the Church of San Rocco (16th c.) and the casino, you arrive in **Piazza Indipendenza** which commemorates Lugano's achievement of independence from the northern cantons in 1798 before it joined the Swiss Confederation in 1803. The elegant **city park★** lies along the lakeshore and is the shady setting for outdoor concerts in the summer. **Villa Ciani**, once owned by the Ciani brothers, who initiated Lugano's first steps in the tourist industry in the second half of the 19th c. Today it houses the **Museo delle Culture** (*Villa Malpensata, Riva Caccia 5, for information, www.mcl.lugano.ch*). The end of the walk offers a fine panorama of the city.

*A walkway over the river Cassarate leads to the port and beach.*

### Monte San Salvatore★★★

*Alt. 912 m, 45 min. return journey, of which 10 min. by cable railway from Paradiso, ℰ 0041 (0)91 98 52 828, www.montesansalvatore.ch.* The views over Lugano, the lake, the Bernese Alps and Vallese are spectacular. You can choose to walk down to Lugano (*75 min.*) or continue to Carona (*40 min.*) and Morcote (*3 h*).

### Monte Brè★★

*Alt. 933 m. 1 h return journey, of which 30 min. by cable railway from Cassarate. You can also reach the top by car through Castagnola, Brè, then head for the Ristorante*

**THE TERROIR**

**Area:** 2812,15 km$^2$, of which approximately 1040 hectares are planted to vine, divided equally between Sopraceneri and Sottoceneri

**Average annual production of Merlot:** approximately 55,000 quintals

**Geography:** climate mild and sunny due to the proximity of the Mediterranean; rainy at some periods of the year

**USEFUL ADDRESSES AND WINE ROUTES**

Ticino Wine - Ente di Promozione della Vitivinicoltura del Canton Ticino – ℰ 0041 (0)91 69 01 353, www.ticinowine.ch

Ferdeviti - Federazione dei Viticoltori Ticinesi – Via Gorelle, Sant'Antonio ℰ 0041 (0)91 85 19 090, www.federviti.ch

Associazione Viticoltori Vinificatori Ticinesi – www.viticoltori.ch

*Ticino vineyards*

*Vetta along a narrow, unpaved road.* In 20 min. you arrive at Brè where you can admire outdoor works of art.

## Lake Lugano★★

*You can choose between boat trips on the lake lasting between 1 hour and half a day. The ferries offer a regular service between Gandria, Cantine di Gandria, Morcote, Porlezza, Ponte Tresa and Campione. The "Tour of the Lake" starts in Lugano.* Irregular in shape, the lake is 35 km long and has a max. depth of 279 m. Most of it lies in Switzerland but the north-east branch (Porlezza), a part of the south-west shore (Porto Ceresio) and an enclave on the east side (Campione d'Italia) fall in Italian territory, where the lake is called Lake Ceresio. Wilder in appearance than lakes Maggiore or Como, it is ringed by the steep but harmonious slopes of the Prealps and the silver leaves of olive trees. It is separated into two sections by a dam that carries the Gotthard rail and road crossings. Ferries connect the two sections.

If you arrive at **Gandria**★ (*6 km east of Lugano*) by boat, you are offered the colourful spectacle of terraces in bloom with geraniums and pergolas, and a maze of tiny stepped streets, porticoed houses and a small Baroque church. The "Olive Path" follows the lakeside and will take you back to Lugano (*1 h*). Nusera Olive Grove was recreated in 2001 on ancient terraces supported by dry stone walls.

## Malcantone and Monte Lema★

*Circular itinerary of 35 km starting from Lugano.*

The Malcantone valleys run west of Lugano between one arm of the lake, the Gulf of Agno, the river Tresa, and the mountains that mark the border with Italy. The region is well equipped for outdoor activities and is dominated by Monte Lema. To reach the mountain, leave Lugano in the direction of Agno (*6 km west*). From Bioggio, take the road that climbs through the woods to Cademario, then to Miglieglia.

The town of **Miglieglia** (*20 km northwest of Lugano*) stands in the shadow of the Church of Santo Stefano (15th c.), decorated with frescoes from the 16th and 17th c.

The ascent to **Monte Lema**★ (*by cable car from Miglieglia*) gives excellent views over the village and church. A path runs from the highest restaurant to the top of the mountain (*20 min. return on a steep path*) from where the **views**★ range from Lake Maggiore and Monte Rosa in the west to Lake Lugano and Monte Generoso in the east. To the north-west you can see the Jungfrau and Eiger.

On the way back down from Miglieglia you can pass through **Bedigliora**, one of the most characteristic villages in the region.

**CANTON TICINO**

## Mendrisio and the region of Mendrisiotto

*Itinerary of 20 km from Capolago (15 km south of Lugano) to Meride.*

The district of Mendrisio forms the southern tip of Italian Switzerland. It is industrial and highly urbanised, particularly along the motorway, but the side valleys, such as Muggio and the nearby hills around Meride, are truly enchanting.

On clear days from the top of **Monte Generoso★★★** (alt. 1701 m, rack railway from Capolago) you have fantastic **views★★★** of the Alps, Lugano, the lakes and right across the Lombard plain to the Apennines.

**Riva San Vitale**, just 1 km from **Capolago**, should be visited just to see its 5th c. baptistery in a room next to the parish church. It has a large font used to immerse babies during baptism, and

© fotoember/iStock

## Grottoes – Ticino style

**Grottoes** are one of the best Ticino inventions! Originally they were cool, natural caves that were used as wine cellars and summer residences. Today the name signifies a rustic, out-of-town restaurant where traditional cuisine is offered. The atmosphere of grottoes is halfway between a rural celebration and a mountain inn! The menu typically offers cold meats, polenta, braised beef, risottoes, mushrooms, desserts, *dolce di pane* (desserts made using old bread mixed with eggs, fruit, etc.), and mulled peaches. The wine (Merlot, Nostrano or Barbera drunk with lemon juice) used to be served in small cups.

the remains of 11th c. frescoes on the walls. At the other end of the village, the Church of Santa Croce (16th c.) is recognisable by its octagonal dome. On the walls of its four-sided interior there are beautiful murals.

Once you penetrate the modern commercial section of **Mendrisio** ♟, you discover a fascinating historic centre in the middle of which stands the Neoclassical domed Church of Santissimi Cosma e Damiano (19th c.). At the bottom of the monumental flight of steps outside stands a square tower, a remnant of the medieval city walls. Walk down the picturesque Via San Damiano and Via Stella to the Oratory of the Madonna delle Grazie (13th c.). The internal decoration is naïf in style. The ancient Convent of the Servi di Maria houses an art museum devoted to temporary exhibitions in Piazza dei Serviti behind the oratory. Continuing down Via Carla Pasta, you come to the Viale alle Cantine on the right where a row of houses that used to be old wine and cheese cellars stand at the foot of the cliff. The restaurants in the grotto offer local cooking.

A treat is in store in **Ligornetto**, the birthplace of the sculptor Vincenzo Vela (1820-91). His elegant villa-atelier, which was turned into a museum of his family's artworks in the 1920s, has been attractively renovated by architect Mario Botta (**Vela Museum★★**, *open 10-17, till 18 in Jun.-Sept. and Sun., closed Mon., ☏ 0041 (0)58 481 30 44, www.museo-vela.ch*). A gallery brings together the extraordinary plaster casts of almost all the monumental sculptural works of this uncontested champion of realism. The large octagonal room that contains the pantheon of illustrious individuals Vela portrayed is quite astonishing.

**Rancate** deserves a visit for the **Giovanni Züst Museum**, which exhibits a collection of paintings by Ticinese and Lombard artists from the 17th to 20th c. An important place is allotted to Antonio Rinaldi (1816-1875), born in the Mendrisio area, with his gracious and romantic portraits. *Open Mar.-Jun. 9-12 and 14-17 Jul.-Aug. 14-18, Oct.-Jan. 10-12 and 14-18, closed working Mon., ☏ 091 81 64 791, facebook.com/pinacotecazuest.*

Pass through **Besazio** ♟ to arrive at **Arzo**. At the entrance to this hillside town there is a marble quarry that provided the material to line the church's bell tower.

Surrounded by vineyards, **Meride** is interesting for its houses with porticoes and internal courtyards. As you wander through its narrow streets, you will note decorations left by the village's stucco workers who emigrated to France, Germany and Russia in the 16th and 17th c.

## 2. LOCARNO AND LAKE MAGGIORE

### Locarno★

The world's most beautiful cinema is to be found in Locarno, when the city's annual international open-air film festival is held in the marvellous **Piazza Grande★** in August. Throughout the rest of the year (and especially on Thursdays, market day) the square is the beating heart of Locarno. Built on the shore of Lake Maggiore by the fan-shaped delta of the tributary, the river Maggia, Locarno enjoys a warm climate. In the heat of the summer, cool is to be found under the porticoes, in the narrow streets of the historic centre or in the valleys inland.

*To visit the historic centre, wander down Via Cittadella and Via Sant'Antonio.* Consecrated in 1230, the Church of **San Francesco** underwent serious alterations in the 16th c. Note the wooden vault over the nave and the Romanesque cross vaults over the aisles. The upper wall in the choir is decorated with a large fresco of the *Annunciation*.

**Casa Rusca★**, which houses the **municipal picture gallery**, is a fine example of an 18th-c. patrician residence. Three storeys of elliptical arches look onto the internal courtyard. The temporary exhibitions focus on modern and contemporary art. Enrico Baj, the Ticinese artist Claude Baccalà, Jean Arp and Giovanni Bianconi, who were linked to Locarno, have all given works to the museum. *Piazza Sant'Antonio. Open 10-12 and 14-17, closed Mon., ☏ 091 75 63 185.*

On Via al Castello you will find the **Visconti Castle**, which was fortified from the 13th c. and turned into a residential palace a century later.

**Madonna del Sasso★★** – *At Orselina. The recommended way to arrive is via cable railway from Via della Stazione,* or by car on the twisting *Via ai Monti della Trinità*. This shrine, which is popular with tourists and pilgrims, is perched on the top of a spur of rock (355 m). On 15 August 1480 the Virgin Mary appeared to Brother Bartolomeo d'Ivrea, a monk at the convent of San Francesco di Locarno, who had come to live as a hermit on the Sasso della Rocca. Following this vision a chapel was built, which marked the start of the construction of the sanctuary. The Church dell'Annunciazione has an imposing entrance, the loggias of its gallery painted with murals. There are frescoes inside and works of art like the *Flight into Egypt* by Bramantino (1522, right altar). There is an excellent **view★** of Locarno and Lake Maggiore from the loggiato. *You can walk back down to the city by following the sign "Locarno via Crucis". It is fairly steep but panoramic.*

**Camellia Park** – *2 km south, near the public swimming pool. Open 9-17.* Enjoying the shade of poplars and oaks, a collection of 520 varieties of camellia benefits from the humidity and mild temperatures offered by the lake. March and April are the best months to see them in bloom but some rare varieties are in flower as late as autumn.

### Ascona★★ ♚

*4 km south-west of Locarno.* Ascona is a sort of St Tropez on the banks of Lake Maggiore. An old fishing village, it began to become chic during the 1950s and has since extended into the

*Madonna del Sasso*

© PeJo/Shutterstock

473

*Lakeside promenade in Ascona*

Maggia delta, close to Locarno. The best positions on the bay are taken by luxury hotels, and the lakeside promenade, which is known humorously as **Piazza Motta** as it is lined with bars and restaurants, remains lively until late at night. By day people visit the beach or take the ferry to the islands of Brissago. The Church of **Santa Maria della Misericordia** (*Via delle Cappelle*), which forms one side of the Collegio Papio, was founded in 1399 and modernised in the 15th c. except for the choir, which remained Gothic. The church is known for its polychrome frescoes (15th-16th c.) in the nave and choir, and for the lovely altarpiece illustrating the life of the Virgin (1519). The Lombard-style cloister surrounds an elegant, tranquil court.

Standing at the heart of a maze of small streets, the parish Church of **Santi Pietro e Paolo** (*Piazza San Pietro*) contains a fine altarpiece and several lovely canvases by Giovanni Serodine, who was born in Ascona and studied under Caravaggio (*Coronation of the Virgin* above the high altar). In the same square, the **Casa Serodine** has a magnificent Baroque façade (1620) decorated with stuccoes by the brother of the painter. As was common in the past among the local artists, builders and decorators, who often moved to Rome or Tuscany where they might make their fortune, the Serodines emigrated from Ascona.

## Monte Verità

The name of the hill that looks down on Ascona was given to it by the Monte Verità community that settled there at the start of the 20th c. in search of a new lifestyle. They were vegetarians, naturists, classless and moneyless. In this period Ascona became a counter-cultural centre where artists, psychoanalysts and anarchists stayed. The land of Monte Verità was bought in 1926 by Baron Edouard Von der Heydt, a banker for the former Emperor Wilhelm II. A sanatorium was built there in Bauhaus style, but this was later transformed into a hotel. The park and terrace of the restaurant are islands of peace and very pleasant in summer.

## Islands of Brissago★

*Reached by boat from Locarno, Ascona, Brissago and Porto Ronco (www.navigazionelaghi.it).* The tiny islands of San Pancrazio and Sant'Apollinare, which enjoy a superb climate, were purchased in 1885 by Baroness Antoinette de Saint Léger, a passionate botanist, who turned San Pancrazio into an exotic garden that later became the **Botanic Garden** of Canton Ticino. Species grow there that are suited to a temperate climate, such as the Japanese banana tree from the Riukiu islands, whereas the blue palms, agaves and bald cypresses are typical of the tropics. Peacocks wander freely between the tall eucalyptuses, the oldest in Ticino, which tower above everything else on this tiny island. *℘ 0041 (0)91 791 43 61, isoledibrissago@ti.ch, www.isolebrissago.ch.*

## Verzasca valley★ and the Contra Dam

*Itinerary of 20 km from Locarno to Corippo.*

The valley runs north-east from Locarno and is named after the "green water" of its river. Just outside Locarno lies **Tenero** 🍷 (*8 km east*), a small village surrounded by vineyards, after which the road climbs up to the gigantic Contra dam. *The road winds around the dam, then rises and passes through several tunnels to reach the terracing and houses of Vogomo on the mountainside. After 2 km take a left turn to* ***Corippo★*** *on the facing slope.* This perched village is one of the most visited in Ticino. It has a magnificent situation with impressive views onto the valley floor and the reservoir.

## 3. BELLINZONA★★★ 🍷

The crenellated walls and three castles visible from far off are like sentinels in the centre of the valley. This remarkable example of a late-medieval stronghold is a UNESCO World Heritage site. Contrary to appearances, the city is not at all austere – to convince yourself just take a walk on a Saturday morning (market day) in the historic centre. The atmosphere is bustling and the cheeses and cold meats on the stalls are inviting.

*From Piazza del Sole, a large square in the north of the city, you arrive at the castle walls. Further on there is a lift in the rock that will carry you up to the castle.*

**Castelgrande★★** – *Open 9-22 (Mon.10-18), walls 10-19 (10-17 in win.); museum Apr.-Nov. 10-18, rest of the year 10.30-16, ☏ 0041 (0)91 82 58 145, www.bellinzonese-altoticino.ch.* This is the oldest of the three castles and the central element of the city's defences. It is protected by a steep crag on one side and the White and Black Towers. The site was restored between 1982 and 1992 to create a contemporary complex and transform the building into a city park. The buildings in the south court now house a restaurant (where you can try the "castle wine" produced by vines grown at the foot of the crag), and a history and archaeology museum. An interesting view over the city is seen from the Terrazza del Castagno.

To the west of the castle, the **panorama** of the city and castle can be admired from the long fortified walls (the Murata).

*You can return to the city down steep streets to Piazza della Collegiata.*

The **Collegiata★** (Collegiate Church) has an imposing Renaissance façade decorated with a rose window. The Baroque interior includes a lovely stucco pulpit and sculpted stoup. The side chapels are decorated by frescoes, the best known being the 5th on the right (painted in 1770 by Cherubini).

To the right of the Collegiate Church are two interesting houses on **Via Nosetto**. One has a façade decorated with busts of famous men (Galileo, Dante, Petrarch, Aristotle, Volta), and at no. 1, "Casa Rossa" has terracotta decorations. On Saturday mornings a market is held in **Piazza Nosetto★** and the surrounding streets.

Inspired by Italian Renaissance architecture, **Palazzo Civico** has an elegant internal court in which two rows of loggias with elliptical arches are decorated with images of the city's history. The third floor has the form of a gallery with columns topped by capitals. The stone stairway ends with a fine lacunar ceiling.

*To the right of Palazzo Civico, Via del Teatro leads to* **Teatro Sociale**. This, the city theatre, was built in 1846-47 as a small-scale La Scala. It is the only Italian-style Neoclassical theatre in Switzerland.

© Valeria/Shutterstock

*Castelgrande*

© Alistair Scott/Shutterstock

*Vineyards in autumn*

**Montebello Castle★★** – *Can be reached by car from the road that leaves from Viale della Stazione. Alternatively on foot in 15 min. up a road to the right of the Collegiate Church. Open castle Apr.-Nov. 10-18, museum 10-18, ℘ 091 82 51 342, www. bellinzonaturismo.ch.* The plan of this formidable citadel is shaped like a diamond. It is a fortress built following the rules of Lombard military architecture. Constructed in the 13th c. by the powerful Rusca family, the castle became the property of the Visconti at the end of the 14th c. A drawbridge over the moat leads to the nucleus of the site, around which fortifications were built in the 14th and 15th c. The top of the tower is a stunning lookout point.

**Sasso Corbaro Castle★** – *Leave Montebello Castle by car and take Via Artore upwards. Turn right into Via Benedetto Ferrini and then Via Sasso Corbaro. Open Apr.-Nov. 10-18, ℘ 091 82 55 906, www. bellinzonaturismo.ch.* This, the last and highest castle, is like an isolated fortress set amongst chestnut trees. Ordered by the Duke of Milan, it was built on a square plan in just 6 months in the 15th c. to reinforce Bellinzona's defences. The guard tower is now a lookout point. **Views★** of the city and the lower Ticino valley as far as Lake Maggiore can be had from the terrace of the first courtyard. From here it is easy to understand the strategic position of Bellinzona: up the valley, there are paths to the St Gotthard and St Bernard passes; down the valley lies the Magadino plain, which at one time was marshy.

## Ravecchia

*Ravecchia lies just 15 min. on foot from Bellinzona: take Via Lugano from Piazza Indipendenza, then first left in Via Ospedale.* This will take you into the quiet suburb of Ravecchia. The old church in the Convent of the Friars Minor (15th c.), the Church of **Santa Maria delle Grazie**, has interesting frescoes, including a *Crucifixion* surrounded by 15 paintings illustrating the life of Christ. The fresco was painted in the late 15th-early 16th c., probably by a Lombard artist.

The small medieval Church of **San Biagio** has a four-sided bell tower and lovely frescoes. The church's façade is adorned with a large St Christopher and a *Virgin and Child* (14th c.) in pinkish tones. As soon as you enter, your gaze will be drawn towards the choir decorated with murals illuminated by indirect light.

## Monte Carasso

*About 2 km west of Bellinzona.* This village of 2300 people on the edge of Bellinzona is an exemplary case in Europe of an innovative urbanisation project. It was drawn up by the Ticinese architect Luigi Snozzi in 1978. What remains visible are the public spaces around the old convent, which was itself turned into a state school.

Other buildings, like the Raiffeisen Bank, the gym and the new cemetery have helped transform the village centre. The private houses too demonstrate an open, creative approach in both their designs and materials.

# Addresses

## Tourist information

**To call** – From Italy dial 0041 followed by the regional area code without the 0. To call within Switzerland dial the area code (including the 0) followed by the number.

**Bellinzona Tourism** – Palazzo Civico, **Bellinzona**, ☎ 0041 (0)91 82 52 131, www.bellinzonaturismo.ch

**Canton Ticino Tourism** – Via Ghiringhelli 7, **Bellinzona** ☎ 0041 (0)91 82 57 056, www.ticino.ch

**Lake Lugano Tourist Board** – Palazzo Civico, Piazza della Riforma or Piazzale della Stazione, **Lugano**, ☎ 0041 (0)58 22 06 500-504, www.luganoregion.com

**Lake Maggiore Tourist Board** – Piazza Stazione, **Locarno**, ☎ 0041 (0)848 09 10 91, www.ascona-locarno.com

## The wineries

*The addresses are listed in alphabetical order by location.*

### BELLINZONA

**Chiericati** – *Via Convento 10* - **Bellinzona** - ☎ 0041 (0)91 82 51 307 - www.chiericati.ch - info@chiericati.ch - *Winery tours by reservation, closed Sat. pm and Sun.* Chiericati, founded in 1950 to sell wines, has been making its own since 1987. The grapes are brought in by local growers. Thanks to state-of-the art cellar work, Chiericati produces top-quality wine. There is also a wine shop on the premises that has become an attraction for connoisseurs.
**Wines**: Ticino DOC Merlot Luca, Merlot del Sole, Al Mercaa Riserva, Convento, La Riviera del Gambarogno and Nobile della Turrita, Ticino DOC Chardonnay Carolina, Ticino DOC

Bianco di Merlot Sinfonia in Bianco Barrique and Confessore. Other products: grappa and nocino liqueur.

**Cagi - Cantina di Giubiasco** – *Via Linoleum 11* - **Giubiasco**, *3 km S of Bellinzona* - ☎ 0041 (0)91 85 72 531 - www.cagivini.ch - info@cagivini.ch - *Winery tours by reservation Mon.-Fri. 7.30-12.00 and 13.30 - 17.30 (Fri. 17.15).* Since 1929 it has been producing wine using grapes harvested by approximately 450 growers. Selection of the grapes is very important to the winery, and they must be rich in sugar and dry extract. The versatility of Merlot, the winery's preferred variety, yields whites and rosés with an intriguing bouquet, and reds with a good structure. Bondola also yields a key product.
**Wines**: IGT Bianco Svizzera Italiana Due Vigne, Ticino DOC Bianco di Merlot Riserva, Ticino DOC Chardonnay Bohème and Vigna Noverasca, Ticino DOC Bianco di Merlot Bucaneve, Bianco Del Ticino DOC Chardor, Ticino DOC Merlot Camorino, Riserva, Monte Carasso, Corte Rossa, Locarnese, 1929, Alba Viti and Bucaneve, Ticino DOC Bondola Tera Negra, Ticino DOC Rosato di Merlot Tre Rose. Other products: grappa and aqua vitae.

### LOCARNO AND LAKE MAGGIORE

**Terreni alla Maggia** – *Via Muraccio 105* - **Ascona** - ☎ 0041 (0)79 23 311 - www.terreniallamaggia.ch - info@terreniallamaggia.ch - *Winery tours with food and wine tasting by reservation.* Established in 1930, Terreni alla Maggia covers an area of about 150 hectares in the municipalities of Ascona, Locarno and Gordola. The estate has fields, vineyards and orchards, and it uses integrated cultivation methods. Hectares under vine: 10,5.
**Wines**: Bianco di Merlot Lepre, Kerner Ticino Lepre Black, Il Castagneto, Merlot Ticino Ascona Riserva, Ticino DOC Rosato di Merlot Pernice, Bondola Rosè, Terra Bella, Merlot rosso L'Usignolo, Merlot Barbarossa. Other products: gin, rice, cornmeal, durum-wheat pasta, Bondola verjuice, mustard.

**Delea** – *Via Zandone 11* - **Losone**, *3 km NW of Ascona* - ☎ 0041 (0)91 79 10 817 - www.delea.ch - vini@delea.ch - *Winery tours by reservation, closed Sun.* Angelo Delea's winery, founded in 1983, was modelled after Bordeaux winemaking techniques, with ageing in casks of prized Alliers and Nevers oak from France. The new complex includes a wine shop, the modern winemaking facilities and the distillery built in 1932, which produces various types of grappa and fruit spirits. Meals and accommodation available at the Fattoria L'Amorosa guest farm (*Via Moyar, Sementina-Gudo, 20 km S of Losone,*

# ADDRESSES

*091 84 02 950, amorosa.ch, 10 rooms)* and enoteca La Bottega del Vino *(www. bottegavino.ch)* in Locarno. Hectares under vine: 20.

**Wines**: Ticino DOC Merlot Carato, MòMò, Merlot del Mago, Merlot Ismaro, Saleggi San Carlo, Marengo, Cabernet Syrah Tiziano, Diamante Rosso Del Ticino DOC, Bianco del Ticino DOC Carato, L'Apocalisse, Chardonnay del Ticino DOC, Sauvignon Blanc Ticino DOC. Other products: grappa and balsamic vinegar.

**Matasci** – *Via Verbano 6* - **Tenero** - *0041 (0)91 73 56 011 - www.matasci-vini.ch - info@ matasci-vini.ch - Winery tours Apr.-Sept. Fri. h16.* The Matasci winery was established back in 1921. The family business is now in its third generation of vignerons. In addition to producing excellent wines, it also has the large "Le Caveau" wine shop, designed to welcome guests and host tastings, the Matasci Arte space and the Wine Museum.

**Wines**: Sirio Barrique, Terra Matta, Selezione d'Ottobre, Le Mimose, Sassariente. Other products: spirits.

## THE LUGANO AREA

**Zanini Vinattieri**– *Via Comi* - **Ligornetto** - *0041 (0)91 64 72 332 - www.zanini-vinattieri.ch - info@zanini-vinattieri.ch- Winery tours by reservation.* Luigi Zanini's viticulture and winemaking activities began in 1964 when Luigi, inspired by his passion for wine, travelled to Italy and France to discover the ancient art of winemaking. Today Zanini Vinattieri manages around 50 hectares of vineyards. His son Luigi has also joined him in this project. They were among the first in Switzerland to use casks to age wine. The Zaninis have also established Castello Luigi and Aristocrazia dei Vini. Hectares under vine: 53.

**Wines**: Bianco del Ticino Vinattieri, Ticino Merlot Riserva Roncaia, Ticino Merlot Ronco dell'Angelo, Ticino Merlot Ligornetto, Ticino Merlot Bianco Vinattieri.

**Tamborini** – *Via Serta 18* - **Lamone**, *6 km N of Lugano* - *0041 (0)91 93 57 545 - www. tamborinivini.ch - info@tamborinivini.ch - Winery tours by reservation, closed Sat. pm (also Sat. am Jan.-Easter) and Sun.* The family business, established by Carlo Tamborini in 1944, has been run by Claudio Tamborini since 1969. The vineyards are situated in particularly fine winegrowing areas such as Comano, Lamone, Vico Morcote, Gudo, Neggio and Castelrotto. Castelrotto (15 km to the south-west) is also the location of Tenuta Vallombrosa, which has a charming B&B *(www.vallombrosa.ch, 10 rooms)* with restaurant. Hectares under vine: 27.

**Wines**: Ticino DOC Riserva Comano, Mosaico Bianco del Ticino SanZeno, Bianco Ticino DOC Vallombrosa, Ticino DOC San Domenico. Other products: grappa.

**Fattoria Moncucchetto** – *Via Crivelli Torricelli 27* - **Lugano** - *0041 (0)91 96 77 060 - www.moncucchetto.ch - info@ moncucchetto.ch - Winery tours by reservation, closed Sun.* The estate, purchased by the Lucchini family in 1919, was already under vine in the 15th c. In 1963 Lucchini, a lawyer and passionate winegrower, planted Merlot. Since the 1970s Lisetta and Niccolò Lucchini have run the estate. A turning point was 2009 with the project for a new winery conceived by the architect Mario Botta. In 2016 the Moncucchetto Riserva 2013 won the gold medal at the Grand Prix du Vin Suisse. Hectares under vine: 15.

**Wines**: Bianco dell'Arco DOC, Sauvignon Bianco Ticino DOC Collina d'oro-Agra, Bianco/Rosso IGT Il Murchì, Lacrima d'Oro, Merlot del Ticino DOC L'Arco, Bianco/Merlot del Ticino DOC Moncucchetto and Moncucchetto Riserva Lugano, Spumante Brut Ticino DOC Refolo. Other products: grappa, nocino liqueur.

**Agriloro** – *Via Prella 14* – **Genestrerio** *(CH 6852)* - *0041 (0)91 64 05 454 - www. agriloro.ch - info@agriloro.ch - Winery tours and tasting by reservation, closed Sun.* Founded in 1981, Agriloro owns both Tenimento dell'Ör (11 hectares, 8 of which are cultivated) and Tenimento La Prella (23 hectares, 12 of which are cultivated). The company produces 28 different wines. The impressive number of prizes these wines have won in international events, along with recognition in the 2019 Mondial du Merlot & Assemblages, all testify to the superior quality standards the company has striven to achieve since its foundation. Hectares under vine: 22.

**Wines**: Ticino DOC Merlot Riserva dell'Ör; Ticino DOC Merlot Riserva La Prella; Rosso del Ticino DOC Sottobosco, Svizzera Italiana IGT Casimiro, Bianco del Ticino Granito. Other products: grappa, spirits.

**Cantina Sociale di Mendrisio** – *Via Bernasconi 22* - **Mendrisio** - *0041 (0)91 64 64 621 - www.cantinamendrisio.ch - info@cantinamendrisio.ch - Winery tours by reservation, closed Sat. and Sun.* The Cantina Sociale di Mendrisio was established in 1949 by a group of local vignerons and it is the Canton's only co-operative winery. It has 300 members with a total of 130 hectares under vine, spread throughout the Mendrisio district, the Blenio Valley and the Riviera Valley. The co-operative has also had its own vineyard since 1962: Tenuta Montalbano, planted with Merlot, Gamaret, Diolinoir, Carminoir and Chardonnay. Meals are also served at the Tenuta Montalbano *(www.montalbano.ch, 0041 (0)91 64 71 206)*. Hectares under vine: 130.

**Wines**: Ticino Bianco di Merlot Tenuta Montalbano, Ticino Chardonnay Tenuta Montalbano, Ticino Merlot Riserva Tenuta Montalbano, La Trosa, Ticino DOC Merlot Riserva Racconti. Other products: grappa.

**F.lli Valsangiacomo** – *Viale alle Cantine 6 - **Mendrisio** - ☏ 0041 (0)91 68 36 053 - www. valswine.ch - info@valswine.ch - Winery tours by reservation.* Giovanni Valsangiacomo established the winery in 1831 and it has been handed down from generation to generation. It started to work its own vineyards in 1954. Today it is known for the production of high-quality Ticino wine and excellent grappa. In 2005 it moved the entire business to the winery in Mendrisio, carved out of the natural rock at the foot of Mount Generoso. Hectares under vine: 25.
**Wines**: Ticino DOC Merlot L'Ariete, Il Mattirolo Rosso, Roncobello; Ticino DOC Merlot Riserva Piccolo Ronco, Don Giovanni, Rubro; Ticino DOC Chardonnay Gransegreto Fondo Del Bosco, Ticino DOC Bianco di Merlot L'Ariete and Il Mattirolo. Other products: honey, grappa.

**Gialdi Vini** – *Via Vignoo 3 - **Mendrisio** - ☏ 0041 (0)91 64 03 030 - www.gialdi.ch - Wine tasting by reservation.* Gialdi Vini was established in 1953 by Guglielmo Gialdi, father of its current director Feliciano, and it started out as a wine importer. It was not until the 1980s that it began to produce its own wine – and with excellent results. The acquisition of numerous other winegrowing concerns has allowed it to expand.
**Wines**: Ticino DOC Bianco/Rosato/Rosso Terre Alte, Chardonnay Ticino DOC Carisma, Bianco del Ticino DOC Ramolo and Biancospino, Ticino DOC Merlot Serravalle and Biasca Premium, Trentasei, Arzo, Giornico Oro and Sassi Grossi, Svizzera Italiana IGT Estro. Other products: grappa.

**Brivio** – *Via Vignoo 3 - **Mendrisio** - ☏ 0041 (0)91 64 03 030 - www.brivio.ch - info@gialdi. ch - Wine tasting at Foresteria "Le Palme" Mon.-Fri. 8-12 and 13.30-18, Sat. 9-13.* Enologist Guido Brivio boasts a long family tradition in the wine trade. In the late 1980s he seized the opportunity to purchase an old winery, which he renovated and equipped with a cellar carved into the rock of Monte Generoso, creating the perfect conditions for ageing and storing wine. In just a short time Guido has made the winery one of the most renowned in Canton Ticino.
**Wines**: Ticino DOC Bianco di Merlot Bianco Rovere and Contrada, Bianco del Ticino DOC Prà Bianco, Ticino DOC Sauvignon Ronco Bain, Ticino DOC Chardonnay Donnay, Ticino DOC Rosato di Merlot Gran Rosé, Ticino DOC Merlot Prà Rosso, Platinum and Baiocco, Touché, Rosso del Ticino DOC Dogaia and Vigna d'Antan, Ticino DOC Merlot Riflessi d'Epoca. Other products: grappa, liquors.

**Cormano Vini** – *Via Maestri Comacini 51 - **Morbio Inferiore**, 5 km SE of Mendrisio - ☏ 0041 (0)91 68 28 940 - www.cormano vini.ch - Winery tours by reservation.* The Cormano winery was founded in 1965, when Pasquale Cormano and his family moved from the Campania region to Canton Ticino and started to grow grapes. However, it was not until 1992, with Giuliano Cormano, that the family built the cellar for producing wine. Today Giuliano, assisted by his wife Patrizia, has established the reputation of his wines, all of which are excellent. Hectares under vine: 6.
**Wines**: Ticino Merlot Beatrice, Carrara and Cormano, Merlot/Cabernet Sauvignon/ Petit Verdot Caronte.

**Vini Rovio Ronco** – *Via in Basso 21 - **Rovio**, 4.5 km N of Capolago - ☏ 0041 (0)91 64 95 831 - www.vinirovio.ch - vini.rovio@bluewin. ch - Winery tours by reservation.* Vini Rovio Ronco uses only the grapes grown in its own vineyards. It currently has vineyards situated in three different municipalities: Rovio, Pugerna and Ligornetto. The 2016 Ticino DOC Merlot San Giorgio was awarded a gold medal at the 2019 Mondial du Merlot. The Merlot, Gamaret, Cabernet Franc, Cabernet Sauvignon, Syrah, Magliasina, Chasselas and Chardonnay varieties are grown. Hectares under vine: 6.5.
**Wines**: Chardonnay and Merlot di Rovio, Rosato Americana, Rosato di Merlot, Bianco and Merlot di Pugerna, Vincenzo Vela. Other products: grappa.

## Where to stay

### BELLINZONA

**Hotel Cereda** – *Via Locarno 10, Sementina, 3 km south-west of Bellinzona - ☏ 0041 (0)91 85 18 080 - www.hotelcereda.ch - 18 rooms, doubles from CHF160.* An intriguing mix of ancient and modern, with a lovely patio with a pergola, and traditional materials.

### LOCARNO

**Hotel Garni Muralto** – *Via Sempione 10, Loc. Muralto, Locarno - ☏ 0041 (0)91 73 53 060 - www.hotelmuralto.ch - Closed 23 Dec.- 6 Jan. - 34 rooms, doubles from CHF129.* The hotel is set in a lovely flower garden with palm trees, offering rooms with a view.

### LUGANO

**Hotel Colibrì** – *Via Aldesago 91 - Aldesago, 6 km east of Lugano, towards Brè - ☏ 0041 (0)91 97 14 242 - www.hotelcolibri.ch - 30 rooms, doubles from CHF175.* The hotel affords magnificent views of the city, the lake and the Alps, especially from the terrace with a swimming pool.

*Italianate appearance of Rovinj*
© Igor Plotnikov/Shutterstock

# Istria

# ISTRIA

With an area of approximately 2820 square kilometres, Istria is the largest peninsula in the Adriatic Sea. Most of it lies in Croatia, but there are also municipalities in Slovenia (Koper, Izola, Piran and Portorož) and in Italy (Muggia and Dolina). The relaunch of winemaking in Istria has been relatively recent. It dates to the mid-1990s when a small number of determined grape-growers began a renewal process that gave the sector a decided boost. Since then giant steps have been taken and the combination of tradition and innovation has brought excellent results. The wine production is based predominantly on traditional native varieties, like Malvasia, Momjan Muscat and Teran.

© Janoka82/iStock

*Rovinj port*

## The terroir

### Istrian wine

Istrian wine has always been appreciated by the greatest connoisseurs. The Roman empress Julia Augusta attributed her longevity to it, while the great traveller Casanova recorded in his memoirs how he fell under the spell of a wine that went by the name of *Refosc*. As for the rulers of the Austro-Hungarian empire, their enthusiasm was such that in 1902 they had a stretch of railway built to join Poreć to Trieste so that the precious liquid could be more easily transported to their table.

The new wave in Istrian viticulture was triggered by a policy that disincentivised the abandonment of vines, partly through economic subsidies. The sparkling results of this measure have aided the region to place greater emphasis on food and wine tourism. One by one the domain owners, from the largest to the smallest, are opening their doors to visitors. And then there are wine festivals, open days, tastings and banquets arranged. The tasting and sales fair – **Vinistra** – is attended by the best winemakers in Istria and is well worth a visit. In particular, an interesting circuit is taking shape in **Verteneglio**, which lies in the wine district where Malvasia is most commonly planted. Here cultural and artistic traditions are being combined successfully with gastronomic tourism. Verteneglio has been included in the Italian Association of Wine Cities for years, and in 2008 the towns of **Buje**, **Umag**, **Novigrad**, **Oprtalj**, and **Groznjan** also joined.

The vine that most symbolises Istrian winemaking is naturally **Malvasia**, which represents more than 50% of the land planted to vine. This generous and versatile vine gives dry wines, with a slightly bitter, almond-like taste. They appear in various tones of straw colour, and offer scents of acacia flowers and fresh fruit. When the grapes are grown in an especially sunny zone, the wines have great body, are suited to laying down and impart intense aromas of ripe fruit. The soil too has a profound effect on the grapes and therefore on the wine: along the coast the soil is "red" and the wines are full-bodied and complex, while inland it is marly and produces lighter, more delicate wines. The western area of Istria is more suited to the cultivation of Malvasia.

The vine is also the subject of the **Istrian Malvasia Festival**, which is held every June at Brtonigla. *For more information, contact Brtonigla Tourist Board, ℘ 00385 (0)52 77 43 07, www.coloursofistria.com.*

**Refosc** (**Refošk**) enjoys the place of honour on Croatian tables. Light, faintly sparkling, and the colour of cherries, this wine happily accompanies both red and white meats. **Teran** is a red wine that the Istrians refer to as "black" for its dark colour. It is a wine of character with an alcohol content of between 12% and 13.5% and is suited ideally to fatty foods, cheeses and Istrian omelettes with asparagus.

## Truffles

Damp and shady and washed by the river Mirna, the grey earth of **Motovun forest** is particularly appropriate for truffles, which have delighted everyone since the days of the Roman emperors. Motovun is the only place in the world where the two most important varieties of this fungus can be found: white and black truffles. Beginning in 1990 after years of oblivion, the Istrian truffle regained its dominant position on the market, in particular the white truffle (*Tuber magnatum*), the larger and more appreciated variety, which is gathered in autumn. The black (or summer) truffle is not held in such high esteem.

## Olive oil (Maslinovo ulje)

Known for its olive oil since time immemorial, the west coast of Istria has many old oil presses along its entire length. Abandoned for centuries, the oil industry has been reborn since 1990. Today Istria produces one of the best olive oils in the world. In addition to its excellent nutritional properties, it is distinguished by its taste, which incorporates hints of grass and flowers of unmatched freshness. Try it with ham and sheep's cheese, the way it is served during tastings by its producers.

© Hipproductions/Shutterstock

# Itineraries

*Sites with a winery are indicated by the symbol ♟; for the addresses of the wineries, see p. 490.*

## 1. POREČ AND THE SURROUNDING AREA

### Poreč★★ ♟

Roman and Venetian Poreč is a much appreciated tourist destination. There are many palaces that were built during the late Renaissance and Baroque periods, when the Venetian nobility chose Poreč as its summer resort. During Austrian domination, the city was the home of the Istrian parliament from 1861. Today Poreč lives from tourism and is able to welcome 100,000 visitors in its many hotels, campsites, tourist villages and guesthouses.

---

**PRINCIPAL VARIETIES CULTIVATED**

**WHITE GRAPES**
Chardonnay
Malvasia
Moscato
Pinot Bianco
Pinot Grigio

**BLACK GRAPES**
Cabernet Franc
Cabernet Sauvignon
Croata Nera
Merlot
Moscato Rosa
Refosco
Terrano

Portico of the Euphrasian Basilica

From the Decumanus, turn right into Via Sv. Eleuterija, which takes you to Eufrazijeva opposite the basilica.

## Euphrasian Basilica★★★ (Eufrazijeva bazilika)

The **Canonica★** is a wonderful example of civil Romanesque architecture (1251) that has a set of twin-light windows along the side that faces Via Sant'Eufrasio. On the left a mosaic lined vault leads to the passage to the **atrium★★** of the Euphrasian Basilica. Built on a square plan, this lovely courtyard, with marble columns imported from Byzantium, has exquisite proportions. Set around the atrium are the **baptistery** (built in the same period as the basilica except for the upper part, which was reconstructed in 1935), the access to the pre-Euphrasian basilica, episcopal palace and mosaic museum (*opposite*), and the basilica itself (*right*).

A splendid **view★★** is given from the top of the bell tower.

**Basilica** – The basilica's façade and mosaics restored in the 19th c. are best admired from the entrance to the baptistery. This remarkable monument was built between 543 and 554 by Bishop Euphrasius in the early Christian style of the churches in Ravenna, combining strong Byzantine influences with a Western tradition inherited from ancient architecture. The aisles in this enormous building are separated from the nave by two rows of arches resting on marble columns imported from Constantinople and given finely sculpted capitals. The out-standing set of **mosaics in the apse★★★** depict hieratic figures typical of the Byzantine school set against a gold ground. The geometric decorative patterns at the bottom were probably taken from a 1st-c. temple and reused. Above the altar the **baldachin★** is a 13th-c. work covered with a Venetian-style mosaic depiction of the Annunciation.

**Basilica Museum (Muzejska zbirka)** – *Reached from the atrium, open 9-21 (9-18 in win.), closed Sun., ℘ 00385 (0)52 45 17 84.* A visit to the museum allows you to examine the **pre-Euphrasian basilica** built at the start of the 5th c. The only remnants of this rectangular construction are a few sections of wall, columns with capitals, and above all a fine **geometric mosaic★**, probably of local manufacture.

The oldest sections of the **episcopal palace** were probably built in the 6th c., making it contemporary with the basilica. The ground floor holds most of the museum collections. The mosaic section exhibits fragments of Ravenna-style mosaics inspired by Roman antiquity.

## The peninsula★★

*Leave the car in the car-park, skirt round the covered market from the right, and arrive in Trg J. Rakovca. From there take Zagrebačka to Trg Slobode.*

The **decumanus★**, the main street of the ancient Roman city, runs the length of the peninsula from Trg Slobode (Freedom Square) to Trg Marafor (Forum Square). r). It is lined by beautiful Gothic-Renaissance and Baroque houses as well as souvenir, ice-cream and jewellery shops. Built in 1447 by Niccolò Lion, the pentagonal tower (Peterokutna kula) on the left of the Decumanus marks the entrance to old Poreč. The **Gothic house★** (Gotička kuća) is a lovely, two-storey Venetian residence with ornamental Gothic windows and a Renaissance entrance.

*Turn left into Trg Matija Gubec (Matija Gubec Square).*

The **Roman house★** (Romanička kuća) was built in the 13th c. over the foundations of a Roman villa. It has an external staircase and a wooden balcony (the one you see was made in 1930).

*Return to the Decumanus.*

In this last section of the main street, around the junction with the Cardo (the main cross street), you will see several superb 15th-c. residences with Gothic façades. Note in particular the lovely **House of the Lions**, named after the lion heads carved above the windows.

Baroque and Gothic palaces stand around **Trg Matite Gupca** (Matite Gupca Square), the square known as "Piazza dei Signori" when ruled by the Venetian Republic.

The rectangular **Trg Marafor** (Forum Square), which has managed to retain some of the Roman paving, occupies the site of the ancient forum of the city of Parentium. This was where the most magnificent buildings in the ancient city stood. Visible in the greenery on the west side of the square are the remains of the Temple of Neptune and the Great Temple, both built in the 2nd c.

*Walk around the garden from Via M. Bernobić and return to Trg Matija Gupca. Now take the street opposite,* **Ulica Sv. Maura★** *(Sv. Maura Street).* Less than 10 m from the noisy Decumanus you can enjoy the peace of a street lined with beautiful houses yet ignored by the tourists. The **Lapidarium** is a large court set with commemorative plaques.

*Continue down the Ulica Sv. Maura to F. Glavinića and turn right to arrive on the seafront (Obala) from Narodni trg (People's Square).*

**Riva Maresciallo Tito** (Obala Maršala Tita) is the centre of summer life in Poreč. The moored boats offer trips to the islands or along the coast. **Otok Sv. Nikola** (St Nicholas Island) off-shore has

© kubais/Shutterstock

## THE TERROIR

**Area:** 15.200 hectares distributed as follows: 14.430 acres hectares in the west (Poreč, Buje, Pula and Rovinj), 515 hectares in the centre (Buzet, Pazin) and 255 hectares to the east (Labin).

**Geography:** the climate is mild and Mediterranean, the soil is a mixture of minerals and marl.

## WINE ROUTES

Istria has the 6 following Wine Routes:

Buje district Wine Route

Poreč district Wine Route

Buzet district Wine Route

Pazin district Wine Route

Rovinj and Vodnjan district Wine Route

Labin district Wine Route

For information, contact the Istria Tourist Board, Pionirska 1, 52440 Poreč - ℰ 00385 (0)52 452797 - www.istria.hr

## USEFUL ADDRESSES

Istra Gourmet, www.istria-gourmet.com, ℰ 00385 (0)52 88 00 88

Vinistra, www.vinistra.com, ℰ 00385 (0)52 62 16 98

*Leme Fjord*

the remains of Croatia's oldest lighthouse (1403) and a Neo-Gothic castle (1886).

*Follow the Riva around the tip of the peninsula, passing by a medieval bulwark in front of the Hotel Adriatic.*

At the foot of the **walls** behind the Euphrasian Basilica there is a pleasant and less frequented spot that offers a lovely view of the sea.

## Istria, land and sea★★

*Circular itinerary of 195 km starting from Poreč. Leave Poreč south in the direction of Vrsar.*

### Vrsar★

This small port was once the residence of the bishops of Poreč but has developed into an important seaside resort. It has kept its ancient centre, which stands on a hill overlooking the sea. Wandering through the alleys you will discover the remains of the Bishops Palace, with its 13th-c. towers and two Romanesque doorways, one of which bears a relief of the winged lion of St Mark. Concerts of classical music are held in summer in the 19th-c. parish church dedicated to St Martin (Župna crkva sv. Martina). In a lovely bay protected by the small island of Sv. Juraj stands the Romanesque Basilica of the Madonna of the Sea (bazilika sv. Marije od Mora).

The hotels and campsites are out of town, on the headlands between Vrsar and Leme fjord. The immense Koversada camp, which is joined by a walkway to the island of the same name, is one of Europe's largest naturist centres.

*The road begins to twist as it moves away from the sea. Be careful of the many buses because the road is narrow and curving.*

### Leme Fjord★★ (Limski zaljev)

This extraordinary fjord once separated the territories of the cities of Poreč and Rovinj. Long and narrow, it forms a gash into the mainland 9 km long and 100 m high. The water is protected (bathing is prohibited) and noted for its purity: it contains farms for breeding oysters, mussels and fish. Picnic areas, the occasional restaurant and small wooden houses selling farm honey, oil and cheese are sprinkled along the fjord's banks.

*Follow the signs as far as Sveti Lovreč (3.5 km, on the right of the road).*

### Sveti Lovreč Pazenatički★ ♞

This lovely medieval fortified village was once a major Venetian military command point. To reach the main beach, where the village pillory post still stands, you pass through an ogival gateway in the 14th/15th-c. walls. A small loggia containing a lapidarium stands in front of the gateway against the sidewall of the 11th-c. St Martin's Church (crkva sv. Martina). The church interior contains a number of frescoes and, close to the door, the 15th-c. Chapel of St Blaise (kapela sv. Blaža). With its houses often adorned with window-boxes and flowers, the village is very pretty.

*Continue for 10 km, then go left at the crossroads (follow the signs to Poreč road) as far as Višnjan.*

## Višnjan ♟

Known for its astronomical observatory, Višnjan is a large, typically Mediterranean village, its houses built with dry-stone walls and tiled roofs. Life in the village mainly happens in the cafés and shops in the lower section but it is worth the trouble to visit the part up on the hill. You will immediately notice the Gothic Chapel of St Antony (crkva sv. Antuna) decorated with Glagolitic graffiti and frescoes by a painter originally from Udine. Follow the main road to the square where there is a well, a Neoclassical church, and a loggia that looks straight down onto the plain (the sea can be seen in the distance).

## Vižinada ♟

The immense Church of St Jerome (crkva sv. Jeronima) is dedicated to the translator of the Bible into Latin, who is said to have been Istrian by birth. Contrasting with this large Neoclassical construction is the Church of St Barnabas (crkva sv. Barnabe). This was originally Romanesque (13th c.) but rebuilt in the Baroque period. It retains some 15th-c. frescoes restored in 2000 that depict the life of Jesus.

## Grožnjan★★

This enchanting hillside town still has some of its ancient walls. With the sea and coastline in the distance, the **views★★** are marvellous and the impression of peace that it gives is all the greater for the contrast with the bustle on the coast. The architectural harmony of the fortified town is striking: its flights of steps, vaulted passageways and small,

tree-lined squares make a pleasing ensemble. Note the lovely Renaissance **loggia**, whose name, **Fontik** (from the Arab *fonduk*) indicates that it used to be a grain store. The interior of the 16th-c. Chapel of Sts Cosmas and Damian was decorated in 1990 by Ivan Lovrenčić, one of the many artists who have moved to the town.

## Buje ♟

Perched on a hill 222 m high, this busy town is surrounded by vineyards and olive groves. Houses of a certain nobility, despite showing signs of wear, flank a small paved street that leads to the 16th-c. Church of St Servilus (crkva sv. Servola), with an incomplete façade and Baroque portal.

*On leaving Buje, follow the signs to Momjan.* With its high hills facing south-west, the district of Momjan is well-known for its wines and in particular its **Muscat (Momjanski muškat)**. The mix of red and grey soils and the alternation of northerly and southerly winds creates a unique microclimate that benefits the local wines. The medieval town of **Momjan** ♟ has a 15th-c. medieval church dedicated to St Martin and an ancient castle in which one of the earliest legal documents written in Croat has been found.

*Leaving Buje in the direction of Koper, you will pass for a while through* **Slovenia** *when you cross the border at Kaštel.*

## Koper★

This small industrial port unexpectedly conceals the lovely, Italianate Titov trg

Historical centre of Piran

© Baldovina/Shutterstock

(Tito Square. It is lined by the cathedral, its bell tower, a loggia and the castle, which now contains a museum.

### Piran★★

Piran is an elegant little town on a rocky peninsula dominated by the walls of its ancient castle (Kaštel). Everything converges on the circular Tartini trg (Tartini Square) that opens onto the port. Standing at its centre is a statue of the famous violinist Giuseppe Tartini, and all around are ancient palaces. One of these, bearing an image of St Mark's lion, is the Town Hall. High up, the Church of St George (crkva sv. Jurja) has a Venetian bell tower and baptistery.

### Portorož

Portorož is a gracious town lying on the north shore of the Gulf of Piran, with a pleasant seaside promenade.

As you return towards the Croatian border, the road passes the bottom of the Gulf of Piran where the salt pans are. *Head right in the direction of Savudrija.* Although you are travelling alongside the sea, you only catch the occasional glimpse of it through the dense tamarisks and other vegetation.

### Savudrija ♀

This little fishing port on a point at the northern tip of Istria marks the start of the "Umag riviera". A lighthouse, a small port sheltered by a bay, and two or three fish restaurants are the features of this pretty and simple town.

*Take the coast road in the direction of Poreč.*

### Umag ♀

You enter the old town on Ulica Garibaldi (Garibaldi Street), which leads into Trg Slobode (Freedom Square). Note the bell tower with low reliefs (a St Mark's lion and the town's patron saint, St Peregrine). The Neoclassical church has an oddly truncated pediment and, inside, an overabundance of Baroque decoration. Riječka ulica (Riječka ulica Street) leads from the square into the tiny peninsula where you will find some houses in Gothic-Renaissance style, fish restaurants, cafés and lace shops.

### Novigrad

Novigrad still has its embattled walls though they have been heavily restored. The road leads to the port where you will have to leave your car to explore the town. Take Velika ulica (High Street) and admire the lovely sculpted façade of Palazzo Rigo at number 5, built in 1760. The street takes you to the pleasant Veliki trg (the Great Square), which looks onto the sea. This is the setting for the Church of St Pelagius (crkva sv. Pelagija), originally Romanesque but heavily renovated in the Baroque period. An 8th-c. crypt beneath the church contains a 12th-c. sarcophagus.

There is a shady park of umbrella pines at the tip of the peninsula from where you can take the promenade lined with cafés and guesthouses.

### 2. ROVINJ★★

Rovinj is perhaps the prettiest town in Istria. Its port lies at the end of a bay lined with warm-tinted houses that face

*Rovinj, an ideal destination for a pleasant holiday*

© Igor Plotnikov/Shutterstock

onto the deep blue sea and throng of dancing boats. Overlooking them all is a Venetian bell tower.

Leave your car in Istarska car-park and walk towards the port down ulica Mattea Benussija (Matthew Benussi St), where the shops and administrative offices are clustered. You come to the three-sided Trg na Lokvi (Lake Square) where the small, octagonal Baptistery of the Holy Trinity (Krstionca Sv. Trojstva) stands (8th c.). You arrive in the port from Trg Tabakina ("Tobacco Square"), named after the nearby tobacco factory, the town's largest employer.

At the Riva Aldo-Negri, turn right and at the end of the seashore you suddenly find yourself presented with a **magnificent view★★★** of the peninsula on which the old city stands.

**St Catherine's Port (Luka sv. Katarina)** – protected by St Catherine Island, the port is where most of the town's tourist activities take place. Walk alongside the port and its many cafés until, at the feet of the old town, you reach the vast square named after Marshal Tito (Trg Maršala Tita) and the obala Budičina (Budicin Promenade), the animated centre of Rovinj.

**Pignaton Square (Trg G. Pignatona)** – a long square lined with café terraces. It opens onto Piazza Valdibora, which in turn looks out over the sea on the other side of the peninsula. This is where the outdoor market is held each morning.

**Marshal Tito Square★ (Trg Maršala Tita)** – a triangular plaza that looks onto the fishing port, this lovely Italian-style square is also lined with café terraces and the odd beautiful palazzo. The old **Town Hall★** is a fine Baroque building with a red ochre façade (1654) reminiscent of Venetian palaces. It is also home to the Civic Museum.

Built in 1680 on the place of a medieval fortified port, the Baroque **Balbi Arch★** is embellished with a turbaned Turk's head and a low relief of the winged lion of Venice.

The **Clock Tower★** (on the left of Marshal Tito Square) is a lovely Venetian tower in red brick, also with a winged lion.

**Circle the old town★★** – continuing your visit, take the wide Budicin Promenade from the square and then Ulica Sv. Križa. This will take you around the hill

on which old Rovinj stands. On the right, flights of steps climb the hill. Continue as far as the church.

Once in Via Vladimir Švalbe note the Hotel Angelo d'Oro on the right.

*The street comes out into Trg na Mostu, from where you can reach Marshal Tito Square or wander down ul. Karera on the left.* This long shopping street runs parallel to the seafront and will take you back to Piazzale del Laco (Trg na Lokvi).

*From Marshal Tito Square enter the* **old town★★** *(Starigrad) through the Balbi Arch.*

**Great Square (Veli trg)** – the square is filled with old houses, many very beautiful. On the right ulica Arsenale passes beneath a vault. The steeply climbing **Grisia★** ("church" in the local dialect) is lined by attractive façades and internal courtyards. Carved steps, vaulted passageways and Gothic windows contribute to the Venetian atmosphere.

**Cathedral of St Euphemia (Katedrala Sv. Eufemije)** – standing on a vast esplanade overlooking the sea in the upper part of the town, the cathedral has a Venetian bell tower crowned by a copper statue of St Euphemia. Standing 63 m high, she indicates the direction of the wind to those about to go out to sea. Construction began of this, the largest Baroque church in Istria, in 1725. There is a fine altarpiece in carved marble depicting St George, St Roch and St Mark. In the right aisle the sarcophagus (4th-5th c.) of St Euphemia attracts pilgrims. Entrance to the bell tower is through the left aisle, from where the **vista★★** over the town, port, sea and coastline is magnificent.

# Addresses

## Tourist information

**To call** – From Italy dial 00385 followed by the regional area code without the 0. To call within Istria dial the 6- or 7-digit number; to call another region in Croatia the area code (including the 0). Numbers starting with 091/095 and 098 are mobile phones.

**Istria Tourist Board** – Pionirska 1, 52440 Poreč, ✆ (0)52 45 27 97, www.istra.hr, call centre (0)52 88 00 88, info@istria.hr

## The wineries

*The addresses are listed in alphabetical order by location.*

### POREČ

**Clai Bijele Zemlje** – *Brajki 104 - Krasica -* **Buje** - ✆ *(0)91 577 6364 - www.clai.hr - info@clai.hr - Winery tours by reservation* ✆ *(0)91 60 26 109*. Giorgio Clai is a winemaker with definite ideas: wine must express the grape variety and terroir. Consequently, he has eliminated the use of chemicals and adopted an approach that respects the environment, following the dictates of biological and biodynamic agriculture. Hectares under vine: 8.
**Wines**: Sv. Jakov Malvasia, white Ottocento, red Ottocento, Pjenušac Brut nature, Tasel slatko vino, Baracija Malvasia, Baracija Refošk. Other products: olive oil, grappa.

**Kabola** – *Kanedolo 90 - Momjan -* **Buje** ✆ *(0)52 77 92 08 - www.kabola.hr - info@kabola.hr - Winery tours and tasting by reservation, closed Sun.* The vigneron Marino Markežić has rapidly made a name for himself as a top-quality winemaker. He has won a number of awards. Along with Malvasia, however, he also makes a memorable Pinot Grigio that is elegant and appealing. A great experimenter, Markežić has also tried his hand at wines aged in amphorae, with excellent results.
The estate has a accommodation (*www.villa-kabola.com*). Hectares under vine: 17.
**Wines**: Re Brut, Istrian Malvasia, Amfora Malvasia, Unica Malvasia, Rosa Teran, Momjan Muscat, Cabernet Sauvignon, Merlot, Cuvee Supremo. Other products: olive oil.

**Kozlović** – *Vale 78 - Momjan -* **Buje** ✆ *(0)52 77 91 77 - www.kozlovic.hr - info@kozlovic.hr - Winery tours and tasting by reservation, closed Sun.* Following the "Istrian wine revolution" of the 1990s, Gianfranco Kozlović was the first winemaker to gain major recognition on a national scale. In 1998 his white Malvasia was acknowledged as the best in Croatia. Today his winery is venerated by connoisseurs of Istrian enology. His Moscato is also widely respected. Hectares under vine: 20.
**Wines**: Valle, Violetta, Malvasia, Momjan Muscat, Dry Teran, Santa Lucia, Santa Lucia Noir, Akacia, Muscat Rose, Svinjon, Sorbus, Mediteran. Other products: grappa, olive oil.

**Misal** – *Peršurići 5 - Višnjan -* **Poreč** - ✆ *(0)52 431 586 or* ✆ *(0)98 195 70 37 - www.misal.hr - ana@misal.hr - Winery tours by reservation.* The Peršurić family has been in the winemaking business for over five centuries: Đordano Peršurić was considered an atypical Istrian vigneron, as he devoted his talent to sparkling wine. His daughters, Katarina and Ana, are today in charge of the family business and do an excellent job. Hectares under vine: 4.
**Wines**: Blanc des Blancs, Prestige, Blanc de noirs, Millennium, Royal, Istra, Rose, Rouge, Amor, Ostalo.

**Roxanich** – *Kosinožići 26 - Nova Vas -* **Poreč** - ✆ *(0)91 61 70 700 - www.roxanich.hr - info@roxanich.hr- Winery tours and tasting by reservation.* Roxanich offers winery tours, a boutique hotel and a restaurant but, first of all, makes excellent wines. Along with traditional Istrian grapes, the winery grows and vinifies varieties such as Merlot and Chardonnay. Hectares under vine: 23.
**Wines**: Malvazija, Chardonnay, Teran, Refošk, Merlot, Pinot, Cabernet Sauvignon.

**Degrassi** – *Podrumarska 3 - Bašanja -* **Savudrija** - ✆ *(0)52 75 92 50 - www.degrassi.hr - info@degrassi.hr - Winery tours by reservation.* Whereas most of his Istrian colleagues have gained a reputation for producing white wine, Moreno Degrassi has established his image thanks to barrel-aged reds: he was the 2019 Istrian champion of Cabernet Franc and Cabernet Sauvignon. Nevertheless, he also produces award-winning whites. Hectares under vine: 25.
**Wines**: Merlot Contarini, Cabernet Franc Contarini, Refosco, Terran, Cabernet Sauvignon Contarini, Chardonnay Ferné, Moscato Bianco San Pellegrin, Malvasia Bomarchese. Other products: grappa.

**Vina Matošević** – *Krunčići 2, Krunčići -* **Sveti Lovreč Pazenatički** - ✆ *(0)52 44 85 58 - www.matosevic.com - info@matosevic.com - Winery tours and wine tasting by reservation.* Ivica Matošević first began to make wine in the mid-1990s as a hobby. Within a relatively short period of time and without a family tradition of winemaking behind him, he achieved excellent results, inaugurating a cosy tasting room over the winery in Krunčići. His Malvasia has won numerous awards, but his entire range is excellent. Hectares under vine: 10.

**Wines**: Istrian Malvasia Alba, Alba Barrique, Alba Robinia, Chardonnay Aura, Merlot Mora, White Grimalda, Red Grimalda.

**Coronica - ATC** – *Koreniki 86* - **Umag** - ℘ *(0)98 334 378 or* ℘ *(0)52 73 03 57 - www. coronica.eu - atc@coronica.eu - Winery tours by reservation.* Moreno Coronica became involved in winemaking by following in the footsteps of his forebears. Today he is one of Istria's most important enologist and producer. Many consider his Malvasia – and above all his Gran Malvasia, aged in barriques – to be among Istria's finest white wines. His Teran is equally good, and his Gran Teran Barrique is one of the region's most interesting reds. Hectares under vine: 20.

**Wines**: Istrian Malvasia; Gran Malvasia, Gran Teran, Teran, Grabar.

**Franko Radovan** – *Radovani 14* - **Višnjan** - ℘ *(0)52 462 166 -vinaradovan.com - info@ vinaradovan.com - Winery tours by reservation.* Franko Radovan is a young vintner who has rapidly gained an enthusiastic following for both his whites and reds. This success has been confirmed by the array of gold medals he has won at wine shows for his Malvasia, Chardonnay, Sauvignon and Teran. Hectares under vine: 9.

**Wines**: Istrian Malvasia, Teran, Cabernet Sauvignon, Sauvignon Blanc, Merlot, Refošk, Rosé, Chardonnay, Capeletto.

⬆ **Vina Poletti** – *Markovac 14* - **Višnjan** - ℘ *(0)91 44 92 510 - www.vina-poletti.hr - vina.poletti@gmail.com - Wine tasting by reservation.* At Vinistra, the regional wine show, Peter Poletti has recently won many gold medals for his Malvasia and Cabernet Sauvignon. Poletti is one of the few here to make wine from an almost forgotten Moscato variety: Moscato Rosa. At his winery, visitors can learn a great deal about Istria's winemaking and culinary traditions. Accommodation available in Villa Bellavista Poletti. Hectares under vine: 7.

**Wines**: Istrian Malvasia, Chardonnay, Teran, Red Rose Muscat, Cabernet Sauvignon, Merlot. Other products: olive oil.

**Franc Arman** – *Narduči 5* - **Vižinada** - ℘ *(0)52 44 62 26 or* ℘ *(0)91 446 22 66 - www.francarman.hr - info@francarman.hr - Winery tours by reservation.* The family tradition of making wine has been handed down for generations: Franco Arman learned from his father Edoardo, and young Oliver is already preparing to inherit the family business. Their Teran recently won a gold medal at Vinistra and their Malvasia is equally outstanding; the winery's Chardonnay and Pinot Grigio are especially famous. Hectares under vine: 8.

**Wines**: Malvasia, Teran, Chardonnay, Cabernet Franc, Pinot Grigio, Merlot.

**Marijan Arman** – *Narduči 3* - **Vižinada** - ℘ *(0)52 44 60 94 - www.arman.hr - info@ arman.hr - Winery tour and tasting by reservation.* For the second year in a row Marijan Arman proudly boasts that his 2018 G Cru was named the best wine in the young Malvasia category at 2019 Vinistra fair in Poreč. Second place for his 2015 Malvasia reserve. Just a few years later, he gained similar recognition for his red wine, Teran. Hectares under vine: 9.

**Wines**: Istrian Malvasia, Chardonnay, Muscat, Sauvignon Blanc, Teran, Cabernet Sauvignon.

⬆ **Pilato** – *Lašići 2* - **Vižinada** - ℘ *(0)52 44 62 81 - www.vina-pilato.com - info@villa-pilato. com - Winery tours by reservation -.* Eligio Pilato debuted among the country's top winemakers in 2002, after his Chardonnay was proclaimed the best white wine in Croatia at the national wine fair Vinovita in 2001. Pilato made the most of this opportunity and his wines have become the guarantee of high standards. There is a villa *(villa-pilato.com)* and charming tasting room by the winery. Hectares under vine: 12.

**Wines**: Istrian Malvasia, Chardonnay, Cabernet Sauvignon, White Pinot, Teran, White Muscat.

### ROVINJ

⬆ **Meneghetti** – *52 211* **Bale** - *14 km SE of Rovinj* - ℘ *(0)91 2431 600 - www.meneghetti.hr - info@meneghetti.hr - Wine tasting by reservation.* Modern winery with annual production of more than 100,000 bottles of first-class wine. Meneghetti is also a charming resort with 10 rooms and suites, 15 maisonettes and a restaurant idyllically situated among vineyards and olive trees. The estate also produces outstanding extra virgin olive oil. Hectares under vine: 4.5.

**Wines**: Malvasia, Chardonnay, Cabernet Franc, Merlot, Pinot Blanc. Other products: olive oil.

## Where to stay

### POREČ

**Agriturismo Baladur** – *Rakvoci 22, Baderna, 14 km east of Poreč* - ℘ *(0)52 462 293 - www. baladur.com - 2 apts., from €60.* This lovely *agriturizam*, or guest farm, reflects traditional architecture and has a garden, bowling facilities and barbecue.

### ROVINJ

**Hotel Adriatic** – *P. Budičina 16, Rovinj* - ℘ *(0)52 800 250 -www.maistra.com/ hotel-adriatic-rovinj - Closed 15 Oct.-Mar. - 14 rooms and 4 suites from €104.* This small and charming hotel with well-appointed rooms is in the main square.

# INDEX OF SITES

# APPENDIX

# APPENDIX

## P

# LIST OF MAPS

## Vineyards and Geographical Areas

## City Maps

# THE**GREEN**GUIDE

## France
- Alsace  Lorraine  Champagne
- Auvergne  Rhone Valley
- Brittany
- Burgundy  Jura
- Châteaux of the Loire
- Dordogne  Berry  Limousin
- France
- French Alps
- French Riviera
- Languedoc  Roussillon  Tarn Gorges
- Normandy
- Northern France and the Paris Region
- Paris
- Provence
- Wine Regions of France

## North America
- Canada
- Charleston
- Chicago
- Montreal & Quebec City
- New England
- New York City
- Portland
- San Francisco
- Savannah
- USA East
- USA West
- Washington, DC

## British Isles
- Great Britain
- Ireland
- London
- Scotland

## Rest of Europe
- Andalucia
- Austria
- Germany
- Grand Tour of Switzerland
- Greece
- Hungary
- Italy
- Lake Balaton
- Milan and the Italian Lakes
- Portugal  Madeira  The Azores
- Reykjavik
- Rome
- Sicily
- Spain
- Switzerland
- Tuscany
- Venice and the Veneto
- Wine Trails of Italy

## Asia
- Japan
- South Korea

**YOUR OPINION IS ESSENTIAL
TO IMPROVING OUR PRODUCTS**

*Help us by answering the
questionnaire on our website:*
**satisfaction.michelin.com**

## Michelin Travel Partner

Société par actions simplifiées au capital de 15 044 940 EUR
27 cours de l'Ile Seguin - 92100 Boulogne Billancourt (France)
R.C.S. Nanterre 433 677 721

No part of this publication may be reproduced in any form
without the prior permission of the publisher.

© Michelin Travel Partner
ISBN 978-2-067243-24-8
Printed: July 2020
Printed and bound in France : Imprimerie CHIRAT, 42540 Saint-Just-la-Pendue - N° 202007.0245